(Continued on reverse) ⟶

The Little, Brown Handbook

Ninth Edition

H. Ramsey Fowler
St. Edward's University

Jane E. Aaron

Daniel Anderson
Technology Consultant
*University of North Carolina,
Chapel Hill*

PEARSON
Longman

New York   Boston   San Francisco
London   Toronto   Sydney   Tokyo   Singapore   Madrid
Mexico City   Munich   Paris   Cape Town   Hong Kong   Montreal

Senior Vice President and Publisher: Joseph Opiela
Acquisitions Editor: Susan Kunchandy
Development Manager: Janet Lanphier
Development Editor: Carol Hollar-Zwick
Senior Supplements Editor: Donna Campion
Media Supplements Editor: Nancy Garcia
Executive Marketing Manager: Ann Stypuloski
Senior Production Manager: Bob Ginsberg
Project Coordination, Text Design, and Electronic Page Makeup:
    Nesbitt Graphics, Inc.
Cover Design Manager: Wendy Ann Fredericks
Cover Designer: Kay Petronio
Jr. Manufacturing Buyer: Roy L. Pickering
Printer and Binder: RR Donnelley & Sons Company
Cover Printer: Phoenix Color Corporation

The authors and publisher are grateful to the many students who allowed their work to be reprinted here and to the copyright holders who are listed on pages 957–58, which are hereby made part of this copyright page.

CIP data is on file with the Library of Congress.

Please visit our Web site at *http://www.ablongman.com/littlebrown*.

ISBN 0-321-10350-5

1 2 3 4 5 6 7 8 9 10—DOC—06 05 04 03

Preface for Students: Using This Book

The Little, Brown Handbook is a basic resource that will answer almost any question you have about writing. Here you can find out how to get ideas, punctuate quotations, search the Internet, cite sources, or write a résumé. The handbook can help you not only in writing courses but also in other courses and beyond school.

Don't let the size of the handbook put you off. You need not read the whole book to get something out of it, and no one expects you to know everything included. Primarily a reference tool, the handbook is written and arranged to help you find the answers you need when you need them, quickly and easily.

Using this book will not by itself make you a good writer; for that, you need to care about your work at every level, from finding a subject to spelling words. But learning how to use the handbook and the information in it can give you the means to write *what* you want in the *way* you want.

Reference aids and content

The next two pages detail the many ways you can find information in the handbook. You'll want to be familiar with two symbols that highlight special information appearing throughout the book:

- The mouse icon shown here signals tips for using computers productively for all kinds of writing activities, and it marks blue boxes that lead directly to the handbook's Web site.
- The symbol ᵔ CULTURE LANGUAGE ᵓ flags material for students who are using standard American English as a second language or a second dialect. A guide to all this material appears inside the back cover of the book.

An overview of the handbook's contents appears inside the front cover. Briefly, the book divides into the following sections:

- Chapters 1–4 deal with the big picture: the writing process and paragraphs.
- Chapters 5–7 discuss critical thinking, reading arguments, and writing arguments.

(Continued on p. vi)

Finding what you need

Use the directory.

Plan of the Book, inside the front cover, displays the book's entire contents.

Use a glossary.

- **Glossary of Usage** (pp. 914–31) clarifies more than 275 words that are commonly confused and misused.
- **Glossary of Terms** (pp. 932–56) defines more than 350 words used in discussing writing.

Use the index.

On the last pages of the book, the extensive index includes every term, concept, and problem word or expression mentioned in the book.

Use a list.

- **Guide to ⟨CULTURE-LANGUAGE⟩ Topics,** inside the back cover, pulls together all the book's material for students using standard American English as a second language or a second dialect.
- **Editing Symbols,** also inside the back cover, explains abbreviations often used to mark papers.
- **Useful Lists and Summaries,** just before the back endpapers, indexes topics that students frequently ask about.

Use the elements of the page.

① **Running head (header),** showing the topic being discussed on this page.

② **Section heading,** a main convention or topic labeled with the section code, **15b:** chapter number (**15**) and section letter (**b**).

③ **Examples,** always indented. Blue-green underlining and red annotations highlight sentence elements and revisions.

④ **Summary or checklist box,** in yellow.

⑤ **Page tab,** containing the nearest section code (**15b**) and the editing symbol for the topic being discussed (**agr**).

⑥ **Computer tip,** signaled by a mouse icon. (See also the previous page.)

⑦ **Web box,** in light blue, linking to the handbook's companion Web site and its specific coverage of the topic being discussed: here, a video tutorial, exercises, and links to other Web sites.

⑧ **Culture-language connection,** in yellow and blue: a pointer for students using standard American English as a second language or a second dialect.

⑨ **Exercise,** with gold vertical line.

1 Pronoun and antecedent **327**

2 **15b** **Make pronouns and their antecedents agree in person, number, and gender.**

The **antecedent** of a pronoun is the noun or other pronoun to which the pronoun refers.

3
Homeowners fret over their tax bills.
antecedent   pronoun

Its constant increases make the tax bill a dreaded document.
pronoun   antecedent

Since a pronoun derives its meaning from its antecedent, the two must agree in person, number, and gender.

4 **Person, number, and gender in pronoun-antecedent agreement**

5 agr 15b

	Number	
Person	Singular	Plural
First	I	we
Second	you	you
Third	he, she, it, indefinite pronouns, singular nouns	they, plural nouns

Gender	
Masculine	he, nouns naming males
Feminine	she, nouns naming females
Neuter	it, all other nouns

6 Note Grammar and style checkers cannot help with agreement between pronoun and antecedent because they cannot recognize the intended relation between the two. You'll need to check for errors on your own.

7 http://www.ablongman.com/littlebrown
For added help and practice with pronoun-antecedent agreement, click on
➤ Sentences
➤ Video tutorials ➤ Recognizing pronoun-antecedent problems
➤ Exercises ➤ Exers. 26 and 27
➤ Web links ➤ Pronoun-antecedent agreement

Collective nouns such as *army, committee, family, group,* and *team* have singular form but may be referred to by singular or plural pronouns, depending on the meaning intended. When the group acts as a unit, the pronoun is singular:

The committee voted to disband itself.

When the members of the group act separately, the pronoun is plural:

The old group have gone their separate ways.

In the last example, note that the verb and pronoun are consistent in number (see also pp. 375–76).

Inconsistent   The old group has gone their separate ways.
Consistent   The old group have gone their separate ways.

8 CULTURE LANGUAGE English collective nouns that are noncount nouns (they don't form plurals) usually take singular pronouns: *The mail sits in its own basket.* A few noncount nouns take plural pronouns, including *clergy, military, people, police, the rich,* and *the poor: The police support their unions.* (See also pp. 323–24.)

9 EXERCISE 2
Revising: Pronoun-antecedent agreement
Revise the following sentences so that pronouns and their antecedents agree in person and number. Some items have more than one possible answer. Try to avoid the generic *he* (see p. 329). If you

(Continued from p. iii)

- Chapters 8–11 treat computer skills for writers, such as file management, e-mail, document design, Web composition, and online collaboration.
- Chapters 12–26 cover sentence basics: the system of English grammar and its conventions, errors that affect clarity, and techniques of effective sentences.
- Chapters 27–37 treat two technical elements of sentences and words: punctuation and mechanics (meaning capital letters, underlining, and the like).
- Chapters 38–43 move to words—how to choose them, look them up, learn them, spell them.
- Chapters 44–50 cover research writing from planning through revising, with a complete guide to citing sources.
- Chapters 51–55 introduce writing in the academic disciplines: literature, the other humanities, the social sciences, and the natural and applied sciences.
- Chapters 56–58 contain practical information on taking essay exams, writing business letters and job applications, and delivering oral presentations.
- Two glossaries—one of problem words and expressions, the other of terms—and a detailed index finish the book.

Recommended usage

The conventions described and illustrated in this handbook are those of standard American English—the label given the dialect of business and the professions. (See also pp. 17–18.) The handbook stresses written standard English, which is more conservative than the spoken dialect in matters of grammar and usage. A great many words and constructions that are widely spoken remain unaccepted in careful writing.

When clear distinctions exist between the language of conversation and that of careful writing, the handbook provides examples of each and labels them *spoken* and *written*. When usage in writing itself varies with the level of formality intended, the handbook labels examples *formal* and *informal*. When usage is mixed or currently changing, the handbook recommends that you choose the more conservative usage because it will be acceptable to all readers.

Preface for Instructors

The Little, Brown Handbook always aims to address both the current and the recurrent needs of writing students and teachers. This ninth edition is no exception. Writing and its teaching are changing dramatically because of electronic media, and the handbook has changed in response. At the same time, much about writing does not change, and the handbook remains a comprehensive, clear, and accessible guide to a host of writing situations and challenges.

The Little, Brown Handbook is actually many books in one, and each is stronger in this edition. The revisions—highlighted below with New—affect most pages.

A guide to writing with computers

The handbook integrates computers into all stages of writing, explaining how they can help and also when they cannot.

- More than 150 computer tips are signaled by the mouse icon shown here.
- Specific, problem-centered advice helps students use spelling and grammar/style checkers effectively.
- Concise, rhetorically focused chapters cover key computer skills, such as file management and e-mail, as well as document design, Web composition, and online collaboration.
- New Special Web boxes point to specific video tutorials, exercises, Web links, and other help on the handbook's companion Web site (see also pp. ix–x).

A guide to research writing

With detailed advice and two sample MLA papers, the handbook always gives close attention to research writing while keeping pace with changes in the methods and challenges of research.

- The discussion emphasizes managing information, evaluating and synthesizing sources, integrating sources, and avoiding plagiarism.
- New A focus on the library as Web gateway includes using the library's Web site (with a case study on navigating a subscrip-

tion service) and distinguishing between library and other on-line sources.

- ■ **New** A detailed case study illustrates evaluating a Web site.
- ■ **New** A section on gathering information from sources includes pros and cons of photocopies, printouts, and downloads.
- ■ **New** A section covers integrating quotations in the humanities, the social sciences, and the natural sciences.
- ■ **New** A separate chapter on avoiding plagiarism includes a section on Internet term-paper sites and detection software, more examples of plagiarism and its correction, and special advice on using sources in Web compositions.

A guide to documenting sources

Often cited for its meticulous coverage of source documentation, the handbook includes extensive sections on four major styles: MLA, Chicago, APA, and CSE.

- ■ **New** Updated MLA style reflects the sixth edition of the *MLA Handbook* (2003) and includes thorough explanations and annotated examples for electronic sources.
- ■ **New** Updated APA style reflects the fifth edition of the APA *Publication Manual* (2001).

A guide to the writing process

The handbook takes a practical approach to assessing the writing situation, generating ideas, writing the thesis statement, revising, and other elements of the writing process.

- ■ Numerous examples, including a student work-in-progress on Internet communication, illustrate every stage.
- ■ **New** A section on academic writing discusses subject, purpose, and audience and establishes a context for college writing.

A guide to critical thinking, reading, and writing

The handbook details techniques of critical reading, focuses on reading arguments critically, and provides concrete suggestions for writing arguments.

- ■ **New** A section on critically viewing images includes a step-by-step method of analysis and a case study using an ad for *Time* magazine.
- ■ **New** An annotated sample argument asserts the virtues of television.

A guide for culturally and linguistically diverse writers

The handbook provides extensive rhetorical and grammatical help for writers whose first language or dialect is not standard American English.

- New Notes labeled 🌐 **CULTURE LANGUAGE** ❯ supplant former ESL notes and now cover dialect as well as language differences.
- Fully integrated coverage, instead of a separate section, means that students can find what they need without having to know which problems they do and don't share with native SAE speakers.
- "Guide to 🌐 **CULTURE LANGUAGE** ❯ Topics," inside the back cover, pulls all the integrated coverage together in one place.

A guide to usage, grammar, and punctuation

The handbook's core reference material continues to be reliable and accessible.

- Concise text explains all basic concepts and common errors.
- Annotated examples from across the curriculum represent college writers and writing.
- Frequent exercises in connected discourse include end-of-part exercises that combine several kinds of problems.

A guide to writing in the disciplines

The handbook offers specific advice on writing about literature and in other humanities, the social sciences, and the natural and applied sciences.

- Discussions emphasize distinctive methods and evidence, writing assignments, tools and language, and documentation and format.
- Extensive guidelines cover documentation and format in MLA, Chicago, APA, and CSE styles, illustrated with sample papers.

An accessible reference guide

The handbook is uncommonly easy to use.

- Helpful endpapers offer several paths to the book's content.
- More than 150 boxes provide summaries and checklists.
- A clean, uncluttered page design makes clear use of color.
- A preface just for students outlines the book's contents, details reference aids, and explains the page layout.

A reference for college and beyond

With chapters on document design, writing across the curriculum, taking essay exams, writing for business, and making oral presentations, the handbook is a resource that students keep. With a cloth cover and sturdy binding, it is a book that lasts.

An integrated text and Web site

New Throughout the handbook, newly designed Web boxes point to specific pages on the handbook's vastly expanded Web site, a powerful online resource for students and teachers:

- More than thirty video tutorials provide explanations, examples, tips, and student interviews to help students understand concepts and techniques. Topics include narrowing a subject online, finding an argument topic, using e-mail, recognizing comma splices, conducting online keyword searches, and designing a *PowerPoint* presentation.
- More than a thousand interactive exercises provide immediate feedback for every answer and are cross-referenced to the text.
- Students can download checklists from the text to generate ideas and revise their work.
- Hundreds of Web links direct students to helpful sites on the writing process, critical thinking, argument, grammar, research, writing in the disciplines, and more.
- The online Glossary of Usage allows students to test their knowledge and practice usage.
- A database includes nine student papers from across the disciplines.
- A password-protected copy of the instructor's manual can be found under Instructors' Resources.

Supplements

An extensive package of supplements accompanies *The Little, Brown Handbook* for both instructors and students. An asterisk (*) precedes any item that is complimentary to qualified adopters of the handbook.

For students

- **CompSolutions Plus Interactive E-Book for The Little, Brown Handbook* offers a complete, searchable version of the handbook, video and audio clips on key topics, interactive exercises, writing-related Web links, and links through an access code to the *CompSolutions* Web site.
- **CompSolutions* Web site offers one convenient portal to several of Longman's most popular multimedia resources for composition (described below). An access card comes with the interactive e-book CD featuring the entire contents of the handbook.

  Longman Writer's Warehouse for Composition provides guided assistance through the writing process, access to Web-based journals and writing portfolios, diagnostic tests, exercises, and video-based writing assignments.

  Avoiding Plagiarism Tutorial consists of interactive modules on plagiarism, common knowledge, paraphrase, and summary. The tutorial also covers both MLA and APA documentation.

  Research Navigator provides access to a database of thousands of academic journals and general-interest periodicals, *The*

New York Times online archives, and several online research tools.

Longman ExerciseZone offers diagnostic tests to help students identify where they need help along with more than 2500 exercises on grammar, style, usage, and punctuation.

The Student Bookshelf is an online library of brief e-books in PDF format, including *Public Literacy, Academic Literacy, Workplace Literacy, Visual Communication, Analyzing Literature,* and *Reading Critically.*

- *The Little, Brown Workbook,* Ninth Edition, by Donna Gorrell, St. Cloud University, parallels the handbook's organization but provides briefer instructional text and many more exercises. This edition includes a new section on writing with computers. A separate answer key is available.

- *ESL Worksheets,* Third Edition, by Dawn Schmid, California State University, San Marcos, provides nonnative speakers with extra practice in the areas that tend to be more troublesome for them.

- **Research Navigator Guide for English,* by H. Eric Branscomb, Salem State College, and Linda R. Barr, University of the Virgin Islands, teaches students how to conduct high-quality online research and to document it properly, provides discipline-specific academic resources and helpful tips on the writing process, and links through an access code to the *Research Navigator* on *CompSolutions* (see opposite).

- *Take Note!* is a cross-platform CD-ROM that integrates note taking, outlining, and bibliography management in one easy-to-use package.

Additional supplements for students include *Eighty Readings,* Second Edition; the *Literacy Library Series (*Public Literacy, Workplace Literacy,* and *Academic Literacy*); **Visual Communication,* by Susan Hilligoss; **Analyzing Literature: A Guide for Students,* by Sharon James McGee; **Reading Critically: Text, Charts, Graphs,* Second Edition, by Judith Olson-Fallon; and two guides to collaborative learning, **Learning Together,* by Tori Haring-Smith, and **A Guide for Peer Response,* by Tori Haring-Smith and Helon Raines.

The handbook may also be packaged with other books at a discount. Two dictionaries are available: *Merriam-Webster's Collegiate Dictionary,* Tenth Edition, a hardcover desk dictionary; and *The New American Webster Handy College Dictionary,* Third Edition, a briefer paperback. And the Penguin Program, through Penguin Putnam, offers a variety of Penguin titles, such as Arthur Miller's *Death of a Salesman* and Julia Alvarez's *How the Garcia Girls Lost Their Accents.*

For instructors

- **Instructor's Manual to Accompany The Little, Brown Handbook*, Ninth Edition, by Janice Okoomian, Brown University, is a comprehensive, spiral-bound, two-color volume that includes answers to all exercises, helpful essays and suggested readings for new and experienced teachers, and hundreds of classroom discussion topics, activities, computer and collaborative exercises, and tips for integrating the handbook and its Web site.
- *An answer key provides answers to all the exercises in the handbook. It is available both in print and online (password-protected).
- **Course Compass* is a proprietary version of *Blackboard*, the course-management resource, augmented with Longman's *CompSolutions* (p. x). For instructors already using *Blackboard* or *WebCT*, the *CompSolutions* resources are available as content cartridges for either platform.
- *On the handbook's companion Web site, instructors can download the password-protected instructor's manual and answer key as well as more than a hundred transparency masters and *PowerPoint* slides that reproduce key boxes and lists from the text.
- **Teaching Online: Internet Research, Conversation, and Composition*, Second Edition, is an accessible introduction to Internet resources for teaching writing. Written by Daniel Anderson, Bret Benjamin, Christopher Busiel, and Bill Paredes-Holt, the book offers basic definitions and information on Internet access and shows how to integrate a variety of Internet tools in writing courses.
- **Diagnostic Editing Tests and Exercises*, by Trudy Zimmerman, Hutchinson Community College, helps instructors assess students' standard American English for placement or to gauge progress. The package is available on reproducible sheets or on TestGen EQ, Longman's online testing program.
- *An extensive assessment package includes TASP and CLAST exams. All items are keyed to the handbook. The tests are available on reproducible sheets or on TestGen EQ, Longman's online testing program.
- *The Longman resources for instructors include six valuable works: *Teaching in Progress: Theories, Practices, and Scenarios*, Third Edition, by Josephine Koster-Tarvers; *Using Portfolios*, by Kathleen McClelland; *Comp Tales*, writing teachers' reports on their teaching experiences, edited by Richard Haswell; and the videos *Writing, Teaching, and Learning*, by David Jolliffe, and *Writing Across the Curriculum: Making It Work*, produced by Robert Morris College and the Public Broadcasting System.

Acknowledgments

We could not keep *The Little, Brown Handbook* fresh and useful without the help of many instructors who talk with sales representatives and editors, answer questionnaires, write detailed reviews, and send us personal notes.

For the ninth edition, we are especially grateful to the many instructors who communicated with us directly or through reviews, drawing on their rich experience to offer insights into the handbook and suggestions for its improvement: James El Allen, College of DuPage; E. Ferol Benavides, Anne Arundel Community College; Mark Bernier, Blinn College; Peggy Cole, Arapahoe Community College; Barbara H. Cole, Sandhills Community College; Catherine S. Cox, University of Pittsburgh at Johnstown; Tracy Duckart, Humboldt State University; Larnell Dunkley, Jr., Benedictine University; Linda Girard, Parkland College; Ellen Redding Kaler, Northwest Missouri State University; Judith Mara Kish, the University of Findlay; Patricia Medeiros, Scottsdale Community College; Kevin Nebergall, Kirkwood Community College; Stacy Oberle, Blinn College; Diane Orsini, Valencia Community College; J. Lisa Ray, Thomas Nelson Community College; David Satran, University of Delaware; Beverly J. Slaughter, Brevard Community College; Julie Wakeman-Linn, Montgomery College; Xiao Wang, Broward Community College; and Noelle Williams, San Jose State University.

In responding to the ideas of these thoughtful critics, we had the help of many creative people. Daniel Anderson, University of North Carolina, Chapel Hill, served as invaluable and patient technology consultant. Barbara Schneider, University of Toledo, offered detailed suggestions for broadening the second-language material to encompass dialect differences. Susan Hollar, University of Michigan, guided us through the labyrinth of the contemporary library. And Sylvan Barnet, Tufts University, continued to lend his expertise in the chapter "Reading and Writing About Literature," which is adapted from his *Short Guide to Writing About Literature* and *Introduction to Literature* (with Morton Berman, William Burto, and William E. Cain).

In and around Longman, too, support was unstinting. Susan Kunchandy sponsored the book in-house and responded enthusiastically to our many needs. Carol Hollar-Zwick, development editor, brought her can-do attitude to plugging holes, serving as a sounding board, and offering creative suggestions. She and Kimberly Rossi, William Russo, and Nancy Garcia created the terrific companion Web site. Ann Stypuloski devised and managed a vibrant marketing effort. Susan McIntyre gave calm and meticulous attention to turning manuscript into bound book, despite a crushing schedule. Catherine Bradish provided the striking new design. Tara Masih copyedited to catch our lapses. And Dorothy Bungert worked her usual miracles in page make-up. We are grateful to all these collaborators.

Contents

PART I

The Writing Process

CHAPTER 1

Assessing the Writing Situation

"Writing is easy," snarled the late sportswriter Red Smith. "All you do is sit down at the typewriter and open a vein." Most writers would smile in agreement, and so might you. Like anything worthwhile, writing well takes hard work. This chapter and the next two will show you some techniques that successful writers use to ease the discomfort of writing and produce effective compositions.

1a   Understanding how writing happens

Every time you sit down to write, you embark on a **writing process**—the term for all the activities, mental and physical, that go into creating what eventually becomes a finished piece of work. Even for experienced writers the process is usually messy, which is one reason that it is sometimes difficult. Though we may get a sense of ease and orderliness from a well-crafted magazine article, we can safely assume that the writer had to work hard to achieve those qualities, struggling to express half-formed thoughts, shaping and reshaping paragraphs to make a point convincingly.

There is no *one* writing process: no two writers proceed in the same way, and even an individual writer adapts his or her process to the task at hand. Still, most experienced writers pass through certain stages that overlap and circle back on each other:

- *Analyzing the writing situation:* considering subject, purpose, audience, and other elements of the project (pp. 4–18).
- *Developing or planning:* gathering information, focusing on a central theme, and organizing material (pp. 19–46).

http://www.ablongman.com/littlebrown

For added help with the writing process, click on
- ➤ The writing process
  - ➤ Video tutorials
  - ➤ Exercises
  - ➤ Downloads
  - ➤ Web links

- *Drafting:* expressing and connecting ideas (pp. 47–51).
- *Revising and editing:* rethinking and improving structure, content, style, and presentation (pp. 51–65).

With experience, as you complete varied assignments and try the varied techniques described in this book, you will develop your own basic writing process.

Note Like many others, you may believe that writing is only, or even mainly, a matter of correctness. True, any written message will find a more receptive audience if it is correct in grammar, spelling, and similar matters. But these concerns should come late in the writing process, after you've allowed yourself to discover what you want to say, freeing yourself to make mistakes along the way. As one writer put it, you need to get the clay on the potter's wheel before you can shape it into a bowl, and you need to shape the bowl before you can perfect it. So get your clay on the wheel, and work with it until it looks like a bowl. Then worry about correctness.

EXERCISE 1
Starting a writing journal
Recall several writing experiences that you have had—a letter you had difficulty composing, an essay you enjoyed writing, an all-nighter spent happily or miserably on a term paper, a posting to an online newsgroup that received a surprising response. What do these experiences reveal to you about writing, particularly your successes and problems with it? For instance:

Do you like to experiment with language?
Are some kinds of writing easier than others?
Do you have trouble getting ideas or expressing them?
Do you worry about grammar and spelling?
Do your readers usually understand what you mean?

Record these thoughts as part of continuing journal entries that track your experiences as a writer. (See pp. 20–22 on keeping a journal, and see the exercises titled "Considering your past work" in Chapters 1–4.) As you complete writing assignments for your composition course and other courses, keep adding to the journal, noting especially which procedures seem most helpful to you. Your aim is to discover your feelings about writing so that you can develop a dependable writing process of your own.

1b Analyzing the writing situation

Any writing you do for others occurs in a context that both limits and clarifies your choices. You are communicating something about a particular subject to a particular audience of readers for a specific reason. You may need to conduct research. You'll be up against a length requirement and a deadline. And you may be expected to present your work in a certain format.

These are the elements of the **writing situation,** and analyzing them at the very start of a project can tell you much about how to proceed. (For more information about these elements, refer to the page numbers given below.)

Subject (pp. 5–8)

- What does your writing assignment instruct you to write about? If you don't have a specific assignment, what do you want to write about?
- What interests you about the subject? What do you already know about it? What questions do you have about it?
- What does the assignment require you to do with the subject?

Audience (pp. 9–12)

- Who will read your writing? What do your readers already know and think about your topic?
- Do your readers have any characteristics—such as educational background, experience in your field, or political views—that could influence their reception of your writing?
- What is your relationship to your readers? How formal or informal should your writing be?
- What do you want readers to do or think after they read your writing?

Purpose (pp. 13–15)

- What aim does your assignment specify? For instance, does it ask you to explain something or argue a point?
- Why are you writing? What effect do you intend your work to have on readers? What do you want your work to accomplish?
- How can you best achieve your purpose?

Research (pp. 606–89)

- What kinds of evidence—such as facts, examples, and the opinions of experts—will best suit your topic, audience, and purpose?
- Does your assignment require you to consult sources of information or conduct other research, such as interviews, surveys, or experiments?
- Besides the requirements of the assignment, what additional information do you need to develop your topic? How will you obtain it?
- What documentation style should you use to cite your sources? (See pp. 688–89 on source documentation in the academic disciplines.)

Deadline and length

- When is the assignment due? How will you apportion the work you have to do in the time available?
- How long should your writing be? If no length is assigned, what seems appropriate for your topic, audience, and purpose?

Document design

- What organization and format does the assignment require? (See pp. 199–200 on format in the academic disciplines and pp. 893–904 on format in business.)
- Even if no particular format is required, how might you use margins, headings, illustrations, and other elements to achieve your purpose? (See pp. 200–12.)

EXERCISE 2
Analyzing a writing situation
The following assignment was given in a survey course in psychology. What does the assignment specify about the elements of the writing situation? What does it imply? Given this assignment, how would you answer the questions opposite and above?

> When is psychotherapy most likely to work? That is, what combinations of client, therapist, and theory tend to achieve good results? In your paper, cite studies supporting your conclusions. Length: 1500 to 1800 words. Post your paper online to me and your discussion group by March 30.

1c   Discovering and limiting a subject

For most college and business writing, you will write in response to an assignment. The assignment may specify your subject, or it may leave the choice to you. (If you're stuck, you can use the discovery techniques on pp. 19–30 to think of subjects.) Whether the subject is assigned or not, it will probably need some thought if it is to achieve these aims:

- The subject should be suitable for the assignment.

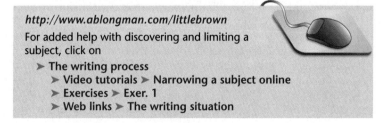

http://www.ablongman.com/littlebrown
For added help with discovering and limiting a subject, click on
➤ **The writing process**
  ➤ **Video tutorials** ➤ **Narrowing a subject online**
  ➤ **Exercises** ➤ **Exer. 1**
  ➤ **Web links** ➤ **The writing situation**

- It should be neither too general nor too limited for the length of project and deadline assigned.
- It should be something you care about.

1 ■ Responding to a specific assignment

Many assignments will set boundaries for your subject. For instance, you might be asked to discuss what makes psychotherapy effective, to prepare a lab report on a physics experiment, or to analyze a character in a short story.

Such assignments may seem to leave little room for you to move around, but in fact you'll have several questions to answer:

- *What's wanted from you?* Writing assignments often contain words such as *discuss, describe, analyze, report, interpret, explain, define, argue,* and *evaluate.* These words specify the way you are to approach your subject, what kind of thinking is expected of you, and what your general purpose is. (See pp. 13–15 for more on purpose.)
- *For whom are you writing?* Some assignments will specify your readers, but usually you will have to figure out for yourself who your audience is and what it expects from you. (For more on analyzing audience, see pp. 9–12.)
- *What kind of research is required?* Sometimes an assignment specifies the kinds of sources you are expected to consult, and you can use such information to choose your subject. (If you are unsure whether research is required, check with your instructor.)
- *How can you narrow the assigned subject to do it justice in the length and time required?* (See the next page.)

2 ■ Responding to a general assignment

Some assignments specify features such as length or amount of research, but they leave the choice of subject entirely to you. Others are somewhat more focused—for instance, "Respond to a reading assigned in this course" or "Discuss a proposal for solving a local social problem"—but still give you much leeway in choosing a particular reading or a particular proposal. To find your approach, consider your experiences, interests, or curiosities:

- What subject do you already know something about or have you been wondering about? Athletic scholarships? Unemployment in your town?
- Have you recently participated in a lively discussion about a controversial topic, such as a change in relations between men and women or an event in the fight against terrorism?
- Do you find a current technological trend, such as the use of cell phones or the Internet, especially exciting or disturbing?

- What have you read or seen lately? A shocking book? A violent or funny movie? An effective television commercial?
- What topic in the reading or class discussion for a course has intrigued you or seemed especially relevant to your own experiences? An economic issue such as taxes? A psychological problem such as depression?
- What makes you especially happy or especially angry? A hobby? The behavior of your neighbors?
- Which of your own or others' dislikes and preferences would you like to understand better? The demand for sport-utility vehicles? A taste for vegetarian cuisine?

Once you have a subject, you'll also need to answer the questions in the bulleted list opposite.

3 ■ Narrowing a subject to a question

Let's say you've decided to write about communication on the Internet or about a particular character in a short story. You've got a subject, but it's still broad, worthy of a lengthy article if not a whole book. For a relatively brief paper, you'll need a narrow focus in order to provide the specific details that make writing significant and interesting—all within the length and deadline specified by the assignment.

One helpful technique for narrowing a subject is to ask focused questions about it, seeking one that seems appropriate for your assignment and that promises to sustain your interest through the writing process. The following examples illustrate how questioning can scale down broad subjects to specific subjects that are limited and manageable:

Broad subjects	Specific subjects
Communication on the Internet	What are the advantages of online communication?
	How, if at all, should the government regulate Internet content?
	How might the Internet contribute to social and economic equality?
Mrs. Mallard in Kate Chopin's "The Story of an Hour"	What changes does Mrs. Mallard undergo?
	Why does Mrs. Mallard respond as she does to news of her husband's death?
	What does the story's irony contribute to the character of Mrs. Mallard?
Lincoln's weaknesses as President	What was Lincoln's most significant error as commander-in-chief of the Union army?
	Why did Lincoln delay emancipating the slaves?
	Why did Lincoln have difficulties controlling his cabinet?

| Federal aid to college students | Which students should be entitled to federal aid? How adequate are the kinds of federal aid available to college students? Why should the federal government aid college students? |

As these examples illustrate, your questions should not lend themselves to yes-or-no answers but should require further thinking.

Here are some guidelines for posing questions:

- Pursue your interests, and consider what the assignment tells you about purpose, audience, sources, length, and deadline.
- Ask as many questions as you can think of. Make a list as described on pages 24–26, or use a tree diagram as shown on pages 38–39.
- Test the question that seems most interesting and appropriate by roughly sketching out the main ideas. Consider how many paragraphs or pages of specific facts, examples, and other details you would need to pin those ideas down. This thinking should give you at least a vague idea of how much work you'd have to do and how long the resulting paper might be.
- If your chosen question is still too broad, break it down further and repeat the previous step.

The Internet can also help you limit a general subject. On the Web, browse a directory such as *BUBL LINK* (*http://bubl.ac.uk/link*). As you pursue increasingly narrow categories, you may find a suitably limited topic.

Don't be discouraged if the perfect question does not come easily or early. You may find that you need to do some planning and writing, exploring different facets of the general subject and pursuing your specific interests, before you hit on the best question. And the question you select may require further narrowing or may shift subtly or even dramatically as you move through the writing process.

EXERCISE 3
Narrowing subjects

Following are some general writing assignments. Use the given information and your own interests to pose specific questions for three of these assignments.

1. For a writing course, consider how the World Wide Web could alter the experience of popular culture. Length: three pages. Deadline: one week.
2. For a course in sociology, research and analyze the dynamics of a particular group of people. Length: unspecified. Deadline: four weeks.
3. For a writing course, read and respond to an essay in a text you are using. Length: three pages. Deadline: two weeks.

4. For a government course, consider possible restrictions on legislators. Length: five pages. Deadline: two weeks.
5. For a letter to the editor of the town newspaper, describe the effects of immigration on your community. Length: two pages. Deadline: unspecified.

EXERCISE 4
Considering your past work: Discovering and limiting a subject
Think of something you've recently written—perhaps an application essay, a business report, or a term paper. How did your subject evolve from beginning to end? In retrospect, was it appropriate for your writing situation? How, if at all, might it have been modified?

EXERCISE 5
Finding and narrowing a subject for your essay
As the first step in developing a three- to four-page essay for the instructor and the other students in your writing course, choose a subject and narrow it. Use the guidelines in the previous section to come up with a question that is suitably interesting, appropriate, and specific.

1d Considering the audience

Who are your readers? Why will they read your writing? What will they need and expect from you? These questions are central to any writing project, and they will crop up again and again. Except in writing meant only for yourself, you are always trying to communicate with readers—something about a particular subject, for a particular purpose.

Your audience will generally be specified or implied in a writing assignment. When you write an editorial for the student newspaper, your audience is fellow students. When you write a report on a physics experiment, your audience is your physics instructor. (See p. 16 for more on audience in academic writing.) Whatever the audience, considering its needs and expectations can help you form or focus a question about your subject, gather answers to the question, and ultimately decide what to say and how to say it.

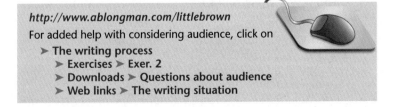

http://www.ablongman.com/littlebrown
For added help with considering audience, click on
➤ **The writing process**
  ➤ Exercises ➤ Exer. 2
  ➤ **Downloads** ➤ **Questions about audience**
  ➤ **Web links** ➤ **The writing situation**

Questions about audience

Identity and expectations

- Who *are* my readers?
- Why are readers going to read my writing? What will they expect?
- What do I want readers to know or do after reading my work, and how should I make that clear to them?
- What is my relationship to my readers? How formal or informal will they expect me to be? What role and tone should I assume?

Characteristics, knowledge, and attitudes

- What characteristic(s) of readers are relevant for my topic and purpose? For instance:

  Age and sex
  Occupation: students, professional colleagues, etc.
  Social or economic role: adult children, car buyers, potential employers, etc.
  Economic or educational background
  Ethnic background
  Political, religious, or moral beliefs and values
  Hobbies or activities

- How will the characteristic(s) of readers influence their attitudes toward my topic?
- What do readers already know and *not* know about my topic? How much do I have to tell them?
- If my topic involves specialized language, how much should I use and define?
- What ideas, arguments, or information might surprise readers? excite them? offend them? How should I handle these points?
- What misconceptions might readers have of my topic and/or my approach to the topic? How can I dispel these misconceptions?

Uses and format

- What will readers do with my writing? Should I expect them to read every word from the top, to scan for information, to look for conclusions? Can I help with a summary, headings, or other aids? (See pp. 199–212 on document design.)

---

1 ■ Knowing what readers need

As a reader yourself, you know what readers need:

- *Context:* a link between what they read and their own knowledge and experiences.
- *Predictability:* an understanding of the writer's purpose and how it is being achieved.
- *Information:* the specific facts, examples, and other details that make the subject clear, concrete, interesting, and convincing.

- *Respect:* a sense that the writer respects their values and beliefs, their background, and their intelligence.
- *Voice:* a sense that the writer is a real person.
- *Clarity and correctness:* writing free of unnecessary stumbling blocks and mistakes.

For much academic and business writing, readers have definite needs and expectations. Thus, pages 15–18 in this chapter discuss academic writing in general, and Chapters 51–55 and 57 discuss writing in various disciplines and in business. Even in these areas, you must make many choices based on audience. In other areas where the conventions of structure and presentation are vaguer, the choices are even more numerous. The box on the previous page contains questions that can help you define and make these choices.

You can download the questions about audience from this book's Web site: see the box on page 9. Store the questions in a file of their own, and duplicate the file for each writing project. Insert appropriate answers for that project between the questions, and print a copy for reference while you develop your paper.

2 ■ Pitching your writing to your audience

Your sense of your audience will influence three key elements of what you write:

- *The specific information you use to gain and keep the attention of readers and to guide them to accept your conclusions.* This information may consist of concrete details, facts, examples, or any other evidence that makes your ideas clear, supports your assertions, and suits your readers' background, biases, and special interests.
- *The role you choose to play in relation to your readers.* Depending on your purpose and your attitude toward your topic, you will want readers to perceive you in a certain way. The possible roles are many and varied—for instance, scholar, storyteller, lecturer, guide, reporter, advocate, inspirer.
- *The tone you use.* **Tone** in writing is like tone of voice in speaking: words and sentence structures on the page convey some of the same information as pitch and volume in the voice. Depending on your writing situation and what you think your readers will expect and respond to, your tone may be formal or informal. The attitude you convey may be serious or light, forceful or calm, irritated or cheerful.

Even when you're writing on the same topic, your information, role, and tone may change substantially for different audiences. Both memos on the next page were written by a student who worked part-time in a small company and wanted to get the company to conserve paper. But the two memos address different readers.

dev

1d

To coworkers

Ever notice how much paper collects in your trash basket every day? Well, most of it can be recycled with little effort, I promise. Basically, all you need to do is set a bag or box near your desk and deposit wastepaper in it. I know, space is cramped in these little cubicles. But what's a little more crowding when the earth's at stake? . . .

Information: how employees could handle recycling; no mention of costs

Role: cheerful, equally harried colleague

Tone: informal, personal (*Ever notice; Well; you; I know, space is cramped; what's*)

To management

In my four months here, I have observed that all of us throw out baskets of potentially recyclable paper every day. Considering the drain on our forest resources and the pressure on landfills that paper causes, we could make a valuable contribution to the environmental movement by helping to recycle the paper we use. At the company where I worked before, employees separate clean wastepaper from other trash at their desks. The maintenance staff collects trash in two receptacles, and the trash hauler (the same one we use here) makes separate pickups. I do not know what the hauler charges for handling recyclable material. . . .

Information: specific reasons; view of company as a whole; reference to another company; problem of cost

Role: serious, thoughtful, responsible employee

Tone: formal, serious (*Considering the drain; forest resources; valuable contribution;* no *you* or contractions)

Typically for business reports and memos, the information grows more specific and the tone more formal as the rank and number of readers rise.

If you are writing online—for instance, to an Internet newsgroup—you may not know enough about your audience to pitch your writing to particular expectations and needs. Consider, then, providing more information than you otherwise might, assuming the role of an equal (perhaps a colleague), and using a level tone (neither hostile nor chummy, neither very formal nor very informal).

EXERCISE 6
Considering audience

Choose one of the following topics, and, for each audience specified, ask the questions on page 10. Decide on four points you would make, the role you would assume, and the tone you would adopt for each audience. Then write a paragraph for each based on your decisions.

1. The effects of smoking: for elementary school students and for adult smokers
2. Your opposition to a proposed law requiring adult bicyclists to wear helmets: for cyclists who oppose the law and for people who favor it

3. Why your neighbors should remove the wrecked truck from their front yard: for your neighbors and for your town zoning board

EXERCISE 7
Considering your past work: Writing for a specific audience

How did audience figure in a piece of writing you've done in the recent past—perhaps an essay for an application or a paper for a course? Who were your readers? How did your awareness of them influence your choice of information, your role, and your tone? At what point in the writing process did you find it most productive to consider your readers consciously?

EXERCISE 8
Analyzing the audience for your essay

Use the questions on page 10 to determine as much as you can about the probable readers of your essay-in-progress (see Exercise 5). What does your analysis reveal about the specific information your readers need? What role do you want to assume, and what tone will best convey your attitude toward your topic?

1e Defining a purpose

When you write, your **purpose** is your chief reason for communicating something about a topic to a particular audience. Purpose thus links both the specific situation in which you are working and the goal you hope to achieve.

1 ■ Defining a general purpose

Your purpose may fall into one of four general categories: entertainment, self-expression, explanation, or persuasion. These purposes may overlap in a single piece of writing, but usually one predominates. And the dominant purpose will influence your particular slant on your topic, the supporting details you choose, even the words you use.

In most college or business writing, by far the most common purposes are explanation and persuasion:

- *Writing that is mainly explanatory is often called **exposition*** (from a Latin word meaning "to explain or set forth"). Using examples, facts, and other evidence, you present an idea about your subject so that readers understand it as you do. Almost

http://www.ablongman.com/littlebrown

For added help with defining a purpose for writing, click on

➤ **The writing process** ➤ **Web links** ➤ **The writing situation**

The general purposes for writing

- To entertain readers
- To express your feelings or ideas
- To explain something to readers (exposition)
- To persuade readers to accept or act on your opinion (argument)

---

any topic is suitable for exposition: how to pitch a knuckleball, why you want to major in business, the implications of a new discovery in computer science, the interpretation of a short story, the causes of an economic slump. Exposition is the kind of writing encountered most often in newspapers, magazines, and textbooks.

- *Writing that is primarily persuasive is often called **argument**.* Using examples, facts, and other evidence, you support your position on a debatable topic so that readers will at least consider your view and perhaps agree with it or act on it. A newspaper editorial favoring city council reform, a business proposal for a new personnel policy, a student paper recommending more required courses or defending a theory about human psychological development—all these are arguments. (Chapters 6 and 7 discuss argument in some detail and provide illustrative essays.)

2 ■ Defining a specific purpose

Purpose can be conceived more specifically, too, in a way that incorporates your particular topic and the outcome you intend— what you want readers to do or think as a result of reading your writing.

To explain how to pitch a knuckleball so that readers can do it themselves

To explain how Annie Dillard's "Total Eclipse" builds to its climax so that readers appreciate the author's skill

To explain why the county has been unable to attract new businesses so that readers better understand the local economic slump

To persuade readers to support the college administration's plan for more required courses

To argue against additional regulation of health-maintenance organizations so that readers will perceive the disadvantages for themselves

To argue for additional gun-control laws so that readers will agree on their necessity

Often, a writing assignment will specify or imply both a general and a specific purpose. Say, for instance, that a psychology teacher assigns a review of the research on infants' perception of color. You know that the purpose is generally to explain, more specifically to summarize and analyze the established findings on the topic. You want readers to come away understanding the current state of the investigation into the topic. In addition, you want your instructor to see that you can competently read others' work and write about it. (See below for more on purpose in academic writing.)

With any writing assignment, try to define your specific purpose as soon as you have formed a question about your subject. Don't worry, though, if you feel uncertain of your purpose at the start. Sometimes you may not discover your purpose until you begin drafting, or you may find that your initial sense of purpose changes as you move through the writing process.

EXERCISE 9
Finding purpose in assignments

For each of your questions from Exercise 3 (pp. 8–9), suggest a likely general purpose (entertainment, self-expression, explanation, persuasion) and try to define a specific purpose as well. Make audience part of your suggestions: what would you want readers to do or think in each case?

EXERCISE 10
Considering your past work: Defining a purpose

Look over two or three things you've written in the past year or so. What was your specific purpose in each one? How did the purpose influence your writing? Did you achieve your purpose?

EXERCISE 11
Defining a purpose for your essay

For your essay-in-progress, use your thinking so far about topic (Exercise 5, p. 9) and audience (Exercise 8, p. 13) to define a general and specific purpose for your writing.

1f   Writing in academic situations

When you write for your college courses, you work within a culture of teachers and students who have specific expectations. As noted earlier, these expectations and the particular writing assignment will likely shape your choice of subject and your purpose. The expectations should also shape the structure of your writing, the

http://www.ablongman.com/littlebrown
For added help with academic writing, click on
➤ **The writing process**
  ➤ **Web links** ➤ **The writing situation**

mix of general statements and specific information, the tone you assume, even the fine points of grammar and usage.

One caution: Generalizations about "academic writing" go only so far because each discipline has its own conventions for ideas, support, organization, and presentation. See Chapters 52–55 on the humanities, social sciences, and natural and applied sciences.

CULTURE LANGUAGE Language and culture interact, each influencing the other. American academic prose serves and shapes the culture of US higher education and is in turn influenced by its use in that culture. Its expectations may differ from the ways you are used to speaking, writing, and reading, especially if your first language is not English or if it is a dialect of English besides that used for academic writing. Throughout the handbook, the symbol opening this paragraph highlights common trouble spots in academic writing.

1 ■ Writing for the instructor

Much of your academic writing will have only one reader besides you: the instructor of the course for which you are writing. Like everyone else, instructors have preferences and pet peeves, but you'll waste time and energy trying to anticipate them. Do attend to written and spoken directions for assignments, of course. But otherwise view your instructor as a representative of a larger culture whose response will be guided by the culture's expectations.

- In a composition course the instructor will represent the audience specified by the assignment or (if no audience was specified) the group you evidently intend to address—perhaps your classmates or the school administration or readers of the town newspaper. The instructor's evaluation of your work will depend on how well you communicate with your target readers.
- In courses such as literature, psychology, management, or chemistry, the instructor will represent practitioners of the discipline. He or she will look for your command of the discipline's research methods, principles, and vocabulary, as well as your ability to organize and express ideas appropriately for the discipline.

In each of your courses, your instructor will also be serving as a coach, guiding you toward achieving the goals of the course. But you'll need to do your part, too, presenting yourself as a serious student of your subject, alert to your readers' expectations.

2 ■ Considering content and structure

Unless you write papers in only one discipline, you will find wide variation in what your instructors expect for the content and structure of your papers. However, you will also find important similarities because all academic writing shares the broad aim of exchanging and often creating knowledge. Mixed with traditions of prose in the United States, this aim results in writing with distinctive features, including the following:

- The organization and presentation are straightforward, as simple as the content and purpose allow.
- A central idea or claim, called a **thesis,** controls the entire paper. (See p. 31.)
- The thesis is clearly stated, usually near the beginning.
- The thesis is supported with evidence drawn from research and sometimes from the writer's own experience.
- Paragraphs break content into chunks. Each paragraph usually focuses on a stated idea supporting the thesis and provides specific evidence for the idea.
- Sentences, paragraphs, and sections are clearly related so that readers always know where they are in the paper's development.

CULTURE LANGUAGE ❧ These features are far from universal. In other cultures, academic writers may be indirect, may expect readers to discover the thesis, or may work mainly from support to thesis instead of the other way around. Recognizing such differences between practices in your native culture and in the United States can help you adapt to US academic writing.

3 ▪ Using language

American academic writing relies on a dialect called **standard American English.** The dialect is also used in business, the professions, government, the media, and other sites of social and economic power where people of diverse backgrounds must communicate with one another. It is "standard" not because it is better than other forms of English, but because it is accepted as the common language, much as the dollar bill is accepted as the common currency.

You'll recognize standard American English as the dialect used in this handbook, in magazines and newspapers, and on television news. But you might also notice that the dialect varies a lot, from the formal English of a President's State of the Union address through the middle formality of this handbook to the informal chitchat between anchors on morning TV. Even in academic writing, standard American English allows much room for the writer's own voice, as these two passages on the same topic show:

More formal

One technique for heightening the emotional appeal of advertisements is "color engineering." Adding color to a product or the surrounding advertisement can increase sales despite the fact that the color serves no practical purpose. For example, until the 1920s manufacturers made fountain pens of hard black rubber. When they suddenly introduced colorful pens, sales rose dramatically.

Less formal

"Color engineering" can intensify the emotional appeal of advertisements. New color in a product or the surrounding ad can boost sales even when the color serves no other use. In the 1920s, for example, fountain-pen makers introduced colorful pens along with the familiar ones of hard black rubber. Sales shot up.

Both examples illustrate several common features of standard American English as it is used in academic writing:

- They follow the rules and conventions of grammar and usage described in guides to the dialect, such as this handbook.
- They use a standard vocabulary, not one that only some groups understand, such as slang, an ethnic or regional dialect, or another language. (See pp. 542–46 for more on specialized vocabularies.)
- The examples create some distance between writer and reader with the third person (*he, she, it, they*). The first person (*I, we*) is sometimes appropriate to express personal opinions or invite readers to think along, but not with a strongly explanatory purpose (*I discovered that "color engineering" can intensify* . . .). The second person (*you*) is appropriate only in addressing readers directly (as in this handbook), and even then it may seem condescending or too chummy (*You should know that "color engineering" can heighten* . . .).

CULTURE LANGUAGE ⟩ If your first language is not English or is an English dialect besides standard American, you know well the power of communicating with others who share your language. Learning to write standard American English in no way requires you to abandon your first language. Like most multilingual people, you are probably already adept at switching between languages as the situation demands—speaking one way with your relatives, say, and another way with an employer. As you practice academic writing, you'll develop the same flexibility.

EXERCISE 12
Considering your past work: Writing in academic situations
Look back at a paper you wrote for a course in high school or college. To what extent does it share the features of academic writing discussed in the preceding section? How does it differ?

EXERCISE 13
Considering your native language or dialect **CULTURE LANGUAGE** ⟩
What main similarities and differences do you notice between writing in your native language or dialect and writing for US college courses? Consider especially content, structure, and the expression of ideas. Which differences do you think are easiest to bridge? Which are most difficult? Why?

CHAPTER 2

Developing and Shaping Ideas

Once you have assessed your writing situation, or even while you're assessing it, you'll begin answering the question you posed about your subject (p. 7). As you generate ideas and information, they in turn may cause you to rephrase your lead question, which will open up new areas to explore. Throughout this stage, you'll bring order to your thoughts, eventually focusing and organizing them so that readers will respond as you intend.

2a Discovering ideas

For some writing projects, you may have little difficulty finding what you have to say about your topic: possible answers to your starting question will tumble forth as ideas on paper or screen. But when you're stuck for what to say, you'll have to coax answers out. Instead of waiting around for inspiration to strike, use a technique to get your mind working. Anything is appropriate: if you like to make drawings or take pictures, for instance, then try that.

The following pages describe some strategies for discovering ideas. These strategies are to be selected from, not followed in sequence: some may help you during early stages of the writing process, even before you're sure of your topic; others may help you later on; and one or two may not help at all. Experiment to discover which strategies work best for you.

Note *Whatever strategy or strategies you use, do your work in writing, not just in your head.* Your work will be retrievable, and the act of writing will help you concentrate and lead you to fresh, sometimes surprising, insights. If you participate in online collaboration to develop topics, your activities will probably be stored electroni-

---

http://www.ablongman.com/littlebrown
For added help with discovering ideas, click on
➤ **The writing process**
  ➤ **Downloads** ➤ **Questions about patterns**
    ➤ **Web links** ➤ **Discovering and shaping ideas**

Techniques for developing a topic

- Keep a journal (below).
- Observe your surroundings (p. 22).
- Freewrite (p. 23).
- Make a list or brainstorm (p. 24).
- Cluster (p. 26).
- Ask the journalist's questions (p. 26).
- Use the patterns of development (p. 27).
- Read (p. 29).
- Think critically (p. 29).

cally so that you can review and use the work. Ask your instructor how to reach the online files.

  CULTURE LANGUAGE ⤷ The discovery process encouraged here rewards rapid writing without a lot of thinking beforehand about what you will write or how. If your first language is not standard American English, you may find it helpful initially to do this exploratory writing in your native language or dialect and then to translate the worthwhile material for use in your drafts. This process can be productive, but it is extra work. You may want to try it at first and gradually move to composing in standard American English.

1 ■ Keeping a journal

A place to record thoughts and observations, a **journal** can be a good source of ideas for writing. It is a kind of diary, but one more concerned with ideas than with day-to-day events. *Journal* comes from the Latin for "daily," and many journal keepers do write faithfully every day; others make entries less regularly, when the mood strikes or an insight occurs or they have a problem to work out.

Advantages of a journal

Writing in a journal, you are writing to yourself. That means you don't have to worry about main ideas, organization, correct grammar and spelling, or any of the other requirements of public writing. You can work out your ideas and feelings without the pressure of an audience "out there" who will evaluate your thinking and expression. The freedom and flexibility of a journal can be liberating. Like many others, you may find writing easier, more fun, and more rewarding than you thought possible.

You can keep a journal either on paper (such as a notebook) or on a computer. If you write in the journal every day, or almost, even just for a few minutes, the routine will loosen up your writing muscles and improve your confidence. Indeed, journal keepers often become dependent on the process for the writing practice it gives them, the concentrated thought it encourages, and the connection it fosters between personal, private experience and public information and events.

Usually for the same reasons, teachers of writing and other subjects sometimes require students to keep journals. The teachers may even collect students' journals to monitor progress, but they read the journals with an understanding of purpose (in other words, they do not evaluate work that was not written to be evaluated), and they usually just credit rather than grade the work.

CULTURE LANGUAGE ⤷   A journal can be especially helpful if your first language is not standard American English. You can practice writing to improve your fluency, try out sentence patterns, and experiment with vocabulary words. Equally important, you can experiment with applying what you know from experience to what you read and observe.

Uses of a journal

Two uses of a journal are discussed elsewhere in this book: a reading journal, in which you think critically (in writing) about what you read (pp. 116–17, 787–88); and a research journal, in which you record your activities and ideas while you pursue a research project (pp. 607–08). But you can use a journal for other purposes as well. Here are just a few:

- Confide your hopes.
- Write about your own history: an event in your family's past, a troubling incident in your life, a change you've seen.
- Analyze a relationship that disturbs you.
- Explore your reactions to current events, movies, television, music, or Web sites.
- Prepare for or respond to a course you're taking by puzzling over a reading or a class discussion.
- Build ideas for specific writing assignments.
- Sketch possible designs for a Web composition you are developing, or track the progress of the site's development.
- Practice various forms or styles of writing—for instance, poems or songs, reviews of movies, or reports for TV news.

The writing you produce in your journal will help you learn and grow, and even the personal and seemingly nonacademic entries can supply ideas when you are seeking a subject to write about or are developing an essay. A thought you recorded months ago about a chemistry lab may provide direction for a research paper on the history of science. Two entries about arguments with your brother may suggest what you need to anchor a psychology paper on sibling relations. If you keep your journal on a computer, you can even copy passages from it directly into your drafts.

The following student samples give a taste of journal writing for different purposes. In the first, Charlie Gabnes tries to work out a personal problem with his child:

> Will's tantrums are getting worse—more often, more intense. Beginning to realize it's affecting my feelings for him. I feel resentment sometimes, and it's not as easy for me to cool off afterward as for him. Also I'm afraid of him sometimes for fear a tantrum will start, so treat him with kid gloves. How do we break this cycle?

In the next example Megan Polanyis ponders something she learned from her biology textbook:

> *Ecology* and *economics* have the same root—Greek word for house. Economy = managing the house. Ecology = studying the house. In ecology the house is all of nature, ourselves, the other animals, the plants, the earth, the air, the whole environment. Ecology has a lot to do with economy: study the house in order to manage it.

In the next example Sara Ling responds to an experience. (We'll follow Ling's writing process in this chapter and the next.)

> Had an exchange today on the snowboarding forum with a woman who joined the forum a while ago. She says she signed on at first with a screen name that didn't give away her gender, and she didn't tell anyone she was a woman. She was afraid the guys on the forum might shout her down. She waited until she'd established herself as an experienced snowboarder. Then she revealed her gender, and no one reacted badly. She asked me about my experiences, since my screen name says Sara. Had to admit I'd had problems of the what-does-a-girl-know sort. Wish I'd taken her approach.

2 ■ Observing your surroundings

Sometimes you can find a good subject or good ideas by looking around you, not in the half-conscious way most of us move from place to place in our daily lives but deliberately, all senses alert. On a bus, for instance, are there certain types of passengers? What seems to be on the driver's mind? On campus, which buildings stand out? Are bicyclists and pedestrians at peace with each other?

To get the most from observation, you should have a notepad and pen or pencil handy for notes and sketches. If you have a camera, you may find that the lens sees things your unaided eyes do not notice. (When observing or photographing people, though, keep some distance, take photographs quickly, and avoid staring. Otherwise, your subjects will feel uneasy.) Back at your desk, study your notes, sketches, or photographs for oddities or patterns that you'd like to explore further.

In some academic writing, you'll be expected to formalize observation with surveys, interviews, or experiments. See pages 648 and 831.

3 ■ Freewriting

Writing into a subject

Many writers find subjects or discover ideas by **freewriting:** writing without stopping for a certain amount of time (say, ten minutes) or to a certain length (say, one page). The goal of freewriting is to generate ideas and information from *within* yourself by going around the part of your mind that doesn't want to write or can't think of anything to write. You let words themselves suggest other words. *What* you write is not important; that you *keep* writing is. Don't stop, even if that means repeating the same words until new words come. Don't go back to reread, don't censor ideas that seem dumb or repetitious, and above all don't stop to edit: grammar, punctuation, vocabulary, spelling, and the like are irrelevant at this stage.

The physical act of freewriting may give you access to ideas you were unaware of. For example, the following freewriting by a student, Robert Benday, drew him into the subject of writing as a disguise:

> Write to write. Seems pretty obvious, also weird. What to gain by writing? never anything before. Writing seems always—always— Getting corrected for trying too hard to please the teacher, getting corrected for not trying hard enuf. Frustration, nail biting, sometimes getting carried away making sentences to tell stories, not even true stories, *esp.* not true stories, *that* feels like creating something. Writing just pulls the story out of me. The story lets me be someone else, gives me a disguise.

(A later phase of Benday's writing appears on p. 26.)

If you write on a computer, try this technique for moving forward while freewriting: turn off your computer's monitor, or turn its brightness control all the way down so that the screen is dark. The computer will record what you type but keep it from you and thus prevent you from tinkering with your prose. This **invisible writing** may feel uncomfortable at first, but it can free the mind for very creative results. When you've finished freewriting, simply turn the monitor on or turn up the brightness control to read what you've written, and then save or revise it as appropriate. Later, you may be able to transfer some of your freewriting directly into your draft.

CULTURE LANGUAGE Invisible writing can be especially helpful if you are uneasy writing in standard American English and you tend to worry about errors while writing. The blank computer screen leaves you no choice but to explore ideas without giving attention to the way you are expressing them. If you choose to write with the monitor on, concentrate on *what* you want to say, not *how* you're saying it.

Focused freewriting

Focused freewriting is more concentrated: you start with your question about your subject and answer it without stopping for, say, fifteen minutes or one full page. As in all freewriting, you push to bypass mental blocks and self-consciousness, not debating what to say or editing what you've written. With focused freewriting, though, you let the physical act of writing take you into and around your subject.

An example of focused freewriting can be found in the work of Sara Ling, whose journal entry appears on page 22. In a composition course, Ling's instructor had distributed "Welcome to Cyberbia," an essay by M. Kadi about communication on the Internet. The instructor then gave the following assignment:

> M. Kadi's "Welcome to Cyberbia" holds that the Internet will do little to bridge differences among people because its users gravitate toward other users who are like themselves in most respects. Nearly ten years after Kadi wrote, do her concerns seem valid? Can the Internet serve as a medium for positive change in the way people of diverse backgrounds relate to each other? If so, how? If not, why not? In an essay of 500–700 words, respond to Kadi's essay with a limited and well-supported opinion of your own. The first draft is due Monday, April 4, for class discussion.

On first reading Kadi's essay, Ling had been impressed with its tight logic but had found unconvincing its pessimistic view of the Internet's potential. She reread the essay and realized that some of Kadi's assertions did not correspond to her own Internet experiences. This discovery led Ling to a question: *How might the Internet help to break down barriers between people?* Her focused freewriting began to develop an answer:

> Kadi says we only meet people like ourselves on the Internet, but I've met lots who have very different backgrounds and interests— or "turned out to have" is more like it, since I didn't know anything about them at first. There's the anonymity thing, but Kadi ignores it. You can be anyone or no one. People can get to know me and my ideas without knowing I'm female or Asian American or a student. Then they can find out the facts about me, but the facts will be less likely to get in the way of communication. Communication without set identity, especially physical appearance. This could make for more tolerance of others, of difference.

With this freewriting, Ling moved beyond her initial response to Kadi's essay into her own views of how anonymity on the Internet could improve communication among diverse groups.

4 ▪ Making a list

Like focused freewriting, list making requires opening yourself to everything that seems even remotely connected to your topic, without concern for order or repetition or form of expression. You can let your topic percolate for a day or more, recording thoughts on it whenever they occur. (For this approach to work, you need to keep paper or a computer with you at all times.) Or, in a method more akin to freewriting, you can **brainstorm** about the topic—that is, focus intently on the topic for a fixed amount of time (say, fifteen minutes), pushing yourself to list every idea and detail that comes to mind.

Like freewriting, brainstorming requires turning off your internal editor so that you keep moving ahead instead of looping back over what you have already written to correct it. It makes no difference whether the ideas and details are expressed in phrases or complete sentences. It makes no difference if they seem silly or irrelevant. Just keep pushing. If you are working on a computer, the technique of invisible writing, described on page 23, can help you move forward.

Here is an example of brainstorming by a student, Johanna Abrams, answering *What can a summer job teach?*

> summer work teaches—
>> how to look busy while doing nothing
>> how to avoid the sun in summer
>> seriously: discipline, budgeting money, value of money
>
> which job? Burger King cashier? baby-sitter? mail-room clerk?
> mail room: how to sort mail into boxes: this is learning??
> how to survive getting fired—humiliation, outrage
> Mrs. King! the mail-room queen as learning experience
> the shock of getting fired: what to tell parents, friends?
> Mrs. K was so rigid—dumb procedures
> Mrs. K's anger, resentment: the disadvantages of being smarter than your boss
> The odd thing about working in an office: a world with its own rules for how to act
> what Mr. D said about the pecking order—big chick (Mrs. K) pecks on little chick (me)
> probably lots of Mrs. Ks in offices all over—offices are all barnyards
> Mrs. K a sad person, really—just trying to hold on to her job, preserve her self-esteem
> a job can beat you down—destroy self-esteem, make you desperate enough to be mean to other people
> how to preserve/gain self-esteem from work??
> if I'd known about the pecking order, I would have been less showoffy, not so arrogant

(A later phase of Abrams's writing appears on pp. 38–39.)

When you think you've exhausted the ideas on your topic, you can edit and shape the list into a preliminary outline of your paper (see pp. 35–38). Working on a computer makes this step fairly easy:

you can delete weak ideas, expand strong ones, and rearrange items with a few keystrokes. You can also freewrite from the list if you think some items are especially promising and deserve more exploration.

5 ■ Clustering

Like freewriting and list making, **clustering** draws on free association and rapid, unedited work. But it also emphasizes the *relations* between ideas by combining writing and nonlinear drawing. When clustering, you radiate outward from a center point—your topic. When an idea occurs, you pursue related ideas in a branching structure until they seem exhausted. Then you do the same with other ideas, staying open to connections, continuously branching out or drawing arrows.

The example of clustering below shows how Robert Benday used the technique for ten minutes to expand on the topic of creative writing as a means of disguise, an idea he arrived at through freewriting (see p. 23). Though he ventured into one dead end, Benday also circled into the interesting possibility (at the bottom) that the fiction writer is like a god who forgives himself by creating characters that represent his good and bad qualities.

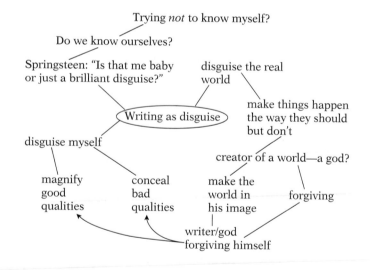

6 ■ Using the journalist's questions

Asking yourself a set of questions about your topic—and writing out the answers—can help you look at the topic objectively and see fresh possibilities in it. Asking questions can also provide some structure to the development of ideas.

One such set of questions is that posed by a journalist with a story to report:

Who was involved?
What happened and what were the results?
When did it happen?
Where did it happen?
Why did it happen?
How did it happen?

These questions can also be useful in probing an essay topic, especially if you are telling a story or examining causes and effects. (See also the next page.)

7 ■ Using the patterns of development

The **patterns of development**—such as narration, definition, comparison and contrast, and classification—are ways we think about and understand a vast range of subjects, from our own daily experiences to the most complex scientific theories. They also serve as strategies and patterns for writing about these subjects, as illustrated by the discussions and paragraph-length examples on pages 92–101.

To see your subject from many angles and open up ideas about it, you can ask the following questions based on the patterns of development. Not all these questions will be productive, but at least a few should open up new possibilities.

You can download the questions from this book's Web site: see the box on page 19. Save the list in a file of its own, duplicate it for each writing project, and insert appropriate answers between the questions. Print your answers so they're handy while you develop your paper. You can also move passages from the answers directly into your draft.

How did it happen?

In **narration** you develop the subject as a story, with important events usually arranged chronologically (as they occurred in time): for instance, an exciting basketball game or the steps leading to a war.

How does it look, sound, feel, smell, taste?

In **description** you use sensory details to give a clear impression of a person, place, thing, or feeling, such as a friend, a favorite room, a building, or an experience.

What are examples of it or reasons for it?

The pattern of **illustration** or **support** suggests development with one or more examples of the subject (one couple's efforts to adopt a child, say, or three television soap operas) or with the reasons for believing or doing something (three reasons for major-ing in English, four reasons for driving defensively).

What is it? What does it encompass, and what does it exclude?

These questions lead to **definition:** specifying what the subject is and is not to give a precise sense of its meaning. Abstract terms—such as *justice, friendship,* and *art*—especially need defining. (See p. 146.)

What are its parts or characteristics?

Using the pattern of **division** or **analysis,** you separate a subject such as a bicycle or a short story into its elements and examine the relations between elements. The first step in critical thinking, analy-sis is also discussed on pages 125–26.

What groups or categories can it be sorted into?

Classification involves separating a large group (such as cars) into smaller groups (subcompact, compact, and so on) based on the characteristics of the individual items (the sizes of the cars). Another example: academic, business, personal, literary, and other types of writing.

How is it like, or different from, other things?

With **comparison and contrast** you point out the similarities and differences between ideas, objects, people, places, and so on: the differences between two similar computer systems, for instance, or the similarities between two opposing political candidates.

Is it comparable to something that is in a different class but more familiar to readers?

This question leads to **analogy,** an extended comparison of un-like subjects. Analogy is often used to explain a topic that may be unfamiliar to readers (for instance, the relation of atoms in a mole-cule) by reference to a familiar topic (two people slow dancing).

Why did it happen, or what results did it have?

With **cause-and-effect analysis,** you explain why something happened or what its consequences were or will be, or both: the causes of cerebral palsy, the effects of a Supreme Court decision, the causes and effects of a gradual change in the climate.

How do you do it, or how does it work?

In **process analysis** you explain how the subject happens (how a plant grows, how a robot works) or how it is accomplished (how to write an essay).

As you can see on pages 92–101, the patterns of development also provide a means of introducing information in paragraphs. Further discussion of how the patterns may combine in an essay ap-pears on pages 110–12.

8 ▪ Reading

Many assignments require reading. To respond to M. Kadi's essay about the Internet, for instance, Sara Ling had to digest Kadi's work. Essays on literary works as well as research papers also demand reading. But even when reading is not required by an assignment, it can help you locate or develop your subject by introducing you to ideas you didn't know or expanding on what you do know.

Say you were writing in favor of amateur athletics, a subject to which you had given a lot of thought. You might be inclined to proceed entirely on your own, drawing on facts, examples, and opinions already in your head. But a little digging in sources might open up more. For instance, an article in *Time* magazine could introduce you to an old rule for amateur status, or a posting to an online newsgroup could suggest a pro-amateurism argument that hadn't occurred to you.

People often read passively, absorbing content like blotters, not interacting with it. To read for ideas, you need to be more active, probing text and illustrations with your mind, nurturing any sparks they set off. Always write while you read, taking notes on content and—just as important—on what the content makes you *think*. (See pp. 115–32 for specific guidelines on the process of active reading.)

Note Whenever you use the information or ideas of others in your writing, you must acknowledge your sources in order to avoid the serious offense of plagiarism. (See Chapter 47.)

9 ▪ Thinking critically

Even if you do not read for information and ideas on your subject, you can still think critically about it. Critical thinking (discussed on pp. 114–32) can produce creative ideas by leading you to see what is not obvious. It can also lead you systematically to conclusions about your subject.

Sara Ling, writing about communication on the Internet, used the operations of critical thinking to explore her topic:

- **Analysis:** What are the subject's elements or characteristics? Ling looked at the ways Internet users can communicate because of their anonymity.
- **Interpretation:** What is the meaning or significance of the elements? Ling saw that the anonymity of Internet users could help them transcend their physical differences.
- **Synthesis:** How do the elements relate to each other, or how does this subject relate to another one? Ling perceived important and hopeful differences between anonymous Internet communication and face-to-face interaction.
- **Evaluation:** What is the value or significance of the subject? Ling concluded that by making people more tolerant of one

another, the Internet could help build community out of diversity.

EXERCISE 1
Considering your past work: Developing a topic

In the past how have you generated the ideas for writing? Have you used any of the techniques described on the preceding pages (perhaps not called by the same names)? Have you found the process of generating ideas to be especially enjoyable or difficult? If some writing tasks have been easier than others, what do you think made the difference?

EXERCISE 2
Keeping a journal

If you haven't already started a journal on your own or in response to Chapter 1, Exercise 1 (p. 3), try to do so now. Every day for at least a week, write for a minimum of fifteen minutes about anything on your mind—or consult the list on page 21 for ideas of what to write about. At the end of the week, review and write about your experience and your journal entries. What did you like about journal writing? What didn't you like? What did you learn about yourself or the world from the writing? What use can you put this knowledge to?

EXERCISE 3
Using freewriting, brainstorming, or clustering

If you haven't tried any of them before, experiment with freewriting, brainstorming, or clustering. Continue with the topic you selected in Chapter 1, Exercise 5 (p. 9), or begin with a new topic. Write or draw for at least ten minutes without stopping to reread and edit. (Try using invisible writing as described on p. 23 if you're freewriting or brainstorming on a computer.) When you finish your experiment, examine what you have written for ideas and relationships that could help you develop the topic. What do you think of the technique you tried? Did you have any difficulties with it? Did it help you loosen up and generate ideas?

EXERCISE 4
Sending an online query

When you have spent some time developing your topic, consider any doubts you may have or any information you still need. Send an online message to your classmates posing your questions and asking for their advice and insights.

EXERCISE 5
Developing your topic

Use at least two of the discovery techniques discussed on the preceding pages to develop the topic you selected in Chapter 1, Exercise 5 (p. 9). (If you completed Exercise 3, then use one additional technique.) Later exercises for your essay-in-progress will be based on the ideas you generate in this exercise.

2b Developing a thesis

Your readers will expect an essay you write to be focused on a central idea, or **thesis,** to which all the essay's paragraphs, all its general statements and specific information, relate. The thesis is the controlling idea, the main point, the conclusion you have drawn about the evidence you have accumulated. It is the answer to the question you have been posing about your subject.

A thesis will probably not leap fully formed into your head. You may begin with an idea you want to communicate, but you will need to refine that idea to fit the realities of the paper you write. And often you will have to write and rewrite before you come to a conclusion about what you have. Still, it's wise to try to pin down your thesis when you have a fairly good stock of ideas. Then the thesis can help you start drafting, help keep you focused, and serve as a point of reference when changes inevitably occur.

1 ■ Conceiving a thesis statement

A thesis is an idea. Spelling out the idea in a **thesis statement** gives you something concrete to work with. Eventually you may place your thesis statement or (more likely) a revised version in the introduction of your final essay as a promise to readers of what they can expect.

As an expression of the thesis, the thesis statement serves three crucial functions and one optional one.

Functions of the thesis statement

- The thesis statement **narrows your subject** to a single, central idea that you want readers to gain from your essay.
- It **claims something specific and significant** about your subject, a claim that requires support.
- It **conveys your purpose,** your reason for writing.
- It often concisely **previews the arrangement of ideas.**

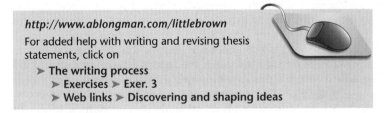

http://www.ablongman.com/littlebrown
For added help with writing and revising thesis statements, click on
➤ **The writing process**
  ➤ **Exercises** ➤ **Exer. 3**
  ➤ **Web links** ➤ **Discovering and shaping ideas**

Here are some examples of questions and answering thesis statements. As assertions, the thesis statements each consist of a topic (usually naming the general subject) and a claim about the topic.

Question	Thesis statement
1. What are the advantages of direct distribution of music via the Web?	Because artists can now publish their music directly via the Web, consumers have many more choices than traditional distribution allows. [*Topic:* consumers. *Claim:* have many more choices.]
2. How did Home Inc. survive the scandal over its hiring practices?	After Home Inc.'s hiring practices were exposed in the media, the company avoided a scandal with policy changes and a well-publicized outreach to employees and consumers. [*Topic:* the company. *Claim:* avoided a scandal in two ways.]
3. What steps can prevent juvenile crime?	Juveniles can be diverted from crime by active learning programs, full-time sports, and intervention by mentors and role models. [*Topic:* juveniles. *Claim:* can be diverted from crime in three ways.]
4. Why did Abraham Lincoln delay in emancipating the slaves?	Lincoln delayed emancipating any slaves until 1863 because his primary goal was to restore and preserve the Union, with or without slavery. [*Topic:* Lincoln's delay. *Claim:* was caused by his goal of preserving the Union.]
5. Which college students should be entitled to federal aid?	As an investment in its own economy, the United States should provide a tuition grant to any college student who qualifies academically. [*Topic:* United States. *Claim:* should provide a tuition grant to any college student who qualifies academically.]
6. Why should strip-mining be controlled?	Strip-mining should be tightly controlled in this region to reduce its pollution of water resources, its destruction of the land, and its devastating effects on people's lives. [*Topic:* strip-mining. *Claim:* should be tightly controlled for three reasons.]

Notice that statements 3 and 6 clearly predict the organization of the essay that will follow. Notice, too, that every statement conveys the purpose of its writer. Statements 1–4 announce that the writers mainly want to explain something to readers: music choices for consumers, a company's success in avoiding a scandal, and so on. Statements 5 and 6 announce that the authors mainly want to convince readers of something: the federal government should aid qualified college students; strip-mining should be controlled.

 CULTURE LANGUAGE ⟩ In some cultures it is considered rude or unnecessary for a writer to state his or her main idea outright or to state it near the beginning. When writing in American schools or work-places, you can assume that your readers expect a clear and early idea of what you think.

2 ■ Drafting and revising a thesis statement

To draft a thesis statement, begin with your question about your subject. If you have updated the question as you generated ideas and information, answering it can get you started.

Question   Why did Lincoln delay in emancipating the slaves?

Answer   Lincoln's goal was primarily to restore and preserve the Union.

Question   How might the Internet help to break down barriers between people?

Answer   Anonymous Internet communication can bypass physi-cal differences.

The next step is to spell out the answer in a sentence that names the topic and makes a claim about it. Creating this sentence may re-quire several drafts.

Sara Ling went through a common process in writing and re-vising her thesis statement on Internet communication. She first answered her starting question, as shown in the second pair of ex-amples above. Then she tried a statement derived from her answer:

Internet communication that is anonymous can bypass physical differences.

Ling saw that this statement focused on her starting topic (*Internet communication*) but somewhat buried the crucial quality of ano-nymity. And the claim lacked significance: So what? Ling first tried to emphasize her intended subject:

The anonymity of Internet communication . . .

Then she worked on her claim:

. . . can bypass physical differences, and it could build diversity into community.

This statement said why the subject was significant (*it could build diversity into community*) but the idea was tacked on with *and,* not integrated into the statement. Ling tried again, emphasizing cause and effect:

Through bypassing physical differences, the unique anonymity of Internet communication could build diversity into community.

For her final revision, Ling responded to a friend's comment that *bypassing physical differences* was too vague. She spelled out her meaning:

By lowering the barriers of physical appearance, the unique anonymity of Internet communication could build diversity into community.

When you are writing and revising your thesis statement, check
it against the following questions:

Checklist for revising the thesis statement

- How well does the **subject** of your statement capture the subject of
  your paper?
- What **claim** does your statement make about your subject?
- What is the **significance** of the claim? How does it answer "So what?"
  and convey your purpose?
- How can the claim be **limited** or made more **specific**? Does it state a
  single idea and clarify the boundaries of the idea?
- How **unified** is the statement? How does each word and phrase contribute to a single idea?

Here are other examples of thesis statements revised to meet
these requirements:

Original	Revised
This new product brought in over $300,000 last year. [A statement of fact, not a claim about the product: what is significant about the product's success?]	This new product succeeded because of its innovative marketing campaign, including widespread press coverage, in-store entertainment, and a consumer newsletter.
People should not go on fad diets. [A vague statement that needs limiting with one or more reasons: what's wrong with fad diets?]	Fad diets can be dangerous when they deprive the body of essential nutrients or rely excessively on potentially harmful foods.
Televised sports are different from live sports. [A general statement: how are they different, and why is the difference significant?]	Although television cannot transmit all the excitement of a live game, its close-ups and slow-motion replays more than compensate.
Seat belts can save lives, but now carmakers are installing air bags. [Not unified: how do the two parts of the sentence relate?]	If drivers had used lifesaving seat belts more often, carmakers might not have needed to install air bags.

Note You may sometimes need more than one sentence for
your thesis statement, particularly if it requires some buildup:

Modern English, especially written English, is full of bad habits that interfere with clear thinking. Getting rid of these habits is a first step to political regeneration.

—Adapted from GEORGE ORWELL,
"Politics and the English Language"

However, don't use this leeway to produce a wordy, general, or dis-unified statement. The two (or more) sentences must build on each other, and the final one must present the key assertion of your paper.

EXERCISE 6
Evaluating thesis statements
Evaluate the following thesis statements, considering whether each one is sufficiently significant, specific, and unified. Rewrite the statements as necessary to meet these goals.

1. Aggression usually leads to violence, injury, and even death, and we should use it constructively.
2. Electronic mail is invaluable.
3. One evening of a radio talk show amply illustrates both the appeal of such shows and their silliness.
4. Good manners make our society work.
5. The poem is about motherhood.

EXERCISE 7
Considering your past work: Developing a thesis
Have you been aware in the past of focusing your essays on a central idea, or thesis? Have you found it more efficient to try to pin down your idea early or to let it evolve during drafting? To what extent has a thesis helped or hindered you in shaping your draft?

EXERCISE 8
Drafting and revising your own thesis statement
Continuing from Exercise 5 (p. 9), write a significant, specific, and unified thesis statement for your essay-in-progress.

2c Organizing ideas

An effective essay has a recognizable shape—an arrangement of parts that guides readers, helping them see how ideas and details relate to each other and contribute to the whole. You may sometimes let an effective organization emerge over one or more drafts.

http://www.ablongman.com/littlebrown
For added help with organizing ideas, click on
➤ **The writing process**
➤ Video tutorials ➤ Outlining with a word processor
➤ Web links ➤ Discovering and shaping ideas

But many writers find that organizing ideas to some extent before drafting can provide a helpful sense of direction, as a map can help a driver negotiate a half-familiar system of roads. If you feel uncertain about the course your essay should follow or have a complicated topic with many parts, devising a shape for your material can clarify your options.

Before you begin organizing your material, look over all the writing you've done so far—freewriting, notes from reading, whatever. Either on paper or on a computer, pull together a master list of all the ideas and details you think you might want to include. You can add to or subtract from the list as you think about shape.

1 ■ Distinguishing the general and the specific

To organize material for an essay, you need to distinguish general and specific ideas and see the relations between ideas. **General** and **specific** refer to the number of instances or objects included in a group signified by a word. The "ladder" below illustrates a general-to-specific hierarchy.

Most general
↑ life form
| plant
| flowering plant
| rose
| American Beauty rose
↓ Uncle Dan's prize-winning American Beauty rose
Most specific

Here are some tips for arranging your ideas:

■ *Underline, boldface, or circle the most general ideas.* These are the ideas that offer the main support for your thesis statement. They will be more general than the evidence that in turn supports them.

■ *Make connections between each general idea and the more specific details that support it.* On paper, start with a fresh sheet, write each general idea down with space beneath it, and add specific information in the appropriate spaces. On a computer, rearrange supporting information under more general points. Your word processor may include a Comment function that allows you to add notes about connections.

■ *Respect the meanings of ideas.* Think through the implications of ideas as you sort them. Otherwise, your hierarchies could become jumbled, with *rose* illogically subordinated to *animal,* or *life form* somehow subordinated to *rose.*

■ *Remove information that doesn't fit.* If you worry about losing deleted information, transfer the notes to a separate sheet of paper or word-processing file.

■ *Fill holes where support seems skimpy.* If you recognize a hole but don't know what to fill it with, try using a discovery technique such as freewriting or clustering, or go back to your research sources.

■ *Experiment with various arrangements of general ideas and supporting information.* Seek an order that presents your material clearly and logically. On paper, you can cut the master list apart and paste or tape each general idea and its support on a separate piece of paper. Then try different orders for the pages. On a computer, first save the master list and duplicate it. To move material around, select a block of text and either copy and then paste it where you want it or (a little quicker) drag the selected text to where you want it.

dev

2c

2 ■ Choosing an organizing tool

Some writers view outlines as chores and straitjackets, but they need not be dull or confining. There are different kinds of outlines, some more flexible than others. All of them can enlarge and clarify your thinking, showing you patterns of general and specific, suggesting proportions, highlighting gaps or overlaps in coverage.

Many writers use outlines not only before but also after drafting—to check the underlying structure of the draft when revising it (see p. 53). No matter when it's made, though, an outline can change to reflect changes in your thinking. View any outline you make as a tentative sketch, not as a fixed paint-by-numbers diagram.

A scratch or informal outline

For many essays, especially those with a fairly straightforward structure, a simple listing of ideas and perhaps their support may provide adequate direction for your writing.

A **scratch outline** lists the key points of the paper in the order they will be covered. Here is Sara Ling's scratch outline for her essay on Internet communication:

Thesis statement

By lowering the barriers of physical appearance, the unique anonymity of Internet communication could build diversity into community.

Scratch outline

No fear of prejudgment
    Physical attributes unknown—age, race, gender, etc.
    We won't be shut out because of appearance
Inability to prejudge others
    Assumptions based on appearance
    Meeting of minds only
    Finding shared interests and concerns

Ling put more into this outline than its simplicity might imply, not only working out an order for her ideas but also sketching their implications.

An **informal outline** is usually more detailed than a scratch outline, including key general points and the specific evidence for them. A student's informal outline appears below.

Thesis statement

After Home Inc.'s hiring practices were exposed in the media, the company avoided a scandal with policy changes and a well-publicized outreach to employees and consumers.

Informal outline

Background on scandal
   Previous hiring practices
   Media exposure and public response (brief)
Policy changes
   Application forms
   Interviewing procedures
   Training of personnel
Outreach to employees
   Signs and letters
   Meetings and workshops
Outreach to consumers
   Press conference
   Store signs
   Advertising—print and radio

A tree diagram

In a **tree diagram,** ideas and details branch out in increasing specificity. Like any outline, the diagram can warn of gaps, overlaps, and digressions. But unlike more linear outlines, it can be supplemented and extended indefinitely, so it is easy to alter for new ideas and arrangements discovered during drafting and revision.

On the facing page is Johanna Abrams's tree diagram, based on her earlier list of ideas on a summer job (p. 25) and the following thesis statment:

Thesis statement

Two months working in a large government agency taught me that an office's pecking order should be respected.

Each main part of the four-part diagram represents a different general idea about the summer-job experience. Within each part, information grows more specific as it branches downward.

A tree diagram or other visual map can be especially useful for planning a project for the World Wide Web. The diagram can help you lay out the organization of your project and its links and then later can serve as a site map for your readers. (For more on composing for the Web, see pp. 220–30.)

Tree diagram

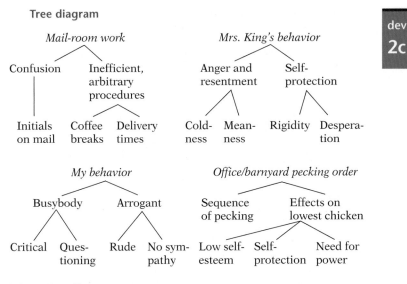

A formal outline

For complex topics requiring complex arrangements of ideas and support, you may want or be required to construct a **formal outline.** More rigidly arranged and more detailed than other outlines, a formal outline not only lays out main ideas and their support but also shows the relative importance of all the essay's elements and how they connect with one another.

Note Because of its structure, a formal outline can be an excellent tool for checking the arrangement of a draft before revising it. (See p. 52.)

On the basis of her scratch outline (p. 37), Sara Ling prepared this formal outline for her essay on the Internet:

Thesis statement
By lowering the barriers of physical appearance, the unique anonymity of Internet communication could build diversity into community.

Formal outline
I. No fear of being prejudged
   A. Unknown physical attributes
      1. Gender
      2. Age
      3. Race
      4. Style
   B. Freer communication
   C. No automatic rejection
II. Inability to prejudge others
   A. No assumptions based on appearance
      1. Body type

   2. Physical disability
   3. Race
 B. Discovery of shared interests and concerns
   1. Sports and other activities
   2. Family values
   3. Political views
 C. Reduction of physical bias

Ling's outline illustrates several principles of outlining that can help ensure completeness, balance, and clear relationships. (These principles largely depend on distinguishing between the general and the specific. See pp. 36–37.)

- *All the outline's parts are systematically indented and labeled.* Roman numerals (I, II) label primary divisions of the essay, indented capital letters (A, B) label secondary divisions, and further indented Arabic numerals (1, 2) label principal supporting points and examples. A fourth level would be indented further still and labeled with small letters (a, b). Each succeeding level contains more specific information than the one before it.
- *The outline divides the material into several groups.* An uninterrupted listing of ideas like the one following would indicate a need for tighter, more logical relationships among ideas. (Compare this example with part II of Ling's actual outline.)

 II. Inability to prejudge others
  A. Body type
  B. Physical disability
  C. Race
  D. Sports and other activities
  E. Family values
  F. Political views
  G. Reduction of physical bias

- *Within each part of the outline, distinct topics of equal generality appear in parallel headings* (with the same indention and numbering or lettering). In the following example, points B, C, and D are more specific than point A, not equally general, so they should be subheadings 1, 2, and 3 under it. (See section IIA of Ling's outline.)

  A. No assumptions based on appearance
  B. Body type
  C. Physical disability
  D. Race

- *All subdivided headings in the outline break into at least two parts* because a topic cannot logically be divided into only one part. The following example violates this principle:

  B. Discovery of shared views
   1. Interests and concerns

Principles of the formal outline

- Labels and indentions indicate order and relative importance.
- Sections and subsections reflect logical relationships.
- Topics of equal generality appear in parallel headings.
- Each subdivision has at least two parts.
- Headings are expressed in parallel grammatical form.
- The introduction and conclusion may be omitted (though not, of course, from the essay).

Any single subdivision should be combined with the heading above it (as in section IIB of Ling's actual outline), matched with another subdivision, or rechecked for its relevance to the heading above it.

- *All headings are expressed in parallel grammatical form* (see pp. 428–31 on parallelism). Ling's is a **topic outline,** in which the headings consist of a noun (*fear, attributes, gender,* and the like) with modifiers (*no, unknown physical, no automatic,* and the like). In a **sentence outline** all headings are expressed as full sentences, as in this rewrite of part II of Ling's outline:

II. On the Internet, we are unable to prejudge others.
   A. We cannot make common assumptions based on physical appearance.
      1. People with athletic builds must be unintelligent.
      2. People in wheelchairs must be unapproachable or pathetic.
      3. People of other races must hold views different from our own.
   B. We discover shared interests and concerns.
      1. We find common ground in sports and other activities.
      2. We see that we all feel much the same about our families.
      3. We learn the similarities in each other's political views.
   C. The Internet could reduce physical bias in the world.

See pages 744–45 for a complete sentence outline.

- *The outline covers only the body of the essay, omitting the introduction and the conclusion.* The beginning and the ending are important in the essay itself, but you need not include them in the outline unless you are required to do so or anticipate special problems with their organization.

3 ■ Choosing a structure

Introduction, body, and conclusion

Most essays share a basic shape:

- The **introduction,** usually a paragraph or two, draws readers into the world of the essay. At a minimum, it announces and clarifies the topic. Often, it ends with the thesis statement, making a commitment that the rest of the essay delivers on. (See pp. 103–06 for more on introductions.)

- The **body** of the essay is its long center, the part that develops the thesis and thus fulfills the commitment of the introduction. The paragraphs in the body develop the general points that support the thesis—the items that would be labeled with Roman numerals and capital letters in a formal outline like the one on pages 39–40. These general points are like the legs of a table supporting the top, the thesis. Each general point may take a paragraph or more, with the bulk of the content providing the details, examples, and reasons (the wood of the table) to support the general point and thus the thesis.

- The **conclusion** generally gives readers something to take away from the essay—a summary of ideas, for instance, or a suggested course of action. (See pp. 106–08 for more on conclusions.)

This basic shape applies mainly to traditional essays. A composition for the World Wide Web probably will have a more flexible structure and will lack a formal conclusion. See pages 220–30 for more on composing for the Web.

 CULTURE LANGUAGE If you are not used to reading and writing American academic prose, its pattern of introduction-body-conclusion and the particular schemes discussed below may seem unfamiliar. For instance, instead of introductions that focus quickly on the topic and thesis, you may be used to openings that establish personal connections with readers or that approach the thesis indirectly. And instead of body paragraphs that first emphasize general points and then support those points with specific evidence, you may be used to general statements without support (because writers can assume that readers will supply the evidence themselves) or to evidence without explanation (because writers can assume that readers will infer the general points). When writing American academic prose, you need to take into account readers' expectations for directness and for the statement and support of general points.

The body of an essay

In most writing situations at least one of the schemes listed in the box opposite will be appropriate for organizing the body of an essay. These schemes are so familiar that readers expect them and look for them. Thus the schemes both help you arrange your material and help readers follow you.

Organizing by space or time

Two organizational schemes—spatial and chronological—grow naturally out of the topic. A **spatial organization** is especially appropriate for essays that describe a place, an object, or a person. Following the way people normally survey something, you move through

---

Schemes for organizing ideas in an essay

- Space
- Time
- Emphasis

General to specific	Increasing importance
Specific to general	Decreasing familiarity
Problem-solution	Increasing complexity

---

space from a chosen starting point to other features of the subject. Describing a friend, for instance, you might begin with his shoes and move upward or begin with his face and move downward.

A **chronological organization** reports events as they occurred in time, usually from first to last. This pattern, like spatial organization, corresponds to readers' own experiences and expectations. It suits an essay in which you do one of the following:

- Tell a story about yourself or someone else.
- Explain a process from beginning to end—for instance, how to run a marathon or how a tree converts carbon dioxide to oxygen.
- Recount a sequence of events, such as a championship baseball game or the Battle of Gettysburg.
- Explain the causes that led to an effect, such as a bill passed by the legislature or a car model's design. Alternatively, explain how a cause, such as a flood or a book, had multiple effects.
- Provide the background to a situation—for instance, the separate lives of a group of friends who gather to help in a soup kitchen or the making of a movie that turned out to be a hit.

A chronological organization structures the essay on pages 69–70.

Organizing for emphasis

Some organizational schemes must be imposed on ideas and information to aid readers' understanding and achieve a desired emphasis. Two of these depend on the distinction between the general and the specific, discussed on pages 36–37. The **general-to-specific scheme** is common in expository and argumentative essays that start with a general discussion of the main points and then proceed to specific examples, facts, or other evidence. The following thesis statement forecasts a general-to-specific organization:

> As an investment in its own economy, the United States should provide a tuition grant to any college student who qualifies academically.

The body of the essay might first elaborate on the basic argument and then provide the supporting data.

Sometimes you may anticipate that readers will not appreciate or agree with your general ideas before they see the support for them—for instance, in an expository essay that presents a novel way of looking at common experience, or in an argumentative essay that takes an unpopular view. In these cases a **specific-to-general scheme** can arouse readers' interest in specific examples or other evidence, letting the evidence build to statements of more general ideas. The following thesis statement could be developed in this way:

> Although most of us are unaware of the public relations campaigns directed at us, they can significantly affect the way we think and live.

The writer might devote most of the essay to a single specific example of a public relations campaign and then explain more generally how the example typifies public relations campaigns.

Many argumentative essays use a **problem-solution scheme:** first outline a problem that needs solving; then propose a solution. (If the solution involves steps toward a goal, it may be arranged chronologically.) The following thesis statement announces a problem-solution paper:

> To improve workflow and quality, the data-processing department should add one part-time staffer and retrain three others in the new systems.

A common scheme in both explanations and arguments is the **climactic organization,** in which ideas unfold in order of increasing drama or importance to a climax. For example, the following thesis statement lists three effects of strip-mining in order of their increasing severity, and the essay would cover them in the same order:

> Strip-mining should be tightly controlled in this region to reduce its pollution of water resources, its destruction of the land, and its devastating effects on people's lives.

As this example suggests, the climactic organization works well in arguments because it leaves readers with the most important point freshest in their minds. In exposition such an arrangement can create suspense and thus hold readers' attention.

Expository essays can also be arranged in variations of the climactic pattern. An essay on the effects of air pollution might proceed from **most familiar to least familiar**—from effects readers are likely to know to ones they may not know. Similarly, an essay on various computer languages might proceed from **simplest to most complex,** so that the explanation of each language provides a basis for readers to understand the more difficult one following.

4 ■ Checking for unity and coherence

In conceiving your organization and writing your essay, you should be aware of two qualities of effective writing that relate to organization: unity and coherence. When you perceive that some-one's writing "flows well," you are probably appreciating these two qualities. An essay has **unity** if all its parts relate to and support the thesis statement. Check for unity with these questions:

- Is each main section relevant to the main idea (thesis) of the essay?
- Within main sections of the outline, does each example or detail support the principal idea of that section?

An essay has **coherence** if readers can see the relations among parts and move easily from one thought to the next. Check for coherence with these questions:

- Do the ideas follow in a clear sequence?
- Are the parts of the essay logically connected?
- Are the connections clear and smooth?

A unified and coherent outline will not necessarily guide you to a unified and coherent essay, because so much can change during drafting. Thus you shouldn't be too hard on your outline, in case a seemingly wayward idea proves useful. But do cut obvious digressions and rearrange material that clearly needs moving.

The unity and coherence of an essay begin in its paragraphs, so these two concepts are treated in greater detail in Chapter 4. You may want to consult several sections in particular before you begin drafting:

- The topic sentence and unity (pp. 73–76)
- Transitions and coherence (pp. 78–88, 108–09)
- Linking paragraphs in the essay (pp. 110–12)

Unity and coherence may seem unimportant in compositions for the World Wide Web, in which entire documents are linked to each other so that it's easy to move among them. However, precisely because the Web is such a fluid medium, you risk losing or confusing your readers if you don't consider unity and coherence. Your project should have a clear purpose and clear ideas relating to that purpose, and the connections between ideas should be spelled out to orient readers. (For more on composing for the Web, see pp. 220–30.)

EXERCISE 9
Organizing ideas
The following list of ideas was extracted by a student from freewriting he did for a brief paper on soccer in the United States. Using his thesis statement as a guide, pick out the general ideas and

arrange the relevant specific points under them. In some cases you may have to infer general ideas to cover specific points in the list.

Thesis statement

Despite increasing interest within the United States, soccer may never be the sport here that it is elsewhere because both the potential fans and the potential backers resist it.

List of ideas

Sports seasons are already too crowded for fans.
Soccer rules are confusing to Americans.
A lot of kids play soccer in school, but the game is still "foreign."
Sports money goes where the money is.
Backers are wary of losing money on new ventures.
Fans have limited time to watch.
Fans have limited money to pay for sports.
Backers are concerned with TV contracts.
Previous attempts to start a pro soccer league failed.
TV contracts almost matter more than live audiences.
Failure of the US Football League was costly.
Baseball, football, hockey, and basketball seasons already overlap.
Soccer fans couldn't fill huge stadiums.
American soccer fans are too few for TV interest.

EXERCISE 10
Creating a formal outline

Use your arrangement of general ideas and specific points from Exercise 9 as the basis for a formal topic or sentence outline. Follow the principles given on pages 39–41.

EXERCISE 11
Considering your past work: Organizing ideas

What has been your experience with organizing your writing? Many writers find it difficult. If you do, too, can you say why? What kinds of outlines or other organizing tools have you used? Which have been helpful and which not?

EXERCISE 12
Organizing your own essay

Continuing from Exercise 8 (p. 35), choose an appropriate organization for your essay-in-progress. Then experiment with organizing tools by preparing a tree diagram or other visual map or a scratch, informal, or formal outline.

CHAPTER 3

Drafting and Revising

The separation of drafting and revising from the planning and development discussed in Chapters 1 and 2 is somewhat artificial because the stages almost always overlap during the writing process. Indeed, if you compose on a computer, you may not experience any boundaries between stages at all. Still, your primary goal during the writing process will usually shift from gathering and shaping information to forming connected sentences and paragraphs in a draft and then restructuring and rewriting the draft.

3a Writing the first draft

The only correct drafting style is the one that works for you. Generally, though, the freer and more fluid you are, the better. Some writers draft and revise at the same time, but most let themselves go during drafting and *especially* do not worry about errors. Drafting is the occasion to find and convey meaning through the act of writing. If you fear making mistakes while drafting, that fear will choke your ideas. You draft only for yourself, so errors do not matter. Write freely until you have worked out what you want to say; *then* focus on any mistakes you may have made.

Starting to draft sometimes takes courage, even for seasoned professionals. Students and pros alike find elaborate ways to procrastinate—rearranging shelves, napping, lunching with friends. Such procrastination may actually help you if you let ideas for writing simmer at the same time. At some point, though, enough is enough: the deadline looms; you've got to get started. If the blankness still stares back at you, then try one of the techniques for unblocking given on the next page.

---

http://www.ablongman.com/littlebrown
For added help with drafting, click on
➤ **The writing process**
  ➤ **Video tutorials** ➤ **Overcoming writer's block**
  ➤ **Web links** ➤ **Drafting, revising, editing**

Ways to start drafting

- **Read over what you've already written**—notes, outlines, and so on. Immediately start your draft with whatever comes to mind.
- **Freewrite** (see p. 23).
- **Write scribbles or type nonsense** until words you can use start coming.
- **Pretend you're writing to a friend about your subject.**
- **Describe an image that represents your subject**—a physical object, a facial expression, two people arguing over something, a giant machine gouging the earth for a mine, whatever.
- **Write a paragraph.** Explain what you think your essay will be about when you finish it.
- **Skip the opening and start in the middle.** Or write the conclusion.
- **Start writing the part that you understand best or feel most strongly about.** Using your outline, divide your essay into chunks— say, one for the introduction, another for the first point, and so on. One of these chunks may call out to be written.

You should find some momentum once you've started writing. If not, however, or if your energy flags, try one or more of the following techniques to keep moving ahead:

Ways to *keep* drafting

- **Set aside enough time for yourself.** For a brief essay, a first draft is likely to take at least an hour or two.
- **Work in a quiet place.**
- **Make yourself comfortable.**
- **If you must stop working, write down what you expect to do next.** Then you can pick up where you stopped with minimal disruption.
- **Be as fluid as possible, and don't worry about mistakes.** Spontaneity will allow your attitudes toward your subject to surface naturally in your sentences, and it will also make you receptive to ideas and relations you haven't seen before. Mistakes will be easier to find and correct later, when you're not also trying to create.
- **Keep going.** Skip over sticky spots; leave a blank if you can't find the right word; put alternative ideas or phrasings in brackets so that you can consider them later without bogging down. If an idea pops out of nowhere but doesn't seem to fit in, quickly jot it down on a separate sheet, or write it into the draft and bracket or boldface it for later attention. You can use an asterisk (*) or some other symbol to mark places where you feel blocked or uncertain. (With a word processor, you can later return to these places by using the Find command to locate the symbol.)

- **Resist self-criticism.** Don't worry about your style, grammar, spelling, punctuation, and the like. Don't worry about what your readers will think. These are very important matters, but save them for revision. On a word processor, help yourself resist self-criticism by turning off automatic spelling- or grammar-checking functions (see p. 187) or by trying invisible writing (p. 23).
- **Use your thesis statement and outline** to remind you of your planned purpose, organization, and content.
- **But don't feel constrained by your thesis and outline.** If your writing leads you in a more interesting direction, follow.

If you write on a computer, frequently save the text you're drafting—at least every five or ten minutes or every couple of paragraphs and certainly every time you leave the computer. (Many word processors will automatically save your text as you're writing. See p. 186.) After each writing session, back up your drafts on a separate disk or server. If you can't back up your files, print out paper copies (so-called hard copy).

Whether you compose on paper or on a computer, you may find it difficult to tell whether a first draft is finished. The distinction between drafts can be significant because creating text is different from rethinking it and because your instructor may ask you and your classmates to submit your drafts, either on paper or over a computer network, so that others can give you feedback on them. For your own revision or others' feedback, you might consider a draft finished for any number of reasons: perhaps you've reached the assigned length and have run out of ideas; perhaps you find yourself writing the conclusion; perhaps you've stopped adding content and are just tinkering with words.

Sara Ling's first draft on Internet communication appears below. As you read the draft, mark the thesis statement and each key idea developing the thesis. Note places where you think the ideas could be clearer or better supported.

First draft

Title?

In "Welcome to Cyberbia," written in 1995, M. Kadi predicts that the Internet will lead to more fragmentation in society because people just seek out others like themselves. But Kadi fails to foresee how the unique anonymity of Internet communication could actually build diversity into community by lowering the barriers of physical appearance.

Anonymity on the Internet. It's one of the best things about technology. No one knows your age or gender or race. Whether your fat or thin or neat or sloppy. What kind of clothes you wear. (Maybe your not wearing clothes at all). People who know you personally don't even know who you are with an invented screen name.

We can make ourselves known without first being prejudged because of our physical attributes. For example, I participate in a snowboarding forum that has mostly men. I didn't realize what I was getting into when I used my full name as my screen name. Before long, I had received unfriendly responses such as "What does a girl know?" and "Why don't you go back to knitting?" I guess I had run into a male prejudice against female snowboarders. However, another woman on the forum had no such problems. At first she signed on with a screen name that did not reveal her gender, and no one responded negatively to her messages. When she had contributed for a while, she earned respect from the other snowboarders. When she revealed that she was a woman at that point, no one responded negatively in the way I had experienced. She posed at first as someone different from who she really was and could make herself heard.

We also cannot prejudge others because of their appearance. Often in face-to-face interaction we assume we know things about people just because of the way they look. Assumptions prevent people from discovering their shared interests and concerns, and this is particularly true where race is concerned. The anonymity of the Internet makes physical barriers irrelevant, and only people's minds meet. Because of this, the Internet could create a world free of physical bias.

Logged on to the Internet we can become more tolerant of others. We can become a community.

EXERCISE 1
Analyzing a first draft
Compare Ling's draft with the previous step in her planning (her formal outline) on pages 39–40. List the places in the draft where the act of drafting led Ling to rearrange her information, add or delete material, or explore new ideas.

EXERCISE 2
Considering your past work: Drafting
Think back over a recent writing experience. At what point in the writing process did you begin drafting? How did drafting go—

smoothly, haltingly, painfully, painlessly? If you had difficulties, what were they? If you didn't, why do you think not?

EXERCISE 3
Drafting your essay
Prepare a draft of the essay you began in Chapters 1 and 2. Use your thesis statement and your outline as guides, but don't be unduly constrained by them. Concentrate on opening up options, not on closing them down. Do not, above all, worry about mistakes.

3b   Revising the first draft

Revision literally means "re-seeing"—looking anew at ideas and details, their relationships and arrangement, the degree to which they work or don't work for the thesis. While drafting, you focus inwardly, concentrating on pulling your topic out of yourself. In revising, you look out to your readers, trying to anticipate how they will see your work. You adopt a critical perspective toward your work (see Chapter 5), examining your draft as a pole-vaulter or dancer would examine a videotape of his or her performance. (Writing teachers often ask students to read each other's drafts partly to train the students in using and benefiting from this critical perspective. See p. 65 for more on such collaboration.)

Word processors have removed the mechanical drudgery of revision. With a few keystrokes you can add, delete, and move words, lines, or whole passages. Writers disagree, though, over whether it's better to consider revisions on paper or on screen:

- Working on a paper copy allows you to see the whole draft at once and may be easier to read accurately, but if your work is stored on a computer you then have to key in your changes.
- Working on a computer allows you to see changes as you make them and to experiment with different versions of the same passage, but it can prevent you from seeing your work as a whole.

You may prefer one method over the other, or you may combine methods, reading a paper copy to find problems and then using the computer to try out revisions.

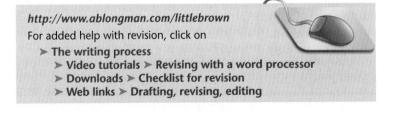

http://www.ablongman.com/littlebrown
For added help with revision, click on
➤ **The writing process**
　　➤ **Video tutorials** ➤ **Revising with a word processor**
　　➤ **Downloads** ➤ **Checklist for revision**
　　➤ **Web links** ➤ **Drafting, revising, editing**

Take a couple of precautions when using a computer for any part of revision:

- Work on a duplicate of your latest draft so that the original remains intact until you're truly finished with it. On the duplicate you can use your word processor's Track Changes function, which shows changes alongside the original text and allows you to accept or reject alterations later.
- Save each draft under its own file name in case you need to consult it for ideas or phrasings. (See p. 185 on naming and managing files.)

1 ■ Gaining distance from your work

Reading your own work critically requires that you create some distance between it and yourself—not always an easy task. The following techniques may help:

Ways to gain distance from your work

- **Take a break after finishing the draft.** A few hours may be enough; a whole night or day is preferable. The break will clear your mind, relax you, and give you some objectivity.
- **Ask someone to read and react to your draft.** Many writing instructors ask their students to submit their first drafts so that the instructor and, often, the other members of the class can serve as an actual audience to help guide revision. (See also pp. 67–68 on receiving and benefiting from comments.)
- **Type a handwritten draft.** The act of transcription can reveal gaps in content or problems in structure.

- **Print out a word-processed draft.** You'll be able to view all pages of the draft at once, and the different medium can reveal weaknesses you didn't see on screen.
- **Outline your draft.** Highlight the main points supporting the thesis, and write these sentences down separately in outline form. (If you're working on a word processor, you can copy and paste these sentences.) Then examine the outline you've made for logical order, gaps, and digressions. A formal outline can be especially illuminating because of its careful structure. (See pp. 39–41 for a discussion of outlining.)
- **Listen to your draft.** Read the draft out loud to yourself or a friend or classmate, read it into a tape recorder and play the tape, or have someone read the draft to you. Experiencing your words with ears instead of eyes can alter your perceptions.
- **Ease the pressure.** Don't try to re-see everything in your draft at once. Use a checklist like the one on p. 55, making a separate pass through the draft for each item.

---

2 ■ Revising, then editing

Strictly speaking, revision includes editing—refining the manner of expression to improve clarity or style or to correct errors. In this chapter, though, revision and editing are treated separately to stress their differences: in revision you deal with the underlying meaning and structure of your essay; in editing you deal with its surface. By making separate drafts beyond the first—a revised one and then an edited one (p. 58)—you'll be less likely to waste time tinkering with sentences that you end up cutting, and you'll avoid the temptation to substitute editing for more substantial revision.

The temptation to edit while revising can be especially attractive on a word processor because it's easy to alter copy. Indeed, writers sometimes find themselves editing compulsively, spinning their wheels with changes that cease to have any marked effect on meaning or clarity and that may in fact sap the writing of energy. Planning to revise and then to edit encourages you to look beyond the confines of the screen so that deeper issues of meaning and structure aren't lost to surface matters such as word choice and sentence arrangement.

3 ■ Titling your essay

The revision stage is a good time to consider a title. After drafting, you have a clearer sense of your direction, and the attempt to sum up your essay in a title phrase can help you focus sharply on your topic, purpose, and audience.

Here are some suggestions for titling an essay:

- *A **descriptive title** is almost always appropriate and is often expected for academic writing.* It announces the topic clearly, accurately, and as briefly as possible. The final title of Sara Ling's essay—"The Internet: Fragmentation or Community?"—is an example, as are "Images of Lost Identity in *North by Northwest,*" "An Experiment in Small-Group Dynamics," "Why Lincoln Delayed Emancipating the Slaves," and "Food Poisoning Involving *E. coli* Bacteria: A Review of the Literature."
- *A **suggestive title**—the kind often found in popular magazines—may be appropriate for more informal writing.* Examples include "Making Peace" (for an essay on the Peace Corps) and "Anyone for Soup?" (for an essay on working in a soup kitchen). For a more suggestive title, Ling might have chosen something like "What We Don't Know Can Help Us" or "Secrets of the Internet." Such a title conveys the writer's attitudes and main concerns but not the precise topic, thereby pulling readers into the essay to learn more. A source for such a title may be a familiar phrase, a fresh image, or a significant expression from the essay itself.

■ *A title tells readers how big the topic is.* For Ling's essay, the title "The Internet" or "Anonymity" would have been too broad, whereas "Lose Your Body" or "Discovering Common Ground" would have been too narrow because each deals with only part of the paper's content.

■ *A title should not restate the assignment or the thesis statement,* as in "The Trouble with M. Kadi's Picture of the Internet" or "What I Think About Diversity on the Internet."

For more information on essay titles, see pages 370–71 (avoiding reference to the title in the opening of the paper), 519 (capitalizing words in a title), and 738–39 (the format of a title in the final paper).

4 ■ Using a revision checklist

Set aside at least as much time to revise your essay as you took to draft it. Plan on going through the draft several times to answer the questions in the checklist on the facing page and to resolve any problems. (If you need additional information on any of the topics in the checklist, refer to the page numbers given in parentheses.) Note that the checklist can also help you if you have been asked to comment on another writer's draft (see p. 66).

If you work on a computer, you can download the revision checklist from this book's Web site: see the box on page 51. Save the list in a file, and duplicate it for each writing project. Then insert your answers to the questions along with related ideas for changes. Print the expanded list so it's handy while you revise.

5 ■ Examining a sample revision

In revising her first draft, Sara Ling had the help of her instructor and several of her classmates, to whom she showed the draft as part of her assignment. Based on the revision checklist, she thought that she wanted to stick with her initial purpose and thesis statement and that they had held up well in the draft. But she also knew without being told that her introduction and conclusion were too hurried, that the movement between paragraphs was too abrupt, that the example of the snowboarding forum went on too long, and that the fourth paragraph was thin: she hadn't supplied enough details to support her ideas and convince her readers.

Ling's readers confirmed her self-evaluation. A few, however, raised a point that she had not considered, reflected in this comment by a classmate:

> I would have an easier time agreeing with you about the Internet if you weren't quite so gung-ho. For instance, what about the dangers of the Internet, as when adults prey on children or men prey on women? In your third paragraph, you don't acknowledge that such things can and do happen. Also, is a bias-free world (fourth para-

Checklist for revision

See also specific revision checklists for arguments (p. 178), research papers (p. 697), and literary analyses (p. 801).

Purpose

What is the essay's purpose? Does that purpose conform to the assignment? Is it consistent throughout the paper? (See pp. 13–15.)

Thesis

What is the thesis of the essay? Where does it become clear? How well do thesis and paper match: Does the paper stray from the thesis? Does it fulfill the commitment of the thesis? (See pp. 31–34.)

Structure

What are the main points of the paper? (List them.) How well does each support the thesis? How effective is their arrangement for the paper's purpose? (See pp. 35–37, 41–45.)

Development

How well do details, examples, and other evidence support each main point? Where, if at all, might readers find support skimpy or have trouble understanding the content? (See pp. 19–30, 91–92.)

Tone

What is the tone of the paper? How appropriate is it for the purpose, topic, and intended readers? Where is it most and least successful? (See pp. 11–12.)

Unity

What does each sentence and paragraph contribute to the thesis? Where, if at all, do digressions occur? Should these be cut, or can they be rewritten to support the thesis? (See pp. 45, 73–76.)

Coherence

How clearly and smoothly does the paper flow? Where does it seem rough or awkward? Can any transitions be improved? (See pp. 45, 78–88.)

Title, introduction, conclusion

How accurately and interestingly does the title reflect the essay's content? (See pp. 53–54.) How well does the introduction engage and focus readers' attention? (See pp. 103–06.) How effective is the conclusion in providing a sense of completion? (See pp. 106–08.)

rev
3b

graph) really such a sure thing? People will still meet in person, after all.

For her revision, Ling printed out a paper copy and then made changes directly on the draft. The main changes are explained in the following list and are keyed to the revision by numbers (some numbers are used more than once).

1. With a descriptive title, Ling named her topic and forecast how she would approach it.

2. Ling rewrote and expanded the previous abrupt introduction to draw readers into the question she would explore and to give a fuller summary of Kadi's essay.

3. Ling rewrote the transitions between paragraphs to make each paragraph relate clearly to her thesis statement and to make the essay flow more smoothly.

4. At these points Ling added examples to support her general statements. This and the following two categories of changes occupied most of Ling's attention during revision.

5. Ling condensed the example from her experience. Some readers commented that it overwhelmed the paragraph, and Ling realized that she had given more background than needed.

6. In response to her classmates, Ling twice qualified her ideas to acknowledge complexities she had previously ignored. (The first qualification created an overlong paragraph, so Ling broke the paragraph in two.)

7. Ling's energy had flagged when she came to her conclusion, and all her readers found it too rushed. In response, she pulled in the final ideas of the preceding paragraph, spelling one out and qualifying the other, and she summarized her main point more fully.

8. Ling added a work-cited entry for Kadi's essay, using MLA style. (See pp. 688–89 for more on documentation in general and Chapter 49 for more on MLA style.)

Revised first draft

The Internet: Fragmentation or Community?   1
~~Title?~~

We hear all sorts of predictions about how the Internet will enrich our lives   2
*and promote equality, tolerance, and thus community in our society. But are
these promises realistic? In her 1995 essay "Welcome to Cyberbia," M. Kadi
argues that they are not. Instead, she*
~~In "Welcome to Cyberbia," written in 1995, M. Kadi~~ predicts that
          not community,   *users merely*
the Internet will lead to more fragmentation ˏin society because ~~people~~ˏ
with the same biases, needs, and concerns as their own. The point is an interesting
~~just~~ seek out others,~~like themselves.~~ But Kadi fails to foresee   *one,*
that
~~how~~ the unique anonymity of Internet communication could actually

build diversity into community by lowering the barriers of physical

appearance.

    Writing on the Internet, you can be as anonymous as you like. Unless you
~~Anonymity on the Internet.~~ It's one of the best things about ~~tech-~~   3
tell them, the people you communicate with do not   *you're*
~~nology.~~ No one knows ˏ your age or gender or race. Whether ~~your~~ fat or

                                       you're
thin or neat or sloppy. What kind of clothes you wear. (Maybe ~~your~~ not

Even p
wearing clothes at all). ~~P~~eople who know you personally don't ~~even~~
if you conceal your identity
know who you are with an invented screen name.

Because of this anonymity, we
~~We~~ can make ourselves known without first being prejudged   3

because of our physical attributes. For example, *a high school student*   4
can participate in a physics discussion group, and not be ignored at first
by professional physicists in the group just because of her age. An adult man
can chat about music with teenagers, who might be inclined to dismiss him until
they hear what he has to say.

~~I participate in a snowboarding forum that has mostly men. I didn't realize what I was getting into when I used my full name as my screen
name. Before long, I had received unfriendly responses such as "What
does a girl know?" and "Why don't you go back to knitting?" I guess I
had run into a male prejudice against female snowboarders. However,
another woman on the forum had no such problems. At first she
signed on with a screen name that did not reveal her gender, and no
one responded negatively to her messages. When she had contributed
for a while, she earned respect from the other snowboarders. When she
revealed that she was a woman at that point, no one responded negatively in the way I experienced. She posed at first as someone different
from who she really was and could make herself heard.~~

When I joined a snowboarding forum using my full name, I received hostile   5
responses such as "What does a girl know?" When a woman I know later joined
the same forum, she established herself first before revealing her gender. The
absence of hostile responses in her case implies that the male participants had
learned not to judge women just for being women.

Granted, concealing or altering identities on the Internet can be a problem,   6
as when adults pose as children to seduce or harm them. These well-publicized
occurrences say a great deal about the need to monitor the use of the Internet
by children, and being cautious about getting together with Internet
correspondents. However, they do not undermine the value of people being able to
make themselves heard in situations where normally (in the real world) they
would be shut out.

The Internet's anonymity has a flip side too. We cannot be prejudged   3
and w
We also cannot prejudge others because of their appearance. Often
in face-to-face interaction we assume we know things about people just
because of the way they look. *Someone with an athletic build must be dumb.*   4
Someone who is heavy must be uninteresting. Someone in a wheelchair must be
unapproachable or pathetic. Perhaps most significant, someone of another race
must have fixed and contrary views about family values, crime, affirmative action
and all sorts of other issues as well.

like these
Assumptions prevent people from discovering their shared interests

and concerns/ ~~and this is particularly true where race is concerned.~~ *. But with*

~~The anonymity of the Internet, makes physical barriers irrelevant/ and~~ *t* *such* *to understanding are .*

~~only people's minds meet. Because of this, the Internet could create a~~

~~world free of physical bias.~~

~~Logged on to the Internet we can become more tolerant of others.~~

~~We can become a community.~~

A world free of physical bias is a long way off, but the more we   6, 7
communicate with just our minds the more likely it is that our minds will find
common ground. Logged on, we can become more accepted and accepting, more
tolerated and tolerant. We can become a community.

Work Cited   8
Kadi, M. "Welcome to Cyberbia." <u>Utne Reader</u> Mar.-Apr. 1995: 57-59.

EXERCISE 4
Analyzing a revised draft

Compare Ling's revised draft with her first draft on pages 49–50. Based on the discussion of her intentions for revision (p. 56), can you see the reasons for most of her changes? Where would you suggest further revisions, and why?

EXERCISE 5
Considering your past work: Revising

In the past, have you usually revised your drafts extensively? Do you think your writing would benefit from more revision of the sort described in this chapter? Why or why not? Many students who don't revise much explain that they lack the time. Is time a problem for you? Can you think of ways to resolve the problem?

EXERCISE 6
Revising your own draft

Revise your own first draft from Exercise 3 (p. 51). Use the checklist for revision on page 55 as a guide. Concentrate on purpose, content, and organization, leaving smaller problems for the next draft.

3c   Editing the revised draft

Editing for style, clarity, and correctness may come second to more fundamental revision, but it is still very important. A carefully

---

http://www.ablongman.com/littlebrown

For added help with editing, click on
- ➤ The writing process
  - ➤ Downloads ➤ Checklist for editing
  - ➤ Web links ➤ Drafting, editing, revising

developed essay will fall flat with readers if you overlook awkward-ness and errors.

When you have revised your first draft, try the following approaches to editing:

Ways to find what needs editing

- **Take a break,** even fifteen or twenty minutes, to clear your head.
- **Work on a paper copy if possible,** even if you compose and revise on a computer. Most people find it much harder to spot errors on a computer screen than on paper. (Print your draft double-spaced so you have room for changes.)
- **Read the draft** *slowly,* **and read what you** *actually see.* Otherwise, you're likely to read what you intended to write but didn't.
- **Read as if you are encountering the draft for the first time.** Put yourself in the reader's place.
- **Have a classmate, friend, or relative read your work.** Make sure you understand and consider the reader's suggestions, even if eventually you decide not to take them.
- **Read the draft aloud,** preferably into a tape recorder, listening for awkward rhythms, repetitive sentence patterns, and missing or clumsy transitions.
- **Learn from your own experience.** Keep a record of the problems that others have pointed out in your writing. (See p. 68 for a suggested format.) When editing, check your work against this record.
- **Don't rely on a spelling or grammar and style checker to find what needs editing.** See the discussion of these checkers on pp.186–89.

In your editing, work for clarity and a smooth movement among sentences and for correctness. Use the questions in the checklist on the next page to guide your editing. (Page numbers indicate where you can look in the handbook for more information.) You can download the editing checklist from this book's Web site: see the box opposite. Save the list in a file, and duplicate it for each writing project. Then insert your answers to the questions along with notes on specific changes you need or want to make. Print the expanded list so it's handy while you edit.

Editing on a computer presents distinct advantages and disadvantages, whether you edit on screen or work on printed copy and transfer corrections onto the computer. Try these approaches:

- If you edit printed copy, the Find command can help you locate the passages to change in the computer copy.
- If you're aware of mistakes or stylistic problems that tend to crop up in your writing—certain misspellings, overuse of *there is,* wordy phrases such as *the fact that,* and so on—you can use the Find command to locate and correct them.

Checklist for editing

Clarity

How well do words and sentences convey their intended meanings? Which words and sentences are confusing? Check the paper especially for these:

Exact language (pp. 552–63)

Parallelism (pp. 428–33)

Clear modifiers (pp. 381–90)

Clear reference of pronouns (pp. 366–72)

Complete sentences (pp. 348–55)

Sentences separated correctly (pp. 357–64)

Effectiveness

How well do words and sentences engage and direct readers' attention? Where, if at all, does the writing seem wordy, choppy, or dull? Check the paper especially for these:

Emphasis of main ideas (pp. 404–13)

Smooth and informative transitions (pp. 86–88, 110–12)

Variety in sentence length and structure (pp. 435–42)

Appropriate language (pp. 542–50)

Concise sentences (pp. 564–71)

Correctness

How little or how much do surface errors interfere with clarity and effectiveness? Check the paper especially for these:

Spelling (pp. 589–602)

Pronoun forms, especially subjective (*he, she, they, who*) vs. objective (*him, her, them, whom*) (pp. 275–83)

Verb forms, especially *-s* and *-ed* endings, correct forms of irregular verbs, and appropriate helping verbs (pp. 284–301)

Verb tenses, especially consistency (pp. 303–10, 376–77)

Agreement between subjects and verbs, especially when words come between them or the subject is *each, everyone,* or a similar word (pp. 318–25)

Agreement between pronouns and antecedents, especially when the antecedent contains *or* or the antecedent is *each, everyone, person,* or a similar word (pp. 326–30)

Sentence fragments (pp. 348–55)

Commas, especially with comma splices (pp. 357–62), with *and* or *but* (455), with introductory elements (457), with nonessential elements (459–63), and with series (465)

Apostrophes in possessives but not plural nouns (*Dave's/witches,* pp. 488–90) and in contractions but not possessive personal pronouns (*it's/its,* p. 491)

- Your word processor may have spelling and grammar/style checkers that highlight misspellings or possible flaws such as very long sentences or mismatched subjects and verbs. The checkers may point you toward areas of your work that need editing, and you can set them to focus on your own frequent errors. But the checkers are far from foolproof. See pages 186–89 on what they can and can't do, and plan on reading your drafts yourself to locate problems in spelling, grammar, or style.

- The ease of editing on a computer can lead to overediting and steal the life from your prose. Resist any temptation to rewrite sentences over and over. (If your computer's grammar and style checker contributes to the temptation, consider turning it off.)

- Inserting or deleting text on a computer requires special care not to omit needed words or leave in unneeded words.

- A computer printout may look perfect just because it's clean. To make sure it's perfect, read the printout carefully. (See the suggestions on pp. 59 and 62.)

Using an editing checklist and her own sense of clarity and effectiveness, Sara Ling edited her revised draft. The second paragraph appears below. One change Ling made throughout the essay shows up here: she resolved an inconsistency in references to *you*, *people*, and *we*, settling on a consistent *we*. In addition, Ling corrected several sentence fragments in the middle of the paragraph.

Edited draft (excerpt)

      Writing on the Internet, ~~you~~ _we_ can be as anonymous as ~~you~~ _we_ like. Unless ~~you~~ _we_ tell them, the people ~~you~~ _we_ communicate with do not know ~~your~~ _our_ age or gender or race~~,~~/ ~~W~~_w_hether ~~you're~~ _we're_ fat or thin or neat or sloppy~~,~~/ ~~W~~_or w_hat kind of clothes ~~you~~ _we_ wear~~.~~/ (~~Maybe you're not~~ _if we're_ wearing clothes at all). Even people who know ~~you~~ _us_ personally don't know who ~~you~~ _we_ are if ~~you~~ _we_ conceal ~~your~~ _our_ identit~~y~~_ies_ with ~~an~~ invented screen name~~.~~_s_

EXERCISE 7
Considering your past work: Editing
How do you find what needs editing in your drafts? What kinds of changes do you make most often? Have you tried focusing on particular kinds of changes, such as correcting mistakes you made in previous writing? If your readers often comment on editing concerns in your work, what can you do to reduce such comments?

EXERCISE 8
Editing your own draft
Use the checklist for editing and your own sense of your essay's needs to edit the revised draft of your essay-in-progress.

3d   Preparing and proofreading the final draft

After editing your essay, retype or print it once more for submission to your instructor. You may be required to use one of the following formats: MLA (pp. 736–39), Chicago (pp. 828–30), APA (pp. 856–59), or CSE (pp. 878–79). If no format is specified, consult the document-design guidelines in Chapter 9. If you've composed on a word processor, use the Print Preview function under the File menu to check for formatting problems that may not otherwise show up on your screen.

Be sure to proofread the final essay several times to spot and correct errors. To increase the accuracy of your proofreading, you may need to experiment with ways to keep yourself from relaxing into the rhythm and the content of your prose. The box below gives a few tricks, including some used by professional proofreaders.

Techniques for proofreading

- **Read printed copy,** even if you will eventually submit the paper electronically. Most people proofread more accurately when reading type on paper than when reading it on a computer screen. (At the same time, don't view the printed copy as necessarily error-free just because it's clean. Clean-looking copy may still harbor errors.)
- **Read the paper aloud.** Slowly and distinctly pronounce exactly what you see.
- **Place a ruler under each line as you read it.**
- **Read "against copy."** Compare your final draft one sentence at a time against the edited draft you copied it from.
- **Ignore content.** To keep the content of your writing from distracting you while you proofread, read the essay backward, end to beginning, examining each sentence as a separate unit. Or, taking advantage of a computer, isolate each paragraph from its context by printing it on a separate page. (Of course, reassemble the paragraphs before submitting the paper.)

Sara Ling's final essay begins on the next page, typed in MLA format except for page breaks. Comments in the margins point out key features of the essay's content.

Final draft

Sara Ling

Professor Nelson

English 120A

14 April 2003

The Internet: Fragmentation or Community?   Descriptive title

We hear all sorts of predictions about how the Inter-   Introduction
net will enrich our individual lives and promote communication, tolerance, and thus community in our society.
But are these promises realistic? In her 1995 essay "Wel-   1. Question to
come to Cyberbia," M. Kadi argues that they are not.   be addressed
Instead, she predicts that the Internet will lead to more   2. Summary of
fragmentation, not community, because users merely   Kadi's essay
seek out others with the same biases, concerns, and needs
as their own. The point is an interesting one, but Kadi   3. Thesis
fails to foresee that the unique anonymity of Internet   statement
communication could actually build diversity into community by lowering the barriers of physical appearance.

Writing on the Internet, we can be as anonymous   Explanation
as we like. Unless we tell them, the people we communi-   of Internet's
anonymity
cate with do not know our age or gender or race,
whether we're fat or thin or neat or sloppy, or what kind
of clothes we wear (if we're wearing clothes at all). Even
people who know us personally don't know who we are
if we conceal our identities with invented screen names.

Because of this anonymity, we can communicate   First main point:
freely on the Internet without being prejudged because   We are not prejudged by others.
of our physical attributes. For example, a high school   1. Examples
student can participate in a physics discussion group
without fear of being ignored by the group's professional physicists just because of her age. An adult man
can chat about music with teenagers who might otherwise dismiss him. When I joined a snowboarding forum
using my full name, I received hostile responses such as
"What does a girl know?" When a woman I know later
joined the same forum, she established herself first
before revealing her gender. The absence of hostile re-

sponses in her case implies that the male participants had learned not to judge women just for being women.

Granted, concealing or altering identities on the Internet can be a problem, as when adults pose as children to seduce or harm them. These well-publicized occurrences say much about the need to monitor children's use of the Internet and be cautious about meeting Internet correspondents. However, they do not undermine the value of being able to make ourselves heard in situations where normally (in the real world) we would be shut out.

> 2. Qualification of first main point

> 3. Conclusion of first main point

The Internet's anonymity has a flip side, too: just as we cannot be prejudged, so we cannot prejudge others because of their appearance. Often in face-to-face interaction, we assume we know things about people just because of the way they look. Someone with an athletic build must be unintelligent. Someone who is heavy must be uninteresting. Someone in a wheelchair must be unapproachable or pathetic. Perhaps most significant, someone of another race must have fixed and contrary views about all kinds of issues, from family values to crime to affirmative action. Assumptions like these prevent us from discovering the interests and concerns we share with people who merely look different. But with the anonymity of the Internet, such physical barriers to understanding are irrelevant.

> Second main point: We cannot prejudge others.
> 1. Clarification of second main point
> 2. Examples

> 3. Effects

> 4. Conclusion of second main point

A world without physical bias may be an unreachable ideal. However, the more we communicate with just our minds, the more likely it is that our minds will find common ground and put less emphasis on physical characteristics. Logged on, we can begin to become more accepted and more accepting, more tolerated and more tolerant. We can begin to become a community.

> Conclusion, summarizing essay

Work Cited

Kadi, M. "Welcome to Cyberbia." <u>Utne Reader</u> Mar.-Apr. 1995: 57-59.

> Work cited in MLA style (see p. 700)

EXERCISE 9
Proofreading

Proofread the following passage, using any of the techniques listed on page 62 to bring errors into the foreground. There are thirteen errors in the passage: missing and misspelled words, typographical errors, and the like. If you are in doubt about any spellings, consult a dictionary.

An envirnmental group, Natural Resources Defense Council, has estimated that 5,500 to 6,200 children who are preschool today may contract cancer durng there lives becuase of the pesticides they consume in there food In addition, these children will be at greater risk for kidney damage, problems with immunity, and other serious imparments. The government bases it's pesticide-safety standards on adults, but childen consume many more the fruits and fruit products likely too contain pestcides.

EXERCISE 10
Preparing your final draft

Prepare the final draft of the essay you have been working on throughout Chapters 1–3. Proofread carefully and correct all errors before submitting your essay for review.

3e   Giving and receiving comments

1 ■ Working collaboratively

Almost all the writing you do in college will generate responses from an instructor. In courses that stress writing, you may submit early drafts as well as your final paper, and your readers may include your classmates as well as your instructor. Like Sara Ling's, such courses may feature **collaborative learning,** in which students work together on writing, from completing exercises to commenting on each other's work to producing whole papers. (At more and more schools this group work occurs over a computer network. See pp. 231–36.)

Whether you participate as a writer or as a writing "coach," collaboration can give you experience in reading written work and in reaching readers through writing. You may at first be anxious about

http://www.ablongman.com/littlebrown
For added advice on working collaboratively, click on
➤ **The writing process** ➤ **Web links** ➤ **Drafting, editing, revising**

criticizing others' work or sharing your own rough drafts, but you'll soon grow to appreciate the interaction and the confidence it gives you in your own reading and writing.

CULTURE LANGUAGE In some cultures writers do not expect criticism from readers, or readers do not expect to think critically about what they read. If critical responses are uncommon in your native culture, collaboration may at first be uncomfortable for you. As a writer, consider that readers are responding to your draft or even your final paper more as an exploration of ideas than as the last word on your subject; then you may be more receptive to readers' suggestions. As a reader, allow yourself to approach a text skeptically, and know that your tactful questions and suggestions will usually be considered appropriate.

2 ■ Responding to the writing of others

If you are the reader of someone else's writing, keep the following principles in mind:

Commenting on others' writing

- **Be sure you know what the writer is saying.** If necessary, summarize the paper to understand its content. (See pp. 123–24.)
- **Address only your most significant concerns with the work.** Use the revision checklist on p. 55 as a guide to what is significant. Unless you have other instructions, ignore mistakes in grammar, punctuation, spelling, and the like. (The temptation to focus on such errors may be especially strong if the writer is less experienced than you are with standard American English.) Emphasizing mistakes will contribute little to the writer's revision.
- **Remember that you are the reader, not the writer.** Don't edit sentences, add details, or otherwise assume responsibility for the paper.
- **Be specific.** If something confuses you, say *why*. If you disagree with a conclusion, say *why*.
- **Be supportive as well as honest.** Tell the writer what you like about the paper. Word comments positively: instead of *This paragraph doesn't interest me,* say *You have an interesting detail here that I almost missed.* Comment in a way that emphasizes the effect of the work on you, the reader: *This paragraph confuses me because. . . .* And avoid measuring the work against a set of external standards: *This essay is poorly organized. Your thesis statement is inadequate.*
- **While reading, make your comments in writing.** Even if you will be delivering your comments in person later on, the written record will help you recall what you thought.
- **Link comments to specific parts of a paper.** Especially if you are reading the paper on a computer, be clear about what part of the paper each comment relates to. You can embed your comments directly into the paper, distinguishing them with highlighting or color. If you're re-

viewing a word-processor document, you may be able to use the Comment function to annotate the paper. (See p. 190 for more on this function.)

- **Phrase your comments carefully.** Avoid misunderstandings by making sure comments are both clear and respectful. If you are responding on paper or online, not face to face with the writer, remember that the writer has nothing but your written words to go on. He or she can't ask you for immediate clarification and can't infer your attitudes from gestures, facial expressions, and tone of voice.

3 ▪ Responding to comments on your own writing

When you *receive* comments from others, whether your classmates or your instructor, you will get more out of the process if you follow the guidelines below.

Benefiting from comments on your writing

- **Think of your readers as counselors or coaches.** They can help you see the virtues and flaws in your work and sharpen your awareness of readers' needs.
- **Read or listen to comments closely.**
- **Know what the critic is saying.** If you need more information, ask for it, or consult the appropriate section of this handbook.
- **Don't become defensive.** Letting comments offend you will only erect a barrier to improvement in your writing. As one writing teacher advises, "Leave your ego at the door."
- **Revise your work in response to appropriate comments.** Whether or not you are required to act on comments, you will learn more from actually revising than from just thinking about it.
- **Remember that you are the final authority on your work.** You should be open to suggestions, but you are free to decline advice when you think it is inappropriate.
- **Keep track of both the strengths and the weaknesses others identify.** Then in later assignments you can build on your successes and give special attention to problem areas.

As the last item in the preceding box indicates, you'll gain the most from collaboration if you carry your learning from one assignment into the next. To keep track of things to work on, try a chart like the one on the next page, with a vertical column for each assignment (or draft) and a horizontal row for each weakness. The handbook section is noted for each problem, and check marks indicate how often the problem occurs in each essay. The chart also provides a convenient place to keep track of words you misspell so that you can master their spellings.

	Assignment		
Weaknesses	**1**	**2**	**3**
not enough details for readers (1d)	✓	✓	✓
unity—wanders away from thesis (2c)	✓		
agreement (15a)	✓		✓
comma splice (18)	✓✓	✓	✓
misspellings	*among* *deceive*	*rebel* *seize*	*omission* *cruelty*

3f   Preparing a writing portfolio

Your writing teacher may ask you to assemble samples of your writing into a portfolio, or folder, once or more during the course. Such a portfolio gives you a chance to consider all your writing over a period and to showcase your best work.

Teachers' requirements for portfolios vary. For instance, some teachers ask students to choose their five or so best papers and to submit final drafts only. Others ask for final papers illustrating certain kinds of writing—say, one narrative, one critique, one argument, one research paper, and so on. Still others ask for notes and drafts along with selected papers. If your class is using online writing tools, your work may be archived as part of the course site and you may be asked to submit your portfolio electronically.

Just as teachers' requirements differ, so do their purposes. But most are looking for a range of writing that demonstrates your progress and strengths as a writer. You, in turn, see how you have advanced from one assignment to the next, as you've had time for new knowledge to sink in and time for practice. Teachers often allow students to revise papers before placing them in the portfolio, even if the papers have already been submitted earlier. In that case, every paper in the portfolio can benefit from all your learning.

http://www.ablongman.com/littlebrown
For added help with preparing a writing portfolio, click on
➤ **The writing process** ➤ **Web links** ➤ **Drafting, revising, editing**

An assignment to assemble a writing portfolio will probably also provide guidelines for what to include, how the portfolio will be evaluated, and how (or whether) it will be weighted for a grade. Be sure you understand the purpose of the portfolio and who will read it. For instance, if your composition teacher will be the only reader and her guidelines urge you to show evidence of progress, you might include a paper that took big risks but never entirely succeeded. In contrast, if a committee of teachers will read your work and the guidelines urge you to demonstrate your competence as a writer, you might include only papers that did succeed.

Unless the guidelines specify otherwise, provide error-free copies of your final drafts, label all your samples with your name, and assemble them all in a folder. Add a cover letter or memo that lists the samples, explains why you've included each one, and evaluates your progress as a writer. The self-evaluation involved should be a learning experience for you and will help your teacher assess your development as a writer.

EXERCISE 11
Analyzing an essay

Carefully read the essay below by Johanna Abrams, a student. Answer the following questions about the essay:

1. What is Abrams's purpose?
2. Who do you think constitutes Abrams's intended audience? What role does she seem to be assuming? What does the tone reveal about her attitude toward the topic?
3. How well does the thesis statement convey Abrams's purpose and attitude? What assertion does it make? How specific is the thesis statement? How well does it preview Abrams's ideas and organization?
4. What organization does Abrams use? Is it clear throughout the essay?
5. What details, examples, and reasons does Abrams use to support her ideas? Where is supporting evidence skimpy?
6. How successful is Abrams in making you care about the topic and her views of it?

Working in the Barnyard

Until two months ago I thought summer jobs occupied time and helped pay the next year's tuition but otherwise provided no useful training. Then I took a temporary job in a large government agency. Two months there taught me the very valuable lesson that the hierarchy of supervisor to employee should be respected.

Last May I was hired by the personnel department of the agency to fill in for vacationing workers in the mail room. I had seven coworkers and a boss, Mrs. King. Our job was to sort the huge morning and afternoon mail shipments into four hundred slots, one for every employee in the agency. Then we delivered the sorted mail out of grocery carts that we wheeled from office to office along assigned corridors, picking up outgoing mail as we went along. Each mail delivery took an entire half-day to sort and deliver.

My troubles began almost as soon as I arrived. Hundreds of pieces of mail were dumped on a shallow table against a wall of mail slots. I was horrified to see that the slots were labeled not with people's names but with their initials—whereas the incoming letters, of course, contained full names. Without thinking, I asked why this was a good idea, only to receive a sharp glance from Mrs. King. So I repeated the question. This time Mrs. King told me not to question what I didn't understand. It was the first of many such exchanges, and I hadn't been on the job a half-hour.

I mastered the initials and the sorting and delivery procedures after about a week. But the longer I worked at the job, the more I saw how inefficient all the procedures were, from delivery routes to times for coffee breaks. When I asked Mrs. King about the procedures, however, she always reacted the same way: it was none of my business.

I pestered Mrs. King more and more over the next seven weeks, but my efforts were fruitless, even counterproductive. Mrs. King began calling me snide names. Then she began picking on my work and singling me out for reprimands, even though I did my best and worked faster than most of the others.

Two months after I had started work, the personnel manager called me in and fired me. I objected, of course, calling up all the deficiencies I had seen in Mrs. King and her systems. The manager interrupted to ask if I had ever heard of the barnyard pecking order: the top chicken pecks on the one below it, the second pecks on the third, and so on all the way down the line to the lowliest chicken, whose life is a constant misery. Mrs. King, the manager said, was that lowliest chicken at the bottom of the pecking order in the agency's management. With little education, she had spent her entire adult life building up her small domain, and she had to protect it from everyone, especially the people who worked for her. The arbitrariness of her systems was an assertion of her power, for no one should doubt for a moment that she ruled her roost.

I had a month before school began again to think about my adventure. At first it irritated me that I should be humiliated while Mrs. King continued on as before. But eventually I saw how arrogant, and how unsympathetic, my behavior had been. In my next job, I'll learn the pecking order before I become a crusader, *if* I do.

—JOHANNA ABRAMS (student)

CHAPTER 4

Writing and Revising Paragraphs

A **paragraph** is a group of related sentences set off by a beginning indention or, sometimes, by extra space. For you and your readers, paragraphs provide breathers from long stretches of text and indicate key changes in the development of your thesis. They help to organize and clarify ideas.

In the body of an essay, you may use paragraphs for any of these purposes:

- To introduce one of the main points supporting your essay's central idea (its thesis) and to develop the point with examples, facts, or other supporting evidence. (See pp. 31–35 for a discussion of an essay's thesis.)
- Within a group of paragraphs centering on one main point, to introduce and develop a key example or other important evidence.
- To shift approach—for instance, from pros to cons, from problem to solution, from questions to answers.
- To mark movement in a sequence, such as from one reason or step to another.

In addition, you will use paragraphs for special purposes:

- To introduce or to conclude an essay. (See pp. 103 and 106.)
- Occasionally, to give strong emphasis to an important point or to mark a significant transition from one point to another. (See p. 108.)
- In dialog, to indicate that a new person has begun speaking. (See p. 109.)

---

http://www.ablongman.com/littlebrown
For added help with writing and revising paragraphs, click on
➤ The writing process
   ➤ Video tutorials ➤ Maintaining paragraph unity
   ➤ Exercises ➤ Exers. 4–6
   ➤ Web links ➤ Paragraphs

¶
4

The following paragraph illustrates simply how an effective body paragraph works to help both writer and reader. The thesis of the essay in which this paragraph appears is that a Texas chili championship gives undue attention to an unpleasant food.

> Some people really like chili, apparently, but nobody can agree how the stuff should be made. C. V. Wood, twice winner at Terlingua, uses flank steak, pork chops, chicken, and green chilis. My friend Hughes Rudd of CBS News, who imported five hundred pounds of chili powder into Russia as a condition of accepting employment as Moscow correspondent, favors coarse-ground beef. Isadore Bleckman, the cameraman I must live with on the road, insists upon one-inch cubes of stew beef and puts garlic in his chili, an Illinois affectation. An Indian of my acquaintance, Mr. Fulton Batisse, who eats chili for breakfast when he can, uses buffalo meat and plays an Indian drum while it's cooking. I ask you.
>
> —CHARLES KURALT, *Dateline America*

General statement relating to thesis: announces topic of paragraph

Four specific examples, all providing evidence for general statement

While you are drafting, conscious attention to the requirements of the paragraph may sometimes help pull ideas out of you or help you forge relationships. But don't expect effective paragraphs like Kuralt's to flow from your fingertips while you are grappling with what you want to say. Instead, use the following checklist to guide your revision of paragraphs so that they work to your and your readers' advantage.

Checklist for revising paragraphs

- Is the paragraph **unified?** Does it adhere to one general idea that is either stated in a **topic sentence** or otherwise apparent? (See opposite.)
- Is the paragraph **coherent?** Do the sentences follow a clear sequence? Are the sentences linked as needed by parallelism, repetition or restatement, pronouns, consistency, and transitional expressions? (See p. 78.)
- Is the paragraph **developed?** Is the general idea of the paragraph well supported with specific evidence such as details, facts, examples, and reasons? (See p. 91.)

On the World Wide Web, the paragraphing conventions described here do not always apply. Web readers sometimes skim text instead of reading word for word, and they are accustomed to embedded links that may take them from the paragraph to another page. Writing for the Web, you may want to write shorter paragraphs than you would in printed documents, and save embedded links for the ends of paragraphs lest readers miss important information. (For more on composing for the Web, see Chapter 10.)

CULTURE LANGUAGE Not all cultures share the paragraphing conventions of American academic writing. The conventions are not universal even among users of standard American English: for instance, US newspaper writers compose very short paragraphs that will break up text in narrow columns. In some other languages, writing moves differently from English—not from left to right, but from right to left or down rows from top to bottom. Even in languages that move as English does, writers may not use paragraphs at all. Or they may use paragraphs but not state the central ideas or provide transitional expressions to show readers how sentences relate. If your native language is not English and you have difficulty with paragraphs, don't worry about paragraphing during drafting. Instead, during a separate step of revision, divide your text into parts that develop your main points. Mark those parts with indentions.

4a Maintaining paragraph unity

Readers generally expect a paragraph to explore one idea. They will be alert for that idea and will patiently follow its development. In other words, they will seek and appreciate paragraph **unity,** clear identification and clear elaboration of one idea and of that idea only.

In an essay the thesis statement often asserts the main idea as a commitment to readers (see p. 31). In a paragraph a **topic sentence** often alerts readers to the essence of the paragraph by asserting the central idea and expressing the writer's attitude toward it. In a brief essay each body paragraph will likely treat one main point supporting the essay's thesis statement; the topic sentences simply elaborate on parts of the thesis. In longer essays paragraphs tend to work in groups, each group treating one main point. Then the topic sentences will tie into that main point, and all the points together will support the thesis.

1 ■ Focusing on the central idea

Like the thesis sentence, the topic sentence is a commitment to readers, and the rest of the paragraph delivers on that commit-

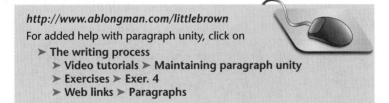

http://www.ablongman.com/littlebrown
For added help with paragraph unity, click on
➤ **The writing process**
  ➤ Video tutorials ➤ **Maintaining paragraph unity**
  ➤ Exercises ➤ **Exer. 4**
  ➤ Web links ➤ **Paragraphs**

¶ un

4a

ment. Look again at Kuralt's paragraph on chili on page 72: the opening statement conveys the author's promise that he will describe various ways to make chili, and the following sentences keep the promise. But what if Kuralt had written this paragraph instead?

> Some people really like chili, apparently, but nobody can agree how the stuff should be made. C. V. Wood, twice winner at Terlingua, uses flank steak, pork chops, chicken, and green chilis. My friend Hughes Rudd, who imported five hundred pounds of chili powder into Russia as a condition of accepting employment as Moscow correspondent, favors coarse-ground beef. He had some trouble finding the beef in Moscow, though. He sometimes had to scour all the markets and wait in long lines. For any American used to overstocked supermarkets and department stores, Russia can be quite a shock.

Topic sentence: general statement

Two examples supporting statement

Digression

By wandering off from chili ingredients to consumer deprivation in Russia, the paragraph fails to deliver on the commitment of its topic sentence.

You should expect digressions while you are drafting: if you allow yourself to explore ideas, as you should, then of course every paragraph will not be tightly woven, perfectly unified. But spare your readers the challenge and frustration of repeatedly shifting focus to follow your rough explorations: revise each paragraph so that it develops a single idea.

While revising your paragraphs for unity, you may want to highlight the central idea of each paragraph to be sure it's stated and then focus on it. On paper, you can bracket or circle the idea. On a computer, you can format the idea in color or highlight it with a color background. Just be sure to remove the color or highlighting before printing the final draft.

2 ■ Placing the topic sentence

The topic sentence of a paragraph and its supporting details may be arranged variously, depending on how you want to direct readers' attention and how complex your central idea is. In the most common arrangements, the topic sentence comes at the beginning of the paragraph, comes at the end, or is not stated at all but is nonetheless apparent. The advantages of each approach are described on the next two pages. If you write on a computer, you can easily experiment by moving the topic sentence around (or deleting it) to see the effect. (The sentence will probably take some editing to work smoothly into various positions.)

Topic sentence at the beginning

When the topic sentence appears first in a paragraph, it can help you select the details that follow. For readers, the topic-first model establishes an initial context in which all the supporting details can be understood. Reading Kuralt's paragraph on page 72, we easily relate each detail or example back to the point made in the first sentence.

The topic-first model is common not only in expository paragraphs, such as Kuralt's, but also in argument paragraphs, such as the one following:

> It is a misunderstanding of the American retail store to think we go there necessarily to buy. Some of us shop. There's a difference. Shopping has many purposes, the least interesting of which is to acquire new articles. We shop to cheer ourselves up. We shop to practice decision-making. We shop to be useful and productive members of our class and society. We shop to remind ourselves how much is available to us. We shop to remind ourselves how much is to be striven for. We shop to assert our superiority to the material objects that spread themselves before us.
>
> —Phyllis Rose, "Shopping and Other Spiritual Adventures"

Topic sentence: statement of misconception

Correction of misconception

Topic sentence at the end

In some paragraphs the central idea may be stated at the end, after supporting sentences have made a case for the general statement. Since this model leads the reader to a conclusion by presenting all the evidence first, it can prove effective in argument. And because the point of the paragraph is withheld until the end, this model can be dramatic in exposition, too, as illustrated by the following example from an essay about William Tecumseh Sherman, a Union general during the US Civil War:

> Sherman is considered by some to be the inventor of "total war": the first general in human history to carry the logic of war to its ultimate extreme, the first to scorch the earth, the first to consciously demoralize the hostile civilian population in order to subdue its army, the first to wreck an economy in order to starve its soldiers. He has been called our first "merchant of terror" and seen as the spiritual father of our Vietnam War concepts of "search and destroy," "pacification," "strategic hamlets," and "free-fire zones." As such,

Information supporting and building to topic sentence

he remains a cardboard figure of our history: a monstrous arch-villain to unreconstructed Southerners, and an embarrassment to Northerners.

⎤ Topic sentence

—Adapted from JAMES RESTON, JR., "You Cannot Refine It"

Expressing the central idea at the end of the paragraph does not eliminate the need to unify the paragraph. The idea in the topic sentence must still govern the selection of all the preceding details.

Central idea not stated

Occasionally, a paragraph's central idea will be stated in the previous paragraph or will be so obvious that it need not be stated at all. The following is from an essay on the actor Humphrey Bogart:

Usually he wore the trench coat unbuttoned, just tied with the belt, and a slouch hat, rarely tilted. Sometimes it was a captain's cap and a yachting jacket. Almost always his trousers were held up by a cowboy belt. You know the kind: one an Easterner waiting for a plane out of Phoenix buys just as a joke and then takes a liking to. Occasionally, he'd hitch up his slacks with it, and he often jabbed his thumbs behind it, his hands ready for a fight or a dame.

Details adding up to the unstated idea that Bogart's character could be seen in his clothing

—PETER BOGDANOVICH, "Bogie in Excelsis"

Paragraphs in descriptive writing (like the one above) and in narrative writing (relating a sequence of events) often lack stated topic sentences. But a paragraph without a topic sentence still should have a central idea, and its details should develop that idea.

EXERCISE 1
Finding the central idea

What is the central idea of each paragraph below? In what sentence or sentences is it expressed?

1.   Today many black Americans enjoy a measure of economic se- 1 curity beyond any we have known in the history of black America. But if they remain in a nasty blue funk, it's because their very exis- 2 tence seems an affront to the swelling ranks of the poor. Nor have 3 black intellectuals ever quite made peace with the concept of the black bourgeoisie, a group that is typically seen as devoid of cultural authenticity, doomed to mimicry and pallid assimilation. I 4 once gave a talk before an audience of black academics and educators, in the course of which I referred to black middle-class culture. Afterward, one of the academics in the audience, deeply affronted, 5 had a question for me. "Professor Gates," he asked rhetorically, his 6

voice dripping with sarcasm, "what *is* black middle-class culture?" I suggested that if he really wanted to know, he need only look 7 around the room. But perhaps I should just have handed him a 8 mirror: for just as nothing is more American than anti-American- ism, nothing is more characteristic of the black bourgeoisie than the sense of shame and denial that the identity inspires.

—HENRY LOUIS GATES, JR., "Two Nations . . . Both Black"

2.   Though they do not know why the humpback whale sings, 1 scientists do know something about the song itself. They have 2 measured the length of a whale's song: from a few minutes to over half an hour. They have recorded and studied the variety 3 and complex arrangements of low moans, high squeaks, and slid- ing squeals that make up the song. And they have learned that 4 each whale sings in its own unique pattern.

—JANET LIEBER (student), "Whales' Songs"

EXERCISE 2
Revising a paragraph for unity

The following paragraph contains ideas or details that do not sup- port its central idea. Identify the topic sentence in the paragraph and delete the unrelated material.

In the southern part of the state, some people still live much as they did a century ago. They use coal- or wood-burning stoves for heating and cooking. Their homes do not have electricity or indoor bathrooms or running water. The towns they live in don't receive adequate funding from the state and federal governments, so the schools are poor and in bad shape. Beside most homes there is a garden where fresh vegetables are gathered for canning. Small pas- tures nearby support livestock, including cattle, pigs, horses, and chickens. Most of the people have cars or trucks, but the vehicles are old and beat-up from traveling on unpaved roads.

EXERCISE 3
Considering your past work: Paragraph unity

For a continuing exercise in this chapter, choose a paper you've written in the past year. Examine the body paragraphs for unity. Do they have clear topic sentences? If not, are the paragraphs' cen- tral ideas still clear? Are the paragraphs unified around their cen- tral ideas? Should any details be deleted for unity? Should other, more relevant details be added in their stead?

EXERCISE 4
Writing a unified paragraph

Develop the following topic sentence into a unified paragraph by using the relevant information in the supporting statements. Delete each statement that does not relate directly to the topic, and then rewrite and combine sentences as appropriate. Place the topic sen- tence in the position that seems most effective to you.

Topic sentence
Mozart's accomplishments in music seem remarkable even today.

Supporting information
Wolfgang Amadeus Mozart was born in 1756 in Salzburg, Austria.
He began composing music at the age of five.
He lived most of his life in Salzburg and Vienna.
His first concert tour of Europe was at the age of six.
On his first tour he played harpsichord, organ, and violin.
He published numerous compositions before reaching adolescence.
He married in 1782.
Mozart and his wife were both poor managers of money.
They were plagued by debts.
Mozart composed over six hundred musical compositions.
His most notable works are his operas, symphonies, quartets, and
    piano concertos.
He died at the age of thirty-five.

EXERCISE 5
Turning topic sentences into unified paragraphs
Develop three of the following topic sentences into detailed and
unified paragraphs.

1. Men and women are different in at least one important respect.
2. The best Web search engine is [*name*].
3. Fans of _____ music [*country, classical, rock, rap, jazz, or
   another kind*] come in [*number*] varieties.
4. Professional sports have [or have not] been helped by extending the regular season with championship play-offs.
5. Working for good grades can interfere with learning.

4b Achieving paragraph coherence

A paragraph is unified if it holds together—if all its details and
examples support the central idea. A paragraph is **coherent** if readers can see *how* the paragraph holds together—how the sentences
relate to each other—without having to stop and reread.

Incoherence gives readers the feeling of being yanked around,
as the following example shows.

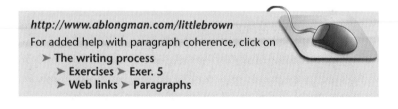

http://www.ablongman.com/littlebrown
For added help with paragraph coherence, click on
➤ **The writing process**
  ➤ **Exercises** ➤ **Exer. 5**
  ➤ **Web links** ➤ **Paragraphs**

Ways to achieve paragraph coherence

- Organize effectively (p. 80).
- Use parallel structures (p. 84).
- Repeat or restate words and word groups (p. 84).
- Use pronouns (p. 85).
- Be consistent in nouns, pronouns, and verbs (p. 85).
- Use transitional expressions (p. 86).

The ancient Egyptians were masters of preserving dead people's bodies by making mummies of them. Mummies several thousand years old have been discovered nearly intact. The skin, hair, teeth, finger- and toenails, and facial features of the mummies were evident. It is possible to diagnose the diseases they suffered in life, such as smallpox, arthritis, and nutritional deficiencies. The process was remarkably effective. Sometimes apparent were the fatal afflictions of the dead people: a middle-aged king died from a blow on the head, and polio killed a child king. Mummification consisted of removing the internal organs, applying natural preservatives inside and out, and then wrapping the body in layers of bandages.

— Topic sentence

Sentences related to topic sentence but disconnected from each other

The paragraph as it was actually written appears below. It is much clearer because the writer arranged information differently and also built links into his sentences so that they would flow smoothly:

- After stating the central idea in a topic sentence, the writer moves to two more specific explanations and illustrates the second with four sentences of examples.
- (Circled) words repeat or restate key terms or concepts.
- [Boxed] words link sentences and clarify relationships.
- Underlined phrases are in parallel grammatical form to reflect their parallel content.

The ancient Egyptians were masters of preserving dead people's bodies by (making mummies) of them. [Basically,] (mummification) consisted of removing the internal organs, applying natural preservatives inside and out, and then wrapping the body in layers of ban-

— Topic sentence

Explanation 1: What mummification is

¶ coh
4b

dages. And the process was remarkably effective. Indeed, mummies several thousand
years old have been discovered nearly intact.

> Explanation 2: Why
> the Egyptians were
> masters

Their skin, hair, teeth, finger- and toenails,
and facial features are still evident. Their diseases in life, such as smallpox, arthritis, and
nutritional deficiencies, are still diagnosable.
Even their fatal afflictions are still apparent: a
middle-aged king died from a blow on the
head; a child king died from polio.

> Specific examples of
> explanation 2

—MITCHELL ROSENBAUM (student),
"Lost Arts of the Egyptians"

Though some of the connections in this paragraph were added in
revision, the writer attended to them while drafting as well. Not only
superficial coherence but also an underlying clarity of relationships
can be achieved by tying each sentence to the one before—generalizing from it, clarifying it, qualifying it, adding to it, illustrating it.
Each sentence in a paragraph creates an expectation of some sort in
the mind of the reader, a question such as "How was a mummy
made?" or "How intact are the mummies?" or "What's another example?" When you recognize these expectations and try to fulfill them,
readers are likely to understand relationships without struggle.

1 ■ Organizing the paragraph

The paragraphs on mummies illustrate an essential element of
coherence: information must be arranged in an order that readers
can follow easily and that corresponds to their expectations. The
common organizations for paragraphs correspond to those for entire essays: by space, by time, and for emphasis. (In addition, the
patterns of development also suggest certain arrangements. See
pp. 92–101.)

If you want to try rearranging a paragraph to achieve different
emphases, you can copy it, paste the duplicate into your document,
and then experiment by moving sentences around. To evaluate the
versions, however, you'll need to edit each one so that sentences
flow smoothly, attending to parallelism, repetition, transitions, and
the other techniques discussed in this section.

Organizing by space or time

A paragraph organized **spatially** focuses readers' attention on
one point and scans a person, object, or scene from that point. The
movement usually parallels the way people actually look at things,

¶ coh

4b

from top to bottom, from side to side, from near to far. Virginia Woolf follows the last pattern in this paragraph:

> The sun struck straight upon the house, making the white walls glare between the dark windows. Their panes, woven thickly with green branches, held circles of impenetrable darkness. Sharp-edged wedges of light lay upon the window-sill and showed inside the room plates with blue rings, cups with curved handles, the bulge of a great bowl, the criss-cross pattern in the rug, and the formidable corners and lines of cabinets and bookcases. Behind their conglomeration hung a zone of shadow in which might be a further shape to be disencumbered of shadow or still denser depths of darkness.
>
> —VIRGINIA WOOLF, *The Waves*

Description moving from outside (closer) to inside (farther)

Unstated central idea: sunlight barely penetrated the house's secrets.

Another familiar way of organizing the elements of a paragraph is **chronologically**—that is, in order of their occurrence in time. In a chronological paragraph, as in experience, the earliest events come first, followed by more recent ones.

> Nor can a tree live without soil. A hurricane-born mangrove island may bring its own soil to the sea. But other mangrove trees make their own soil—and their own islands—from scratch. These are the ones which interest me. The seeds germinate in the fruit on the tree. The germinated embryo can drop anywhere—say, onto a dab of floating muck. The heavy root end sinks; a leafy plumule unfurls. The tiny seedling, afloat, is on its way. Soon aerial roots shooting out in all directions trap debris. The sapling's networks twine, the interstices narrow, and water calms in the lee. Bacteria thrive on organic broth; amphipods swarm. These creatures grow and die at the tree's wet feet. The soil thickens, accumulating rainwater, leaf rot, seashells, and guano; the island spreads.
>
> —ANNIE DILLARD, "Sojourner"

Topic sentence

Details in order of their occurrence

Organizing for emphasis

Some organizational schemes are imposed on paragraphs to achieve a certain emphasis. The most common is the **general-to-specific** scheme, in which the topic sentence often comes first and then the following sentences become increasingly specific. The paragraph on mummies (pp. 79–80) illustrates this organization: each

¶ coh

4b

sentence is either more specific than the one before it or at the same level of generality. Here is another illustration:

> Perhaps the simplest fact about sleep is that individual needs for it vary widely. Most ⎤ Topic sentence
>
> adults sleep between seven and nine hours, but occasionally people turn up who need twelve hours or so, while some rare types can get by on three or four. Rarest of all are those legendary types who require almost no sleep at all; respected researchers have recently studied three such people. One of them—a healthy, happy woman in her seventies— sleeps about an hour every two or three days. The other two are men in early middle age, who get by on a few minutes a night. One of them complains about the daily fifteen min- utes or so he's forced to "waste" in sleeping.
>
> Supporting examples, increasingly specific
>
> —LAWRENCE A. MAYER,
> "The Confounding Enemy of Sleep"

In the less common **specific-to-general** organization, the ele- ments of the paragraph build to a general conclusion:

> It's disconcerting that so many college women, when asked how their children will be cared for if they themselves work, refer with vague confidence to "the day care cen- ter" as though there were some great amor- phous kiddie watcher out there that the state provides.
>
> Common belief
>
> But such places, adequately funded, well run, and available to all, are still scarce in this country, particularly for middle-class women. And figures show that when she takes time off for family-connected reasons (births, child care), a woman's chances for ca- reer advancement plummet. In a job market that's steadily tightening and getting more competitive, these obstacles bode the kind of danger ahead that can shatter not only professions, but egos.
>
> Actual situation
>
> A hard reality is that there's not much more support for our daugh- ters who have family-plus-career goals than there was for us; there's simply a great deal more self and societal pressure.
>
> General conclusion: topic sentence
>
> —JUDITH WAX, *Starting in the Middle*

As its name implies, the **problem-solution** arrangement intro- duces a problem and then proposes or explains a solution. The next paragraph explains how to gain from Internet newsgroups despite their limitations:

Even when you do find a newsgroup with apparently useful material, you have no assurance of a correspondent's authority because of e-mail's inherent anonymity. Many people don't cite their credentials. Besides, anyone can pose as an expert. | Topic sentence and clarification: statement of the problem

The best information you can get initially is apt to be a reference to something of which you were not aware but can then investigate for yourself. Internet newsgroups can be valuable for that alone. I have been directed to software-problem solutions, owners of out-of-print books, and important people who know nothing about communicating through electronic communities. It is best to start with the assumption that you are conversing with peers, people who know things that you don't, while you probably know things that they don't. Gradually, by trading information, you develop some virtual relationships and can assess the relative validity of your sources. Meanwhile, you will probably have learned a few things along the way. | Solution to the problem

—Adapted from JOHN A. BUTLER,
Cybersearch

When your details vary in significance, you can arrange them in a **climactic** order, from least to most important or dramatic:

Nature has put many strange tongues into the heads of her creatures. | Topic sentence

There is the frog's tongue, rooted at the front of the mouth so it can be protruded an extra distance for nabbing prey. | Least dramatic example

There is the gecko lizard's tongue, so long and agile that the lizard uses it to wash its eyes. But the ultimate lingual whopper has been achieved in the anteater. The anteater's head, long as it is, is not long enough to contain the tremendous tongue which licks deep into ant-hills. Its tongue is not rooted in the mouth or throat: it is fastened to the breastbone. | Most dramatic example

—ALAN DEVOE, "Nature's Utmost"

In other organizations, you can arrange details according to how you think readers are likely to understand them. In discussing the virtues of public television, for instance, you might proceed from **most familiar to least familiar,** from a well-known program your readers have probably seen to less well-known programs they may not have seen. Or in defending the right of government employees to strike, you might arrange your reasons from **simplest to most complex,** from the employees' need to be able to redress grievances to more subtle consequences for relations between employers and employees.

2 ■ Using parallel structures

Another way to achieve coherence is through **parallelism**—the use of similar grammatical structures for similar elements of meaning within a sentence or among sentences. (See Chapter 25 for a detailed discussion of parallelism.) Parallel structures help tie together the last three sentences in the paragraph on mummies (p. 80). In the following paragraph, underlining highlights the parallel structures linking sentences. Aphra Behn (lived 1640–89) was the first Englishwoman to write professionally.

> In addition to her busy career as a writer, Aphra Behn also found time to briefly marry and spend a little while in debtor's prison. She found time to take up a career as a spy for the English in their war against the Dutch. She made the long and difficult voyage to Suriname [in South America] and became involved in a slave rebellion there. She plunged into political debate at Will's Coffee House and defended her position from the stage of the Drury Lane Theater. She actively argued for women's rights to be educated and to marry whom they pleased, or not at all. She defied the seventeenth-century dictum that ladies must be "modest" and wrote freely about sex.   —ANGELINE GOREAU, "Aphra Behn"

3 ■ Repeating or restating words and word groups

Repeating or restating key words or word groups is an important means of achieving paragraph coherence and of reminding your readers what the topic is. In the next example, notice how the circled words tie the sentences together and stress the important ideas of the paragraph:

> Having listened to both Chinese and English, I also tend to be suspicious of any comparisons between the two languages. Typically, one language—that of the person doing the comparing—is often used as the standard, the benchmark for a logical form of expression. And so the language being compared is always in danger of being judged deficient or superfluous, simplistic or unnecessarily complex, melodious or cacophonous. English speakers point out that Chinese is extremely difficult because it relies on variations in tone barely discernible to the human ear. By the same token, Chinese speakers tell me English is extremely difficult because it is inconsistent, a language of too many broken rules, of Mickey Mice and Donald Ducks.   —AMY TAN, "The Language of Discretion"

¶ coh

4b

Note Though planned repetition can be effective, careless or excessive repetition weakens prose (see p. 568).

4 ■ Using pronouns

Pronouns, such as *she, he, it, they,* and *who,* refer to and function as nouns (see p. 242). Thus pronouns naturally help relate sentences to one another. In the following paragraph the pronouns and the nouns they refer to are circled:

> After dark, on the warrenlike streets of Brooklyn where I live, I often see women who fear the worst from me. They seem to have set their faces on neutral, and with their purse straps strung across their chests bandolier-style, they forge ahead as though bracing themselves against being tackled. I understand, of course, that the danger they perceive is not a hallucination. Women are particularly vulnerable to street violence, and young black males are drastically overrepresented among the perpetrators of that violence. Yet these truths are no solace against the kind of alienation that comes of being ever the suspect, a fearsome entity with whom pedestrians avoid making eye contact.
> —BRENT STAPLES, "Black Men and Public Space"

5 ■ Being consistent

Being consistent is the most subtle way to achieve paragraph coherence because readers are aware of consistency only when it is absent. Consistency (or the lack of it) occurs primarily in the tense of verbs and the number and person of nouns and pronouns (see Chapter 20). Although some shifts will be necessary because of meaning, inappropriate shifts, as in the following passages, will interfere with a reader's ability to follow the development of ideas:

Shifts in tense

In the Hopi religion, water <u>is</u> the driving force. Since the Hopi <u>lived</u> in the Arizona desert, they <u>needed</u> water urgently for drinking, cooking, and irrigating crops. Their complex beliefs <u>are</u> focused in part on gaining the assistance of supernatural forces in obtaining water. Many of the Hopi kachinas, or spirit essences, <u>were</u> directly concerned with clouds, rain, and snow.

Shifts in number

<u>Kachinas</u> represent the things and events of the real world, such as clouds, mischief, cornmeal, and even death. A <u>kachina</u> is not worshiped as a god but regarded as an interested friend. <u>They</u> visit the Hopi from December through July in the form of men who dress in kachina costumes and perform dances and other rituals.

¶ coh

4b

Shifts in person

Unlike the man, the Hopi woman does not keep contact with kachinas through costumes and dancing. Instead, one receives a small likeness of a kachina, called a *tihu*, from the man impersonating the kachina. You are more likely to receive a tihu as a girl approaching marriage, though a child or older woman sometimes receives one, too.

The grammar checker on a word processor cannot help you locate shifts in tense, number, or person among sentences. Shifts are sometimes necessary (as when tenses change to reflect actual differences in time), and even a passage with needless shifts may still consist of sentences that are grammatically correct (as all the sentences are in the preceding examples). The only way to achieve consistency in your writing is to review it yourself.

6 ■ Using transitional expressions

Specific words and word groups, called **transitional expressions,** can connect sentences whose relationships may not be instantly clear to readers. Notice the difference in these two versions of the same paragraph:

> Medical science has succeeded in identifying the hundreds of viruses that can cause the common cold. It has discovered the most effective means of prevention. One person transmits the cold viruses to another most often by hand. An infected person covers his mouth to cough. He picks up the telephone. His daughter picks up the telephone. She rubs her eyes. She has a cold. It spreads. To avoid colds, people should wash their hands often and keep their hands away from their faces.

Paragraph is choppy and hard to follow

> Medical science has thus succeeded in identifying the hundreds of viruses that can cause the common cold. It has also discovered the most effective means of prevention. One person transmits the cold viruses to another most often by hand. For instance, an infected person covers his mouth to cough. Then he picks up the telephone. Half an hour later, his daughter picks up the same telephone. Immediately afterward, she rubs her eyes. Within a few days, she, too, has a cold.

Transitional expressions (boxed) remove choppiness and spell out relationships

And thus it spreads. To avoid colds, therefore, people should wash their hands often and keep their hands away from their faces.
                              —KATHLEEN LAFRANK (student),
                              "Colds: Myth and Science"

There are scores of transitional expressions on which to draw. The box below shows many common ones, arranged according to the relationships they convey.

Transitional expressions

To add or show sequence
again, also, and, and then, besides, equally important, finally, first, further, furthermore, in addition, in the first place, last, moreover, next, second, still, too

To compare
also, in the same way, likewise, similarly

To contrast
although, and yet, but, but at the same time, despite, even so, even though, for all that, however, in contrast, in spite of, nevertheless, notwithstanding, on the contrary, on the other hand, regardless, still, though, yet

To give examples or intensify
after all, an illustration of, even, for example, for instance, indeed, in fact, it is true, of course, specifically, that is, to illustrate, truly

To indicate place
above, adjacent to, below, elsewhere, farther on, here, near, nearby, on the other side, opposite to, there, to the east, to the left

To indicate time
after a while, afterward, as long as, as soon as, at last, at length, at that time, before, earlier, formerly, immediately, in the meantime, in the past, lately, later, meanwhile, now, presently, shortly, simultaneously, since, so far, soon, subsequently, then, thereafter, until, when

To repeat, summarize, or conclude
all in all, altogether, as has been said, in brief, in conclusion, in other words, in particular, in short, in simpler terms, in summary, on the whole, that is, therefore, to put it differently, to summarize

To show cause or effect
accordingly, as a result, because, consequently, for this purpose, hence, otherwise, since, then, therefore, thereupon, thus, to this end, with this object

Note Draw carefully on the preceding list of transitional expressions because the ones in each group are not interchangeable. For instance, *besides, finally,* and *second* may all be used to add information, but each has its own distinct meaning.

To see where transitional expressions might be needed in your paragraphs, examine the movement from each sentence to the next. (On a computer or on paper, you can highlight the transitional expressions already present and then review the sentences that lack them.) Abrupt changes are most likely to need a transition: a shift from cause to effect, a contradiction, a contrast. (You can smooth and clarify transitions *between* paragraphs, too. See pp. 108 and 110–12.)

 CULTURE LANGUAGE ➤ If transitional expressions are not common in your native language, you may be tempted to compensate when writing in English by adding them to the beginnings of most sentences. But such explicit transitions aren't needed everywhere, and in fact too many can be intrusive and awkward. When inserting transitional expressions, consider the reader's need for a signal: often the connection from sentence to sentence is already clear from the context, or it can be made clear by relating the content of sentences more closely (see pp. 84–85). When you do need transitional expressions, try varying their positions in your sentences, as shown in the sample paragraph on pages 86–87.

Punctuating transitional expressions

A transitional expression is usually set off by a comma or commas from the rest of the sentence:

> <u>Immediately afterward,</u> she rubs her eyes. <u>Within a few days,</u> she, too, has a cold.

See pages 461–62 for more on this convention and its exceptions.

7 ■ Combining devices to achieve coherence

The devices for achieving coherence rarely appear in isolation in effective paragraphs. As any example in this chapter shows, writers usually combine sensible organization, parallelism, repetition, pronouns, consistency, and transitional expressions to help readers follow the development of ideas. And the devices also figure, naturally, in the whole essay (see pp. 110–13 for an example of paragraphs linked in an essay).

> **EXERCISE 6**
> **Analyzing paragraphs for coherence**
> Study the paragraphs by Janet Lieber (p. 77), Hillary Begas (p. 92), and Freeman Dyson (p. 94) for the authors' use of various devices

to achieve coherence. Look especially for organization, parallel structures and ideas, repetition and restatement, pronouns, and transitional expressions.

EXERCISE 7
Arranging sentences coherently

After the topic sentence (sentence 1), the sentences in the student paragraph below have been deliberately scrambled to make the paragraph incoherent. Using the topic sentence and other clues as guides, rearrange the sentences in the paragraph to form a well-organized, coherent unit.

We hear complaints about the Postal Service all the time, but 1 we should not forget what it does *right*. The total volume of mail 2 delivered by the Postal Service each year makes up almost half the total delivered in all the world. Its 70,000 employees handle 3 140,000,000,000 pieces of mail each year. And when was the last 4 time they failed to deliver yours? In fact, on any given day the Postal 5 Service delivers almost as much mail as the rest of the world combined. That huge number means over 2,000,000 pieces per employee 6 and over 560 pieces per man, woman, and child in the country.

EXERCISE 8
Eliminating inconsistencies

The following paragraph is incoherent because of inconsistencies in person, number, or tense. Identify the inconsistencies and revise the paragraph to give it coherence. (For further exercises in eliminating inconsistencies, see pp. 376, 377–78, and 380.)

The Hopi tihu, or kachina likeness, is often called a "doll," but its owner, usually a girl or woman, does not regard them as a plaything. Instead, you treated them as a valued possession and hung them out of the way on a wall. For its owner the tihu represents a connection with the kachina's spirit. They are considered part of the kachina, carrying a portion of the kachina's power.

EXERCISE 9
Using transitional expressions

Transitional expressions have been removed from the following paragraph at the numbered blanks. Fill in each blank with an appropriate transitional expression (1) to contrast, (2) to intensify, and (3) to show effect. Consult the list on page 87 if necessary.

All over the country, people are swimming, jogging, weightlifting, dancing, walking, playing tennis—doing anything to keep fit. ___(1)___ this school has consistently refused to construct and equip a fitness center. The school has ___(2)___ refused to open existing athletic facilities to all students, not just those playing organized sports. ___(3)___ students have no place to exercise except in their rooms and on dangerous public roads.

EXERCISE 10
Considering your past work: Paragraph coherence
Continuing from Exercise 3 (p. 77), examine the body paragraphs of your essay to see how coherent they are and how their coherence could be improved. Do the paragraphs have a clear organization? Do you use parallelism, repetition and restatement, pronouns, and transitional expressions to signal relationships? Are the paragraphs consistent in person, number, and tense? Revise two or three paragraphs in ways you think will improve their coherence.

EXERCISE 11
Writing a coherent paragraph
Write a coherent paragraph from the following information, combining and rewriting sentences as necessary. First, begin the paragraph with the topic sentence given and arrange the supporting sentences in a climactic order. Then combine and rewrite the supporting sentences, helping the reader see connections by introducing parallelism, repetition and restatement, pronouns, consistency, and transitional expressions.

Topic sentence
Hypnosis is far superior to drugs for relieving tension.

Supporting information
Hypnosis has none of the dangerous side effects of the drugs that relieve tension.
Tension-relieving drugs can cause weight loss or gain, illness, or even death.
Hypnosis is nonaddicting.
Most of the drugs that relieve tension do foster addiction.
Tension-relieving drugs are expensive.
Hypnosis is inexpensive even for people who have not mastered self-hypnosis.

EXERCISE 12
Turning topic sentences into coherent paragraphs
Develop three of the following topic sentences into coherent paragraphs. Organize your information by space, by time, or for emphasis, as seems most appropriate. Use parallelism, repetition and restatement, pronouns, consistency, and transitional expressions to link sentences.

1. The most interesting character in the book [or movie] was _____.
2. Of all my courses, _____ is the one that I think will serve me best throughout life.
3. Although we in the United States face many problems, the one we should concentrate on solving first is _____.
4. The most dramatic building in town is the _____.
5. Children should not have to worry about the future.

4c Developing the paragraph

In an essay that's understandable and interesting to readers, you will provide plenty of solid information to support your general statements. You work that information into the essay through the paragraph, as you build up each point relating to the thesis.

A paragraph may be unified and coherent but still be inadequate if you skimp on details. Take this example:

> Untruths can serve as a kind of social oil when they smooth connections between people. In preventing confrontation and injured feelings, they allow everyone to go on as before.

General statements needing examples to be clear and convincing

This paragraph lacks **development**, completeness. It does not provide enough information for us to evaluate or even care about the writer's assertions.

1 ■ Using specific information

If they are sound, the general statements you make in any writing will be based on what you have experienced, observed, read, and thought. Readers will assume as much and will expect you to provide the evidence for your statements—sensory details, facts, statistics, examples, quotations, reasons. Whatever helps you form your views you need, in turn, to share with readers.

Here is the actual version of the preceding sample paragraph. With examples, the paragraph is more interesting and convincing.

> Untruths can serve as a kind of social oil when they smooth connections between people. Assuring a worried friend that his haircut is flattering, claiming an appointment to avoid an aunt's dinner invitation, pretending interest in an acquaintance's children—these lies may protect the liar, but they also protect the person lied to. In preventing confrontation and injured feelings, the lies allow everyone to go on as before.
> —JOAN LAR (student), "The Truth of Lies"

Examples specifying kinds of lies and consequences

http://www.ablongman.com/littlebrown

For added help with developing paragraphs, click on
➤ **The writing process**
   ➤ **Exercises ➤ Exer. 6**
   ➤ **Downloads ➤ Questions about patterns**
   ➤ **Web links ➤ Paragraphs**

If your readers often comment that your writing needs more specifics, you should focus on that improvement in your revisions. Try listing the general statements of each paragraph on lines by themselves with space underneath. Then use one of the discovery techniques discussed on pages 19–31 (freewriting, brainstorming, and so on) to find the details to support each sentence. Write these into your draft. If you write on a computer, you can do this revision directly on your draft. First create a duplicate of your draft, and then, working on the copy, separate the sentences and explore their support. Rewrite the supporting details into sentences, reassemble the paragraph, and edit it for coherence.

2 ■ Using a pattern of development

If you have difficulty developing an idea or shaping your information, then try asking yourself questions derived from the patterns of development. (The same patterns can help with essay development, too. See pp. 27–28.)

You can download the following questions from this book's Web site: see the box on page 91. When you're having difficulty with a paragraph, you can duplicate the list and explore answers. You may be able to import what you write directly into your draft.

How did it happen? (Narration)

Narration retells a significant sequence of events, usually in the order of their occurrence (that is, chronologically):

> Jill's story is typical for "recruits" to religious cults. She was very lonely in college and appreciated the attention of the nice young men and women who lived in a house near campus. They persuaded her to share their meals and then to move in with them. Between intense bombardments of "love," they deprived her of sleep and sometimes threatened to throw her out. Jill became increasingly confused and dependent, losing touch with any reality besides the one in the group. She dropped out of school and refused to see or communicate with her family. Before long she, too, was preying on lonely college students.
>
> —Hillary Begas (student),
> "The Love Bombers"

Important events in chronological order

As this paragraph illustrates, a narrator is concerned not just with the sequence of events but also with their consequence, their importance to the whole. Thus a narrative rarely corresponds to real time; instead, it collapses transitional or background events and focuses on events of particular interest. In addition, writers sometimes rearrange events, as when they simulate the workings of memory by flashing back to an earlier time.

How does it look, sound, feel, smell, taste? (Description)

Description details the sensory qualities of a person, place, thing, or feeling. You use concrete and specific words to convey a dominant mood, to illustrate an idea, or to achieve some other purpose. Some description is **subjective:** the writer filters the subject through his or her biases and emotions. In the subjective description by Virginia Woolf on page 81, the *glare* of the walls, the *impenetrable darkness,* the *bulge of a great bowl,* and the *formidable corners and lines* all indicate the author's feelings about what she describes.

In contrast to subjective description, journalists and scientists often favor description that is **objective,** conveying the subject without bias or emotion:

The two toddlers, both boys, sat together for half an hour in a ten-foot-square room with yellow walls (one with a two-way mirror for observation) and a brown carpet. The room was unfurnished except for two small chairs and about two dozen toys. The boys' interaction was generally tense. They often struggled physically and verbally over several toys, especially a large red beach ball and a small wooden fire engine. The larger of the two boys often pushed the smaller away or pried his hands from the desired object. This larger boy never spoke, but he did make grunting sounds when he was engaging the other. In turn, the smaller boy twice uttered piercing screams of "No!" and once shouted "Stop that!" When he was left alone, he hummed and muttered to himself.

> Objective description: specific record of sensory data without interpretation

—RAY MATTISON (student),
"Case Study: Play Patterns of Toddlers"

What are examples of it or reasons for it? (Illustration or support)

Some ideas can be developed simply by **illustration or support**—supplying detailed examples or reasons. The writer of the paragraph on lying (p. 91) developed her idea with several specific examples of her general statements. You can also supply a single extended example:

The language problem that I was attacking loomed larger and larger as I began to learn more. When I would describe in English certain concepts and objects enmeshed in Korean emotion and imagination, I became slowly aware of nuances, of differences be-

> Topic sentence (assertion to be illustrated)

tween two languages even in simple expression. The remark "Kim entered the house" seems to be simple enough, yet, unless a reader has a clear visual image of a Korean house, his understanding of the sentence is not complete. When a Korean says he is "in the house," he may be in his courtyard, or on his porch, or in his small room! If I wanted to give a specific picture of entering the house in the Western sense, I had to say "room" instead of house—sometimes. I say "sometimes" because many Koreans entertain their guests on their porches and still are considered to be hospitable, and in the Korean sense, going into the "room" may be a more intimate act than it would be in the English sense. Such problems!
—KIM YONG IK, "A Book-Writing Venture"

Single detailed example

Sometimes you can develop a paragraph by providing your reasons for stating a general idea:

There are three reasons, quite apart from scientific considerations, that mankind needs to travel in space. The first reason is the need for garbage disposal: we need to transfer industrial processes into space, so that the earth may remain a green and pleasant place for our grandchildren to live in. The second reason is the need to escape material impoverishment: the resources of this planet are finite, and we shall not forgo forever the abundant solar energy and minerals and living space that are spread out all around us. The third reason is our spiritual need for an open frontier: the ultimate purpose of space travel is to bring to humanity not only scientific discoveries and an occasional spectacular show on television but a real expansion of our spirit.
—FREEMAN DYSON, "Disturbing the Universe"

Topic sentence

Three reasons arranged in order of increasing drama and importance

What is it? What does it encompass, and what does it exclude? (Definition)

A **definition** says what something is and is not, specifying the characteristics that distinguish the subject from the other members of its class. You can easily define concrete, noncontroversial terms in a single sentence: *A knife is a cutting instrument* (its class) *with a sharp blade set in a handle* (the characteristics that set it off from, say, scissors or a razor blade). But defining a complicated or controversial topic often requires extended explanation, and you may need to devote a whole paragraph or even an essay to it. Such a definition may provide examples to identify the subject's characteristics. It may also involve other methods of development discussed here, such as classification or comparison and contrast.

The following definition of the word *quality* comes from an essay asserting that "quality in product and effort has become a vanishing element of current civilization":

> In the hope of possibly reducing the hail of censure which is certain to greet this essay (I am thinking of going to Alaska or possibly Patagonia in the week it is published), let me say that quality, as I understand it, means investment of the best skill and effort possible to produce the finest and most admirable result possible.

— General definition

> Its presence or absence in some degree characterizes every man-made object, service, skilled or unskilled labor—laying bricks, painting a picture, ironing shirts, practicing medicine, shoemaking, scholarship, writing a book.

— Activities in which quality may figure

> You do it well or you do it half-well. Materials are sound and durable or they are sleazy; method is painstaking or whatever is easiest. Quality is achieving or reaching for the highest standard as against being satisfied with the sloppy or fraudulent. It is honesty of purpose as against catering to cheap or sensational sentiment. It does not allow compromise with the second-rate.

— Contrast between quality and nonquality

> —BARBARA TUCHMAN,
> "The Decline of Quality"

What are its parts or characteristics? (Division or analysis)

Division and **analysis** both involve separating something into its elements, the better to understand it. Here is a simple example:

> A typical daily newspaper compresses considerable information into the top of the first page, above the headlines.

— The subject being divided

> The most prominent feature of this space, the newspaper's name, is called the *logo* or *nameplate*. Under the logo and set off by rules is a line of small type called the *folio line*, which contains the date of the issue, the volume and issue numbers, copyright information, and the price. To the right of the logo is a block of small type called a *weather ear*, a summary of the day's forecast. And above the logo is a *skyline*, a kind of advertisement in which the paper's editors highlight a special feature of the issue.

— Elements of the subject, arranged spatially

> —KANSHA STONE (student),
> "Anatomy of a Paper"

Generally, analysis goes beyond simply identifying elements. Often used as a synonym for *critical thinking,* analysis also involves interpreting the elements' meaning, significance, and relationships. You identify and interpret elements according to your particular interest in the subject. (See pp. 114–32 for more on critical thinking and analysis.)

The following paragraph comes from an essay about soap operas. The analytical focus of the whole essay is the way soap operas provide viewers with a sense of community missing from their own lives. The paragraph itself has a narrower focus related to the broader one.

> The surface realism of the soap opera conjures up an illusion of "liveness." The domestic settings and easygoing rhythms encourage the viewer to believe that the drama, however ridiculous, is simply an extension of daily life. The conversation is so slow that some have called it "radio with pictures." (Advertisers have always assumed that busy housewives would listen, rather than watch.) Conversation is casual and colloquial, as though one were eavesdropping on neighbors. There is plenty of time to "read" the character's face; close-ups establish intimacy. The sets are comfortably familiar: well-lit interiors of living rooms, restaurants, offices, and hospitals. Daytime soaps have little of the glamour of their prime-time relations. The viewer easily imagines that the conversation is taking place in real time.
>
> —RUTH ROSEN, "Search for Yesterday"

Topic and focus: how "liveness" seems an extension of daily life

Elements:
Slow conversation

Casual conversation

Intimate close-ups
Familiar sets

Absence of glamour
Appearance of real time

What groups or categories can it be sorted into? (Classification)

Classification involves sorting many things into groups based on their similarities. Using the pattern, we scan a large group composed of many members that share at least one characteristic—office workers, say—and we assign the members to smaller groups on the basis of some principle—salary, perhaps, or dependence on computers. Here is an example:

> In my experience, the parents who hire daytime sitters for their school-age children tend to fall into one of three groups. The first group includes parents who work and want someone to be at home when the children return from school. These parents are looking for an extension of themselves, someone who will give the care they would give if they were at home. The second group includes parents who may be home all day themselves but are

Topic sentence

Three groups:
   Alike in one way (all hire sitters)

   No overlap in groups (each has a different attitude)

too disorganized or too frazzled by their children's demands to handle child care alone. They are looking for an organizer and helpmate. The third and final group includes parents who do not want to be bothered by their children, whether they are home all day or not. Unlike the parents in the first two groups, who care for their children whenever and however they can, these parents are looking for a permanent substitute for themselves.

Classes arranged in order of increasing drama

—NANCY WHITTLE (student),
"Modern Parenting"

How is it like, or different from, other things? (Comparison and contrast)

Asking about similarities and differences leads to **comparison and contrast:** comparison focuses on similarities, whereas contrast focuses on differences. The two may be used separately or together to develop an idea or to relate two or more things. Commonly, comparisons are organized in one of two ways. In the first, **subject by subject,** the two subjects are discussed separately, one at a time:

Consider the differences also in the behavior of rock and classical music audiences. At a rock concert, the audience members yell, whistle, sing along, and stamp their feet. They may even stand during the entire performance. The better the music, the more active they'll be. At a classical concert, in contrast, the better the performance, the more *still* the audience is. Members of the classical audience are so highly disciplined that they refrain from even clearing their throats or coughing. No matter what effect the powerful music has on their intellects and feelings, they sit on their hands.

Subjects: rock and classical audiences

Rock audience

Classical audience

—TONY NAHM (student),
"Rock and Roll Is Here to Stay"

In the second comparative organization, **point by point,** the two subjects are discussed side by side and matched feature for feature:

The first electronic computer, ENIAC, went into operation just over fifty years ago, yet the differences between it and today's home computer are enormous. ENIAC was enormous itself, consisting of forty panels, each two feet wide and four feet deep. Today's PC or Macintosh, by contrast, can fit easily on one's desk or even lap. ENIAC had to be configured by hand, with its programmers taking

Subjects: ENIAC and home computer

Size: ENIAC, home computer

Ease of programming: ENIAC, home computer

up to two days to reset switches and cables. Today, the average home user can change programs in an instant. And for all its size and inconvenience, ENIAC was also slow. In its time, its operating speed of 100,000 pulses per second seemed amazingly fast. However, today's home machine can operate at 1 billion pulses per second or faster.

> Speed: ENIAC, home computer

—SHIRLEY KAJIWARA (student),
"The Computers We Deserve"

The following examples show the two organizing schemes in outline form. The one on the left corresponds to the point-by-point paragraph about computers. The one on the right uses the same information but reorganizes it to cover the two subjects separately: first one, then the other.

Point by point
I. Size
   A. ENIAC
   B. Home computer
II. Ease of programming
   A. ENIAC
   B. Home computer
III. Speed
   A. ENIAC
   B. Home computer

Subject by subject
I. ENIAC
   A. Size
   B. Ease of programming
   C. Speed
II. Home computer
   A. Size
   B. Ease of programming
   C. Speed

Is it comparable to something that is in a different class but more familiar to readers? (Analogy)

Whereas we draw comparisons and contrasts between elements in the same general class (audiences, computers), we link elements in different classes with a special kind of comparison called **analogy**. Most often in analogy we illuminate or explain an unfamiliar, abstract class of things with a familiar and concrete class of things:

> We might eventually obtain some sort of bedrock understanding of cosmic structure, but we will never understand the universe in detail; it is just too big and varied for that. If we possessed an atlas of our galaxy that devoted but a single page to each star system in the Milky Way (so that the sun and all its planets were crammed on one page), that atlas would run to more than ten million volumes of ten thousand pages each. It would take a library the size of Harvard's to house the atlas, and merely to flip through it, at the rate of a page per second, would require over ten thousand years.   —TIMOTHY FERRIS,
> *Coming of Age in the Milky Way*

Abstract subject: the universe, specifically the Milky Way

Concrete subject: an atlas

Why did it happen, or what results did it have? (Cause-and-effect analysis)

When you use analysis to explain why something happened or what is likely to happen, then you are determining causes and effects. **Cause-and-effect analysis** is especially useful in writing about social, economic, or political events or problems. In the next paragraph the author looks at the causes of Japanese collectivism, which he elsewhere contrasts with American individualism:

The *shinkansen* or "bullet train" speeds across the rural areas of Japan giving a quick view of cluster after cluster of farmhouses surrounded by rice paddies. This particular pattern did not develop purely by chance, but as a consequence of the technology peculiar to the growing of rice, the staple of the Japanese diet. The growing of rice requires the construction and maintenance of an irrigation system, something that takes many hands to build. More importantly, the planting and the harvesting of rice can only be done efficiently with the cooperation of twenty or more people. The "bottom line" is that a single family working alone cannot produce enough rice to survive, but a dozen families working together can produce a surplus. Thus the Japanese have had to develop the capacity to work together in harmony, no matter what the forces of disagreement or social disintegration, in order to survive.

> Effect: pattern of Japanese farming

> Causes: Japanese dependence on rice, which requires collective effort

> Effect: working in harmony

—WILLIAM OUCHI, *Theory Z*

Cause-and-effect paragraphs tend to focus either on causes, as Ouchi's does, or on effects, as this paragraph does:

At each step, with every graduation from one level of education to the next, the refrain from bystanders was strangely the same: "Your parents must be so proud of you." I suppose that my parents were proud, although I suspect, too, that they felt more than pride alone as they watched me advance through my education. They seemed to know that my education was separating us from one another, making it difficult to resume familiar intimacies. Mixed with the instincts of parental pride, a certain hurt also communicated itself—too private ever to be adequately expressed in words, but real nonetheless.

> Cause: education

> Effects:
>   Pride

>   Separation
>   Loss of intimacies

>   Hurt

—RICHARD RODRIGUEZ,
"Going Home Again"

¶ dev

4c

How does one do it, or how does it work? (Process analysis)

When you analyze how to do something or how something works, you explain the steps in a **process.** Paragraphs developed by process analysis are usually organized chronologically, as the steps in the process occur. Some process analyses tell the reader how to do a task:

As a car owner, you waste money when you pay a mechanic to change the engine oil. ⎤ Process: changing oil

The job is not difficult, even if you know little about cars. All you need is a wrench to remove the drain plug, a large, flat pan to collect the ⎱ Equipment needed draining oil, plastic bottles to dispose of the ⎰ used oil, and fresh oil. First, warm up the car's engine so that the oil will flow more easily. When the engine is warm, shut it off and re-move its oil-filler cap (the owner's manual shows where this cap is). Then locate the drain plug under the engine (again consulting the owner's manual for its location) and place the ⎱ Steps in process flat pan under the plug. Remove the plug with the wrench, letting the oil flow into the pan. When the oil stops flowing, replace the plug and, at the engine's filler hole, add the amount and kind of fresh oil specified by the owner's manual. Pour the used oil into the plastic bot-tles and take it to a waste-oil collector, which any garage mechanic can recommend.

—ANTHONY ANDREAS (student),
"Do-It-Yourself Car Care"

Other process analyses explain how processes are done or how they work in nature. Annie Dillard's paragraph on mangrove islands (p. 81) is one example. Here is another:

What used to be called "laying on of ⎱ Process: therapeutic hands" is now practiced seriously by nurses ⎰ touch and doctors. Studies have shown that thera-peutic touch, as it is now known, can aid re-laxation and ease pain, two effects that may ⎱ Benefits in turn cause healing. A "healer" must first ⎰ concentrate on helping the patient. Then, hands held a few inches from the patient's body, the healer moves from head to foot. Healers claim that they can detect energy dis- ⎱ Steps in process turbances in the patient that indicate tension, pain, or sickness. With further hand move-ments, the healer tries to redirect the energy. Patients report feeling heat from the healer's hands, perhaps indicating an energy transfer ⎱ How process works between healer and patient.

—LISA KUKLINSKI (student),
"Old Ways to Noninvasive Medicine"

Diagrams, photographs, and other figures can do much to clarify process analyses. See pages 208–11 for guidelines on creating and clearly labeling figures.

Combining patterns of development

Whatever pattern you choose as the basis for developing a paragraph, other patterns may also prove helpful. Combined patterns have appeared often in this section: Dyson analyzes causes and effects in presenting reasons (p. 94); Tuchman uses contrast to define *quality* (p. 95); Nahm uses description to compare (p. 97); Ouchi uses process analysis to explain causes (p. 99).

As you will see on pages 110–12, the paragraphs within an essay inevitably will be developed with a variety of patterns, even when one controlling pattern develops and structures the entire essay.

3 ▪ Checking length

The average paragraph contains between 100 and 150 words, or between four and eight sentences. The actual length of a paragraph depends on the complexity of its topic, the role it plays in developing the thesis of the essay, and its position in the essay. Nevertheless, very short paragraphs are often inadequately developed; they may leave readers with a sense of incompleteness. And very long paragraphs often contain irrelevant details or develop two or more topics; readers may have difficulty following, sorting out, or remembering ideas.

When you are revising your essay, reread the paragraphs that seem very long or very short, checking them especially for unity and adequate development. If the paragraph wanders, cut everything from it that does not support your main idea (such as sentences that you might begin with *By the way*). If it is underdeveloped, supply the specific details, examples, or reasons needed, or try one of the methods of development we have discussed here.

EXERCISE 13
Analyzing paragraph development
Examine the paragraphs by Henry Louis Gates, Jr. (pp. 76–77), and Judith Wax (p. 82) to discover how the authors achieve paragraph development. What pattern or patterns of development does each author use? Where does each author support general statements with specific evidence?

EXERCISE 14
Analyzing and revising skimpy paragraphs
The following paragraphs are not well developed. Analyze them, looking especially for general statements that lack support or leave questions in your mind. Then rewrite one into a well-developed paragraph, supplying your own concrete details or examples.

1.   One big difference between successful and unsuccessful teachers is the quality of communication. A successful teacher is sensitive to students' needs and excited by the course subject. In contrast, an unsuccessful teacher seems uninterested in students and bored by the subject.

2.   Gestures are one of our most important means of communication. We use them instead of speech. We use them to supplement the words we speak. And we use them to communicate some feelings or meanings that words cannot adequately express.

3.   I've discovered that a word processor can do much—but not everything—to help me improve my writing. I can easily make changes and try out different versions of a paper. But I still must do the hard work of revising.

EXERCISE 15
Considering your past work: Paragraph development
Continuing from Exercises 3 (p. 77) and 10 (p. 90), examine the development of the body paragraphs in your writing. Where does specific information seem adequate to support your general statements? Where does support seem skimpy? Revise the paragraphs as necessary to make your ideas clearer and more interesting. It may help you to pose the questions on pages 92–100.

EXERCISE 16
Writing with the patterns of development
Write at least three unified, coherent, and well-developed paragraphs, each one developed with a different pattern. Draw on the topics provided here, or choose your own topics.

1. *Narration*
   An experience of public
     speaking
   A disappointment
   Leaving home
   Waking up
2. *Description (objective or subjective)*
   Your room
   A crowded or deserted
     place
   A food
   An intimidating person
3. *Illustration or support*
   Why study
   Having a headache
   The best sports event
   Usefulness (or uselessness)
     of a self-help book
4. *Definition*
   Humor
   An adult

   Fear
   Authority
5. *Division or analysis*
   A television news show
   A barn
   A Web site
   A piece of music
6. *Classification*
   Factions in a campus con-
     troversy
   Styles of playing poker
   Types of Web sites
   Kinds of teachers
7. *Comparison and contrast*
   Surfing the Web and watch-
     ing TV
   AM and FM radio an-
     nouncers
   High school and college
     football
   Movies on TV and in a
     theater

8. *Analogy*
   Paying taxes and giving
     blood
   The US Constitution and a
     building's foundation
   Graduating from high
     school and being
     released from prison
9. *Cause-and-effect analysis*
   Connection between ten-
     sion and anger

   Causes of failing a course
   Connection between credit
     cards and debt
   Causes of a serious accident
10. *Process analysis*
    Preparing for a job interview
    Setting up an e-mail account
    Protecting your home from
      burglars
    Making a jump shot

4d Writing special kinds of paragraphs

Several kinds of paragraphs do not always follow the guidelines for unity, coherence, development, and length because they serve special functions. These are the essay introduction, the essay conclusion, the transitional or emphatic paragraph, and the paragraph of spoken dialog.

1 ■ Opening an essay

Most of your essays will open with a paragraph that draws readers from their world into your world. A good opening paragraph usually satisfies several requirements:

- It focuses readers' attention on your subject and arouses their curiosity about what you have to say.
- It specifies what your topic is and implies your attitude.
- Often it provides your thesis statement.
- It is concise and sincere.

The box on the next page provides a range of options for achieving these goals.

If you are composing on the World Wide Web, you'll want to consider the expectations of Web readers. Your opening page may take the place of a conventional introduction, providing concise text indicating your site's subject and purpose, a menu of its contents, and links to other pages. (See pp. 228–30 for more on composing for the Web.)

CULTURE LANGUAGE ➤ The requirements and options for essay introductions may not be what you are used to if your native language is not

http://www.ablongman.com/littlebrown
For added help with introductions and conclusions, click on
➤ **The writing process** ➤ **Web links** ➤ **Paragraphs**

¶
4d

Some strategies for opening paragraphs

- Ask a question.
- Relate an incident.
- Use a vivid quotation.
- Offer a surprising statistic or other fact.
- State an opinion related to your thesis.
- Outline the argument your thesis refutes.
- Provide background.

- Create a visual image that represents your subject.
- Make a historical comparison or contrast.
- Outline a problem or dilemma.
- Define a word central to your subject.
- In some business or technical writing, summarize your paper.

English. In other cultures, readers may seek familiarity or reassurance from an author's introduction, or they may prefer an indirect approach to the subject. In academic and business English, however, writers and readers prefer concise, direct expression.

The funnel introduction

One reliably effective introduction forms a kind of funnel. The writer starts with a statement or question about the subject, a hook that forms a transition between readers' experience or knowledge and the subject of the essay. Then the writer clarifies or narrows the subject in one or more sentences. And finally, in the thesis statement, the writer asserts the central idea of the essay (see pp. 31–35). Here are two examples:

> Can your home or office computer make you sterile? Can it strike you blind or dumb? — Questions about subject
>
> The answer is: probably not. Nevertheless, reports of side effects relating to computer use should be examined, especially in the area of birth defects, eye complaints, and postural difficulties. — Clarification of subject: bridge to thesis statement
>
> Although little conclusive evidence exists to establish a causal link between computer use and problems of this sort, the circumstantial evidence can be disturbing. — Thesis statement
>
> —THOMAS HARTMANN, "How Dangerous Is Your Computer?"

> The Declaration of Independence is so widely regarded as a statement of American ideals that its origins in practical politics tend to be forgotten. — Statement about subject
>
> Thomas Jefferson's draft was intensely debated and then revised in the Continental Congress. Jefferson was disappointed — Clarification of subject: bridge to thesis statement

with the result. However, a close reading of both the historical context and the revisions themselves indicates that the Congress improved the document for its intended purpose.
—Ann Weiss (student), "The Editing of the Declaration of Independence"

⎤ Thesis statement

Other effective introductions

Several other types of introduction can be equally effective, though they are sometimes harder to invent and control. You can begin with a quotation that leads into the thesis statement:

> "It is difficult to speak adequately or justly of London," wrote Henry James in 1881. "It is not a pleasant place; it is not agreeable, or cheerful, or easy, or exempt from reproach. It is only magnificent." Were he alive today, James, a connoisseur of cities, might easily say the same thing about New York or Paris or Tokyo, for the great city is one of the paradoxes of history. In countless different ways, it has almost always been an unpleasant, disagreeable, cheerless, uneasy and reproachful place; in the end, it can only be described as magnificent.   —*Time*

You can relate an incident or convey a visual image that sets the stage for the thesis:

> Canada is pink. I knew that from the map I owned when I was six. On it, New York was green and brown, which was true as far as I could see, so there was no reason to distrust the map maker's portrayal of Canada. When my parents took me across the border and we entered the immigration booth, I looked excitedly for the pink earth. Slowly it dawned on me; this foreign, "different" place was not so different. I discovered that the world in my head and the world at my feet were not the same.
> —Robert Ornstein, *Human Nature*

You can open with a startling question or opinion:

> Caesar was right. Thin people need watching. I've been watching them for most of my adult life, and I don't like what I see. When these narrow fellows spring at me, I quiver to my toes. Thin people come in all personalities, most of them menacing. You've got your "together" thin person, your mechanical thin person, your condescending thin person, your tsk-tsk thin person. All of them are dangerous.   —Suzanne Britt, "That Lean and Hungry Look"

When some background to the essay is useful, you can begin with a historical comparison or contrast:

> Throughout the first half of this century, the American Medical Association, the largest and most powerful medical organization in the world, battled relentlessly to rid the country of quack

potions and cure-alls; and it is the AMA that is generally credited with being the single most powerful force behind the enactment of the early pure food and drug laws. Today, however, medicine's guardian seems to have done a complete about-face and become one of the pharmaceutical industry's staunchest allies—often at the public's peril and expense.   —MAC JEFFERY,
"Does Rx Spell Rip-off?"

An effective introductory paragraph need not be long, as the following opener shows:

> I've often wondered what goes into a hot dog. Now I know and I wish I didn't.   —WILLIAM ZINSSER, *The Lunacy Boom*

Ineffective introductions

When writing and revising an introductory paragraph, avoid the following approaches that are likely to bore readers or make them question your sincerity or control:

Openings to avoid

- **A vague generality or truth.** Don't extend your reach too wide with a line such as *Throughout human history . . .* or *In today's world. . . .* You may have needed a warm-up paragraph to start drafting, but your readers can do without it.
- **A flat announcement.** Don't start with *The purpose of this essay is . . . , In this essay I will . . . ,* or any similar presentation of your intention or topic.
- **A reference to the essay's title.** Don't refer to the title of the essay in the first sentence—for example, *This is a big problem* or *This book is about the history of the guitar.*
- *According to Webster. . . .* Don't start by citing a dictionary definition. A definition can be an effective springboard to an essay, but this kind of lead-in has become dull with overuse.
- **An apology.** Don't fault your opinion or your knowledge with *I'm not sure if I'm right, but . . . , I don't know much about this, but . . . ,* or a similar line.

---

2 ■ Closing an essay

Most of your compositions will end with a closing statement or conclusion, a signal to readers that you have not simply stopped writing but have actually finished. The conclusion completes an essay, bringing it to a climax while assuring readers that they have understood your intention.

Note that compositions for the Web usually do not provide the kind of closure featured in essays. In fact, you'll need to ensure that your Web pages don't dead-end, leaving the reader stranded without options for moving backward or forward through your material. (For more on Web composition, see Chapter 10.)

Effective conclusions

An essay conclusion may consist of a single sentence or a group of sentences, usually set off in a separate paragraph. The conclusion may take one or more of the following approaches:

Some strategies for closing paragraphs

- Strike a note of hope or despair.
- Give a symbolic or powerful fact or other detail.
- Give an especially compelling example.
- Create a visual image that represents your subject.

- Use a quotation.
- Recommend a course of action.
- Summarize the paper.
- Echo the approach of the intro-duction.
- Restate your thesis and reflect on its implications.

The following paragraph concludes the essay on the Declaration of Independence (the introduction appears on pp. 104–05):

> The Declaration of Independence has come to be a statement of this nation's political philosophy, but that was not its purpose in 1776. Jefferson's passionate expression had to bow to the goals of the Congress as a whole to forge unity among the colonies and to win the support of foreign nations.
>
> —Ann Weiss (student), "The Editing of the Declaration of Independence"

Echo of introduction: contrast between past and present

Restatement and elaboration of thesis

Maxine Hong Kingston uses a different technique—a vivid image—to conclude an essay on her aunt, a suicide by drowning:

> My aunt haunts me—her ghost drawn to me because now, after fifty years of neglect, I alone devote pages of paper to her, though not origamied into houses and clothes. I do not think she always means me well. I am telling on her, and she was a spite suicide, drowning herself in the drinking water. The Chinese are always very frightened of the drowned one, whose weeping ghost, wet hair hanging and skin bloated, waits silently by the water to pull down a substitute.
>
> —Maxine Hong Kingston, "No Name Woman"

Summary

Image

In the next paragraph the author concludes an essay on environmental protection with a call for action:

Until we get the answers, I think we had better keep on building power plants and growing food with the help of fertilizers and such insect-controlling chemicals as we now have. The risks are well known, thanks to the environmentalists. If they had not created a widespread public awareness of the ecological crisis, we wouldn't stand a chance. } Summary and opinion

But such awareness by itself is not enough. Flaming manifestos and prophecies of doom are no longer much help, and a search for scapegoats can only make matters worse. The time for sensations and manifestos is about over. Now we need rigorous analysis, united effort and very hard work. } Call for action

—PETER F. DRUCKER, "How Best to Protect the Environment"

Ineffective conclusions

The preceding three examples illustrate ways of avoiding several pitfalls of conclusions:

Closings to avoid

- **A repeat of the introduction.** Don't simply replay your introduction. The conclusion should capture what the paragraphs of the body have added to the introduction.
- **A new direction.** Don't introduce a subject different from the one your essay has been about. If you arrive at a new idea, this may be a signal to start fresh with that idea as your thesis.
- **A sweeping generalization.** Don't conclude more than you reasonably can from the evidence you have presented. If your essay is about your frustrating experience trying to clear a parking ticket, you cannot reasonably conclude that *all* local police forces are tied up in red tape.
- **An apology.** Don't cast doubt on your essay. Don't say, *Even though I'm no expert* or *This may not be convincing, but I believe it's true* or anything similar. Rather, to win your readers' confidence, display confidence.

3 ■ Using short emphatic or transitional paragraphs

A short emphatic paragraph can give unusual stress to an important idea, in effect asking the reader to pause and consider before moving on.

In short, all those who might have taken responsibility ducked it, and catastrophe was inevitable.

A transitional paragraph, because it is longer than a word or phrase and set off by itself, moves a discussion from one point to

¶
4d

another more slowly or more completely than does a single transitional expression or even a transitional sentence attached to a larger paragraph.

> These, then, are the causes of the current contraction in hospital facilities. But how does this contraction affect the medical costs of the government, private insurers, and individuals?

> So the debates were noisy and emotion-packed. But what did they accomplish? Historians have identified at least three direct results.

Use transitional paragraphs only to shift readers' attention when your essay makes a significant turn. A paragraph like the following one betrays a writer who is stalling:

> Now that we have examined these facts, we can look at some others that are equally central to an examination of this important issue.

4 ■ Writing dialog

When recording a conversation between two or more people, start a new paragraph for each person's speech. The paragraphing establishes for the reader the point at which one speaker stops talking and another begins.

> The dark shape was indistinguishable. But once I'd flooded him with light, there he stood, blinking.
> "Well," he said eventually, "you're a sight for sore eyes. Should I stand here or are you going to let me in?"
> "Come in," I said. And in he came.
>
> —LOUISE ERDRICH, *The Beet Queen*

Though dialog appears most often in fictional writing (the source of the preceding example), it may occasionally freshen or enliven narrative or expository essays. (For guidance in using quotation marks and other punctuation in passages of dialog, see pp. 468–70 and 498.)

EXERCISE 17
Analyzing an introduction and conclusion
Analyze the introductory and concluding paragraphs in the first and final drafts of the student essay in Chapter 3, pages 49–50 and 63–64. What is wrong with the first-draft paragraphs? Why are the final-draft paragraphs better? Could they be improved still further?

EXERCISE 18
Considering your past work: Introductions and conclusions
Examine the opening and closing paragraphs of the essay you've been analyzing in Exercises 3, 10, and 15. Do the paragraphs fulfill the requirements and avoid the pitfalls outlined on pages

¶
4e

103–08? Revise them as needed for clarity, conciseness, focus, and interest.

4e   Linking paragraphs in the essay

Your paragraphs do not stand alone: each one is a key unit of a larger piece of writing. Though you may draft paragraphs or groups of paragraphs almost as mini-essays, you will eventually need to stitch them together into a unified, coherent, well-developed whole. The techniques parallel those for linking sentences in paragraphs:

- Make sure each paragraph contributes to your thesis.
- You will probably use varied patterns of development for individual paragraphs, even when the whole essay is developed and structured by another pattern. Just be sure to follow through on your overall pattern.
- Arrange the paragraphs in a clear, logical order. See pages 35–45 for advice on essay organization.
- Create links between paragraphs. Use repetition and restatement to stress and connect key terms, and use transitional expressions and transitional sentences to indicate sequence, direction, contrast, and other relationships.

The following essay illustrates the way effective paragraphs can build an effective essay. The overall pattern of development is analysis. The overall organization is climactic. Sentences and paragraphs are linked by repetition, restatement, and pronouns (circled words); transitional expressions (boxed words); parallelism (underlined); and transitional sentences (noted in marginal comments).

A Picture of Hyperactivity

A hyperactive committee member can contribute to efficiency. A hyperactive salesperson can contribute to profits. When a child is hyperactive, though, people—even parents—may wish he had never been born. A collage of those who must cope with this disorder in children is a dark picture of frustration, anger, and loss.

⎦ Thesis statement

The first part of the collage is the doctors. In their terminology the word hyperactivity has been replaced by ADHD, attention-deficit

⎤ Transitional topic sentence

hyperactivity disorder. They apply the term to children and adults who are inattentive, impulsive, and excessively restless or busy. But doctors do not fully understand the problem and thus differ over how to treat it. For example, some recommend a special diet; others, behavior-modifying drugs; and still others, who do not consider ADHD to be a medical problem, a psychiatrist for the entire family. The result is a merry-go-round of tests, confusion, and frustration for the parents and the child.

Paragraph developed by definition, example, and cause-and-effect analysis

¶
4e

As the parent of an ADHD child, I can say what ADHD means to the parents who form the second part of the collage. It means worry that is deep and enduring. It means despair that is a companion on dark and sleepless nights. It means fear that is heart twisting and constant, for the ADHD child is most destructive toward himself. It means a mixture of frustration, guilt, and anger. And finally, since there are times when that anger goes out of control and the child is in danger from the parent, it means self-loathing.

Transitional topic sentence

Paragraph developed by definition and cause-and-effect analysis

The weight of ADHD, however, rests not on the doctors or the parents but on the child. For him is reserved the final and darkest part of the collage because he is most affected. From early childhood he is dragged from doctor to doctor, is attached to strange and frightening machines, and is tested or discussed by physicians, parents, neighbors, teachers, peers. His playmates dislike him because of his temper and his unwillingness to follow rules. Even his pets fear and mis-

Transitional sentence

Topic sentence

Paragraph developed by narration and cause-and-effect analysis trust him because he treats them erratically, often hurting them without meaning to. As time goes on, he sees his parents more and more often in tears and anger, and he knows that he is the cause. He is highly intelligent, but he does poorly when he enters school because of his short attention span. He is fond of sports and games, but he never joins the other children on the playground because he has an uncontrollable temper and poor coordination. By the time he reaches age seven or eight, he is obsessed with one thought: "Mama," my son asks me repeatedly, "why do I have to be this way?"

At last the collage is completed, and it is dark and somber. ADHD, as applied to children, is a term with uncertain, unattractive, and bitter associations. But the picture does have a bright spot, for inside every ADHD child is a loving, trustful, calm person waiting to be recognized.

⎤ — Transitional sentence

—LINDA DEVEREAUX (student)

EXERCISE 19
Analyzing paragraphs in essays
Analyze the ways in which paragraphs combine in the two student essays in Chapter 3, pages 63–64 and 69–70. With what techniques does each writer link paragraphs to the thesis statement and to each other? Where, if at all, does the writer seem to stray from the thesis or fail to show how paragraphs relate to it? How would you revise the essays to solve any problems they exhibit?

EXERCISE 20
Considering your past work: Paragraphs in the essay
Examine the overall effect of the essay you've been analyzing in Exercises 3, 10, 15, and 18. Do all the paragraphs relate to your thesis? Are they arranged clearly and logically? How do repetition and restatement, transitional expressions, or transitional sentences connect the paragraphs? Can you see ways to improve the essay's unity, coherence, and development?

PART II

Critical Thinking, Reading, and Writing

CHAPTER 5

Taking a Critical Perspective

Throughout college and beyond, you will be expected to think, read, and write critically. **Critical** here means "skeptical," "exacting," "creative." When you operate critically, you question, test, and build on what others say and what you yourself think. The word *critical* does not mean "negative" in this context: you can think critically about something you like, don't like, or just view neutrally.

You already operate critically every day of your life, as when you probe a friendship ("What did she mean by that?") or when you discuss a movie you just saw ("Don't you think the bad guy was too obvious?"). Such questioning helps you figure out why things happen to you or what your experiences mean.

This chapter introduces more formal methods for thinking and reading critically (opposite), viewing images critically (p. 133), and writing critically (p. 137). Learning and applying these methods will both engage you in and prepare you for school courses, career, and life in a democratic society:

- Teachers and employers in every field, from the arts to social work to zoology, will expect you to assess what you read, see, and hear and to make a good case for your own ideas.
- In daily life, critical thinking helps you understand your own actions and ideas, weigh them against opposing views, and persuasively articulate your reasoning and motivations.
- Your very independence and freedom depend on your ability to think, read, and write critically. An open democracy allows as much play for stupid and false claims as for sound ones, and the claims that seem sound often conflict with each other. Crit-

http://www.ablongman.com/littlebrown
For added help with critical thinking, reading, and writing, click on
➤ Critical thinking and argument
   ➤ Video tutorials
   ➤ Exercises
   ➤ Downloads
   ➤ Web links

ical thinking empowers you to decide for yourself what's useful, fair, and wise—and what's not.

There's no denying that critical thinking, reading, and writing require discipline and hard work. Besides channeling your curiosity, paying attention, and probing, you will often need to consult experts, interpreting and evaluating their ideas. Such an approach also requires a healthy tolerance for doubt or uncertainty—that feeling you may have when the old rules don't seem to apply or when a change is frightening but still attractive. Out of uncertainty, though, comes creativity—the capacity to organize and generate knowledge, to explain, resolve, illuminate, play. Compared to passive, rote learning, creative work is more involving, more productive, and more enjoyable.

crit

5a

5a   Thinking and reading critically

In college much of your critical thinking will focus on written texts (a short story, a journal article, an Internet posting, a site on the Web) or on visual objects (a photograph, a chart, a film). Like all subjects worthy of critical consideration, such works operate on at least three levels: (1) what the creator actually says or shows, (2) what the creator does not say or show but builds into the work (intentionally or not), and (3) what you think. Discovering each level of the work, even if it is visual, involves a number of reading techniques that are discussed in this chapter and summarized in the box below.

The techniques of critical reading are not steps in a firm sequence. You will not use all of them for all the reading you do. On some occasions, even when a close, critical reading is required, you

Techniques of critical reading

For reading a work of literature, which requires a somewhat different approach, see pp. 786–94.

- **Writing:** making notes on your reading throughout the process (next page)
- **Previewing:** getting background; skimming (p. 117)
- **Reading:** interacting with and absorbing the text (p. 118)
- **Summarizing:** distilling and understanding content (p. 123)
- **Forming your critical response** (p. 124)

  Analyzing: separating into parts
  Interpreting: inferring meaning and assumptions
  Synthesizing: reassembling parts; making connections
  Evaluating: judging quality and value

may simply lack the time to preview, read, and reread. (But if your reading time is continually squeezed by your schedule, you may need to rethink your schedule.) On other occasions your reason for reading (your purpose) will determine which techniques you use.

Even a work like *People* magazine is open to different methods of reading for different purposes:

| Purpose | Learn some gossip while filling time in the dentist's office. |
| Kind of reading | Quick, uncritical |

| Purpose | Examine *People* as an artifact of our popular culture that reflects and perhaps even molds contemporary values. |
| Kind of reading | Close, critical |

Course assignments, too, differ in their requirements. A book report may require writing, previewing, reading, and summarizing but not intense critical reading. An evaluation of a journal article, in contrast, requires all the techniques discussed here.

CULTURE LANGUAGE The idea of reading critically may require you to make some adjustments if readers in your native culture tend to seek understanding or agreement more than engagement from what they read. Readers of English use texts for all kinds of reasons, including pleasure, reinforcement, information, and many others. But they also read skeptically, critically, to see the author's motives, test their own ideas, and arrive at new knowledge.

1 ▪ Writing while reading

There are two good reasons to write while you read: to record information and ideas for future use, and to get more out of the work. The first is discussed as part of research writing (see pp. 607–08). The second has more to do with critical reading.

Critical reading is *active* reading. You interact with the work, getting involved with it, bringing to it *your* experiences, knowledge, and questions. When you use a pen or pencil or keyboard while reading, you create writing in response to writing. In this way you "translate" the work into your own words and reconstruct it for yourself.

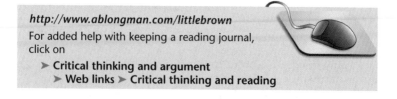

http://www.ablongman.com/littlebrown
For added help with keeping a reading journal, click on
➤ **Critical thinking and argument**
  ➤ **Web links** ➤ **Critical thinking and reading**

Many readers keep a **reading journal,** a notebook or computer file in which they regularly work out questions and thoughts about what they read. One technique for keeping such a journal is to divide a page or computer screen into two vertical columns, the left side for the work itself, such as summary and questions, and the right side for what the work makes you think, such as agreements or doubts based on your own experiences, comparisons with other works, and ideas for writing. A two-column journal can encourage you to go beyond summarizing what you read to interacting critically with it because the blank right column will beckon you to respond. See page 120 for an example of this technique.

crit
5a

If you don't keep a regular reading journal, you can still benefit from writing while reading in other ways:

- If you're reading a printed work that you own, you may opt to write directly on the pages as you read them (see pp. 119–20).
- If you don't own the material, make your notes on a separate sheet or a photocopy or in a computer file.
- If you're reading a Web page or another online source, you have several options: print out a copy of the material and annotate that; open your word processor at the same time and make notes in the word-processing document; copy and paste the material into a word-processing document and insert your own comments in color or with the Comment function (see p. 190); or compose electronic mail while you're reading and then send it to yourself.

Note Whenever you download a document or take notes separately from the text you're reading, be sure to record all necessary information about the text's location so that you can find it again and cite it fully if you use it. (See p. 617 for a list of information to record.) Online sources sometimes restrict downloading, so check the source's copyright notice to see whether any restrictions apply. See pages 686–88 for more on copying and acknowledging online sources.

2 ■ Previewing the material

When you're reading a work of literature, such as a story or a poem, it's often best just to plunge right in (see p. 787). But for critical reading of other works, it's worthwhile to form some expectations and even some preliminary questions before you start reading word for word. The preview will make your reading more informed and fruitful.

One way to preview is to **skim,** looking for clues about content, author, and how you will interact with the work. Not the same as idly turning pages or scrolling through screens, skimming is a focused, concentrated activity in which you seek information. Use the questions below as a guide. In your journal write down any impressions that you may want to return to later.

Questions for previewing

- **Length:** Is the material brief enough to read in one sitting, or will you need more time? To gauge the length of an online source such as a Web site, study any menus for an indication of the source's complexity. Then scroll through a couple of pages and follow a couple of links to estimate the overall length.
- **Facts of publication:** Does the date of publication suggest currency or datedness? Does the publisher or publication specialize in a particular kind of material—scholarly articles, say, or popular books? For a Web source, who or what sponsors the site: an individual? a nonprofit organization? an academic institution? a corporation? a government body? (See pp. 654 and 659 on locating the authors of online sources.)
- **Content cues:** What do the title, summary or abstract, headings, illustrations, and other features tell you? What questions do they raise in your mind?
- **Author:** What does the biographical information tell you about the author's publications, interests, biases, and reputation in the field? For an online message, which may be posted by an unfamiliar or anonymous author, what can you gather about the author from his or her words? If possible, trace unfamiliar authors to learn more about them.
- **Yourself:** Do you anticipate particular difficulties with the content? What biases of your own may influence your response to the text—for instance, anxiety, curiosity, boredom, or an outlook similar or opposed to that of the author?

3 ■ Reading

Reading is itself more than a one-step process. Your primary goal is to understand the first level on which the text operates—what the author actually says.

First reading

The first time through new material, read as steadily and smoothly as possible, trying to get the gist of what the author is saying and a sense of his or her tone.

- To help your concentration, read in a quiet place away from distractions such as music or talking.
- Give yourself time. Rushing yourself or worrying about something else you have to do will prevent you from grasping what you read.
- Try to enjoy the work. Seek connections between it and what

you already know. Appreciate new information, interesting relationships, forceful writing, humor, good examples.

- Make notes sparingly during this reading. Mark major stumbling blocks—such as a paragraph you don't understand—so that you can try to resolve them before rereading.
- If you're browsing a Web site with multiple pages and links to other sites, use the Bookmarks or Favorites function of your Web browser to mark interesting pages and links so that you can return to them. Then, when reading pages, proceed steadily without taking frequent or extensive notes, reserving that work for the next reading.

CULTURE LANGUAGE ➤ If English is not your first language and you come across unfamiliar words, don't stop and look up every one. You will lose more in concentration than you will gain in understanding. Instead, try to guess the meanings of unfamiliar words from their contexts (see pp. 586–87), circle them, and look them up later.

Rereadings

After the first reading, plan on at least one other. This time read *slowly*. Your main concern should be to grasp the content and how it is constructed. That means rereading a paragraph if you didn't get the point, looking up key words in a dictionary, or following more links at a Web site.

Use your pen, pencil, or keyboard freely to question and comment on the text:

- If you can't write directly on the material (because you don't own it or it's online), make separate notes as suggested on page 117.
- If you can write directly on the material, use any system of annotations that works for you—perhaps "?" in the margin next to passages you don't understand, circles around unfamiliar words, underlining or brackets for main points, "*" for passages you agree with, "!" for those you find startling, "So what?" for those you can't see the point of.
- If you're reading an online source that you can download onto your word processor, use the Highlight function to mark text you have questions or comments on. Then insert your annotations in color (so they're distinct from the original) or with your word processor's Comment function.

Following are examples of active reading from a student, Charlene Robinson. She was responding to Thomas Sowell's "Student Loans," an essay beginning on page 121. First Robinson annotated a photocopy of the essay (the first four paragraphs appear on the next page):

The first lesson of economics is scarcity: There is never enough of anything to fully satisfy all those who want it.

The first lesson of politics is to disregard the first lesson of economics. When politicians discover some group that is being vocal about not having as much as they want, the "solution" is to give them more. Where do politicians get this "more"? They rob Peter to pay Paul.

After a while, of course, they discover that Peter doesn't have enough. Bursting with compassion, politicians rush to the rescue. Needless to say, they do not admit that robbing Peter to pay Paul was a dumb idea in the first place. On the contrary, they now rob Tom, Dick, and Harry to help Peter.

The latest chapter in this long-running saga is that politicians have now suddenly discovered that many college students graduate heavily in debt. To politicians it follows, as the night follows the day, that the government should come to their rescue with the taxpayers' money.

Basic contradiction between economics and politics

← *biblical reference?*

ironic and dismissive language

politicians = fools? or irresponsible

After reading the text, Robinson wrote about it in the journal she kept on her computer. She divided the journal into two columns, one each for the text and her responses. Here is the portion pertaining to the paragraphs above:

Text	Responses
Economics teaches lessons (1), and politics (politicians) and economics are at odds	Is economics truer or more reliable than politics? More scientific?
Politicians don't accept econ. limits--always trying to satisfy "vocal" voters by giving them what they want (2)	Politicians do spend a lot of our money. Is that what they're elected to do, or do they go too far?
"Robbing Peter to pay Paul" (2)--from the Bible (the Apostles)?	
Politicians support student loan program with taxpayer funds bec. of "vocal" voters (2-4): another ex. of not accepting econ. limits	I support the loan program, too. Are politicians being irresponsible when they do? (Dismissive language underlined on copy.)

You should try to answer the questions about meaning that you raise in your annotations and your journal, and that may take another reading or some digging in other sources, such as dictionaries and encyclopedias. Recording in your journal what you think the author means will help you build an understanding of the text, and a focused attempt to summarize will help even more (see p. 123). Such efforts will resolve any confusion you feel, or they will give you the confidence to say that your confusion is the fault of the author, not the reader.

crit

5a

EXERCISE 1
Reading

Reprinted below is an essay by Thomas Sowell on the federal government's student-loan program. A respected conservative economist, Sowell is also a newspaper columnist and the author of many books on economics, politics, and education. This essay appeared in Sowell's collection *Is Reality Optional?*

Read this essay at least twice, until you think you understand what the author is saying. Either on these pages or separately, note your questions and reactions in writing. Look up any words you don't know, and try to arrive at answers to your questions. (It may help to discuss the selection with classmates.)

Student Loans

The first lesson of economics is scarcity: There is never 1
enough of anything to fully satisfy all those who want it.

The first lesson of politics is to disregard the first lesson of 2
economics. When politicians discover some group that is being vocal about not having as much as they want, the "solution" is to give them more. Where do politicians get this "more"? They rob Peter to pay Paul.

After a while, of course, they discover that Peter doesn't have 3
enough. Bursting with compassion, politicians rush to the rescue. Needless to say, they do not admit that robbing Peter to pay Paul was a dumb idea in the first place. On the contrary, they now rob Tom, Dick, and Harry to help Peter.

The latest chapter in this long-running saga is that politicians 4
have now suddenly discovered that many college students graduate heavily in debt. To politicians it follows, as the night follows the day, that the government should come to their rescue with the taxpayers' money.

How big is this crushing burden of college students' debt that 5
we hear so much about from politicians and media deep thinkers? For those students who graduate from public colleges owing money, the debt averages a little under $7,000. For those who graduate from private colleges owing money, the average debt is a little under $9,000.

Buying a very modestly priced automobile involves more debt 6
than that. And a car loan has to be paid off faster than the ten years that college graduates get to repay their student loans. Moreover, you have to keep buying cars every several years, while one college education lasts a lifetime.

College graduates of course earn higher incomes than other 7
people. Why, then, should we panic at the thought that they have

to repay loans for the education which gave them their opportunities? Even graduates with relatively modest incomes pay less than 10 percent of their annual salary on the loan the first year—with declining percentages in future years, as their pay increases.

Political hysteria and media hype may focus on the low-income student with a huge debt. That is where you get your heart-rending stories—even if they are not at all typical. In reality, the soaring student loans of the past decade have resulted from allowing high-income people to borrow under government programs. 8

Before 1978, college loans were available through government programs only to students whose family income was below some cut-off level. That cut-off level was about double the national average income, but at least it kept out the Rockefellers and the Vanderbilts. But, in an era of "compassion," Congress took off even those limits. 9

That opened the floodgates. No matter how rich you were, it still paid to borrow money through the government at low interest rates. The money you had set aside for your children's education could be invested somewhere else, at higher interest rates. Then, when the student loan became due, parents could pay it off with the money they had set aside—pocketing the difference in interest rates. 10

To politicians and the media, however, the rapidly growing loans showed what a great "need" there was. The fact that many students welshed when time came to repay their loans showed how "crushing" their burden of debt must be. In reality, those who welsh typically have smaller loans, but have dropped out of college before finishing. People who are irresponsible in one way are often irresponsible in other ways. 11

No small amount of the deterioration of college standards has been due to the increasingly easy availability of college to people who are not very serious about getting an education. College is not a bad place to hang out for a few years, if you have nothing better to do, and if someone else is paying for it. Its costs are staggering, but the taxpayers carry much of that burden, not only for state universities and city colleges, but also to an increasing extent even for "private" institutions. 12

Numerous government subsidies and loan programs make it possible for many people to use vast amounts of society's resources at low cost to themselves. Whether in money terms or in real terms, federal aid to higher education has increased several hundred percent since 1970. That has enabled colleges to raise their tuition by leaps and bounds and enabled professors to be paid more and more for doing less and less teaching. 13

Naturally all these beneficiaries are going to create hype and hysteria to keep more of the taxpayers' money coming in. But we would be fools to keep on writing blank checks for them. 14

When you weigh the cost of things, in economics that's called "trade-offs." In politics, it's called "mean-spirited." Apparently, if we just took a different attitude, scarcity would go away. 15

—THOMAS SOWELL

4 ■ Summarizing

Before you can see what is beneath the surface of a text and figure out what you think of it, you need to understand exactly what the author is actually saying. A good way to master the content of a text and see its strengths and weaknesses is to **summarize** it: distill it to its main points, in your own words.

Some assignments call for brief summaries, as when you summarize the plot in a critical essay about a novel (p. 799). Summary is also an essential tool in research papers and other writing that draws on sources (p. 667). Here, though, we're concerned with summarizing for yourself—for your own enlightenment.

crit

5a

A summary should state in as few words as possible the main ideas of a passage. When you need to summarize a few paragraphs or a brief article, your summary should not exceed one-fifth the length of the original. For longer works, such as chapters of books or whole books, your summary should be quite a bit shorter in proportion to the original. A procedure for drafting a summary appears in the box on the next page. (You've seen the beginning of this process in Charlene Robinson's journal on p. 120.)

Summarizing even a single paragraph can be tricky. Here is one attempt to summarize paragraphs 1–4 of Thomas Sowell's "Student Loans" (p. 121):

Draft summary   As much as politicians would like to satisfy voters by giving them everything they ask for, the government cannot afford a student loan program.

This sentence "misreads" the four paragraphs because it asserts that the government cannot afford student loans. Sowell's point is more complicated than that. This accurate summary captures it:

Revised summary   As their support of the government's student loan program illustrates, politicians ignore the economic reality that using resources to benefit one group (students in debt) involves taking the resources from another group (taxpayers).

Using your own words when writing a summary not only helps you understand the meaning but also constitutes the first step in avoiding plagiarism. The second step is to cite the source when you use it in something written for others. See Chapter 47.

http://www.ablongman.com/littlebrown
For added help with writing summaries, click on
  ➤ **Critical thinking and argument**
    ➤ **Web links** ➤ **Critical thinking and reading**

Writing a summary

- **Understand the meaning.** Look up words or concepts you don't know so that you understand the author's sentences and how they relate to one another.
- **Understand the organization.** Work through the text to identify its sections—single paragraphs or groups of paragraphs focused on a single topic, related pages or links on a Web site. To understand how parts of a work relate to one another, try drawing a tree diagram or creating an outline (pp. 37–41). Both tools work well for straight text; the tree diagram may work better for nonlinear material such as a Web site.
- **Distill each section.** Write a one- or two-sentence summary of each section you identify. Focus on the main point of the section, omitting examples, facts, and other supporting evidence.
- **State the main idea.** Write a sentence or two capturing the author's central idea.
- **Support the main idea.** Write a full paragraph (or more, if needed) that begins with the central idea and supports it with the sentences that summarize sections of the work. The paragraph should concisely and accurately state the thrust of the entire work.
- *Use your own words.* By writing, you re-create the meaning of the work in a way that makes sense for you.

Note Many word processors include an AutoSummarize function that can distill a paragraph or a whole document to a few sentences. Do not count on this tool for summarizing texts that you may have copied onto your computer. The summaries are rarely accurate, and you will not gain the experience of interacting with the text on your own.

EXERCISE 2
Summarizing

Start where the preceding summary of Thomas Sowell's essay ends (at paragraph 5) to summarize the entire essay. Your summary, in your own words, should not exceed one paragraph. (For additional exercises in summarizing, see p. 673.)

5 ■ Forming your critical response

Once you've grasped the content of what you're reading—what the author says—then you can turn to understanding what the author does not say outright but suggests or implies or even lets slip. At this stage you are concerned with the purpose or intention of the author and with how he or she carries it out. Depending on what you are reading and why, you may examine evidence, organization, attitude, use of language, and other elements of the text.

Critical thinking and reading consist of four operations: analyzing, interpreting, synthesizing, and (often) evaluating. Although we'll look at them one by one, these operations interrelate and overlap. Indeed, the first three are often combined under the general label *analysis,* and evaluation is sometimes taken for granted as a result of the process.

In the following pages, we use three quite different examples to show how critical reading can work: *People* magazine, Sowell's "Student Loans," and a Web site.

Analyzing

Analysis is the separation of something into its parts or elements, the better to understand it. To see these elements in what you are reading, begin with a question that reflects your purpose in analyzing the text: why you're curious about it or what you're trying to make out of it. This question will serve as a kind of lens that highlights some features and not others.

Here are some questions you might ask about *People* magazine, listed along with the elements of the magazine that each question highlights:

Questions for analysis	Elements
Does *People* challenge or perpetuate stereotypes?	Stereotypes: explicit and implicit stereotypes or challenges in the magazine
Does the magazine offer positive role models for its readers?	Role models: text and photographs presenting positive or negative role models
Does the magazine's editorial material (articles and accompanying photographs) encourage readers to consume goods and entertainment?	Encouragement of consumption: references to goods and entertainment, focus on consumers, equation of consumption with happiness or success

As these examples show, a question for analysis concentrates your attention on relevant features and eliminates irrelevant features. To answer the question about *People*'s encouragement of consump-

---

http://www.ablongman.com/littlebrown
For added help with the operations of critical thinking and reading, click on
➤ **Critical reading and argument**
  ➤ **Video tutorials** ➤ **Investigating assumptions**
  ➤ **Exercises** ➤ **Exer. 1**
  ➤ **Downloads**
    ➤ **Guidelines for analysis, interpretation, and synthesis**
    ➤ **Guidelines for evaluation**
  ➤ **Web links** ➤ **Critical thinking and argument**

tion, you would focus on items that feature consumption and the products consumed: photographs of designer clothes and celebrities' well-appointed homes, articles on the authors of best-selling books and the stars of new movies. At the same time, you would skip over items that have little or no relevance to consumption, such as uplifting stories about families or the physically challenged.

Analyzing Thomas Sowell's "Student Loans" (pp. 121–22), you might ask these questions:

Questions for analysis	Elements
What is Sowell's attitude toward politicians?	References to politicians: content, words, tone
How does Sowell support his assertions about the loan program's costs?	Support: evidence, such as statistics and examples

The screen shot below shows the opening page of a Web site that promises relief from student-loan debt. Analyzing this page, you might ask these questions:

Questions for analysis	Elements
What kind of organization is the Federated Loan Consolidation Corporation?	Information about the corporation: address, name, text
What are the intentions of the Federated Loan Consolidation Corporation?	Information about the corporation (as above) as well as features of the site design: type, color, art

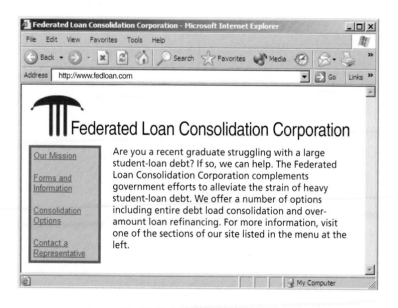

A difference in the kinds of questions asked is a key distinction among academic disciplines. A sociologist neatly outlined three disciplines' approaches to poverty:

> Political science does a wonderful job looking at poverty as a policy issue. Economics does an equally wonderful job looking at it from an income-distribution perspective. But sociology asks how people in poverty live and what they aspire to.

crit

5a

Even within disciplines, approaches may differ. The sociologist quoted above may focus on how people in poverty live, but another may be more interested in the effects of poverty on cities or the changes in the poor population over the last fifty years. (See Chapters 51–55 for more on the disciplines' analytical questions.)

Interpreting

Identifying the elements of something is of course only the beginning: you also need to interpret the meaning or significance of the elements and of the whole. Interpretation usually requires you to infer the author's **assumptions,** opinions or beliefs about what is or what could or should be. (**Infer** means to draw a conclusion based on evidence.)

The word *assumption* here has a more specific meaning than it does in everyday usage, where it may stand for expectation ("I assume you'll pay"), speculation ("It was a mere assumption"), or error ("The report was riddled with assumptions"). Defined more strictly as what a person *supposes* to be true, assumptions are unavoidable. We all adhere to certain values and beliefs; we all form opinions. We live our lives by such assumptions.

Though pervasive, assumptions are not always stated outright. Speakers and writers may judge that their audience already understands and accepts their assumptions; they may not even be aware of their assumptions; or they may deliberately refrain from stating their assumptions for fear that the audience will disagree. That is why your job as a critical thinker is to interpret what the assumptions are.

Reasonable inferences

Like an author deciding what to say in an article, the publishers of *People* magazine make assumptions that guide their selection of content for the magazine. One set of assumptions, perhaps the most important, concerns what readers want to see: as a for-profit enterprise, the magazine naturally aims to maintain and even expand its readership (currently about 3.4 million each week). If your analysis of the magazine's editorial material reveals that much of it features consumer products, you might infer the following:

> **Reasonable** The publishers of *People* assume that the magazine's readers are consumers who want to see and hear about goods and entertainment.

Guidelines for analysis, interpretation, and synthesis

crit
5a

- **What is the purpose of your reading?**
- **What questions do you have about the work,** given your purpose?
- **What elements does the most interesting question highlight?** What elements might you ignore as a result?
- **How do you interpret the meaning and significance of the elements?** What are your assumptions about the work? What do you infer about the author's assumptions?
- **What patterns can you see in (or synthesize from) the elements?** How do the elements relate? How does this whole work relate to other works?
- **What do you conclude about the work?** What does this conclusion add to the work?

 You can download these guidelines from this book's Web site: see the box on p. 125. Create a copy each time you're reading a work critically, and use the questions to prompt your written responses.

Nowhere in *People* will you find a statement of this assumption, but the evidence implies it.

Similarly, Thomas Sowell's "Student Loans" (pp. 121–22) is based on certain assumptions, some obvious, some not so obvious. If you were analyzing Sowell's attitude toward politicians, as suggested earlier, you would focus on his statements about them. Sowell says that they "disregard the first lesson of economics" (paragraph 2), which implies that they ignore important principles (knowing that Sowell is an economist himself makes this a reasonable assumption on your part). Sowell also says that politicians "rob Peter to pay Paul," are "[b]ursting with compassion," "do not admit . . . a dumb idea," are characters in a "long-running saga," and arrive at the solution of spending taxes "as the night follows the day"—that is, inevitably (paragraphs 2–4). From these statements and others, you can infer the following:

> **Reasonable** Sowell assumes that politicians become compassionate when a cause is loud and popular, not necessarily just, and they act irresponsibly by trying to solve the problem with other people's (taxpayers') money.

Interpreting the screen shot on page 126 to discover the nature of the Federated Loan Consolidation Corporation, you would look at the site's address, where *com* indicates that the organization is a commercial entity. (See pp. 653–54 for more on interpreting electronic addresses.) Yet you might also notice that the site does not resemble other corporate sites, which typically have flashier designs incorporating more images, color, and boxes, among other elements. Instead, the site's look is rather plain—the sort of design you might expect from a government site. The prominent *Federated* in the organization's name and *complements government efforts* in the text reinforce the appearance of a government connection. These findings might lead you to infer the following:

crit
5a

Reasonable The Federated Loan Consolidation Corporation assumes that its readers (potential customers) will be more willing to explore its refinancing options if they believe that it is a reliable organization somehow affiliated with the government.

Unreasonable inferences

Interpreting assumptions gives you greater insight into an author's intentions. But it's crucial that inferences fit the evidence of the text, as those above about *People,* Sowell's essay, and the Web site do. Sometimes it's tempting to read too much into the text, as in the next examples:

Faulty *People*'s publishers deliberately skew the magazine's editorial material to promote products on which they receive kickbacks. [The inference is far-fetched, even absurd. It would be reasonable only if there were hard evidence of kickbacks.]

Faulty Sowell thinks that politicians should not be entrusted with running the country. [The inference misreads Sowell. Although he does not outline a solution for politicians' irresponsibility, there's no evidence that he would overhaul our democratic political system.]

Faulty The Federated Loan Consolidation Corporation claims that it is a government-sponsored agency in order to exploit graduates with heavy student-loan debt. [The inference takes an unwarranted leap. The site does not claim government affiliation or sanction, and it contains no evidence of exploitation.]

Faulty inferences like those above are often based on the reader's *own* assumptions about the text or its subject. When thinking and reading critically, you need to look hard at *your* ideas, too.

Synthesizing

If you stopped at analysis and interpretation, critical thinking and reading might leave you with a pile of elements and possible meanings but no vision of the whole. With **synthesis** you make connections among parts *or* among wholes. You create a new whole by drawing conclusions about relationships and implications.

The following conclusion pulls together the earlier analysis of *People* magazine's editorial content and the interpretation of the publisher's assumptions about readers:

> Conclusion *People* magazine appeals to its readers' urge to consume by displaying, discussing, and glamorizing consumer goods.

The statement below about Thomas Sowell's essay "Student Loans" connects his assumptions about politicians to a larger idea also implied by the essay:

> Conclusion Sowell's view that politicians are irresponsible with taxpayers' money reflects his overall opinion that the laws of economics, not politics, should drive government.

The next statement draws on elements of the Federated Loan Consolidation Corporation Web site and the inference about the company's understanding of its readers:

> Conclusion The Federated Loan Consolidation Corporation uses its name, a mention of the government, and a restrained design to appeal to potential customers who may be wary of commercial lending operations.

You can also synthesize your critical readings of a number of sources, again drawing your own conclusions:

> Conclusion In *People, Lifestyles, Vanity Fair,* and other magazines aimed at consumers, the line between advertising and editorial material is sometimes almost invisible.

(Synthesizing several sources is important in research writing. See pp. 660–62.)

To create your own links between experiences, ideas, and entire sources, it helps (again) to write while reading and thinking. The active reading recommended earlier (pp. 119–21) is the place to start, as you note your questions and opinions about the text. You can also create connections with a combination of writing and drawing: start with your notes, or write your ideas out fresh, and draw connections between related thoughts with lines and arrows. (On a word processor you can use the Highlight function or different colors to link related ideas, or use the Comment function to annotate connections.) You want to open up your thinking, so experiment freely.

With synthesis, you create something different from what you started with. To the supermarket shopper reading *People* while standing in line, the magazine may be entertaining and inconsequential. To you—after a critical reading in which you analyze, interpret, and synthesize—the magazine is (at least in part) a significant vehicle of our consumer culture. The difference depends entirely on the critical reading.

Evaluating

Many critical reading and writing assignments end at analysis, interpretation, and synthesis: you explain your understanding of what the author says and doesn't say. Only if you are expected to **evaluate** the work will you state and defend the judgments you've made about its quality and its significance.

You'll inevitably form judgments while reading the work: *What a striking series of images* or *That just isn't enough evidence*. In evaluating, you collect your judgments, determine that they are generally applicable and are themselves not trivial, and turn them into assertions: *The poet creates fresh, intensely vivid images. The author does not summon the evidence to support his case.* And you support these statements with citations from the text.

Evaluation takes a certain amount of confidence. You may think that you lack the expertise to cast judgment on another's writing, especially if the text is difficult or the author well known. True, the more informed you are, the better a critical reader you are. But conscientious reading and analysis will give you the internal authority to judge a work *as it stands* and *as it seems to you*, against your own unique bundle of experiences, observations, and attitudes.

The box below gives questions that can help you evaluate many kinds of works. There's more on evaluation (including evaluation of online sources) on pages 651–59. For arguments and in academic

---

Guidelines for evaluation

- **What are your reactions to the work?** What in the work are you responding to?
- **How sound are the work's central idea and evidence?**
- **How well does the author achieve his or her purpose?** How worthwhile is the purpose?
- **How authoritative, trustworthy, and sincere is the author?**
- **How unified and coherent is the work?** Do its parts all support a central idea and clearly relate to one another?
- **What do color, graphics, or (online) sound or video contribute to the work?** Do such elements add meaning or merely decoration?
- **What is the overall quality and significance of the work?**
- **Do you agree or disagree with the work?** Can you support, refute, or extend it?

 You can download these guidelines from this book's Web site: see the box on p. 125. Create a copy each time you're evaluating a work, and use the questions to prompt your written responses.

disciplines, you'll require additional, more specific criteria. See Chapters 6 and 51–55.

EXERCISE 3
Thinking critically

Following are some statements about the communications media. Use systematic critical thinking to understand not only what the statement says but also why its author might have said it. As in the example, do your thinking in writing: the act of writing will help you think, and your notes will help you discuss your ideas with your classmates. (Additional exercises in critical reading appear on pp. 459–60 and 662–63.)

Example:

Statement: Every year sees the disappearance of more book publishers because the larger companies gobble up the smaller ones.

Analysis: Why did the author make this statement? Certain words reveal the author's purpose: *disappearance of more book publishers; because; larger companies gobble up smaller ones.*

Interpretation: More book publishers means others have disappeared. *Because* specifies cause. *Gobble up* implies consumption, predator to prey. Author's assumptions: Large publishers behave like predators. The predatory behavior of large companies causes the disappearance of small companies. The more publishing companies there are, the better.

Synthesis: The author objects to the predatory behavior of large publishing companies, which he or she holds responsible for eliminating small companies and reducing the total number of companies.

Evaluation: This biased statement against large publishers holds them responsible for the shrinking numbers of book publishers. But are the large companies solely responsible? And why is the shrinking necessarily bad?

1. Newspapers and newsmagazines are better news sources than television because they demand reading, not just viewing.
2. Radio call-in shows are the true democratic forum, giving voice to people of all persuasions.
3. Online communication threatens to undermine our ability to interact face to face.

EXERCISE 4
Reading an essay critically

Reread Thomas Sowell's "Student Loans" (pp. 121–22) in order to form your own critical response to it. Follow the guidelines for analysis, interpretation, synthesis, and evaluation in the boxes on pages 128 and 131. Focus on any elements suggested by your question about the text: possibilities are assumptions, evidence, organization, use of language, tone, authority, vision of education or students. Be sure to write while reading and thinking; your notes will help your analysis and enhance your creativity, and they will be essential for writing about the selection (Exercise 10, p. 140).

EXERCISE 5
Reading a magazine critically

Do your own critical reading of *People* or another magazine. What do you see beyond the obvious? What questions does your reading raise? Let the guidelines on pages 128 and 131 direct your response, and do your work in writing. (A writing suggestion based on this exercise appears on p. 140.)

crit
5b

EXERCISE 6
Reading a Web site critically

Use your Web browser to find the Web site of a corporation or other commercial organization with which you are familiar, such as the manufacturer of a car, television, computer, or other product you own; the bank where you have your account; or the online store where you buy books or music. Examine the site's layout, color, images, sound, video, and interactive features as well as the content of the text. What do the elements tell you about the site's purpose or purposes—for instance, does the site aim to sell something, to give advice, to provide services? What assumptions does it make about readers? How well do the elements achieve the site's purposes? Refer to the boxes on pages 128 and 131 for additional questions to consider, and do your thinking in writing. (A writing suggestion based on this exercise appears on p. 141.)

5b   Viewing images critically

Every day we are bombarded with images—pictures on billboards, commercials on television, graphs and charts in newspapers and textbooks, to name just a few examples. Most images slide by without our noticing them, or so we think. But images, sometimes even more than text, can influence us covertly. Their creators have purposes, some worthy, some not, and understanding those purposes requires that we think critically.

The methods of viewing images critically parallel those for reading text critically: preview, analyze, interpret, synthesize, and (often) evaluate. In the next few pages, we'll apply these methods to the illustration on page 135, an advertisement for *Time* magazine that appeared in the magazine itself.

1 ▪ Previewing

Look at the work as a whole:

- ▪ What can you tell about the source of the work? Who created it?
- ▪ What does the work show?
- ▪ What is the work's overall effect?
- ▪ What questions do you have about the work?

The *Time* advertisement, like most ads, has two significant sources: the site where the ad appeared and the company promoting its product. In this case, the sources are the same: the magazine is advertising itself.

The ad consists of three parts: a photograph depicting a boy being scanned by an airport security person, a *Time* cover superimposed on the photograph, and text asking a question and issuing an invitation. Overall, the ad pinpoints the significant controversy over US national security in the aftermath of the terrorist attacks of September 11, 2001, using this controversy to promote the magazine. The ad also raises at least two questions besides the one it poses directly: Does *Time* take any position on the controversy? And why is the magazine promoting itself to people who are already reading the magazine?

2 ▪ Analyzing

Study the work closely to begin answering your questions about it. Look not just at the obvious content but at the features that may seem unimportant. Assume that everything in the work appears there for a reason.

- ▪ Which elements stand out the most? Which are less prominent?
- ▪ What do color, composition, and similar features emphasize?
- ▪ If words accompany the image, what do they contribute in relation to the image?

In the *Time* ad the most prominent element is the photograph: the blond boy, the man, the scanning tool, the "Baggage Claim" sign overhead, the clutter of people and activity in the background. Color, type, and shape form the familiar image of a *Time* cover, with the scanner centered in it like the bull's-eye on a target.

Beneath the visual elements, the ad's text guides readers' impression of the photograph and *Time* cover. Positioned on a white background, the words attract attention even though they are set in small type. They encourage readers to question what they see and to seek (or continue seeking) answers in *Time* magazine.

3 ▪ Interpreting

Consider what the elements of the work convey about the assumptions and intentions of its creator.

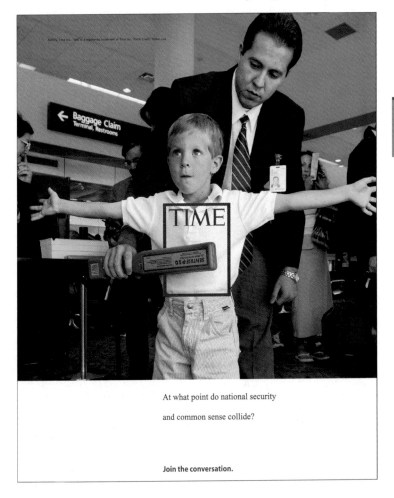

At what point do national security

and common sense collide?

Join the conversation.

- What do the various elements of the work say, in images or in words?
- What appeals do the elements make to viewers? Do they emphasize reason or feelings or a combination?
- What does the creator seem to assume about viewers' interests, beliefs, and needs?
- What seems to be the purpose of the work?

The *Time* ad appeals partly to reason: to the interest of readers in current news and opinion, to their grasp of the need for national security, to the value of "common sense" solutions, and to "conversation" as a way to reach solutions. But the ad also appeals strongly to emotion. Treating a boy as if he were a security threat is absurd, even humorous. The boy's innocent, patient, nervous expression arouses sympathy, while the man's serious attention to his work arouses disdain. The disorderly scene behind the main figures evokes the frustration and anxiety of air travel today. Most subtly, the ad plucks feelings about so-called profiling, or singling out people as suspicious solely because of physical characteristics such as gender or hair and skin color. Many people, reluctantly or not, favor profiling over the waste and inconvenience caused by searching everyone, even small blond-haired boys.

Time clearly assumes that readers are both rationally and emotionally concerned about national security. The ad uses the controversy to attract readers' notice and to define the magazine as cutting edge, with the purpose of increasing sales.

4 ■ Synthesizing

Consider how the work's elements mesh to achieve an overall meaning or effect.

- How do the elements relate to and reinforce one another?
- What point or points do the elements make together? What is the message?
- How does the work relate to similar works—for instance, works in the same medium, by the same creator, or with the same purpose?

The *Time* ad represents an image of the magazine: a site of questioning and dialog, up-to-the-minute in its coverage, calm, humorous, alert to readers' concerns, aware that readers may favor profiling but not want to say so outright.

The ultimate aim of this message is complicated by its appearing in *Time:* readers are already holding the magazine they're being urged to buy. Generally, advertisements appear in places where they are likely to attract new customers. This ad seems to assume little permanence in readers: perhaps they picked up the magazine at a newsstand or doctor's office; perhaps even subscribers need selling on the magazine's virtues. The ad tells readers what they can get in *Time,* assures them that the magazine understands their attitudes, and whets their desire for the promised "conversation"—not just in this week's issue but in the issues to come with a paid subscription.

5 ■ Evaluating

Judge the reasonableness, significance, or value of the work.

- How accurate and fair is the work, or how distorted and biased?
- How successful is the work? Does it achieve its apparent purpose? Is the purpose worthwhile?
- How does the work affect you? Do you find it informative, inviting, dull, objectionable, or what?

The *Time* ad can be evaluated both as a work of persuasion and, within that category, as a work of advertising. As persuasion, advertising rarely meets high standards of reasonableness and accuracy. Its promotional purpose encourages one-sidedness and selective use of evidence, when evidence is offered. *Time* makes a central claim: that it provides dialog about difficult issues. The claim is not supported directly, although readers could seek support in the rest of the magazine. They would have to decide for themselves whether to be engaged or provoked by the ad's subtle message about profiling.

Judged solely as an advertisement, the *Time* piece fares well. Eye-catching, humorous, and concise, it entices the reader to study the photograph and nod in response to the question. The ad plants a memorable idea about the magazine that may strengthen the loyalty of current subscribers and induce occasional readers to become subscribers.

EXERCISE 7
Writing about the *Time* advertisement

In a paragraph, write your own evaluation of the *Time* ad on page 135. Base your evaluation on analysis, interpretation, and synthesis, as outlined on the preceding pages. What do you see in the ad? How effective is it?

EXERCISE 8
Viewing an image critically

Look in a magazine or book for an image that interests you. Or search the wide array of images at the Corbis photograph collection (*http://corbis.com*) or the *WebMuseum* (*http://www.ibiblio.org/wm*). Using the questions on the preceding pages, "read" the image methodically and critically, writing down your responses. (A writing suggestion based on this exercise appears on p. 141.)

5c Writing critically

Critical writing is largely influenced by the discipline or profession in which it occurs. Thus the topic is covered more extensively in Chapters 7 (argument), 52 (literature), 53 (other humanities), 54 (social sciences), and 55 (natural and applied sciences). In this introduction, we'll look at some fundamentals and an illustration.

http://www.ablongman.com/littlebrown
For added help with critical writing, click on
➤ **Critical thinking and argument**
➤ **Web links** ➤ **Critical writing**

crit
5c

Remember that critical writing is *not* summarizing. You may write a summary to clarify for yourself what the author says, and you may briefly summarize a work in your own larger piece of writing. But your job in critical writing is not just to report what a text says; it is to transmit your analysis, interpretation, synthesis, and perhaps evaluation of the text.

The following essay by Charlene Robinson, a student, is a response to Thomas Sowell's "Student Loans." Robinson arrived at her response through the process of critical reading outlined in this chapter and then by gathering and organizing her ideas, developing her own central idea (or thesis) about Sowell's text, and drafting and revising until she believed she had supported her central idea.

Robinson does not assume that her readers see the same things in Sowell's essay or share her views, so she offers evidence of Sowell's ideas in the form of direct quotations, summaries, and paraphrases (restatements in her own words). (See pp. 667–72 for more on these techniques.) Robinson then documents these borrowings from Sowell using the style of the Modern Language Association (MLA): the numbers in parentheses are page numbers in the book containing Sowell's essay, listed at the end as a "work cited." (See Chapter 49 for more on MLA style.)

Weighing the Costs

In his essay "Student Loans," the economist Thomas Sowell challenges the US government's student-loan program for several reasons: a scarce resource (taxpayers' money) goes to many undeserving students, a high number of recipients fail to repay their loans, and the easy availability of money has led to both lower academic standards and higher college tuitions. Sowell wants his readers to "weigh the costs of things" (133) in order to see, as he does, that the loan program should not receive so much government funding. But does he provide the evidence of cost and other problems to lead the reader to agree with him? The answer is no, because hard evidence is less common than debatable and unsupported assumptions about students, scarcity, and the value of education.

> Introduction:
>
> 1. Summary of Sowell's essay
>
> 2. Robinson's critical question
>
> 3. Thesis statement

Sowell's portrait of student-loan recipients is questionable. It is based on averages, some statistical and some not, but averages are often deceptive. For example, Sowell cites college graduates' low average debt of $7,000 to $9,000 (131) without acknowledging the fact that many students' debt is much higher or giving the full range of statistics. Similarly, Sowell dismisses "heart-rending stories" of "the low-income student with a huge debt" as

> First main point
>
> Evidence for first point:
>
> 1. Paraphrases and quotations from Sowell's text (with source citations in MLA style)

"not at all typical" (132), yet he invents his own exaggerated version of the typical loan recipient: an affluent slacker ("Rockefellers" and "Vanderbilts") for whom college is a "place to hang out for a few years" sponging off the government, while his or her parents clear a profit from making use of the loan program (132). While such students (and parents) may well exist, are they really typical? Sowell does not offer any data one way or the other—for instance, how many loan recipients come from each income group, what percentage of loan funds go to each group, how many loan recipients receive significant help from their parents, and how many receive none.

Another set of assumptions in the essay has to do with "scarcity": "There is never enough of anything to fully satisfy all those who want it," Sowell says (131). This statement appeals to readers' common sense, but does the "lesson" of scarcity necessarily apply to the student-loan program? Sowell omits many important figures needed to prove that the nation's resources are too scarce to support the program, such as the total cost of the program, its percentage of the total education budget and the total federal budget, and its cost compared to the cost of defense, Medicare, and other expensive programs. Moreover, Sowell does not mention the interest paid by loan recipients, even though the interest must offset some of the costs of running the program and covering unpaid loans.

The most fundamental and most debatable assumption underlying Sowell's essay is that higher education is a kind of commodity that not everyone is entitled to. In order to diminish the importance of graduates' average debt from education loans, Sowell claims that a car loan will probably be higher (131). This comparison between education and an automobile implies that the two are somehow equal as products and that an affordable higher education is no more a right than a new car is. Sowell also condemns the "irresponsible" students who drop out of school and "the increasingly easy availability of college to people who are not very serious about getting an education" (132). But he overlooks the value of encouraging education, including education of those who don't finish college or who aren't scholars. For many in the United States, education has a greater value than that of a mere commodity like a car. And even from an economic perspective such as Sowell's, the cost to

2. Sowell's omissions

Transition to second main point

Second main point

Evidence for second point: Sowell's omissions

Third main point

Evidence for third point: paraphrases and quotations of Sowell's text (with source citations in MLA style) society of an uneducated public needs to be taken into account.

Sowell writes with conviction, and his concerns are valid: high taxes, waste, unfairness, declining educational standards, obtrusive government. However, the essay's flaws make it unlikely that Sowell could convince readers who do not already agree with him. He does not support his portrait of the typical loan recipient, he fails to demonstrate a lack of resources for the loan program, and he neglects the special nature of education compared to other services and products. Sowell may have the evidence to back up his assumptions, but by omitting it he himself does not truly weigh the costs of the loan program.

Conclusion:

1. Acknowledgment of Sowell's concerns

2. Summary of three main points

3. Return to theme of introduction: weighing costs

Work Cited

Sowell, Thomas. "Student Loans." <u>Is Reality Optional? and Other Essays</u>. Stanford: Hoover, 1993. 131–33.

—CHARLENE ROBINSON (student)

Reference to complete source for Sowell's essay (in MLA style)

EXERCISE 9
Responding to critical writing

Read Charlene Robinson's essay carefully. What is Robinson's critical question about Sowell's essay? How does it relate to her thesis statement? What assumptions does she identify in Sowell's essay? What conclusions does she reach about the essay? Do you think her response is accurate and fair? Is it perceptive? Does Robinson provide enough evidence from Sowell's essay to convince you of her points? Does she miss anything you would have mentioned? Write your responses in a brief essay.

EXERCISE 10
Writing critically about an essay

Write an essay based on your own critical reading of Thomas Sowell's essay (Exercise 4, pp. 132–33). Your critique may be entirely different from Charlene Robinson's, or you may have developed some of the same points. If there are similarities, they should be expressed and supported in your own way, in the context of your own approach.

EXERCISE 11
Writing critically about a magazine

Write an essay based on your critical response to *People* magazine or another magazine (Exercise 5, p. 133). Follow the guidelines on page 138 for developing and organizing your essay.

EXERCISE 12
Writing critically about a Web site

Write an essay based on your critical response to a commercial Web site (Exercise 6, p. 133). Be sure to use specific examples of the site's elements to support your ideas about the site. Follow the guidelines on page 138 for developing and organizing your essay.

EXERCISE 13
Writing critically about an image

Write an essay based on your critical response to an image (Exercise 8, p. 137). Follow the guidelines on page 138 for developing and organizing your essay.

crit

5c

CHAPTER 6

Reading Arguments Critically

Argument is writing that attempts to open readers' minds to an opinion, change readers' own opinions, or move readers to action. A good argument is neither a cold exercise in logic nor an attempt to beat others into submission. It is a work of negotiation and problem solving in which both writer and reader search for the knowledge that will create common ground between them.

Of course, not all arguments are "good." Whether deliberately or not, some are unclear, incomplete, misleading, or downright false. The negotiation fails; the problem remains unsolved. This chapter will help you recognize good arguments when you read them, and the following chapter will help you write good arguments when you need to.

CULTURE LANGUAGE The ways of reading and writing arguments described in this chapter and the next may be uncomfortable to you if your native culture approaches such writing differently. In some cultures, for example, a writer is expected to begin indirectly, to avoid asserting his or her opinion outright, to rely for evidence on appeals to tradition, or to establish a compromise rather than argue a position. In American academic and business settings, readers and writers look or aim for a well-articulated opinion, evidence gathered from many sources, and a direct and concise argument for the opinion.

6a Recognizing the elements of argument

Few arguments are an easy read. Most demand the attentive critical reading discussed in the previous chapter. (If you haven't read pp. 115–32, you should do so before continuing.) As a reader of

http://www.ablongman.com/littlebrown
For added help with reading arguments, click on
➤ Critical thinking and argument
➤ Video tutorials
➤ Exercises
➤ Downloads
➤ Web links

Questions for critically reading an argument

- What **claims** does the writer make?
- What kinds and quality of **evidence** does the writer provide to support the claims?
- What **assumptions** underlie the argument, connecting evidence to claims?
- What is the writer's **tone?** How does the writer use **language?**
- Is the writer **reasonable?**
- Is the argument logical? Has the writer committed any **fallacies?**
- Are you convinced? Why or why not?

 You can download these questions from this book's Web site: see the box on the previous page. Create a copy for each argument you are reading, and use the questions to prompt your written responses.

arg

6a

argument, your purpose will almost always be the same: you'll want to know whether you should be convinced by the argument. This purpose focuses your attention on the elements that make an argument convincing, or not.

In a scheme adapted from the work of the British philosopher Stephen Toulmin, an argument has three main elements:

- **Claims:** positive statements that require support. In an argument the central claim is stated outright as the **thesis** (see p. 31); it is what the argument is about. For instance:

  The college needs a new chemistry laboratory to replace the existing outdated lab.

  Several minor claims, such as that the present equipment is inadequate, will contribute to the central assertion.
- **Evidence:** the facts, examples, expert opinions, and other information that support the claims. (Toulmin calls evidence *data* or *grounds*, terms that indicate both its specificity and its work as an argument's foundation.) Evidence to support the preceding claim might include the following:

  The present lab's age
  An inventory of equipment
  The testimony of chemistry professors

  Like the claims, the evidence is always stated outright.
- **Assumptions:** the writer's underlying (and often unstated) beliefs, opinions, principles, or inferences that tie the evidence to the claims. (Toulmin calls these assumptions *warrants:* they justify making the claims on the basis of the evidence provided.) For instance, the following assumption might connect

the evidence of professors' testimony with the claim that a new lab is needed:

Chemistry professors are the most capable of evaluating the present lab's quality.

In the following pages, we'll examine each of these elements along with several others: tone and language, reasonableness, and common errors in reasoning. The student paper in the previous chapter, Charlene Robinson's "Weighing the Costs" (pp. 138–40), provides a good example of critically reading an argument for its claims, evidence, and assumptions.

Note Online arguments often differ considerably from conventional written arguments and may require different ways of reading and evaluating. A Web site, for instance, may partly support claims with links to other pages or sites rather than directly in the main document itself. And online discussions tend to build arguments gradually from the give and take of the participants, so that no one contribution is definitive. In reading such arguments, you may have to do more work than with conventional arguments to put opinions in context and locate the backbone of claims, evidence, and assumptions.

6b   Testing claims

The claims or assertions in an argument carry specific burdens: they should state arguable opinions, and they should define their terms.

1 ■ Distinguishing facts, opinions, beliefs, and prejudices

Most statements we hear, read, or make in speaking and writing are claims of fact, opinion, belief, or prejudice. In an argument the acceptability of a claim depends partly on which of these categories it falls into.

Facts

A **fact** is verifiable—that is, one can determine whether it is true:

World War II ended in 1945.
The football field is 100 yards long.

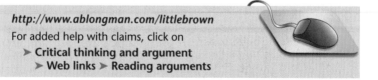

Facts provide crucial evidence for the claims of an argument, and as evidence they may be problematic because they can be misinterpreted or distorted (see pp. 149–50). But they are ultimately verifiable, so they do not make worthwhile arguments by themselves.

Opinions

An **opinion** is a judgment *based* on facts, an honest attempt to draw a reasonable conclusion from evidence. For example:

> Mandatory drug testing in workplaces is essential to increase employees' productivity.
>
> Mandatory drug testing in workplaces does not substantially increase employees' productivity.
>
> Mandatory drug testing in workplaces violates constitutional freedoms.

All three of these opinions share certain features:

- They express viewpoints based on an interpretation of facts.
- They are arguable. Indeed, they argue with each other, though each writer had access to the same facts.
- They are potentially changeable. With more evidence the writers might alter their opinions partly or wholly.

The main claim, or thesis, of an argument is always an opinion. Other, more specific claims of opinion generally form the backbone of the argument supporting the thesis. By themselves, however, opinions do not make arguments. As a critical reader, you must satisfy yourself that the writer has specified the evidence for the opinions and that the assumptions linking claims and evidence are clear and believable.

Beliefs

An opinion is not the same as a **belief,** a conviction based on cultural or personal faith, morality, or values:

> Abortion is legalized murder.
>
> Capital punishment is legalized murder.
>
> The primary goal of government should be to provide equality of opportunity for all.

Such statements are often called opinions because they express viewpoints, but they are not based on facts and other evidence. Since they cannot be disproved by facts or even contested on the basis of facts, they cannot serve as the central claim of an argument. Statements of belief do figure in argument, however: they can serve as a kind of evidence, and they often form the assumptions linking claims and evidence. See pages 148 and 151.

Prejudices

One kind of assertion that has no place in argument is a prejudice, an opinion based on insufficient or unexamined evidence:

> Women are bad drivers.
> Fat people are jolly.
> Teenagers are irresponsible.

arg
6b

Unlike a belief, a prejudice is testable: it can be contested and disproved on the basis of facts. Very often, however, we form prejudices or accept them from others—parents, friends, the communications media—without questioning their meaning or testing their truth. Writers who display prejudice do not deserve the confidence and agreement of readers. Readers who accept prejudice are not thinking critically.

Note When reading arguments that appear online, you should be especially vigilant for claims of belief or prejudice that pose as considered opinions. Anyone with a computer and an Internet connection can post anything on the Internet, without passing it through an editorial screening like that undergone by books and articles in journals and magazines. The filtering of such material is entirely up to the reader.

2 ■ Looking for defined terms

In any argument, but especially in arguments about abstract ideas, clear and consistent definition of terms is essential. In the following claim, the writer is not clear about what she means by the crucial term *justice:*

> Over the past few decades, justice has deteriorated so badly that it almost does not exist anymore.

The word *justice* is **abstract:** it does not refer to anything specific or concrete and in fact has varied meanings. (The five definitions in *The American Heritage Dictionary* include "the principle of moral rightness" and "the administration and procedure of law.") When the writer specifies her meaning, her assertion is much clearer:

> If by *justice* we mean treating people fairly, punishing those who commit crimes, and protecting the victims of those crimes, then justice has deteriorated badly over the past few decades.

Writers who use highly abstract words such as *justice, equality, success,* and *maturity* have a responsibility to define them. If the word is important to the argument, such a definition may take an entire paragraph. As a reader you have the obligation to evaluate the writer's definitions before you accept his or her assertions. (See pp. 94–95 for more on definition and a paragraph defining the abstract word *quality.*)

6c   Weighing evidence

In argument, evidence demonstrates the validity of the writer's claims. If the evidence is inadequate or questionable, the claims are at best doubtful.

1 ■ Recognizing kinds of evidence

Writers draw on several kinds of evidence to support their claims.

Evidence for argument

- **Facts:** verifiable statements
- **Statistics:** facts expressed in numbers
- **Examples:** specific cases
- **Expert opinions:** the judgments of authorities
- **Appeals to readers' beliefs or needs**

Facts

Facts are statements whose truth can be verified by observation or research (see p. 144). Facts employing numbers are **statistics:**

Of those polled, 62 percent stated a preference for a flat tax.

In 2002 there were 1,370,237 men and women on active duty in the US armed forces.

The average American household consists of 2.58 persons.

Numbers may be implied:

The earth is closer to the sun than Saturn is.
The cost of medical care is rising.

Or a fact may involve no numbers at all:

The city council adjourned without taking a vote.
The President vetoed the bill.

Examples

Examples are specific instances of the point being made, including historical precedents and personal experiences. The passage

---

http://www.ablongman.com/littlebrown
For added help with evidence, click on
  ➤ **Critical thinking and argument**
    ➤ **Web links** ➤ **Reading arguments**

arg
6c

below uses a personal narrative as partial support for the claim in the first sentence:

> Besides broadening students' knowledge, required courses can also introduce students to possible careers that they otherwise would have known nothing about. Somewhat reluctantly, I enrolled in a psychology course to satisfy the requirement for work in social science. But what I learned in the course about human behavior has led me to consider becoming a clinical psychologist instead of an engineer.

Expert opinions

Expert opinions are the judgments formed by authorities on the basis of their own examination of the facts. In the following passage the writer cites the opinion of an expert to support the claim in the first sentence:

> Despite the fact that affirmative action places some individuals at a disadvantage, it remains necessary to right the wrongs inflicted historically on whole groups of people. Howard Glickstein, a past director of the US Commission on Civil Rights, maintains that "it simply is not possible to achieve equality and fairness" unless the previous grounds for discrimination (such as sex, race, and national origin) are now considered as grounds for admission to schools and jobs (26).

As this passage illustrates, a citation of expert opinion should always refer the reader to the source, here indicated by the page number in parentheses, "(26)." Such a citation is also generally accompanied by a reference to the expert's credentials. See pages 677 and 688–89.

CULTURE LANGUAGE In some cultures a person with high standing in government, society, or organized religion may be considered an authority on many different subjects. In American academic and business settings, authority tends to derive from study, learning, and experience: the more knowledge a person can demonstrate about a subject, the more authority he or she has. See page 150 on relevant evidence.

Appeals to beliefs or needs

An **appeal to beliefs or needs** asks readers to accept an assertion in part because they already accept it as true without evidence or because it coincides with their needs. Each of the following examples combines such an appeal (second sentence) with a summary of factual evidence (first sentence).

> Thus the chemistry laboratory is outdated in its equipment. In addition, its shabby, antiquated appearance shames the school, making it seem a second-rate institution. [Appeals to readers' belief that their school is or should be first-rate.]

That police foot patrollers reduce crime has already been demonstrated. Such officers might also restore our sense that our neighborhoods are orderly, stable places. [Appeals to readers' need for order and stability.]

(For more on beliefs, see p. 145. For more on appeals to emotion, see pp. 172–73.)

arg

6c

2 ■ Judging the reliability of evidence

To support claims and convince readers, evidence must be reliable. The tests of reliability for appeals to readers' beliefs and needs are specific to the situation: whether they are appropriate for the argument and correctly gauge how readers actually feel (see p. 173). With the other kinds of evidence, the standards are more general, applying to any argument.

Note If you are reading an argument that cites online sources (and their addresses) for its evidence, you can easily use your Web browser to find the sources and see for yourself how reliable the evidence is. (See p. 639 for advice on finding the originals of sites that have changed or disappeared.)

Accuracy

Accurate evidence is true:

- It is drawn from trustworthy sources.
- It is quoted exactly.
- It is presented with the original meaning undistorted.

In an essay favoring gun control, a writer should not rely exclusively on procontrol sources, which are undoubtedly biased. Instead, the writer should also cite anticontrol sources (representing the opposite bias) and neutral sources (attempting to be unbiased). If the writer quotes an expert, the quotation should present the expert's true meaning, not just a few words that happen to support the writer's argument. (As a reader you may have difficulty judging the accuracy of quotations if you are not familiar with the expert's opinions.)

Not just opinions but also facts and examples may be misinterpreted or distorted. Suppose you were reading an argument for extending a three-year-old law allowing the police to stop vehicles

---

Criteria for weighing evidence

- Is it **accurate**: trustworthy, exact, undistorted?
- Is it **relevant**: authoritative, pertinent, current?
- Is it **representative**: true to context?
- Is it **adequate**: plentiful, specific?

randomly as a means of apprehending drunk drivers. If the author cited statistics showing that the number of drunk-driving accidents dropped in the first two years of the law but failed to note that the number rose back to the previous level in the third year, then the evidence would be distorted and thus inaccurate. You or any reader would be justified in questioning the entire argument, no matter how accurate the rest seemed.

Relevance

Relevant evidence pertains to the argument:

- It comes from sources with authority on the subject.
- It relates directly to the point the writer is making.
- It is current.

In an argument against a method of hazardous-waste disposal, a writer should not offer his church minister's opinion as evidence unless she is an authority on the subject and her expertise is up to date. If she is an authority on Method A and not Method B, the writer should not use her opinion as evidence against Method B. Similarly, the writer's own experience of living near a hazardous-waste site may be relevant evidence *if* it pertains to his thesis. His authority in this case is that of a close observer and a citizen. (See also p. 158 on the fallacy of false authority.)

Representativeness

Representative evidence is true to its context:

- It reflects the full range of the sample from which it is said to be drawn.
- It does not overrepresent any element of the sample.

In an essay arguing that dormitories should stay open during school holidays, a writer might say that "the majority of the school's students favor leaving the dormitories open." But that writer would mislead you and other readers if the claim were based only on a poll of her roommates and dormitory neighbors. A few dormitory residents could not be said to represent the entire student body, particularly the nonresident students. To be representative, the poll would have to take in many more students in proportions that reflect the numbers of resident and nonresident students on campus.

Adequacy

Adequate evidence is sufficient:

- It is plentiful enough to support the writer's assertions.
- It is specific enough to support the writer's assertions.

A writer arguing against animal abuse cannot hope to win over readers solely with statements about her personal experiences and claims of her opinions. Her experience may indeed be relevant evidence if, say, she has worked with animals or witnessed animal abuse. And her opinions are indeed important to the argument, to let readers know what she thinks. But even together these are not adequate evidence: they cannot substitute entirely for facts, nonpersonal examples, and the opinions of experts to demonstrate abuse and describe the scope of the problem.

6d Discovering assumptions

Assumptions connect evidence to claims: they are the opinions or beliefs that explain why a particular piece of evidence is relevant to a particular claim. As noted in the preceding chapter on critical thinking, assumptions are not flaws in arguments but necessities: we all acquire beliefs and opinions that shape our view of the world. Here are some examples that you, or people you know, may hold:

> Criminals should be punished.
> Hard work is virtuous.
> Teachers' salaries are too low.

Assumptions are inevitable in argument, but they aren't neutral. For one thing, an assumption can weaken an argument. Say that a writer claims that real estate development should be prevented in your town. As evidence for this claim, the writer offers facts about past developments that have replaced older buildings. But the evidence is relevant to the claim only if you accept the writer's extreme assumptions that old buildings are always worthy and new development is always bad.

In such a case, the writer's bias may not even be stated. Hence a second problem: in arguments both sound and unsound, assumptions are not always explicit. Following are a claim and evidence forming a reasonable argument. What is the unstated assumption?

Claim

The town should create a plan to manage building preservation and new development.

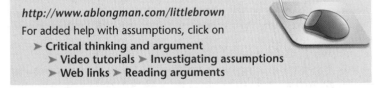

arg
6e

Evidence

Examples of how such plans work; expert opinions on how and why both preservation and development are needed.

In this instance the assumption is that neither uncontrolled development nor zero development is healthy for the town. If you can accept this assumption, you should be able to accept the writer's claim (though you might still disagree over particulars).

Here are some tips for dealing with assumptions:

Guidelines for analyzing assumptions

- **What are the assumptions underlying the argument?** How does the writer connect claims with evidence?
- **Are the assumptions believable?** Do they express your values? Do they seem true in your experience?
- **Are the assumptions consistent with each other?** Is the argument's foundation solid, not slippery?

6e Watching language, hearing tone

Tone is the expression of the writer's attitudes toward himself or herself, toward the subject, and toward the reader (see pp. 11–12 for a discussion). Tone can tell you quite a bit about the writer's intentions, biases, and trustworthiness. For example:

> Some women cite personal growth as a reason for pursuing careers while raising children. Of course, they are equally concerned with the personal growth of the children they relegate to "child-care specialists" while they work.

In the second sentence this writer is being **ironic,** saying one thing while meaning another. The word *relegate* and the quotation marks with *child-care specialists* betray the writer's belief that working mothers may selfishly neglect their children for their own needs. Irony can sometimes be effective in argument, but here it marks the author as insincere in dealing with the complex issues of working parents and child care.

When reading arguments, you should be alert for the author's language. Look for words that **connote,** or suggest, certain attitudes and evoke certain responses in readers. (Notice your own responses to these word pairs with related meanings but different connotations: *daring/foolhardy, dislike/detest, glad/joyous, angry/rabid, freedom/license.*) Connotative language is no failure in argument; indeed, the strongest arguments use it skillfully to appeal to readers' hearts as well as their minds (see pp. 172–73). But be suspicious if the language runs counter to the substance of the argument.

Look also for evasive words. **Euphemisms,** such as *attack of a sexual nature* for "rape" or *peace-keeping force* for a warmaking army, are supposedly inoffensive substitutes for words that may frighten or offend readers (see p. 546). In argument, though, they are sometimes used to hide or twist the truth. An honest, forthright arguer will avoid them.

Finally, watch carefully for sexist, racist, and other biased language that reveals deep ignorance or, worse, entrenched prejudice on the part of the writer. Obvious examples are *broad* for woman and *fag* for homosexual. (See pp. 547–50 for more on such language.)

Note Online arguments are sometimes hotter, less tempered, than printed arguments. An author whose language seems harsh or biased may be taking advantage of the Internet's openness to push a one-sided view. But he or she may also be writing too quickly and informally to take the necessary care with language. You'll need to decide for yourself what the author's motives are, perhaps asking him or her for clarification.

6f   Judging reasonableness

The **reasonableness** of an argument is the sense you get as a reader that the author is fair and sincere. The reasonable writer does not conceal or distort facts, hide prejudices, mask belief as opinion, manipulate you with language, or resort to any of dozens of devices used unconsciously by those who don't know better and deliberately by those who do.

Reasonableness involves all the elements of argument examined so far: claims, evidence, assumptions, and language. In addition, the fair, sincere argument always avoids so-called fallacies (covered in the next section), and it acknowledges the opposition.

Judging whether a writer deals adequately with his or her opposition is a fairly simple matter for the reader of argument. By definition, an arguable issue has more than one side. Even if you have no preconceptions about a subject, you will know that another side exists. If the writer pretends otherwise, or dismisses the opposition too quickly, you are justified in questioning the honesty and fairness of the argument. (For the more complicated business of *writing* an acknowledgment of opposing views, see pp. 174–75.)

EXERCISE 1
Reading arguments critically
Following are two brief arguments. Though not directly opposed, the two arguments do represent different stances on environmental issues. Read each argument critically, following the process outlined in the previous chapter (pp. 115–33) and answering the questions in the box on page 143 (questions about claims, evidence, assumptions, and the other elements of argument). Develop your

responses in writing so that you can refer to them for later exercises and class discussion.

The Environmental Crisis Is Not Our Fault

I am as responsible as most eco-citizens: I bike everywhere; I don't own a car; I recycle newspapers, bottles, cans, and plastics; I have a vegetable garden in the summer; I buy organic products; and I put all vegetable waste into my backyard compost bin, probably the only one in all of Greenwich Village. But I don't at the same time believe that I am saving the planet, or in fact doing anything of much consequence about the various eco-crises around us. What's more, I don't even believe that if "all of us" as individuals started doing the same it would make any but the slightest difference.

Leave aside ozone depletion and rain forest destruction— those are patently corporate crimes that no individual actions can remedy to any degree. Take, instead, energy consumption in this country. In the most recent figures, residential consumption was 7.2 percent of the total, commercial 5.5 percent, and industrial 23.3 percent; of the remainder, 27.8 percent was transportation (about one-third of it by private car) and 36.3 percent was electric generation (about one-third for residential use). Individual energy use, in sum, was something like 28 percent of total consumption. Although you and I cutting down on energy consumption would have some small effect (and should be done), it is surely the energy consumption of industry and other large institutions such as government and agribusiness that needs to be addressed first. And it is industry and government that must be forced to explain what their consumption is for, what is produced by it, how necessary it is, and how it can be drastically reduced.

The point is that the ecological crisis is essentially beyond "our" control, as citizens or householders or consumers or even voters. It is not something that can be halted by recycling or double-pane insulation. It is the inevitable by-product of our modern industrial civilization, dominated by capitalist production and consumption and serviced and protected by various institutions of government, federal to local. It cannot possibly be altered or reversed by simple individual actions, even by the actions of the millions who take part in Earth Day—even if they all go home and fix their refrigerators and from then on walk to work. Nothing less than a drastic overhaul of this civilization and an abandonment of its ingrained gods—progress, growth, exploitation, technology, materialism, anthropocentricity, and power—will do anything substantial to halt our path to environmental destruction, and it's hard to see how life-style solutions will have an effect on that.

What I find truly pernicious about such solutions is that they get people thinking they are actually making a difference and doing their part to halt the destruction of the earth: "There, I've taken all the bottles to the recycling center and used my string bag at the grocery store; I guess that'll take care of global warming." It is the kind of thing that diverts people from the hard truths and hard choices and hard actions, from the recognition that they have to take on the larger forces of society—corporate and governmental—where true power, and true destructiveness, lie.

And to the argument that, well, you have to start somewhere 5 to raise people's consciousness, I would reply that this individualistic approach does not in fact raise consciousness. It does not move people beyond their old familiar liberal perceptions of the world, it does nothing to challenge the belief in technofix or write-your-Congressperson solutions, and it does not begin to provide them with the new vocabulary and modes of thought necessary for a true change of consciousness. We need, for example, to think of recycling centers not as the answer to our waste problems, but as a confession that the system of packaging and production in this society is out of control. Recycling centers are like hospitals; they are the institutions at the end of the cycle that take care of problems that would never exist if ecological criteria had operated at the beginning of the cycle. Until we have those kinds of understandings, we will not do anything with consciousness except reinforce it with the same misguided ideas that created the crisis.

—KIRKPATRICK SALE

Myths We Wouldn't Miss

There are tall tales and legends. There are fables and apocryphal 1 stories. And there are myths—a number of which we would like to see disappear. Here are some myths that would not be missed:

MYTH: Offshore drilling would be an ecological disaster.   2

Truth is, there hasn't been a serious spill in US waters result- 3 ing from offshore drilling operations in more than thirty years—and even that one, in Santa Barbara Channel in 1969, caused no permanent damage to the environment.

This is why we always have such a problem with the reasoning 4 of those who call for moratoriums or outright bans on such activity while the nation continues to import foreign oil. The fact is, oil industry offshore drilling operations cause less pollution than urban runoff, atmospheric phenomena, municipal discharges or natural seeps.

Why this nation would choose *not* to drill for oil and *not* to 5 provide the jobs, profits and taxes such activity would mean for the American economy when there are no better alternatives is a mystery we hope puzzles others as much as it does us.

MYTH: America is a profligate waster of energy.   6

The myth makers like to throw around numbers that read like 7 this: with only 5 percent of the world's population, the US uses about 25 percent of the world's energy. But ours is a big country—three thousand miles from one ocean to the next. Transportation accounts for more than 60 percent of US oil use. We could probably cut down if we moved everybody into one corner of the country, but where is the waste?

It certainly isn't the automobiles that are inefficient. They are 8 twice as efficient as the ones we used thirty years ago. If American drivers use more gasoline than their counterparts in Europe and Japan, it may just have something to do with the country's size.

In fact, proof of the country's size may be in our economic 9
output—and may also hold a clue as to why we use the energy we
do. Despite having only 5 percent of the world's population, America may indeed use 25 percent of the world's energy. However,
according to the latest statistics, we also produce about 25 percent
of the world's goods and services. Again, where's the waste?

arg
6g

MYTH: Conservation is *the answer* to America's energy problems. 10

No doubt about it, we all need to be careful of the amount of 11
energy we use. But as long as this nation's economy needs to grow,
we are going to need energy to fuel that growth.

For the foreseeable future, there are no viable alternatives to 12
petroleum as the major source of energy, especially for transportation fuels. Let's face it. Over the past thirty years we *have* learned
to conserve—in our factories, our homes, our cars. We probably
can—and should—do more. But conservation and new exploration
should not be mutually exclusive, because even without an increase in energy consumption, we are using up domestic reserves
of oil and gas and must replace them. For the good of the economy, those reserves should be replaced with new domestic production, to the extent economically possible. Otherwise, the only
solutions would be additional imports or no growth. And stifling
growth would be a gross disservice to the people for whom such
growth would provide the opportunity for a better life.

Simply put, America is going to need more energy for all its 13
people.

And that is no myth. 14

—Oil corporation advertisement

6g Recognizing fallacies

You'll need to know **fallacies**—errors in argument—as both a
reader (to spot them) and a writer (to avoid them). The many common fallacies fall into two groups. Some evade the issue of the argument. Others treat the argument as if it were much simpler than it is.

1 ■ Recognizing evasions

The central claim of an argument defines an issue or question:
Should real estate development be controlled? Should drug testing

Checklist of fallacies

Evasions

- **Begging the question:** treating an opinion that is open to question as if it were already proved or disproved.
- **Non sequitur** ("it does not follow"): drawing a conclusion from irrelevant evidence.
- **Red herring:** introducing an irrelevant issue to distract readers.
- **False authority:** citing as expert opinion the views of a person who is not an expert.
- **Inappropriate appeals:**

  Appealing to readers' fear or pity.

  Snob appeal: appealing to readers' wish to be like those who are more intelligent, famous, rich, and so on.

  Bandwagon: appealing to readers' wish to be part of the group.

  Flattery: appealing to readers' intelligence, taste, and so on.

  Argument ad populum ("to the people"): appealing to readers' general values, such as patriotism or love of family.

  Argument ad hominem ("to the man"): attacking the opponent rather than the opponent's argument.

Oversimplifications

- **Hasty generalization (jumping to a conclusion):** asserting an opinion based on too little evidence.
- **Sweeping generalization:** asserting an opinion as applying to all instances when it may apply to some, or to none. **Absolute statements** and **stereotypes** are variations.
- **Reductive fallacy:** generally, oversimplifying causes and effects.
- **Post hoc fallacy:** assuming that *A* caused *B* because *A* preceded *B.*
- **Either/or fallacy (false dilemma):** reducing a complicated question to two alternatives.
- **False analogy:** exaggerating the similarities in an analogy or ignoring key differences.

be mandatory in the workplace? An effective argument faces the central issue squarely with relevant opinions, beliefs, and evidence. An ineffective argument dodges the issue.

Begging the question

A writer **begs the question** by treating an opinion that is open to question as if it were already proved or disproved. (In essence, the writer begs readers to accept his or her ideas from the start.)

> The college library's expenses should be reduced by cutting subscriptions to useless periodicals. [Begged questions: Are some of the library's periodicals useless? Useless to whom?]

The fact is that the welfare system is too corrupt to be reformed. [Begged questions: How corrupt is the welfare system? Does corruption, even if extensive, put the system beyond reform?]

Non sequitur

A **non sequitur** occurs when no logical relation exists between two or more connected ideas. In Latin *non sequitur* means "it does not follow." In the sentences below, the second thought does not follow from the first:

If high school English were easier, fewer students would have trouble with the college English requirement. [Presumably, if high school English were easier, students would have *more* trouble.]

Kathleen Newsome has my vote for mayor because she has the best-run campaign organization. [Shouldn't one's vote be based on the candidate's qualities, not the campaign's organization?]

Red herring

A **red herring** is literally a kind of fish that might be drawn across a path to distract a bloodhound from a scent it's following. In argument, a red herring is an irrelevant issue intended to distract readers from the relevant issues. The writer changes the subject rather than pursue the argument.

A campus speech code is essential to protect students, who already have enough problems coping with rising tuition. [Tuition costs and speech codes are different subjects. What protections do students need that a speech code will provide?]

Instead of developing a campus speech code that will infringe on students' First Amendment rights, administrators should be figuring out how to prevent another tuition increase. [Again, tuition costs and speech codes are different subjects. How would the code infringe on rights?]

False authority

Arguments often cite as evidence the opinions of people who are experts on the subject (see p. 148). But writers use **false authority** when they cite as an expert someone whose expertise is doubtful or nonexistent.

Jason Bing, a recognized expert in corporate finance, maintains that pharmaceutical companies do not test their products thoroughly enough. [Bing's expertise in corporate finance bears no apparent relation to the testing of pharmaceuticals.]

According to Helen Liebowitz, the Food and Drug Administration has approved sixty dangerous drugs in the last two years alone. [Who is Helen Liebowitz? On what authority does she make this claim?]

Inappropriate appeals

Appeals to readers' emotions are common in effective arguments. But such appeals must be relevant and must supplement rather than substitute for facts, examples, and other evidence.

Writers sometimes ignore the question with **appeals to readers' fear or pity.**

> By electing Susan Clark to the city council, you will prevent the city's economic collapse. [Trades on people's fears. Can Clark single-handedly prevent economic collapse? Is collapse even likely?]

> She should not have to pay taxes, because she is an aged widow with no friends or relatives. [Appeals to people's pity. Should age and loneliness, rather than income, determine a person's tax obligation?]

Sometimes writers ignore the question by appealing to readers' sense of what other people believe or do. One approach is **snob appeal,** inviting readers to accept an assertion in order to be identified with others they admire.

> As any literate person knows, James Joyce is the best twentieth-century novelist. [But what qualities of Joyce's writing make him a superior novelist?]

> Michael Jordan banks at Big City, and so should you. [A celebrity's endorsement of course does not automatically guarantee the worth of a product, a service, an idea, or anything else.]

A similar tactic invites readers to accept an assertion because everybody else does. This is the **bandwagon approach.**

> As everyone knows, marijuana use leads to heroin addiction. [What is the evidence?]

Yet another diversion involves **flattery** of readers, in a way inviting them to join in a conspiracy.

> We all understand campus problems well enough to see the disadvantages of such a backward policy. [What are the disadvantages of the policy?]

The **argument ad populum** ("argument to the people") asks readers to accept a conclusion based on shared values or even prejudices and nothing else.

> Any truly patriotic American will support the President's action. [But why is the action worth taking?]

One final and very common kind of inappropriate emotional appeal addresses *not* the pros and cons of the issue itself but the real or imagined negative qualities of the people who hold the opposing view. This kind of argument is called **ad hominem,** Latin for "to the man."

One of the scientists has been treated for emotional problems, so his pessimism about nuclear waste merits no attention. [Do the scientist's previous emotional problems invalidate his current views?]

2 ■ Recognizing oversimplifications

To **oversimplify** is to conceal or ignore complexities in a vain attempt to create a neater, more convincing argument than reality allows.

Hasty generalization

A **hasty generalization**, also called **jumping to a conclusion**, is a claim based on too little evidence or on evidence that is unrepresentative. (See also p. 150.)

It is disturbing that several of the youths who shot up schools were users of violent video games. Obviously, these games can breed violence, and they should be banned. [A few cases do not establish the relation between the games and violent behavior. Most youths who play violent video games do not behave violently.]

From the way it handled this complaint, we can assume that the consumer protection office has little intention of protecting consumers. [One experience with the office does not demonstrate its intention or overall performance.]

Sweeping generalization

Whereas a hasty generalization comes from inadequate evidence, a **sweeping generalization** probably is not supportable at all. One kind of sweeping generalization is the **absolute statement** involving words such as *all, always, never,* and *no one* that allow no exceptions. Rarely can evidence support such terms. Moderate words such as *some, sometimes, rarely,* and *few* are more reasonable.

Another common sweeping generalization is the **stereotype**, a conventional and oversimplified characterization of a group of people.

People who live in cities are unfriendly.
Californians are fad-crazy.
Women are emotional.
Men can't express their feelings.

(See also pp. 547–50 on sexist and other biased language.)

Reductive fallacy

The **reductive fallacy** oversimplifies (or reduces) the relation between causes and their effects. The fallacy (sometimes called **oversimplification**) often involves linking two events as if one caused the other directly, whereas the causes may be more complex or the relation may not exist at all. For example:

> Poverty causes crime. [If so, then why do people who are not poor commit crimes? And why aren't all poor people criminals?]

> The better a school's athletic facilities are, the worse its academic programs are. [The sentence assumes a direct cause-and-effect link between athletics and scholarship.]

Post hoc fallacy

Related to the reductive fallacy is the assumption that because *A* preceded *B*, then *A* must have caused *B*. This fallacy is called in Latin *post hoc, ergo propter hoc,* meaning "after this, therefore because of this," or the **post hoc fallacy** for short.

> In the two months since he took office, Mayor Holcomb has allowed crime in the city to increase 12 percent. [The increase in crime is probably attributable to conditions existing before Holcomb took office.]

> The town council erred in permitting the adult bookstore to open, for shortly afterward two women were assaulted. [It cannot be assumed without evidence that the women's assailants visited or were influenced by the bookstore.]

Either/or fallacy

In the **either/or fallacy** (also called **false dilemma**), the writer assumes that a complicated question has only two answers, one good and one bad, both bad, or both good.

> City police officers are either brutal or corrupt. [Most city police officers are neither.]

> Either we permit mandatory drug testing in the workplace or productivity will continue to decline. [Productivity is not necessarily dependent on drug testing.]

False analogy

An **analogy** is a comparison between two essentially unlike things for the purpose of definition or illustration. In arguing by analogy, a writer draws a likeness between things on the basis of a single shared feature and then extends the likeness to other features. For instance, the "war on drugs" equates a battle against a foe with a program to eradicate (or at least reduce) sales and use of illegal drugs. Both involve an enemy, a strategy of overpowering the enemy, a desired goal, officials in uniform, and other similarities.

Analogy can only illustrate a point, never prove it: just because things are similar in one respect, they are not *necessarily* alike in other respects. In the fallacy called **false analogy,** the writer assumes such a complete likeness. Here is the analogy of the war on drugs taken to its false extreme:

> To win the war on drugs, we must wage more of a military-style operation. Prisoners of war are locked up without the benefit of a trial by jury, and drug dealers should be, too. Soldiers shoot their enemy on sight, and officials who encounter big drug operations should, too. Military traitors may be executed, and corrupt law enforcers could be, too.

arg

6g

EXERCISE 2
Analyzing advertisements

Leaf through a magazine or watch commercial television for half an hour, looking for advertisements that attempt to sell a product not on the basis of its worth but by snob appeal, flattery, or other inappropriate appeals to emotions. Be prepared to discuss the advertisers' techniques.

EXERCISE 3
Identifying and revising fallacies

Identify at least one fallacy illustrated by each of the following sentences. Then revise the sentence to make it more reasonable.

1. A successful marriage demands a maturity that no one under twenty-five possesses.
2. Students' persistent complaints about the grading system prove that it is unfair.
3. The United States got involved in World War II because the Japanese bombed Pearl Harbor.
4. People watch television because they are too lazy to talk or read or because they want mindless escape from their lives.
5. Racial tension is bound to occur when people with different backgrounds are forced to live side by side.

EXERCISE 4
Identifying fallacies in arguments

Analyze the two arguments on pages 154–56 for fallacies. To what extent do any fallacies weaken either argument? Explain.

EXERCISE 5
Identifying fallacies online

Use a Web browser to reach the online conversations at *http://groups.google.com*. Find a conversation about drug testing in the workplace, environmental pollution, violence in the media, or any other subject that interests you and that is debatable. Read through the arguments made in the conversation, noting the fallacies you see. List the fallacious statements as well as the types of fallacies they illustrate, keeping in mind that a given statement may illustrate more than a single type.

CHAPTER 7

Writing an Argument

In composing an argument, you try to clarify an issue or solve a problem by finding the common ground between you and others who will read your work. Using critical thinking, you develop and test your own ideas. Using a variety of techniques, you engage readers in an attempt to narrow the distance between your views and theirs.

7a Finding a subject

An argument subject must be arguable—that is, reasonable people will disagree over it and be able to support their positions with evidence. This sentence implies the *do*s and *don't*s listed in the box on the next page. Help with writing subjects appears earlier in this book:

- Working with a specific assignment, page 6.
- Working with a general assignment, pages 6–7.
- Narrowing a subject to a question, pages 7–8.

CULTURE LANGUAGE The guidelines for an argument subject may make you uncomfortable if your native language is something other than English and you're not accustomed to the kinds of arguments discussed here. One way to find a subject for argument is to read a newspaper every day for at least a week, looking for issues that involve or interest you. Following the development of the issues in articles, editorials, and letters to the editor will give you a sense of how controversial they are, what the positions are, and what your position might be.

---

http://www.ablongman.com/littlebrown
For added help with writing arguments, click on
➤ **Critical thinking and argument**
  ➤ Video tutorials
  ➤ Exercises
  ➤ Downloads
  ➤ Web links

Tests for an argument subject

A good subject:

- Concerns a matter of opinion—a conclusion drawn from evidence.
- Can be disputed: others might take a different position.
- *Will* be disputed: it is controversial.
- Is something you care about and know about or want to research.
- Is narrow enough to argue in the space and time available.

A bad subject:

- Cannot be disputed because it concerns a fact, such as the distance to Saturn or the functions of the human liver.
- Cannot be disputed because it concerns a personal preference or belief, such as a liking for a certain vacation spot or a moral commitment to vegetarianism.
- *Will not* be disputed because few if any disagree over it—the virtues of a secure home, for instance.

EXERCISE 1
Finding a subject for argument

Explain why each subject below is or is not appropriate for argument. (Refer to the box above if you need help.)

1. Granting of athletic scholarships
2. Care of automobile tires
3. Censoring the Web sites of hate groups
4. History of the town park
5. Housing for the homeless
6. Billboards in urban residential areas or in rural areas
7. Animal testing for cosmetics research
8. Cats versus dogs as pets
9. Ten steps in recycling wastepaper
10. Benefits of being a parent

7b Conceiving a thesis statement

The **thesis** is the main idea of your paper (see pp. 31–35). In an argument the **thesis statement** makes the claim that you want your

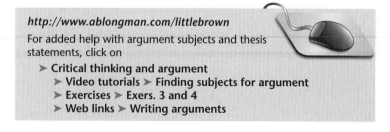

http://www.ablongman.com/littlebrown

For added help with argument subjects and thesis statements, click on

➤ **Critical thinking and argument**
  ➤ **Video tutorials** ➤ **Finding subjects for argument**
  ➤ **Exercises** ➤ **Exers. 3 and 4**
  ➤ **Web links** ➤ **Writing arguments**

readers to accept or act on. Here are two thesis statements on the same subject:

> The new room fees are unjustified given the condition of the dormitories.
>
> The administration should postpone the new room fees at least until conditions in the dormitories are improved.

Your thesis statement must satisfy the same requirements as your subject (see the box opposite). But it must also specify the basis for your claim. In both thesis statements above, the basis for protesting the room fees is that the dormitories are in poor condition.

Note that the writer of either of these arguments must clarify the definition of *condition(s)* if the argument is to be clear and reasonable. Always take pains to define abstract and general terms that are central to your argument, preferably in or just after the thesis statement. (See p. 146.)

EXERCISE 2
Conceiving a thesis statement
For each subject in Exercise 1 that you deemed arguable, draft a tentative thesis statement that specifies the basis for an argument. If you prefer, choose five arguable subjects of your own and draft a thesis statement for each one. One thesis statement should interest you enough to develop into a complete argument in later exercises.

7c   Analyzing your purpose and your audience

Your purpose in argument is, broadly, to engage readers in order to convince them of your position or persuade them to act. But arguments have more specific purposes as well, such as the following:

> To strengthen the commitment of existing supporters
> To win new supporters from the undecided or uninformed
> To get the opposition to reconsider
> To inspire supporters to act
> To deter the undecided from acting

It's no accident that each of these purposes characterizes the audience (*existing supporters, the undecided,* and so on). In argument,

---

even more than in other kinds of writing, achieving your purpose depends on the response of your readers, so you need a sense of who they are and where they stand. The "Questions About Audience" on page 10 can help you identify readers' knowledge, beliefs, and other pertinent information. In addition, you need to know how readers stand on your subject—not only whether they agree or disagree generally, but also which specific assertions they will find more or less convincing.

Your purpose can help you fill in this information. If you decide to address supporters or opponents, you essentially select readers with certain inclinations and ignore other readers who may tune in. If you decide to win new supporters from those who are undecided on your topic, you'll have to imagine skeptical readers who will be convinced only by an argument that is detailed, logical, and fair. Like you when you read an argument critically, these skeptical readers seek to be reasoned with, not manipulated into a position or hammered over the head.

> **EXERCISE 3**
> **Analyzing purpose and audience**
> Specify a purpose and likely audience for the thesis statement you chose to develop in Exercise 2. What do purpose and audience suggest about the way you should develop the argument?

7d   Using reason

As a reader of argument, you seek evidence for the writer's claims and clear reasoning about the relationship of evidence to claims. As a writer of argument, you seek to provide what the reader needs in a way that furthers your case.

The thesis of your argument is a conclusion you reach by reasoning about evidence. Two common processes of reasoning are induction and deduction—methods of thinking that you use all the time even if you don't know their names. You can think of induction and deduction as two different ways of moving among claims, evidence, and assumptions—the elements of argument derived from Stephen Toulmin's work and discussed on pages 143–52.

http://www.ablongman.com/littlebrown
For added help with methods of reasoning, click on
➤ **Critical thinking and argument**
   ➤ **Web links** ➤ **Writing arguments**

1 ▪ Reasoning inductively

When you're about to buy a used car, you consult friends, relatives, and consumer guides before deciding what kind of car to buy. Using **inductive reasoning**, you make specific observations about cars (your evidence) and you induce, or infer, a **generalization** (or claim) that Model X is the most reliable. Writing a paper on the effectiveness of print advertising, you might also use inductive reasoning:

First analyze statistics on advertising in print and in other media (evidence).

Then read comments by advertisers and publishers (more evidence).

Finally, form a conclusion that print is the most cost-effective advertising medium (generalization).

This reasoning builds from the evidence to the claim, with assumptions connecting evidence to claim.

Evidence

Data and opinions on advertising media.

Assumption

What is true in one set of circumstances (one set of print ads) is true in a similar set of circumstances (other print ads).

Claim

Generalization: Print is the most cost-effective advertising medium.

With induction, you predict something about the unknown based on what you know: you create new knowledge out of old.

The more evidence you accumulate, the more probable it is that your generalization is true. Note, however, that absolute certainty is not possible. At some point you must *assume* that your evidence justifies your generalization, for yourself and your readers. Most errors in inductive reasoning involve oversimplifying either the evidence or the generalization. See pages 156–62 on fallacies.

2 ▪ Reasoning deductively

You use **deductive reasoning** when you proceed from your generalization that Model X is the most reliable used car to your own specific circumstances (you want to buy a used car) to the conclusion (or claim) that you should buy a Model X car. Like induction, deduction uses the elements of argument—claims, evidence, and assumptions—but differently. The diagram on page 168 corresponds to the one for induction above, picking up the example of print advertising.

arg

7d

Assumption

A fact, a principle, a belief, or (as here) a generalization from induction: Print is the most cost-effective advertising medium.

Evidence

New information: Companies on lean budgets should advertise in the most cost-effective medium.

Claim

Conclusion: Companies on lean budgets should advertise in print.

arg
7d

With deduction, you apply old information to new.

The conventional way of displaying a deductive argument is in a **syllogism:**

> *Premise:* All human beings are mortal. [A generalization, fact, principle, or belief that you assume to be true.]
> *Premise:* I am a human being. [New information: a specific case of the first premise.]
> *Conclusion:* Therefore, I am mortal.

As long as the premises of a syllogism are true, the conclusion derives logically and certainly from them. If you want the school administration to postpone new room fees for one dormitory, your deductive argument might be expressed in this syllogism:

> *Premise:* The administration should not raise fees on dorm rooms in poor condition.
> *Premise:* The rooms in Polk Hall are in poor condition.
> *Conclusion:* Therefore, the administration should not raise fees on the rooms in Polk Hall.

The force of deductive reasoning depends on the reliability of the premises and the care taken to apply them in drawing conclusions. The reasoning process is **valid** if the premises lead logically to the conclusion. It is **true** if the premises are believable. Sometimes the reasoning is true but *not* valid:

> *Premise:* The administration should not raise fees on dorm rooms in poor condition.
> *Premise:* Tyler Hall is a dormitory.
> *Conclusion:* Therefore, the administration should not raise fees on the rooms in Tyler Hall.

Both premises may be true, but the first does not *necessarily* apply to the second, so the conclusion is invalid.

Sometimes, too, the reasoning is valid but *not* true:

> *Premise:* All college administrations are indifferent to students' needs.
> *Premise:* The administration of Central State is a college administration.

Tests for inductive and deductive reasoning

Induction

- Have you stated your evidence clearly?
- Is your evidence complete enough and good enough to justify your claim? What is the assumption that connects evidence and claim? Is it believable?
- Have you avoided fallacies?

Deduction

- What are the premises leading to your conclusion? Look especially for unstated premises.
- What does the first premise assume? Is the assumption believable?
- Does the first premise necessarily apply to the second premise?
- Is the second premise believable?
- Have you avoided fallacies?

> *Conclusion:* Therefore, the administration of Central State is indifferent to students' needs.

This syllogism is valid but useless: the first premise is an untrue assumption, so the entire argument is untrue. Invalid and untrue syllogisms underlie many of the fallacies discussed on pages 156–62.

A particular hazard of deductive reasoning is the **unstated premise:** the basic assumption linking evidence and conclusion is not stated but implied. Here the unstated premise is believable and the argument is reasonable:

> Ms. Stein has worked with drug addicts for fifteen years, so she knows a great deal about their problems. [Unstated premise: Anyone who has worked fifteen years with drug addicts knows about their problems.]

But when the unstated premise is wrong or unfounded, the argument is false. For example:

> Since Jane Lightbow is a senator, she must receive money illegally from lobbyists. [Unstated premise: All senators receive money illegally from lobbyists.]

To avoid such false conclusions, you may be tempted to make your claims sound more reasonable. But even a conclusion that sounds reasonable must be supportable. For instance, changing *must* to *might* modifies the unstated assumption about Senator Lightbow:

> Since Jane Lightbow is a senator, she might receive money illegally from lobbyists. [Unstated premise: *Some* senators receive money illegally from lobbyists.]

But it does not necessarily follow that Senator Lightbow is one of the "some." The sentence, though logical, is not truly reasonable unless evidence demonstrates that Senator Lightbow should be linked with illegal activities.

EXERCISE 4
Reasoning inductively

Study the facts below and then evaluate each of the numbered conclusions following them. Which of the generalizations are reasonable given the evidence, and which are not? Why?

In 2000–01 each American household viewed an average of 49 hours and 16 minutes of television weekly.

Each individual viewed an average of 30 hours and 16 minutes per week.

Those viewing the most television per week (42 hours and 10 minutes) were women over age 55.

Those viewing the least television per week (19 hours and 9 minutes) were children ages 6 to 11.

Households earning under $30,000 a year watched an average of 52 hours and 31 minutes a week.

Households earning more than $60,000 a year watched an average of 47 hours and 27 minutes a week.

1. Households with incomes under $30,000 tend to watch more television than average.
2. Women watch more television than men.
3. Nonaffluent people watch less television than affluent people.
4. Women over age 55 tend to watch more television than average.
5. Children watch less television than critics generally assume.

EXERCISE 5
Reasoning deductively

Convert each of the following statements into a syllogism. (You may have to state unstated assumptions.) Use the syllogism to evaluate both the validity and the truth of the statement.

> *Example:*
> DiSantis is a banker, so he does not care about the poor.
>
> *Premise:* Bankers do not care about the poor.
> *Premise:* DiSantis is a banker.
> *Conclusion:* Therefore, DiSantis does not care about the poor.
>
> The statement is untrue because the first premise is untrue.

1. The mayor opposed pollution controls when he was president of a manufacturing company, so he may not support new controls or vigorously enforce existing ones.
2. Information on corporate Web sites is unreliable because the sites are sponsored by for-profit entities.
3. Schroeder is a good artist because she trained at Parsons, like many other good artists.

4. Wealthy athletes who use their resources to help others deserve our particular appreciation.
5. Jimson is sexist because she has hired only one woman.

7e Using evidence

Whether your argument is reasonable or not depends heavily on the evidence you marshal to support it. The kinds of evidence and the criteria for evaluating evidence are discussed in detail on pages 147–51. Finding evidence is discussed under research writing on pages 621–49. Evaluating sources of evidence, including online sources, is discussed under research writing on pages 651–59.

The kind and quantity of evidence you use should be determined by your purpose, your subject, and the needs of your audience. Some arguments, such as an appeal for volunteer help in a soup kitchen, will rely most heavily on examples (including perhaps a narrative of your own experience) and on appeals to readers' beliefs. Other arguments, such as a proposal for mandatory side air bags in cars, will rely much more on statistics and expert opinions. Most arguments, including these, will mingle facts, examples, expert opinions, and appeals to readers' beliefs and needs.

In using evidence for argument, you'll need to be especially wary of certain traps that carelessness or zeal can lure you into. These are listed in the following box.

Responsible use of evidence

- **Don't distort.** You mislead readers when you twist evidence to suit your argument—for instance, when you claim that crime in your city occurs five times more often than it did in 1955, without mentioning that the population is also seven times larger.
- **Don't stack the deck.** Ignoring damning evidence is like cheating at cards. You must deal forthrightly with the opposition. (See pp.174–75.)
- **Don't exaggerate.** Watch your language. Don't attempt to manipulate readers by characterizing your own evidence as *pure* and *rock-solid* and the opposition's as *ridiculous* and *half-baked.* Make the evidence speak for itself.
- **Don't oversimplify.** Avoid forcing the evidence to support more than it can. (See also p. 160.)
- **Don't misquote.** When you cite experts, quote them accurately and fairly.

---

http://www.ablongman.com/littlebrown
For added help with evidence, click on
➤ **Critical thinking and argument**
➤ **Web links** ➤ **Writing arguments**

EXERCISE 6
Using reason and evidence in your argument

Develop the structure and evidence for the argument you began in Exercises 2 and 3 (pp. 165 and 166). (You may want to begin drafting at this stage.) Is your argument mainly inductive or mainly deductive? Use the box on page 169 to test the reasoning of the argument. Use the boxes on pages 149 and 171 to test your evidence.

7f   Reaching your readers

To reach your readers in argument, you appeal directly to their reason and emotions, you present yourself as someone worth heeding, and you account for views opposing your own.

1 ■ Appealing to readers

In forming convictions about arguable issues, we generally interpret the factual evidence through the filter of our values, beliefs, tastes, desires, and feelings. You may object to placing the new town dump in a particular wooded area because the facts suggest that the site is not large enough and that prevailing winds will blow odors back through the town. But you may also have fond memories of playing in the wooded area as a child, feelings that color your interpretation of the facts and strengthen your conviction that the dump should be placed elsewhere. Your conviction is partly rational, because it is based on evidence, and partly emotional, because it is also based on feelings.

Rational and emotional appeals

In most arguments you will combine **rational appeals** to readers' capacities for reasoning logically between evidence and claim with **emotional appeals** to readers' beliefs and feelings. The following passages, all arguing the same view on the same subject, illustrate how either a primarily rational or a primarily emotional appeal may be weaker than an approach that uses both:

Rational appeal
Advertising should show more physically challenged people. The millions of disabled Americans have considerable buying power,

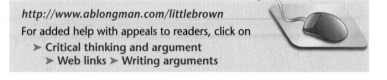

http://www.ablongman.com/littlebrown
For added help with appeals to readers, click on
➤ Critical thinking and argument
  ➤ Web links ➤ Writing arguments

yet so far advertisers have made no attempt to tap that power. [Appeals to the logic of financial gain.]

Emotional appeal

Advertising should show more physically challenged people. By keeping the physically challenged out of the mainstream depicted in ads, advertisers encourage widespread prejudice against disability, prejudice that frightens and demeans those who hold it. [Appeals to the sense of fairness, open-mindedness.]

arg

7f

Rational and emotional appeals

Advertising should show more physically challenged people. The millions of disabled Americans have considerable buying power, yet so far advertisers have made no attempt to tap that power. Further, by keeping the physically challenged out of the mainstream depicted in ads, advertisers encourage widespread prejudice against disability, prejudice that frightens and demeans those who hold it.

The third passage, in combining both kinds of appeal, gives readers both rational and emotional bases for agreeing with the writer.

For an emotional appeal to be successful, it must be appropriate for the audience and the argument:

- It must not misjudge readers' actual feelings.
- It must not raise emotional issues that are irrelevant to the claims and the evidence. (See pp. 159–60 for a discussion of specific inappropriate appeals, such as the bandwagon approach.)

One further caution: When you compose an argument for the Web, you may be tempted to use images, video, or sound to reinforce your claims. Multimedia elements can have a strong emotional appeal, to be sure. But in argument you have a particular responsibility to ensure that such elements are relevant to your claims and to explain their relevance in your text.

Ethical appeal

A third kind of approach to readers, the **ethical appeal,** is the sense you give of being a competent, fair, trustworthy person. A sound argument backed by ample evidence—a rational appeal—will convince readers of your knowledge and reasonableness. (So will your acknowledging the opposition. See the next page.) Appropriate emotional appeals will demonstrate that you share readers' beliefs and needs. An argument that is concisely written and correct in grammar, spelling, and other matters will underscore your competence. In addition, a sincere and even tone will assure readers that you are a balanced person who wants to reason with them.

A sincere and even tone need not exclude language with emotional appeal—words such as *frightens* and *demeans* at the end of the third example on the previous page. But avoid certain forms of expression that will mark you as unfair:

- Insulting words such as *idiotic* or *fascist*.
- Biased language such as *rednecks* or *fags*. (See pp. 547–50.)
- Sarcasm—for instance, using the sentence *What a brilliant idea* to indicate contempt for the idea and its originator.
- Exclamation points! They'll make you sound shrill!

See also pages 152–53 on tone.

2 ■ Answering opposing views

A good test of your fairness in argument is how you handle possible objections. Assuming your thesis is indeed arguable, then others can marshal their own evidence to support a different view or views. You need to find out what these other views are and what the support is for them. Then, in your argument, you need to take these views on, refute those you can, grant the validity of others, and demonstrate why, despite their validity, the opposing views are less compelling than your own.

The student who wrote the following paragraph first stated an opposing view, then conceded its partial validity, and finally demonstrated its irrelevance:

> The athletic director argues against reducing university support for athletic programs on the grounds that they make money that goes toward academic programs. It is true that here at Springfield the surpluses from the football and basketball programs have gone into the general university fund, and some of that money may have made it into academic departments (the fund's accounting methods make it impossible to say for sure). But the athletic director misses the point. The problem is not that the athletic programs may cost more than they take in but that they demand too much to begin with. For an institution that hopes to become first-rate academically, too many facilities, too much money, too much energy, and too many people are tied up in the effort to produce championship sports teams.

Before or while you draft your essay, list for yourself all the opposing views you can think of. You'll find them in your research, by

http://www.ablongman.com/littlebrown
For added help with answering opposing views, click on
 ➤ Critical thinking and argument
  ➤ Video tutorials ➤ Answering opposing views
  ➤ Web links ➤ Writing arguments

talking to friends and classmates, and by critically thinking about your own ideas. You can also look for a range of views in a discussion group that deals with your subject. (The archive at *http:// groups.google.com* is a place to start.)

To deal with opposing views, figure out which ones you can refute (do more research if necessary), and prepare to concede those views you can't refute. It's not a mark of weakness or failure to admit that the opposition has a point or two. Indeed, by showing yourself to be honest and fair, you strengthen your ethical appeal and thus your entire argument.

arg
7f

EXERCISE 7
Identifying appeals

Identify each passage below as primarily a rational appeal or primarily an emotional appeal. Which passages make a strong ethical appeal as well?

1. Web surfing may contribute to the global tendency toward breadth rather than depth of knowledge. Using those most essential of skills—pointing and clicking—our brightest minds may now never encounter, much less read, the works of Plato, Shakespeare, and Darwin.
2. Thus the data collected by these researchers indicate that a mandatory sentence for illegal possession of handguns may lead to reduction in handgun purchases.
3. Most broadcasters worry that further government regulation of television programming could breed censorship—certainly, an undesirable outcome. Yet most broadcasters also accept that children's television is a fair target for regulation.
4. Anyone who cherishes life in all its diversity could not help being appalled by the mistreatment of laboratory animals. The so-called scientists who run the labs are misguided.
5. Many experts in constitutional law have warned that the rule violates the right to free speech. Yet other experts have viewed the rule, however regretfully, as necessary for the good of the community as a whole.

EXERCISE 8
Reaching your readers

Continuing your argument-in-progress from Exercise 6 (p. 172), analyze whether your claims are rational or emotional and whether the mix is appropriate for your audience and argument. Analyze your ethical appeal, too, considering whether it can be strengthened. Then make a list of possible opposing views. Think freely at first, not stopping to censor views that seem far-fetched or irrational. When your list is complete, decide which views must be taken seriously and why, and develop a response to each one.

7g   Organizing your argument

All arguments include the same parts:

- The **introduction** establishes the significance of the subject and provides background. The introduction generally includes the thesis statement. However, if you think your readers may have difficulty accepting your thesis statement before they see at least some support for it, then it may come later in the paper. (See pp. 103–06 for more on introductions.)
- The **body** states claims relating to the thesis and, in one or more paragraphs, develops each claim with clearly relevant evidence. See below for more on organizing the body.
- The **response to opposing views** details those views and either demonstrates your argument's greater strengths or concedes the opponents' points. See below for more on organizing this response.
- The **conclusion** restates the thesis, summarizes the argument, and makes a final appeal to readers. (See pp. 106–08 for more on conclusions.)

The structure of the body and the response to opposing views depend on your subject, purpose, audience, and form of reasoning. The box opposite shows several possible arrangements.

You may want to experiment with various organizations—for instance, trying out your strongest claims first or last in the body, stating claims outright or letting the evidence build to them, answering the opposition near the beginning or near the end or claim by claim. You can do this experimentation on paper, of course, but it's easier on a computer. Try rearranging your outline as described on page 37. Or try rearranging your draft (work with a copy) by cutting and pasting parts of it for different emphases.

EXERCISE 9
Organizing your argument
Continuing from Exercise 8 (p. 175), develop a structure for your argument. Consider especially how you will introduce it, how you will arrange your claims, where you will place your responses to opposing views, and how you will conclude.

http://www.ablongman.com/littlebrown
For added help with organizing an argument, click on
➤ **Critical thinking and argument**
  ➤ **Web links** ➤ **Writing arguments**

Organizing an argument's body and response to opposing views

The traditional scheme
Claim 1 and evidence
Claim 2 and evidence
Claim X and evidence
Response to opposing views

The problem-solution scheme
The problem: claims and evidence
The solution: claims and evidence
Response to opposing views

arg

7h

Variations on the traditional scheme
Use a variation if you believe your readers will reject your argument without an early or intermittent response to opposing views.

Response to opposing views
Claim 1 and evidence
Claim 2 and evidence
Claim X and evidence

Claim 1 and evidence
Response to opposing views
Claim 2 and evidence
Response to opposing views
Claim X and evidence
Response to opposing views

7h   Revising your argument

When you revise your argument, do it in at least two stages—revising underlying meaning and structure, and editing more superficial elements. The checklists on pages 55 and 60 can be a guide. Supplement them with the checklist on the next page, which encourages you to think critically about your own argument. (You can download the checklist from this book's Web site: see the box below. Then use a copy for each argument you write, providing written responses to the questions.)

EXERCISE 10
Writing and revising your argument
Draft and revise the argument you have developed in the exercises in this chapter. Use the revision checklists on page 55 and on the next page to review your work.

http://www.ablongman.com/littlebrown
For added help with revising an argument, click on
➤ **Critical thinking and argument**
➤ **Downloads** ➤ **Checklist for revising an argument**
➤ **Web links** ➤ **Writing arguments**

Checklist for revising an argument

Thesis

- What is your thesis? Where is it stated?
- In what ways is your thesis statement an arguable claim?

Reasoning

- If your thesis derives from induction, where have you related the evidence to your generalization?
- If your thesis derives from deduction, is your syllogism both true and valid?
- Have you avoided fallacies in reasoning?

Evidence

- Where have you provided the evidence readers need?
- Where might your evidence not be accurate, relevant, representative, or adequate? (Answer this question from the point of view of a neutral or even skeptical reader.)

Appeals

- Where have you considered readers' probable beliefs and values?
- How are your rational appeals and emotional appeals appropriate for your readers?
- What is your ethical appeal? How can you improve it?

Opposing views

- What opposing views have you answered?
- How successfully have you refuted opposing views? (Again, consider the neutral or skeptical reader.)

Organization

- How clearly does your argument move from one point to the next?
- How appropriate is your organization given your readers' likely views?

7i Examining a sample argument

The following essay by Craig Holbrook, a student, illustrates the principles discussed in this chapter. As you read the essay, notice especially the structure, the relation of claims and supporting evidence, the kinds of appeals Holbrook makes, and the ways he responds to opposing views.

TV Can Be Good for You

Television wastes time, pollutes minds, destroys brain cells, and turns some viewers into murderers. Thus runs the prevailing talk about the medium, supported by serious research as well as simple belief. But television has at least one strong virtue, too, which helps to explain its endurance as a cultural force. In an era when people often have little time to speak with one another, television provides replacement voices that ease loneliness, spark healthful laughter, and even educate young children.

Most people who have lived alone understand the curse of silence, when the only sound is the buzz of unhappiness or anxiety inside one's own head. Although people of all ages who live alone can experience intense loneliness, the elderly are especially vulnerable to solitude. For example, they may suffer increased confusion or depression when left alone for long periods but then rebound when they have steady companionship (Bondevik and Skogstad 329–30).

A study of elderly men and women in New Zealand found that television can actually serve as a companion by assuming "the role of social contact with the wider world," reducing "feelings of isolation and loneliness because it directs viewers' attention away from themselves" ("Television Programming"). Thus television's replacement voices can provide comfort because they distract from a focus on being alone.

The absence of real voices can be most damaging when it means a lack of laughter. Here, too, research shows that television can have a positive effect on health. Laughter is one of the most powerful calming forces available to human beings, proven in many studies to reduce heart rate, lower blood pressure, and ease other stress-related ailments (Burroughs, Mahoney, and Lippman 172; Griffiths 18). Television offers plenty of laughter for all kinds of viewers: the recent listings for a single Friday night included more than twenty comedy programs running on the networks and on basic cable between 6 and 9 PM.

A study reported in a health magazine found that laughter inspired by television and video is as healthful as the laughter generated by live comedy. Volunteers laughing at a video comedy routine "showed significant improvements in several immune functions, such as natural killer-cell activity" (Laliberte 78). Further, the effects of the comedy

arg

7i

Introduction:

Identification of prevailing view

Disagreement with prevailing view

Thesis statement making three claims for television

Background for claim 1: effects of loneliness

Evidence for effects of loneliness

Evidence for effects of television on loneliness

Statement of claim 1

Background for claim 2: effects of laughter

Evidence for effects of laughter

Evidence for comedy on television

Evidence for effects of laughter in response to television

were so profound that "merely anticipating watching a funny video improved mood, depression, and anger as much as two days beforehand" (Laliberte 79). Even for people with plenty of companionship, television's replacement voices can have healthful effects by causing laughter.

> Statement of claim 2

Television also provides information about the world. This service can be helpful to everyone but especially to children, whose natural curiosity can exhaust the knowledge and patience of their parents and caretakers. While the TV may be baby-sitting children, it can also enrich them. For example, educational programs such as those on the Discovery Channel, the Disney Channel, and PBS offer a steady stream of information at various cognitive levels. Even many cartoons, which are generally dismissed as mindless or worse, familiarize children with the material of literature, including strong characters enacting classic narratives.

> Background for claim 3: educational effects
>
> Evidence for educational programming on television

Two researchers studying children and television found that TV is a source of creative and psychological instruction, inspiring children "to play imaginatively and develop confidence and skills" (Colman and Colman 9). Instead of passively watching, children "interact with the programs and videos" and "sometimes include the fictional characters they've met into reality's play time" (Colman and Colman 8). Thus television's replacement voices both inform young viewers and encourage exchange.

> Evidence for educational effects of television on children

The value of these replacement voices should not be oversold. For one thing, almost everyone agrees that too much TV does no one any good and may cause much harm. Many studies show that excessive TV watching increases violent behavior, especially in children, and can cause, rather than ease, other antisocial behaviors and depression (Reeks 114; Walsh 34). In addition, human beings require the give and take of actual interaction. Steven Pinker, an expert in children's language acquisition, warns that children cannot develop language properly by watching television. They need to interact with actual speakers who respond directly to their specific needs (282). Replacement voices are not real voices and in the end can do only limited good.

> Statement of claim 3
>
> Anticipation of objections
>
> 1. Harm of television
>
> 2. Need for actual interaction
>
> Qualification of claims in response to objections

But even limited good is something, especially for those who are lonely, angry, or neglected. Television is not an entirely positive force, but neither is it an entirely negative one. Its voices stand by to provide company, laughter, and information whenever they're needed.

> Conclusion

PART III

Using Computers Critically

CHAPTER 8

Using Key
Computer Skills

Knowing how to operate computers is essential for most students and in most careers. Yet operating the machines is only part of the requirement. Even more important is being a critical producer and consumer of electronic information.

This handbook treats computer work that is especially relevant to writers. Throughout Chapters 1–3, tips for using a word processor appear at the mouse symbol above. (If you need help with basic word-processing operations, use the box below to reach the book's Web site.) This chapter discusses other fundamental skills for writers: managing files, working critically with options such as spelling and grammar/style checkers, writing electronic mail, and using the Web. Then the following three chapters cover document design, Web composition, and online collaboration.

8a Managing files

A major advantage of writing with a computer is the ability to save your work in different forms and files. The challenge is to keep the original document intact and to keep track of all the versions by labeling and organizing them. The following screen shots and explanations (keyed to each other by number) demonstrate these file-management basics.

1. A word processor's File menu is the key to file management. From it you can create new documents, save and rename them, and open them.

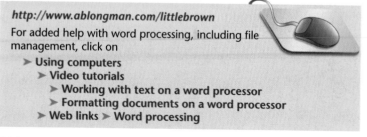

http://www.ablongman.com/littlebrown

For added help with word processing, including file management, click on
➤ **Using computers**
  ➤ **Video tutorials**
    ➤ **Working with text on a word processor**
    ➤ **Formatting documents on a word processor**
  ➤ **Web links** ➤ **Word processing**

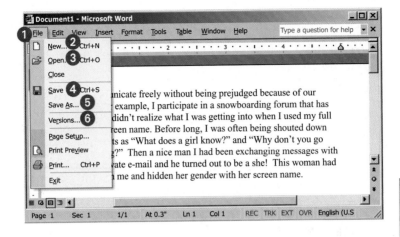

2. Select New to start composing a new document. You'll be able to choose the kind of document, such as a blank word-processing document (for papers) or a letter. Save your new document right away using the Save command (4).

3. Select Open to view or edit a document that you have already saved.

4. Select Save to save and name a new document or to save changes you have made to an existing document. A dialog box will let you name the document and decide where to place it in your file structure (see the next page).

5. Select Save As for either of two file-management purposes: to copy a document and rename the copy, or to copy a document in a new location. As with the Save function, a dialog box will let you rename the file and decide where to place it. The Save As function leaves the original intact, so it's one way to record successive drafts of a paper, each with a different name (for instance, *netcom, netcom2,* and so on). You'll see each name in your file structure.

6. Select Versions to save different stages of a particular document. The word processor will store and time-stamp each version, and you'll be able to compare and select revisions. Unlike with the Save As function, only one file name will be displayed in your file structure.

Using the File menu commands is only part of file management. You can also name documents and use the computer's file spaces to organize your work and make documents easy to retrieve. The next screen shot and following explanations demonstrate this process.

1. When you first save a document or copy one using Save As, the word processor will prompt you to name the document. Give

each new document a name that you'll be able to recognize later—perhaps a shortened version of the document's subject (as here: *netcom*), a reference to the assignment (such as *Paper 1*), or a format that matches the file-naming conventions of a course with your name and other information (such as *LingAsnmnt1* or *Ling.p1d1*). For a copied document, the name might relate to the original—for a revision, say, *netcom2, Paper 1.2,* or *Ling.p1d2*.

2. The same dialog box will ask you to decide where to put your file within your file structure. Select an existing folder if the document relates to others in the same folder—for instance, the papers for a particular course or the drafts of a particular paper. Open the folder and then click Save to save your file.

3. Select the New Folder icon to create and name a new folder—if, for instance, you're saving the first paper for a course (as in the screen shot) or you're saving the first draft of a paper (in which case the folder name can reflect the paper's name, such as *NetcomPaper*).

Note Two precautions can prevent significant loss of work if the computer malfunctions:

- Save your work every five to ten minutes. Most word processors have an Auto Save function that will save your work automatically as you type, at the interval you specify. Still, get in the habit of saving manually whenever you make major changes.
- After doing any major work on a project, create a backup version of the file on a second drive or diskette.

8b Working with spelling and grammar/style checkers

A word processor can remove much of the drudgery of writing, but it can't help much with the important decisions you must make to communicate effectively. It cannot know your purpose for writing, your audience, or anything else about your writing situation.

These limitations affect the spelling and grammar/style checkers that work with word processors. Although they will flag many basic errors, they will also miss many problems and may even flag items that are actually correct. These tools can help you only if you use them critically:

- Read your work yourself to ensure that it's clear and error-free. (See pp. 58–62 for editing and proofreading tips.)
- Consider a checker's suggestions carefully, weighing each one against your intentions. If you aren't sure whether to accept a checker's suggestion, consult a dictionary, writing handbook, or other source. Your version may be fine.

Note Spelling and grammar/style checkers can usually be set to flag possible errors as soon as you type them. But many writers find this function distracting when they are trying to generate ideas or do in-depth revision. To avoid attending too much to the flagged surface problems in your writing, use the Tools menu to turn off the checkers. You can always instruct the computer to check for errors when you are ready to do so. (If you compose with the checkers on, you can instruct most word processors to ignore flags by selecting them with the right mouse button.)

8b

1 ■ Using a spelling checker

Your word processor's spelling checker can be a great ally: it will flag words that are spelled incorrectly and usually suggest alternative spellings that resemble what you've typed. However, this ally also has the potential to undermine you because of its limitations:

- The checker flags all words that don't match entries in its dictionary. Thus it may flag a word that you've spelled correctly just because it doesn't recognize the word.
- In providing a list of alternative spellings for your word, the checker may highlight the one it considers most likely to be correct. You need to verify that this alternative is actually what you intend before selecting it. Keep in mind, too, that the checker's list may not provide a correct alternative at all. Consult an online or printed dictionary when you aren't sure of the checker's recommendations (see Chapter 41).

---

http://www.ablongman.com/littlebrown
For added help with using spelling and grammar/style checkers, click on
➤ **Using computers** ➤ **Video tutorials** ➤ **Using spelling and grammar/style checkers**

- Most important, a spelling checker will not flag words that appear in its dictionary but you have misused. The jingle shown in the screen shot below has circulated widely as a warning about spelling checkers (we found it in the *Bulletin of the Missouri Council of Teachers of Mathematics*). The jingle contains thirteen misspellings, not one of them flagged by the spelling checker. Can you spot the errors?

8b

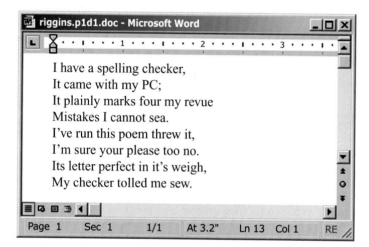

You can supplement a spelling checker by maintaining a file of your frequent misspellings and selecting Find under the Edit menu to check for them. But in the end *the only way to rid your papers of spelling errors is to proofread your papers yourself.* See page 62 for proofreading tips. And see Chapter 43 for more advice on spelling.

2 ▪ Using a grammar and style checker

Word processors' grammar and style checkers can flag incorrect grammar or punctuation and wordy or awkward sentences. However, these programs can call your attention only to passages that *may* be faulty. They miss many errors because they are not yet capable of analyzing language in all its complexity (for instance, they can't accurately distinguish a word's part of speech when there are different possibilities, as *light* can be a noun, a verb, or an adjective). And they often question passages that don't need editing, such as an appropriate passive verb or a deliberate and emphatic use of repetition.

In the screen shot on the facing page, the checker has flagged a direct repetition of *light* in the first sentence but left unflagged the other intrusive repetitions of the word. And the checker has flagged the entire second sentence because it is long, but in fact the sentence is grammatically correct and clear.

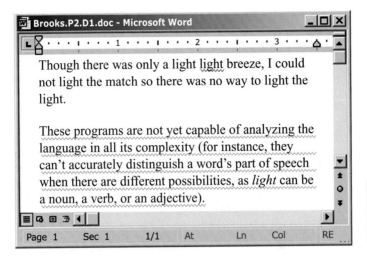

You can customize a grammar and style checker to suit your needs and habits as a writer. (Select Options under the Tools menu.) Most checkers allow you to specify whether to check grammar only or grammar and style. Some style checkers can be set to the level of writing you intend, such as formal, standard, and informal. (For academic writing choose formal.) You can also instruct the checker to flag specific grammar and style problems that tend to occur in your writing, such as mismatched subjects and verbs, apostrophes in plural nouns, overused passive voice, or a confusion between *its* and *it's*.

As with a spelling checker, so with a grammar and style checker: it will not do your editing for you. Each time it questions something, you must determine whether a change is needed at all and what change will be most effective, and you must read your papers carefully on your own to find any errors the program missed.

8c   Using other word-processing tools

1 ■ Selecting optional programs

Word processors either come with or are compatible with a number of optional programs. These programs, too, can both help and hurt your writing depending on how critically you use them.

■ *Thesaurus programs* help with word choices by responding to your word with a display of several synonyms (words that have similar meanings). A single keystroke allows you to replace your word with a displayed word. Thesaurus programs are limited because they display only some synonyms, not all, and even a narrow list may contain words that do not suit your meaning. Neither an electronic nor a printed thesaurus will be any help if it leads you to misuse words whose meanings you don't know. Before you use a word suggested by a thesaurus, always check its meaning in a dictionary. (See pp. 554 and 576 for more on thesauruses.)

- *Outlining programs* help you organize your work by providing automatic indentions, easy resequencing, and other features. However, some writers find these programs too rigid. To experiment with whether an outlining program can help you, select Outline or Bullets and Numbering/Outline from the Insert or Format menu of your word processor.

- *Graphics programs* allow you to create charts and graphs or images to be inserted into your documents. You can also use the programs to resize and crop images that you wish to add to your documents. (See p. 208 for more on these programs.)

- *Documentation programs* help you format your source citations in many disciplines' styles. (See p. 689 for more on these programs.)

2 ■ Commenting on documents and tracking changes

Your word processor may provide two additional functions that can significantly affect the way you draft and revise: Comment and Track Changes.

Commenting on documents

The Comment function creates something like a sticky Post-it note: it allows you to comment on your own or others' writing without inserting words into the document text. Usually you can add comments to a document by selecting Comment from the Insert menu and then composing your commentary. Color brackets or highlights in the text will indicate that comments have been added, and readers can view the commentary by selecting the bracketed or highlighted item. In the screen shot at the top of the facing page, clicking on the bracketed phrase at the bottom of the document has produced the pop-up comment you see.

When using the Comment function, also use some of the file-management techniques discussed on pages 184–86. Copy the original document, and rename it with an addition that indicates its status. In the screen shot, the reviewer, Franklin Potter, added *RevPotter* to the name of Riggins's original document.

See pages 65–67 for tips on reviewing others' writing. Your instructor may also have specific instructions.

8c

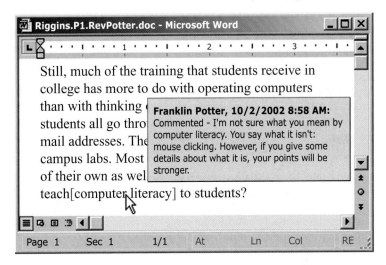

Still, much of the training that students receive in college has more to do with operating computers than with thinking [...] students all go thro[...] mail addresses. The[...] campus labs. Most [...] of their own as wel[...] teach[computer literacy] to students?

> **Franklin Potter, 10/2/2002 8:58 AM:**
> Commented - I'm not sure what you mean by computer literacy. You say what it isn't: mouse clicking. However, if you give some details about what it is, your points will be stronger.

Page 1   Sec 1   1/1   At   Ln   Col   RE

8c

Tracking changes

You can keep track of the revisions you make in a document with an option usually found under the Tools or File menu. In the screen shot below, the revisions are in red: deleted copy crossed out and added copy underlined. (Changes may appear differently in your documents, depending on how you set them.)

Tracking changes may encourage you to revise more freely because you can always revert to your original text. It allows you to

Riggins.P1D2.doc - Microsoft Word

Overall, basic computer skills are most useful for improving communication. It is important, however, not to confuse computer literacy with knowing how to save a file or copy a selection of text. ~~Computer literacy is more than knowing how to click a mouse. To be literate, students must know why and when to click the mouse.~~ <u>Computer literacy has more to do with learning how to be a critical consumer and producer of electronic information than with understanding the workings of computers.</u>

Page 1   Sec 1   1/1   At   Ln   Col   RE

weigh the relative effectiveness of the original and revised versions as you view them side by side (you can then easily accept or reject changes). It also gives you a way to evaluate the kinds of changes you are making. For instance, if during revision you see only minor surface alterations (word substitutions, added punctuation, and the like), then you might consider whether and where to read more deeply for more fundamental changes.

8d Using electronic mail

You may be using electronic mail, or e-mail, every day to converse quickly and casually with friends and family. In college you'll also use e-mail for a host of academic reasons, from collaborating with classmates to conducting research, and you'll want to communicate both purposefully and efficiently. This section covers composing and responding to messages and observing Internet etiquette. For more on using e-mail to interact with the other students in a course, see pages 233–36. For more on using e-mail as a research tool, see page 645.

Note The e-mail program at your school may differ from the one used for the screen shots here. If you aren't sure how to use your school's e-mail, ask your instructor or one of the school's technology advisers.

1 ■ Composing messages

To use e-mail productively for writing, pause to weigh each element of the message, as illustrated in the screen shot opposite and the explanations following.

1. *Think about the readers listed in the To or Recipient field.* Consider whether you're addressing an individual or a group, what the audience knows or needs to know about your subject and purpose, and what tone is appropriate for addressing this audience. (See p. 10 for a list of questions to ask about audience.)
2. *Describe the content of your message in the Subject heading.* Then your audience will know what to expect and what priority to assign the message.
3. *Use attachments to share your work and to respond to the writing of others.* In the screen shot, the writer is sending a draft to

http://www.ablongman.com/littlebrown
For added help with electronic mail, click on
➤ **Using computers**
  ➤ **Video tutorials** ➤ **Using e-mail**
  ➤ **Web links** ➤ **E-mail**

flashbob@cncu.edu, 01:13 PM 10/17/2002-0400, Student Loan Project: My Sections

Arial

1 T̲o̲: flashbob@cncu.edu<Bob Riggins>
F̲rom: Franklin Potter <fpotter@cncu.edu>
2 S̲ubject: Student Loan Project: My Sections
3 A̲ttached: D:\My Documents\english120\Potter.P1.doc;

4 Hi gang. I've attached the draft of my sections of our paper to this message. One thing I'm a bit unsure about in my sections is how evenhanded I am when I talk about the private loan consolidation companies. I want to make sure that I point out problems while still recognizing that they are businesses and have a right to operate for a profit. Anyway, keep that in mind as you read the sections.

I also e-mailed the people at Federated Loan Consolidation Corporation and asked them whether they were affiliated with a federal agency and about the kinds of guarantees they provide for fixed interest rates. I guess one issue I really want to get at is how these private corporations represent themselves. I'll pass on any information they send me. See you in class, Frank.

8d

his classmates for feedback. Be aware that attachments are not always readable: different word processors (such as *Word-Perfect* and *Microsoft Word*) use different, often incompatible, file formats; and documents sent over the Internet are sometimes encoded in special formats (such as MIME) that may need to be decoded at the recipient's end. See the box below for help with attachments.

Dealing with incompatible or encoded files

If you have trouble sending or receiving readable electronic documents by electronic mail, try these strategies:

- Send your documents in rich text format (RTF) or in text-only format, both of which can be read by most word processors. RTF offers the significant advantage of preserving most formatting, such as bold, italic, underlining, and tabs. Documents saved in text-only format lose all formatting. With either option, save a *copy* of your document (not the original) in the new format. In your word processor's File menu, first choose Save to preserve the original document. Then choose Save As, give the document a new name, go to the Save As Type option, and choose Rich Text Format or Text Only.
- If your recipient can't read your RTF or text-only document, use the word processor's Copy and Paste commands to copy the document into the body of an e-mail message. You will lose most, if not all, of your document's formatting.
- To read an encoded file, such as one in MIME, you may need to use a special decoding program. Your school's technology advisers can help you obtain and use such a program.

---

4. *Pitch the content and tone of your message to your audience.* In the message shown in the screen shot, the writer knows the recipients well and yet has serious information to convey to them, so he writes informally but states his points and concerns carefully. Writing to the corporation mentioned in the message, the writer would be more formal in both tone and approach. Although e-mail is typically more casual than printed correspondence, in academic settings a crafted message is more likely to achieve the intended purpose. Use short paragraphs with blank lines between them. For long messages—which recipients can review only one screen at a time—provide a tight structure, a clear forecast of the content, and a clear division into parts (using headings if necessary). Proofread all but the most informal messages for errors in grammar, punctuation, and spelling.

8d

Note Some e-mail programs don't allow underlining, italics, and boldface. Even if you can use such highlighting, you should assume that your recipients will not be able to see it in your messages. For alternatives, use underscores to indicate _underlining_ or asterisks to provide *emphasis*.

2 ■ Responding to messages

When you respond to a message, rely on the strategies discussed above and heed some special concerns.

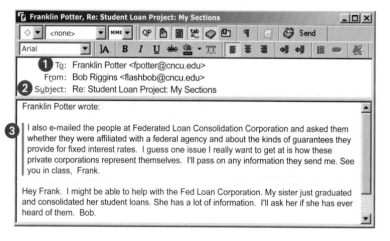

1. *Check that the response addresses the appropriate person or people.* Using the Reply or Respond function can be tricky because some programs address only the original sender while others address all recipients of the original message.
2. *Check that the reply has an appropriate subject heading.* Most e-mail programs label a response with the same subject heading

as the original, preceded by *Re:* (from Latin, meaning "In reference to"). If your response indeed continues the same subject, then *Re:* indicates as much. However, if you raise a new issue, you should rewrite the subject heading to say so.

3. *Use quoted material from earlier messages critically.* Most e-mail programs can copy the original message into your response, setting off the quoted material with a vertical line (as in the screen shot) or some other device. By weaving your replies into the quoted material, you can respond to the author point by point, as you would in conversation. However, delete from the original anything you are not responding to so that your recipient can focus on what you have to say without wading through his or her own words. (In the screen shot opposite, Riggins selected only the part of Potter's message that he wanted to comment on, deleting the rest.)

8d

3 ■ Observing netiquette

To communicate effectively online, you'll need to abide by some rules of behavior and simple courtesies. You won't always see others observing this **netiquette,** or Internet etiquette, but you will see that those who do observe it receive the more thoughtful and considerate replies.

Addressing messages

- *Avoid spamming.* With a few keystrokes, you can broadcast a message to many recipients at once—all the students in a course, say, or all the participants in a discussion group. Occasionally, you may indeed have a worthwhile idea or important information that everyone on the list will want to know. But flooding whole lists with irrelevant messages—called **spamming**—is rude and irritating.
- *Avoid sending frivolous messages to all the members of a group.* Instead of dashing off "I agree" and distributing the two-word message widely, put some time into composing a thoughtful response and send it only to those who will be interested.

Composing messages

- *Remember that the messages you receive represent individuals.* Don't say or do anything that you wouldn't say or do face to face.
- *Use names.* In the body of your message, address your reader(s) by name if possible and sign off with your own name and information on how to contact you. Your own name is especially important if your e-mail address does not spell it out.
- *Pay careful attention to tone.* Refrain from **flaming,** or attacking, correspondents. Don't use all-capital letters, which SHOUT. And use irony or sarcasm only cautiously: in the absence of facial

expressions, they can lead to misunderstandings. To indicate irony and emotions, you can use **emoticons,** such as the smiley :-). These sideways faces can easily be overused, though, and should not substitute for thoughtfully worded opinions.

- *Avoid saying anything in e-mail that you would not say in a printed document such as a letter or memo.* E-mail can usually be retrieved from the server, and in business and academic settings it may well be retrieved in disputes over contracts, grades, and other matters.

Reading and responding to messages

- *Be a forgiving reader.* Avoid nitpicking over spelling or other surface errors. And because attitudes are sometimes difficult to convey, give authors an initial benefit of the doubt: a writer who at first seems hostile may simply have tried too hard to be concise; a writer who at first seems unserious may simply have failed at injecting humor into a worthwhile message.

- *Forward messages only with permission.* You may want to send a message you've received to someone else, but do so only if you know that the author of the message won't mind.

- *Avoid participating in flame "wars,"* overheated dialogs that contribute little or no information or understanding. If a war breaks out in a discussion, ignore it: don't rush to defend someone who is being attacked, and don't respond even if you are under attack yourself.

8e

8e Going places on the Web

As a writer, you'll use the World Wide Web to launch writing, collaborate with others, and conduct research. This section explains

---

http://www.ablongman.com/littlebrown
For added help with browsing and using the Internet, click on

- ➤ Using computers ➤ Web links ➤ Using the Internet
- ➤ Research writing
  - ➤ Video tutorials
    - ➤ Finding source information
    - ➤ Using keywords with a search engine
    - ➤ Evaluating online sources
  - ➤ Exercises ➤ Exers. 1–3
  - ➤ Web links
    - ➤ Finding sources
    - ➤ Sources in literature and other humanities
    - ➤ Sources in the social sciences
    - ➤ Sources in the natural and applied sciences

important Web-browser skills and directs you to all of this book's Web resources.

1 ▪ Using a Web browser

To reach a Web site and its files, you need a program called a browser: *Microsoft Internet Explorer* and *Netscape* are the most common, and one of them is probably in use at your school. The screen shot below demonstrates some of the features of most Web browsers.

1. To reach a Web site, first enter its address, or URL, in the Address or Location field. (For more on URLs, see pp. 653–54.) Then select Go or press Enter on your keyboard.
2. To return to a page you have just visited, select Back. To move forward again, select Forward. The Back function is especially useful when a Web site dead-ends, leaving you stranded on a page.
3. To stop the browser from loading a page or file, select Stop. Stop the browser if a page is taking too long to load or if you have selected a link by mistake. Select Refresh or Reload if a page fails to load completely or if you believe its content may have changed since your last visit.
4. To record a site's address for future visits, select Favorites or Bookmarks. The browser will maintain a list of sites you record in this way, so that you can easily return to them later.
5. To see a list of sites you have visited during recent browsing sessions, select History. The History list can return you to a site you may have neglected to bookmark and can locate a site not easily reached with the Back function.

2 ▪ Consulting Web resources

Both in this book and on the Web itself, you can find resources that will help you become a proficient Web user:

- Information about composing for the Web appears in Chapter 10.
- Information about conducting research on the Web, including using search engines and evaluating Web sources, appears on pages 639–45 and 653–58.

- Web sites for specific disciplines appear on pages 796–97 (literature), 816–18 (history, art, and other humanities), 836–38 (social sciences), and 867–69 (natural and applied sciences).
- Documentation models for electronic sources appear on pages 721–32 (MLA style), 824–26 (Chicago style), 849–53 (APA style), and 875–78 (CSE style).
- Information about the workings and possibilities of the Internet appears on many Web sites, including the one for this book (see the box on p. 196), Learn the Net's *Internet Basics* (*http://www.learnthenet.com/english/section/intbas.html*), and the Public Broadcasting Service's *Understanding and Using the Internet* (*http://www.pbs.org/uti*).

8e

CHAPTER 9

Designing Documents

Imaginehowharditwouldbetoreadandwriteiftextlookedlikethis. To make reading and writing easier, we place a space between words. This convention and many others—such as page margins, page numbers, and paragraph breaks—have evolved over time to help writers communicate clearly with readers.

This chapter looks at principles and elements of design that can help you present your documents effectively. The documents discussed include academic papers, reports, flyers, newsletters, and brochures. More information on business formats appears in Chapter 56. Information on designing for the World Wide Web appears in Chapter 10.

9a Formatting academic papers

Many academic disciplines prefer specific formats for students' papers. This book details four such formats:

- MLA, used in English, foreign languages, and some other humanities (pp. 736–39).
- Chicago, used in history, art history, religion, and some other humanities (pp. 828–30).
- APA, used in the social sciences (pp. 856–59).
- CSE, used in some natural and applied sciences (pp. 878–79).

Other academic formats can be found in the style guides listed on pages 818, 838, and 869.

The design guidelines in this chapter extend the range of elements and options covered by most academic styles. Your instructors

http://www.ablongman.com/littlebrown
For added help with document design, click on
➤ Using computers
   ➤ Video tutorials ➤ Formatting documents on a word processor
   ➤ Web links ➤ Document design

may want you to adhere strictly to a particular style or may allow some latitude in design. Ask them for their preferences.

9b   Considering principles of design

Most of the principles of design respond to the ways we read. White space, for instance, relieves our eyes and helps to lead us through a document. Groupings or lists help to show relationships. Type sizes, images, and color add variety and help to emphasize important elements.

The sample documents below and on the facing page illustrate quite different ways of presenting a report for a marketing course.

Ineffective design

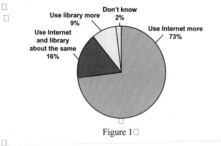

Ready or Not, Here They Come: College Students and the Internet

College life once meant classrooms of students listening to teachers or groups of students talking over lunch in the union. But the reality today is more complex: students interact with their peers and professors by computer as much as face to face. As these students graduate and enter the workforce, all of society will be affected by their experience.

According to the Pew Internet Research Center (2002), today's college students are practiced computer and Internet users. The Pew Center reports that 20 percent of students in college today started using computers between ages five and eight. By age eighteen all students were using computers. Almost all college students, 86 percent, rely on the Internet, with 66 percent of students using more than one e-mail address. Computer ownership among this group is also very high: 85 percent have purchased or have been given at least one computer.

Students are eager to tap into the Internet's benefits and convenience.

Don't know 2%
Use library more 9%
Use Internet and library about the same 16%
Use Internet more 73%

Figure 1

Figure 1, from the Pew Report, shows that the Internet has eclipsed the library as the site of college students' research. In fact, a mere 9 percent of students report relying more on the

Runs title and subtitle together. Does not distinguish title from text.

Crowds the page with minimal margins.

Downplays paragraph breaks with small indentions.

Buries statistics in a paragraph. Obscures relationships with nonparallel wording.

Does not introduce the figure, leaving readers to infer its meaning and purpose.

Leaves large white space that overemphasizes the figure.

Presents the figure undynamically, flat on.

Does not caption the figure to explain what it shows, offering only a figure number and a partial text explanation.

Even at a glance, the second document is easier to scan and read. It makes better use of white space, groups similar elements, uses bullets and fonts for emphasis, and more successfully integrates the visual data of the chart.

As you design your own documents, think about your purpose, the expectations of your readers, and how readers will move through your document. Also consider the following general principles of design, noting how they overlap and support each other.

Creating flow

Many of the other design principles work in concert with the larger goal of conducting the reader through a document by establishing flow, a pattern for the eye to follow. In text-heavy docu-

Effective design

Distinguishes title from subtitle and both from text.	**Ready or Not, Here They Come** **College Students and the Internet**
Provides adequate margins.	College life once meant classrooms of students listening to teachers or groups of students talking over lunch in the union. But the reality today is more complex: students interact with their peers and professors by computer as much as face to face. As these students graduate and enter the workforce, all of society will be affected by their experience.
Emphasizes paragraph breaks with white space.	According to the Pew Internet Research Center (2002), today's college students are practiced computer users and Internet users.
Groups statistics in a bulleted list set off with white space. Uses parallel wording for parallel information.	• They started young: 20 percent were using computers between ages five and eight, and all were using them by age eighteen. • They rely on the Internet: 86 percent have used the network, and 66 percent use more than one e-mail address. • They own computers: 85 percent have purchased or have been given at least one computer.
Introduces the figure to indicate its meaning and purpose.	Students are eager to tap into the Internet's benefits and convenience. Figure 1, from the Pew Report, shows that the Internet has eclipsed the library as the site of college students' research.
Reduces white space with shorter labels and a key.	
Presents the figure dynamically, emphasizing the most significant segment.	16% 9% 2% 73% ■ Use Internet more ■ Use Internet and library about the same □ Use library more □ Don't know
Captions the figure so that it can be read separately from the text.	*Figure 1.* College students' use of the Internet and the library for research

---

Principles of document design

- **Create flow** to conduct the reader through the document.
- **Space elements** to give the reader's eye a rest and to focus the reader's attention.
- **Group related elements** in lists or under similar headings.
- **Emphasize important elements.**
- **Standardize elements** to match appearance with content and to minimize variations.

---

des

9b

ments like that on the previous page, flow may be achieved mainly with headings, lists, and illustrations. In other documents, such as the flyer on page 215, flow will come from the arrangement and spacing of information as well as from headings.

Spacing

The white space on a page eases crowding and focuses readers' attention. On an otherwise full page, just the space indicating paragraphs (an indention or a line of extra space) gives readers a break and reassures them that ideas are divided into manageable chunks.

In papers, reports, and other formal documents, spacing appears mainly in paragraph breaks, in margins, and around headings and lists. In publicity documents, such as flyers and brochures, spacing is usually more generous between elements and helps boxes, headings, and the like pop off the page.

Grouping

Grouping information shows relationships visually, reinforcing the sense of the text itself. Here in this discussion, we group the various principles of design under visually identical headings to emphasize them and their similar importance. In the effectively designed document on the previous page, the bulleted list details statistics about students' computer use. The list uses similar wording for each item to reinforce the similarities in the data. Thinking of likely groups as you write can help you organize your material so that it makes sense to you and your readers.

Emphasizing

Part of a critical reader's task is to analyze and interpret the meaning of a document, and design helps the reader by stressing what's important. Type fonts and sizes, headings, indentions, color, boxes, white space—all of these establish hierarchies of information, so that the reader almost instinctively grasps what is crucial, what is less so, and what is merely supplementary. In this book, for example, the importance of headings is clear from their size and color and from the presence or absence of decorative elements, such as the box around 9c below; and boxes like the one opposite clearly mark summaries and other key information. As you design a document, considering where and how to emphasize elements can actually help you determine your document's priorities.

Standardizing

As we read a document, the design of its elements quickly creates expectations in us. We assume, for instance, that headings in the same size and color signal information of the same importance or that a list contains items of parallel content. Just as the design creates expectations, so it should fulfill them, treating similar elements similarly. Anticipating design standards as you write a document can help you develop a consistent approach to its elements.

Standardizing also creates clear, uncluttered documents. Even if they are used consistently, too many variations in type fonts and sizes, colors, indentions, and the like overwhelm readers as they try to determine the significance of the parts. Most formal documents, such as papers and reports, need no more than a single type font for text and headings, with type size and highlighting (such as CAPITAL LETTERS, **boldface,** or *italics*) distinguishing the levels of headings. Publicity documents, such as flyers and brochures, generally employ more variation to arrest readers' attention. (See pp. 215 and 219.)

des
9c

9c   Using the elements of design

Applying the preceding design principles involves seven main elements of document design: print quality, margins, text, lists, headings, illustrations (tables, figures, images), and color. You won't use all these elements for every project, however, and in many writing situations you will be required to follow a prescribed format (see p. 199 on formats in academic writing).

Note Your word processor may provide wizards or templates for many kinds of documents, such as letters, memos, reports, agendas, résumés, and brochures. **Wizards** guide you through setting up and writing complicated documents. **Templates** are preset forms to which you add your own text, headings, and other elements. Wizards and templates can be helpful, but not if they lead you to create cookie-cutter documents no matter what the writing situation. Always keep in mind that a document should be appropriate for your subject, audience, and purpose.

1 ■ Print quality

The cartridge on your printer should be fresh enough to produce a dark impression. A printer that forms characters out of tiny dots may be acceptable for your academic papers, but make sure the tails on letters such as *j, p,* and *y* fall below the line of type, as they do here. For documents that are complex or that will be distributed to the public, use an inkjet or laser printer, which creates characters more like the ones you see here.

2 ■ Margins

Margins at the top, bottom, and sides of a page help to prevent the pages from overwhelming readers with unpleasant crowding. Most academic and business documents use a minimum one-inch margin on all sides. Publicity documents, such as the flyer on page 215, often use narrower margins, compensating with white space between elements.

des
9c

3 ■ Text

A document must be readable. You can make text readable by attending to line spacing, type fonts and sizes, highlighting, word spacing, and line breaks.

Line spacing

Most academic documents are double-spaced, with an initial indention for paragraphs, while most business documents are single-spaced, with an extra line of space between paragraphs. Double or triple spacing sets off headings in both. Publicity documents, such as flyers and brochures, tend to use more line spacing to separate and group distinct parts of the content.

Type fonts and sizes

The readability of text also derives from the type fonts (or faces) and their sizes. For academic and business documents, choose a type size of 10 or 12 points, as in these samples:

```
10-point Courier      10-point Times New Roman
12-point Courier      12-point Times New Roman
```

http://www.ablongman.com/littlebrown
For added information about typography and fonts, click on
➤ **Using computers** ➤ **Web sites** ➤ **Document design**

For text, generally use a font with **serifs**—the small lines finishing the letters in the preceding samples and in the font you're reading now. **Sans serif** fonts (*sans* means "without" in French) include this one found on many word processors:

10-point Arial   **12-point Arial**

Though fine for headings, sans serif type can be more difficult than serif type to read in extended text.

Your word processor probably offers many decorative fonts as well:

10-point Bodega Sans   10-point Tekton
10-POINT STENCIL   10-point Ruzicka Freehand
10-point Lucinda Sans   10-point Park Avenue

Decorative fonts are generally inappropriate in academic and business writing, where letter forms should be conventional and regular. But in publicity documents like the flyer on page 215, decorative fonts can attract attention, create motion, and reinforce a theme. (In publicity documents, too, font sizes are often much larger than 10 or 12 points, even for passages of text.)

Note The point size of a type font is often an unreliable guide to its actual size, as the decorative fonts above illustrate: all the samples are 10 points, but they vary considerably. Before you use a font, print out a sample to be sure it is the size you want.

Highlighting

Within a document's text, underlined, *italic,* **boldface,** or even color type can emphasize key words or sentences. Underlining is rarest these days, having been replaced by italics in all but a few disciplines. (It remains called for in MLA style. See p. 711.) Both academic and business writing sometimes use boldface to give strong emphasis—for instance, to a term being defined—and publicity documents often rely extensively on boldface to draw the reader's eye. Neither academic nor business writing generally uses color within passages of text. In publicity documents, however, color may be effective if the color is dark enough to be readable. (See pp. 211–12 for more on color in document design.)

No matter what your writing situation, use highlighting selectively to complement your meaning, not merely to decorate your work. Many readers consider type embellishments to be distracting.

Word spacing

In most writing situations, follow these guidelines for spacing within and between words:

■ Leave one space between words.

des
9c

- Leave one space after all punctuation, with these exceptions:

Dash (two hyphens or the so-called em dash on a computer)	book--its	book—its
Hyphen	one-half	
Apostrophe within a word	book's	
Two or more adjacent marks	book.")	
Opening quotation mark, parenthesis, or bracket	("book	[book

- Leave one space before and after an ellipsis mark. In the examples below, ellipsis marks indicate omissions within a sentence and at the end of a sentence. See pages 511–13 for additional examples.

book . . . in
book. . . . The

Line breaks

Your word processor will generally insert appropriate breaks between lines of continuous text: it will not, for instance, automatically begin a line with a comma or period, and it will not end a line with an opening parenthesis or bracket. However, you will have to prevent it from breaking a two-hyphen dash or a three-dot ellipsis mark by spacing to push the beginning of each mark to the next line.

When you instruct it to do so (usually under the Tools menu), your word processor will also automatically hyphenate words to prevent very short lines. If you must decide yourself where to break words, follow the guidelines in Chapter 37.

4 ■ Lists

Lists give visual reinforcement to the relations between like items—for example, the steps in a process or the elements of a proposal. A list is easier to read than a paragraph and adds white space to the page.

When wording a list, work for parallelism among items—for instance, all complete sentences or all phrases (see also p. 431). Set the list with space above and below. Number the items, or mark them with bullets: centered dots or other devices, such as the squares used in the list opposite about headings. On most word processors you can format a numbered or bulleted list automatically using the Format menu.

5 ■ Headings

Headings are signposts: they direct the reader's attention by focusing the eye on a document's most significant content.

Academic and business documents

You won't always need headings in academic and business writing: a three-page paper or a one-page letter, for instance, probably will not require signposts. But in many longer documents, headings are useful to break the text into discrete parts, create emphasis, and orient the reader. See the example on page 213.

When you use headings in academic and business writing, follow these guidelines:

- *Use one, two, or three levels of headings* depending on the needs of your material and the length of your document. Some level of heading every two or so pages will help keep readers on track.
- *Create an outline of your document to plan where headings should go.* Reserve the first level of heading for the main points (and sections). Use a second and perhaps a third level of heading to mark subsections of supporting information.

des
9c

- *Keep headings as short as possible* while making them specific about the material that follows.
- *Word headings consistently*—for instance, all questions (*What Is the Scientific Method?*), all phrases with *-ing* words (*Understanding the Scientific Method*), or all phrases with nouns (*The Scientific Method*).
- *Indicate the relative importance of headings* with type size, positioning, and highlighting, such as capital letters or boldface.

FIRST-LEVEL HEADING

Second-Level Heading

Third-Level Heading

Generally, you can use the same type font and size for headings as for the text. Avoid very decorative fonts like those shown on page 205.

- *Don't break a page immediately after a heading.* Push the heading to the next page.

Note Document format in psychology and some other social sciences requires a particular treatment of headings. See page 858.

Publicity documents

In publicity documents, headings not only direct but capture the reader's attention, and they work with white space and other elements to organize the flow of information. Some of the preceding guidelines for academic and business writing apply to publicity documents, too: headings should be as short as possible, and their relative importance should be clear. But publicity headings are usually in a font different from and considerably larger than the document's text, they may use decorative fonts that reinforce the document's message, and they often use color. See pages 215–19 for examples.

6 ■ Tables, figures, and images

Tables, figures, and images can often make a point for you more efficiently than words can. Tables present data. Figures (such as graphs and charts) usually recast data in visual form. Images (such as diagrams, drawings, photographs, and clip art) can explain processes, represent what something looks like, add emphasis, or convey a theme.

Note Many computer programs can help you create tables, graphs, charts, and other illustrations. Your word processor may include such a program. However, if you use many illustrations in your writing, you may want to learn a spreadsheet program such as *Excel* or *Quattro* (for graphs and charts) or a graphics program such as *Photoshop, CorelDraw, FreeHand,* or *Canvas* (for images). Your word processor may also include files of clip art, and the Web can be an excellent resource for photographs and other images. (See also pp. 229–30.)

Illustrations and the writing situation

Academic and many business documents tend to use tables, figures, and images differently from publicity documents. In the latter, illustrations are generally intended to attract readers' attention, enliven the piece, or emphasize a point, and they may not be linked directly to the document's text. In academic and business writing, however, illustrations directly reinforce and amplify the text. Follow these guidelines when using tables, figures, or images in academic and most business writing:

- *Focus on a purpose for your illustration*—a reason for including it and a point you want it to make. Otherwise, readers may find it irrelevant or confusing.
- *Provide a source note* whenever the data or the entire illustration is someone else's independent material (see p. 683). Each

des
9c

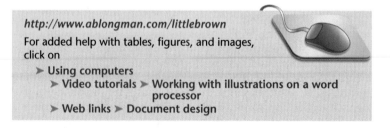

http://www.ablongman.com/littlebrown
For added help with tables, figures, and images,
click on
➤ Using computers
➤ Video tutorials ➤ Working with illustrations on a word
processor
➤ Web links ➤ Document design

discipline has a slightly different style for such source notes: those in the table below and the figures on the next two pages reflect the style of the social sciences. See also Chapters 49 and 53–55.

- *Number figures and images together*, and label them as figures: Figure 1, Figure 2, and so on.
- *Number and label tables separately from figures:* Table 1, Table 2, and so on.
- *Refer to each illustration* (for instance, "See Figure 2") at the point(s) in the text where readers will benefit by consulting it.
- *Place each illustration on a page by itself* immediately after the page that refers to it.

Note Many businesses and academic disciplines have preferred styles for illustrations that differ from those given here. When in doubt about how to prepare and place tables and figures, ask your instructor or supervisor.

des
9c

Tables

Tables usually summarize raw data, displaying the data concisely and clearly:

- *Provide a self-explanatory title above the table.* Readers should see what the table shows without having to refer to the body of your document.
- *Provide self-explanatory headings for horizontal rows and vertical columns.* Use abbreviations only if you are certain readers will understand them.
- *Lay out rows and columns for maximum clarity.* In the sample below, lines divide the table into parts, headings align with their data, and numbers align vertically down columns.

Table 1

Percentage of Young Adults Living at Home, 1960–2000

	1960	1970	1980	1990	2000
Males					
Age 18–24	52	54	54	58	57
Age 25–34	9	9	10	15	13
Females					
Age 18–24	35	41	43	48	47
Age 25–34	7	7	7	8	8

Note: Data from U.S. Bureau of Census, *Census 2000 Summary Tables,* retrieved July 1, 2002, from http://www.census.gov/servlet/QTTTable?_ts=30543101060

Figures

Figures represent data graphically. They include the three kinds presented below and on the facing page: pie charts (showing percentages making up a whole), bar graphs (showing comparative data), and line graphs (showing change).

- *Provide a self-explanatory caption or legend below the figure.* Readers should see what the figure shows without having to refer to the body of your document.
- *Provide self-explanatory labels for all parts of the figure.*
- *Draw the figure to reflect its purpose and the visual effect you want it to have.* For instance, shortening the horizontal date axis in Figure 3 opposite emphasizes the dramatic movement of the line over time.
- *Take special care with graphs.* Generally make the width greater than the height, and always show a zero point so that the values are clear.

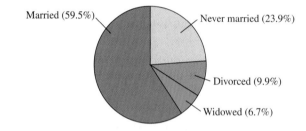

Figure 1. Marital status in 2000 of US adults aged eighteen and over. Data from *Statistical Abstract of the United States, 2001.*

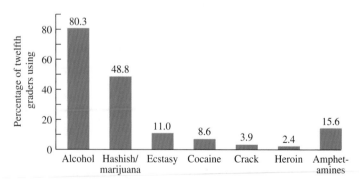

Figure 2. Lifetime prevalence of use of alcohol, compared with other drugs, among twelfth graders in 2000. Data from Monitoring the Future, Institute for Social Research, University of Michigan, published in Lloyd D. Johnston et al., *Monitoring the Future: National Survey Results on Drug Use, 1975–2000. Vol. 1: Secondary School Students.* Bethesda, MD: National Institute on Drug Abuse, 2001.

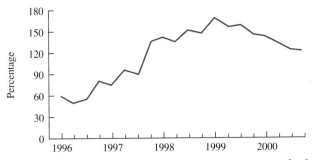

Figure 3. Five-year cumulative return for equities in Standard & Poor's 500 Index, 1996–2000.

Photographs, clip art, and other images

Images can either add substance to a document or simply enliven it. In a psychology paper, for instance, a photograph may illustrate a key experiment, while in a brochure a photograph may add the visual interest of, say, people working together or a cityscape. In academic and most business documents, images may include not only photographs but also diagrams and drawings. They are not sufficient by themselves to represent your ideas: you need to consider carefully how they relate and add to your text, you need to explain their significance, and you need to label, number, and caption them (see opposite).

One kind of image rarely appears in academic and business writing: **clip art,** icons and drawings such as the writing hand used in the flyer on page 215. Many word processors provide files of clip art, and they are also available from CD-ROMs and Web sites (links appear on this book's Web site: see the box on p. 208). Be selective in using these resources: clip art is mostly decorative (which is why it seldom appears in academic and business documents), and an overdecorated document is not only cluttered but unemphatic. In a publicity document, use only clip art that is relevant to your theme and content, directing readers' attention to elements you want to stress.

Note When using an image prepared by someone else—for instance, a photograph downloaded from the Web or an item of clip art from a CD-ROM—you must verify that the source permits reproduction of the image before you use it. In most documents but especially academic papers, you must also cite the source of any borrowed image. See pages 687–88 on copyright issues with Internet sources.

7 ▪ Color

With a color printer, many word processors and most desktop publishers can produce documents that use color for bullets, headings, borders, boxes, illustrations, and other elements. Publicity documents generally use color, whereas academic and business documents consisting only of text and headings may not need color. (Ask your instructor or supervisor for his or her preferences.) If you do use color, follow these guidelines:

- *Employ color to clarify and highlight your content.* Too much color or too many colors on a page will distract rather than focus readers' attention.
- *Make sure that color type is readable.* For text, where type is likely to be relatively small, use only dark colors. For headings, lighter colors may be readable if the type is large and bold-faced.
- *Stick to the same color for all headings at the same level*—for instance, red for primary headings, black for secondary headings.
- *Use color for bullets, lines, and other nontext elements.* But use no more than a few colors to keep pages clean.
- *Use color to distinguish the parts of illustrations*—the segments of charts, the lines of graphs, and the parts of diagrams. Use only as many colors as you need to make your illustration clear.

EXERCISE
Redesigning a paper
Save a duplicate copy of a recent paper or one you are currently working on. Then format the duplicate using appropriate elements of design, such as type fonts, lists, and headings. (For a new paper, be sure your instructor will accept your new design.) When you have finished the redesign, share the work with your instructor.

9d Designing reports, flyers, newsletters, and brochures

You can use the design principles and elements discussed on the preceding pages to good effect in long and complex reports and in documents such as flyers, newsletters, and brochures. Here we illustrate each kind of document, with comments on the facing pages that highlight some of their most important design features.

A report

Reports are text-heavy documents, sometimes lengthy, that convey information such as the results of research. They usually contain tables or figures and may contain images as well. They may employ color. Other key design elements include headings (often in varied fonts) and lists.

The page shown opposite opens a business report intended to outline a problem and propose a solution. In keeping with a formal business-writing situation, the document is single-spaced (with

Canada Geese at ABC Institute: An Environmental Problem

Summary

The flock of Canada geese on and around ABC Institute's grounds has grown dramatically in recent years. What was once a source of pleasure for institute employees and others using the grounds has become a nuisance and an environmental problem. This report reviews the problem, considers the options for reducing the flock, and proposes as a solution the cooperation of ABC Institute, the municipalities around Taylor Lake, and the US Fish and Wildlife Service to reduce the flock by humane means.

The Problem

Canada geese began living at Taylor Lake, adjacent to ABC Institute, when they were relocated there in 1985 by the state game department. As a nonmigratory flock, the geese are present year-round, with the highest population each year occurring in fall, winter, and early spring, after the young have fledged.

In recent years the flock of geese at Taylor Lake has grown dramatically. The Audubon Society's annual Christmas bird census shows a thirty-fold increase from the 37 geese counted in 1986 to the 1125 counted in 2002 (see Figure 1).

Figure 1. Goose population of Taylor Lake, 1991–2002.

The principal environmental problem caused by the geese is pollution of grass and water by defecation. During high-population months, geese droppings cover the ABC Institute's grounds as well as the park's athletic fields and picnicking areas. The runoff from these droppings into Taylor Lake has substantially affected the quality of the lake's water, so that local authorities have twice (2001 and 2002) issued warnings against swimming.

The Solution

Several possible solutions to the goose overpopulation and resulting environmental problems are *not viable alternatives*:

- Harass the geese with dogs and audiovisual effects (light and noise) so that the geese choose to leave. This solution is inhumane to the geese and unpleasant for human neighbors.
- Feed the geese a chemical that will weaken the shells of their eggs and thus reduce growth of the flock. This solution is inhumane to the geese and also impractical, because geese are long-lived.
- Kill adult geese. This solution is, obviously, inhumane to the geese.

The most appropriate and humane solution is to thin the goose population by trapping and removing many geese (perhaps 600) to areas less populated by humans, such as wildlife preserves and wilderness areas. Though costly (see figures below), this solution would be efficient and harmless to the geese, provided that sizable netted enclosures are used for traps. [Discussion of solution continues, followed by "Recommendations."]

des

9d

double spacing between paragraphs and around the list), and the overall appearance is restrained. Color appears only in headings and in the figure. The document uses two type fonts, one for the text and headings and one for the figure. Headings clearly delineate the structure of the page: first a summary, then an outline of the problem, and then a discussion of the solution. The figure is visually pleasing and clear, with a caption and labels that explain its content. A bulleted list emphasizes the group of alternative solutions.

Note In many academic disciplines and business organizations, reports have specific formatting requirements: in psychology, for instance, a report should include an abstract (see p. 856). If you are unsure about the formatting requirements for your reports, ask your instructor or supervisor.

des
9d

A flyer

Flyers advertise meetings, events, election candidates, items for sale. They are usually designed to be seen at some distance and to convey simple messages.

Flyers usually make generous use of space to focus viewers' eyes on the main message in large type. Space also promotes flow, directing readers' eyes over the document's supporting information.

The flyer here announces an event sponsored by a volunteer organization. The event title is large to attract attention. The white space and arrangement of elements create a familiar zigzag movement: information flows down and across from left to right. Color and a box emphasize crucial information about the event. The flyer looks simple, but it achieves its purpose through flow and emphasis.

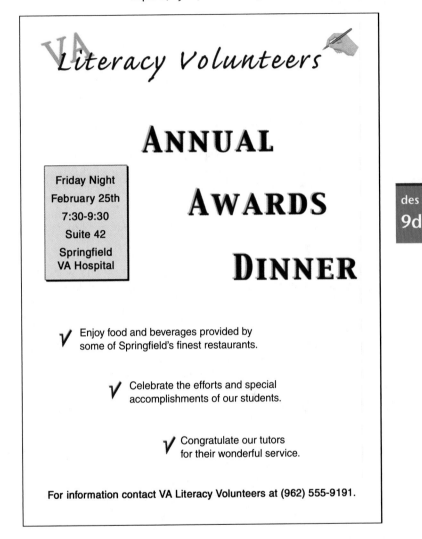

Literacy Volunteers

ANNUAL

**Friday Night
February 25th
7:30-9:30
Suite 42
Springfield
VA Hospital**

AWARDS

DINNER

✓ Enjoy food and beverages provided by
   some of Springfield's finest restaurants.

   ✓ Celebrate the efforts and special
      accomplishments of our students.

      ✓ Congratulate our tutors
         for their wonderful service.

For information contact VA Literacy Volunteers at (962) 555-9191.

des
9d

A newsletter

Newsletters provide channels of communication for the members of organizations such as corporations, special-interest or professional groups, or charitable foundations.

Newsletters generally rely on columns, which create more room for text and headings and allow variations in the length and emphasis of sections. (See p. 203 on using templates and wizards, which can be very helpful for newsletters.) Within the columnar format, careful spacing and varied type fonts and sizes help readers skim for highlights and also read whole articles. In addition, boxes and lists often group and emphasize information; color often highlights headings, lines, and other features; and images often emphasize or decorate. With all these elements in play, standardizing can be difficult: similar elements should be treated similarly, and the overall appearance should be eye-catching but not so cluttered that it confuses the reader.

The page shown here comes from a newsletter that is designed to engage, motivate, and inform volunteer tutors who work with military veterans. To suit its purpose, the newsletter is lively in appearance, using extra-large type for title and headings, devices such as lines and borders to separate sections, and color to catch readers' eyes and focus their attention. The most important article on the page, the report on the awards dinner, spreads across two columns. A colored box in the first column provides information readers can use to work through the rest of the document. And a bulleted list (with decorative bullets) highlights and groups related items.

des

9d

Literacy Volunteers

Springfield Veterans Administration Hospital   **SPRING 2003**

From the director

Can you help us? With more and more learners in the VA's literacy program, we need more and more tutors. You may know people who would be interested in participating in the program, if only they knew about it.

Those of you who have been tutoring VA patients in reading and writing know both the great need you fulfill and the great benefits you bring to your students. New tutors need no special skills (we'll provide the training), only patience and an interest in helping others.

We've scheduled an orientation meeting for Friday, June 6, at 6:30 PM. Please come and bring a friend who is willing to contribute a couple of hours a week to our work.

Thanks,
Nancy Thomas

IN THIS ISSUE

AWARDS FOR STUDENTS AND TUTORS AT ANNUAL DINNER

The annual SVAH literacy awards dinner on February 25 was a great success. George Bello obtained food and beverage contributions from area restaurants and suppliers, and the students decorated the dining room on the theme of books and reading. In all, eighty-six people attended.

The highlight of the night was the awards ceremony. Ten students, recommended by their tutors, received certificates recognizing their efforts and special accomplishments in learning to read and write:

Ramon Berva
Edward Byar
David Dunbar
Tony Garnier
Chris Giugni
Akili Haynes
Pat Laird
Jim Livingston
Paul Obeid
B.J. Resnansky

In addition, nine tutors received certificates commemorating five years of service at SVAH:

Anita Crumpton
Felix Cruz-Rivera
Bette Eigen
Kelly Bortoluzzi
Harriotte Henderson
Andy Obiso
Carla Puente
Robert Smith
Sara Villante

Congratulations to all!

New Guidelines on PTSD

Most of us are working with veterans who have been diagnosed with post-traumatic stress disorder. Because this disorder is often complicated by alcoholism, depression, anxiety, and other problems, the National Center for PTSD has issued some guidelines for helping PTSD patients in a way that reduces their stress.

- The hospital must know your tutoring schedule, and you need to sign in and out before and after each tutoring session.

- Cancellations are stressful for patients. Stick to your schedule.

- To protect patients' privacy, meet them only in designated visiting and tutoring areas, never in their rooms.

- Treat patients with dignity and respect, even when (as sometimes happens) they grow frustrated and angry. Seek help from a nurse or orderly if you need it.

des
9d

A brochure

Brochures advertise and inform: they are usually targeted to a specific audience, such as visitors to a historic site or potential clients for a business, and their designs convey both an attractive and a readable message. Brochures almost always use color and varied type fonts, and they often contain images and lists. They are often printed in three columns on both sides of a single sheet of paper, which is then folded in thirds. The result is three panels, each with an inner and an outer face, for six pages total.

Perhaps the most difficult challenge in brochure design is formatting the panels. Do some initial planning by folding a sheet of paper in thirds from top to bottom, turning the folded paper sideways, and sketching ideas and copy on each panel. When you have a plan, you can implement it on your computer by orienting a document horizontally on the screen and dividing the page into a column for each panel. Your word processor may include a brochure template (see p. 203), or you may have access to a desktop publishing program that provides several templates and makes it easy to arrange elements on a page.

As you format the panels, imagine readers looking at the final product. With a three-panel, two-sided brochure, readers see the cover first, then lift it to reveal two inside panels. Most readers will look first to the right, so your most immediate message should go there. The inside left then reinforces and elaborates on that message. The reinforcement is important because the inside left panel remains visible as readers continue to examine the brochure. On the innermost two panels you can put the details—information on your organization's accomplishments, the people involved, how readers can reach you, and so on. The outside middle panel (the back cover when the brochure is folded) usually resembles an envelope, with a return address in the upper left and the rest blank for a recipient's address and postage.

The sample here shows the cover and inside left panel of a brochure for the literacy group whose newsletter appears on the previous page. The cover's very simple layout and extensive white space draw readers to the group's name. Spaced out below, in smaller type, is a brief description of the group; and at the bottom, in still smaller type, is its affiliation. In contrast to the cover, the inside left panel contains more type, using headings to highlight its two parts and a list to outline and emphasize the group's activities. (The right panel facing this one included less text, briefly defining the problem of illiteracy among veterans and summarizing the group's approach to solving the problem.)

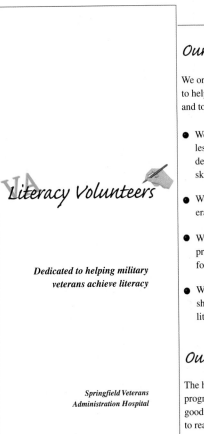

Our Mission

We organize and empower volunteers to help military veterans achieve literacy and to prepare them for lifelong learning.

- We provide workshops and formal lessons for veterans wishing to develop their reading and writing skills.

- We train volunteers to tutor veterans one on one.

- We maintain outreach programs to provide access to literacy training for all veterans.

- We create literacy resources and share them with others who promote literacy for veterans.

Our Volunteers

The heart of the VA Literacy program is our volunteers. Their goodwill and generosity allow us to reach out to those who have served our country.

Literacy Volunteers

Dedicated to helping military veterans achieve literacy

Springfield Veterans Administration Hospital

des
9d

CHAPTER 10

Composing
for the Web

Increasingly, students are using the World Wide Web for their own writing, from personal sites to projects for courses. This chapter provides advice for composing Web pages. It notes some key differences between Web compositions and printed documents (below); describes HTML editors, the software used to create Web compositions (p. 222); and discusses the content and design of papers posted as Web documents (p. 223) and of original sites (p. 224).

10a Distinguishing Web compositions from printed documents

A Web site is often called a **hypertext** because it provides more options for navigation than a traditional printed document does. We generally read printed documents **linearly**—that is, straight through from first page to last. Reference aids such as tables of contents, indexes, and cross-references can help us find material out

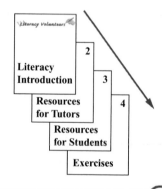

http://www.ablongman.com/littlebrown
For added help with Web composition, click on
➤ Using computers
  ➤ Video tutorials ➤ Balancing Web design and content
  ➤ Web links ➤ Web composition

of the linear order, but the text and any illustrations are usually intended to be read in sequence.

In contrast, a hypertext such as a Web site is intended to be examined in the order readers choose as they follow electronic links among the pages of the site and often to related sites.

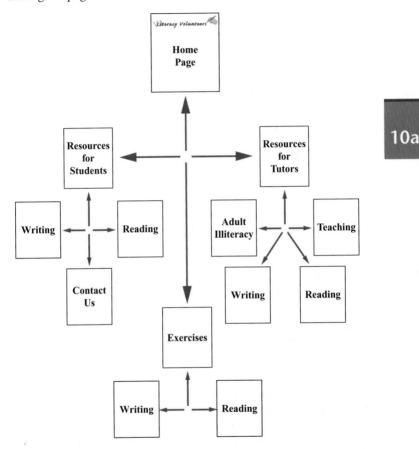

This illustration shows the structure of a fairly simple Web site: readers can move in any direction signaled by arrows or back to the home page with a single click of the mouse.

Creating a Web hypertext requires several considerations:

- *Plan the site carefully.* A hypertext can disorient readers as they scroll up and down and pursue various links. Page length, links, menus, and other cues should work to keep readers oriented.
- *Anticipate what readers may see on their screens.* Each reader's screen frames and organizes the experience of a Web composition. Screen space is limited and varies from one computer to

another. Text and visual elements should be managed for maximum clarity and effectiveness on a variety of screens.

■ *Integrate visual and sound elements into the text.* Web compositions can include not only tables, figures, and images (which printed documents may also have) but also video (such as animation or film clips) and audio (such as music or excerpts from speeches). However, graphics, photographs, sound, and other multimedia elements should not merely embellish the text but contribute to it. See pages 228–30 for more on multimedia.

■ *Acknowledge your sources.* It's easy to incorporate material from other sources into a Web site, but you have the same obligation to cite your sources as you do in a printed document (see pp. 680–85). Further, your Web site is a form of publication, like a magazine or a book. Unless the material you are using explicitly allows copying without permission, you may need to seek the copyright holder's permission, just as print publishers do. (See pp. 687–88 for more on copyright.)

10b

EXERCISE 1
Comparing printed documents and Web compositions
Either online or face to face, work with a partner or a small group of classmates to compare the strengths and weaknesses of printed documents and Web compositions. Consider ease of access, readability, flexibility, stability, visual appeal, organization, and other features. When your team has compiled a list of differences and similarities, discuss your findings with the rest of the class.

10b   Using HTML

Most Web pages are created using hypertext markup language, or HTML, and an HTML editor. The HTML editing program inserts command codes into your document that achieve the effects you want when the material appears on the Web.

From the user's point of view, most HTML editors work much as word processors do, with similar options for sizing, formatting, and highlighting copy and with a display that shows what you will see in the final version. Indeed, you can compose a Web page without bothering at all about the behind-the-scenes HTML coding. As you gain experience with Web building, however, you may want to create more sophisticated pages by editing the codes themselves.

http://www.ablongman.com/littlebrown
For access to HTML editors and help with using HTML, click on
➤ **Using computers** ➤ **Web links** ➤ **HTML editors**

There are many HTML editors on the market. *FrontPage, Go-Live,* and *Dreamweaver* are three of the most popular. The *Netscape* Web browser includes *Composer,* which you can also download for free from *http://channels.netscape.com/ns/browsers.* In addition, the Web site for this book (see the facing page) provides links to free or low-cost HTML editors.

10c Creating online papers

When you create a composition for the Web, it will likely fall into one of two categories: pages such as class papers that resemble printed documents in being linear and text-heavy and that call for familiar ways of writing and reading (discussed below); or "native" hypertext documents that you build from scratch, which call for screen-oriented writing and reading (pp. 224–26).

10c

If an instructor asks you to post a paper to a Web site, you can compose it on your word processor and then use the Save As HTML function available on most word processors to translate it into a Web page. After translating the paper, your word processor should allow you to modify some of the elements on the page, or you can open the translated document in an HTML editor.

The illustration below shows the opening screen of a student's project for a composition course. The project incorporates many of

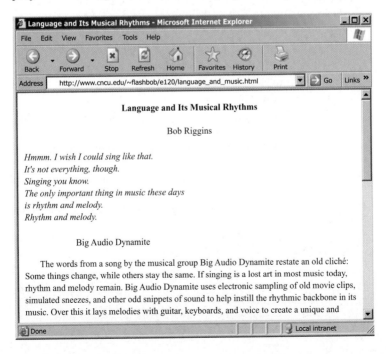

the design features that make any text-heavy document more accessible to Web readers:

- *Use a white- or cream-colored background for pages.* It is more difficult to read text on a computer screen than on paper, and bright or dark background colors compound the problem.
- *Use a standard type font and size for text.* (See pp. 204–05 on fonts.) With standard fonts, a size of at least 12 points should ensure that pages are readable on most systems.
- *Use a maximum line length of seventy or eighty characters.* Longer lines are hard to read. You may have to increase the margins for shorter lines.
- *Use headings as signposts* in documents that require scrolling through several screens. Otherwise, readers may lose track of the document's overall organization.

10d Creating original sites

When you create an original Web site, you need to be aware that Web readers generally alternate between skimming pages for highlights and focusing intently on sections of text. To facilitate this kind of reading, you'll want to consider the guidelines above for handling text and also your site's structure and content, flow, ease of navigation, and use of images, video, and sound. You'll manipulate these elements to suit your audience and purpose, as the two samples in this section illustrate.

1 ■ Developing structure and content

Organize your site so that it efficiently arranges your content and also orients readers:

- *Sketch possible site plans before getting started.* (See p. 221 for an example.) Your aim is to develop a sense of the major components of your project and to create a logical space for each component.
- *As you conceive the organization of your site, consider how menus on the site's pages can provide overviews of the organization as well as direct access to the pages* (see also pp. 226–27). The screen

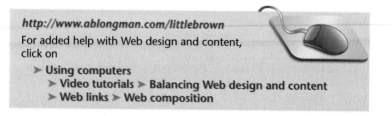

http://www.ablongman.com/littlebrown

For added help with Web design and content, click on
- ➤ **Using computers**
  - ➤ **Video tutorials** ➤ **Balancing Web design and content**
  - ➤ **Web links** ➤ **Web composition**

shots below, from the site of a volunteer organization, include two menus: a box near the top provides an overview of the site, and a set of icons at the bottom of each page directs readers home or elsewhere.

- *Treat the first few sentences of any page as a get-acquainted space for you and your readers.* On the page below, the text hooks readers with an interesting situation and then orients them with general information.
- *Compose descriptive links.* As you create links within your own site or to other sites on the Web, indicate what's at the other locations. Instead of just *Click here,* for instance, say *Click here for writing exercises* or *Further information about snowboarding.* When you provide a list of links to related sites, annotate each one with information about its contents.
- *Distill your text so that it includes only essential information.* Concise prose is essential in any writing situation, of course. But Web readers expect to scan text quickly and, in any event, have difficulty following long text passages on a computer screen. (See Chapter 40 for advice on writing concisely.)

10d

2 ■ Achieving flow

Beginning Web authors sometimes start at the top of the page and then add element upon element until information proceeds down the screen much as it would in a printed document. However, by thinking about how information will flow on a page, you can take better advantage of the Web's visual nature.

The screen shot below shows the opening page of a personal Web site. Though simple in content and design, the page illustrates how the arrangement of elements can invite readers in and direct their attention.

To achieve flow on your Web pages, follow these guidelines:

- *Standardize elements of your design to create expectations in readers and to fulfill those expectations.* For instance, develop a uniform style for the main headings of pages, for headings within pages, and for menus. The personal page below reflects the theme of the title in purple type and berry images. (For more on standardizing, see p. 203.)
- *Make scanning easy for readers.* Focus them on crucial text by adding space around it. Use icons and other images to empha-

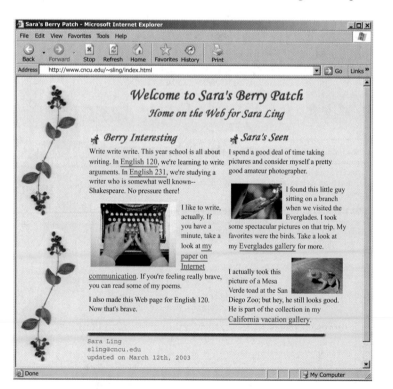

size text. Add headings to break up text and to highlight content. Use lists to reinforce the parallel importance of items. (See pp. 203–12 for more on all these design elements.)

- *Position boxes, illustrations, and other elements to help conduct readers through a page.* The personal page opposite presents information in columns, each with a different focus, and arranges images for variety and interest.

3 ■ Ensuring easy navigation

A Web site of more than a few pages requires a menu on every page so that readers can navigate the site. Like the table of contents in a book, a menu lists the features of the site, giving its plan at a glance. By clicking on any item in the list, readers can go directly to a page that interests them. The screen shots on page 225 show a text menu in the tinted box on the top right and an icon menu along the bottom. As in the illustration, always supplement icons with verbal descriptions of the links to be sure readers understand where each link leads.

You can embed a menu at the top, side, or bottom of a page. Menus at the top or side are best on short pages because they will not scroll off the screen as readers move down the page. On longer pages, menus at the bottom prevent readers from dead-ending— that is, reaching a point where they can't easily move forward or backward. You can also use a combination of menus, as in the illustration on page 225.

A more complicated approach is to divide a page into separate **frames,** or windows, and to place a menu within one frame. Menus within frames add stability to complex sites because they remain at the same spot on the screen no matter where readers go in the site. Frames can cause problems, though—for instance, they sometimes prevent readers from printing or saving pages from a Web site.

In designing a menu, keep it simple: many different type fonts and colors will overwhelm readers instead of orienting them. And make the menus look the same from one page to the next so that readers recognize them easily.

10d

> **EXERCISE 2**
> **Mapping a Web site**
> As the first step in creating a Web site, use paper and a pencil to sketch possible Web structures for a project you have recently completed or one you are currently working on. (You can use boxes to represent pages, as in the illustration on p. 221.) Consider what the site's home page should cover, how many pages you'll need and what they should cover, and how you will link the pages. Use the plan you like best as the basis for creating the site in Exercise 3, next page, and Exercise 4, page 230.

EXERCISE 3
Examining and creating menus

Explore various Web sites for examples of navigation menus at the tops, bottoms, and sides of pages and in frames. Compare the examples you find, considering how clear the menus are and how their placement influences your movement through the site. Sketch possible menu designs for the Web project you began in the previous exercise. Where will you place your menu, and why? What will it contain?

4 ▪ Using images

10d

The Web makes it easy to incorporate visual elements such as lines, circles, icons, graphs, drawings, photographs, and artwork. Exploring the Web, you'll see that site designers have taken advantage of these capabilities—so much so that Web readers often expect at least some visual enhancement of text.

Several guidelines can help you use images effectively in your Web compositions:

- *Use visual elements for a purpose.* They should supplement or replace text, highlight important features, and direct the flow of information. Don't use them for their own sake, as mere decoration.
- *Make the size of your files a central concern* so that readers don't have to wait forever for your site to download. If you are using lines or other icons, choose a limited number. If you are using photographs or other images, try to keep the file size below thirty kilobytes (30k). Consider reducing large files to thumbnail size on a single page and linking the thumbnails to larger reproductions on other pages or sites. Readers can then decide which images they wish to see larger.
- *Compose descriptions of images that relate them to your text.* Don't ask the elements to convey your meaning by themselves.
- *Provide alternative descriptions of images* to give a sense of them to readers with disabilities or readers whose Web browsers can't display them.
- *Observe any copyright restrictions on the use of images* (see pp. 687–88).

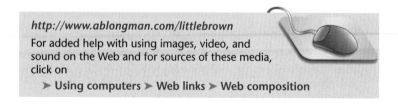

http://www.ablongman.com/littlebrown

For added help with using images, video, and sound on the Web and for sources of these media, click on

➤ **Using computers** ➤ **Web links** ➤ **Web composition**

5 ■ Using video and sound

Video and sound files can provide information that is simply unavailable in printed documents. For instance, as part of a film review you might place a short clip from the film on your Web page and then provide a close reading of the clip. Or as part of a project on a controversial issue you might provide links to sound files containing political speeches. You may be able to link directly to a video or sound file with your HTML editor, or you can learn about embedding these elements into your pages through one of the links at this book's Web site: see the box on the facing page.

The advantages of video and sound in Web compositions are offset by their many complications:

- ■ You and your readers need the right computer equipment. Readers' systems must have programs that can read video and sound files.
- ■ The files are generally so large that readers using modems may not bother to wait for them to download. A so-called streaming program reduces the download time substantially, but preparing files for the program requires considerable experience.
- ■ Most video and sound files on the Web are copyrighted, so you'll probably need to seek the permission of the copyright holder before using multimedia that you have downloaded from another site. (See also pp. 687–88.)

Before you incorporate multimedia elements into your Web compositions, make certain that they have a legitimate purpose. They should add essential information that can't be provided in any other medium, and they should be well integrated with the rest of your composition.

10d

6 ■ Finding sources for images, video, and sound

To use multimedia elements in a Web composition, you can create your own or obtain them from other sources. Most advanced word processors include graphics programs with which you can draw charts, graphs, diagrams, and logos; and many computers come with a simple painting or drawing program. More sophisticated graphics programs are available, too, such as *Photoshop, Corel-Draw, FreeHand,* or *Canvas*. Any graphics program requires learning and practice to be used efficiently, but the investment pays off in professional-looking illustrations.

You can also incorporate your own artwork, photographs, video clips, and sound recordings into Web compositions. You'll need additional equipment: a scanner for art and photographs, and multimedia capture equipment for video and sound. You'll also need some specialized software. You may be able to find the right machines and get advice at your campus computer lab, or consult the Web links at this book's Web site (see the box on p. 228).

CD-ROMs and especially the Web itself provide vast collections of icons, drawings, photographs, video, and sound. Sometimes these resources are not restricted by copyright. When they are restricted, you will have to obtain the copyright holders' permission (see pp. 687–88), but this obligation should not deter you from taking advantage of the offerings. In addition to the links at this book's Web site, you can find images through most search engines. Try the Images search option at *Google* (*http://www.google.com*).

10d

EXERCISE 4
Creating a Web site
Building on the site map and navigation menu that you created in Exercises 2 and 3 (pp. 227–28), create the Web site for your project. Make links between pages, and incorporate the navigation menu into each page. Add appropriate images and other design elements as you refine each page of the site. When you're finished, ask classmates, your instructor, or your school's technology advisers for revision suggestions. Then post the revised site on the Web.

EXERCISE 5
Creating a personal Web page
Design a personal Web page—perhaps a site for family and friends that demonstrates your interests and activities or a site for potential employers that includes your résumé. (See pp. 899–902 on creating a résumé.) Compose the page with your purpose and audience in mind, using text, links, design elements, images, video, or sound as appropriate for your writing situation. Seek the advice of classmates, your instructor, or your school's technology advisers if you need help along the way or to test the final version. Then post the revised site on the Web.

CHAPTER 11

Collaborating Online

Writing often involves collaborating with others as much as it does working in solitude. Indeed, many businesses and teachers expect writers to collaborate on generating ideas and producing and revising drafts. (See also pp. 65–68.) Computers have vastly expanded the options for collaboration, ranging from simple e-mail exchanges to videoconferencing and virtual environments.

In this chapter we look at strategies for online collaboration in your courses, whether you use e-mail, real-time conversation, or courseware such as *WebCT* or *Blackboard*. Your instructors or your school's technology advisers will introduce you to the system and help set you up. Here we focus on nontechnical matters: working well in a group (below), participating in discussions (p. 232), and working on drafts (p. 234).

11a Working well in a group

To collaborate effectively, a group needs to work productively and efficiently. The members form bonds with one another, develop procedures for their work, and continually assess how the work is proceeding.

1 ■ Forming bonds

As the members of your group get to know one another, they'll be forming ties that will help the group cohere. To facilitate this bonding, the group may want to encourage some purely social interactions—comments on weekend plans, movies, and the like. Exchanges that do not contribute information or ideas to the group's project may still be worthwhile if they help create a social foundation and don't overwhelm or undermine the project.

---

http://www.ablongman.com/littlebrown
For added help with online collaboration, click on
➤ **Using computers** ➤ **Web links** ➤ **Online collaboration**

Ideally, the group members will grow to like and respect one another. But a certain friction between members should be tolerable and undamaging if the group has agreed on a common purpose and shared goals. Defining these aims early on, as part of getting acquainted, will facilitate the group's work.

2 ▪ Developing procedures

As the group works, it will need procedures for *how* to work. The procedures may be logistical and technical—for instance, requiring responses to e-mail messages within twelve hours and using a particular format for exchanging drafts. The procedures may also relate to the group's project—for instance, assigning specific tasks to members or establishing guidelines for review of drafts.

The group should also develop conventions for members' behavior so that work remains agreeable—for instance, requiring that messages be sent privately when they don't address the project or banning offensive language and personal attacks. These precautions may seem unnecessary at first, but they can prevent distractions and injured feelings.

3 ▪ Assessing group dynamics

At agreed-upon intervals, the group should reflect on how well it's working: Have goals been met as planned? Are members satisfied with their responsibilities? Is miscommunication causing problems? Are procedures breaking down or getting in the way? With periodic self-assessment, the group can deal with obstacles before they become insurmountable.

After the project is finished, a final self-assessment can help members as they participate in other collaborations. One technique is to imagine that a hidden observer has been watching the group throughout its work. What would the observer say about the group's interactions and output? How well did the group start up? Which stages went most or least smoothly? What roles did the members play? How successful was the result?

11b Participating in discussions

Many instructors use online conversations for discussing class readings and other topics and to help students generate ideas for writing. There are two basic types of online conversation: real-time **chat** (also called **synchronous communication**), which occurs immediately, like a telephone conversation; and e-mail or discussion forums, in which messages are somewhat delayed.

Note For any discussion method, follow the guidelines in the previous section on forming bonds, developing procedures, and assessing group dynamics.

1 ■ Using online chat

You may be familiar with chat conversations from using instant messaging with friends and family. In academic settings, chat will likely occur with courseware such as *WebCT* or *Blackboard*.

Collaborating via chat discussions will be more productive if you follow these tips:

- *Use the chat space for brainstorming topics and exchanging impressions.* The pace of online chat rarely allows lengthy consideration and articulation of messages.
- *Focus on a thread or common topic.* Online chat can be the electronic equivalent of a busy hallway outside a classroom, with different conversations occurring in the same space. If you have trouble keeping up with all the messages, concentrate on the ones that relate to your interest.
- *Write as quickly and fluidly as possible.* Don't worry about producing perfect prose.
- *Observe the standards of conduct expected in your group.* If someone upsets or irritates you, remember that the person is, like you, an individual deserving of respect.
- *Save transcripts of online chats.* Then you'll be able to refer to them later. (If you are unsure how to save transcripts, ask your instructor.)

11b

2 ■ Using e-mail

Your class may have an e-mail discussion list that you can use to gather information, generate and test ideas for assignments, or respond to readings. Once you subscribe to the class list (your instructor will tell you how), you will receive other list members' messages in your incoming e-mail. Messages addressing the same topic form a thread. Your message may start a new thread, or it may join a thread already in progress, as does the example below.

When participating in an e-mail discussion list, observe the net-iquette guidelines on pages 195–96. And always double-check the addressees on your messages before sending them. It can be easy (and embarrassing) to send a message intended for only one person to the entire list instead.

3 ■ Using Web forums

Like e-mail lists, **Web forums** allow participants to develop threads of messages on related topics. (Web forums are sometimes called **message forums** or **discussion boards.**) The screen shots opposite show the index of messages for one such thread as well as the messages themselves.

With Web forums, as with e-mail discussions, participants can take the time to digest messages and compose thoughtful responses. In the conversation shown opposite, the second and third writers respond thoughtfully to the first. The third, Potter, actually chal-lenges the assumption in the first message, but he frames the chal-lenge productively in the context of the issue being discussed. Since most online conversations aim to explore and test ideas, there are bound to be disagreements. They need not be unpleasant, however, if everyone adheres to a code of reasonable conduct.

11c   Working on drafts

Computers can both streamline and complicate the collabora-tive work of sharing, responding to, and revising papers. The me-dium for exchanging drafts will likely be e-mail or courseware—both discussed below.

Note Whichever medium you use, respond to the deep issues in others' drafts, especially early drafts: thesis, purpose, audience, organization, and support for the thesis. (See p. 55 for a revision checklist that can guide your reading.) Hold comments on style, grammar, punctuation, and other surface matters until you're re-viewing late drafts, if indeed you are expected to comment on them at all.

1 ■ Using e-mail

To share drafts and comments by e-mail, you can copy and paste text into your e-mail messages or send word-processor files as attachments. Your group may need to experiment a bit to see which option works better, and you can then agree on procedures.

If your group pastes drafts into e-mail messages, take the fol-lowing steps:

- *Decide on a convention for adding comments.* For instance, you can break the lines of the draft to insert bracketed comments.

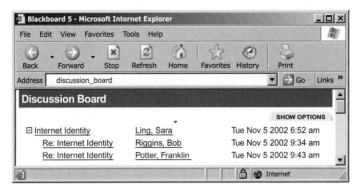

Author: Ling, Sara <sling@cncu.edu>

Subject: Internet Identity

Hi everyone. I'm hoping you can give me some advice about my topic and maybe share some of your experiences. I disagree with Kadi's argument that the Internet will lead to more fragmentation, not community. On the snowboarding forum that I sometimes participate in, I received a lot of hostile responses when I logged on as a woman. But another member of the group wrote to tell me that when she logged on as a man, she was welcomed into the group. It made me realize that the anonymity of the Internet could be used to bring people together, not split them apart.

Have any of you had similar experiences when you've been online? Do you think that anonymity can bring people together?

Author: Riggins, Bob <flashbob@cncu.edu>

Subject: Re: Internet Identity

I had a similar experience when I tried to post a question to a newsgroup. I logged on with my e-mail account as my name, "flashbob." Nobody responded to my question at all. I think part of it was because the name I used was so playful that nobody took me seriously. You may be on to something, Sara.

Author: Potter, Franklin <fpotter@cncu.edu>

Subject: Re: Internet Identity

I think you and Bob both have a point about the names used on the Internet having a lot to do with how people relate. But I'm not sure that your experience totally challenges what Kadi is saying. When I've been online, I've found that people who are a lot alike tend to hang out and encourage each other. Even if the other woman on the snowboarding forum was able to change her identity, she still ended up confiding in you. I guess I would just be careful about claiming that anonymity will automatically bring different kinds of people together. Hope this helps. Frank.

(Comments in all-capital letters are difficult to read and can be seen as overly insistent.)

- *Avoid breaking up the text repeatedly with detailed comments.* Instead, focus on the parts that you think need the most attention or comment paragraph by paragraph.

If your group shares files as e-mail attachments, follow these guidelines:

- *Use a word processor's Comment function to append questions and suggestions.* See pages 190–91 for more on the Comment function, which allows detailed remarks without interrupting the text.
- *Ensure that participants use compatible systems and word processors.* File sharing can be tricky. If you can't read one another's files, see page 193 for troubleshooting tips.

2 ▪ Using courseware

Web-based courseware such as *WebCT* or *Blackboard* allows exchange of texts and information with just a few mouse clicks. Participants upload files from their computers into a shared file space, and others can then download the files into their own computers. (As with e-mail attachments, incompatible files can be a problem. See p. 193 for tips.) Courseware encourages users to see and practice writing as a public exchange of ideas.

The screen shot below shows file sharing on one courseware program: two students are sharing drafts and providing feedback. The writers have used a system for naming files in order to clarify who wrote what and to preserve past work. (Some programs overwrite and thus erase an older file when a user uploads a new file with exactly the same name.) Your instructor may establish a file-naming system for the course, or you and your classmates can develop one. See pages 184–86 for more on file management, including file naming.

PART IV

Grammatical Sentences

CHAPTER 12

Understanding Sentence Grammar

Grammar describes how language works. Following the rules of standard English grammar is what allows you to communicate with others across barriers of personality, region, class, or ethnic origin. If you are a native English speaker, you follow these rules mostly unconsciously. But when you're trying to improve your ability to communicate, it can help to make the rules conscious and learn the language used to describe them.

Grammar reveals a lot about a sentence, even if you don't know the meanings of all the words:

The rumfrums prattly biggled the pooba.

You don't know what this sentence means, but you can infer that some things called *rumfrums* did something to a *pooba*. They *biggled* it, whatever that means, in a *prattly* way. Two grammatical cues, especially, make this sentence like *The students easily passed the test*:

- *Word forms.* The ending *-s* means more than one *rumfrum*. The ending *-ed* means that *biggled* is an action that happened in the past. The ending *-ly* means that *prattly* probably describes *how* the *rumfrums biggled*.
- *Word order. Rumfrums biggled pooba* resembles a common sequence in English: something (*rumfrums*) performed some action (*biggled*) to or on something else (*pooba*). Since *prattly* comes right before the action, it probably describes the action.

This chapter explains how such structures work and shows how practicing with them can help you communicate more effectively.

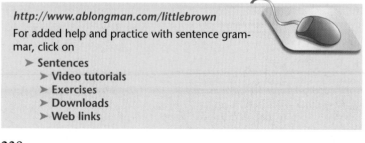

http://www.ablongman.com/littlebrown
For added help and practice with sentence grammar, click on
➤ Sentences
   ➤ Video tutorials
   ➤ Exercises
   ➤ Downloads
   ➤ Web links

Note Grammar and style checkers can both offer assistance and cause problems as you compose sentences. Look for the cautions and tips for using such checkers in this and the next five parts of this book. For more information about grammar and style checkers, see page 186.

12a   Understanding the basic sentence

The **sentence** is the basic unit of thought. Its grammar consists of words with specific forms and functions arranged in specific ways.

1 ■ Identifying subjects and predicates

Most sentences make statements. First they name something; then they make an assertion about or describe an action involving that something. These two sentence parts are the **subject** and the **predicate:**

Subject	Predicate
Art	can be controversial.
It	has caused disputes in Congress and in artists' studios.
Its meaning and value to society	are often the focus of debate.

gr
12a

CULTURE LANGUAGE The subject of an English sentence may be a noun (*art*) or a pronoun that refers to a noun (*it*), but not both: <u>Art</u> [not <u>Art it</u>] *can be controversial.* See page 394.

2 ■ Identifying the basic words: Nouns and verbs

The following five simple sentences consist almost entirely of two quite different kinds of words:

Subject	Predicate
The earth	trembled.
The earthquake	destroyed the city.
The result	was chaos.
The government	sent the city aid.
The citizens	considered the earthquake a disaster.

http://www.ablongman.com/littlebrown
For added help and practice with the parts of speech, click on
➤ **Sentences**
  ➤ **Exercises** ➤ **Exer. 1**
  ➤ **Web links** ➤ **Sentence grammar**

The parts of speech

Nouns name persons, places, things, ideas, or qualities: *Roosevelt, girl, Kip River, coastline, Koran, table, strife, happiness.* (See below.)

Pronouns usually substitute for nouns and function as nouns: *I, you, he, she, it, we, they, myself, this, that, who, which, everyone.* (See p. 242.)

Verbs express actions, occurrences, or states of being: *run, bunt, inflate, become, be.* (See the facing page.)

Adjectives describe or modify nouns or pronouns: *gentle, small, helpful.* (See p. 247.)

Adverbs describe or modify verbs, adjectives, other adverbs, or whole groups of words: *gently, helpfully, almost, really, someday.* (See p. 248.)

Prepositions relate nouns or pronouns to other words in a sentence: *about, at, down, for, of, with.* (See p. 250.)

Conjunctions link words, phrases, and clauses. **Coordinating conjunctions** and **correlative conjunctions** link words, phrases, or clauses of equal importance: *and, but, or, nor; both . . . and, not only . . . but also, either . . . or.* (See pp. 265–66.) **Subordinating conjunctions** introduce subordinate clauses and link them to main clauses: *although, because, if, whenever.* (See p. 259.)

Interjections express feeling or command attention, either alone or in a sentence: *hey, oh, darn, wow.*

gr
12a

The words in the subject position name things, such as *earth, earthquake,* and *government.* In contrast, the words in the predicate position express states or actions, such as *trembled, destroyed,* and *sent.*

These two groups of words work in different ways. *Citizen* can become *citizens,* but not *citizened. Destroyed* can become *destroys,* but not *destroyeds.* Grammar reflects such differences by identifying the **parts of speech** or **word classes** shown in the box above. Except for *the* and *a,* which simply point to and help identify the words after them, the five sentences about the earthquake consist entirely of nouns and verbs.

Nouns

Meaning

Nouns name. They may name a person (*Rosie O'Donnell, Jesse Jackson, astronaut*), a thing (*chair, book, Mt. Rainier*), a quality (*pain, mystery, simplicity*), a place (*city, Washington, ocean, Red Sea*), or an idea (*reality, peace, success*).

Form

Most nouns form the **possessive** to indicate ownership or source. Singular nouns usually add an apostrophe plus *-s* (*Auden's poems*); plural nouns usually add just an apostrophe (*citizens' rights*).

Nouns also change form to distinguish between singular (one) and plural (more than one). Most nouns add *-s* or *-es* for the plural:

earthquake, earthquakes; city, cities. Some nouns have irregular plurals: *woman, women; child, children.*

CULTURE LANGUAGE Some useful rules for forming noun plurals appear on pages 595–96. The irregular plurals must be memorized. Note that some nouns (noncount nouns) do not form plurals in English—for instance, *equality, anger, oxygen, equipment.* (See pp. 341–42.)

Nouns with *the, a,* and *an*

Nouns are often preceded by *the* or *a* (*an* before a vowel sound: *an apple*). These words are usually called **articles** or **determiners** and always indicate that a noun follows.

CULTURE LANGUAGE See pages 340–44 for the rules governing the use of *the, a/an,* or no article at all before a noun.

Verbs

Meaning

Verbs express an action (*bring, change, grow*), an occurrence (*become, happen*), or a state of being (*be, seem*).

gr

12a

Form

Most verbs can be recognized by two changes in form:

- To indicate a difference between present and past time, most verbs add *-d* or *-ed* to the form listed in the dictionary: *They play today. They played yesterday.* Some verbs indicate past time irregularly: *eat, ate; begin, began* (see p. 286).
- When their subjects are singular nouns or some singular pronouns, all present-time verbs except *be* and *have* add *-s* or *-es* to the dictionary form: *The bear escapes. It runs. The woman begins. She sings.* The *-s* forms of *be* and *have* are *is* and *has.*

(See Chapter 14, pp. 284–302, for more on verb forms.)

Helping verbs

Certain forms of all verbs can combine with other words such as *do, have, can, might, will,* and *must.* These other words are called **helping verbs** or **auxiliary verbs.** In verb phrases such as *could run, will be running,* and *has escaped,* they help to convey time and other attributes. (See Chapter 14, pp. 286, 292–97.)

A note on form and function

In different sentences an English word may serve different functions, take correspondingly different forms, and belong to different word classes. For example:

The government sent the city aid. [*Aid* functions as a noun.]
Governments aid citizens. [*Aid* functions as a verb.]

Because words can function in different ways, we must always determine how a particular word works in a sentence before we can identify what part of speech it is. **The *function* of a word in a sentence always determines its part of speech in that sentence.**

Pronouns

Most **pronouns** substitute for nouns and function in sentences as nouns do. In the following sentence all three pronouns—*who, they, their*—refer to *nurses:*

> Some nurses who have families prefer the night shift because they have more time with their children.

The most common pronouns are the **personal pronouns** (*I, you, he, she, it, we, they*) and the **relative pronouns** (*who, whoever, which, that*). Most of these change form to indicate their function in the sentence—for instance, *He called me. I called him back.* (See Chapter 13 for a discussion of these form changes.)

gr
12a

EXERCISE 1
Identifying subjects and predicates
Identify the subject and the predicate of each sentence below. Then use each sentence as a model to create a sentence of your own.

> *Example:*
>
>   subject   predicate
> An important scientist | spoke at commencement.
> *Sample imitation:* The hungry family ate at the diner.

1. The leaves fell.
2. October ends soon.
3. The orchard owners made apple cider.
4. They examined each apple carefully before using it.
5. Over a hundred people will buy cider at the roadside stand.

EXERCISE 2
Identifying nouns, verbs, and pronouns
In the following sentences identify all words functioning as nouns with *N*, all words functioning as verbs with *V*, and all pronouns with *P*.

> *Example:*
>
> P   V   N   N
> We took the tour through the museum.

1. The trees died.
2. They caught a disease.
3. The disease was a fungus.
4. It ruined a grove that was treasured.
5. Our great-grandfather planted the grove in the last century.

EXERCISE 3
Using nouns and verbs

Identify each of the following words as a noun, as a verb, or as both. Then create sentences of your own, using each word in each possible function.

> *Example:*
> fly
> Noun and verb.
> The fly sat on the meat loaf. [Noun.] The planes fly low. [Verb.]

1. wish
2. tie
3. swing
4. mail

5. spend
6. label
7. door

8. company
9. whistle
10. glue

3 ■ Forming sentence patterns with nouns and verbs

English builds all sentences on the five basic patterns shown in the box on the next page. As the diagrams indicate, the patterns differ in their predicates because the relation between the verb and the remaining words is different.

CULTURE LANGUAGE The word order in English sentences may not correspond to word order in the sentences of your native language. English, for instance, strongly prefers subject first, then verb, then any other words, whereas some other languages prefer the verb first. The main exceptions to the word patterns discussed below appear on pages 269–71. See also pages 381–88 on positioning modifiers in sentences.

gr
12a

Pattern 1: The earth trembled.

In the simplest pattern the predicate consists only of the verb. Verbs in this pattern do not require following words to complete their meaning and thus are called **intransitive** (from Latin words meaning "not passing over").

Subject	Predicate
	Intransitive verb
The earth	trembled.
Mosquitoes	buzz.
The hospital	may close.

---

http://www.ablongman.com/littlebrown

For added help and practice with basic sentence patterns, click on

➤ **Sentences**
  ➤ **Exercises** ➤ **Exers. 2 and 3**
  ➤ **Web links** ➤ **Sentence grammar**

The five basic sentence patterns

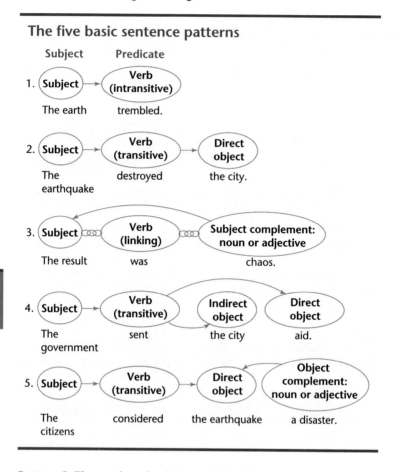

gr
12a

Pattern 2: The earthquake destroyed the city.

In pattern 2 the predicate consists of a verb followed by a noun that identifies who or what receives the action of the verb. This noun is a **direct object.** Verbs that require direct objects to complete their meaning are called **transitive** ("passing over"): the verb transfers the action from subject to object.

Subject	Predicate	
	Transitive verb	*Direct object*
The earthquake	destroyed	the city.
The people	wanted	peace.
Education	opens	doors.

CULTURE / LANGUAGE The distinction between transitive verbs and intransitive verbs like those in pattern 1 is important because only transitive verbs can be used in the passive voice (*The city was destroyed*). (See p. 270.) Your dictionary says whether a verb is transitive or intransitive. Some verbs (*begin, learn, read, write,* and others) are both.

Pattern 3: The result was chaos.

In pattern 3 the predicate also consists of a verb followed by a noun, but here the noun renames or describes the subject. We could write the sentence *The result = chaos.* The verb serving as an equal sign is a **linking verb** because it links the subject and the following description. The linking verbs include *be, seem, appear, become, grow, remain, stay, prove, feel, look, smell, sound,* and *taste.* The word that describes the subject is called a **subject complement** (it complements, or completes, the subject).

Subject	Predicate Linking verb	Subject complement
The result	was	chaos.
The trees	are	elms.
The man	became	an accountant.

Subject complements in this sentence pattern may also be adjectives, words such as *tall* and *hopeful* (see p. 247):

Subject	Predicate Linking verb	Subject complement
The result	was	chaotic.
Rents	are	high.
The apartments	seem	expensive.

Pattern 4: The government sent the city aid.

In pattern 4 the predicate consists of a verb followed by two nouns. The second noun, *aid,* is a direct object (see pattern 2). But the first noun, *city,* is an **indirect object,** identifying to or for whom the action of the verb is performed. The direct object and indirect object refer to different things, people, or places.

Subject	Predicate Transitive verb	Indirect object	Direct object
The government	sent	the city	aid.
Businesses	gave	the museum	money.
One company	offered	its employees	bonuses.

A number of verbs can take indirect objects, including those above and *allow, bring, buy, deny, find, get, leave, make, pay, read, sell, show, teach,* and *write.*

gr
12a

CULTURE LANGUAGE With some verbs expressing action done to or for someone, the indirect object must be turned into a phrase beginning with *to* or *for*. These verbs include *admit, announce, demonstrate, explain, introduce, mention, prove, recommend, say,* and *suggest*. The *to* or *for* phrase then falls after the direct object.

Faulty	The manual explains <u>workers</u> the new procedure.
Revised	The manual explains the new procedure <u>to workers</u>.

Pattern 5: The citizens considered the earthquake a disaster.

In pattern 5, as in pattern 4, the predicate consists of a verb followed by two nouns. But in pattern 5 the first noun is a direct object and the second noun renames or describes it. Here the second noun is an **object complement** (it complements, or completes, the object):

Subject	Predicate		
	Transitive verb	*Direct object*	*Object complement*
The citizens	considered	the earthquake	a disaster.
The class	elected	Joan O'Day	president.
Reporters	declared	her	the winner.

Just as a subject complement (pattern 3) renames or describes a subject, so an object complement renames or describes a direct object. Like a subject complement, an object complement may be a noun or an adjective, as below:

Subject	Predicate		
	Transitive verb	*Direct object*	*Object complement*
The citizens	considered	the earthquake	disastrous.
The results	proved	Sweeney	wrong.
Success	makes	some people	nervous.

EXERCISE 4
Identifying sentence patterns

In the following sentences, identify each verb as intransitive, transitive, or linking. Then identify each direct object (DO), indirect object (IO), subject complement (SC), and object complement (OC).

> *Example:*
>
> transitive
> verb   IO   DO   DO
> Children <u>give</u> their <u>parents</u> both <u>headaches</u> and <u>pleasures</u>.

1. Many people find New Orleans exciting.
2. Tourists flock there each year.
3. Usually they visit the French Quarter first.
4. The Quarter's old buildings are magnificent.
5. In the Quarter, artists sell tourists their paintings.

gr

12a

EXERCISE 5
Creating sentences

Create sentences by using each of the following verbs in the pattern indicated. (For the meanings of the abbreviations, see the directions for Exercise 4.) You may want to change the form of the verb.

Example:
give (S-V-IO-DO)
Sam gave his brother a birthday card.

1. laugh (S-V)
2. elect (S-V-DO-OC)
3. steal (S-V-DO)
4. catch (S-V-DO)
5. bring (S-V-IO-DO)

6. seem (S-V-SC)
7. call (S-V-DO-OC)
8. become (S-V-SC)
9. buy (S-V-IO-DO)
10. study (S-V)

12b   Expanding the basic sentence with single words

gr
12b

Most of the sentences we read, write, or speak are more complex and also more informative and interesting than those examined so far. Most sentences contain one or more of the following: (1) modifying words (discussed here); (2) word groups, called phrases and clauses (p. 249); and (3) combinations of two or more words or word groups of the same kind (p. 265).

1 ■ Using adjectives and adverbs

The simplest expansion of sentences occurs when we add modifying words to describe or limit the nouns and verbs. Modifying words add details:

Recently, the earth trembled.
The earthquake nearly destroyed the old city.
The federal government soon sent the city aid.
The grant was a very generous one but disappeared too quickly.

The underlined words represent two different parts of speech:

■ **Adjectives** describe or modify nouns and pronouns. They specify which one, what quality, or how many.

old   city   generous   one   two   pears
adjective noun   adjective pronoun   adjective noun

- **Adverbs** describe or modify verbs, adjectives, other adverbs, and whole groups of words. They specify when, where, how, and to what extent.

An *-ly* ending often signals an adverb, but not always: *friendly* is an adjective; *never, not,* and *always* are adverbs. The only way to tell whether a word is an adjective or an adverb is to determine what it modifies.

Adjectives and adverbs appear in three forms:

- The **positive** form is the basic form, the one listed in the dictionary: *good, green, angry; badly, quickly, angrily.*
- The **comparative** form indicates a greater degree of the quality named by the word: *better, greener, angrier; worse, more quickly, more angrily.*
- The **superlative** form indicates the greatest degree of the quality named: *best, greenest, angriest; worst, most quickly, most angrily.*

(For further discussion of these forms, see p. 336.)

2 ■ Using other words as modifiers

Nouns and special forms of verbs may sometimes serve as modifiers of other nouns. In combinations such as *office buildings, Thanksgiving prayer,* and *shock hazard,* the first noun modifies the second. In combinations such as *singing birds, corrected papers,* and *broken finger,* the first word is a verb form modifying the following noun. (These modifying verb forms are discussed in more detail on pp. 253–56.) Again, the part of speech to which we assign a word always depends on its function in a sentence.

EXERCISE 6
Identifying and using adjectives and adverbs
Identify the adjectives and adverbs in the following sentences. Then use each sentence as a model for creating a sentence of your own.

Example:

    adjective   adverb   adjective
The red barn sat uncomfortably among modern buildings.

Sample imitation: The little girl complained loudly to her busy mother.

1. The blue water glistened in the hot afternoon sunlight.
2. Happily, children dipped their toes in the cool lake.
3. Excitedly, some of the children hopped into the water.

gr
12b

4. Cautious parents watched from their shady porches.
5. The children played contentedly until the day finally ended.

EXERCISE 7
Using verb forms as modifiers
Use each of the following verb forms to modify a noun in a sentence of your own.

Example:
smoking
Only a <u>smoking cigar</u> remained.

1. scrambled
2. twitching
3. rambling
4. typed

5. painted
6. written
7. charging

8. ripened
9. known
10. driven

EXERCISE 8
Sentence combining: Single-word modifiers
To practice expanding the basic sentence patterns with single-word modifiers, combine each group of sentences below into one sentence. You will have to delete and rearrange words.

gr
12c

Example:
New Orleans offers tourists food. New Orleans offers food proudly. The food is delicious.
New Orleans <u>proudly</u> offers tourists <u>delicious</u> food.

1. The turn of the century ushered in technology and materials. The century was the twentieth. The technology was improved. The materials were new.
2. A skeleton made the construction of skyscrapers possible. The skeleton was sturdy. It was made of steel.
3. By 1913 the Woolworth Building, with its ornaments, stood 760 feet (55 stories). The building was towering. The ornaments were Gothic.
4. At 1450 feet the Sears Tower in Chicago doubles the height of the Woolworth Building. The doubling is now. The Woolworth height is puny. The puniness is relative.
5. Skyscrapers would not have been practical if Elisha Graves Otis had not built the elevator in 1857. It was the first elevator. The elevator was safe. It served passengers.

12c Expanding the basic sentence with word groups

Most sentences we read or write contain whole word groups that serve as nouns and modifiers. Such word groups enable us to combine several bits of information into one sentence and to make the relations among them clear, as in the following sentence:

subject

When the experiment succeeded, the researchers, excited by the re-

verb   object

sults, expanded the study to enroll more patients.

Attached to *researchers expanded the study,* the skeleton of this sentence, are three groups of words that add related information: *When the experiment succeeded, excited by the results, to enroll more patients.* These constructions are phrases and clauses:

- A **phrase** is a group of related words that lacks either a subject or a predicate or both: *excited by the results, to enroll more patients.*
- A **clause** contains both a subject and a predicate: *When the experiment succeeded* and *the researchers expanded the study* are both clauses, though only the second can stand alone as a sentence.

1 ■ Using prepositional phrases

Prepositions are connecting words. Unlike nouns, verbs, and modifiers, which may change form, prepositions never change form. As the box opposite shows, many prepositions signal relationships of time or space; others signal relationships such as addition, comparison or contrast, cause or effect, concession, condition, opposition, possession, and source. Notice that some prepositions consist of more than one word.

Note Some of the prepositions listed as signaling time or space also serve other functions and could be listed in the third column as well. *By,* for instance, may signal time (*by tomorrow*) and source (*by William Faulkner*).

A preposition connects a noun or pronoun to another word in the sentence: *Robins nest in trees.* The noun or pronoun so connected (*trees*) is the **object of the preposition.** The preposition plus its object and any modifiers is a **prepositional phrase:**

Preposition	Object
on	the surface
with	great satisfaction
upon	entering the room
from	where you are standing
except for	ten employees

http://www.ablongman.com/littlebrown
For added help and practice with prepositions and prepositional phrases, click on
➤ **Sentences**
  ➤ **Exercises** ➤ **Exer. 4**
  ➤ **Web links** ➤ **Sentence grammar**

gr
12c

Common prepositions

Time or space (position or direction)			Other relationships (addition, comparison, etc.)	
about	by	out of	according to	in spite of
above	down	outside	as	instead of
across	during	over	as for	like
after	for	past	aside from	of
against	from	since	because of	on account of
along	in	through	concerning	regarding
along with	inside	throughout	despite	regardless of
among	inside of	till	except	unlike
around	into	to	except for	with
at	near	toward	excepting	without
before	next to	under	in addition to	
behind	off	underneath		
below	on	until		
beneath	onto	up		
beside	on top of	upon		
between	out	within		
beyond				

gr
12c

Prepositions normally come before their objects. But in speech and informal writing the preposition sometimes comes after its object: *What do you want to see him about?*

Prepositional phrases function as adjectives (modifying nouns) or as adverbs (modifying verbs, adjectives, or other adverbs). As modifiers, they add details that make sentences clearer and more interesting for readers.

Life on a raft was an opportunity for adventure.
    adjective phrase   adjective phrase

Huck Finn rode the raft by choice.
                       adverb phrase

CULTURE LANGUAGE The meanings and idiomatic uses of English prepositions can be difficult to master; most must be memorized or looked up in a dictionary. (A list of dictionaries for English as a second language appears on p. 574.) See pages 300–01 for the uses of prepositions in two-word verbs such as *look after* and pages 558–59 for the uses of prepositions in idioms.

Punctuating prepositional phrases

Since a prepositional phrase lacks a subject and a predicate, it should not be punctuated as a complete sentence. If it is, the result is a **sentence fragment** (Chapter 17):

Fragment   Toward the sun.

The phrase must be attached to another group of words containing both a subject and a predicate:

Revised   The plane turned <u>toward the sun</u>.

A prepositional phrase that introduces a sentence is set off with punctuation, usually a comma, unless it is short (see p. 457):

<u>According to the newspaper and other sources</u>, the governor has reluctantly decided to veto the bill.

<u>In 1865</u> the Civil War finally ended.

A prepositional phrase that interrupts or concludes a sentence is *not* set off with punctuation when it is essential to the meaning of the word or words it modifies (see p. 459):

The announcement <u>of a tuition increase</u> surprised no one.

Students expected new fees <u>for the coming year</u>.

When an interrupting or concluding prepositional phrase is *not* essential to meaning, but merely adds information to the sentence, then it *is* set off with punctuation, usually a comma or commas (see p. 459):

The governor, <u>according to the newspaper and other sources</u>, has reluctantly decided to veto the bill.

As all the preceding examples illustrate, a preposition and its object are not separated by a comma.

EXERCISE 9
Identifying prepositional phrases

Identify the prepositional phrases in the following passage. Indicate whether each phrase functions as an adjective or as an adverb, and name the word that the phrase modifies.

Example:

After an hour I finally arrived at the home of my professor.

On July 3, 1863, at Gettysburg, Pennsylvania, General Robert E. Lee gambled unsuccessfully for a Confederate victory in the American Civil War. Called Pickett's Charge, the battle was one of the most disastrous conflicts of the war. Confederate and Union forces faced each other on parallel ridges separated by almost a mile of open fields. After an artillery bombardment of the Union position, about 12,000 Confederate infantry marched toward the Union ridge. The Union guns had been silent but suddenly roared, mowing the approaching Confederates. Within an hour, perhaps half of the Confederate soldiers lay wounded or dead.

EXERCISE 10
Sentence combining: Prepositional phrases
To practice writing sentences with prepositional phrases, combine each group of sentences below into one sentence that includes one or two prepositional phrases. You will have to add, delete, and re-arrange words. Some items have more than one possible answer.

> *Example:*
> I will start working. The new job will pay the minimum wage.
> I will start working <u>at a new job</u> <u>for the minimum wage</u>.

1. The slow loris protects itself well. Its habitat is Southeast Asia. It possesses a poisonous chemical.
2. To frighten predators, the loris exudes the chemical. The chemical comes from a gland. The gland is on the loris's upper arm.
3. The loris's chemical is highly toxic. The chemical is not like a skunk's spray. Even small quantities of the chemical are toxic.
4. A tiny dose can affect a human. The dose would get in the mouth. The human would be sent into shock.
5. Predators probably can sense the toxin. They detect it at a distance. They use their nasal organs.

gr
12c

2 ▪ Using verbals and verbal phrases

Verbals are special verb forms such as *smoking* or *hidden* or *to win* that can function as nouns (*smoking* is dangerous) or as modifiers (*the hidden money, the urge to win*).

Note A verbal *cannot* stand alone as the complete verb in the predicate of a sentence. For example, *The man smoking* and *The money hidden* are not sentences but sentence fragments (see p. 348). Any verbal must combine with a helping verb to serve as the predicate of a sentence: *The man was smoking. The money is hidden.*

Because verbals cannot serve alone as sentence predicates, they are sometimes called **nonfinite verbs** (in essence, they are "unfinished"). **Finite verbs**, in contrast, can make an assertion or express a state of being without a helping verb (they are "finished"). Either of the two tests on the next page can distinguish finite and nonfinite verbs.

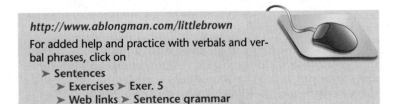

http://www.ablongman.com/littlebrown
For added help and practice with verbals and verbal phrases, click on
  ➤ Sentences
    ➤ Exercises ➤ Exer. 5
    ➤ Web links ➤ Sentence grammar

Tests for finite and nonfinite verbs (verbals)

Test 1 Does the word require a change in form when a third-person subject changes from singular to plural?

> Yes   Finite verb: *It sings. They sing.*
>
> No   Nonfinite verb (verbal): *bird singing, birds singing*

Test 2 Does the word require a change in form to show the difference in present, past, and future?

> Yes   Finite verb: *It sings. It sang. It will sing.*
>
> No   Nonfinite verb (verbal): *The bird singing is/was/will be a robin.*

There are three kinds of verbals: participles, gerunds, and infinitives.

Participles

All verbs have two participle forms, a present and a past. The **present participle** consists of the dictionary form of the verb plus the ending *-ing: beginning, completing, hiding.* The **past participle** of most verbs consists of the dictionary form plus *-d* or *-ed: believed, completed.* Some common verbs have an irregular past participle, such as *begun* or *hidden.* (See pp. 287–89.)

Both present and past participles function as adjectives to modify nouns and pronouns:

Shopping malls sometimes frustrate shoppers.

Shoppers may feel trapped.

⟨ **CULTURE LANGUAGE** ⟩ For English verbs expressing feeling, the present and past participles have different meanings: *It was a boring lecture. The bored students slept.* See page 339.

Gerunds

Gerund is the name given to the *-ing* form of the verb when it serves as a noun:

subject
Strolling through stores can exhaust the hardiest shopper.

object
Many children learn to hate shopping.

Present participles and gerunds can be distinguished *only* by their function in a sentence. If the *-ing* form functions as an adjective (*a teaching degree*), it is a present participle. If the *-ing* form functions as a noun (*Teaching is difficult*), it is a gerund.

⟨ **CULTURE LANGUAGE** ⟩ In English, always use a gerund, not any other verb form, as the object of a preposition: *Diners are prohibited from smoking.* See also the culture-language note on the facing page.

Infinitives

The **infinitive** is the *to* form of the verb, the dictionary form preceded by the infinitive marker *to: to begin, to hide, to run.* Infinitives may function as adjectives, nouns, or adverbs:

The question to answer is why shoppers endure mall fatigue.
adjective

The solution for mall fatigue is to leave.
noun

Still, shoppers find it difficult to quit.
adverb

CULTURE LANGUAGE Infinitives and gerunds may follow some English verbs and not others and may differ in meaning after a verb: *The singer stopped to sing. The singer stopped singing.* (See pp. 298–300.)

Verbal phrases

Participles, gerunds, and infinitives—like other forms of verbs —may take subjects, objects, or complements, and they may be modified by adverbs. The verbal and all the words immediately related to it make up a **verbal phrase.** With verbal phrases, we can create concise sentences packed with information.

Like participles, **participial phrases** always serve as adjectives, modifying nouns or pronouns:

Buying things, most shoppers feel themselves in control.

They make selections determined by personal taste.

Gerund phrases, like gerunds, always serve as nouns:

subject
Shopping for clothing and other items satisfies personal needs.

object of preposition
Malls are good at creating such needs.

Infinitive phrases may serve as nouns, adverbs, or adjectives:

sentence subject   subject complement
To design a mall is to create an artificial environment.
noun phrase   noun phrase

Malls are designed to make shoppers feel safe.
adverb phrase

The environment supports the impulse to shop for oneself.
adjective phrase

Note When an infinitive or infinitive phrase serves as a noun after verbs such as *hear, help, let, make, see,* and *watch,* the infinitive marker *to* is omitted: *We all heard her tell* [not *to tell*] *the story.*

gr
12c

Punctuating verbals and verbal phrases

Verbal phrases punctuated as complete sentences are sentence fragments (Chapter 17). A complete sentence must contain a subject and a finite verb (p. 254):

| **Fragment** | <u>Treating</u> the patients kindly. |
| **Revised** | <u>She treats</u> the patients kindly. |

A verbal or verbal phrase serving as a modifier is almost always set off with a comma when it introduces a sentence (see p. 459):

<u>To pay tuition,</u> some students work at two jobs.

A modifying verbal or verbal phrase that interrupts or concludes a sentence is *not* set off with punctuation when it is essential to the meaning of the word or words it modifies (see p. 459):

Jobs <u>paying well</u> are hard to find.

When an interrupting or concluding verbal modifier is *not* essential to meaning but merely adds information to the sentence, it *is* set off with punctuation, usually a comma or commas (see p. 459):

One good job, <u>paying twelve dollars an hour,</u> was filled in fifteen minutes.

gr
12c

EXERCISE 11
Identifying verbals and verbal phrases

The following sentences contain participles, gerunds, and infinitives as well as participial, gerund, and infinitive phrases. First identify each verbal or verbal phrase. Then indicate whether it is used as an adjective, an adverb, or a noun.

> *Example:*
>
>   adjective   adverb
> <u>Laughing</u>, the talk-show host prodded her guest <u>to talk</u>.

1. Written in 1850 by Nathaniel Hawthorne, *The Scarlet Letter* tells the story of Hester Prynne.
2. Shunned by the community, Hester endures her loneliness.
3. Hester is humble enough to withstand her Puritan neighbors' cutting remarks.
4. Despite the cruel treatment, the determined young woman refuses to leave her home.
5. By living a life of patience and unselfishness, Hester eventually becomes the community's angel.

EXERCISE 12
Sentence combining: Verbals and verbal phrases

To practice writing sentences with verbals and verbal phrases, combine each of the following pairs of sentences into one sentence. You will have to add, delete, change, and rearrange words. Each item has more than one possible answer.

Example:

My father took pleasure in mean pranks. For instance, he hid the neighbor's cat.

My father took pleasure in mean pranks such as <u>hiding the neighbor's cat</u>.

1. Air pollution is a health problem. It affects millions of Americans.
2. The air has been polluted mainly by industries and automobiles. It contains toxic chemicals.
3. Environmentalists pressure politicians. They think politicians should pass stricter laws.
4. Many politicians waver. They are not necessarily against environmentalism.
5. The problems are too complex. They cannot be solved easily.

3 ▪ Using absolute phrases

Absolute phrases consist of a noun or pronoun and a participle, plus any modifiers:

┌──────── absolute phrase ────────┐
Many ethnic groups, <u>their own place established</u>, are making way for new arrivals.

┌──────── absolute phrase ────────┐ ┌──────── absolute phrase ────────┐
<u>Their native lands left behind</u>, <u>an uncertain future looming</u>, immigrants face many obstacles.

gr
12c

These phrases are called *absolute* (from a Latin word meaning "free") because they have no specific grammatical connection to a noun, verb, or any other word in the rest of the sentence. Instead, they modify the entire rest of the sentence, adding information or clarifying meaning.

Notice that absolute phrases, unlike participial phrases, always contain a subject. Compare the following:

┌─── participial phrase
For many immigrants <u>learning English</u>, the language introduces American culture.

┌──────── absolute phrase ────────┐
<u>The immigrants having learned English</u>, their opportunities widen.

We often omit the participle from an absolute phrase when it is some form of *be,* such as *being* or *having been:*

<u>Two languages [being] at hand</u>, bilingual citizens in fact have many cultural and occupational advantages.

http://www.ablongman.com/littlebrown
For added help with absolute phrases, click on
➤ **Sentences** ➤ **Web links** ➤ **Sentence grammar**

Punctuating absolute phrases

Absolute phrases are always set off from the rest of the sentence with punctuation, usually a comma or commas (see also p. 464):

<u>Their future more secure,</u> these citizens will make room for new arrivals.

These citizens, <u>their future more secure,</u> will make room for new arrivals.

EXERCISE 13
Sentence combining: Absolute phrases

To practice writing sentences with absolute phrases, combine each pair of sentences below into one sentence that contains an absolute phrase. You will have to add, delete, change, and rearrange words.

Example:
The flower's petals wilted. It looked pathetic.
<u>Its petals wilted</u>, the flower looked pathetic.

1. Geraldine Ferraro's face beamed. She enjoyed the crowd's cheers after her nomination for Vice President.
2. A vacancy had occurred. Sandra Day O'Connor was appointed the first female Supreme Court justice.
3. Her appointment was confirmed. Condoleezza Rice became the first female national security adviser.
4. The midterm elections were over. Nancy Pelosi was elected the first female minority leader of the House of Representatives.
5. The election was won. Elizabeth Dole was a US senator from North Carolina.

gr
12c

4 ■ Using subordinate clauses

A **clause** is any group of words that contains both a subject and a predicate. There are two kinds of clauses, and the distinction between them is important:

■ A **main** or **independent clause** makes a complete statement and can stand alone as a sentence: *The sky darkened.*

■ A **subordinate** or **dependent clause** is just like a main clause *except* that it begins with a subordinating word: *<u>when</u> the sky darkened; <u>whoever</u> calls.* The subordinating word reduces the clause to a single part of speech—an adjective, an adverb, or a noun—that supports the idea in a main clause. Because it only

http://www.ablongman.com/littlebrown
For added help and practice with clauses, click on
➤ **Sentences**
   ➤ **Exercises** ➤ **Exer. 6**
   ➤ **Web links** ➤ **Sentence grammar**

modifies or names something, a subordinate clause cannot stand alone as a sentence (see the discussion of punctuation on p. 261). (The word *subordinate* means "secondary" or "controlled by another." It comes from the Latin *sub,* "under," and *ordo,* "order.")

The following examples show the differences between main and subordinate clauses:

```
┌─────── main clause ───────┬─ main clause ┐
The school teaches parents. It is unusual.
┌─────── subordinate clause ───────┬─ main clause ┐
Because the school teaches parents, it is unusual.
```

```
┌─────────── main clause ───────────┬─────── main clause ───────┐
Some parents avoid their children's schools. They are often illiterate.
┌─────────────── main clause ───────────────┐
Parents who are illiterate often avoid their children's schools.
       └ subordinate clause ┘
```

Two kinds of subordinating words introduce subordinate clauses: subordinating conjunctions and relative pronouns.

Subordinating conjunctions

Subordinating conjunctions, like prepositions, never change form in any way. In the following box they are arranged by the relationships they signal. (Some fit in more than one group.)

Common subordinating conjunctions

Cause or effect	Condition	Comparison or contrast	Space or time
as	even if	as	after
because	if	as if	as long as
in order that	if only	as though	before
since	provided	rather than	now that
so that	since	than	once
	unless	whereas	since
Concession	when	whether	till
although	whenever	while	until
as if	whether		when
even if		**Purpose**	whenever
even though		in order that	where
though		so that	wherever
		that	while

---

http://www.ablongman.com/littlebrown
For added help with subordinating conjunctions, click on
➤ **Sentences** ➤ **Web links** ➤ **Sentence grammar**

CULTURE LANGUAGE Subordinating conjunctions convey their meaning without help from other function words, such as the coordinating conjunctions *and, but, for,* or *so* (p. 265).

Faulty <u>Even though</u> the parents are illiterate, <u>but</u> their children may read well. [*Even though* and *but* have the same meaning, so both are not needed.]

Revised <u>Even though</u> the parents are illiterate, their children may read well.

Relative pronouns

Unlike subordinating conjunctions, **relative pronouns** usually act as subjects or objects in their own clauses, and two of them (*who* and *whoever*) change form accordingly (see pp. 280–81).

Relative pronouns

| which | what | who (whose, whom) |
| that | whatever | whoever (whomever) |

---

gr
12c

Subordinate clauses

Subordinate clauses function as adjectives, adverbs, or nouns.

Adjective clauses

Adjective clauses modify nouns and pronouns. They usually begin with the relative pronoun *who, whom, whose, which,* or *that,* although a few adjective clauses begin with *when* or *where* (standing for *in which, on which,* or *at which*). The pronoun is the subject or object of the clause it begins. The clause ordinarily falls immediately after the noun or pronoun it modifies:

Parents <u>who are illiterate</u> often have bad memories of school.

Schools <u>that involve parents</u> are more successful with children.

One school, <u>which is open year-round</u>, helps parents learn to read.

The school is in a city <u>where the illiteracy rate is high</u>.

Adverb clauses

Like adverbs, **adverb clauses** modify verbs, adjectives, other adverbs, and whole groups of words. They usually tell how, why, when, where, under what conditions, or with what result. They always begin with subordinating conjunctions.

The school began teaching parents <u>when adult illiteracy gained national attention</u>.

At first the program was not as successful as its founders had hoped.

Because it was directed at people who could not read, advertising had to be inventive.

An adverb clause can often be moved around in a sentence with no loss of clarity. Compare the preceding example and this one:

Advertising had to be inventive because it was directed at people who could not read.

Noun clauses

Noun clauses function as subjects, objects, and complements in sentences. They begin with *that, what, whatever, who, whom, whoever, whomever, when, where, whether, why,* or *how.* Unlike adjective and adverb clauses, noun clauses *replace* a word (a noun) within a clause; therefore, they can be difficult to identify.

―――――― sentence subject ――――――
Whether the program would succeed depended on door-to-door advertising.

―――――― direct object ――――――
Teachers explained in person how the program would work.

―――――― sentence subject ――――――
Whoever seemed slightly interested was invited to an open meeting.

―――――― object of preposition ――――――
A few parents were anxious about what their children would think.

Elliptical clauses

A subordinate clause that is grammatically incomplete but clear in meaning is an **elliptical clause** (*ellipsis* means "omission"). The meaning of the clause is clear because the missing element can be supplied from the context. Most often the elements omitted are the relative pronouns *that, which,* and *whom* from adjective clauses or the predicate from the second part of a comparison.

The parents knew their children could read better than they [could read].

Skepticism and fear were among the feelings [that] the parents voiced.

Though [they were] often reluctant at first, about a third of the parents attended the meeting.

Punctuating subordinate clauses

Subordinate clauses punctuated as complete sentences are sentence fragments (Chapter 17). Though a subordinate clause contains a subject and a predicate and thus resembles a complete sentence, it also begins with a subordinating word that makes it into an adjective, adverb, or noun. A single part of speech cannot stand alone as a complete sentence.

> **Fragment**   Because a door was ajar.
> **Revised**   A door was ajar.
> **Revised**   The secret leaked because a door was ajar.

A subordinate clause serving as an adverb is almost always set off with a comma when it introduces a sentence (see p. 457):

> Although the project was almost completed, it lost its funding.

A modifying subordinate clause that interrupts or concludes a main clause is *not* set off with punctuation when it is essential to the meaning of the word or words it modifies (see p. 459):

> The woman who directed the project lost her job.
> The project lost its funding because it was not completed on time.

When an interrupting or concluding subordinate clause is *not* essential to meaning, but merely adds information to the sentence, it *is* set off with punctuation, usually a comma or commas (see p. 459):

> The project lost its funding, although it was almost completed.
> The director, who holds a PhD, sought new funding.

gr
12c

EXERCISE 14
Identifying subordinate clauses

Identify the subordinate clauses in the following sentences. Then indicate whether each is used as an adjective, an adverb, or a noun. If the clause is a noun, indicate what function it performs in the sentence.

> *Example:*
>   noun
> The article explained how one could build an underground house. [Object of *explained*.]

1. Scientists who want to catch the slightest signals from space use extremely sensitive receivers.
2. Even though they have had to fight for funding, these scientists have persisted in their research.
3. The research is called SETI, which stands for Search for Extraterrestrial Intelligence.
4. The theory is that intelligent beings in space are trying to get in touch with us.
5. The challenge is to guess what frequency these beings would use to send signals.

EXERCISE 15
Sentence combining: Subordinate clauses

To practice writing sentences with subordinate clauses, combine each pair of main clauses into one sentence. Use either subordinating conjunctions or relative pronouns as appropriate, referring to the lists on pages 259 and 260 if necessary. You will have to add, delete, and rearrange words. Each item has more than one possible answer.

Example:

She did not have her tire irons with her. She could not change her bicycle tire.

<u>Because</u> she did not have her tire irons with her, she could not change her bicycle tire.

1. Moviegoers expect something. Movie sequels should be as exciting as the original films.
2. A few sequels are good films. Most are poor imitations of the originals.
3. A sequel to a blockbuster film arrives in the theater. Crowds quickly line up to see it.
4. Viewers pay to see the same villains and heroes. They remember these characters fondly.
5. Afterward, viewers often grumble about filmmakers. The filmmakers rehash tired plots and characters.

5 ▪ Using appositives

gr
12c

An **appositive** is usually a noun that renames another noun nearby, most often the noun just before the appositive. (The word *appositive* derives from a Latin word that means "placed near to" or "applied to.") An appositive phrase includes modifiers as well.

Bizen ware, a dark stoneware, has been produced in Japan since the fourteenth century.

The name Bizen comes from the location of the kilns used to fire the pottery.

All appositives can replace the words they refer to: *A dark stoneware has been produced in Japan.*

Appositives are often introduced by words and phrases such as *or, that is, such as, for example,* and *in other words:*

Bizen ware is used in the Japanese tea ceremony, <u>that is, the Zen Buddhist observance that links meditation and art.</u>

Appositives are economical alternatives to adjective clauses containing a form of *be,* as shown in the next example.

http://www.ablongman.com/littlebrown
For added help and practice with appositives, click on
➤ Sentences
   ➤ Exercises ➤ Exer. 7
      ➤ Web links ➤ Sentence grammar

Bizen ware, [which is] a dark stoneware, has been produced in Japan since the fourteenth century.

Although most appositives are nouns that rename other nouns, they may also be and rename other parts of speech, such as the verb *thrown* in the sentence below:

The pottery is thrown, or formed on a potter's wheel.

Punctuating appositives

Appositives punctuated as complete sentences are sentence fragments (see Chapter 17). To correct such fragments, you can usually connect the appositive to the main clause containing the word referred to:

Fragment	An exceedingly tall man with narrow shoulders.
Revised	He stood next to a basketball player, an exceedingly tall man with narrow shoulders.

An appositive is *not* set off with punctuation when it is essential to the meaning of the word it refers to (see p. 461):

The verb *howl* comes from the Old English verb *houlen.*

When an appositive is *not* essential to the meaning of the word it refers to, it *is* set off with punctuation, usually a comma or commas (see p. 461):

An aged elm, the tree was struck by lightning.
The tree, an aged elm, was struck by lightning.
Lightning struck the tree, an aged elm.

A nonessential appositive is sometimes set off with a dash or dashes, especially when it contains commas (see p. 506):

Three people—Will, Carolyn, and Tom—object to the new procedure.

A concluding appositive is sometimes set off with a colon (see p. 504):

Two principles guide the judge's decisions: justice and mercy.

> **EXERCISE 16**
> ### Sentence combining: Appositives
> To practice writing sentences with appositives, combine each pair of sentences into one sentence that contains an appositive. You will have to delete and rearrange words. Some items have more than one possible answer.
>
> *Example:*
> The largest land animal is the elephant. The elephant is also one of the most intelligent animals.
>
> The largest land animal, the elephant, is also one of the most intelligent animals.

gr
12c

1. Some people perform amazing feats when they are very young. These people are geniuses from birth.
2. John Stuart Mill was a British philosopher. He had written a history of Rome by age seven.
3. Two great artists began their work at age four. They were Paul Klee and Gustav Mahler.
4. Mahler was a Bohemian composer of intensely emotional works. He was also the child of a brutal father.
5. Paul Klee was a Swiss painter. As a child he was frightened by his own drawings of devils.

12d   Compounding words, phrases, and clauses

A **compound construction** combines words that are closely related and equally important. It makes writing clearer and more economical because it pulls together linked information.

Headaches can be controlled by biofeedback. Heart rate can be controlled by biofeedback.

┌——— compound subject ———┐
Headaches and heart rate can be controlled by biofeedback.

Without medication, biofeedback cures headaches. It steadies heart rate. It lowers blood pressure. It relaxes muscles.

┌——— compound predicate ———┐
Without medication, biofeedback cures headaches, steadies heart rate, lowers blood pressure, and relaxes muscles.

1 ■ Using coordinating conjunctions and correlative conjunctions

Two kinds of words create compound constructions: coordinating and correlative conjunctions. **Coordinating conjunctions** are few and do not change form. In the following box the relationship that each conjunction signals appears in parentheses:

Coordinating conjunctions

and (*addition*)	nor (*alternative*)	for (*cause*)	yet (*contrast*)
but (*contrast*)	or (*alternative*)	so (*effect*)	

To remember the coordinating conjunctions, use the word *fanboys: for, and, nor, but, or, yet, so.*

http://www.ablongman.com/littlebrown
For added help with coordinating and correlative conjunctions, click on
➤ **Sentences** ➤ **Web links** ➤ **Sentence grammar**

The coordinating conjunctions *and, but, nor,* and *or* always connect words or word groups of the same kind—that is, two or more nouns, verbs, adjectives, adverbs, phrases, subordinate clauses, or main clauses:

Biofeedback or simple relaxation can relieve headaches.
Biofeedback is effective but costly.
Relaxation also works well, and it is inexpensive.
Relaxation is effective yet inexpensive.

The conjunctions *for* and *so* connect only main clauses. *For* indicates cause; *so* indicates effect.

Biofeedback can be costly, for the training involves technical equipment and specialists.

Relaxation can be difficult to learn alone, so some people do seek help from specialists.

Some coordinating conjunctions pair up with other words to form **correlative conjunctions.** In the following box the relationship each conjunction signals appears in parentheses:

gr

12d

Common correlative conjunctions

both . . . and (*addition*)   neither . . . nor (*negation*)
not only . . . but also (*addition*)   whether . . . or (*alternative*)
not . . . but (*substitution*)   as . . . as (*comparison*)
either . . . or (*alternative*)

Both biofeedback and relaxation can relieve headaches.

The techniques require neither psychotherapy nor medication.

The headache sufferer learns not only to recognize the causes of headaches but also to control those causes.

Punctuating compounded words, phrases, and clauses

Two words, phrases, or subordinate clauses that are connected by a coordinating conjunction are *not* separated by a comma (see p. 472):

The library needs renovation and rebuilding.

The work will begin after the spring term ends but before the fall term begins.

When two *main* clauses are joined into one sentence with a coordinating conjunction, a comma precedes the conjunction (see p. 455):

The project will be lengthy, and everyone will suffer some inconvenience.

When two main clauses are joined *without* a coordinating conjunction, they must be separated with a semicolon to avoid the error called a comma splice (see p. 477):

> The work cannot be delayed; it's already overdue.

In a series of three or more items, commas separate the items, with *and* usually preceding the last item (see p. 465):

> The renovated library will feature <u>new study carrels, new shelving, and a larger reference section.</u>

Semicolons sometimes separate the items in a series if they are long or contain commas (see p. 482).

A comma also separates two or more adjectives when they modify a noun equally and are not joined by a coordinating conjunction (see p. 465):

> <u>Cracked, crumbling</u> walls will be repaired.

The comma does *not* separate adjectives when the one nearer the noun is more closely related to it in meaning (see p. 466):

> <u>New reading</u> lounges will replace the old ones.

gr
12d

2 ■ Using conjunctive adverbs

One other kind of connecting word, called a **conjunctive adverb**, relates only main clauses, not words, phrases, or subordinate clauses. In the following box the conjunctive adverbs are arranged by the relationships they signal:

Common conjunctive adverbs

Addition	Comparison or contrast	Cause or effect
also	however	accordingly
besides	in comparison	as a result
further	in contrast	consequently
furthermore	instead	hence
in addition	likewise	similarly
incidentally	nevertheless	therefore
moreover	nonetheless	thus
	otherwise	
Emphasis		**Time**
certainly		finally
indeed		meanwhile
in fact		next
still		now
undoubtedly		then
		thereafter

It's important to distinguish between conjunctive adverbs and conjunctions (coordinating and subordinating) because they demand different punctuation (see the discussion below). Conjunctive adverbs are *adverbs:* they describe the relation of ideas in two clauses, and, like most adverbs, they can move around in their clause:

> Relaxation techniques have improved; <u>however</u>, few people know them.

> Relaxation techniques have improved; few people know them, <u>however</u>.

In contrast, conjunctions bind two clauses into a single grammatical unit, and they cannot be moved:

> <u>Although</u> few people know them, relaxation techniques have improved. [The subordinating conjunction can't be moved: *Few people know them <u>although</u>, relaxation techniques have improved.*]

> Relaxation techniques have improved, <u>but</u> few people know them. [The coordinating conjunction can't be moved: *Relaxation techniques have improved, few people know them <u>but</u>.*]

gr
12d

Note Some connecting words have more than one use. *After, until,* and some other words may be either prepositions or subordinating conjunctions. Some prepositions, such as *behind* and *in,* can serve also as adverbs, as in *He trailed <u>behind</u>.* And some conjunctive adverbs, particularly *however,* may also serve simply as adverbs in sentences such as *<u>However</u> much it costs, we must have it.* Again, the part of speech of a word depends on its function in a sentence.

Punctuating sentences containing conjunctive adverbs

Because the two main clauses related by a conjunctive adverb remain independent units, they must be separated by a semicolon (see p. 480). If they are separated by a comma, the result is a comma splice (Chapter 18):

Comma splice	Interest rates rose, <u>therefore</u>, real estate prices declined.
Revised	Interest rates rose; <u>therefore</u>, real estate prices declined.

A conjunctive adverb is almost always set off from its clause with a comma or commas (see p. 461):

> The decline was small; <u>however</u>, some investors were badly hurt.
> The decline was small; some investors, <u>however</u>, were badly hurt.

EXERCISE 17
Sentence combining: Compound constructions

To practice compounding words, phrases, and clauses, combine each of the following pairs of sentences into one sentence that is as short as possible without altering meaning. Use an appropriate connecting word of the type specified in parentheses, referring to the lists on pages 265–67 as necessary. You will have to add, delete, and rearrange words, and you may have to change or add punctuation.

> *Example:*
> The encyclopedia had some information. It was not detailed enough. (*Conjunctive adverb.*)
> The encyclopedia had some information; <u>however</u>, it was not detailed enough.

1. All too often people assume that old age is not a productive time. Many people in their nineties have had great achievements. (*Conjunctive adverb.*)
2. In his nineties the philosopher Bertrand Russell spoke vigorously for international peace. He spoke for nuclear disarmament. (*Correlative conjunction.*)
3. Grandma Moses did not retire to an easy chair. She began painting at age seventy-six and was still going at one hundred. (*Conjunctive adverb.*)
4. The British general George Higginson published his memoirs after he was ninety. The British archaeologist Margaret Murray published her memoirs after she was ninety. (*Coordinating conjunction.*)
5. The architect Frank Lloyd Wright designed his first building at age twenty. He designed his last building at age ninety. (*Coordinating conjunction.*)

gr
12e

12e Changing the usual order of the sentence

So far, all the examples of basic sentence grammar have been similar: the subject of the sentence comes first, naming the performer of the predicate's action, and the predicate comes second. This arrangement of subject and predicate describes most sentences that occur in writing, but four other kinds of sentences alter the basic pattern.

1 ■ Forming questions

The following are the most common ways of forming questions from statements. Remember to end a question with a question mark (p. 449).

■ Move the verb or a part of it to the beginning of the question. The verb may be a form of *be:*

The rate <u>is</u> high.	<u>Is</u> the rate high?
We <u>are</u> going now.	<u>Are</u> we going now?

Or the verb may consist of a helping verb and a main verb. Then move the helping verb—or the first helping verb if there's more than one—to the front of the question:

Rates <u>can</u> rise.   <u>Can</u> rates rise?
Rates <u>have</u> been rising.   <u>Have</u> rates been rising?

Questions formed this way can be answered *yes* or *no*.

- If the verb consists of only one word and is not a form of *be*, start the question with a form of *do* and use the plain form of the verb. (These questions can also be answered *yes* or *no*.)

Interest rates <u>rose</u>.   <u>Did</u> interest rates <u>rise</u>?

- Add a question word—*how, what, who, when, where, which, why*—to the beginning of a yes-or-no question. Such a question requires an explanatory answer.

Did rates rise today?   <u>Why</u> did rates rise today?
Is the rate high?   <u>Why</u> is the rate high?
Can rates rise?   <u>How</u> can rates rise?

gr
12e

- Add *who, what,* or *which* to the beginning of a question as the subject. Then the subject-verb order remains the same as in a statement.

Something is the answer.   <u>What</u> is the answer?
Someone can answer.   <u>Who</u> can answer?

2 ▪ Forming commands

We construct commands very simply: we merely delete the subject of the sentence, *you:*

Think of options.   Eat your spinach.
Watch the news.   Leave me alone.

3 ▪ Writing passive sentences

When the subject of a sentence performs the action of the verb, the verb is in the **active voice:**

                active
subject   verb   object
<u>Kyong</u> <u>wrote</u> the <u>paper</u>.

We can change the form of the verb and make the object into the subject. The verb in this new sentence is in the **passive voice** because the subject *receives* the action:

subject   passive verb
The <u>paper</u> <u>was written</u> by Kyong.

Only transitive verbs (verbs that take objects) can be expressed in the passive voice. The passive verb consists of a form of *be* plus the past participle of the main verb (*paper was written, absences were excused*). The actual actor (the person performing the action of the verb) may be expressed in a prepositional phrase (as in the earlier example: *by Kyong*) or may be omitted entirely if it is unknown or unimportant: *The house was flooded.*

(For more on formation of the passive voice, see Chapter 14, pp. 314–16. Also see p. 316 on overuse of the passive voice.)

4 ■ Writing sentences with postponed subjects

The subject follows the predicate in two sentence patterns that are not questions, commands, or passive sentences. In one pattern the normal word order is reversed for emphasis:

Henry comes here. [Normal order.]
Here comes Henry. [Reversed order.]

This pattern occurs most often when the normal order is subject–intransitive verb–adverb. Then the adverb moves to the front of the sentence while subject and predicate reverse order.

A second kind of sentence with a postponed subject begins with either *it* or *there*, as in the following:

verb   subject
There will be eighteen people attending the meeting.

verb   subject
It was surprising that Marinetti was nominated.

gr
12e

The words *there* and *it* in such sentences are **expletives.** Their only function is to postpone the sentence subject. Expletive sentences do have their uses (see p. 570), but they can be unemphatic because they add words and delay the sentence subject. Usually, the normal subject-predicate order is more effective: *Eighteen people will attend the meeting. Marinetti's nomination was surprising.*

CULTURE LANGUAGE ❧ When you use an expletive construction, be careful to include *there* or *it*. Only commands and some questions can begin with verbs (see pp. 269–70).

Faulty No one predicted the nomination. Were no polls showing Marinetti ahead.

Revised No one predicted the nomination. There were no polls showing Marinetti ahead.

EXERCISE 18
Forming questions and commands

Form a question and a command from the following noun and verb pairs.

Example:
wood, split
Did you <u>split</u> all this <u>wood</u>?
<u>Split</u> the <u>wood</u> for our fire.

1. water, boil
2. music, stop
3. table, set
4. dice, roll
5. telephone, use

EXERCISE 19
Rewriting passives and expletives
Rewrite each passive sentence below as active, and rewrite each expletive construction to restore normal subject-predicate order. (For additional exercises with the passive voice and with expletives, see pp. 316, 567–68, and 571.)

Example:
All the trees in the park were planted by the city.
<u>The city planted</u> all the trees in the park.

1. The screenplay for *Monster's Ball* was cowritten by Milo Addica and Will Rokos.
2. The film was directed by Marc Foster.
3. There was only one performance in the movie that received an Academy Award.
4. It was Halle Berry who won the award for best actress.
5. Berry was congratulated by the press for being the first African American to win the award.

gr
12f

12f Classifying sentences

We describe and classify sentences in two different ways: by function (statement, question, command, exclamation, and so on) or by structure. Four basic sentence structures are possible: simple, compound, complex, and compound-complex. Each structure gives different emphasis to the sentence's main idea or ideas and to any supporting information.

http://www.ablongman.com/littlebrown
For added help and practice with sentence classification, click on
➤ Sentences
　➤ Exercises ➤ Exer. 8
　➤ Web links ➤ Sentence grammar

1 ■ Writing simple sentences

A **simple sentence** consists of a single main clause and no subordinate clause:

┌──────── main clause ────────┐
Last summer was unusually hot.

┌─────────────── main clause ───────────────────┐
The summer made many farmers leave the area for good or reduced
────────────────────
them to bare existence.

2 ■ Writing compound sentences

A **compound sentence** consists of two or more main clauses and no subordinate clause. The clauses may be joined by a coordinating conjunction and a comma, by a semicolon alone, or by a conjunctive adverb and a semicolon.

┌── main clause ──┐   ┌──── main clause ────┐
Last July was hot, but August was even hotter.

┌────── main clause ──────┐ ┌────── main clause ──────┐
The hot sun scorched the earth; the lack of rain killed many crops.

3 ■ Writing complex sentences

A **complex sentence** contains one main clause and one or more subordinate clauses:

┌── main clause ──┐ ┌────── subordinate clause ──────┐
Rain finally came, although many had left the area by then.

┌─────────────── main clause ───────────────┐ ┌─ subordinate clause ─┐
Those who remained were able to start anew because the govern-
       subordinate clause
ment came to their aid.

Notice that length does not determine whether a sentence is complex or simple; both kinds can be short or long.

4 ■ Writing compound-complex sentences

A **compound-complex sentence** has the characteristics of both the compound sentence (two or more main clauses) and the complex sentence (at least one subordinate clause):

┌────── subordinate clause ──────┐┌────── main clause ──────┐
Even though government aid finally came, many people had already
──────────────────────   ┌────── main clause ──────┐
been reduced to poverty, and others had been forced to move.

gr
12f

EXERCISE 20
Identifying sentence structures
Mark the main clauses and subordinate clauses in the following sentences. Identify each sentence as simple, compound, complex, or compound-complex.

Example:

┌────────────── main clause ──────────────┐ ┌── subordinate clause ──┐
The police began patrolling more often when crime in the neigh-

borhood increased. [Complex sentence.]

1. Joseph Pulitzer endowed the Pulitzer Prizes.
2. Pulitzer, incidentally, was the publisher of the New York news-paper *The World*.
3. Although the first prizes were for journalism and letters only, Pulitzers are now awarded in music and other areas.
4. For example, Berke Breathed won for his *Bloom County* comic strip, and Roger Reynolds won for his musical composition *Whispers Out of Time*.
5. Although only one prize is usually awarded in each category, in 1989 Taylor Branch's *Parting the Waters* won a history prize, and it shared the honor with James M. McPherson's *Battle Cry of Freedom*.

EXERCISE 21
Sentence combining: Sentence structures

Combine each set of simple sentences below to produce the kind of sentence specified in parentheses. You will have to add, delete, change, and rearrange words.

Example:

The traffic passed the house. It never stopped. (*Complex.*)
The traffic that passed the house never stopped.

1. Recycling takes time. It reduces garbage in landfills. (*Compound.*)
2. People begin to recycle. They generate much less trash. (*Complex.*)
3. White tissues and paper towels biodegrade more easily than dyed ones. People still buy dyed papers. (*Complex.*)
4. The cans are aluminum. They bring recyclers good money. (*Simple.*)
5. Environmentalists have hope. Perhaps more communities will recycle newspaper and glass. Many citizens refuse to participate. (*Compound-complex.*)

gr
12f

CHAPTER 13

Case of Nouns and Pronouns

Case is the form of a noun or pronoun that shows the reader how it functions in a sentence—that is, whether it functions as a subject, as an object, or in some other way. As shown in the box on the next page, only *I, we, he, she, they,* and *who* change form for each case. Thus these pronouns are the focus of this chapter.

The **subjective case** generally indicates that the word is a subject or a subject complement. (See pp. 239 and 245.)

> subject
> She and Novick discussed the proposal.

> subject
> The proposal ignores many who need help.

> subject complement
> The disgruntled planners were she and Novick.

The **objective case** generally indicates that the word is the object of a verb or preposition. (See pp. 244–46 and 250.)

> object of verb
> The proposal disappointed her and Novick.

> object   object
> of verb   of verb
> A colleague whom they respected let them down.

> object of
> preposition
> Their opinion of him suffered.

The **possessive case** generally indicates ownership or source:

> Her counterproposal is in preparation.
> Theirs is the more defensible position.
> The problem is not his.

http://www.ablongman.com/littlebrown

For added help and practice with noun and pronoun case, click on
➤ **Sentences**
  ➤ **Video tutorials** ➤ **Understanding pronouns**
  ➤ **Exercises** ➤ **Exers. 9–11**
  ➤ **Web links** ➤ **Case of nouns and pronouns**

Case forms of nouns and pronouns

	Subjective	Objective	Possessive
Nouns	boy	boy	boy's
	Jessie	Jessie	Jessie's

Personal pronouns
Singular

1st person	I	me	my, mine
2nd person	you	you	your, yours
3rd person	he	him	his
	she	her	her, hers
	it	it	its

Plural

1st person	we	us	our, ours
2nd person	you	you	your, yours
3rd person	they	them	their, theirs

Relative and interrogative pronouns

	who	whom	whose
	whoever	whomever	—
	which, that, what	which, that, what	—

Indefinite pronouns

	everybody	everybody	everybody's

ca
13a

Do not use an apostrophe to form the possessive of personal pronouns: *yours* (not *your's*); *theirs* (not *their's*). (See p. 409. See also p. 488 for the possessive forms of nouns, which do use apostrophes.)

Note Some grammar and style checkers can't spot any problems with pronoun case. Others do flag mistakes, but they also miss a lot. For instance, one checker spotted the error in *We asked whom would come* (should be *who would come*), but it overlooked *We dreaded them coming* (should be *their coming*). To be sure you catch possible errors in case, review your sentences on your own, deciding for yourself which are correct.

LANGUAGE In standard American English, *-self* pronouns do not change form to show function. Their only forms are *myself, yourself, himself, herself, itself, ourselves, yourselves, themselves*. Avoid nonstandard forms such as *hisself, ourself,* and *theirselves*.

13a   Use the subjective case for compound subjects and for subject complements.

In compound subjects use the same pronoun form you would use if the pronoun stood alone as a subject:

subject
She and Novick will persist.

subject
The others may lend their support when she and Novick get a hearing.

If you are in doubt about the correct form, try the test in the box below.

After a linking verb, such as a form of *be*, a pronoun renaming the subject (a subject complement) should be in the subjective case:

subject complement
The ones who care most are she and Novick.

subject
complement
It was they whom the mayor appointed.

If this construction sounds stilted to you, use the more natural order: *She and Novick are the ones who care most. The mayor appointed them.*

A test for case forms in compound constructions

1. **Identify a compound construction** (one connected by *and, but, or, nor*).

   [He, Him] and [I, me] won the prize.
   The prize went to [he, him] and [I, me].

2. **Write a separate sentence for each part of the compound.**

   [He, Him] won the prize. [I, Me] won the prize.
   The prize went to [he, him]. The prize went to [I, me].

3. **Choose the pronouns that sound correct.**

   He won the prize. I won the prize. [Subjective.]
   The prize went to him. The prize went to me. [Objective.]

4. **Put the separate sentences back together.**

   He and I won the prize.
   The prize went to him and me.

ca
13b

13b   Use the objective case for compound objects.

In compound objects use the same pronoun form you would use if the pronoun stood alone as an object:

direct object
The mayor nominated Zhu and him.

---

http://www.ablongman.com/littlebrown

For added help and practice with subjective and objective case, click on

➤ Sentences ➤ Exercises ➤ Exers. **9 and 10**

indirect object
The mayor gave <u>Zhu and him</u> awards.

object of preposition
Credit goes equally to <u>them and the mayor</u>.

If you are in doubt about the correct form, try the test in the box on the previous page.

EXERCISE 1
Choosing between subjective and objective pronouns

From the pairs in brackets, select the appropriate subjective or objective pronoun(s) for each of the following sentences.

Example:

"Between you and [I, me]," the seller said, "this deal is a steal."
"Between you and <u>me</u>," the seller said, "this deal is a steal."

1. Lisa and [I, me] were competing for places on the relay team.
2. The fastest runners at our school were [she, her] and [I, me], so [we, us] expected to make the team.
3. [She, Her] and [I, me] were friends but also intense rivals.
4. The time trials went badly, excluding both [she, her] and [I, me] from the team.
5. Next season we are determined to earn at least one place between [she, her] and [I, me].

13c   **Use the appropriate case when the plural pronoun *we* or *us* occurs with a noun.**

Whether to use *we* or *us* with a noun depends on the use of the noun:

object of preposition
Freezing weather is welcomed by <u>us</u> skaters.

subject
<u>We</u> skaters welcome freezing weather.

13d   **In appositives the case of a pronoun depends on the function of the word described or identified.**

object of verb ⟶ appositive identifies object
The class elected two <u>representatives</u>, DeShawn and <u>me</u>.

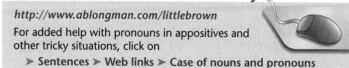

http://www.ablongman.com/littlebrown

For added help with pronouns in appositives and other tricky situations, click on

➤ Sentences ➤ Web links ➤ Case of nouns and pronouns

subject   appositive
identifies subject

Two representatives, DeShawn and I, were elected.

If you are in doubt about case in an appositive, try the sentence without the word the appositive identifies: *The class elected De-Shawn and me; DeShawn and I were elected.*

EXERCISE 2
Choosing between subjective and objective pronouns

From the pairs in brackets, select the appropriate subjective or objective pronoun for each of the following sentences.

Example:
Convincing [we, us] veterans to vote yes will be difficult.
Convincing us veterans to vote yes will be difficult.

1. Obtaining enough protein is important to [we, us] vegetarians.
2. Instead of obtaining protein from meat, [we, us] vegetarians get our protein from other sources.
3. Jeff claims to know only two vegetarians, Helena and [he, him], who avoid all animal products, including milk.
4. Some of [we, us] vegetarians eat fish, which is a good source of protein.
5. [We, Us] vegetarians in my family, my parents and [I, me], drink milk and eat fish.

ca
13f

13e The case of a pronoun after *than* or *as* in a comparison depends on the meaning.

When a pronoun follows *than* or *as* in a comparison, the case of the pronoun indicates what words may have been omitted. When the pronoun is subjective, it must serve as the subject of an omitted verb:

subject
Some critics like Glass more than he [does].

When the pronoun is objective, it must serve as the object of an omitted verb:

object
Some critics like Glass more than [they like] him.

13f Use the objective case for pronouns that are subjects or objects of infinitives.

subject of
infinitive
The school asked him to speak.

object of
infinitive
Students chose to invite him.

13g The case of the pronoun *who* depends on its function in its clause.

To choose between *who* and *whom*, *whoever* and *whomever*, you need to figure out whether the word is a subject or an object. Use *who* where you would use *he* or *she*—all ending in vowels. Use *whom* where you would use *him* or *her*—all ending in consonants.

1 ■ At the beginning of questions use *who* for a subject and *whom* for an object.

subject ⟶
Who wrote the policy?

object ⟵
Whom does it affect?

To help find the correct case of *who* in a question, try the test in the following box:

A test for *who* versus *whom* in questions

1. **Pose the question.**

   [Who, Whom] makes that decision?
   [Who, Whom] does one ask?

2. **Answer the question, using a personal pronoun.** Choose the pronoun that sounds correct, and note its case.

   [She, Her] makes that decision. She makes that decision. [Subjective.]
   One asks [she, her]. One asks her. [Objective.]

3. **Use the same case (*who* or *whom*) in the question.**

   Who makes that decision? [Subjective.]
   Whom does one ask? [Objective.]

Note In speech the subjective case *who* is commonly used whenever it is the first word of a question, regardless of whether it is a subject or an object. But formal writing requires a distinction between the forms:

Spoken	Who should we credit?
Written	object ⟵ Whom should we credit?

http://www.ablongman.com/littlebrown

For added help and practice with *who* versus *whom*, click on

➤ Sentences
  ➤ Exercises ➤ Exer. 11
    ➤ Web links ➤ Case of nouns and pronouns

2 ■ In subordinate clauses use *who* and *whoever* for all subjects, *whom* and *whomever* for all objects.

The case of a pronoun in a subordinate clause depends on its function in the clause, regardless of whether the clause itself functions as a subject, an object, or a modifier:

subject ⟶
Credit <u>whoever</u> wrote the policy.

object ⟵
Research should reveal <u>whom</u> to credit.

If you have trouble determining which form to choose, try the test in the following box:

A test for *who* versus *whom* in subordinate clauses

1. **Locate the subordinate clause.**

   Few people know [who, whom] they should ask.
   They are unsure [who, whom] makes the decision.

2. **Rewrite the subordinate clause as a separate sentence, substituting a personal pronoun for *who, whom*.** Choose the pronoun that sounds correct, and note its case.

   They should ask [she, her]. They should ask <u>her</u>. [Objective.]
   [She, Her] makes the decision. <u>She</u> makes the decision. [Subjective.]

3. Use the same case (*who* or *whom*) in the subordinate clause.

   Few people know <u>whom</u> they should ask. [Objective.]
   They are unsure <u>who</u> makes the decision. [Subjective.]

---

ca
13g

Note Don't let expressions such as *I think* and *she says* confuse you when they come between the subject *who* and its verb:

subject ⟶
He is the one <u>who</u> the polls say will win.

To choose between *who* and *whom* in such constructions, delete the interrupting phrase: *He is the one <u>who</u> will win.*

EXERCISE 3
Choosing between *who* and *whom*
From the pairs in brackets, select the appropriate form of the pronoun in each of the following sentences.

Example:
My mother asked me [who, whom] I was going out with.
My mother asked me <u>whom</u> I was going out with.

1. The judges awarded first prize to Inez, [who, whom] they believed gave the best performance.
2. Inez beat the other contestants [who, whom] competed against her.

3. She is a consummate performer, singing to [whoever, whomever] would listen.
4. [Who, Whom] in the school has not heard Inez sing?
5. [Who, Whom] has she not performed for?

EXERCISE 4
Sentence combining: *Who* versus *whom*
Combine each pair of sentences below into one sentence that contains a clause beginning with *who* or *whom*. Be sure to use the appropriate case form. You will have to add, delete, and rearrange words. Each item may have more than one possible answer.

Example:

David is the candidate. We think David deserves to win.
David is the candidate <u>who</u> we think deserves to win.

1. Some children have undetected hearing problems. These children may do poorly in school.
2. They may not hear important instructions and information from teachers. Teachers may speak softly.
3. Classmates may not be audible. The teacher calls on those classmates.
4. Some hearing-impaired children may work harder to overcome their disability. These children get a lot of encouragement at home.
5. Some hearing-impaired children may take refuge in fantasy friends. They can rely on these friends not to criticize or laugh.

ca
13h

13h Ordinarily, use a possessive pronoun or noun immediately before a gerund.

A **gerund** is the *-ing* form of a verb (*running, sleeping*) used as a noun (p. 254). Like nouns, gerunds are commonly preceded by possessive nouns and pronouns: *our vote* (noun), *our voting* (gerund).

The coach disapproved of their lifting weights.

The coach's disapproving was a surprise.

A noun or pronoun before an *-ing* verb form is not always possessive. Sometimes the *-ing* form will be a present participle modifying the preceding word:

Everyone had noticed him weightlifting. [Emphasis on *him*.]
　　　　　　 objective　participle
　　　　　　 pronoun

Everyone had noticed his weightlifting. [Emphasis on the activity.]
　　　　　　 possessive　gerund
　　　　　　 pronoun

Note that a gerund usually is not preceded by the possessive when the possessive would create an awkward construction:

Awkward	A rumor spread about everybody's on the team wanting to quit.
Less awkward	A rumor spread about everybody on the team wanting to quit.
Better	A rumor spread that everybody on the team wanted to quit.

EXERCISE 5
Revising: Case

Revise all inappropriate case forms in the following paragraph, and explain the function of each case form.

Written four thousand years ago, *The Epic of Gilgamesh* tells of the friendship of Gilgamesh and Enkidu. Gilgamesh was a bored king who his people thought was too harsh. Then he met Enkidu, a wild man whom had lived with the animals in the mountains. Immediately, him and Gilgamesh wrestled to see whom was more powerful. After hours of struggle, Enkidu admitted that Gilgamesh was stronger than him. Now the friends needed adventures worthy of the two strongest men on earth. Gilgamesh said, "Between you and I, mighty deeds will be accomplished, and our fame will be everlasting." Among their acts, Enkidu and him defeated a giant bull, Humbaba, and cut down the bull's cedar forests. Them bringing back cedar logs to Gilgamesh's treeless land won great praise from the people. When Enkidu died, Gilgamesh mourned his death, realizing that no one had been a better friend than him. When Gilgamesh himself died many years later, his people raised a monument praising Enkidu and he for their friendship and their mighty deeds of courage.

ca

13h

Note See page 346 for an exercise involving case along with other aspects of grammar.

CHAPTER 14

Verbs

The verb is the most complicated part of speech in English, changing form to express a wide range of information.

VERB FORMS

All verbs except *be* have five basic forms. The first three are the verb's **principal parts.**

- The **plain form** is the dictionary form of the verb. When the subject is a plural noun or the pronoun *I, we, you,* or *they,* the plain form indicates action that occurs in the present, occurs habitually, or is generally true.

  A few artists <u>live</u> in town today.
  They <u>hold</u> classes downtown.

- The **past-tense form** indicates that the action of the verb occurred before now. It usually adds *-d* or *-ed* to the plain form, although some irregular verbs form it in other ways (see p. 286).

  Many artists <u>lived</u> in town before this year.
  They <u>held</u> classes downtown. [Irregular verb.]

- The **past participle** is usually the same as the past-tense form, except in most irregular verbs. It combines with forms of *have* or *be* (*has <u>climbed</u>, was <u>created</u>*), or by itself it modifies nouns and pronouns (*the <u>sliced</u> apples*).

  Artists have <u>lived</u> in town for decades.
  They have <u>held</u> classes downtown. [Irregular verb.]

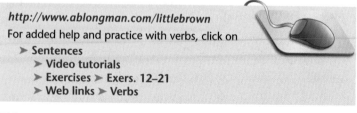

http://www.ablongman.com/littlebrown
For added help and practice with verbs, click on
➤ Sentences
  ➤ Video tutorials
  ➤ Exercises ➤ Exers. 12–21
  ➤ Web links ➤ Verbs

- The **present participle** adds *-ing* to the verb's plain form. It combines with forms of *be* (*is buying*), modifies nouns and pronouns (*the boiling water*), or functions as a noun (*Running exhausts me*).

A few artists are living in town today.
They are holding classes downtown.

- The **-s form** ends in *-s* or *-es*. When the subject is a singular noun, a pronoun such as *everyone*, or the personal pronoun *he, she,* or *it,* the *-s* form indicates action that occurs in the present, occurs habitually, or is generally true.

The artist lives in town today.
She holds classes downtown.

The verb *be* has eight forms rather than the five forms of most other verbs:

Plain form	be		
Present participle	being		
Past participle	been		
	I	*he, she, it*	*we, you, they*
Present tense	am	is	are
Past tense	was	was	were

Terms used to describe verbs

Tense
The time of the verb's action—for instance, present (*kick*), past (*kicked*), future (*will kick*). (See p. 303.)

Mood
The attitude of the verb's speaker or writer—the difference, for example, in *I kick the ball, Kick the ball,* and *I suggest that you kick the ball.* (See p. 312.)

Voice
The distinction between the **active,** in which the subject performs the verb's action (*I kick the ball*), and the **passive,** in which the subject is acted upon (*The ball is kicked by me*). (See p. 314.)

Person
The verb form that reflects whether the subject is speaking (*I/we kick the ball*), spoken to (*You kick the ball*), or spoken about (*She kicks the ball*). (See p. 319.)

Number
The verb form that reflects whether the subject is singular (*The girl kicks the ball*) or plural (*Girls kick the ball*). (See p. 319.)

CULTURE LANGUAGE If standard American English is not your native language or dialect, you may have difficulty with verbs' *-s* forms (including those for *be: is, was*) or with the forms that indicate time (such as the past-tense form). See pages 291–92 and 305–06, respectively, for more on these forms.

Helping verbs

Helping verbs, also called **auxiliary verbs,** combine with some verb forms to indicate time and other kinds of meaning, as in *can run, was sleeping, had been eaten.* These combinations are **verb phrases.** Since the plain form, present participle, or past participle in any verb phrase always carries the principal meaning, it is sometimes called the **main verb.**

Verb phrase
Helping   *Main*
Artists <u>can</u>   <u>train</u> others to draw.
The techniques <u>have</u>   <u>changed</u> little.

These are the most common helping verbs:

be able to	had better	must	used to
be supposed to	have to	ought to	will
can	may	shall	would
could	might	should	

Forms of *be:* be, am, is, are, was, were, been, being
Forms of *have:* have, has, had, having
Forms of *do:* do, does, did

CULTURE LANGUAGE The helping verbs of standard American English may be problematic if you are used to speaking another language or dialect. See pages 292–97 for more on helping verbs.

14a   Use the correct forms of regular and irregular verbs.

Most verbs are **regular**; that is, they form their past tense and past participle by adding *-d* or *-ed* to the plain form.

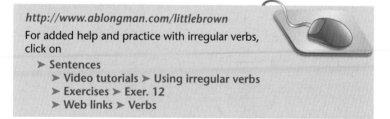

http://www.ablongman.com/littlebrown
For added help and practice with irregular verbs, click on
➤ **Sentences**
  ➤ **Video tutorials** ➤ **Using irregular verbs**
  ➤ **Exercises** ➤ **Exer. 12**
  ➤ **Web links** ➤ **Verbs**

Plain form	Past tense	Past participle
live	lived	lived
act	acted	acted

Since the past tense and past participle are created in the same way, the forms of regular verbs do not often cause problems in speech and writing (but see p. 291).

About two hundred English verbs are **irregular;** that is, they form their past tense and past participle in some irregular way.

Plain form	Past tense	Past participle
begin	began	begun
break	broke	broken
sleep	slept	slept

You can see the difference between a regular and an irregular verb in these examples:

Plain form	Today the birds <u>twitter</u>.
	Today the birds <u>sing</u>.
Past tense	Yesterday the birds <u>twittered</u>.
	Yesterday the birds <u>sang</u>.
Past participle	In the past the birds have <u>twittered</u>.
	In the past the birds have <u>sung</u>.

vb

14a

Check a dictionary under the plain form if you have any doubt about a verb's principal parts. If no other forms are listed, the verb is regular: both the past tense and the past participle add -*d* or -*ed* to the plain form. If the verb is irregular, the dictionary will list the plain form, the past tense, and the past participle in that order (*go, went, gone*). If the dictionary gives only two forms (as in *think, thought*), then the past tense and the past participle are the same.

CULTURE LANGUAGE ◆ Some English dialects use distinctive verb forms that differ from those of standard American English: for instance, *drug* for *dragged, growed* for *grew, come* for *came,* or *went* for *gone.* In situations requiring standard American English, use the forms in the list below or in a dictionary.

Principal parts of common irregular verbs

Plain form	Past tense	Past participle
arise	arose	arisen
become	became	become
begin	began	begun
bid	bid	bid
bite	bit	bitten, bit

(continued)

Principal parts of common irregular verbs
(continued)

Plain form	Past tense	Past participle
blow	blew	blown
break	broke	broken
bring	brought	brought
burst	burst	burst
buy	bought	bought
catch	caught	caught
choose	chose	chosen
come	came	come
cut	cut	cut
dive	dived, dove	dived
do	did	done
draw	drew	drawn
dream	dreamed, dreamt	dreamed, dreamt
drink	drank	drunk
drive	drove	driven
eat	ate	eaten
fall	fell	fallen
find	found	found
flee	fled	fled
fly	flew	flown
forget	forgot	forgotten, forgot
freeze	froze	frozen
get	got	got, gotten
give	gave	given
go	went	gone
grow	grew	grown
hang (suspend)	hung	hung
hang (execute)	hanged	hanged
hear	heard	heard
hide	hid	hidden
hold	held	held
keep	kept	kept
know	knew	known
lay	laid	laid
lead	led	led
leave	left	left
lend	lent	lent
let	let	let
lie	lay	lain
lose	lost	lost
pay	paid	paid
prove	proved	proved, proven
ride	rode	ridden
ring	rang	rung
rise	rose	risen

Plain form	Past tense	Past participle
run	ran	run
say	said	said
see	saw	seen
set	set	set
shake	shook	shaken
shrink	shrank, shrunk	shrunk, shrunken
sing	sang, sung	sung
sink	sank, sunk	sunk
sit	sat	sat
slide	slid	slid
speak	spoke	spoken
spring	sprang, sprung	sprung
stand	stood	stood
steal	stole	stolen
swim	swam	swum
swing	swung	swung
take	took	taken
tear	tore	torn
throw	threw	thrown
wear	wore	worn
write	wrote	written

vb

14a

Note A grammar and style checker may flag incorrect forms of irregular verbs, but it may also fail to do so. For example, a checker flagged *The runner* <u>*stealed*</u> *second base* (*stole* is correct) but not *The runner had* <u>*steal*</u> *second base* (*stolen* is correct). When in doubt about the forms of irregular verbs, refer to the preceding list, consult a dictionary, or consult the links at this book's Web site (see the box on p. 286).

EXERCISE 1
Using irregular verbs

For each irregular verb in brackets, give either the past tense or the past participle, as appropriate, and identify the form you used.

> *Example:*
> Though we had [hide] the cash box, it was [steal].
> Though we had <u>hidden</u> the cash box, it was <u>stolen</u>. [Two past participles.]

1. The world population has [grow] by two-thirds of a billion people in less than a decade.
2. Recently it [break] the 6 billion mark.
3. Experts have [draw] pictures of a crowded future.
4. They predict that the world population may have [slide] up to as much as 10 billion by the year 2050.
5. Though the food supply [rise] in the last decade, the share to each person [fall].

14b   Distinguish between *sit* and *set, lie* and *lay,* and *rise* and *raise*.

The forms of *sit* and *set, lie* and *lay,* and *rise* and *raise* are easy to confuse:

Plain form	Past tense	Past participle
sit	sat	sat
set	set	set
lie	lay	lain
lay	laid	laid
rise	rose	risen
raise	raised	raised

In each of these confusing pairs, one verb is **intransitive** (it does not take an object) and one is **transitive** (it does take an object). (See pp. 243–44 for more on this distinction.)

Intransitive

The patients lie in their beds. [*Lie* means "recline" and takes no object.]

Visitors sit with them. [*Sit* means "be seated" or "be located" and takes no object.]

Patients' temperatures rise. [*Rise* means "increase" or "get up" and takes no object.]

Transitive

Orderlies lay the dinner trays on tables. [*Lay* means "place" and takes an object, here *trays.*]

Orderlies set the trays down. [*Set* means "place" and takes an object, here *trays.*]

Nursing aides raise the shades. [*Raise* means "lift" or "bring up" and takes an object, here *shades.*]

EXERCISE 2
Distinguishing *sit/set, lie/lay, rise/raise*
Choose the correct verb from the pair given in brackets. Then supply the past tense or past participle, as appropriate.

> *Example:*
> After I washed all the windows, I [lie, lay] down the squeegee and then I [sit, set] the table.
> After I washed all the windows, I laid down the squeegee and then I set the table.

1. Yesterday afternoon the child [lie, lay] down for a nap.
2. The child has been [rise, raise] by her grandparents.
3. Most days her grandfather has [sit, set] with her, reading her stories.

4. She has [rise, raise] at dawn most mornings.
5. Her toys were [lie, lay] out on the floor.

14c Use the -s and -ed forms of the verb when they are required. ⟨CULTURE LANGUAGE⟩

Speakers of some English dialects and nonnative speakers of English sometimes omit the -s and -ed verb endings when they are required in standard American English.

Note A grammar and style checker will flag many omitted -s and -ed endings from verbs, such as in *he ask* and *was ask*. But it will miss many omissions, too. You'll need to proofread your papers carefully on your own to catch missing endings.

Required -s ending

Use the -s form of a verb when *both* of these situations hold:

- The subject is a singular noun (*boy*), an indefinite pronoun (*everyone*), or *he, she,* or *it.* (These subjects are **third person,** used when someone or something is being spoken about.)
- The verb's action occurs in the present.

The letter <u>asks</u> [not <u>ask</u>] for a quick response.
Delay <u>costs</u> [not <u>cost</u>] money.

Be especially careful with the -s forms of *be* (*is*), *have* (*has*), and *do* (*does, doesn't*). These forms should always be used to indicate present time with third-person singular subjects.

The company <u>is</u> [not <u>be</u>] late in responding.
It <u>has</u> [not <u>have</u>] problems.
It <u>doesn't</u> [not <u>don't</u>] have the needed data.
The contract <u>does</u> [not <u>do</u>] depend on the response.

In addition, *be* has an -s form in the past tense with *I* and with third-person singular subjects:

The company <u>was</u> [not <u>were</u>] in trouble before.

I, you, and plural subjects do *not* take the -s form of verbs:

I <u>am</u> [not <u>is</u>] a student.
You <u>are</u> [not <u>is</u>] also a student.
They <u>are</u> [not <u>is</u>] students, too.

vb
14c

http://www.ablongman.com/littlebrown
For added practice with -s and -ed verb endings, click on
➤ Sentences ➤ Exercises ➤ Exer. 13

Required -ed or -d ending

The -ed or -d verb form is required in *any* of these situations:

- The verb's action occurred in the past:

  Yesterday the company <u>asked</u> [not <u>ask</u>] for more time.

- The verb form functions as a modifier:

  The data <u>concerned</u> [not <u>concern</u>] should be retrievable.

- The verb form combines with a form of *be* or *have*:

  The company is <u>supposed</u> [not <u>suppose</u>] to be the best.
  It has <u>developed</u> [not <u>develop</u>] an excellent reputation.

Watch especially for a needed -ed or d ending when it isn't pronounced clearly in speech, as in *asked, discussed, mixed, supposed, walked,* and *used.*

vb
14d

EXERCISE 3
Using -s and -ed verb endings   CULTURE LANGUAGE

Supply the correct form of each verb in brackets. Be careful to include -s and -ed (or -d) endings where they are needed for standard English.

A teacher sometimes [<u>ask</u>] too much of a student. In high school I was once [<u>punish</u>] for being sick. I had [<u>miss</u>] some school, and I [<u>realize</u>] that I would fail a test unless I had a chance to make up the classwork. I [<u>discuss</u>] the problem with the teacher, but he said I was [<u>suppose</u>] to make up the work while I was sick. At that I [<u>walk</u>] out of the class. I [<u>receive</u>] a failing grade then, but it did not change my attitude. Today I still balk when a teacher [<u>make</u>] unreasonable demands or [<u>expect</u>] miracles.

14d   Use helping verbs with main verbs appropriately.   CULTURE LANGUAGE

Helping verbs combine with main verbs to form verb phrases (see p. 286).

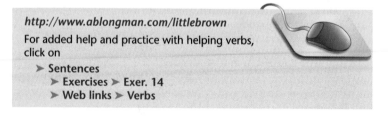

http://www.ablongman.com/littlebrown
For added help and practice with helping verbs, click on
➤ **Sentences**
  ➤ **Exercises** ➤ **Exer. 14**
  ➤ **Web links** ➤ **Verbs**

Note Grammar and style checkers often spot omitted helping verbs and incorrect main verbs with helping verbs, but sometimes they do not. A checker flagged *Many been fortunate* and *She working* but overlooked other examples on the following pages, such as *The conference will be occurred.* Careful proofreading is the only insurance against missing helping verbs and incorrect main verbs.

1 ■ Use helping verbs when they are required.

Standard American English requires helping verbs in certain situations:

■ The main verb ends in *-ing:*

Researchers <u>are</u> conducting fieldwork all over the world. [Not Researchers <u>conducting</u>. . . .]

■ The main verb is *been* or *be:*

Many <u>have</u> been fortunate in their discoveries. [Not <u>Many been</u>. . . .]
Some <u>could</u> be real-life Indiana Joneses. [Not <u>Some be</u>. . . .]

■ The main verb is a past participle, such as *talked, begun,* or *thrown.*

Their discoveries <u>were</u> covered in newspapers and magazines. [Not Their discoveries <u>covered</u>. . . .]

The researchers <u>have</u> done TV interviews. [Not <u>The researchers done</u>. . . .]

In every example above, omitting the helping verb would create an incomplete sentence, or **sentence fragment** (see Chapter 17). In a complete sentence, some part of the verb (helping or main) must be capable of changing form to show changes in time: *I <u>run</u>, I <u>ran;</u> you <u>are</u> running, you <u>were</u> running* (see p. 349). But a present participle (*conducting*), an irregular past participle (*been*), and the infinitive *be* cannot change form in this way. They need helping verbs to work as sentence verbs.

2 ■ Combine helping verbs and main verbs appropriately for your meaning.

Helping verbs and main verbs combine into verb phrases in specific ways.

Note The main verb in a verb phrase (the one carrying the main meaning) does not change to show a change in subject or time: *she has <u>sung</u>, you had <u>sung</u>.* Only the helping verb may change, as in these examples.

vb
14d

Form of *be* + present participle

The **progressive tenses** indicate action in progress (see p. 305). Create them with *be, am, is, are, was, were,* or *been* followed by the main verb's present participle:

> She is working on a new book.

Be and *been* always require additional helping verbs to form the progressive tenses:

can	might	should			have	
could	must	will	}	be working	has	} been working
may	shall	would			had	

When forming the progressive tenses, be sure to use the *-ing* form of the main verb:

> **Faulty**   Her ideas are grow more complex. She is developed a new approach to ethics.
>
> **Revised**   Her ideas are growing more complex. She is developing a new approach to ethics.

vb
14d

Form of *be* + past participle

The **passive voice** of the verb indicates that the subject *receives* the action of the verb (see p. 314). Create the passive voice with *be, am, is, are, was, were, being,* or *been* followed by the main verb's past participle:

> Her latest book was completed in four months.

Be, being, and *been* always require additional helping verbs to form the passive voice:

have			am	was	
has	}	been completed	is	were	} being completed
had			are		

will be completed

Be sure to use the main verb's past participle for the passive voice:

> **Faulty**   Her next book will be publish soon.
> **Revised**   Her next book will be published soon.

Note Use only transitive verbs to form the passive voice:

> **Faulty**   A philosophy conference will be occurred in the same week. [*Occur* is not a transitive verb.]
> **Revised**   A philosophy conference will occur in the same week.

See pages 314–16 for advice on when to use and when to avoid the passive voice.

vb

14d

Forms of *have*

Four forms of *have* serve as helping verbs: *have, has, had, having.* One of these forms plus the main verb's past participle creates one of the **perfect tenses,** those expressing action completed before another specific time or action (see p. 305):

> Some students have complained about the laboratory.
> Others had complained before.

Will and other helping verbs sometimes accompany forms of *have* in the perfect tenses:

> Several more students will have complained by the end of the week.

Forms of *do*

Do, does, and *did* have three uses as helping verbs, always with the plain form of the main verb:

- To pose a question: *How did the trial end?*
- To emphasize the main verb: *It did end eventually.*
- To negate the main verb, along with *not* or *never: The judge did not withdraw.*

Be sure to use the main verb's plain form with any form of *do:*

Faulty	The judge did remained in court.
Revised	The judge did remain in court.

Modals

The modal helping verbs include *can, could, may,* and *might,* along with several two- and three-word combinations, such as *have to* and *be able to.* (See p. 286 for a list of helping verbs.)

Modals convey various meanings, with these being most common:

- **Ability:** *can, could, be able to*

  The equipment can detect small vibrations. [Present.]
  The equipment could detect small vibrations. [Past.]
  The equipment is able to detect small vibrations. [Present. Past: was able to. Future: will be able to.]

- **Possibility:** *could, may, might, could/may/might have* + past participle

  The equipment could fail. [Present.]
  The equipment may fail. [Present or future.]
  The equipment might fail. [Present or future.]
  The equipment may have failed. [Past.]

■ **Necessity or obligation:** *must, have to, be supposed to*

The lab must purchase a backup. [Present or future.]
The lab has to purchase a backup. [Present or future. Past: had to.]
The lab will have to purchase a backup. [Future.]
The lab is supposed to purchase a backup. [Present. Past: was supposed to.]

■ **Permission:** *may, can, could*

The lab may spend the money. [Present or future.]
The lab can spend the money. [Present or future.]
The lab could spend the money. [Present or future, more tentative.]
The school then announced that the lab could spend the money. [Past.]

■ **Intention:** *will, shall, would*

The lab will spend the money. [Future.]
Shall we offer advice? [Future. Use *shall* for questions requesting opinion or consent.]
We knew we would offer advice. [Past.]

■ **Request:** *could, can, would*

Could [or can or would] you please obtain a bid? [Present or future.]

■ **Advisability:** *should, had better, ought to, should have* + past participle

You should obtain three bids. [Present or future.]
You had better obtain three bids. [Present or future.]
You ought to obtain three bids. [Present or future.]
You should have obtained three bids. [Past.]

■ **Past habit:** *would, used to*

In years past we would obtain five bids.
We used to obtain five bids.

The following conventions govern the combination of modals and main verbs shown in the examples:

■ One-word modals do not change form to show a change in subject: *I could run, she could run.* Most two- and three-word modals do change form, like other helping verbs: *I have to run, she has to run.*

■ Modals can sometimes indicate past, present, or future time, occasionally with a word change (*can* to *could,* for instance) or with a form change in a two- or three-word modal (such as *is/was able to*).

■ For present or future time, modals are used with the plain form of the main verb: *he can go, I might drive, I will be able to drive.*

For past time, some modals change spelling (especially *can* to *could*), and others add *have* before the past participle of the main verb: *might have driven.*

- Don't use *to* between a one-word modal and the main verb: *can drive,* not *can to drive.* (Most of the two- and three-word modals do include *to: ought to drive.*)
- Don't use two one-word modals together: *I will be able to drive,* not *I will can drive.*

EXERCISE 4
Using helping verbs   CULTURE LANGUAGE

Add helping verbs in the following sentences where they are needed for standard English.

> *Example:*
> The story been told for many years.
> The story has been told for many years.

1. Each year thousands of new readers been discovering Agatha Christie's mysteries.
2. The books written by a prim woman who had worked as a nurse during World War I.
3. Christie never expected that her play *The Mousetrap* be performed for decades.
4. During her life Christie always complaining about movie versions of her stories.
5. Readers of her stories been delighted to be baffled by her.

vb

14d

EXERCISE 5
Revising: Helping verbs plus main verbs   CULTURE LANGUAGE

Revise the following sentences so that helping verbs and main verbs are used correctly. Circle the number of any sentence that is already correct.

> *Example:*
> The college testing service has test as many as five hundred students at one time.
> The college testing service has tested as many as five hundred students at one time.

1. A report from the Bureau of the Census has confirm a widening gap between rich and poor.
2. As suspected, the percentage of people below the poverty level did increased over the last decade.
3. More than 17 percent of the population is make 5 percent of all the income.
4. About 1 percent of the population will keeping an average of $500,000 apiece after taxes.
5. The other 99 percent all together may retain about $300,000.

14e Use a gerund or an infinitive after a verb as appropriate.

Nonnative speakers of English sometimes stumble over using a gerund or an infinitive after a verb. A **gerund** is the *-ing* form of a verb used as a noun (*opening*). An **infinitive** is the plain form of a verb preceded by *to* (*to open*). (See pp. 254–55 for more on these forms.)

Gerunds and infinitives may follow certain verbs but not others. And sometimes the use of a gerund or infinitive with the same verb changes the meaning.

Note A grammar and style checker will spot some but not all errors in matching gerunds or infinitives with verbs. For example, a checker failed to flag *I practice to swim* and *I promise helping out.* Use the lists given here and a dictionary of English as a second language to determine whether an infinitive or a gerund is appropriate. (See p. 574 for a list of ESL dictionaries.)

vb
14e

Either gerund or infinitive

A gerund or an infinitive may follow these verbs with no significant difference in meaning:

begin	hate	love
can't bear	hesitate	prefer
can't stand	intend	start
continue	like	

The pump began working.
The pump began to work.

Meaning change with gerund or infinitive

With four verbs, a gerund has quite a different meaning from an infinitive:

forget	stop
remember	try

The engineer stopped eating. [He no longer ate.]
The engineer stopped to eat. [He stopped in order to eat.]

http://www.ablongman.com/littlebrown
For added help and practice with verbs and gerunds or infinitives, click on
➤ Sentences
  ➤ Exercises ➤ Exer. 15
  ➤ Web links ➤ Verbs

Gerund, not infinitive

Do not use an infinitive after these verbs:

admit	discuss	mind	recollect
adore	dislike	miss	resent
appreciate	enjoy	postpone	resist
avoid	escape	practice	risk
consider	finish	put off	suggest
deny	imagine	quit	tolerate
detest	keep	recall	understand

Faulty   He finished to eat lunch.
Revised   He finished eating lunch.

Infinitive, not gerund

Do not use a gerund after these verbs:

agree	decide	mean	refuse
appear	expect	offer	say
ask	have	plan	wait
assent	hope	pretend	want
beg	manage	promise	wish
claim			

Faulty   He decided checking the pump.
Revised   He decided to check the pump.

vb

14e

Noun or pronoun + infinitive

Some verbs may be followed by an infinitive alone or by a noun or pronoun and an infinitive. The presence of a noun or pronoun changes the meaning.

ask	dare	need	wish
beg	expect	promise	would like
choose	help	want	

He expected to watch.
He expected his workers to watch.

Some verbs *must* be followed by a noun or pronoun before an infinitive:

admonish	encourage	oblige	require
advise	forbid	order	teach
allow	force	permit	tell
cause	hire	persuade	train
challenge	instruct	remind	urge
command	invite	request	warn
convince			

He instructed his workers to watch.

Do not use *to* before the infinitive when it follows one of these verbs and a noun or pronoun:

feel	make ("force")
have	see
hear	watch
let	

He let his workers <u>learn</u> by observation.

EXERCISE 6
Revising: Verbs plus gerunds or infinitives 🔹 **CULTURE LANGUAGE** 🔺

Revise the following sentences so that gerunds or infinitives are used correctly with verbs. Circle the number preceding any sentence that is already correct.

> *Example:*
> A politician cannot avoid to alienate some voters.
> A politician cannot avoid <u>alienating</u> some voters.

1. A program called HELP Wanted tries to encourage citizens take action on behalf of American competitiveness.
2. Officials working on this program hope improving education for work.
3. American businesses find that their workers need learning to read.
4. In the next ten years the United States expects facing a shortage of 350,000 scientists.
5. HELP Wanted suggests creating a media campaign.

vb
14 f

14f   Use the appropriate particles with two-word verbs. 🔹 **CULTURE LANGUAGE** 🔺

Standard American English includes some verbs that consist of two words: the verb itself and a **particle,** a preposition or adverb that affects the meaning of the verb. For example:

<u>Look up</u> the answer. [Research the answer.]
<u>Look over</u> the answer. [Examine the answer.]

The meanings of these two-word verbs are often quite different from the meanings of the individual words that make them up. (There

http://www.ablongman.com/littlebrown
For added practice with verbs plus particles, click on
➤ **Sentences** ➤ **Exercises** ➤ **Exer. 16**

are some three-word verbs, too, such as *put up with* and *run out of*.) A dictionary of English as a second language will define two-word verbs and say whether the verb may be separated in a sentence, as explained below. (See p. 574 for a list of ESL dictionaries.) A grammar and style checker will recognize few if any misuses of two-word verbs. You'll need to proofread on your own to catch and correct errors.

Note Many two-word verbs are more common in speech than in more formal academic or business writing. For formal writing, consider using *research* instead of *look up*, *examine* or *inspect* instead of *look over*.

Inseparable two-word verbs

Verbs and particles that may not be separated by any other words include the following:

call on	go out with	run across	stay away
catch on	go over	run into	stay up
come across	grow up	run out of	take care of
get along	keep on	speak up	turn out
get up	look for	speak with	turn up at
give in	look into	stand up	work for
go on	play around		

Faulty	Children <u>grow</u> quickly <u>up</u>.
Revised	Children <u>grow up</u> quickly.

Separable two-word verbs

Most two-word verbs that take direct objects may be separated by the object:

Parents <u>help out</u> their children.
Parents <u>help</u> their children <u>out</u>.

If the direct object is a pronoun, the pronoun *must* separate the verb from the particle:

Faulty	Parents <u>help out</u> them.
Revised	Parents <u>help</u> them <u>out</u>.

The separable two-word verbs include the following:

bring up	give back	make up	throw out
call off	hand in	point out	try on
call up	hand out	put away	try out
drop off	help out	put back	turn down
fill out	leave out	put off	turn on
fill up	look over	take out	wrap up
give away	look up	take over	

vb

14f

EXERCISE 7
Revising: Verbs plus particles   CULTURE LANGUAGE

Identify any two- or three-word verbs in the sentences below, and indicate whether each is separable (S) or inseparable (I). Then fill the blank with the correct option for placing nouns or pronouns with verbs and particles. Consult an ESL dictionary if necessary.

Example:

Hollywood producers never seem to come up with entirely new plots, but they also never _____ to present the old ones.

a. run out of new ways
b. run new ways out of
c. Either a or b

Hollywood producers never seem to come up with (I) entirely new plots, but they also never (a) run out of new ways to present the old ones.

1. American movies treat everything from going out with someone to making up an ethnic identity, but few people _____.

a. look into their significance
b. look their significance into
c. Either a or b

2. While some viewers stay away from topical films, others _____ simply because a movie has sparked debate.

a. turn up at the theater
b. turn at the theater up
c. Either a or b

3. Some movies aroused such strong responses that theaters were obliged to _____.

a. throw out rowdy spectators
b. throw rowdy spectators out
c. Either a or b

4. Filmmakers have always been eager to _____ to the public.

a. point out their influence
b. point their influence out
c. Either a or b

5. Everyone agrees that filmmakers will _____, if only because it can fill up theaters.

a. keep on creating controversy
b. keep creating controversy on
c. Either a or b

TENSE

Tense shows the time of a verb's action. The table on the next page defines and illustrates the tense forms for a regular verb in the active voice. (See pp. 286 and 314 on regular verbs and voice.)

Note Grammar and style checkers can provide little help with incorrect verb tenses and tense sequences because correctness usually depends on meaning. Proofread carefully yourself to catch errors in tense or tense sequence.

⟨ **CULTURE ⟩ LANGUAGE** In standard American English, a verb conveys time and sequence through its form. In some other languages and English dialects, various markers besides verb form may indicate the time of a verb. For instance, in African American dialect *I be attending class on Friday* means that the speaker attends class every Friday. To a speaker of standard American English, however, the sentence may be unclear: last Friday? this Friday? every Friday? The intended meaning must be indicated by verb tense: *I attended class on Friday. I will attend class on Friday. I attend class on Friday.*

t

14g

14g Use the appropriate tense to express your meaning.

Many errors in verb tense are actually errors in verb form like those discussed earlier. Still, the present tense, the perfect tenses, and the progressive tenses can cause problems.

1 ▪ Observe the special uses of the present tense.

Most academic and business writing uses the past tense (*the rebellion occurred*), but the present tense has several distinctive uses:

Action occurring now
She understands the problem.
We define the problem differently.

Habitual or recurring action
Banks regularly undergo audits.
The audits monitor the banks' activities.

http://www.ablongman.com/littlebrown
For added help and practice with verb tense, click on
➤ Sentences
➤ Exercises ➤ Exers. 17 and 18
➤ Web links ➤ Verbs

Tenses of a regular verb (active voice)

Present Action that is occurring now, occurs habitually, or is generally true

Simple present Plain form or *-s* form

I walk.
You/we/they walk.
He/she/it walks.

Present progressive *Am, is,* or *are* plus *-ing* form

I am walking.
You/we/they are walking.
He/she/it is walking.

Past Action that occurred before now

Simple past Past-tense form (*-d* or *-ed*)

I/he/she/it walked.
You/we/they walked.

Past progressive *Was* or *were* plus *-ing* form

I/he/she/it was walking.
You/we/they were walking.

Future Action that will occur in the future

Simple future Plain form plus *will*

I/you/he/she/it/we/they will walk.

Future progressive *Will be* plus *-ing* form

I/you/he/she/it/we/they will be walking.

Present perfect Action that began in the past and is linked to the present

Present perfect *Have* or *has* plus past participle (*-d* or *-ed*)

I/you/we/they have walked.
He/she/it has walked.

Present perfect progressive *Have been* or *has been* plus *-ing* form

I/you/we/they have been walking.
He/she/it has been walking.

Past perfect Action that was completed before another past action

Past perfect *Had* plus past participle (*-d* or *-ed*)

I/you/he/she/it/we/they had walked.

Past perfect progressive *Had been* plus *-ing* form

I/you/he/she/it/we/they had been walking.

Future perfect Action that will be completed before another future action

Future perfect *Will have* plus past participle (*-d* or *-ed*)

I/you/he/she/it/we/they will have walked.

Future perfect progressive *Will have been* plus *-ing* form

I/you/he/she/it/we/they will have been walking.

A general truth

The mills of the gods <u>grind</u> slowly.
The earth <u>is</u> round.

Discussion of literature, film, and so on (see also p. 795)

Huckleberry Finn <u>has</u> adventures we all envy.
In that article, the author <u>examines</u> several causes of crime.

Future time

Next week we <u>draft</u> a new budget.
Funding <u>ends</u> in less than a year.

(In the last two examples, time is really indicated by *Next week* and *in less than a year*.)

2 ■ Observe the uses of the perfect tenses.

The perfect tenses generally indicate action completed before another specific time or action. (The term *perfect* derives from the Latin *perfectus*, "completed.") The present perfect tense also indicates action begun in the past and continued into the present. The perfect tenses consist of a form of *have* plus the verb's past participle.

present perfect
The dancer <u>has performed</u> here only once. [The action is completed at the time of the statement.]

present perfect
Critics <u>have written</u> about the performance ever since. [The action began in the past and continues now.]

past perfect
The dancer <u>had trained</u> in Asia before his performance. [The action was completed before another past action.]

future perfect
He <u>will have performed</u> here again by next month. [The action begins now or in the future and will be completed by a specified time in the future.]

CULTURE LANGUAGE ✚ With the present perfect tense, the words *since* and *for* are followed by different information. After *since*, give a specific point in time: *The United States has been a member of the United Nations since 1945.* After *for*, give a span of time: *The United States has been a member of the United Nations for over half a century.*

3 ■ Observe the uses of the progressive tenses.   CULTURE LANGUAGE ✚

The progressive tenses indicate continuing (therefore progressive) action. In standard American English the progressive tenses consist of a form of *be* plus the verb's *-ing* form (present participle). (The words *be* and *been* must be combined with other helping verbs. See p. 294.)

t

14g

present progressive
The economy is improving.

past progressive
Last year the economy was stagnating.

future progressive
Economists will be watching for signs of growth.

present perfect progressive
The government has been expecting an upturn.

past perfect progressive
Various indicators had been suggesting improvement.

future perfect progressive
By the end of this month, investors will have been pushing the markets up for half a year.

Note Verbs that express unchanging states (especially mental states) rather than physical actions do not usually appear in the progressive tenses. These verbs include *adore, appear, believe, belong, care, doubt, hate, have, hear, imagine, know, like, love, mean, need, own, prefer, realize, remember, see, sound, taste, think, understand,* and *want.*

Faulty	She is wanting to study ethics.
Revised	She wants to study ethics.

t seq
14h

14h   Use the appropriate sequence of verb tenses.

The term **sequence of tenses** refers to the relation between the verb tense in a main clause and the verb tense in a subordinate clause or phrase. The tenses need not be identical as long as they reflect changes in actual or relative time. For example, the verbs in the following sentence are in clear sequence:

Ramon's father arrived in the United States thirty years ago, after he had married, and now Ramon has decided that he will return to his father's homeland.

The difficulties with tense sequence are discussed below. (For a discussion of tense shifts—changes *not* required by meaning—see pp. 376–77.)

1 ▪ Use the appropriate tense sequence with infinitives.

The tense of an infinitive is determined by the tense of the verb in the predicate. The **present infinitive** is the verb's plain form preceded by *to* (see p. 255). It indicates action *at the same time* as or *later* than that of the verb:

verb: infinitive:
present present
The researcher expects to see change.

verb: infinitive:
present perfect   present
She <u>would have liked</u> <u>to see</u> [not <u>to have seen</u>] change before now.

The verb's **perfect infinitive** consists of *to have* followed by the past participle, as in *to have talked, to have won.* It indicates action *earlier* than that of the verb:

               verb: infinitive:
              present   perfect
Other researchers <u>would like</u> [not <u>would have liked</u>] <u>to have seen</u> change as well.

    verb: infinitive:
  present   perfect
They <u>judge</u> the data <u>to have been interpreted</u> correctly.

2 ■ Use the appropriate tense sequence with participles.

The tense of a participle is determined by the tense of the verb in the predicate. The present participle shows action occurring *at the same time* as that of the verb:

participle: verb:
present   past perfect
<u>Testing</u> a large group, the researcher <u>had posed</u> multiple-choice questions.

The past participle and the present perfect participle show action occurring *earlier* than that of the verb:

participle: verb:
past   past
<u>Prepared</u> by earlier failures, she <u>knew</u> not to ask open questions.

   participle: verb:
present perfect   past
<u>Having tested</u> many people, she <u>understood</u> the process.

3 ■ Use the appropriate tense sequence with the past or past perfect tense.

When the verb in the main clause is in the past or past perfect tense, the verb in the subordinate clause must also be past or past perfect:

main clause: subordinate clause:
past   past
The researchers <u>discovered</u> that people <u>varied</u> widely in their knowledge of public events.

main clause: subordinate clause:
past   past perfect
The variation <u>occurred</u> because respondents <u>had been born</u> in different decades.

main clause: subordinate clause:
past perfect   past
None of them <u>had been born</u> when Warren G. Harding <u>was</u> President.

t seq
14h

Exception Always use the present tense for a general truth, such as *The earth is round:*

main clause: past   subordinate clause: present

Most <u>understood</u> that popular Presidents <u>are</u> not necessarily good Presidents.

4 ■ Use the appropriate tense sequence in conditional sentences.

A **conditional sentence** states a factual relation between cause and effect, makes a prediction, or speculates about what might happen. Such a sentence usually consists of a subordinate clause beginning with *if, when,* or *unless* along with a main clause stating the result. The three kinds of conditional sentences use distinctive verbs.

Factual relation

For statements that something always or usually happens whenever something else happens, use the present tense in both clauses:

subordinate clause: present   main clause: present

When a voter <u>casts</u> a ballot, he or she <u>has</u> complete privacy.

If the linked events occurred in the past, use the past tense in both clauses:

subordinate clause: past   main clause: past

When voters <u>registered</u> in some states, they <u>had</u> to pay a poll tax.

Prediction

For a prediction, generally use the present tense in the subordinate clause and the future tense in the main clause:

subordinate clause: present   main clause: future

Unless citizens <u>regain</u> faith in politics, they <u>will</u> not <u>vote</u>.

Sometimes the verb in the main clause consists of *may, can, should,* or *might* plus the verb's plain form: *If citizens <u>regain</u> faith, they <u>may vote</u>.*

Speculation

Speculations are mainly of two kinds, each with its own verb pattern. For events that are possible in the present, though unlikely, use the past tense in the subordinate clause and *would, could,* or *might* plus the verb's plain form in the main clause:

subordinate clause: past   main clause: *would* + verb

If voters <u>had</u> more confidence, they <u>would vote</u> more often.

Use *were* instead of *was* when the subject is *I, he, she, it,* or a singular noun. (See p. 313 for more on this distinctive verb form.)

> subordinate clause: main clause:
> past   *would* + verb
>
> If the voter <u>were</u> more confident, he or she <u>would vote</u> more often.

For events that are impossible in the present, that are contrary to fact, use the same forms as above (including the distinctive *were* when applicable):

> subordinate clause: main clause:
> past   *might* + verb
>
> If Lincoln <u>were</u> alive, he <u>might inspire</u> confidence.

For events that were impossible in the past, use the past perfect tense in the subordinate clause and *would, could,* or *might* plus the present perfect tense in the main clause:

> subordinate clause: main clause:
> past perfect   *might* + present perfect
>
> If Lincoln <u>had lived</u> past the Civil War, he <u>might have helped</u> stabilize the country.

t seq

14h

5 ■ Use the appropriate tense sequence with indirect quotations.

An **indirect quotation** reports what someone said or wrote but not in the exact words and not in quotation marks: *Lincoln said that events had controlled him* (quotation: "Events have controlled me"). An indirect quotation generally appears in a subordinate clause (underlined above), with certain conventions governing verb tense in most cases.

When the verb in the main clause is in the present tense, the verb in the indirect quotation (subordinate clause) is in the same tense as the original quotation:

> main clause: indirect quotation:
> present   present
>
> Haworth <u>says</u> that Lincoln <u>is</u> our noblest national hero. [Quotation: "Lincoln <u>is</u> our noblest national hero."]

> main clause: indirect quotation:
> present   past
>
> He <u>says</u> that Lincoln <u>was</u> a complicated person. [Quotation: "Lincoln <u>was</u> a complicated person."]

When the verb in the main clause is in the past tense, the verb in the indirect quotation usually changes tense from the original quotation. Present tense changes to past tense.

> main clause: indirect quotation:
> past   past
>
> An assistant to Lincoln <u>said</u> that the President <u>was</u> always generous. [Quotation: "The President <u>is</u> always generous."]

Past tense and present perfect tense change to past perfect tense. (Past perfect tense does not change.)

> main clause: indirect quotation:
>   past   past perfect
> Lincoln <u>said</u> that events <u>had controlled</u> him. [Quotation: "Events <u>have controlled</u> me."]

When the direct quotation states a general truth or reports a situation that is still true, the verb in the indirect quotation remains in the present tense regardless of the verb tense in the main clause:

> main clause: indirect quotation:
>   past   present
> Lincoln <u>said</u> that right <u>makes</u> might. [Quotation: "Right <u>makes</u> might."]

Note As several of these examples show, an indirect quotation differs in at least two additional ways from the original quotation:

- The indirect quotation is usually preceded by *that*.
- The indirect quotation changes pronouns, especially from forms of *I* or *we* to forms of *he, she,* or *they.*

EXERCISE 8
Adjusting tense sequence: Past or past perfect tense

The tenses in each sentence below are in correct sequence. Change the tense of one verb as instructed. Then change the tense of infinitives, participles, and other verbs to restore correct sequence. Some items have more than one possible answer.

> *Example:*
>
> Delgado will call when he reaches his destination. (*Change <u>will call</u> to <u>called</u>.*)
>
> Delgado <u>called</u> when he <u>reached</u> [or <u>had reached</u>] his destination.

1. Diaries that Adolf Hitler is supposed to have written have surfaced in Germany. (*Change <u>have surfaced</u> to <u>had surfaced</u>.*)
2. Many people believe that the diaries are authentic because a well-known historian has declared them so. (*Change <u>believe</u> to <u>believed</u>.*)
3. However, the historian's evaluation has been questioned by other authorities, who call the diaries forgeries. (*Change <u>has been questioned</u> to <u>was questioned</u>.*)
4. They claim, among other things, that the paper is not old enough to have been used by Hitler. (*Change <u>claim</u> to <u>claimed</u>.*)
5. Eventually, the doubters will win the debate because they have the best evidence. (*Change <u>will win</u> to <u>won</u>.*)

EXERCISE 9
Revising: Tense sequence with conditional sentences
Supply the appropriate tense for each verb in brackets below.

Example:

If Babe Ruth or Jim Thorpe [be] athletes today, they [remind] us that even sports heroes must contend with a harsh reality.

If Babe Ruth or Jim Thorpe were athletes today, they might [or could or would] remind us that even sports heroes must contend with a harsh reality.

1. When an athlete [turn] professional, he or she commits to a grueling regimen of mental and physical training.
2. If athletes [be] less committed, they [disappoint] teammates, fans, and themselves.
3. If professional athletes [be] very lucky, they may play until age forty.
4. Unless an athlete achieves celebrity status, he or she [have] few employment choices after retirement.
5. If professional sports [be] less risky, athletes [have] longer careers and more choices after retirement.

t seq

14h

EXERCISE 10
Using verb tenses in indirect quotations
Each passage below comes from the British essayist Charles Lamb (1775–1834). Indirectly quote each passage in a sentence of your own, beginning with the words given in parentheses.

Example:

"The greatest pleasure I know is to do a good action by stealth and to have it found out by accident." (*Charles Lamb said that. . . .*)

Charles Lamb said that the greatest pleasure he knew was to do a good action by stealth and to have it found out by accident.

1. "Coleridge holds that a man cannot have a pure mind who refuses apple-dumplings." (*Lamb cited Coleridge's observation that. . . .*)
2. "The human species, according to the best theory I can form of it, is composed of two distinct races, the men who borrow, and the men who lend." (*Lamb wrote that. . . .*)
3. "Nothing puzzles me more than time and space; and yet nothing troubles me less, as I never think about them." (*He muses that. . . .*)
4. "When I am not walking, I am reading; I cannot sit and think." (*He admitted that. . . .*)
5. "Sentimentally I am disposed to harmony. But organically I am incapable of a tune." (*He confesses that. . . .*)

MOOD

Mood in grammar is a verb form that indicates the writer's or speaker's attitude toward what he or she is saying. The **indicative mood** states a fact or opinion or asks a question:

> The theater <u>needs</u> help. [Opinion.]
> The ceiling <u>is falling</u> in. [Fact.]
> <u>Will</u> you <u>contribute</u> to the theater? [Question.]

The **imperative mood** expresses a command or gives a direction. It omits the subject of the sentence, *you:*

> <u>Help</u> the theater. [Command.]
> <u>Send</u> contributions to the theater. [Direction.]

The **subjunctive mood** expresses a suggestion, a requirement, or a desire, or it states a condition that is contrary to fact (that is, imaginary or hypothetical). The subjunctive mood uses distinctive verb forms.

vb
14i

- **Suggestion or requirement:** plain form with all subjects.

  The manager asked that he <u>donate</u> money. [Suggestion.]
  Rules require that every donation <u>be</u> mailed. [Requirement.]

- **Desire or present condition contrary to fact:** past tense; for *be,* the past tense *were.*

  We wish that the theater <u>had</u> more money. [Desire.]

  It would be in better shape if it <u>were</u> better funded. [Present condition contrary to fact.]

- **Past condition contrary to fact:** past perfect.

  The theater could have been better funded if it <u>had been</u> better managed.

With conditions contrary to fact, the verb in the main clause also expresses the imaginary or hypothetical with the helping verb *could* or *would,* as in the last two sample sentences above.

(For a discussion of keeping mood consistent within and among sentences, see p. 377.)

http://www.ablongman.com/littlebrown

For added help and practice with verb mood, click on

➤ **Sentences**
  ➤ **Exercises** ➤ **Exer. 19**
  ➤ **Web links** ➤ **Verbs**

14i Use the subjunctive verb forms appropriately.

Contemporary English uses distinctive subjunctive verb forms in only a few constructions and idioms. (For the sequence of tenses in many subjunctive sentences, see pp. 308–09.)

Note A grammar and style checker may spot some simple errors in the subjunctive mood, but it may miss others. For example, a checker flagged *I wish I <u>was</u> home* (should be <u>were</u> *home*) but not *If I had a hammer, I <u>will</u> hammer in the morning* (should be <u>would</u> *hammer*). Instead of relying on the checker, proofread your work looking for appropriate uses of subjunctive verbs.

1 ▪ Use the subjunctive in contrary-to-fact clauses beginning with *if* or expressing desire.

If the theater <u>were</u> saved, the town would benefit.
We all wish the theater <u>were</u> not so decrepit.
I wish I <u>were</u> able to donate money.

Note The indicative form *was* (*We all wish the theater <u>was</u> not so decrepit*) is common in speech and in some informal writing, but the subjunctive *were* is usual in formal English.

Not all clauses beginning with *if* express conditions contrary to fact. In the sentence *If Joe <u>is</u> out of town, he hasn't heard the news,* the verb *is* is correct because the clause refers to a condition presumed to exist.

2 ▪ Use *would* or *could* only in the main clause of a conditional statement.

The helping verb *would* or *could* appears in the main clause of a sentence expressing a condition contrary to fact. The helping verb does not appear in the subordinate clause beginning with *if:*

Not Many people would have helped if they <u>would have</u> known.
But Many people would have helped if they <u>had</u> known.

3 ▪ Use the subjunctive in *that* clauses following verbs that demand, request, or recommend.

Verbs such as *ask, demand, insist, mandate, recommend, request, require, suggest,* and *urge* indicate demand or suggestion. They often precede subordinate clauses beginning with *that* and containing the substance of the demand or suggestion. The verb in such a *that* clause should be in the subjunctive mood:

The board urged that everyone <u>contribute</u>.
The members insisted that they themselves <u>be</u> donors.
They suggested that each <u>donate</u> both time and money.

vb
14i

Note These constructions have widely used alternative forms that do not require the subjunctive, such as *The board urged everyone to contribute* or *The members insisted on donating.*

4 ■ Use the subjunctive in some set phrases and idioms.

Several English expressions commonly use the subjunctive. For example:

<u>Come</u> rain or <u>come</u> shine.
<u>Be</u> that as it may.
The people <u>be</u> damned.

> **EXERCISE 11**
> **Revising: Subjunctive mood**
> Revise the following sentences with appropriate subjunctive verb forms.
>
> *Example:*
> I would help the old man if I was able to reach him.
> I would help the old man if I <u>were</u> able to reach him.
>
> 1. If John Hawkins would have known of the dangerous side effects of smoking tobacco, would he have introduced the dried plant to England in 1565?
> 2. Hawkins noted that if a Florida Indian was to travel for several days, he would have smoked tobacco to satisfy his hunger and thirst.
> 3. Early tobacco growers feared that their product would not gain acceptance unless it was perceived as healthful.
> 4. To prevent fires, in 1646 the General Court of Massachusetts passed a law requiring that a colonist smoked tobacco only if he was five miles from any town.
> 5. To prevent decadence, in 1647 Connecticut passed a law mandating that one's smoking of tobacco was limited to once a day in one's own home.

VOICE

The **voice** of a verb tells whether the subject of the sentence performs the action (**active voice**) or is acted upon (**passive voice**). In the passive voice, the actual actor may be named in a prepositional phrase (such as *by the city*) or may be omitted.

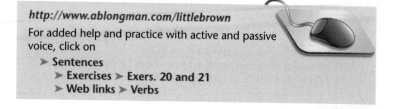

http://www.ablongman.com/littlebrown
For added help and practice with active and passive voice, click on
➤ **Sentences**
  ➤ **Exercises** ➤ **Exers. 20 and 21**
  ➤ **Web links** ➤ **Verbs**

Active and passive voice

Active voice   The subject acts.

| The city | controls | rents. |

Passive voice   The subject is acted upon.

| Rents | are controlled | by the city. |
| Rents | are controlled. | |

⟐ CULTURE / LANGUAGE A passive verb always consists of a form of *be* plus the past participle of the main verb: *rents are controlled.* Other helping verbs must also be used with *be, being,* and *been: rents have been controlled.* Only a transitive verb (one that takes an object) may be used in the passive voice. (See p. 294.)

Converting active to passive

To change a transitive verb from active to passive voice, convert either an indirect object or a direct object into the subject of the sentence, and use the passive verb form:

	subject	transitive verb	indirect object	direct object
Active	The city	gives	tenants	leases.

	new subject	passive verb	direct object	
Passive	Tenants	are given	leases.	

	new subject	passive verb	indirect object	old subject
	Leases	are given	tenants	by the city.

Converting passive to active

To change a passive verb to active, name the verb's actor as subject, use an active verb form, and convert the old subject into an object:

	subject	passive verb	
Passive	Tenants	are protected	by leases.

	new subject	active verb	old subject = object
Active	Leases	protect	tenants.

14j   Generally, prefer the active voice. Use the passive voice when the actor is unknown or unimportant.

Because the passive omits or de-emphasizes the actor (the performer of the verb's action), it can deprive writing of vigor and is often vague or confusing. The active voice is usually stronger, clearer, and more forthright.

| Weak passive | The <u>Internet is used</u> for research by many scholars, and its <u>expansion</u> to the general public <u>has been criticized</u> by some. |
| Strong active | Many <u>scholars use</u> the Internet for research, and <u>some have criticized</u> its expansion to the general public. |

The passive voice is useful in two situations: when the actor is unknown and when the actor is unimportant or less important than the object of the action.

The Internet <u>was established</u> in 1969 by the US Department of Defense. The <u>network has</u> now <u>been extended</u> internationally to governments, foundations, corporations, educational institutions, and private individuals. [In the first sentence the writer wishes to stress the Internet rather than the Department of Defense. In the second sentence the actor is unknown or too complicated to name.]

After the solution <u>had been cooled</u> to 10°C, the acid <u>was added</u>. [The person who cooled and added, perhaps the writer, is less important than the facts that the solution was cooled and acid was added. Passive sentences are common in scientific writing. See pp. 865–66.]

Except in such situations, however, you should prefer the active voice in your writing.

Note Most grammar and style checkers can be set to spot the passive voice. But they will often flag appropriate uses, such as when the actor is unknown. Use a checker to help you see the passive voice in your writing, but decide for yourself whether flagged verbs are appropriate.

EXERCISE 12
Converting between active and passive voices
To practice using the two voices of the verb, convert the following sentences from active to passive or from passive to active. (In converting from passive to active, you may have to add a subject for the new sentence.) Which version of each sentence seems more effective, and why? (For additional exercises with the passive voice, see pp. 272 and 406.)

Example:
The aspiring actor was discovered in a nightclub.
A talent scout discovered the aspiring actor in a nightclub.

1. When the Eiffel Tower was built in 1889, it was thought by the French to be ugly.
2. At that time many people still resisted industrial technology.
3. The tower's naked steel construction epitomized this technology.
4. Beautiful ornament was expected to grace fine buildings.
5. Further, the tower could not even be called a building because it had no solid walls.

EXERCISE 13
Revising: Verb forms, tense, mood

Circle all the verbs and verbals in the following paragraph and correct their form, tense, or mood if necessary.

For centuries the natives of Melanesia, a group of islands laying northeast of Australia, have practice an unusual religion. It began in the eighteenth century when European explorers first have visited the islands. The natives were fascinated by the rich goods or "cargo" possessed by the explorers. They saw the wealth as treasures of the gods, and cargo cults eventually had arisen among them. Over the centuries some Melanesians turned to Christianity in the belief that the white man's religion will bring them the white man's treasures. During World War II, US soldiers, having arrived by boat and airplane to have occupied some of the islands, introduced new and even more wonderful cargo. Even today some leaders of the cargo cults insist that the airplane is worship as a vehicle of the Melanesians' future salvation.

pass

14j

Note See page 346 for an exercise involving verbs along with other aspects of grammar.

CHAPTER 15

Agreement

Agreement helps readers understand the relations between elements in a sentence. Subjects and verbs agree in number and person:

More Japanese Americans live in Hawaii and California than elsewhere.
   subject   verb

Daniel Inouye was the first Japanese American in Congress.
   subject   verb

Pronouns and their **antecedents**—the words they refer to—agree in person, number, and gender:

Inouye makes his home in Hawaii.
antecedent   pronoun

Hawaiians value his work for them.
   antecedent   pronoun

15a Make subjects and verbs agree in number.

Most subject-verb agreement problems arise when endings are omitted from subjects or verbs or when the relation between sentence parts is uncertain.

Note A grammar and style checker will look for problems with subject-verb agreement. Most checkers also allow you to customize settings so that you can turn off other options and look just for agreement problems (see p. 186). Checkers will catch all simple

http://www.ablongman.com/littlebrown
For added help and practice with subject-verb and pronoun-antecedent agreement, click on
➤ Sentences
   ➤ Video tutorials
   ➤ Exercises ➤ Exers. 22–27
   ➤ Web links

Person and number in subject-verb agreement

	Number	
Person	*Singular*	*Plural*
First	I eat.	We eat.
Second	You eat.	You eat.
Third	He/she/it eats.	They eat.
	The bird eats.	Birds eat.

errors such as *Addie and John is late* and many more complicated sentences such as *Is Margaret and Tom going with us?* (should be *are* in both cases). But a checker failed to flag *The old group has gone their separate ways* (should be *have*) and offered the wrong correction for *The old group have gone their separate ways,* which is already correct. Do not automatically accept a checker's points, and proofread your work carefully on your own.

agr

15a

1 ■ The -s and -es endings work differently for nouns and verbs.

An *-s* or *-es* ending does opposite things to nouns and verbs: it usually makes a noun *plural,* but it always makes a present-tense verb *singular.* Thus a singular noun as subject will not end in *-s,* but its verb will. A plural noun as subject will end in *-s,* but its verb will not. **Between them, subject and verb use only one *-s* ending.**

Singular	Plural
The boy plays.	The boys play.
The bird soars.	The birds soar.

The only exceptions to these rules involve the nouns that form irregular plurals, such as *child/children, woman/women.* The irregular plural still requires a plural verb: The *children play.*

 CULTURE LANGUAGE ➤ If your first language is not standard American English, subject-verb agreement may be problematic, especially for the reasons given on the next page.

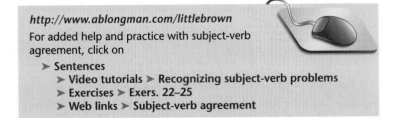

http://www.ablongman.com/littlebrown
For added help and practice with subject-verb agreement, click on
➤ Sentences
  ➤ Video tutorials ➤ Recognizing subject-verb problems
  ➤ Exercises ➤ Exers. 22–25
  ➤ Web links ➤ Subject-verb agreement

- Some English dialects follow different rules for subject-verb agreement, such as omitting the *-s* ending for singular verbs or using the *-s* ending for plural verbs.

Nonstandard	The voter resist change.
Standard	The voter resists change.
Standard	The voters resist change.

The verb *be* changes spelling for singular and plural in both present and past tenses. (See also p. 285.)

| Nonstandard | Taxes is high. They was raised just last year. |
| Standard | Taxes are high. They were raised just last year. |

Have also has a distinctive *-s* form, *has:*

| Nonstandard | The new tax have little chance of passing. |
| Standard | The new tax has little chance of passing. |

- As helping verbs in verb phrases, only *be, have,* and *do* change form for different subjects: *The car does run. The cars do run.* The modal helping verbs—*can, might, should, will,* and others—do not change: *The car should run. The cars should run.* As these examples show, the main verb in a verb phrase (*run*) does not change with different subjects.

agr
15a

2 ■ **Subject and verb should agree even when other words come between them.**

When the subject and verb are interrupted by other words, make sure the verb agrees with the subject:

A catalog of courses and requirements often baffles [not baffle] students.

The requirements stated in the catalog are [not is] unclear.

Note Phrases beginning with *as well as, together with, along with,* and *in addition to* do not change the number of the subject:

The president, as well as the deans, has [not have] agreed to revise the catalog.

If you really mean *and* in such a sentence, use it. Then the subject is compound, and the verb should be plural: *The president and the deans have agreed to revise the catalog.*

3 ■ **Subjects joined by *and* usually take plural verbs.**

Two or more subjects joined by *and* usually take a plural verb, whether one or all of the subjects are singular:

Summary of subject-verb agreement

- **Basic subject-verb agreement** (p. 319):

Singular	Plural
The kite flies.	The kites fly.

- **Words between subject and verb** (opposite):

  The kite with two tails flies badly. The tails of the kite compete.

- **Subjects joined by** *and* (opposite):

  The kite and the bird are almost indistinguishable.

- **Subjects joined by** *or* **or** *nor* (p. 322):

  The kite or the bird dives. Kites or birds fill the sky.

- **Indefinite pronouns as subjects** (p. 322):

  No one knows. All the spectators wonder.

- **Collective nouns as subjects** (p. 323):

  A flock appears. The flock disperse.

- **Inverted word order** (p. 324):

  Is the kite or the bird blue? Are the kite and the bird both blue?

- **Linking verbs** (p. 324):

  The kite is a flier and a dipper.

- ***Who, which, that* as subjects** (p. 324):

  The kite that flies longest wins. Kites that fall lose.

- **Subjects with plural form and singular meaning** (p. 325):

  Aeronautics plays a role in kite flying.

- **Titles and words named as words** (p. 325):

  Kite Dynamics is one title. *Vectors* is a key word.

agr

15a

Frost and Roethke were contemporaries.

Frost, Roethke, Stevens, and Pound are among the great American poets.

Exceptions When the parts of the subject form a single idea or refer to a single person or thing, they take a singular verb:

Avocado and bean sprouts is a California sandwich.

When a compound subject is preceded by the adjective *each* or *every*, the verb is usually singular:

Each man, woman, and child has a right to be heard.

But a compound subject *followed* by *each* takes a plural verb:

The man and the woman each have different problems.

4 ■ When parts of a subject are joined by *or* or *nor*, the verb agrees with the nearer part.

When all parts of a subject joined by *or* or *nor* are singular, the verb is singular; when all parts are plural, the verb is plural.

Either the painter or the carpenter knows the cost.

The cabinets or the bookcases are too costly.

When one part of the subject is singular and the other plural, avoid awkwardness by placing the plural part closer to the verb so that the verb is plural:

Awkward	Neither the owners nor the contractor agrees.
Revised	Neither the contractor nor the owners agree.

When the subject consists of nouns and pronouns of different person requiring different verb forms, the verb agrees with the nearer part of the subject. Reword if this construction is awkward:

Awkward	Either Juarez or I am responsible.
Revised	Either Juarez is responsible, or I am.

5 ■ With an indefinite pronoun, use a singular or plural verb as appropriate.

An **indefinite pronoun** is one that does not refer to a specific person or thing. Most indefinite pronouns take a singular verb, but some take a plural verb and some take a singular *or* a plural verb.

Common indefinite pronouns

Singular			Singular or plural	Plural
anybody	everyone	no one	all	both
anyone	everything	nothing	any	few
anything	much	one	more	many
each	neither	somebody	most	several
either	nobody	someone	some	
everybody	none	something		

(margin: agr 15a)

The singular indefinite pronouns refer to a single unspecified person or thing, and they take a singular verb:

Something smells.   Neither is right.

The plural indefinite pronouns refer to more than one unspecified thing, and they take a plural verb:

Both are correct.   Several were invited.

The other indefinite pronouns take a singular or a plural verb depending on whether the word they refer to is singular or plural. The word may be stated in the sentence:

All of the money is reserved for emergencies.

All of the funds are reserved for emergencies.

Or the word may be implied:

All are planning to attend. [*All* implies "all the people."]

All is lost. [*All* implies "everything."]

CULTURE LANGUAGE See page 344 for the distinction between *few* ("not many") and *a few* ("some").

6 ▪ Collective nouns take singular or plural verbs depending on meaning.

A **collective noun** has singular form but names a group of individuals or things—for example, *army, audience, committee, crowd, family, group, team.* As a subject, a collective noun may take a singular or plural verb, depending on the context. When the group acts as one unit, use a singular verb:

The group agrees that action is necessary.

But when considering the group's members as individuals who act separately, use the plural form of the verb:

The old group have gone their separate ways.

The collective noun *number* may be singular or plural. Preceded by *a*, it is plural; preceded by *the*, it is singular.

A number of people are in debt.

The number of people in debt is very large.

CULTURE LANGUAGE In English some noncount nouns (nouns that don't form plurals) are collective nouns because they name groups: for instance, *furniture, clothing, mail.* These noncount nouns usually take

agr
15a

singular verbs: *Mail arrives daily.* But some of these nouns take plural verbs, including *clergy, military, people, police,* and any collective noun that comes from an adjective, such as *the poor, the rich, the young, the elderly.* If you mean one representative of the group, use a singular noun such as *police officer* or *poor person.*

7 ▪ The verb agrees with the subject even when the normal word order is inverted.

Inverted subject-verb order occurs mainly in questions and in constructions beginning with *there* or *it* and a form of *be:*

Is voting a right or a privilege?

Are a right and a privilege the same thing?

There are differences between them.

In constructions beginning with *there,* you may use *is* before a compound subject when the first element in the subject is singular:

There is much work to do and little time to do it.

Word order may sometimes be inverted for emphasis. The verb still agrees with its subject:

From the mountains comes an eerie, shimmering light.

8 ▪ A linking verb agrees with its subject, not the subject complement.

A linking verb such as *is* or *are* should agree with its subject, usually the first element in the sentence, not with the noun or pronoun serving as a subject complement (see p. 245):

The child's sole support is her court-appointed guardians.

Her court-appointed guardians are the child's sole support.

9 ▪ *Who, which,* and *that* take verbs that agree with their antecedents.

When used as subjects, *who, which,* and *that* refer to another word in the sentence, called the **antecedent.** The verb agrees with the antecedent:

Mayor Garber ought to listen to the people who work for her.

Bardini is the only aide who has her ear.

Agreement problems often occur with relative pronouns when the sentence includes *one of the* or *the only one of the:*

Bardini is one of the aides who work unpaid. [Of the aides who work unpaid, Bardini is one.]

Bardini is the only one of the aides who knows the community. [Of the aides, only one, Bardini, knows the community.]

LANGUAGE In phrases like those above beginning with *one of the,* be sure the noun is plural: *Bardini is one of the aides* [not *aide*] *who work unpaid.*

10 ■ **Nouns with plural form but singular meaning take singular verbs.**

Some nouns with plural form (that is, ending in *-s*) are usually regarded as singular in meaning. They include *athletics, economics, linguistics, mathematics, measles, mumps, news, physics, politics,* and *statistics,* as well as place names such as *Athens, Wales,* and *United States.*

After so long a wait, the news has to be good.

Statistics is required of psychology majors.

A few of these words take plural verbs only when they describe individual items rather than whole bodies of activity or knowledge: *The statistics prove him wrong.*

Measurements and figures ending in *-s* may also be singular when the quantity they refer to is a unit:

Three years is a long time to wait.

Three-fourths of the library consists of reference books.

11 ■ **Titles and words named as words take singular verbs.**

When your sentence subject is the name of a corporation, the title of a work (such as a book), or a word you are defining or describing, the verb should be singular even if the name, title, or word is plural:

Hakada Associates is a new firm.

Dream Days remains a favorite book.

Folks is a down-home word for *people.*

EXERCISE 1
Revising: Subject-verb agreement

Revise the verbs in the following sentences as needed to make subjects and verbs agree in number. If the sentence is already correct as given, circle the number preceding it.

Example:
Each of the job applicants type sixty words per minute.
Each of the job applicants types sixty words per minute.

1. Weinstein & Associates are a consulting firm that try to make businesspeople laugh.
2. Statistics from recent research suggests that humor relieves stress.
3. Reduced stress in businesses in turn reduce illness and absenteeism.
4. Reduced stress can also reduce friction within an employee group, which then work more productively.
5. In special conferences held by one consultant, each of the participants practice making the others laugh.
6. One consultant to many companies suggest cultivating office humor with practical jokes such as a rubber fish in the water cooler.
7. When employees or their manager regularly post cartoons on the bulletin board, office spirit usually picks up.
8. When someone who has seemed too easily distracted is entrusted with updating the cartoons, his or her concentration often improves.
9. In the face of levity, the former sourpuss becomes one of those who hides bad temper.
10. Every one of the consultants caution, however, that humor has no place in life-affecting corporate situations such as employee layoffs.

15b Make pronouns and their antecedents agree in person, number, and gender.

The **antecedent** of a pronoun is the noun or other pronoun to which the pronoun refers.

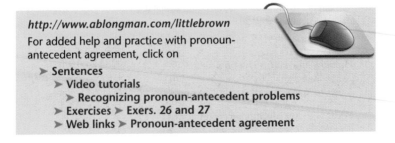

http://www.ablongman.com/littlebrown
For added help and practice with pronoun-antecedent agreement, click on
➤ **Sentences**
  ➤ **Video tutorials**
    ➤ **Recognizing pronoun-antecedent problems**
  ➤ **Exercises** ➤ **Exers. 26 and 27**
  ➤ **Web links** ➤ **Pronoun-antecedent agreement**

Homeowners fret over their tax bills.
antecedent   pronoun

Its constant increases make the tax bill a dreaded document.
pronoun   antecedent

Since a pronoun derives its meaning from its antecedent, the two must agree in person, number, and gender.

Person, number, and gender in pronoun-antecedent agreement

| | Number | |
Person	Singular	Plural
First	I	we
Second	you	you
Third	he, she, it, indefinite pronouns, singular nouns	they, plural nouns

Gender

Masculine	he, nouns naming males
Feminine	she, nouns naming females
Neuter	it, all other nouns

agr
15b

Note Grammar and style checkers cannot help with agreement between pronoun and antecedent because they cannot recognize the intended relation between the two. You'll need to check for errors on your own.

CULTURE LANGUAGE The gender of a pronoun should match its antecedent, not a noun that the pronoun may modify: *Sara Young invited her* [not *his*] *son to join the company's staff.* Also, nouns in English have only neuter gender unless they specifically refer to males or females. Thus nouns such as *book, table, sun,* and *earth* take the pronoun *it.*

1 ■ Antecedents joined by *and* usually take plural pronouns.

Two or more antecedents joined by *and* usually take a plural pronoun, whether one or all of the antecedents are singular:

Mr. Bartos and I cannot settle our dispute.

The dean and my adviser have offered their help.

Summary of pronoun-antecedent agreement

- **Basic pronoun-antecedent agreement:**

  Old Faithful spews its columns of water, each of them over 115 feet high.

- **Antecedents joined by *and* (previous page):**

  Old Faithful and Giant are geysers known for their height.

- **Antecedents joined by *or* or *nor* (below):**

  Either Giant or Giantess ejects its column the highest.

- **Indefinite words as antecedents (opposite):**

  Each of the geysers has its own personality. Each person who visits has his or her memories.

- **Collective nouns as antecedents (p. 330):**

  A crowd amuses itself watching Old Faithful. The crowd go their separate ways.

agr

15b

Exceptions When the compound antecedent refers to a single idea, person, or thing, then the pronoun is singular:

My friend and adviser offered her help.

When the compound antecedent follows *each* or *every*, the pronoun is singular:

Every girl and woman took her seat.

2 ■ When parts of an antecedent are joined by *or* or *nor*, the pronoun agrees with the nearer part.

When the parts of an antecedent are connected by *or* or *nor*, the pronoun should agree with the part closer to it:

Tenants or owners must present their grievances.

Either the tenant or the owner will have her way.

When one subject is plural and the other singular, the sentence will be awkward unless you put the plural one second:

Awkward   Neither the tenants nor the owner has yet made her case.

Revised   Neither the owner nor the tenants have yet made their
case.

3 ■ With an indefinite word as antecedent, use a singular or plural pronoun as appropriate.

Indefinite words do not refer to any specific person or thing.
They include **indefinite pronouns** such as *anyone, everybody, no
one, one, somebody* (see p. 322 for a longer list). They also include
generic nouns, or singular nouns that refer to typical members of a
group, as in *The individual has rights* or *The job requires a person
with computer skills.*

The pronoun referring to a singular generic noun should always be singular: *The wolf nurses its young.* The pronoun referring
to an indefinite pronoun should be singular or plural depending on
the meaning of the indefinite pronoun. Four indefinite pronouns—
both, few, many, several—are always plural in meaning and are referred to with plural pronouns:

Few realize how their athletic facilities have changed.

Five indefinite pronouns—*all, any, more, most, some*—may be singular or plural depending on the word to which they refer:

Few women athletes had changing spaces, so most had to change
in their rooms.

Most of the changing space was dismal, its color a drab olive green.

All other indefinite words—nouns and pronouns—are singular and
take singular pronouns:

Now everyone on the women's teams has her own locker.

Each of the men still has his own locker.

Most agreement problems arise with the singular indefinite
words. We often use these words to mean something like "many" or
"all" rather than "one" and then refer to them with plural pronouns,
as in *Everyone has their own locker* or *A person can padlock their
locker.* Often, too, we mean indefinite words to include both masculine and feminine genders and thus resort to *they* instead of the
generic *he*—the masculine pronoun referring to both genders, as in
Everyone deserves his privacy. (For more on the generic *he*, which
many readers view as sexist, see p. 548.) To achieve agreement in
such cases, you have the options shown in the following box:

agr
15b

Ways to correct agreement with indefinite words

■ **Change the indefinite word to a plural, and use a plural pronoun to match:**

Faulty   Every athlete deserves <u>their</u> privacy.
Revised   <u>Athletes</u> deserve their privacy.

■ **Rewrite the sentence to omit the pronoun:**

Faulty   Everyone is entitled to <u>their</u> own locker.
Revised   Everyone is entitled to <u>a</u> locker.

■ **Use *he or she* (*him or her, his or her*) to refer to the indefinite word:**

Faulty   Now everyone has <u>their</u> private space.
Revised   Now everyone has <u>his or her</u> private space.

However, used more than once in several sentences, *he or she* quickly becomes awkward. (Many readers do not accept the alternative *he/she*.) In most cases, using the plural or omitting the pronoun will not only correct agreement problems but also create more readable sentences.

4 ■ Collective noun antecedents take singular or plural pronouns depending on meaning.

Collective nouns such as *army, committee, family, group,* and *team* have singular form but may be referred to by singular or plural pronouns, depending on the meaning intended. When the group acts as a unit, the pronoun is singular:

The committee voted to disband <u>itself</u>.

When the members of the group act separately, the pronoun is plural:

The old group have gone <u>their</u> separate ways.

In the last example, note that the verb and pronoun are consistent in number (see also pp. 375–76).

Inconsistent   The old group <u>has</u> gone <u>their</u> separate ways.
Consistent   The old group <u>have</u> gone <u>their</u> separate ways.

CULTURE LANGUAGE English collective nouns that are noncount nouns (they don't form plurals) usually take singular pronouns: *The mail sits in its own basket.* A few noncount nouns take plural pronouns, including *clergy, military, people, police, the rich,* and *the poor: The police support their unions.* (See also pp. 323–24.)

EXERCISE 2
Revising: Pronoun-antecedent agreement

Revise the following sentences so that pronouns and their ante-cedents agree in person and number. Some items have more than one possible answer. Try to avoid the generic *he* (see p. 329). If you change the subject of a sentence, be sure to change verbs as neces-sary for agreement. If the sentence is already correct as given, cir-cle the number preceding it.

> *Example:*
> Each of the Boudreaus' children brought their laundry home at Thanksgiving.
>
> All of the Boudreaus' children brought <u>their</u> laundry home at Thanksgiving. *Or:* Each of the Boudreaus' children brought <u>laundry</u> home at Thanksgiving. *Or:* Each of the Boudreaus' children brought <u>his or her</u> laundry home at Thanksgiving.

1. Each girl raised in a Mexican American family in the Rio Grande Valley of Texas hopes that one day they will be given a *quinceañera* party for their fifteenth birthday.
2. Such celebrations are very expensive because it entails a reli-gious service followed by a huge party.
3. A girl's immediate family, unless they are wealthy, cannot af-ford the party by themselves.
4. Her parents will ask each close friend or relative if they can help with the preparations.
5. Surrounded by her family and attended by her friends and their escorts, the *quinceañera* is introduced as a young woman eligi-ble for fashionable Mexican American society.

EXERCISE 3
Adjusting for agreement

In the sentences below, subjects agree with verbs and pronouns agree with antecedents. Make the change specified in parentheses after each sentence, and then revise the sentence as necessary to maintain agreement. Some items have more than one possible an-swer.

> *Example:*
> The student attends weekly conferences with her teacher. (*Change The student to Students.*)
> Students <u>attend</u> weekly conferences with <u>their</u> teacher.

1. A biologist wishes to introduce captive red wolves into the Smoky Mountains in order to increase the wild population of this endangered species. (*Change A biologist to Biologists.*)
2. When freed, the wolf naturally has no fear of humans and thus is in danger of being shot. (*Change wolf to wolves.*)
3. The first experiment to release the wolves was a failure. (*Change experiment to experiments.*)

agr

15b

4. Now researchers pen the wolf puppy in the wooded area that will eventually be its territory. (*Change puppy to puppies.*)
5. The wolf has little contact with people, even its own keeper, during the year of its captivity. (*Change wolf to wolves.*)

EXERCISE 4
Revising: Agreement
Revise the sentences in the following paragraphs to correct errors in agreement between subjects and verbs or between pronouns and their antecedents. Try to avoid the generic *he* (see p. 329).

The writers Richard Rodriguez and Maxine Hong Kingston, despite their differences, shares one characteristic: their parents was immigrants to California. A frequent theme of their writings are the difficulties of growing up with two languages and two cultures.

A child whose first language is not English is often ridiculed because they cannot communicate "properly." Rodriguez learned Spanish at home, but at school everyone expected him to use their language, English. He remembers his childish embarrassment because of his parents' poor English. College and graduate school, which usually expands one's knowledge, widened the gap between Rodriguez and his Latino culture. His essays suggests that he lost a part of himself, a loss that continue to bother him.

Kingston spoke Chinese at home and also learned her first English at school. She sometimes write of these experiences, but more often she write to recover and preserve her Chinese culture. *The Woman Warrior,* which offer a blend of autobiography, family history, and mythic tales, describe the struggle of Kingston's female relatives. *China Men* focus on Kingston's male ancestors; each one traveled to Hawaii or California to make money for their wife back in China. Kingston's work, like Rodriguez's essays, reflect the tension and confusion that the child of immigrants often feel when they try to blend two cultures.

Note See page 346 for an exercise involving agreement along with other aspects of grammar.

CHAPTER 16

Adjectives and Adverbs

Adjectives and adverbs are modifiers that describe, restrict, or otherwise qualify the words to which they relate.

Functions of adjectives and adverbs

Adjectives modify	nouns:	<u>serious</u> student
	pronouns:	<u>ordinary</u> one
Adverbs modify	verbs:	<u>warmly</u> greet
	adjectives:	<u>only</u> three people
	adverbs:	<u>quite</u> seriously
	phrases:	<u>nearly</u> to the edge of the cliff
	clauses:	<u>just</u> when we arrived
	sentences:	<u>Fortunately,</u> she is employed.

Many of the most common adjectives are familiar one-syllable words such as *bad, strange, large,* and *wrong.* Many others are formed by adding endings such as *-al, -able, -ful, -less, -ish, -ive,* and *-y* to nouns or verbs: *optional, fashionable, beautiful, fruitless, selfish, expressive, dreamy.*

Most adverbs are formed by adding *-ly* to adjectives: *badly, strangely, largely, beautifully.* But note that we cannot depend on *-ly* to identify adverbs, since some adjectives also end in *-ly (fatherly, lonely)* and since some common adverbs do not end in *-ly (always, here, not, now, often, there).* Thus the only sure way to distinguish between adjectives and adverbs is to determine what they modify.

Note Grammar and style checkers will spot some but not all problems with misused adjectives and adverbs. For instance, a checker flagged *Some children suffer <u>bad</u>* and *Chang was the most*

http://www.ablongman.com/littlebrown

For added help and practice with adjectives and adverbs, click on
- ➤ **Sentences**
  - ➤ **Exercises** ➤ **Exers. 28–33**
  - ➤ **Web links** ➤ **Adjectives and adverbs**

333

wisest person in town and *Jenny did not feel nothing.* But it did not flag *Educating children good is everyone's focus.* You'll need to proofread your work on your own to be sure you've used adjectives and adverbs appropriately.

CULTURE LANGUAGE In standard American English an adjective does not change along with the noun it modifies to show plural number: *white* [not *whites*] *shoes, square* [not *squares*] *spaces.* Only nouns form plurals.

16a Use adjectives only to modify nouns and pronouns.

Adjectives modify only nouns and pronouns. Using adjectives instead of adverbs to modify verbs, adverbs, or other adjectives is nonstandard:

> Nonstandard The groups view family values different.
>
> Standard   The groups view family values differently.

The adjectives *good* and *bad* often appear where standard English requires the adverbs *well* and *badly:*

> Nonstandard Educating children good is everyone's focus.
>
> Standard   Educating children well is everyone's focus.
>
> Nonstandard Some children suffer bad.
>
> Standard   Some children suffer badly.

CULTURE LANGUAGE To negate a verb or an adjective, use the adverb *not:*

They are not learning. They are not stupid.

To negate a noun, use the adjective *no:*

No child should fail to read.

16b Use an adjective after a linking verb to modify the subject. Use an adverb to modify a verb.

A **linking verb** is one that links, or connects, a subject and its complement: *They are golfers. He is lucky.* (See also p. 245.) Linking verbs are forms of *be,* the verbs associated with our five senses (*look, sound, smell, feel, taste*), and a few others (*appear, seem, become, grow, turn, prove, remain, stay*).

Some of these verbs may or may not be linking, depending on their meaning in the sentence. When the word after the verb modifies the subject, the verb is linking and the word should be an adjective: *He feels strong.* When the word modifies the verb, however, it should be an adverb: *He feels strongly about that.*

Two word pairs are especially troublesome in this context. One is *bad* and *badly:*

The weather grew bad.
    linking adjective
    verb

She felt bad.
    linking adjective
    verb

Flowers grow badly in such soil.
    verb adverb

The other pair is *good* and *well. Good* serves only as an adjective. *Well* may serve as an adverb with a host of meanings or as an adjective meaning only "fit" or "healthy."

Decker trained well.
    verb adverb

She felt well.
    linking adjective
    verb

Her health was good.
    linking adjective
    verb

16c After a direct object, use an adjective to modify the object and an adverb to modify the verb.

ad
16c

After a direct object, an adjective modifies the object, whereas an adverb modifies the verb of the sentence. (See pp. 244–45 for more on direct objects.)

Campus politics made Mungo angry.
    adjective

Mungo repeated the words angrily.
    adverb

You can test whether a modifier should be an adjective or an adverb by trying to separate it from the direct object. If you can separate it, it should be an adverb: *Mungo angrily repeated the words.* If you cannot separate it, it is probably an adjective.

The instructor considered the student's work thorough. [The adjective can be moved in front of *work* (*student's thorough work*), but it cannot be separated from *work.*]

The instructor considered the student's work thoroughly. [The adverb can be separated from *work.* Compare *The instructor thoroughly considered the student's work.*]

http://www.ablongman.com/littlebrown
For added practice with identifying adjectives and adverbs, click on
➤ Sentences ➤ Exercises ➤ Exer. 28

EXERCISE 1
Revising: Adjectives and adverbs

Revise the following sentences so that adjectives and adverbs are used appropriately. If any sentence is already correct as given, circle the number preceding it.

Example:

The announcer warned that traffic was moving very slow.
The announcer warned that traffic was moving very <u>slowly</u>.

1. King George III of England declared Samuel Johnson suitably for a pension.
2. Johnson was taken serious as a critic and dictionary maker.
3. Thinking about his meeting with the king, Johnson felt proudly.
4. Johnson was relieved that he had not behaved badly in the king's presence.
5. After living cheap for over twenty years, Johnson finally had enough money from the pension to eat and dress good.

ad
16d

16d Use the comparative and superlative forms of adjectives and adverbs appropriately.

Adjectives and adverbs can show degrees of quality or amount with the endings *-er* and *-est* or with the words *more* and *most* or *less* and *least*. Most modifiers have three forms:

	Adjectives	Adverbs
Positive The basic form listed in the dictionary	red awful	soon quickly
Comparative A greater or lesser degree of the quality named	redder more/less awful	sooner more/less quickly
Superlative The greatest or least degree of the quality named	reddest most/least awful	soonest most/least quickly

If sound alone does not tell you whether to use *-er/-est* or *more/most*, consult a dictionary. If the endings can be used, the dictionary will list them. Otherwise, use *more* or *most*.

http://www.ablongman.com/littlebrown

For added help and practice with comparatives and superlatives, click on

➤ **Sentences**
  ➤ **Exercises** ➤ **Exer. 29**
  ➤ **Web links** ➤ **Adjectives and adverbs**

1 ■ Use the correct forms of irregular adjectives and adverbs.

The irregular modifiers change the spelling of their positive form to show comparative and superlative degrees:

Degrees of irregular adjectives and adverbs

Positive	Comparative	Superlative
Adjectives		
good	better	best
bad	worse	worst
little	littler, less	littlest, least
many		
some }	more	most
much		
Adverbs		
well	better	best
badly	worse	worst

2 ■ Use either *-er/-est* or *more/most,* not both.

A double comparative or double superlative combines the *-er* or *-est* ending with the word *more* or *most.* It is redundant.

Chang was the wisest [not most wisest] person in town.
He was smarter [not more smarter] than anyone else.

3 ■ Use the comparative for comparing two things and the superlative for comparing three or more things.

It is the shorter of her two books. [Comparative.]
The Yearling is the most popular of the six books. [Superlative.]

In conversation the superlative form is often used to compare only two things: *When two people argue, the angriest one is usually wrong.* But the distinction between the forms should be observed in writing.

4 ■ Use comparative or superlative forms only for modifiers that can logically be compared.

Some adjectives and adverbs cannot logically be compared—for instance, *perfect, unique, dead, impossible, infinite.* These absolute words can be preceded by adverbs like *nearly* and *almost* that mean "approaching," but they cannot logically be modified by *more* or *most* (as in *most perfect*). This distinction is sometimes ignored in speech, but it should always be made in writing:

Not He was the most unique teacher we had.
But He was a unique teacher.

EXERCISE 2
Using comparatives and superlatives
Write the comparative and superlative forms of each adjective or adverb below. Then use all three forms in your own sentences.

> *Example:*
> heavy: heavier (comparative), heaviest (superlative)
> The barbells were too <u>heavy</u> for me. The trunk was <u>heavier</u> than I expected. Joe Clark was the <u>heaviest</u> person on the team.

1. badly   3. good   5. understanding
2. steady   4. well

EXERCISE 3
Revising: Comparatives and superlatives
Revise the sentences below so that the comparative and superlative forms of adjectives and adverbs are appropriate for formal usage. Circle the number preceding any sentence that is already correct.

> *Example:*
> Attending classes full time and working at two jobs was the most impossible thing I ever did.
>
> Attending classes full time and working at two jobs was <u>impossible</u> [or <u>the hardest thing I ever did</u>].

1. Charlotte was the older of the three Brontë sisters, all of whom were novelists.
2. Some readers think Emily Brontë's *Wuthering Heights* is the most saddest novel they have ever read.
3. Of the other two sisters, Charlotte and Anne, Charlotte was probably the more talented.
4. Critics still argue about whether Charlotte or Emily wrote more better.
5. Certainly this family of women novelists was the most unique.

ad
16e

16e Watch for double negatives.

In a **double negative** two negative words such as *no, not, none, neither, barely, hardly,* or *scarcely* cancel each other out. Some double negatives are intentional: for instance, *She was <u>not unhappy</u>* indicates with understatement that she was indeed happy. But most double negatives say the opposite of what is intended: *Jenny did <u>not</u>*

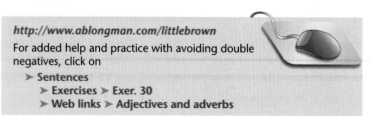

feel nothing asserts that Jenny felt other than nothing, or something. For the opposite meaning, one of the negatives must be eliminated or changed to a positive: *She felt nothing* or *She did not feel anything*.

Faulty	The IRS cannot hardly audit all tax returns. None of its audits never touch many cheaters.
Revised	The IRS cannot audit all tax returns. Its audits never touch many cheaters.

16f Use nouns sparingly as modifiers.

We often use one noun to modify another. For example:

child care   flood control   security guard

Such phrases can be both clear and concise, but overuse of noun modifiers can lead to flat, even senseless, writing. To avoid awkwardness or confusion, observe two principles. First, prefer possessives or adjectives as modifiers:

Not	A student takes the state medical board exams to become a dentist technician.
But	A student takes the state medical board's exams to become a dental technician.

Second, use only short nouns as modifiers and use them only in two- or three-word sequences:

Confusing	Minimex maintains a plant employee relations improvement program.
Revised	Minimex maintains a program for improving relations among plant employees.

ad
16g

16g Distinguish between present and past participles as adjectives. CULTURE LANGUAGE

Both present participles and past participles may serve as adjectives: *a burning building, a burned building*. As in the examples, the two participles usually differ in the time they indicate.

But some present and past participles—those derived from verbs expressing feeling—can have altogether different meanings. The

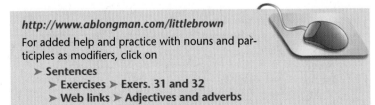

present participle modifies something that causes the feeling: *That was a frightening storm* (the storm frightens). The past participle modifies something that experiences the feeling: *They quieted the frightened horses* (the horses feel fright).

The following participles are among those likely to be confused:

amazing/amazed	fascinating/fascinated
amusing/amused	frightening/frightened
annoying/annoyed	frustrating/frustrated
astonishing/astonished	interesting/interested
boring/bored	pleasing/pleased
confusing/confused	satisfying/satisfied
depressing/depressed	shocking/shocked
embarrassing/embarrassed	surprising/surprised
exciting/excited	tiring/tired
exhausting/exhausted	worrying/worried

EXERCISE 4
Revising: Present and past participles 〔 **CULTURE LANGUAGE** 〕

Revise the adjectives in the following sentences as needed to distinguish between present and past participles. If the sentence is already correct as given, circle the number preceding it.

Example:
The subject was embarrassed to many people.
The subject was <u>embarrassing</u> to many people.

1. Several critics found Alice Walker's *The Color Purple* to be a fascinated book.
2. One confused critic wished that Walker had deleted the scenes set in Africa.
3. Another critic argued that although the book contained many depressed episodes, the overall impact was excited.
4. Since other readers found the book annoyed, this critic pointed out its many surprised qualities.
5. In the end most critics agreed that the book was a satisfied novel.

16h Use *a, an, the,* and other determiners appropriately. 〔 **CULTURE LANGUAGE** 〕

Determiners are special kinds of adjectives that mark nouns because they always precede nouns. Some common determiners are *a, an,* and *the* (called **articles**) and *my, their, whose, this, these, those, one, some,* and *any.* They convey information to readers—for instance, by specifying who owns what, which one of two is meant, or whether a subject is familiar or unfamiliar.

Native speakers of standard American English can rely on their intuition when using determiners, but speakers of other languages and dialects often have difficulty with them. In standard English the use of determiners depends on the context they appear in and the kind of noun they precede:

- **A proper noun** names a particular person, place, or thing and begins with a capital letter: *February, Joe Allen, Red River.* Most proper nouns are not preceded by determiners.
- **A count noun** names something that is countable in English and can form a plural: *girl/girls, apple/apples, child/children.* A singular count noun is always preceded by a determiner; a plural count noun sometimes is.
- **A noncount noun** names something not usually considered countable in English, and so it does not form a plural. A noncount noun is sometimes preceded by a determiner. Here is a sample of noncount nouns, sorted into groups by meaning:

Abstractions: confidence, democracy, education, equality, evidence, health, information, intelligence, knowledge, luxury, peace, pollution, research, success, supervision, truth, wealth, work

Food and drink: bread, candy, cereal, flour, meat, milk, salt, water, wine

Emotions: anger, courage, happiness, hate, joy, love, respect, satisfaction

Natural events and substances: air, blood, dirt, gasoline, gold, hair, heat, ice, oil, oxygen, rain, silver, smoke, weather, wood

Groups: clergy, clothing, equipment, furniture, garbage, jewelry, junk, legislation, machinery, mail, military, money, police, vocabulary

Fields of study: architecture, accounting, biology, business, chemistry, engineering, literature, psychology, science

A dictionary of English as a second language will tell you whether a noun is a count noun, a noncount noun, or both. (See p. 574 for recommended dictionaries.)

Note Many nouns can be both count and noncount nouns:

The library has a room for readers. [*Room* is a count noun meaning "walled area."]

The library has room for reading. [*Room* is a noncount noun meaning "space."]

Partly because the same noun may fall into different groups, grammar and style checkers are unreliable guides to missing or misused articles and other determiners. For instance, a checker flagged the

omitted *a* before *Scientist* in *Scientist developed new processes;* it did not flag the omitted *a* before *new* in *A scientist developed new process;* and it mistakenly flagged the correctly omitted article *the* before *Vegetation* in *Vegetation suffers from drought.* To correct omitted or misused articles, you'll need to proofread carefully on your own.

1 ■ Use *a, an,* and *the* where they are required.

With singular count nouns

A or *an* precedes a singular count noun when the reader does not already know its identity, usually because you have not mentioned it before:

> A scientist in our chemistry department developed a process to strengthen metals. [*Scientist* and *process* are being introduced for the first time.]

The precedes a singular count noun that has a specific identity for the reader, for one of the following reasons:

■ You have mentioned the noun before:

> A scientist in our chemistry department developed a process to strengthen metals. The scientist patented the process. [*Scientist* and *process* were identified in the preceding sentence.]

■ You identify the noun immediately before or after you state it:

> The most productive laboratory is the research center in the chemistry department. [*Most productive* identifies *laboratory. In the chemistry department* identifies *research center.* And *chemistry department* is a shared facility.]

■ The noun names something unique—the only one in existence:

> The sun rises in the east. [*Sun* and *east* are unique.]

■ The noun names an institution or facility that is shared by the community of readers:

> Many men and women aspire to the presidency. [*Presidency* is a shared institution.]
>
> The fax machine has changed business communication. [*Fax machine* is a shared facility.]

The is not used before a singular noun that names a general category:

> Sherman said that war is hell. [*War* names a general category.]
> The war in Croatia left many dead. [*War* names a specific war.]

With plural count nouns

A or *an* never precedes a plural noun. *The* does not precede a plural noun that names a general category. *The* does precede a plural noun that names specific representatives of a category.

Men and women are different. [*Men* and *women* name general categories.]

The women formed a team. [*Women* refers to specific people.]

With noncount nouns

A or *an* never precedes a noncount noun. *The* does precede a noncount noun when it names specific representatives of a general category:

Vegetation suffers from drought. [*Vegetation* names a general category.]

The vegetation in the park withered or died. [*Vegetation* refers to specific plants.]

With proper nouns

A or *an* never precedes a proper noun. *The* generally does not precede a proper noun:

Garcia lives in Boulder.

There are exceptions, however. For instance, we generally use *the* before plural proper nouns (*the Murphys, the Boston Celtics*) and the names of groups and organizations (*the Department of Justice, the Sierra Club*), ships (*the Lusitania*), oceans (*the Pacific*), mountain ranges (*the Alps*), regions (*the Middle East*), rivers (*the Mississippi*), and some countries (*the United States, the Sudan*).

2 ■ Use other determiners appropriately.

The uses of English determiners besides articles also depend on context and kind of noun. The following determiners may be used as indicated with singular count nouns, plural count nouns, or noncount nouns.

With any kind of noun (singular count, plural count, noncount)

my, our, your, his, her, its, their
possessive nouns (*boy's, boys'*)
whose, which(*ever*), *what*(*ever*)
some, any, the other
no

Their account is overdrawn. [Singular count.]

Their funds are low. [Plural count.]

Their money is running out. [Noncount.]

Only with singular nouns (count and noncount)

this, that

This account has some money. [Count.]

That information may help. [Noncount.]

Only with noncount nouns and plural count nouns

> *most, enough, other, such, all, all of the, a lot of*
>
> <u>Most</u> money is needed elsewhere. [Noncount.]
> <u>Most</u> funds are committed. [Plural count.]

Only with singular count nouns

> *one, every, each, either, neither, another*
>
> <u>One</u> car must be sold. [Singular count.]

Only with plural count nouns

> *these, those*
> *both, many, few, a few, fewer, fewest, several*
> *two, three,* and so forth
>
> <u>Two</u> cars are unnecessary. [Plural count.]

Note *Few* means "not many" or "not enough." *A few* means "some" or "a small but sufficient quantity."

> <u>Few</u> committee members came to the meeting.
> <u>A few</u> members can keep the committee going.

ad

16h

Do not use *much* with a plural count noun:

> <u>Many</u> [not <u>much</u>] members want to help.

Only with noncount nouns

> *much, more, little, a little, less, least, a large amount of*
>
> <u>Less</u> luxury is in order. [Noncount.]

Note *Little* means "not many" or "not enough." *A little* means "some" or "a small but sufficient quantity."

> <u>Little</u> time remains before the conference.
> The members need <u>a little</u> help from their colleagues.

Do not use *many* with a noncount noun:

> <u>Much</u> [not <u>many</u>] work remains.

EXERCISE 5
Revising: Articles CULTURE LANGUAGE

For each blank below, indicate whether *a, an, the,* or no article should be inserted.

From _____ native American Indians who migrated from _____ Asia 20,000 years ago to _____ new arrivals who now come by _____ planes, _____ United States is _____ nation of foreigners. It is _____ country of immigrants who are all living under _____ single flag.

Back in _____ seventeenth and eighteenth centuries, at least 75 percent of the population came from _____ England. However, between 1820 and 1975 more than 38 million immigrants came to this country from elsewhere in _____ Europe. Many children of _____ immigrants were self-conscious and denied their heritage; many even refused to learn _____ native language of their parents and grandparents. They tried to "Americanize" themselves. The so-called Melting Pot theory of _____ social change stressed _____ importance of blending everyone together into _____ kind of stew. Each nationality would contribute its own flavor, but _____ final stew would be something called "American."

This Melting Pot theory was never completely successful. In the last half of the twentieth century, _____ ethnic revival changed _____ metaphor. Many people now see _____ American society as _____ mosaic. Americans are once again proud of their heritage, and _____ ethnic differences make _____ mosaic colorful and interesting.

EXERCISE 6
Revising: Adjectives and adverbs

Revise the following paragraph so that it conforms to formal usage of adjectives and adverbs.

Americans often argue about which professional sport is better: basketball, football, or baseball. Basketball fans contend that their sport offers more action because the players are constant running and shooting. Because it is played indoors in relative small arenas, basketball allows fans to be more closer to the action than the other sports do. Fans point to how graceful the players fly through the air to the hoop. Football fanatics say they don't hardly stop yelling once the game begins. They cheer when their team executes a real complicated play good. They roar more louder when the defense stops the opponents in a goal-line stand. They yell loudest when a fullback crashes in for a score. In contrast, the supporters of baseball believe that it might be the most perfect sport. It combines the one-on-one duel of pitcher and batter struggling valiant with the tight teamwork of double and triple plays. Because the game is played slow and careful, fans can analyze and discuss the manager's strategy. Besides, they don't never know when they might catch a foul ball as a souvenir. However, no matter what the sport, all fans feel happily only when their team wins!

Note See the next page for an exercise involving adjectives and adverbs along with other aspects of grammar.

ad
16h

EXERCISE ON CHAPTERS 13–16
Revising: Grammatical sentences

The paragraphs below contain errors in pronoun case, verb forms, subject-verb agreement, pronoun-antecedent agreement, and the forms of adjectives and adverbs. Revise the paragraphs to correct the errors. (To download a double-spaced, editable version of this exercise, go to *http://www.ablongman.com/littlebrown* and click on Sentences > Downloads > Revising: Grammatical Sentences.)

Occasionally, musicians become "crossover artists" whom can perform good in more than one field of music. For example, Wynton and Branford Marsalis was train in jazz by their father, the great pianist Ellis Marsalis. Both of the sons has became successful classical artists. Branford's saxophone captures the richness of pieces by Ravel and Stravinsky. Wynton's albums of classical trumpet music from the Baroque period has brung him many awards. Still, if he was to choose which kind of music he likes best, Wynton would probable choose jazz. In contrast to the Marsalises, Yo-Yo Ma and Jean-Pierre Rampal growed up studying classical music. Then in the 1980s they was invited by Claude Bolling, a French pianist, to record Bolling's jazz compositions. In fact, Rampal's flute blended with Bolling's music so good that the two men have did three albums.

Such crossovers are often more harder for vocalists. Each type of music has their own style and feel that is hard to learn. For example, Luciano Pavarotti and Kiri te Kanawa, two great opera performers, have sang popular music and folk songs in concerts and on albums. On each occasion, their technique was the most perfect, yet each sounded as if he was simply trying to sing proper. It is even more difficulter for pop or country vocalists to sing opera, as Linda Ronstadt and Gary Morris founded when they appear in *La Bohème*. Each of them have a clear, pure voice, but a few critics said that him and her lacked the vocal power necessary for opera. However, Bobby McFerrin been successful singing both pop and classical pieces. He won a Grammy award for his song "Don't Worry, Be Happy." But he is equal able to sing classical pieces *a cappella* (without musical accompaniment). His voice's remarkable range and clarity allows him to imitate many musical instruments.

No matter how successful, all of these musicians has shown great courage by performing in a new field. They are willing to test and stretch their talents, and each of we music fans benefit.

PART V

Clear Sentences

CHAPTER 17

Sentence Fragments

A **sentence fragment** is part of a sentence that is set off as if it were a whole sentence by an initial capital letter and a final period or other end punctuation. Although writers occasionally use fragments deliberately and effectively (see p. 355), readers perceive most fragments as serious errors because, expecting complete sentences, they find partial sentences distracting or confusing. (Before reading further, you may find it helpful to review pp. 239–46 and 258–62 on sentences and clauses.)

Complete sentence versus sentence fragment

A **complete sentence** or **main clause**

- contains a subject and a verb (*The wind blows*)
- and is not a subordinate clause (beginning with a word such as *because* or *who*).

A **sentence fragment**

- lacks a verb (*The wind blowing*)
- or lacks a subject (*And blows*)
- or is a subordinate clause not attached to a complete sentence (*Because the wind blows*).

Note A grammar and style checker can spot many but not all sentence fragments, and it may flag sentences that are actually correct commands, such as *Continue reading*. Repair any actual fragments that a checker finds, but proofread your work yourself to ensure that it's fragment-free.

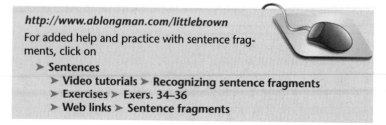

http://www.ablongman.com/littlebrown
For added help and practice with sentence fragments, click on
➤ **Sentences**
  ➤ **Video tutorials** ➤ **Recognizing sentence fragments**
  ➤ **Exercises** ➤ **Exers. 34–36**
  ➤ **Web links** ➤ **Sentence fragments**

17a Test your sentences for completeness, and revise any fragments.

The following three tests will help you determine whether a word group punctuated as a sentence is actually a complete sentence. If the word group does not pass *all three* tests, it is a fragment and needs to be revised.

Tests for complete sentences

Perform *all three* of the following tests to be sure your sentences are complete.

1. Find the verb.
2. Find the subject.
3. Make sure the clause is not subordinate.

Test 1: Find the verb.

Look for a verb in the group of words. If you do not have one, the word group is a fragment:

Fragment Uncountable numbers of sites on the World Wide Web. [Compare a complete sentence: *Uncountable numbers of sites make up the World Wide Web.*]

Any verb form you find must be a **finite verb,** one that changes form as indicated below. A verbal does not change; it cannot serve as a sentence verb without the aid of a helping verb.

	Finite verbs in complete sentences	Verbals in sentence fragments
Singular	The network grows.	The network growing.
Plural	Networks grow.	Networks growing.
Present	The network grows.	
Past	The network grew.	The network growing.
Future	The network will grow.	

CULTURE LANGUAGE Some languages allow forms of *be* to be omitted as helping verbs or linking verbs. But English requires stating forms of *be:*

Fragments The network growing. It already larger than its developers anticipated. [Compare complete sentences: *The network is growing. It is already larger than its developers anticipated.*]

Test 2: Find the subject.

If you find a finite verb, look for its subject by asking who or what performs the action or makes the assertion of the verb. The

frag

17a

subject of the sentence will usually come before the verb. If there is no subject, the word group is probably a fragment:

> **Fragment**   And has great popular appeal. [Compare a complete sentence: *And the Web has great popular appeal.*]

In one kind of complete sentence, a command, the subject *you* is understood: [*You*] *Experiment with the Web.*

▸ CULTURE LANGUAGE ◂ Some languages allow the omission of the sentence subject, especially when it is a pronoun. But in English, except in commands, the subject is always stated:

> **Fragments**   Web commerce is expanding dramatically. Is threatening traditional stores. [Compare a complete sentence: *It is threatening traditional stores.*]

Test 3: Make sure the clause is not subordinate.

A subordinate clause usually begins with a subordinating word:

Subordinating conjunctions			Relative pronouns	
after	once	until	that	who/whom
although	since	when	which	whoever/whomever
as	than	where		whose
because	that	whereas		
if	unless	while		

frag

17a

(See p. 259 for a longer list of subordinating conjunctions.)

Subordinate clauses serve as parts of sentences (nouns or modifiers), not as whole sentences:

> **Fragment**   When the government devised the Internet. [Compare a complete sentence: *The government devised the Internet.* Or: *When the government devised the Internet, no expansive computer network existed.*]
>
> **Fragment**   The reason that the government devised the Internet. [This fragment is a noun (*reason*) plus its modifier (*that . . . Internet*). Compare a complete sentence: *The reason that the government devised the Internet was to provide secure links among departments and defense contractors.*]

Note Questions beginning with *how, what, when, where, which, who, whom, whose,* and *why* are not sentence fragments: *Who was responsible? When did it happen?*

Revising sentence fragments

Almost all sentence fragments can be corrected in one of two ways, the choice depending on the importance of the information in the fragment.

Revision of sentence fragments

- Rewrite the fragment as a complete sentence.
- Combine the fragment with the appropriate main clause.

Rewriting the fragment as a complete sentence gives the information in the fragment the same importance as that in other complete sentences:

Fragment	A major improvement of the Internet occurred with the World Wide Web. Which allows users to move easily between sites.
Revised	A major improvement of the Internet occurred with the World Wide Web. It allows users to move easily between sites.

Two main clauses may be separated by a semicolon instead of a period (see p. 477).

The second method of correcting a fragment, combining it with a main clause, subordinates the information in the fragment to the information in the main clause:

Fragment	The Web is easy to use. Loaded with links and graphics.
Revised	The Web, loaded with links and graphics, is easy to use.

frag

17a

In this example, commas separate the inserted phrase from the rest of the sentence because the phrase is not essential to the meaning of any word in the main clause but simply adds information (see p. 459). When a phrase or subordinate clause *is* essential to the meaning of a word in the main clause, a comma or commas do *not* separate the two elements:

Fragment	With the links, users can move to other Web sites. That they want to consult.
Revised	With the links, users can move to other Web sites that they want to consult.

Sometimes a fragment may be combined with the main clause using a colon or a dash (see pp. 503 and 506, respectively):

Fragment	The Web connects sites from all over the Internet. Different databases, different software, different machines.
Revised	The Web connects sites from all over the Internet: different databases, different software, different machines.

Fragment	The Web is a boon to researchers. <u>A vast and accessible library.</u>
Revised	The Web is a boon to researchers—a vast and accessible library.

EXERCISE 1
Identifying and revising sentence fragments

Apply the tests for completeness to each of the following word groups. If a word group is a complete sentence, circle the number preceding it. If it is a sentence fragment, revise it in two ways: by making it a complete sentence, and by combining it with a main clause written from the information given in other items.

Example:

And could not find his money. [The word group has a verb (*could . . . find*) but no subject.]

Revised into a complete sentence: And <u>he</u> could not find his money.

Combined with a new main clause: <u>He was lost</u> and could not find his money.

1. In an interesting article about vandalism against works of art.
2. The motives of the vandals varying widely.
3. Those who harm artwork are usually angry.
4. But not necessarily at the artist or the owner.
5. For instance, a man who hammered at Michelangelo's *Pietà.*
6. And knocked off the Virgin Mary's nose.
7. Because he was angry at the Roman Catholic Church.
8. Which knew nothing of his grievance.
9. Although many damaged works can be repaired.
10. Usually even the most skillful repairs are forever visible.

17b   A subordinate clause is not a complete sentence.

Subordinate clauses contain both subjects and verbs, but they always begin with a subordinating conjunction (*although, if,* and so on) or a relative pronoun (*who, which, that*). (See p. 258.) Subordinate clauses serve as nouns or modifiers, but they cannot stand alone as complete sentences.

To correct a subordinate clause set off as a sentence, combine it with the main clause or remove or change the subordinating word to create a main clause.

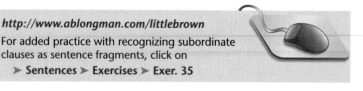

http://www.ablongman.com/littlebrown

For added practice with recognizing subordinate clauses as sentence fragments, click on

➤ **Sentences** ➤ **Exercises** ➤ **Exer. 35**

Fragment	Many pine trees bear large cones. <u>Which appear in August.</u>
Revised	Many pine trees bear large cones**,** which appear in August.
Revised	Many pine trees bear large cones**.** <u>They</u> appear in August.

17c A verbal phrase or a prepositional phrase is not a complete sentence.

A **verbal phrase** consists of an infinitive (*to choose*), a past participle (*chosen*), or a present participle or gerund (*choosing*) together with any objects and modifiers it may have (see p. 255). A verbal phrase is a noun or modifier and cannot serve as the verb in a complete sentence:

Fragment	For many of the elderly, their house is their only asset. <u>Offering some security but no income.</u>
Revised	For many of the elderly, their house is their only asset**,** offering some security but no income.
Revised	For many of the elderly, their house is their only asset**.** <u>It offers</u> some security but no income.

A **prepositional phrase** is a modifier consisting of a preposition (such as *in, on, to,* and *with*) together with its object and any modifiers (see p. 250). A prepositional phrase cannot stand alone as a complete sentence:

frag
17c

Fragment	<u>In a squeeze between a valuable asset and little income.</u> Eventually many elderly people sell their homes.
Revised	In a squeeze between a valuable asset and little income**,** eventually many elderly people sell their homes.
Revised	<u>Many elderly people are</u> in a squeeze between a valuable asset and little income**.** Eventually they may sell their homes.

CULTURE ⟋ LANGUAGE Some English prepositions consist of two or three words: *as well as, along with, in addition to, on top of,* and others. Don't let prepositions of more than one word mislead you into writing sentence fragments.

http://www.ablongman.com/littlebrown

For added practice with verbal-phrase and other sentence fragments, click on

➤ **Sentences** ➤ **Exercises** ➤ **Exer. 36**

Fragment	In today's retirement communities, the elderly may have health care, housekeeping, and new friends. <u>As well as financial security.</u>
Revised	In today's retirement communities, the elderly may have health care, housekeeping, and new friends**,** as well as financial security.

17d Any word group lacking a subject or a verb or both is not a complete sentence.

We often follow a noun with a modifier. No matter how long the noun and its modifier are, they cannot stand alone as a sentence:

Fragments	<u>People waving flags and cheering.</u> <u>Lined the streets for the parade.</u>
Revised	People waving flags and cheering lined the streets for the parade.
Fragment	<u>Veterans who fought in Vietnam.</u> They are finally being honored.
Revised	Veterans who fought in Vietnam are finally being honored.

Appositives are nouns, or nouns and their modifiers, that rename or describe other nouns (see p. 263). They cannot stand alone as sentences:

Fragment	When I was a child, my favorite adult was an old uncle. <u>A retired sea captain who always told me long stories of wild adventures in faraway places.</u>
Revised	When I was a child, my favorite adult was an old uncle**,** a retired sea captain who always told me long stories of wild adventures in faraway places.

Compound predicates are predicates made up of two or more verbs and their objects, if any (see p. 265). A verb or its object cannot stand alone as a sentence:

Fragment	Uncle Marlon drew out his tales. <u>And embellished them.</u>
Revised	Uncle Marlon drew out his tales and embellished them.
Fragment	He described characters he had met. <u>And storms at sea.</u>
Revised	He described characters he had met and storms at sea.

Note Beginning a sentence with a coordinating conjunction such as *and* or *but* can lead to a sentence fragment. Check every

frag
17d

sentence you begin with a coordinating conjunction to be sure it is complete.

EXERCISE 2
Revising: Sentence fragments
Correct any sentence fragment below either by combining it with a main clause or by making it a main clause. If an item contains no sentence fragment, circle the number preceding it.

Example:
Jujitsu is good for self-protection. Because it enables one to overcome an opponent without the use of weapons.

Jujitsu is good for self-protection because it enables one to overcome an opponent without the use of weapons.

1. Human beings who perfume themselves. They are not much different from other animals.
2. Animals as varied as insects and dogs release *pheromones*. Chemicals that signal other animals.
3. Human beings have a diminished sense of smell. And do not consciously detect most of their own species' pheromones.
4. The human substitute for pheromones may be perfumes. Especially musk and other fragrances derived from animal oils.
5. Some sources say that humans began using perfume to cover up the smell of burning flesh. During sacrifices to the gods.
6. Perfumes became religious offerings in their own right. Being expensive to make, they were highly prized.
7. The earliest historical documents from the Middle East record the use of fragrances. Not only in religious ceremonies but on the body.
8. In the nineteenth century chemists began synthesizing perfume oils. Which previously could be made only from natural sources.
9. The most popular animal oil for perfume today is musk. Although some people dislike its heavy, sweet odor.
10. Synthetic musk oil would help conserve a certain species of deer. Whose gland is the source of musk.

frag
17e

17e Be aware of the acceptable uses of incomplete sentences.

A few word groups lacking the usual subject-predicate combination are not sentence fragments because they conform to the expectations of most readers. They include exclamations (*Oh no!*); questions and answers (*Where next? To Kansas.*); and commands (*Move along. Shut the window.*). Another kind of incomplete sentence, occurring in special situations, is the transitional phrase (*So much for the causes, now for the results. One final point.*).

Experienced writers sometimes use sentence fragments when they want to achieve a special effect. Such fragments appear more in informal than in formal writing. Unless you are experienced and thoroughly secure in your own writing, you should avoid all fragments and concentrate on writing clear, well-formed sentences.

EXERCISE 3
Revising: Sentence fragments

Revise the following paragraph to eliminate sentence fragments by combining them with main clauses or rewriting them as main clauses.

Baby red-eared slider turtles are brightly colored. With bold patterns on their yellowish undershells. Which serve as a warning to predators. The bright colors of skunks and other animals. They signal that the animals will spray nasty chemicals. In contrast, the turtle's colors warn largemouth bass. That the baby turtle will actively defend itself. When a bass gulps down a turtle. The feisty baby claws and bites. Forcing the bass to spit it out. To avoid a similar painful experience. The bass will avoid other baby red-eared slider turtles. The turtle loses its bright colors as it grows too big. For a bass's afternoon snack.

Note See page 401 for an exercise involving sentence fragments along with comma splices, fused sentences, and other sentence errors.

frag
17e

CHAPTER 18

Comma Splices and Fused Sentences

A sentence or main clause contains at least a subject and a predicate, which together express a complete thought (see p. 239). We can separate two consecutive main clauses in one of four ways:

- With a period:

  The ship was huge. Its mast stood eighty feet high.

- With a semicolon:

  The ship was huge; its mast stood eighty feet high.

- With a comma preceding a coordinating conjunction that joins the clauses and specifies the relation between them:

  The ship was huge, and its mast stood eighty feet high.

- Occasionally with a colon when the second clause explains the first (see p. 503):

  The ship was huge: its mast stood eighty feet high.

The period, semicolon, or colon alone or the comma plus coordinating conjunction signals readers that one main clause (complete thought) is ending and another is beginning.

The comma splice and the fused sentence deprive readers of this signal and often force them to reread for sense. In a **comma splice** the two main clauses are joined (or spliced) *only* with a comma, not with a coordinating conjunction as well:

Comma splice
The ship was huge, its mast stood eighty feet high.

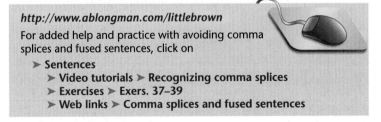

http://www.ablongman.com/littlebrown
For added help and practice with avoiding comma splices and fused sentences, click on
➤ Sentences
  ➤ Video tutorials ➤ Recognizing comma splices
  ➤ Exercises ➤ Exers. 37–39
  ➤ Web links ➤ Comma splices and fused sentences

Situations that may produce comma splices and fused sentences

- **The first clause is negative; the second, positive:**

  Splice   Petric is not a nurse, she is a doctor.
  Revised   Petric is not a nurse; she is a doctor.

- **The second clause amplifies or illustrates the first:**

  Fused   She did well in college her average was 3.9.
  Revised   She did well in college: her average was 3.9.

- **The second clause contains a conjunctive adverb or other transitional expression, such as *however* or *for example* (see p. 361):**

  Splice   She had intended to become a biologist, <u>however</u>, medicine
            seemed more exciting.
  Revised   She had intended to become a biologist; <u>however</u>, medicine
            seemed more exciting.

- **The subject of the second clause repeats or refers to the subject of the first clause:**

  Fused   Petric is an internist <u>she</u> practices in Topeka.
  Revised   Petric is an internist. <u>She</u> practices in Topeka.

- **Splicing or fusing is an attempt to link related ideas or to smooth choppy sentences:**

  Splice   She is very committed to her work, she devotes almost all
            her time to patient care.
  Revised   <u>Because</u> she is very committed to her work, she devotes
            almost all her time to patient care.
  Revised   She is <u>so</u> committed to her work <u>that</u> she devotes almost all
            her time to patient care.

- **Words identifying the speaker divide a quotation between two complete sentences. (See p. 468 for the punctuation to use in this case.)**

  Splice   "Medicine is a human frontier," Petric says, "The boundaries
            are unknown."
  Revised   "Medicine is a human frontier," Petric says. "The boundaries
            are unknown."

cs/fs
18

In a **fused sentence** no punctuation or coordinating conjunction appears between the main clauses.

Fused sentence
The ship was huge its mast stood eighty feet high.

Exception Experienced writers sometimes use a comma without a coordinating conjunction between very brief main clauses that are grammatically parallel:

He's not a person, he's a monster.

However, many readers view such punctuation as incorrect. Unless you are certain that your readers will not object to the comma in a sentence like this one, separate the clauses with periods or semicolons, as described in this chapter.

Note Grammar and style checkers can detect many comma splices, but they will miss most fused sentences. For example, a checker flagged *Money is tight, we need to spend carefully* but not *Money is tight we need to spend carefully.* A checker may also question sentences that are actually correct, such as *Money being tighter now than before, we need to spend carefully.* Verify that revision is actually needed on any flagged sentence, and read your work carefully on your own to be sure it is correct.

CULTURE LANGUAGE An English sentence may not include more than one main clause unless the clauses are separated by a comma and a coordinating conjunction or by a semicolon or colon. If your native language does not have such a rule or has accustomed you to writing long sentences, you may need to edit your English writing especially for comma splices and fused sentences.

COMMA SPLICES

CS
18a

18a **Separate two main clauses with a comma *only* when they are joined by a coordinating conjunction.**

A comma cannot separate main clauses unless they are linked by a coordinating conjunction (*and, but, or, nor, for, so, yet*). Readers expect the same main clause to continue after a comma alone. When they find themselves reading a second main clause before they realize they have finished the first, they may have to reread.

http://www.ablongman.com/littlebrown
For added help and practice with avoiding comma splices, click on
➤ Sentences
  ➤ Video tutorials ➤ Recognizing comma splices
  ➤ Exercises ➤ Exers. 37 and 38
  ➤ Web links ➤ Comma splices and fused sentences

Revision of comma splices and fused sentences

1. **Underline the main clauses in your draft.**
2. **When two main clauses fall in the same sentence, check the connection between them.**
3. **If nothing falls between the clauses or only a comma does, revise in one of the following ways.** The revision depends on the relation you want to establish between the clauses. (See the text discussion for examples.)

    Make the clauses into separate sentences.
    Insert a comma followed by *and, but,* or another coordinating conjunction. Or, if the comma is already present, insert just the coordinating conjunction.
    Insert a semicolon between clauses.
    Subordinate one clause to the other.

You have several options for revising comma splices.

Making separate sentences

Revising a comma splice by making separate sentences from the main clauses will always be correct. The period is not only correct but preferable when the ideas expressed in the two main clauses are only loosely related:

| Comma splice | Chemistry has contributed much to our understanding of foods, many foods such as wheat and beans can be produced in the laboratory. |
| Revised | Chemistry has contributed much to our understanding of foods. Many foods such as wheat and beans can be produced in the laboratory. |

CULTURE / LANGUAGE Making separate sentences may be the best option if you are used to writing very long sentences in your native language and often write comma splices in English.

Inserting a coordinating conjunction

When the ideas in the main clauses are closely related and equally important, you may correct a comma splice by inserting the appropriate coordinating conjunction immediately after the comma to join the clauses:

| Comma splice | Some laboratory-grown foods taste good, they are nutritious. |
| Revised | Some laboratory-grown foods taste good, and they are nutritious. |

Using a semicolon

If the relation between the ideas expressed in the main clauses is very close and obvious without a conjunction, you can separate the clauses with a semicolon.

| Comma splice | Good taste is rare in laboratory-grown vegetables, they are usually bland. |
| Revised | Good taste is rare in laboratory-grown vegetables; they are usually bland. |

Subordinating one clause

When the idea in one clause is more important than that in the other, you can express the less important idea in a phrase or a subordinate clause. (See p. 259 for a list of subordinating conjunctions and pp. 419–23 for more on subordination.) Subordination is often more effective than forming separate sentences because it defines the relation between ideas more precisely:

Comma splice	The vitamins are adequate, the flavor is deficient.
Revised	The vitamins are adequate. The flavor is deficient. [Both ideas receive equal weight.]
Improved	<u>Even though</u> the vitamins are adequate, the flavor is deficient. [Emphasis on the second idea.]

18b Separate main clauses related by *however, for example,* and so on.

cs 18b

Two kinds of words that are not conjunctions describe how one main clause relates to another:

- **Conjunctive adverbs,** such as *consequently, finally, hence, however, indeed, therefore,* or *thus.* (See p. 267 for a longer list.)
- Other **transitional expressions,** such as *even so, for example, in fact, of course, to the right,* and *to this end.* (See p. 87 for a longer list.)

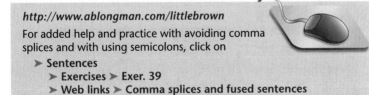

http://www.ablongman.com/littlebrown
For added help and practice with avoiding comma splices and with using semicolons, click on
➤ Sentences
  ➤ Exercises ➤ Exer. 39
  ➤ Web links ➤ Comma splices and fused sentences

When two main clauses are related by a conjunctive adverb or a transitional expression, they must be separated by a period or by a semicolon. The adverb or expression is also generally set off by a comma or commas (see p. 461):

Comma splice	Most Americans refuse to give up unhealthful habits, <u>consequently</u> our medical costs are higher than those of many other countries.
Revised	Most Americans refuse to give up unhealthful habits<u>.</u> <u>Consequently,</u> our medical costs are higher than those of many other countries.
Revised	Most Americans refuse to give up unhealthful habits<u>;</u> <u>consequently,</u> our medical costs are higher than those of many other countries.

Conjunctive adverbs and transitional expressions are different from coordinating conjunctions (*and, but,* and so on) and subordinating conjunctions (*although, because,* and so on):

- Unlike conjunctions, conjunctive adverbs and transitional expressions do not join two clauses into a grammatical unit but merely describe the way two clauses relate in meaning.
- Thus, unlike conjunctions, conjunctive adverbs and transitional expressions can be moved from one place to another in a clause (see also p. 268). No matter where in the clause an adverb or expression falls, though, the clause must be separated from another main clause by a period or semicolon.

cs

18b

Comma splice

The increased time devoted to watching television is not the only cause of the decline in reading ability, <u>however</u>, it is one of the important causes.

Period

The increased time devoted to watching television is not the only cause of the decline in reading ability<u>.</u> <u>However,</u> it is one of the important causes.

Semicolon

The increased time devoted to watching television is not the only cause of the decline in reading ability<u>;</u> <u>however,</u> it is one of the important causes.

The increased time devoted to watching television is not the only cause of the decline in reading ability<u>;</u> it is<u>,</u> <u>however,</u> one of the important causes.

EXERCISE 1
Identifying and revising comma splices
Correct each comma splice below in *two* of the ways described on pages 360–61. If an item contains no comma splice, circle the number preceding it.

Example:

Carolyn still had a headache, she could not get the child-proof cap off the aspirin bottle.

Carolyn still had a headache because she could not get the child-proof cap off the aspirin bottle. [Subordination.]

Carolyn still had a headache, for she could not get the child-proof cap off the aspirin bottle. [Coordinating conjunction.]

1. Money has a long history, it goes back at least as far as the earliest records.
2. Many of the earliest records concern financial transactions, indeed, early history must often be inferred from commercial activity.
3. Every known society has had a system of money, though the objects serving as money have varied widely.
4. Sometimes the objects have had real value, in modern times, however, their value has been more abstract.
5. Cattle, fermented beverages, and rare shells have served as money, each one had actual value for the society.

FUSED SENTENCES

18c **Combine two main clauses only with an appropriate conjunction or punctuation mark between them.**

fs
18c

When two main clauses are joined without a word to connect them or a punctuation mark to separate them, the result is a **fused sentence.** Fused sentences can rarely be understood on first reading, and they are never acceptable in standard written English.

Fused Our foreign policy is not well defined it confuses many countries.

Fused sentences may be corrected in the same ways as comma splices. See pages 360–61.

Separate sentences
Our foreign policy is not well defined. It confuses many countries.

http://www.ablongman.com/littlebrown
For added help and practice with avoiding fused sentences, click on
➤ Sentences
  ➤ Exercises ➤ Exers. 37–39
  ➤ Web links ➤ Comma splices and fused sentences

Comma and coordinating conjunction
Our foreign policy is not well defined**,** and it confuses many countries.

Semicolon
Our foreign policy is not well defined**;** it confuses many countries.

Subordinating conjunction
<u>Because</u> our foreign policy is not well defined**,** it confuses many countries.

EXERCISE 2
Identifying and revising fused sentences
Revise each of the fused sentences below in *two* of the four ways shown above.

Example:
Tim was shy he usually refused invitations.
Tim was shy**,** so he usually refused invitations.
Tim was shy**;** he usually refused invitations.

1. Throughout history money and religion were closely linked there was little distinction between government and religion.
2. The head of state and the religious leader were often the same person all power rested in one ruler.
3. These powerful leaders decided what objects would serve as money their backing encouraged public faith in the money.
4. Coins were minted of precious metals the religious overtones of money were then strengthened.
5. People already believed the precious metals to be divine their use in money intensified its allure.

EXERCISE 3
Sentence combining: Comma splices and fused sentences
Combine each pair of sentences below into one sentence without creating a comma splice or fused sentence. Combine sentences by (1) supplying a comma and coordinating conjunction, (2) supplying a semicolon, or (3) subordinating one clause to the other. You will have to add, delete, or change words as well as punctuation.

Example:
The sun sank lower in the sky. The colors gradually faded.
As the sun sank lower in the sky**,** the colors gradually faded. [The first clause is subordinated to the second.]

1. The exact origin of paper money is unknown. It has not survived as coins, shells, and other durable objects have.
2. Perhaps goldsmiths were also bankers. Thus they held the gold of their wealthy customers.
3. The goldsmiths probably gave customers receipts for their gold. These receipts were then used in trade.

4. The goldsmiths were something like modern-day bankers. Their receipts were something like modern-day money.

5. The goldsmiths became even more like modern-day bankers. They began issuing receipts for more gold than they actually held in their vaults.

EXERCISE 4
Revising: Comma splices and fused sentences

Identify and revise the comma splices and fused sentences in the following paragraph.

All those parents who urged their children to eat broccoli were right, the vegetable really is healthful. Broccoli contains sulforaphane, moreover, this mustard oil can be found in kale and Brussels sprouts. Sulforaphane causes the body to make an enzyme that attacks carcinogens, these substances cause cancer. The enzyme speeds up the work of the kidneys then they can flush harmful chemicals out of the body. Other vegetables have similar benefits however, green, leafy vegetables like broccoli are the most efficient. Thus wise people will eat their broccoli it could save their lives.

Note See page 401 for an exercise involving comma splices and fused sentences along with other sentence errors.

cs/fs

18

CHAPTER 19

Pronoun Reference

A **pronoun** such as *it* or *they* derives its meaning from its **antecedent,** the noun it substitutes for. Therefore, a pronoun must refer clearly and unmistakably to its antecedent in order for the meaning to be clear. A sentence such as *Jim told Mark he was not invited* is not clear because the reader does not know whether *he* refers to Jim or to Mark.

One way to make pronoun reference clear is to ensure that the pronoun and antecedent agree in person, number, and gender (see p. 326). The other way is to ensure that the pronoun refers unambiguously to a single, close, specific antecedent.

Note Grammar and style checkers cannot recognize unclear pronoun reference. For instance, a checker did not spot any of the problems in Exercise 2 on pages 372–73. You must proofread your work to spot unclear pronoun reference.

CULTURE LANGUAGE An English pronoun does need a clear antecedent nearby, but don't use both a pronoun and its antecedent as the subject of the same sentence or clause: *Jim* [not *Jim he*] *told Mark to go alone.* (See also pp. 393–94.)

19a Make a pronoun refer clearly to one antecedent.

When either of two nouns can be a pronoun's antecedent, the reference will not be clear:

> **Confusing** Emily Dickinson is sometimes compared with Jane
> Austen, but she was quite different.

http://www.ablongman.com/littlebrown
For added help and practice with pronoun reference, click on
  ➤ **Sentences**
      ➤ **Video tutorials** ➤ **Recognizing pronoun reference problems**
      ➤ **Exercises** ➤ **Exers. 40 and 41**
      ➤ **Web links** ➤ **Pronoun reference**

Principal causes of unclear pronoun reference

- **More than one possible antecedent** (facing page and below):

  Confusing   To keep birds from eating seeds, soak them in blue food coloring.

  Clear   To keep birds from eating seeds, soak the seeds in blue food coloring.

- **Antecedent too far away** (p. 368):

  Confusing   Employees should consult with their supervisor who require personal time.

  Clear   Employees who require personal time should consult with their supervisor.

- **Antecedent only implied** (p. 369):

  Confusing   Many children begin reading on their own by watching television, but this should be discounted in government policy.

  Clear   Many children begin reading on their own by watching television, but such self-instruction should be discounted in government policy.

See also pages 371–72.

ref
19a

Revise such a sentence in one of two ways:

- Replace the pronoun with the appropriate noun:

  Clear   Emily Dickinson is sometimes compared with Jane Austen, but Dickinson [or Austen] was quite different.

- Avoid repetition by rewriting the sentence. If you use the pronoun, make sure it has only one possible antecedent:

  Clear   Despite occasional comparison, Emily Dickinson and Jane Austen were quite different.

  Clear   Though sometimes compared with her, Emily Dickinson was quite different from Jane Austen.

Sentences that report what someone said, using verbs such as *said* or *told*, often require direct rather than indirect quotation:

  Confusing   Juliet Noble told Ann Torre that she was next in line for the job.

  Clear   Juliet Noble told Ann Torre, "I am next in line for the job."

  Clear   Juliet Noble told Ann Torre, "You are next in line for the job."

Note Avoid the awkward device of using a pronoun followed by the appropriate noun in parentheses, as in the following example:

Weak	Noble and Torre had both hoped for the job, so <u>she (Noble)</u> was disappointed.
Improved	Noble was disappointed because she and Torre had both hoped for the job.

19b Place a pronoun close enough to its antecedent to ensure clarity.

A clause beginning *who, which,* or *that* generally should fall immediately after the word to which it refers:

Confusing	Jody found a lamp in the attic that her aunt had used.
Clear	In the attic Jody found a lamp that her aunt had used.

Even when only one word could possibly serve as the antecedent of a pronoun, the relationship between the two may still be unclear if they are widely separated:

Confusing	Jane Austen had little formal education but was well educated at home. Far from living an isolated life in the English countryside, the Austens were a large family with a wide circle of friends who provided entertainment and cultural enrichment. They also provided material for <u>her</u> stories.
Clear	Jane Austen had little formal education but was well educated at home. Far from living an isolated life in the English countryside, the Austens were a large family with a wide circle of friends who provided entertainment and cultural enrichment. They also provided material for <u>Jane Austen's</u> stories.

The confusing separation of pronoun and antecedent is most likely to occur in long sentences and, as illustrated above, in adjacent sentences within a paragraph.

http://www.ablongman.com/littlebrown
For added help and practice with clear and close pronoun reference, click on
➤ Sentences
  ➤ Exercises ➤ Exer. 40
  ➤ Web links ➤ Pronoun reference

ref
19b

EXERCISE 1
Revising: Ambiguous and remote pronoun reference
Rewrite the following sentences to eliminate unclear pronoun reference. If you use a pronoun in your revision, be sure that it refers to only one antecedent and that it falls close enough to its antecedent to ensure clarity.

> *Example:*
> Saul found an old gun in the rotting shed that was just as his grandfather had left it.
> In the rotting shed Saul found an old <u>gun that</u> was just as his grandfather had left it.

1. There is a difference between the heroes of the twentieth century and the heroes of earlier times: they have flaws in their characters.
2. Sports fans still admire Pete Rose, Babe Ruth, and Joe Namath even though they could not be perfect.
3. Fans liked Rose for having his young son serve as batboy when he was in Cincinnati.
4. Rose's reputation as a gambler and tax evader may overshadow his reputation as a ball player, but it will survive.
5. Rose amassed an unequaled record as a hitter, using his bat to do things no one else has ever done. It stands even though Rose has been banned from baseball.

19c Make a pronoun refer to a specific antecedent, not an implied one.

ref
19c

A pronoun should refer to a specific noun or other pronoun. The reader can only guess at the meaning of a pronoun when its antecedent is implied by the context, not stated outright.

1 ■ Use *this, that, which,* and *it* cautiously.

The most common kind of implied reference occurs when the pronoun *this, that, which,* or *it* refers to a whole idea or situation described in the preceding clause, sentence, or even paragraph. Such reference, often called **broad reference**, is acceptable only when the

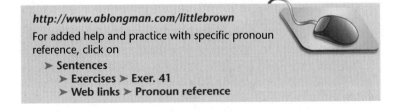

http://www.ablongman.com/littlebrown
For added help and practice with specific pronoun reference, click on
➤ **Sentences**
   ➤ **Exercises** ➤ **Exer. 41**
   ➤ **Web links** ➤ **Pronoun reference**

pronoun refers clearly to the entire preceding clause. In the following sentence, *which* could not possibly refer to anything but the
whole preceding clause:

> I can be kind and civil to people, <u>which</u> is more than you can.
> —George Bernard Shaw

But if a pronoun might confuse a reader, you should avoid using it
or provide an appropriate noun:

Confusing	The faculty agreed on changing the requirements, but <u>it</u> took time.
Clear	The faculty agreed on changing the requirements, but <u>the agreement</u> took time.
Clear	The faculty agreed on changing the requirements, but <u>the change</u> took time.
Confusing	The British knew little of the American countryside, and they had no experience with the colonists' guerrilla tactics. <u>This</u> gave the colonists an advantage.
Clear	The British knew little of the American countryside, and they had no experience with the colonists' guerrilla tactics. This <u>ignorance and inexperience</u> gave the colonists an advantage.

2 ▪ Implied nouns are not clear antecedents.

A noun may be implied in some other word or phrase, such as
an adjective (*happiness* implied in *happy*), a verb (*driver* implied in
drive), or a possessive (*mother* implied in *mother's*). But a pronoun
cannot refer clearly to an implied noun, only to a specific, stated
one:

Confusing	Cohen's report brought <u>her</u> a lawsuit.
Clear	Cohen was sued over <u>her</u> report.
Confusing	Her reports on psychological development generally go unnoticed outside <u>it</u>.
Clear	Her reports on psychological development generally go unnoticed outside <u>the field</u>.

3 ▪ Titles of papers are not clear antecedents.

The title of a paper is entirely separate from the paper itself, so
a pronoun should not be used in the opening sentence of a paper to
refer to the title:

Title	How to Row a Boat
Not	This is not as easy as it looks.
But	Rowing a boat is not as easy as it looks.

19d Use *it* and *they* to refer to definite antecedents.

In conversation we commonly use expressions such as *It says in the paper* or *In Texas they say*. But such indefinite use of *it* and *they* is inappropriate in writing. The constructions are not only unclear but wordy:

Confusing	In Chapter 4 of this book, it describes the early flights of the Wright brothers.
Clear	Chapter 4 of this book describes the early flights of the Wright brothers.
Confusing	In the average television drama, they present a false picture of life.
Clear	The average television drama presents a false picture of life.

19e Use *you* only to mean "you, the reader."

ref
19e

In all but very formal writing, *you* is acceptable when the meaning is clearly "you, the reader." But the context must be appropriate for such a meaning:

Inappropriate	In the fourteenth century you had to struggle simply to survive.
Revised	In the fourteenth century one [or a person] had to struggle simply to survive.

Writers sometimes drift into *you* because *one, a person, the individual,* or a similar indefinite word can be difficult to sustain. Sentence after sentence, the indefinite word may sound stuffy, and it requires the sexist *he* or the awkward *he or she* for pronoun-antecedent agreement (see pp. 326–30). To avoid these difficulties, try using plural nouns and pronouns:

Original	In the fourteenth century one had to struggle simply to survive.
Revised	In the fourteenth century people had to struggle simply to survive.

19f   Use the pronoun *it* only one way in a sentence.

We use *it* idiomatically in expressions such as *It is raining.* We use *it* to postpone the subject in sentences such as *It is true that more jobs are available to women today.* And we use *it* as a personal pronoun in sentences such as *Joan wanted the book, but she couldn't find it.* All these uses are standard, but two of them in the same passage can confuse the reader:

Confusing	It is true that the Constitution sets limits, but it is also flexible.
Clear	The Constitution does set limits, but it is also flexible.

19g   Use *who, which,* and *that* for appropriate antecedents.

The relative pronouns *who, which,* and *that* commonly refer to persons, animals, or things. *Who* refers most often to persons but may also refer to animals that have names:

> Dorothy is the girl who visits Oz.
> Her dog, Toto, who accompanies her, gives her courage.

Which refers to animals and things:

> The Orinoco River, which is 1,600 miles long, flows through Venezuela into the Atlantic Ocean.

That refers to animals and things and occasionally to persons when they are collective or anonymous:

> The rocket that failed cost millions.
> Infants that walk need constant tending.

(See also p. 461 for the use of *which* and *that* in nonessential and essential clauses.)

The possessive *whose* generally refers to people but may refer to animals and things to avoid awkward and wordy *of which* constructions:

> The book whose binding broke was rare. [Compare *The book of which the binding broke was rare.*]

EXERCISE 2
Revising: Indefinite and inappropriate pronoun reference
Many of the pronouns in the following sentences do not refer to specific, appropriate antecedents. Revise the sentences as necessary to make them clear.

Example:

In Grand Teton National Park, they have moose, elk, and trumpeter swans.

<u>Moose, elk, and trumpeter swans live</u> in Grand Teton National Park.

1. "Life begins at forty" is a cliché many people live by, and this may well be true.
2. When she was forty, Pearl Buck's novel *The Good Earth* won the Pulitzer Prize.
3. Buck was a novelist which wrote primarily about China.
4. In *The Good Earth* you have to struggle, but fortitude is rewarded.
5. Buck received much critical praise and earned over $7 million, but she was very modest about it.
6. Kenneth Kaunda, past president of Zambia, was elected to it in 1964, at age forty.
7. When Catherine I became empress of Russia at age forty, they feared more than loved her.
8. At forty, Paul Revere made his famous ride to warn American revolutionary leaders that the British were going to arrest them. This gave the colonists time to prepare for battle.
9. In the British House of Commons they did not welcome forty-year-old Nancy Astor as the first female member when she entered in 1919.
10. In AD 610, Muhammad, age forty, began to have a series of visions that became the foundation of the Muslim faith. Since then, millions of people have become one.

ref

19g

EXERCISE 3
Revising: Pronoun reference
Revise the following paragraph so that each pronoun refers clearly to a single specific and appropriate antecedent.

In Charlotte Brontë's *Jane Eyre,* she is a shy young woman that takes a job as governess. Her employer is a rude, brooding man named Rochester. He lives in a mysterious mansion on the English moors, which contributes an eerie quality to Jane's experience. Eerier still are the fires, strange noises, and other unexplained happenings in the house; but Rochester refuses to discuss this. Eventually, they fall in love. On the day they are to be married, however, she learns that he has a wife hidden in the house. She is hopelessly insane and violent and must be guarded at all times, which explains his strange behavior. Heartbroken, Jane leaves the moors, and many years pass before they are reunited.

Note See page 401 for an exercise involving unclear pronoun reference along with sentence fragments, comma splices, and other sentence errors.

CHAPTER 20

Shifts

Inconsistencies in grammatical elements will confuse your readers and distort your meaning. In the following passage from a first draft, the underlining indicates confusing inconsistencies in verbs and subjects:

First draft

A <u>bank</u> commonly <u>owes</u> more to its customers than <u>is held</u> in reserve. <u>They kept</u> enough assets to meet reasonable withdrawals, but panicked <u>customers</u> may demand all their deposits. Then demands <u>will exceed</u> supplies, and <u>banks failed</u>. These days, <u>a person's</u> losses are not likely to be great because the government insures <u>your</u> deposits.

Revised

A bank commonly owes more to its customers than <u>it holds</u> in reserve. <u>It keeps</u> enough assets to meet reasonable withdrawals, but panicked customers may demand all their deposits. Then demands will exceed supplies, and the <u>bank will fail</u>. These days, the losses of <u>customers</u> are not likely to be great because the government insures <u>their</u> deposits.

Holds to match *owes*

Singular *It* and present-tense *keeps* to match *bank . . . owes*

Singular *bank* to match *bank;* future tense to match *will exceed*

Plural *customers* to match *customers*

Their to match *customers*

Shifts like those in the first draft are likely to occur while you are trying to piece together meaning during drafting. But during editing you should make your sentences consistent in grammatical elements.

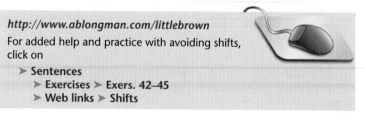

http://www.ablongman.com/littlebrown
For added help and practice with avoiding shifts, click on
➤ Sentences
   ➤ Exercises ➤ Exers. 42–45
   ➤ Web links ➤ Shifts

Note Grammar and style checkers cannot recognize most shifts in sentences. Proofread your work on your own, looking carefully for inconsistencies.

20a Keep a sentence or related sentences consistent in person and number.

Person in grammar refers to the distinction among the person talking (first person), the person spoken to (second person), and the person, object, or concept being talked about (third person). **Number** refers to the distinction between one (singular) and more than one (plural).

Shifts in person

Most shifts in person occur because we can refer to people in general, including our readers, either in the third person (*a person, one; people, they*) or in the second person (*you*):

> People should not drive when they have been drinking.
> One should not drive when he or she has been drinking.
> You should not drive when you have been drinking.

Although any one of these possibilities is acceptable in an appropriate context, a mixture of them is inconsistent:

Inconsistent	If a person works hard, you can accomplish a great deal.
Revised	If you work hard, you can accomplish a great deal.
Revised	If a person works hard, he or she can accomplish a great deal.
Better	If people work hard, they can accomplish a great deal.

shift

20a

Shifts in number

Inconsistency in number occurs most often between a pronoun and its antecedent (see p. 326):

Inconsistent	If a student does not understand a problem, they should consult the instructor.
Revised	If a student does not understand a problem, he or she should consult the instructor.
Better	If students do not understand a problem, they should consult the instructor.
Or	A student who does not understand a problem should consult the instructor.

Note Generic nouns and most indefinite pronouns take singular pronouns with a definite gender: *he, she,* or *it.* When we use a generic noun like *student* or *person* or an indefinite pronoun like *everyone* or *each*, we often mean to include both males and females. To indicate this meaning, use *he or she* rather than *he* (as in the first of the preceding revisions) or, better still, rewrite in the plural or rewrite to avoid the pronoun (as in the second and third of the revisions). See page 330 for more discussion and examples.

Inconsistency in number can also occur between other words (usually nouns) that relate to each other in meaning.

Inconsistent	All the <u>boys</u> have a good <u>reputation</u>.
Revised	All the <u>boys</u> have good <u>reputations</u>.

The consistency in the revised sentence is called **logical agreement** because the nouns are consistent (the *boys* have *reputations*, not a single *reputation*).

EXERCISE 1
Revising: Shifts in person and number

Revise the following sentences to make them consistent in person and number.

Example:

A plumber will fix burst pipes, but they won't repair waterlogged appliances.

<u>Plumbers</u> will fix burst pipes, but they won't repair waterlogged appliances.

1. When a taxpayer is waiting to receive a tax refund from the Internal Revenue Service, you begin to notice what time the mail carrier arrives.
2. If the taxpayer does not receive a refund check within six weeks of filing a return, they may not have followed the rules of the IRS.
3. If a taxpayer does not include a Social Security number on a return, you will have to wait for a refund.
4. When taxpayers do not file their return early, they will not get a refund quickly.
5. If one makes errors on the tax form, they might even be audited, thereby delaying a refund even longer.

20b Keep a sentence or related sentences consistent in tense and mood.

Shifts in tense

Within a sentence or from one sentence to another, certain changes in tense may be required to indicate changes in actual or relative time (see p. 306). For example:

Ramon <u>will graduate</u> from college thirty-one years after his father <u>arrived</u> in the United States.

But changes that are not required by meaning distract readers. Unnecessary shifts between past and present in passages narrating a series of events are particularly confusing:

Inconsistent	Immediately after Booth <u>shot</u> Lincoln, Major Rathbone <u>threw</u> himself upon the assassin. But Booth <u>pulls</u> a knife and <u>plunges</u> it into the major's arm.
Revised	Immediately after Booth <u>shot</u> Lincoln, Major Rathbone <u>threw</u> himself upon the assassin. But Booth <u>pulled</u> a knife and <u>plunged</u> it into the major's arm.

Use the present tense consistently to describe what an author has written, including the action in literature or a film:

Inconsistent	The main character in the novel <u>suffers</u> psychologically because he <u>has</u> a clubfoot, but he eventually <u>triumphed</u> over his disability.
Revised	The main character in the novel <u>suffers</u> psychologically because he <u>has</u> a clubfoot, but he eventually <u>triumphs</u> over his disability.

Shifts in mood

Shifts in the mood of verbs occur most frequently in directions when the writer moves between the imperative mood (*Unplug the appliance*) and the indicative mood (*You should unplug the appliance*). (See p. 312.) Directions are usually clearer and more concise in the imperative, as long as its use is consistent:

shift

20b

Inconsistent	<u>Cook</u> the mixture slowly, and <u>you should stir</u> it until the sugar is dissolved.
Revised	<u>Cook</u> the mixture slowly, and <u>stir</u> it until the sugar is dissolved.

EXERCISE 2
Revising: Shifts in tense and mood

Revise the following sentences to make them consistent in tense and mood.

Example:

Lynn ran to first, rounded the base, and keeps running until she slides into second.

Lynn ran to first, rounded the base, and <u>kept</u> running until she <u>slid</u> into second.

1. When your cholesterol count is too high, adjusting your diet and exercise level reduced it.

2. After you lowered your cholesterol rate, you decrease the chances of heart attack and stroke.
3. First eliminate saturated fats from your diet; then you should consume more whole grains and raw vegetables.
4. To avoid saturated fats, substitute turkey and chicken for beef, and you should use cholesterol-free salad dressing and cooking oil.
5. A regular program of aerobic exercise, such as walking or swimming, improves your cholesterol rate and made you feel much healthier.

20c   Keep a sentence or related sentences consistent in subject and voice.

When a verb is in the **active voice,** the subject names the actor: *Linda passed the peas.* When a verb is in the **passive voice,** the subject names the receiver of the action: *The peas were passed* [*by Linda*]. (See pp. 314–16.)

A shift in voice may sometimes help focus the reader's attention on a single subject, as in *The candidate campaigned vigorously and was nominated on the first ballot.* However, most shifts in voice also involve shifts in subject. They are unnecessary and confusing.

> **Inconsistent**   Internet newsgroups cover an enormous range of topics for discussion. Forums for meeting people with like interests are provided in these groups.
>
> **Revised**   Internet newsgroups cover an enormous range of topics for discussion and provide forums for meeting people with like interests.

EXERCISE 3
Revising: Shifts in subject and voice

Make the following sentences consistent in subject and voice.

Example:
At the reunion they ate hot dogs and volleyball was played.
At the reunion they ate hot dogs and played volleyball.

1. If students learn how to study efficiently, much better grades will be made on tests.
2. Conscientious students begin to prepare for tests immediately after the first class is attended.
3. Before each class all reading assignments are completed, and the students outline the material and answer any study questions.
4. In class they listen carefully and good notes are taken.
5. Questions are asked by the students when they do not understand the professor.

20d Keep a quotation or a question consistently direct or indirect.

Direct quotations or questions report the exact words of a quotation or question:

> "I am the greatest," bragged Muhammad Ali.
> In his day few people asked, "Is he right?"

Indirect quotations or questions report that someone said or asked something, but not in the exact words:

> Muhammad Ali bragged that he was the greatest.
> In his day few people asked whether he was right.

Shifts between direct and indirect quotations or questions are difficult to follow.

Shift in quotation	Kapek reported that the rats avoided the maze and "as of this writing, none responds to conditioning."
Revised (indirect)	Kapek reported that the rats avoided the maze and that as of his writing none responded to conditioning.
Revised (direct)	Kapek reported, "The rats avoid the maze. As of this writing, none responds to conditioning."
Shift in question	The reader wonders whether the experiment failed or did it perhaps succeed?
Revised (indirect)	The reader wonders whether the experiment failed or whether it perhaps succeeded.
Revised (direct)	Did the experiment fail? Or did it perhaps succeed?

shift

20d

For more on quotations, see pages 309–10 (tense and other changes in indirect quotations), 468–70 (commas with signal phrases such as *she said*), 494–501 (quotation marks), and 674–79 (integrating quotations into your writing). For more on questions, see pages 449–50.

EXERCISE 4
Revising: Shifts in direct and indirect quotations and questions

Revise each of the following sentences twice, once to make it consistently direct, once to make it consistently indirect. (You will have to guess at the exact wording of direct quotations and questions that are now stated indirectly.)

Example:

We all wonder what the next decade will bring and will we thrive or not?

Direct: What will the next decade bring? Will we thrive or not?

Indirect: We all wonder what the next decade will bring and whether we will thrive or not.

1. One anthropologist says that the functions of marriage have changed and "nowhere more dramatically than in industrialized cultures."
2. The question even arises of whether siblings may marry and would the union be immoral?
3. The author points out, "Sibling marriage is still illegal everywhere in the United States" and that people are still prosecuted under the law.
4. She says that incest could be considered a universal taboo and "the questions asked about the taboo vary widely."
5. Some ask is the taboo a way of protecting the family or whether it may be instinctive.

EXERCISE 5
Revising: Shifts

Revise the following paragraph to eliminate unnecessary shifts in person, number, tense, mood, and voice.

shift
20d

   Driving in snow need not be dangerous if you practice a few rules. First, one should avoid fast starts, which prevent the wheels from gaining traction and may result in the car's getting stuck. Second, drive more slowly than usual, and you should pay attention to the feel of the car: if the steering seemed unusually loose or the wheels did not seem to be grabbing the road, slow down. Third, avoid fast stops, which lead to skids. One should be alert for other cars and intersections that may necessitate that the brakes be applied suddenly. If you need to slow down, the car's momentum can be reduced by downshifting as well as by applying the brakes. When braking, press the pedal to the floor only if you have antilock brakes; otherwise, the pedal should be pumped in short bursts. If you feel the car skidding, the brakes should be released and the wheel should be turned into the direction of the skid, and then the brakes should be pressed or pumped again. If one repeated these motions, the skid would be stopped and the speed of the car would be reduced.

Note See page 401 for an exercise involving shifts along with sentence fragments, comma splices, and other sentence errors.

CHAPTER 21

Misplaced and Dangling Modifiers

In reading a sentence in English, we depend principally on the arrangement of the words to tell us how they are related. In writing, we may create confusion if we fail to connect modifiers to the words they modify.

Note Grammar and style checkers do not recognize many problems with modifiers. For instance, a checker failed to flag the misplaced modifiers in *Gasoline high prices affect usually car sales* or the dangling modifier in *The vandalism was visible passing the building.* Proofread your work on your own to find and correct problems with modifiers.

MISPLACED MODIFIERS

A modifier is **misplaced** if readers can't easily relate it to the word it modifies. Misplaced modifiers may be awkward, confusing, or even unintentionally funny.

21a Place modifiers where they will clearly modify the words intended.

Readers tend to link a modifying word, phrase, or clause to the nearest word it could modify: *I saw a man in a green hat.* Thus the writer must place the phrase so that it clearly modifies the intended word and not some other.

Confusing He served steak to the men on paper plates.

http://www.ablongman.com/littlebrown

For added help with misplaced modifiers, click on

➤ Sentences
  ➤ Video tutorials ➤ Repairing misplaced modifiers
  ➤ Exercises ➤ Exers. 46–49
  ➤ Web links ➤ Misplaced and dangling modifiers

Revised	He served the men steak on paper plates.
Confusing	Many dogs are killed by automobiles and trucks roaming unleashed.
Revised	Many dogs roaming unleashed are killed by automobiles and trucks.
Confusing	This is the only chocolate chip cookie in a bag that tastes like Mom's. [Actual advertisement.]
Revised	This is the only bagged [or packaged] chocolate chip cookie that tastes like Mom's.

EXERCISE 1
Revising: Misplaced phrases and clauses

Revise the following sentences so that phrases and clauses clearly modify the appropriate words.

> *Example:*
> I came to enjoy flying over time.
> Over time I came to enjoy flying.

1. Women have contributed much to knowledge and culture of great value.
2. Emma Willard founded the Troy Female Seminary, the first institution to provide a college-level education for women in 1821.
3. Sixteen years later Mary Lyon founded Mount Holyoke Female Seminary, the first true women's college with directors and a campus who would sustain the college even after Lyon's death.
4. *Una* was the first US newspaper, which was founded by Pauline Wright Davis in 1853, that was dedicated to gaining women's rights.
5. Mitchell's Comet was discovered in 1847, which was named for Maria Mitchell.

21b Place limiting modifiers carefully.

Limiting modifiers include *almost, even, exactly, hardly, just, merely, nearly, only, scarcely,* and *simply.* They modify the expressions that immediately follow them, as these uses of *just* show:

Just the manuscript was discovered by an archaeologist.
The manuscript was just discovered by an archaeologist.
The manuscript was discovered just by an archaeologist.

In speech several limiting modifiers frequently occur before the verb, regardless of the words they are intended to modify. In writing, however, these modifiers should fall immediately before the word or word group they modify to avoid any ambiguity:

Unclear	He only discovered the manuscript on his last dig.
Revised	He discovered only the manuscript on his last dig.
Revised	He discovered the manuscript only on his last dig.

EXERCISE 2
Using limiting modifiers

Use each of the following limiting modifiers in two versions of the same sentence.

Example:
only
He is the only one I like. He is the one only I like.

1. almost   3. hardly   5. nearly
2. even   4. simply

21c   Make each modifier refer to only one grammatical element.

A modifier can modify only *one* element in a sentence—the subject, the verb, or some other element. A **squinting modifier** seems confusingly to refer to either of two words:

Squinting	Snipers who fired on the soldiers often escaped capture.
Clear	Snipers who often fired on the soldiers escaped capture.
Clear	Snipers who fired on the soldiers escaped capture often.

When an adverb modifies an entire main clause, as in the last example, it can usually be moved to the beginning of the sentence: *Often, snipers who fired on the soldiers escaped capture.*

EXERCISE 3
Revising: Squinting modifiers

Revise each sentence twice so that the squinting modifier applies clearly first to one element and then to the other.

Example:

The work that he hoped would satisfy him completely frustrated him.

The work that he hoped would <u>completely</u> satisfy him frustrated him.

The work that he hoped would satisfy him frustrated him <u>completely</u>.

1. People who sunbathe often can damage their skin.
2. Sunbathers who apply a sunscreen frequently block some of the sun's harmful ultraviolet rays.
3. Men and women who lie out in the sun often have leathery, dry skin.
4. Doctors tell sunbathers when they are older they risk skin cancer.
5. People who stay out of the sun usually will have better skin and fewer chances of skin cancer.

21d   Keep subjects, verbs, and objects together.

English sentences tend to move from subject to verb to object. The movement is so familiar that modifiers between these elements can be awkward.

A subject and verb may be separated by an adjective that modifies the subject: *Kuwait, which has a population of 1.3 million, is a rich nation.* But an adverb of more than a word usually stops the flow of the sentence:

Awkward   subject ┌——— adverb ———┐ verb
Kuwait, <u>after the Gulf War ended in 1991</u>, began returning to normal.

Revised   ┌——— adverb ———┐ subject verb
<u>After the Gulf War ended in 1991</u>, Kuwait began returning to normal.

A modifier between a verb and its direct object is always awkward:

Awkward   ┌— verb —┐ adverb object
The war had damaged <u>badly</u> many of Kuwait's oil fields.

Revised   ┌— verb —┐ object
The war had <u>badly</u> damaged many of Kuwait's oil fields.
        adverb

See the facing page on inserting single-word adverbs between parts of a verb phrase, as in the revision above.

21e Keep parts of infinitives or verb phrases together.

An **infinitive** consists of the marker *to* plus the plain form of a verb: *to produce, to enjoy.* The two parts of the infinitive are widely regarded as a grammatical unit that should not be split:

infinitive

Awkward   The weather service expected temperatures to not rise.

infinitive

Revised   The weather service expected temperatures not to rise.

A split infinitive may sometimes be natural and preferable, though it may still bother some readers:

infinitive

Several US industries expect to more than triple their use of robots.

Here the split infinitive is more economical than the alternatives, such as *Several US industries expect to increase their use of robots by more than three times.*

A **verb phrase** consists of a helping verb plus a main verb, as in *will call, was going, had been writing* (see p. 286). A single-word adverb may be inserted after the helping verb in a verb phrase (or the first helping verb if more than one): *Scientists have lately been using spacecraft to study the sun.* But when longer adverbs interrupt verb phrases, the result is almost always awkward.

helping
verb   adverb

Awkward   The spacecraft *Ulysses* will after traveling near the sun
main verb
report on the sun's energy fields.

adverb

Revised   After traveling near the sun, the spacecraft *Ulysses*
verb phrase
will report on the sun's energy fields.

CULTURE LANGUAGE In an English question, place a one-word adverb after the first helping verb and the subject:

helping   rest of
verb   subject adverb verb phrase
Will spacecraft ever be able to leave the solar system?

mm
21e

EXERCISE 4
Revising: Separated sentence parts

Revise the following sentences to connect separated parts (subject-predicate, verb-object, verb phrase, infinitive).

Example:

Most children have by the time they are seven lost a tooth.
By the time they are seven, most children have lost a tooth.

1. Myra Bradwell founded in 1868 the *Chicago Legal News.*
2. Bradwell was later denied, although she had qualified, admission to the Illinois Bar Association.
3. In an attempt to finally gain admission to the bar, she carried the case to the Supreme Court, but the justices decided against her.
4. Bradwell was determined that no other woman would, if she were qualified, be denied entrance to a profession.
5. The Illinois legislature finally passed, in response to Bradwell's persuasion, a bill ensuring that no one on the basis of gender would be restricted from a profession.

21f   Position adverbs with care. ⟨ CULTURE LANGUAGE ⟩

mm
21f

Most adverbs may fall in several places in a sentence, as long as they clearly modify the intended word (21b, 21c) and do not separate sentence parts awkwardly (21d, 21e). A few adverbs are subject to additional conventions that can trouble nonnative speakers of English.

Adverbs of frequency

Adverbs of frequency include *always, never, often, rarely, seldom, sometimes,* and *usually.* They appear at the beginning of a sentence, before a one-word verb, or after the helping verb in a verb phrase:

	verb phrase adverb
Awkward	Robots have put <u>sometimes</u> humans out of work.

	helping main
	verb adverb verb
Revised	Robots have <u>sometimes</u> put humans out of work.

	adverb verb phrase
Revised	<u>Sometimes</u> robots have put humans out of work.

Adverbs of frequency always follow the verb *be:*

	adverb verb
Awkward	Robots <u>often</u> are helpful to workers.

	verb adverb
Revised	Robots are <u>often</u> helpful to workers.

Adverbs of degree

Adverbs of degree include *absolutely, almost, certainly, completely, especially, extremely, hardly,* and *only.* They fall just before the word modified (an adjective, another adverb, sometimes a verb).

http://www.ablongman.com/littlebrown

For added help and practice with positioning adverbs and adjectives, click on

➤ **Sentences**
   ➤ **Exercises** ➤ **Exer. 48**
   ➤ **Web links** ➤ **Misplaced and dangling modifiers**

	adjective adverb
Awkward	Robots have been useful <u>especially</u> in making cars.

	adverb adjective
Revised	Robots have been <u>especially</u> useful in making cars.

Adverbs of manner

Adverbs of manner include *badly, beautifully, openly, sweetly, tightly, well,* and others that describe how something is done. They usually fall after the verb:

	adverb verb
Awkward	Robots <u>smoothly</u> work on assembly lines.

	verb adverb
Revised	Robots work <u>smoothly</u> on assembly lines.

The adverb *not*

When the adverb *not* modifies a verb, place it after the helping verb (or the first helping verb if more than one):

	helping main verb verb
Awkward	Robots do think <u>not</u>.

	helping main verb verb
Revised	Robots do <u>not</u> think.

Place *not* after a form of *be: Robots are <u>not</u> thinkers.*

When *not* modifies another adverb or an adjective, place it before the other modifier: *Robots are <u>not</u> sleek machines.*

mm
21g

21g Arrange adjectives appropriately. ⟨CULTURE LANGUAGE⟩

English follows distinctive rules for arranging two or three adjectives before a noun. (A string of more than three adjectives before a noun is rare.) The order depends on the meaning of the adjectives, as indicated in the following table:

Determiner	Opinion	Size or shape	Color	Origin	Material	Noun used as adjective	Noun
many						state	**laws**
	striking		green	Thai			**birds**
a	fine			German			**camera**
this		square			wooden		**table**
all						business	**reports**
the			blue		litmus		**paper**

See page 465 for guidelines on punctuating two or more adjectives before a noun.

EXERCISE 5
Revising: Placement of adverbs and adjectives   CULTURE LANGUAGE

Revise the sentences below to correct the positions of adverbs or adjectives. If a sentence is already correct as given, circle the number preceding it.

> *Example:*
> Gasoline high prices affect usually car sales.
> <u>High</u> gasoline prices <u>usually</u> affect car sales.

1. Some years ago Detroit cars often were praised.
2. Luxury large cars especially were prized.
3. Then a serious oil shortage led drivers to value small foreign cars that got good mileage.
4. Now with gasoline ample supplies, consumers are returning to American large cars.
5. However, the large cars not are luxury sedans but vans and sport-utility vehicles.

DANGLING MODIFIERS

21h   Relate dangling modifiers to their sentences.

dm
21h

A **dangling modifier** does not sensibly modify anything in its sentence:

Dangling   Passing the building, the vandalism became visible. [The modifying phrase seems to describe *vandalism*, but vandalism does not pass buildings. Who was passing the building? Who saw the vandalism?]

Dangling modifiers usually introduce sentences, contain a verb form, and imply but do not name a subject: in the preceding example, the implied subject is the someone or something passing the building. Readers assume that this implied subject is the same as the subject of the sentence (*vandalism* in the example). When it is not, the modifier "dangles" unconnected to the rest of the sentence.

The modifiers most likely to dangle are participial, infinitive, and prepositional phrases and elliptical clauses.

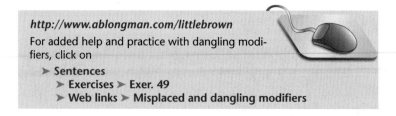

http://www.ablongman.com/littlebrown
For added help and practice with dangling modifiers, click on
➤ Sentences
   ➤ Exercises ➤ Exer. 49
   ➤ Web links ➤ Misplaced and dangling modifiers

- Participial phrases:

  Dangling   <u>Passing the building</u>, the vandalism became visible.
  Revised   <u>As we passed</u> the building, the vandalism became visible.

- Infinitive phrases:

  Dangling   <u>To understand the causes</u>, vandalism has been extensively investigated.
  Revised   To understand the causes, <u>researchers have</u> extensively <u>investigated</u> vandalism.

- Prepositional phrases in which the object of the preposition is a gerund:

  Dangling   <u>After studying the problem</u>, vandals are now thought to share certain characteristics.
  Revised   After studying the problem, <u>researchers think that</u> vandals share certain characteristics.

- Elliptical clauses in which the subject and perhaps the verb are omitted:

  Dangling   <u>When destructive</u>, researchers have learned that vandals are more likely to be in groups.
  Revised   When <u>vandals are</u> destructive, researchers have learned, <u>they</u> are more likely to be in groups.

dm

21h

Dangling modifiers are especially likely when the verb in the main clause is in the **passive voice** instead of the **active voice**—that is, when the verb expresses what is *done to* the subject instead of what the subject *does* (see pp. 314–15). The passive voice appears in the second and third examples above: *vandalism has been investigated; vandals are thought.* The revisions recast the verbs and subjects as active: *researchers have investigated; researchers think.*

Note that a modifier may be dangling even when the sentence elsewhere contains a word the modifier might seem to describe, such as *vandals* below:

Dangling   <u>When destructive</u>, researchers have learned that vandals are more likely to be in groups.

In addition, a dangling modifier may fall at the end of a sentence:

Dangling   The vandalism was visible <u>passing the building</u>.

Revising dangling modifiers

Revise most dangling modifiers in one of two ways, depending on what you want to emphasize in the sentence.

Identifying and revising dangling modifiers

- **Identify the modifier's subject.** If the modifier lacks a stated subject (as *when in diapers* does), identify what the modifier describes.
- **Compare the subject of the modifier and the subject of the sentence.** Verify that what the modifier describes is in fact the subject of the main clause. If it is not, the modifier probably dangles.
- **Revise as needed.** Either (*a*) recast the dangling modifier with a stated subject of its own, or (*b*) change the subject of the main clause to be what the modifier describes.

	┌── modifier ──┐ subject
Dangling	When in diapers, my mother remarried.
Revision *a*	When I was in diapers, my mother remarried.
Revision *b*	When in diapers, I attended my mother's second wedding.

- Change the subject of the main clause to a word the modifier properly describes:

Dangling	To express themselves, graffiti decorate walls.
Revised	To express themselves, some youths decorate walls with graffiti.

- Rewrite the dangling modifier as a complete clause with its own stated subject and verb:

Revised	Because some youths need to express themselves, graffiti decorate walls.

dm
21h

EXERCISE 6
Revising: Dangling modifiers
Revise the following sentences to eliminate any dangling modifiers. Each item has more than one possible answer.

Example:
Driving north, the vegetation became increasingly sparse.
Driving north, we noticed that the vegetation became increasingly sparse.
As we drove north, the vegetation became increasingly sparse.

1. After accomplishing many deeds of valor, Andrew Jackson's fame led to his election to the presidency in 1828 and 1832.
2. By the age of fourteen, both of Jackson's parents had died.
3. To aid the American Revolution, service as a mounted courier was chosen by Jackson.
4. Though not well educated, a successful career as a lawyer and judge proved Jackson's ability.
5. Winning many military battles, the American public believed in Jackson's leadership.

EXERCISE 7
Sentence combining: Placing modifiers

Combine each pair of sentences below into a single sentence by rewriting one as a modifier. Make sure the modifier applies clearly to the appropriate word. You will have to add, delete, and rearrange words, and you may find that more than one answer is possible in each case.

> *Example:*
> Bob demanded a hearing from the faculty. Bob wanted to appeal the decision.
> <u>Wanting to appeal the decision</u>, Bob demanded a hearing from the faculty.

1. Evening falls in the Central American rain forests. The tungara frogs begin their croaking chorus.
2. Male tungara frogs croak loudly at night. The "songs" they sing are designed to attract female frogs.
3. But predators also hear the croaking. They gather to feast on the frogs.
4. The predators are lured by their croaking dinners. The predators include bullfrogs, snakes, bats, and opossums.
5. The frogs hope to mate. Their nightly chorus can result in death instead.

EXERCISE 8
Revising: Misplaced and dangling modifiers

Revise the following paragraph to eliminate any misplaced or dangling modifiers.

mm/dm

21

    Central American tungara frogs silence several nights a week their mating croaks. When not croaking, the chance that the frogs will be eaten by predators is reduced. The frogs seem to fully believe in "safety in numbers." They more than likely will croak along with a large group rather than by themselves. By forgoing croaking on some nights, the frogs' behavior prevents the species from "croaking."

Note See page 401 for an exercise involving misplaced and dangling modifiers along with other sentence errors.

CHAPTER 22

Mixed and Incomplete Sentences

MIXED SENTENCES

A **mixed sentence** contains two or more parts that are incompatible—that is, the parts do not fit together. The misfit may be in grammar or in meaning.

Note Grammar and style checkers may recognize a simple mixed construction such as *reason is because,* but they will fail to flag most mixed sentences. A checker was unable to recognize almost all of the mixed sentences in this chapter. Proofread your work carefully to locate and revise problem sentences.

22a Untangle sentences that are mixed in grammar.

Sentences mixed in grammar combine two or more incompatible grammatical structures.

1 ■ Make sure subject and verb fit together grammatically.

A mixed sentence may occur when you start a sentence with one plan and end it with another:

```
                ─────── modifier (prepositional phrase) ───────┐ verb
Mixed    By paying more attention to impressions than facts leads
         us to misjudge others.
```

This mixed sentence makes a prepositional phrase work as the subject of *leads,* but prepositional phrases function as modifiers, not as nouns, and thus not as sentence subjects. (See p. 250.)

```
                ─────── modifier (prepositional phrase) ───────┐
Revised  By paying more attention to impressions than facts,
         subject + verb
         we misjudge others.
```

http://www.ablongman.com/littlebrown
For added help and practice with mixed sentences, click on
➤ Sentences ➤ Exercises ➤ Exer. 50

Revised
┌─────────── subject (gerund phrase) ───────────┐ verb
Paying more attention to impressions than facts leads us
to misjudge others.

Mixed sentences are especially likely on a word processor when you connect parts of two sentences or rewrite half a sentence but not the other half. Mixed sentences may also occur when you don't focus your sentences on the subject and verb so that these elements carry the principal meaning. (See p. 404.) If you need help identifying the subject and verb, see pages 239 and 241. Otherwise, the cure for grammatically mixed sentences is careful editing and proofreading.

Here are two more examples of mixed grammar:

Mixed
┌─────────── modifier (adverb clause) ───────────┐ verb
Although he was seen with a convicted thief does not make him a thief.

Revised
┌─────────── subject (noun clause) ───────────┐ verb
That he was seen with a convicted thief does not make him a thief.

Revised
┌─────────── modifier (adverb clause) ───────────┐ subject + verb
Although he was seen with a convicted thief, he is not necessarily a thief.

Mixed
subject ┌─────────── modifier (adjective clause) ───────────
The fact that someone may be considered guilty just for associating with someone guilty.

Revised
subject verb
The fact is that someone may be considered guilty just for associating with someone guilty.

Revised
subject ┌─────── verb ───────┐
Someone may be considered guilty just for associating with someone guilty.

In some mixed sentences the grammar is so jumbled that the writer has little choice but to start over:

Mixed
My long-range goal is through law school and government work I hope to help people deal with those problems we all deal with more effectively.

Possible
My long-range goal is to go to law school and then work in government so that I can help people deal more effectively with problems we all face.

2 ■ State parts of sentences, such as subjects, only once. ◖ CULTURE LANGUAGE ◗

In some languages other than English, certain parts of sentences may be repeated. These include the subject in any kind of clause or an object or adverb in an adjective clause. In English, however, these parts are stated only once in a clause.

mixed
22a

Repetition of subject

You may be tempted to restate a subject as a pronoun before the verb. But the subject needs stating only once in its clause.

Faulty   The liquid it reached a temperature of 180°F.
Revised   The liquid reached a temperature of 180°F.

Faulty   Gases in the liquid they escaped.
Revised   Gases in the liquid escaped.

Faulty   The supervisor of the lab she had just left.
Revised   The supervisor of the lab had just left.

Repetition in an adjective clause

Adjective clauses begin with *who, whom, whose, which, that, where,* and *when* (see p. 260). The beginning word replaces another word: the subject (*He is the person who called*), an object of a verb or preposition (*He is the person whom I mentioned*), or a preposition and pronoun (*He knows the office where [in which] the conference will occur*).

Do not state the word that *who, whom,* and so on replace in an adjective clause:

Faulty   The technician whom the test depended on her was burned. [*Whom* should replace *her.*]
Revised   The technician whom the test depended on was burned.

Adjective clauses beginning with *where* or *when* do not need an adverb such as *there* or *then:*

Faulty   Gases escaped at a moment when the technician was unprepared then.
Revised   Gases escaped at a moment when the technician was unprepared.

mixed
22b

22b   Match subjects and predicates in meaning.

In a sentence with mixed meaning, the subject is said to be or do something it cannot logically be or do. Such a mixture is sometimes called **faulty predication** because the predicate conflicts with the subject.

Illogical equation with *be*

When a form of *be* connects a subject and a word that describes the subject (a complement), the subject and complement must be logically related:

Mixed   A compromise between the city and the country would be
the ideal place to live.

Revised   A community that offered the best qualities of both city
and country would be the ideal place to live.

Is when, is where

Definitions require nouns on both sides of *be.* Definition
clauses beginning with *when* or *where* are common in speech but
should be avoided in writing:

Mixed   An examination is when you are tested on what you
know.

Revised   An examination is a test of what you know.

Reason is because

The commonly heard construction *reason is because* is redundant since *because* means "for the reason that":

Mixed   The reason the temple requests donations is because the
school needs expansion.

Revised   The reason the temple requests donations is that the
school needs expansion.

Revised   The temple requests donations because the school needs
expansion.

Other mixed meanings

Mismatched subjects and predicates are not confined to sentences with *be:*

Mixed   The use of emission controls was created to reduce air
pollution.

Revised   Emission controls were created to reduce air pollution.

Mixed   The area of financial mismanagement poses a threat to
small businesses.

Revised   Financial mismanagement poses a threat to small businesses.

mixed

22b

EXERCISE 1
Revising: Sentences mixed in grammar or meaning
Revise the following sentences so that their parts fit together both
in grammar and in meaning. Each item has more than one possible
answer.

Example:

When they found out how expensive pianos are is why they were discouraged.

They were discouraged <u>because</u> they found out how expensive pianos are.

When they found out how expensive pianos are, <u>they</u> were discouraged.

1. A hurricane is when the winds in a tropical depression rotate counterclockwise at more than seventy-four miles per hour.
2. Because hurricanes can destroy so many lives and so much property is why people fear them.
3. Through high winds, storm surge, floods, and tornadoes is how a hurricane can kill thousands of people.
4. Among the hurricanes in history, they have become less deadly since 1950.
5. The reason for the lower death rates is because improved communication systems and weather satellites warn people early enough to escape the hurricane.

EXERCISE 2
Revising: Repeated sentence parts   **CULTURE LANGUAGE**

Revise the following sentences to eliminate any unnecessary repetition of sentence parts.

Example:

Over 79 percent of Americans they have heard of global warming.

Over 79 percent of <u>Americans have</u> heard of global warming.

1. Global warming it is caused by the gradual erosion of the ozone layer that protects the earth from the sun.
2. Scientists who study this problem they say that the primary causes of erosion are the use of fossil fuels and the reduction of forests.
3. Many nonscientists they mistakenly believe that aerosol spray cans are the primary cause of erosion.
4. One scientist whom others respect him argues that Americans have effectively reduced their use of aerosol sprays.
5. He argues that we will stop global warming only when the public learns the real causes then.

mixed

22b

INCOMPLETE SENTENCES

The most serious kind of incomplete sentence is the fragment (see Chapter 17). But sentences are also incomplete when they omit one or more words needed for clarity.

Note Grammar and style checkers will not flag most kinds of incomplete sentences discussed in this section. Only your own careful proofreading can ensure that sentences are complete.

22c Omissions from compound constructions should be consistent with grammar or idiom.

In both speech and writing, we commonly omit words not necessary for meaning, such as those in brackets in the following examples. Notice that all the sentences contain compound constructions (see p. 265):

> By 2010 automobile-emission standards will be tougher, and by 2015 [automobile-emission standards will be] tougher still.

> Some cars will run on electricity and some [will run] on methane or another alternative fuel.

> Environmentalists have hopes for alternative fuels and [for] public transportation.

Such omissions are possible only when you omit words that are common to all the parts of a compound construction. When the parts differ in either grammar or idiom, all words must be included in all parts:

> One new car gets eighty miles per gallon of gasoline; some old cars get as little as five miles per gallon. [One verb is singular, the other plural.]

> Environmentalists were invited to submit proposals and were eager to do so. [Each *were* has a different grammatical function: the first is a helping verb; the second is a linking verb.]

> They believe in and work for fuel conservation. [Idiom requires different prepositions with *believe* and *work.*]

Notice that in the sentence *My brother and friend moved to Dallas,* the omission of *my* before *friend* indicates that *brother* and *friend* are the same person. If two different persons are meant, the modifier or article must be repeated: *My brother and my friend moved to Dallas.*

(See p. 558 for a list of English idioms with prepositions and pp. 428–31 for a discussion of grammatical parallelism.)

inc
22d

22d All comparisons should be complete and logical.

Comparisons make statements about the relation between two or more things, as in *Dogs are more intelligent than cats.*

---

http://www.ablongman.com/littlebrown

For added help and practice with incomplete sentences, click on

➤ Sentences ➤ Exercises ➤ Exer. 51

1 ▪ State a comparison fully enough to ensure clarity.

A comparison must not omit words needed to clarify meaning:

Unclear   Automakers worry about their industry more than envi-
           ronmentalists.

Clear   Automakers worry about their industry more than envi-
           ronmentalists <u>do</u>.

Clear   Automakers worry about their industry more than <u>they
           worry about</u> environmentalists.

2 ▪ The items being compared should in fact be comparable.

A comparison is logical only if it likens items that can sensibly
be compared:

Illogical   The cost of an electric car is greater than a gasoline-
             powered car. [Illogically compares a cost and a car.]

Revised   The cost of an electric car is greater than <u>the cost of</u> [or
             <u>that of</u>] a gasoline-powered car.

3 ▪ Use *any* or *any other* appropriately in comparisons.

Comparing a person or thing with all others in the same group
creates two units: (1) the individual person or thing and (2) all *other*
persons or things in the group. The two units need to be distinguished:

Illogical   Los Angeles is larger than <u>any</u> city in California. [Since
             Los Angeles is itself a city in California, the sentence
             seems to say that Los Angeles is larger than itself.]

Logical   Los Angeles is larger than <u>any other</u> city in California.

Comparing a person or thing with the members of a *different*
group assumes separate units to begin with. The two units do not
need to be distinguished with *other:*

Illogical   Los Angeles is larger than <u>any other</u> city in Canada.
             [The cities in Canada constitute a group to which Los
             Angeles does not belong.]

Logical   Los Angeles is larger than <u>any</u> city in Canada.

4 ▪ Comparisons should state what is being compared.

Brand X gets clothes <u>whiter</u>. [Whiter than what?]
Brand Y is so much <u>better</u>. [Better than what?]

22e Include all needed prepositions, articles, and other words.

In haste or carelessness we sometimes omit small words such
as articles and prepositions that are needed for clarity:

Incomplete	Regular payroll deductions are a type painless savings. You hardly notice missing amounts, and after period of years the contributions can add a large total.
Revised	Regular payroll deductions are a type <u>of</u> painless savings. You hardly notice <u>the</u> missing amounts, and after <u>a</u> period of years the contributions can add <u>up to</u> a large total.

Be careful not to omit *that* when the omission is confusing:

Incomplete	The personnel director expects many employees will benefit from the plan. [*Many employees* seems to be the object of *expects.*]
Revised	The personnel director expects <u>that</u> many employees will benefit from the plan.

Attentive proofreading is the best insurance against the kinds of omissions described in this section. *Proofread all your papers carefully.* See page 62 for tips.

CULTURE LANGUAGE ➤ If your native language or dialect is not standard American English, you may have difficulty knowing when to use the English articles *a, an,* and *the.* For guidelines on using articles, see pages 340–41.

EXERCISE 3
Revising: Incomplete sentences
Revise the following sentences so that they are complete, logical, and clear. Some items have more than one possible answer.

inc

22e

> *Example:*
> Our house is closer to the courthouse than the subway stop.
> Our house is closer to the courthouse than <u>it is</u> to the subway stop.
> Our house is closer to the courthouse than the subway stop <u>is</u>.

1. The first ice cream, eaten in China in about 2000 BC, was more lumpy than the modern era.
2. The Chinese made their ice cream of milk, spices, and overcooked rice and packed in snow to solidify.
3. In the fourteenth century ice milk and fruit ices appeared in Italy and the tables of the wealthy.
4. At her wedding in 1533 to the king of France, Catherine de Médicis offered more flavors of fruit ices than any hostess offered.
5. Modern sherbets resemble her ices; modern ice cream her soft dessert of thick, sweetened cream.

EXERCISE 4
Revising: Mixed and incomplete sentences
Revise the following paragraph to eliminate mixed or incomplete constructions.

The Hancock Tower in Boston is thin mirror-glass slab that rises almost eight hundred feet. When it was being constructed was when its windows began cracking, and some fell crashing to the ground. In order to minimize risks is why the architects and owners replaced over a third the huge windows with plywood until the problem could be found and solved. With its plywood sheath, the building was homelier than any skyscraper, the butt of many jokes. Eventually, however, it was discovered that the reason the windows cracked was because joint between the double panes of glass was too rigid. The solution of thicker single-pane windows was installed, and the silly plywood building crystallized into reflective jewel.

Note See the facing page for an exercise involving mixed and incomplete sentences along with sentence fragments, comma splices, and other sentence errors.

inc
22

EXERCISE ON CHAPTERS 17–22
Revising: Clear sentences

Clarify meaning in the following paragraphs by revising sentence fragments, comma splices, fused sentences, problems with pronoun reference, awkward shifts, misplaced and dangling modifiers, and mixed and incomplete sentences. Most errors can be corrected in more than one way. (To download a double-spaced, editable version of this exercise, go to *http://www.ablongman.com/littlebrown* and click on Sentences > Downloads > Revising: Clear sentences.)

Many people who are physically challenged. They have accomplished much. Which proves that they are not "handicapped." Confined to wheelchairs, successful careers have been forged by Bob Sampson and Stephen Hawking. Despite Sampson's muscular dystrophy, he has earned a law degree he has also worked for United Airlines for more than thirty years. Stephen Hawking most famous for his book *A Brief History of Time.* Unable to speak, Hawking's voice synthesizer allows him to dictate his books and conduct public lectures. And teach mathematics classes at Cambridge University.

Franklin D. Roosevelt, Ann Adams, and Itzhak Perlman all refused let polio destroy their lives. Indeed, Roosevelt led the United States during two of the worst periods of its history as President. The Great Depression and World War II. Reassured by his strong, firm voice, Roosevelt inspired hope and determination in the American people. Ann Adams, who was talented in art before polio paralyzed her, knew she had to continue to be one. Having retrained herself to draw with a pencil grasped in her teeth. She produces sketches of children and pets. That were turned into greeting cards. The profits from the cards sustained her. Roosevelt and Adams were stricken with polio when they were adults; Itzhak Perlman when a child. He was unable to play sports, instead he studied the violin, now many think he is greater than any violinist in the world.

Like Perlman, many physically challenged individuals turn to the arts. Perhaps the reason is because the joy of artistic achievement compensates for other pleasures they cannot experience. Ray Charles, Stevie Wonder, José Feliciano, and Andrea Bocelli all express, through their music, their souls. Although unable to see physically, their music reveals truly how well they see. Hearing impairment struck Ludwig van Beethoven and Marlee Matlin it did not stop them from developing their talents. Already a successful composer, many of Beethoven's most powerful pieces were written after he became deaf. Similarly, Matlin has had excellent acting roles in movies, plays, and television programs, indeed she won an Oscar for *Children of a Lesser God.* She encourages others to develop their ability, and many hearing-impaired actors have been inspired by her.

mng

PART VI

Effective Sentences

CHAPTER 23

Emphasizing Ideas

When you emphasize the main ideas in your sentences, you hold and channel readers' attention.

Note Many grammar and style checkers can spot some problems with emphasis, such as nouns made from verbs, passive voice, wordy phrases, and long sentences that may also be flabby and unemphatic. However, the checkers cannot help you identify the important ideas in your sentences or whether those ideas receive appropriate emphasis.

Ways to emphasize ideas

- Use the subjects and verbs of sentences to state key actors and actions (below).
- Use the beginnings and endings of sentences to pace and stress information (p. 406).
- Arrange series items in order of increasing importance (p. 409).
- Use an occasional balanced sentence (p. 410).
- Carefully repeat key words and phrases (p. 411).
- Set off important ideas with punctuation (p. 411).
- Write concisely (p. 412).

23a Using subjects and verbs effectively

The heart of every sentence is its subject, which usually names the actor, and its verb, which usually specifies the subject's action: *Children* [subject] *grow* [verb]. When these elements do not identify

http://www.ablongman.com/littlebrown
For added help and practice with emphasis, click on
➤ **Sentences**
  ➤ **Exercises** ➤ **Exers. 52 and 53**
  ➤ **Downloads** ➤ **Revising: Emphasizing ideas**
  ➤ **Web links** ➤ **Emphasis**

the sentence's key actor and action, readers must find that information elsewhere and the sentence may be wordy and unemphatic.

In the following sentences, the subjects and verbs are underlined:

| Unemphatic | The <u>intention</u> of the company <u>was</u> to expand its workforce. A <u>proposal</u> <u>was</u> also <u>made</u> to diversify the backgrounds and abilities of employees. |

These sentences are unemphatic because their key ideas (the company's intending and proposing) do not appear in their subjects and verbs. Revised, the sentences are not only clearer but more concise:

| Revised | The <u>company</u> <u>intended</u> to expand its workforce. It also <u>proposed</u> to diversify the backgrounds and abilities of employees. |

The constructions below and on the next page usually drain meaning from a sentence's subject and verb.

Nouns made from verbs

Nouns made from verbs can obscure the key actions of sentences and add words. These nouns include *intention* (from *intend*), *proposal* (from *propose*), *decision* (from *decide*), *expectation* (from *expect*), *persistence* (from *persist*), *argument* (from *argue*), and *inclusion* (from *include*).

| Unemphatic | After the company made a <u>decision</u> to hire more disabled workers, its next step was the <u>construction</u> of wheelchair ramps and other facilities. |
| Revised | After the company <u>decided</u> to hire more disabled workers, it next <u>constructed</u> wheelchair ramps and other facilities. |

Weak verbs

Weak verbs, such as *made* and *was* in the unemphatic sentence above, tend to stall sentences just where they should be moving and often bury key actions:

| Unemphatic | The company <u>is</u> now the leader among businesses in complying with the 1990 Americans with Disabilities Act. Its officers <u>make</u> speeches on the act to business groups. |

emph
23a

http://www.ablongman.com/littlebrown
For added practice using subjects and verbs effectively, click on
➤ Sentences ➤ Exercises ➤ Exer. 52

Revised   The company now <u>leads</u> other businesses in complying with the 1990 Americans with Disabilities
Act. Its officers <u>speak</u> on the act to business groups.

Passive voice

Verbs in the passive voice state actions received by, not performed by, their subjects. Thus the passive de-emphasizes the true
actor of the sentence, sometimes omitting it entirely. Generally,
prefer the active voice, in which the subject performs the verb's action. (See also p. 316.)

Unemphatic   The 1990 <u>law is seen</u> by most businesses as fair, but
the costs of complying <u>have</u> sometimes <u>been exag-
gerated</u>.

Revised   Most <u>businesses see</u> the 1990 law as fair, but some
<u>opponents have exaggerated</u> the costs of complying.

EXERCISE 1
Revising: Emphasis of subjects and verbs

Rewrite the following sentences so that their subjects and verbs
identify their key actors and actions.

Example:

The issue of students making a competition over grades is a
reason why their focus on learning may be lost.

<u>Students</u> who compete over grades <u>may lose</u> their focus on
learning.

1. The work of many heroes was crucial in helping to emancipate
the slaves.
2. The contribution of Harriet Tubman, an escaped slave herself,
included the guidance of hundreds of other slaves to freedom
on the Underground Railroad.
3. A return to slavery was risked by Tubman or possibly death.
4. During the Civil War she was also a carrier of information
from the South to the North.
5. After the war needy former slaves were helped by Tubman's
raising of money for refuges.

emph
23b

23b   Using sentence beginnings and endings

Readers automatically seek a writer's principal meaning in the
main clause of a sentence—essentially, in the subject that names the

http://www.ablongman.com/littlebrown
For added practice beginning and ending sen-
tences effectively, click on
➤ Sentences ➤ Exercises ➤ Exer. 53

actor and the verb that usually specifies the action (see pp. 404–05). Thus you can help readers understand your intended meaning by controlling the information in your subjects and the relation of the main clause to any modifiers attached to it.

Old and new information

Generally, readers expect the beginning of a sentence to contain information that they already know or that you have already introduced. They then look to the sentence ending for new information. In the unemphatic passage below, the subjects of the second and third sentences both introduce new topics (underlined) while the old topics (the controversy and education) appear at the ends of the sentences:

> **Unemphatic** Education almost means controversy these days, with rising costs and constant complaints about its inadequacies. But the value of schooling should not be obscured by the controversy. The single best means of economic advancement, despite its shortcomings, remains education.

In the more emphatic revision, the underlined old information begins each sentence and new information ends the sentence. The passage follows the pattern A→B. B→C. C→D.

> **Revised** Education almost means controversy these days, with rising costs and constant complaints about its inadequacies. But the controversy should not obscure the value of schooling. Education remains, despite its shortcomings, the single best means of economic advancement.

Cumulative and periodic sentences

You can call attention to information by placing it first or last in a sentence, reserving the middle for incidentals:

> **Unemphatic** Education remains the single best means of economic advancement, despite its shortcomings. [Emphasizes shortcomings.]
>
> **Revised** Despite its shortcomings, education remains the single best means of economic advancement. [Emphasizes advancement more than shortcomings.]
>
> **Revised** Education remains, despite its shortcomings, the single best means of economic advancement. [De-emphasizes shortcomings.]

emph

23b

Many sentences begin with the main clause and then add more modifiers to explain, amplify, or illustrate it. Such sentences are called **cumulative** (because they accumulate information as they proceed) or **loose** (because they are not tightly structured). They parallel the way we naturally think.

Cumulative   Education has no equal in opening minds, instilling values, and creating opportunities.

Cumulative   Most of the Great American Desert is made up of bare rock, rugged cliffs, mesas, canyons, mountains, separated from one another by broad flat basins covered with sunbaked mud and alkali, supporting a sparse and measured growth of sagebrush or creosote or saltbush, depending on location and elevation.   —Edward Abbey

The opposite kind of sentence, called **periodic,** saves the main clause until just before the end (the period) of the sentence. Everything before the main clause points toward it.

Periodic   In opening minds, instilling values, and creating opportunities, education has no equal.

Periodic   With people from all over the world—Korean grocers, Jamaican cricket players, Vietnamese fishers, Haitian cabdrivers, Chinese doctors—the American mosaic is continually changing.

The periodic sentence creates suspense for readers by reserving important information for the end. But readers should already have an idea of the sentence's subject—because it was discussed or introduced in the preceding sentence—so that they know what the opening modifiers describe. In a variation of the periodic sentence, you can name the subject at the beginning, follow it with a modifier, and then complete the main clause:

Dick Hayne, who works in jeans and loafers and likes to let a question cure in the air for a while before answering it, bears all the markings of what his generation used to call a laid-back kind of guy.   —George Rush

emph
23b

EXERCISE 2
Sentence combining: Beginnings and endings

Locate the main idea in each group of sentences below. Then combine each group into a single sentence that emphasizes that idea by placing it at the beginning or the end. For sentences 2–5, determine the position of the main idea by considering its relation to the previous sentences: if the main idea picks up a topic that's already been introduced, place it at the beginning; if it adds new information, place it at the end.

Example:

The storm blew roofs off buildings. It caused extensive damage. It knocked down many trees. It severed power lines.

Main idea at beginning: The storm caused extensive damage, blowing roofs off buildings, knocking down many trees, and severing power lines.

Main idea at end: Blowing roofs off buildings, knocking down many trees, and severing power lines, <u>the storm caused extensive damage</u>.

1. Pat Taylor strode into the room. The room was packed. He greeted students called "Taylor's Kids." He nodded to their parents and teachers.
2. This was a wealthy Louisiana oilman. He had promised his "Kids" free college educations. He was determined to make higher education available to all qualified but disadvantaged students.
3. The students welcomed Taylor. Their voices joined in singing. They sang "You Are the Wind Beneath My Wings." Their faces beamed with hope. Their eyes flashed with self-confidence.
4. The students had thought a college education was beyond their dreams. It seemed too costly. It seemed too demanding.
5. Taylor had to ease the costs and the demands of getting to college. He created a bold plan. The plan consisted of scholarships, tutoring, and counseling.

23c Arranging parallel elements effectively

Series

With parallelism, you use similar grammatical structures for ideas linked by *and, but,* and similar words: *Blustery winds and upturned leaves often signal thunderstorms.* (See Chapter 25.) In addition, you should arrange the parallel ideas in order of their importance:

Unemphatic	The storm ripped the roofs off several buildings, killed ten people, and knocked down many trees in town. [Buries the most serious damage—deaths—in the middle.]
Emphatic	The storm knocked down many trees in town, ripped the roofs off several buildings, and killed ten people. [Arranges items in order of increasing importance.]

emph
23c

You may want to use an unexpected item at the end of a series for humor or for another special effect:

Early to bed and early to rise makes a man healthy, wealthy, and dead. —JAMES THURBER

But be careful not to use such a series carelessly. The following series seems thoughtlessly random rather than intentionally humorous:

Unemphatic	The painting has subdued tone, intense feeling, and a length of about three feet.
Emphatic	The painting, about three feet long, has subdued tone and intense feeling.

Balanced sentences

A sentence is **balanced** when its clauses are parallel—that is, matched in grammatical structure (Chapter 25). Read the following examples aloud to hear their rhythm.

> The fickleness of the women I love is equalled only by the infernal constancy of the women who love me.   —GEORGE BERNARD SHAW

In a pure balanced sentence two main clauses are exactly parallel: they match item for item.

> Scratch a lover, and find a foe.   —DOROTHY PARKER

But the term is commonly applied to sentences that are only approximately parallel or that have only some parallel parts:

> If thought corrupts language, language can also corrupt thought.
> —GEORGE ORWELL
>
> As the traveler who has once been from home is wiser than he who has never left his own doorstep, so a knowledge of one other culture should sharpen our ability to scrutinize more steadily, to appreciate more lovingly, our own.   —MARGARET MEAD

Balanced sentences are heavily emphatic but require thoughtful planning. When used carefully, they can be an especially effective way to alert readers to a strong contrast between two ideas.

EXERCISE 3
Revising: Series and balanced elements
Revise the following sentences so that elements in a series or balanced elements are arranged to give maximum emphasis to main ideas.

emph

23c

> *Example:*
>
> The campers were stranded without matches, without food or water, and without a tent.
>
> The campers were stranded without matches, without a tent, and without food or water.

1. Remembering her days as a "conductor" on the Underground Railroad made Harriet Tubman proud, but she got angry when she remembered her years as a slave.
2. Tubman wanted freedom regardless of personal danger, whereas for her husband, John, personal safety was more important than freedom.
3. Tubman proved her fearlessness in many ways: she led hundreds of other slaves to freedom, she was a spy for the North during the Civil War, and she disobeyed John's order not to run away.
4. To conduct slaves north to freedom, Tubman risked being returned to slavery, being hanged for a huge reward, and being caught by Southern patrollers.

5. After the war Tubman worked tirelessly for civil rights and women's suffrage; raising money for homes for needy former slaves was something else she did.

23d Repeating ideas

Repetition of words and phrases often clutters and weakens sentences, as discussed on page 568. But carefully planned repetition can be an effective means of emphasis. Such repetition often combines with parallelism. It may occur in a series of sentences within a paragraph (see p. 84). Or may occur in a series of words, phrases, or clauses within a sentence, as in the following examples:

> There is something uneasy in the Los Angeles air this afternoon, some unnatural stillness, some tension. —JOAN DIDION

> We have the tools, all the tools—we are suffocating in tools—but we cannot find the actual wood to work or even the actual hand to work it. —ARCHIBALD MacLEISH

23e Separating ideas

When you save important information for the end of a sentence, you can emphasize it even more by setting it off from the rest of the sentence, as in the second example below:

> Mothers and housewives are the only workers who do not have regular time off, so they are the great vacationless class.

> Mothers and housewives are the only workers who do not have regular time off. They are the great vacationless class. —ANNE MORROW LINDBERGH

emph
23e

You can vary the degree of emphasis by varying the extent to which you separate one idea from the others. A semicolon provides more separation than a comma, and a period provides still more separation. Compare the following sentences:

> Most of the reading which is praised for itself is neither literary nor intellectual, but narcotic.

> Most of the reading which is praised for itself is neither literary nor intellectual; it is narcotic.

> Most of the reading which is praised for itself is neither literary nor intellectual. It is narcotic. —DONALD HALL

Sometimes a dash or a pair of dashes will isolate and thus emphasize a part of a statement (see also pp. 506–07):

> His schemes were always elaborate, ingenious, and exciting—and wholly impractical.

Athletics—that is, winning athletics—has become a profitable university operation.

EXERCISE 4
Emphasizing with repetition or separation

Emphasize the main idea in each sentence or group of sentences below by following the instructions in parentheses: either combine sentences so that parallelism and repetition stress the main idea, or place the main idea in a separate sentence. Each item has more than one possible answer.

Example:

I try to listen to other people's opinions. When my mind is closed, I find that other opinions open it. And they can change my mind when it is wrong. (*Parallelism and repetition.*)

I try to listen to other people's opinions, for they can open my mind when it is closed and they can change my mind when it is wrong.

1. One of the few worthwhile habits is daily reading. One can read for information. One can read for entertainment. Reading can give one a broader view of the world. (*Parallelism and repetition.*)
2. Reading introduces new words. One encounters unfamiliar styles of expression through reading. (*Parallelism and repetition.*)
3. Students who read a great deal will more likely write vividly, coherently, and grammatically, for they will have learned from other authors. (*Separation.*)
4. Reading gives knowledge. One gets knowledge about other cultures. One will know about history and current events. One gains information about human nature. (*Parallelism and repetition.*)
5. As a result of reading, writers have more resources and more flexibility, and thus reading creates better writers. (*Separation.*)

emph
23f

23f Being concise

Conciseness—brevity of expression—aids emphasis no matter what the sentence structure. Unnecessary words detract from necessary words. They clutter sentences and obscure ideas.

Weak	In my opinion the competition in the area of grades is distracting. It distracts many students from their goal, which is to obtain an education that is good. There seems to be a belief among a few students that grades are more important than what is measured by them.
Emphatic	The competition for grades distracts many students from their goal of obtaining a good education. A few students seem to believe that grades are more important than what they measure.

Some techniques for tightening sentences appear earlier in this chapter (pp. 404–06). These techniques are also covered, along with others, in Chapter 40 on writing concisely.

Ways to achieve conciseness

- **Make the subject and verb of each sentence identify its actor and action** (pp. 404–06, 565):

  Avoid nouns made from verbs.
  Use strong verbs.
  Rewrite the passive voice as active.

- **Cut or shorten empty words or phrases** (p. 566):

  Shorten filler phrases, such as *by virtue of the fact that.*
  Cut all-purpose words, such as *area, factor.*
  Cut unneeded qualifiers, such as *in my opinion, for the most part.*

- **Cut unnecessary repetition** (p. 568).
- **Reduce clauses to phrases and phrases to single words** (p. 569).
- **Avoid constructions beginning with *there is* or *it is*** (p. 570).
- **Combine sentences** (p. 570).
- **Cut or rewrite jargon** (p. 570).

EXERCISE 5
Revising: Conciseness

Revise the following sentences to make them more emphatic by eliminating wordiness.

Example:
The problem in this particular situation is that we owe more money than we can afford under present circumstances.
The <u>problem</u> is that we owe more money than we can afford.

emph

23f

1. As far as I am concerned, customers who are dining out in restaurants in our country must be wary of suggestive selling, so to speak.
2. In suggestive selling, diners are asked by the waiter to buy additional menu selections in addition to what was ordered by them.
3. For each item on the menu, there is another food that will naturally complement it.
4. For example, customers will be presented with the question of whether they want to order french fries along with a sandwich or whether they want to order a salad along with a steak dinner.
5. Due to the fact that customers often give in to suggestive selling, they often find that their restaurant meals are more costly than they had intended to pay.

EXERCISE 6
Revising: Emphasizing ideas

Drawing on the advice in this chapter, rewrite the following paragraph to emphasize main ideas and to de-emphasize less important
information. (You can download a double-spaced, editable version
of this exercise from this book's Web site: see the box at the bottom
of p. 404.)

In preparing pasta, there is a requirement for common sense
and imagination rather than for complicated recipes. The key to
success in this area is fresh ingredients for the sauce and perfectly
cooked pasta. The sauce may be made with just about any fresh
fish, meat, cheese, herb, or vegetable. As for the pasta itself, it may
be dried or fresh, although fresh pasta is usually more delicate and
flavorful, as many experienced cooks find. Dried pasta is fine with
zesty sauces; with light oil and cream sauces fresh pasta is the best
choice. There is a difference in the cooking time for dried and fresh
pasta, with dried pasta taking longer. It is important that the cook
follow the package directions and that the pasta be tested before
the cooking time is up. The pasta is done when the texture is neither tough nor mushy but *al dente*, or "firm to the bite," according
to the Italians, who ought to know.

Note See page 444 for an exercise involving emphasis along
with parallelism and other techniques for effective sentences.

CHAPTER 24

Using Coordination and Subordination

When clearly written, your sentences show the relations between ideas and stress the more important ideas over the lesser ones. Two techniques can help you achieve such clarity:

- **Coordination** shows that two or more elements in a sentence are equally important in meaning. You signal coordination with words such as *and, but,* and *or.*

  equally
  ⟵important⟶
  Car and health insurance are modern necessities.

  ⟵————— equally important —————⟶
  Car insurance is costly, but health insurance seems a luxury.

- **Subordination** shows that some elements in a sentence are less important than other elements for your meaning. Usually, the main idea appears in the main clause, and supporting information appears in single words, phrases, and subordinate clauses.

  less important   more important
  ⟵——— (subordinate clause) ———⟶ ⟵ (main clause) ——⟶
  Because accidents and thefts occur frequently, car insurance is costly.

  more important   less important
  ⟵——— (main clause) ———⟶ ⟵ (phrase) ——⟶
  The health-insurance industry is changing, for better or worse.

Note Grammar and style checkers may spot some errors in punctuating coordinated and subordinated elements, and they can flag long sentences that may contain excessive coordination or subordination. But otherwise they provide little help because they cannot recognize the relations among ideas in sentences. You'll need to weigh and clarify those relations yourself.

http://www.ablongman.com/littlebrown
For added help and practice with coordination and subordination, click on
➤ **Sentences**
  ➤ **Exercises** ➤ **Exers. 54 and 55**
  ➤ **Downloads** ➤ **Revising: Coordination and subordination**
  ➤ **Web links** ➤ **Coordination and subordination**

24a Coordinating to relate equal ideas

By linking equally important information, you can emphasize the relations for readers. Compare the passages below:

String of simple sentences

We should not rely so heavily on oil. Coal and uranium are also overused. We have a substantial energy resource in the moving waters of our rivers. Smaller streams add to the total volume of water. The resource renews itself. Oil and coal are irreplaceable. Uranium is also irreplaceable. The cost of water does not increase much over time. The costs of coal, oil, and uranium rise dramatically.

Ideas coordinated

We should not rely so heavily on oil, coal, and uranium, for we have a substantial energy resource in the moving waters of our rivers and streams. Oil, coal, and uranium are irreplaceable and thus subject to dramatic cost increases; water, however, is self-renewing and more stable in cost.

The information in both passages is essentially the same, but the second is shorter and considerably easier to read and understand because it builds connections among coordinate ideas.

To link ideas, you can use coordinating conjunctions (*and, but, or, nor, for, so, yet*), correlative conjunctions (*both . . . and* and others), and conjunctive adverbs (*however, thus,* and others). These words signal certain relationships, such as addition (*and, both . . . and, moreover*) and contrast (*but, not . . . but, however*). See the full lists of these words on pages 265–66.

coord

24a

Ways to coordinate information in sentences

- **Link main clauses with a comma and a coordinating conjunction:** *and, but, or, nor, for, so, yet* (p. 455).

  Independence Hall in Philadelphia is now restored, but fifty years ago it was in bad shape.

- **Relate main clauses with a semicolon alone or a semicolon and a conjunctive adverb:** *however, indeed, thus,* etc. (pp. 477, 480).

  The building was standing; however, it suffered from neglect.

- **Within clauses, link words and phrases with a coordinating conjunction:** *and, but, or, nor* (p. 265).

  The people and officials of the nation were indifferent to Independence Hall or took it for granted.

- **Link main clauses, words, or phrases with a correlative conjunction:** *both . . . and, not only . . . but also,* etc. (p. 266).

  People not only took the building for granted but also neglected it.

Punctuating coordinated words, phrases, and clauses

Most coordinated words, phrases, and subordinate clauses are not punctuated with commas (see p. 472). The exceptions are items in a series and coordinate adjectives:

> We rely heavily on <u>coal, oil, and uranium</u>. [A series; see p. 465.]
>
> <u>Dirty, unhealthy</u> air is one result. [Coordinate adjectives; see p. 465.]

In a sentence consisting of two main clauses, punctuation depends on whether a coordinating conjunction, a conjunctive adverb, or no connecting word links the clauses:

> Oil is irreplaceable, <u>but</u> water is self-renewing. [See p. 455.]
> Oil is irreplaceable; <u>however</u>, water is self-renewing. [See p. 480.]
> Oil is irreplaceable; water is self-renewing. [See p. 477.]

1 ■ Using coordination effectively

A string of coordinated elements—especially main clauses—creates the same effect as a string of simple sentences: it obscures the relative importance of ideas and details.

> **Excessive**   The weeks leading up to the resignation of Presi-
> **coordination** dent Nixon were eventful, and the Supreme Court
>   and the Congress closed in on him, and the Senate
>   Judiciary Committee voted to begin impeachment
>   proceedings, and finally the President resigned on
>   August 9, 1974.

Such a passage needs editing to stress the important points (underlined below) and to de-emphasize the less important information:

> **Revised**   <u>The weeks leading up to the resignation of Presi-
>   dent Nixon were eventful</u>, as the Supreme Court
>   and the Congress closed in on him and the Senate
>   Judiciary Committee voted to begin impeachment
>   proceedings. Finally, <u>the President resigned</u> on Au-
>   gust 9, 1974.

coord

24a

2 ■ Coordinating logically

Coordinated sentence elements should be logically equal and related, and the relation between them should be the one expressed by the connecting word. If either principle is violated, the result is **faulty coordination**.

http://www.ablongman.com/littlebrown
For added practice with coordination, click on
➤ Sentences ➤ Exercises ➤ Exer. 54

Faulty   John Stuart Mill was a nineteenth-century utilitarian, and he believed that actions should be judged by their useful- ness or by the happiness they cause. [The two clauses are not separate and equal: the second expands on the first by explaining what a utilitarian such as Mill believed.]

Revised   John Stuart Mill, a nineteenth-century utilitarian, believed that actions should be judged by their usefulness or by the happiness they cause.

Faulty   Mill is recognized as a utilitarian, and he did not found the utilitarian school of philosophy. [The two clauses seem to contrast, requiring *but* or *yet* between them.]

Revised   Mill is recognized as a utilitarian, but he did not found the utilitarian school of philosophy.

Sometimes faulty coordination occurs because the writer omits necessary information:

Faulty   Jeremy Bentham founded the utilitarian school, and Mill was precocious. [The two clauses seem unrelated.]

Revised   Jeremy Bentham founded the utilitarian school before Mill was born, and Mill joined at the precocious age of twenty.

EXERCISE 1
Sentence combining: Coordination

Combine sentences in the following passages to coordinate related ideas in the ways that seem most effective to you. You will have to supply coordinating conjunctions or conjunctive adverbs and the appropriate punctuation.

1. Many chronic misspellers do not have the time to master spelling rules. They may not have the motivation. They may rely on dictionaries to catch misspellings. Most dictionaries list words under their correct spellings. One kind of dictionary is designed for chronic misspellers. It lists each word under its common *mis*spellings. It then provides the correct spelling. It also provides the definition.

2. Henry Hudson was an English explorer. He captained ships for the Dutch East India Company. On a voyage in 1610 he passed by Greenland. He sailed into a great bay in today's northern Canada. He thought he and his sailors could winter there. The cold was terrible. Food ran out. The sailors mutinied. The sail- ors cast Hudson adrift in a small boat. Eight others were also in the boat. Hudson and his companions perished.

coord

24a

EXERCISE 2
Revising: Excessive or faulty coordination

Revise the following sentences to eliminate excessive or faulty co- ordination. Relate ideas effectively by adding or subordinating in- formation or by forming more than one sentence. Each item has more than one possible answer.

Example:

My dog barks, and I have to move out of my apartment.

Because my dog's barking <u>disturbs my neighbors</u>, I have to move out of my apartment.

1. Often soldiers admired their commanding officers, and they gave them nicknames, and these names frequently contained the word "old," but not all of the commanders were old.
2. General Thomas "Stonewall" Jackson was also called "Old Jack," and he was not yet forty years old.
3. Another Southern general in the Civil War was called "Old Pete," and his full name was James Longstreet.
4. The Union general Henry W. Halleck had a reputation as a good military strategist, and he was an expert on the work of a French military authority, Henri Jomini, and Halleck was called "Old Brains."
5. General William Henry Harrison won the Battle of Tippecanoe, and he received the nickname "Old Tippecanoe," and he used the name in his presidential campaign slogan "Tippecanoe and Tyler, Too," and he won the election in 1840, but he died of pneumonia a month after taking office.

24b   Subordinating to distinguish main ideas

With **subordination** you use words or word groups to indicate that some elements in a sentence are less important than others. In the following sentence, it is difficult to tell what is most important:

Excessive coordination   In recent years computer prices have dropped, and production costs have dropped more slowly, and computer manufacturers have had to contend with shrinking profits.

The following rewrite places the point of the sentence (shrinking profits) in the main clause and reduces the rest of the information to a subordinate clause (underlined):

Revised   <u>Because production costs have dropped more slowly than prices in recent years</u>, computer manufacturers have had to contend with shrinking profits.

sub 24b

No rules can specify what information in a sentence you should make primary and what you should subordinate; the decision will

http://www.ablongman.com/littlebrown

For added help and practice with subordination, click on

➤ **Sentences**
  ➤ **Exercises** ➤ **Exer. 55**
    ➤ **Web links** ➤ **Coordination and subordination**

Ways to subordinate information in sentences

- **Use a subordinate clause beginning with a subordinating conjunction:** *although, because, if, whereas,* etc. (p. 259).

  <u>Although some citizens had tried to rescue Independence Hall</u>, they had not gained substantial public support.

- **Use a subordinate clause beginning with a relative pronoun:** *who, whoever, which, that* (p. 260).

  The first strong step was taken by the federal government, <u>which made the building a national monument</u>.

- **Use a phrase** (p. 250).

  <u>Like most national monuments</u>, Independence Hall is protected by the National Park Service. [Prepositional phrase.]
  <u>Protecting many popular tourist sites</u>, the service is a highly visible government agency. [Verbal phrase.]

- **Use an appositive** (p. 263).

  The National Park Service, <u>a branch of the Department of Interior</u>, also runs Yosemite and other wilderness parks.

- **Use a modifying word.**

  At the <u>red brick</u> Independence Hall, park rangers give <u>guided</u> tours and protect the <u>irreplaceable</u> building from vandalism.

---

depend on your meaning. But, in general, you should consider using subordinate structures for details of time, cause, condition, concession, purpose, and identification (size, location, and the like). You can subordinate information with the following structures:

sub

24b

- Subordinate clauses beginning with subordinating conjunctions (*because, when,* and others) or relative pronouns (mainly *who, which, that*). (See pp. 259–60 for full lists of these words.) Because subordinate clauses are longer and grammatically more like main clauses than phrases or single words, they tend to place the greatest emphasis on subordinate information.
- Phrases, including appositives renaming nouns (*her son, a man named Carl*), prepositional phrases beginning with a preposition such as *in* or *on* (*in the book*), or verbal phrases beginning with a verb form such as *saving* or *to save*. (See pp. 263, 250, and 253, respectively, for more on these kinds of phrases.) Phrases give less weight than subordinate clauses but more than single words.
- Single words, such as adjectives and adverbs that modify other words. Single words give the least weight to subordinate information.

The following examples show how subordinate structures may convey various meanings with various weights. (Some appropriate subordinating conjunctions, relative pronouns, and prepositions for each meaning appear in parentheses.)

Space or time (*after, before, since, until, when, while; at, in, on, until*)

The mine explosion killed six workers. The owners adopted safety measures.

After the mine explosion killed six workers, the owners adopted safety measures. [Subordinate clause.]

After six deaths, the owners adopted safety measures. [Prepositional phrase.]

Cause or effect (*as, because, since, so that; because of, due to*)

Jones had been without work for six months. He was having trouble paying his bills.

Because Jones had been without work for six months, he was having trouble paying his bills. [Subordinate clause.]

Having been jobless for six months, Jones could not pay his bills. [Verbal phrase.]

Condition (*if, provided, since, unless, whenever; with, without*)

Forecasters predict a mild winter. Farmers hope for an early spring.

Whenever forecasters predict a mild winter, farmers hope for an early spring. [Subordinate clause.]

With forecasts for a mild winter, farmers hope for an early spring. [Prepositional phrase.]

Concession (*although, as if, even though, though; despite, except for, in spite of*)

The horse looked gentle. It proved hard to manage.

Although the horse looked gentle, it proved hard to manage. [Subordinate clause.]

The horse, a gentle-looking animal, proved hard to manage. [Appositive.]

The gentle-looking horse proved hard to manage. [Single word.]

Purpose (*in order that, so that, that; for, toward*)

Congress passed new immigration laws. Many Vietnamese refugees could enter the United States.

Congress passed new immigration laws so that many Vietnamese refugees could enter the United States. [Subordinate clause.]

Congress passed new immigration laws, permitting many Vietnamese refugees to enter the United States. [Verbal phrase.]

sub

24b

Identification (*that, when, where, which, who; by, from, of*)

Old barns are common in New England. They are often painted red.

Old barns, <u>which are often painted red</u>, are common in New England. [Subordinate clause.]

Old barns, <u>often painted red</u>, are common in New England. [Verbal phrase.]

Old <u>red</u> barns are common in New England. [Single word.]

Punctuating subordinate constructions

A modifying word, phrase, or clause that introduces a sentence is usually set off from the rest of the sentence with a comma (see p. 457):

<u>Unfortunately,</u> the bank failed.

<u>In a little over six months,</u> the bank became insolvent.

<u>When the bank failed,</u> many reporters investigated.

A modifier that interrupts or concludes a main clause is *not* set off with punctuation when it is essential to the meaning of a word or words in the clause (see p. 459):

One article <u>about the bank failure</u> won a prize.

The article <u>that won the prize</u> appeared in the local newspaper.

The reporter wrote the article <u>because the bank failure affected many residents of the town.</u>

When an interrupting or concluding modifier is *not* essential to meaning, but simply adds information to the sentence, it *is* set off with punctuation, usually a comma or commas (see p. 459):

The bank, <u>over forty years old,</u> never reopened after its doors were closed.

The bank managers, <u>who were cleared of any wrongdoing,</u> all found new jobs.

Some customers of the bank never recovered all their money, <u>though most of them tried to do so.</u>

Like a modifier, an appositive is set off with punctuation (usually a comma or commas) only when it is *not* essential to the meaning of the word it refers to (see p. 461):

The bank, <u>First City,</u> was the oldest in town.

Our newspaper, <u>the *Chronicle*,</u> was one of several reporting the story.

A dash or dashes may also be used to set off a nonessential appositive, particularly when it contains commas (see p. 506). A concluding appositive is sometimes set off with a colon (see p. 504).

1 ▪ Subordinating logically

Use subordination only for the less important information in a sentence. **Faulty subordination** reverses the dependent relation the reader expects:

Faulty	Ms. Angelo was in her first year of teaching, although she was a better instructor than others with many years of experience. [The sentence suggests that Angelo's inexperience is the main idea, whereas the writer intended to stress her skill *despite* her inexperience.]
Revised	<u>Although Ms. Angelo was in her first year of teaching</u>, she was a better instructor than others with many years of experience.

2 ▪ Using subordination effectively

Subordination can do much to organize and emphasize information. But it loses that power when you try to cram too much loosely related detail into one long sentence:

Overloaded	The boats that were moored at the dock when the hurricane, which was one of the worst in three decades, struck were ripped from their moorings, because the owners had not been adequately prepared, since the weather service had predicted the storm would blow out to sea, which storms do at this time of year.

Such sentences usually have more than one idea that deserves a main clause, so they are best revised by sorting their details into more than one sentence:

Revised	Struck by one of the worst hurricanes in three decades, <u>the boats at the dock were ripped from their moorings. The owners were unprepared</u> because the weather service had said that storms at this time of year blow out to sea.

sub

24b

A common form of excessive subordination occurs with a string of adjective clauses, each beginning with *which, who,* or *that,* as in the following:

Stringy	The company opened a new plant outside Louisville, which is in Kentucky and which is on the Ohio River, which forms the border between Kentucky and Ohio.

To revise such sentences, recast some of the subordinate clauses as other kinds of modifying structures:

Revised	The company opened a new plant outside Louisville, <u>Kentucky,</u> <u>a city</u> <u>across the Ohio River</u> <u>from Ohio.</u>

EXERCISE 3
Sentence combining: Subordination

Combine each of the following pairs of sentences twice, each time using one of the subordinate structures in parentheses to make a single sentence. You will have to add, delete, change, and rearrange words.

Example:

During the late eighteenth century, workers carried beverages in brightly colored bottles. The bottles had cork stoppers. (*Clause beginning that. Phrase beginning with.*)

During the late eighteenth century, workers carried beverages in brightly colored bottles that had cork stoppers.

During the late eighteenth century, workers carried beverages in brightly colored bottles with cork stoppers.

1. The bombardier beetle sees an enemy. It shoots out a jet of chemicals to protect itself. (*Clause beginning when. Phrase beginning seeing.*)
2. The beetle's spray is very potent. It consists of hot and irritating chemicals. (*Phrase beginning consisting. Phrase beginning of.*)
3. The spray's two chemicals are stored separately in the beetle's body and mixed in the spraying gland. The chemicals resemble a nerve-gas weapon. (*Phrase beginning stored. Clause beginning which.*)
4. The tip of the beetle's abdomen sprays the chemicals. The tip revolves like a turret on a World War II bomber. (*Phrase beginning revolving. Phrase beginning spraying.*)
5. The beetle defeats most of its enemies. It is still eaten by spiders and birds. (*Clause beginning although. Phrase beginning except.*)

EXERCISE 4
Revising: Subordination

Rewrite the following paragraph in the way you think most effective to subordinate the less important ideas to the more important ones. Use subordinate clauses, phrases, and single words as you think appropriate.

Fewer students today are majoring in the liberal arts. I mean by "liberal arts" such subjects as history, English, and the social sciences. Students think a liberal arts degree will not help them get jobs. They are wrong. They may not get practical, job-related experience from the liberal arts, but they will get a broad education, and it will never again be available to them. Many employers look for more than a technical, professional education. They think such an education can make an employee's views too narrow. The employers want open-minded employees. They want employees to think about problems from many angles. The liberal arts curriculum instills such flexibility. The flexibility is vital to the health of our society.

EXERCISE 5
Revising: Faulty or excessive subordination
Revise the following sentences to eliminate faulty or excessive subordination. Correct faulty subordination by reversing main and subordinate structures. Correct excessive subordination by coordinating equal ideas or by making separate sentences.

Example:
Terrified to return home, he had driven his mother's car into a cornfield.
<u>Having driven his mother's car into a cornfield</u>, he was terrified to return home.

1. Genaro González is blessed with great writing talent, which means that his novel *Rainbow's End* and his story collection *Only Sons* have been published.
2. He loves to write, although he has also earned a doctorate in psychology.
3. His first story, which reflects his consciousness of his Aztec heritage and place in the world, is entitled "Un Hijo del Sol."
4. González, who writes equally well in English and Spanish, received a large fellowship that enabled him to take a leave of absence from Pan American University, where he teaches psychology, so that he could write without worrying about an income.
5. González wrote the first version of "Un Hijo del Sol" while he was a sophomore at Pan American, which is in the Rio Grande valley of southern Texas, which González calls "el Valle" in the story.

24c   Choosing clear connectors

Most connecting words signal specific and unambiguous relations; for instance, the coordinating conjunction *but* clearly indicates contrast, and the subordinating conjunction *because* clearly indicates cause. A few connectors, however, require careful use, either because they are ambiguous in many contexts or because they are often misused.

sub

24c

1 ■ Using *as* and *while* clearly

The subordinating conjunction *as* can indicate several relations, including comparison and time:

Comparison	The technicians work quickly, <u>as</u> they are required to do.
Time	One shift starts <u>as</u> the other stops.

Avoid using *as* to indicate cause. It is unclear.

Unclear	<u>As</u> the experiment was occurring, the laboratory was sealed. [Time or cause intended?]
Revised	<u>When</u> the experiment was occurring, the laboratory was sealed. [Time.]
Revised	<u>Because</u> the experiment was occurring, the laboratory was sealed. [Cause.]

The subordinating conjunction *while* can indicate either time or concession. Unless the context makes the meaning of *while* unmistakably clear, choose a more exact connector:

Unclear	<u>While</u> technicians work in the next room, they cannot hear the noise. [Time or concession intended?]
Revised	<u>When</u> technicians work in the next room, they cannot hear the noise. [Time.]
Revised	<u>Although</u> technicians work in the next room, they cannot hear the noise. [Concession.]

Do not use *while* in place of *and* or *but:*

| Faulty | The technicians do not think a new study is necessary, <u>while</u> the institute insists on it. |
| Revised | The technicians do not think a new study is necessary, <u>but</u> the institute insists on it. |

2 ■ Using *as* and *like* correctly

The use of *as* as a substitute for *whether* or *that* is considered nonstandard (it does not conform to spoken and written standard English):

| Nonstandard | They are not sure <u>as</u> the study succeeded. |
| Revised | They are not sure <u>whether</u> [or <u>that</u>] the study succeeded. |

Although the preposition *like* is often used as a conjunction in informal speech and in advertising (*Dirt-Away works <u>like</u> a soap should*), writing generally requires the conjunction *as, as if, as though,* or *that:*

| Speech | It seemed <u>like</u> it did succeed. |
| Writing | It seemed <u>as if</u> [or <u>as though</u> or <u>that</u>] it did succeed. |

sub
24c

EXERCISE 6
Revising: Coordination and subordination
The following paragraph consists entirely of simple sentences. Use coordination and subordination to combine sentences in the ways you think most effective to emphasize main ideas. (You can download a double-spaced, editable version of this exercise from this book's Web site: see the box on p. 415.)

Sir Walter Raleigh personified the Elizabethan Age. That was the period of Elizabeth I's rule of England. The period occurred in the last half of the sixteenth century. Raleigh was a courtier and poet. He was also an explorer and entrepreneur. Supposedly, he gained Queen Elizabeth's favor. He did this by throwing his cloak beneath her feet at the right moment. She was just about to step over a puddle. There is no evidence for this story. It does illustrate Raleigh's dramatic and dynamic personality. His energy drew others to him. He was one of Elizabeth's favorites. She supported him. She also dispensed favors to him. However, he lost his queen's goodwill. Without her permission he seduced one of her maids of honor. He eventually married the maid of honor. Elizabeth died. Then her successor imprisoned Raleigh in the Tower of London. Her successor was James I. The king falsely charged Raleigh with treason. Raleigh was released after thirteen years. He was arrested again two years later on the old treason charges. At the age of sixty-six he was beheaded.

Note See page 444 for an exercise involving coordination and subordination along with parallelism and other techniques for effective sentences.

sub

24

CHAPTER 25

Using Parallelism

Parallelism is a similarity of grammatical form between two or more elements.

> The air is dirtied by ‖ factories belching smoke
> and ‖ cars spewing exhaust.

Parallel structure reinforces and highlights a close relation between compound sentence elements, whether words, phrases, or clauses.

The principle underlying parallelism is that form should reflect meaning: since the parts of compound constructions have the same function and importance, they should have the same grammatical form.

Note A grammar and style checker cannot recognize faulty parallelism because it cannot recognize the relations among ideas. You will need to find and revise problems with parallelism on your own.

25a Using parallelism for coordinate elements

Use parallelism in all the situations illustrated in the box opposite.

Note Parallel elements match each other in structure, as in the example above, but they do not always match word for word:

> The pioneers passed ‖ through the town
> and ‖ into the vast, unpopulated desert.

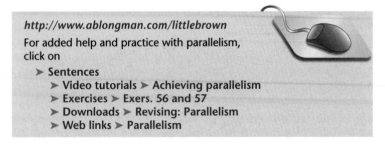

http://www.ablongman.com/littlebrown
For added help and practice with parallelism, click on
➤ Sentences
  ➤ Video tutorials ➤ Achieving parallelism
  ➤ Exercises ➤ Exers. 56 and 57
  ➤ Downloads ➤ Revising: Parallelism
  ➤ Web links ➤ Parallelism

Patterns of parallelism

- **Use parallel structures for elements connected by coordinating conjunctions (*and, but, or,* etc.) or correlative conjunctions (*both . . . and, neither . . . nor,* etc.):**

  In 1988 a Greek cyclist, backed up by ‖ engineers,
  physiologists,
  and ‖ athletes,
  broke the world's record for human flight
  with neither ‖ a boost
  nor ‖ a motor.

- **Use parallel structures for elements being compared or contrasted:**

  ‖ Pedal power
  rather than ‖ horse power
  propelled the plane.

- **Use parallel structures for lists, outlines, or headings:**

  The four-hour flight was successful because
  ‖ (1) the cyclist was very fit,
  ‖ (2) he flew a straight course over water,
  and ‖ (3) he kept the aircraft near the water's surface.

---

1 ▪ Using parallelism for elements linked by coordinating conjunctions

The coordinating conjunctions *and, but, or, nor,* and *yet* always signal a need for parallelism:

The industrial base was <u>shifting</u> and <u>shrinking</u>.

Politicians rarely <u>acknowledged the problem</u> or <u>proposed alternatives</u>.

Industrial workers were understandably disturbed <u>that they were losing their jobs</u> and <u>that no one seemed to care</u>.

If sentence elements linked by coordinating conjunctions are not parallel in structure, the resulting sentence will be awkward and distracting:

Nonparallel	Three reasons why steel companies kept losing money were <u>that their plants were inefficient</u>, <u>high labor costs</u>, and <u>foreign competition was increasing</u>.
Revised	Three reasons why steel companies kept losing money were <u>inefficient plants</u>, high labor costs, and <u>increasing foreign competition</u>.

All the words required by idiom or grammar must be stated in compound constructions (see also p. 397).

//
25a

Nonparallel	Given training, workers can acquire the <u>skills</u> and <u>interest in</u> other jobs. [*Skills* and *interest* require different prepositions, so both must be stated.]
Revised	Given training, workers can acquire the skills <u>for</u> and interest in other jobs.

Often, the same word must be repeated to avoid confusion:

Confusing	Thoreau stood up for his principles <u>by not paying</u> his taxes and <u>spending</u> a night in jail. [Did he spend a night in jail or not?]
Revised	Thoreau stood up for his principles by not paying his taxes and <u>by</u> spending a night in jail.

Be sure that clauses beginning *who* or *which* are coordinated only with other *who* or *which* clauses, even when the pronoun is not repeated:

Nonparallel	Thoreau is the nineteenth-century essayist <u>who retired</u> to the woods and <u>he wrote</u> about nature.
Revised	Thoreau is the nineteenth-century essayist who retired to the woods and [<u>who</u>] <u>wrote</u> about nature.

2 ■ Using parallelism for elements linked by correlative conjunctions

Correlative conjunctions are pairs of connectors. For example:

both . . . and	neither . . . nor	not only . . . but also
either . . . or	not . . . but	whether . . . or

They stress equality and balance and thus emphasize the relation between elements, even long phrases and clauses. The elements should be parallel to confirm their relation:

> It is not <u>a tax bill</u> but <u>a tax relief bill</u>, providing relief not <u>for the needy</u> but <u>for the greedy</u>.   —FRANKLIN DELANO ROOSEVELT

> At the end of the novel, Huck Finn both <u>rejects society's values by turning down money and a home</u> and <u>affirms his own values by setting out for "the territory."</u>

Most errors in parallelism with correlative conjunctions occur when the element after the second connector does not match the element after the first connector.

//
25a

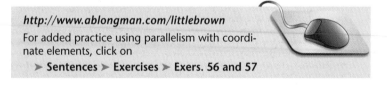

http://www.ablongman.com/littlebrown

For added practice using parallelism with coordinate elements, click on

➤ **Sentences** ➤ **Exercises** ➤ **Exers. 56 and 57**

Nonparallel	Mark Twain refused either <u>to ignore</u> the moral blindness of his society or <u>spare</u> the reader's sensibilities. [*To* follows *either,* so it must also follow *or.*]
Revised	Mark Twain refused either to ignore the moral blindness of his society or <u>to</u> spare the reader's sensibilities.
Nonparallel	Huck Finn learns not only <u>that human beings have an enormous capacity</u> for folly but also <u>enormous dignity</u>. [The first element includes *that human beings have;* the second element does not.]
Revised	Huck Finn learns <u>that human beings have</u> not only <u>an enormous capacity</u> for folly but also enormous dignity.

3 ■ Using parallelism for elements being compared or contrasted

Elements being compared or contrasted should ordinarily be cast in the same grammatical form.

It is better <u>to live rich</u> than <u>to die rich</u>.　　—SAMUEL JOHNSON

Weak	The study found that most welfare recipients wanted <u>to work</u> rather than <u>handouts</u>.
Revised	The study found that most welfare recipients wanted <u>work</u> rather than handouts.
Revised	The study found that most welfare recipients wanted to work rather than <u>to accept</u> handouts.

4 ■ Using parallelism for lists, outlines, or headings

The elements of a list or outline that divides a larger subject are coordinate and should be parallel in structure. Parallelism is essential in the headings that divide a paper into sections (see p. 207) and in a formal topic outline (see p. 41).

//

25a

Faulty	Improved
Changes in Renaissance England	Changes in Renaissance England
1. Extension of trade routes	1. Extension of trade routes
2. <u>Merchant class became</u> more powerful	2. <u>Increased power</u> of the merchant class
3. <u>The</u> death of feudalism	3. <u>Death</u> of feudalism
4. <u>Upsurging</u> of the arts	4. <u>Upsurge</u> of the arts
5. <u>The sciences were encouraged</u>	5. <u>Encouragement</u> of the sciences
6. <u>Religious quarrels began</u>	6. <u>Rise</u> of religious quarrels

EXERCISE 1
Identifying parallel elements
Identify the parallel elements in the following sentences. How does parallelism contribute to the effectiveness of each sentence?

1. Eating an animal has not always been an automatic or an everyday affair; it has tended to be done on solemn occasions and for a special treat.   —MARGARET VISSER

2. They [pioneer women] rolled out dough on the wagon seats, cooked with fires made out of buffalo chips, tended the sick, and marked the graves of their children, their husbands and each other.   —ELLEN GOODMAN

3. The mornings are the pleasantest times in the apartment, exhaustion having set in, the sated mosquitoes at rest on ceiling and walls, sleeping it off, the room a swirl of tortured bedclothes and abandoned garments, the vines in their full leafiness filtering the hard light of day, the air conditioner silent at last, like the mosquitoes.   —E. B. WHITE

4. Aging paints every action gray, lies heavy on every movement, imprisons every thought.   —SHARON CURTIN

EXERCISE 2
Revising: Parallelism
Revise the following sentences to make coordinate, compared, or listed elements parallel in structure. Add or delete words or rephrase as necessary.

Example:

After emptying her bag, searching the apartment, and she called the library, Jennifer realized she had lost the book.

After emptying her bag, searching the apartment, and <u>calling</u> the library, Jennifer realized she had lost the book.

//
25a

1. The ancient Greeks celebrated four athletic contests: the Olympic Games at Olympia, the Isthmian Games were held near Corinth, at Delphi the Pythian Games, and the Nemean Games were sponsored by the people of Cleonae.
2. Each day of the games consisted of either athletic events or holding ceremonies and sacrifices to the gods.
3. In the years between the games, competitors were taught wrestling, javelin throwing, and how to box.
4. Competitors participated in running sprints, spectacular chariot and horse races, and running long distances while wearing full armor.
5. The purpose of such events was developing physical strength, demonstrating skill and endurance, and to sharpen the skills needed for war.
6. Events were held for both men and for boys.
7. At the Olympic Games the spectators cheered their favorites to victory, attended sacrifices to the gods, and they feasted on the meat not burned in offerings.

8. The athletes competed less to achieve great wealth than for gaining honor both for themselves and their cities.
9. Of course, exceptional athletes received financial support from patrons, poems and statues by admiring artists, and they even got lavish living quarters from their sponsoring cities.
10. With the medal counts and flag ceremonies, today's Olympians sometimes seem to be proving their countries' superiority more than to demonstrate individual talent.

25b   Using parallelism to increase coherence

Effective parallelism will enable you to combine in a single, well-ordered sentence related ideas that you might have expressed in separate sentences. Compare the following three sentences with the original single sentence written by H. L. Mencken:

> Slang originates in the effort of ingenious individuals to make the language more pungent and picturesque. They increase the store of terse and striking words or widen the boundaries of metaphor. Thus a vocabulary for new shades and differences in meaning is provided by slang.

> Slang originates in the effort of ingenious individuals to make the language more pungent and picturesque—to increase the store of terse and striking words, to widen the boundaries of metaphor, and to provide a vocabulary for new shades and differences in meaning.   —H. L. Mencken

Parallel structure works as well to emphasize the connections among related sentences in a paragraph:

> *Lewis Mumford stands* high in the company of this century's sages. A scholar of cosmic cultural reach and conspicuous public conscience, a distinguished critic of life, arts, and letters, an unequaled observer of cities and civilizations, *he is* secure in the modern pantheon of great men. *He is* also an enigma and an anachronism. A legend of epic proportions in intellectual and academic circles, *he is* surprisingly little known to the public.   —Ada Louise Huxtable

Here, Huxtable tightly binds her sentences with two layers of parallelism: the subject-verb patterns of all four sentences (italic and underlined) and the appositives of the second and fourth sentences (underlined). (See p. 84 for another illustration of parallelism among sentences.)

//
25b

http://www.ablongman.com/littlebrown
For added practice using parallelism for coherence, click on
> Sentences > Exercises > Exer. 57

EXERCISE 3
Sentence combining: Parallelism
Combine each group of sentences below into one concise sentence in which parallel elements appear in parallel structures. You will have to add, delete, change, and rearrange words. Each item has more than one possible answer.

Example:
The new process works smoothly. It is efficient, too.
The new process works smoothly <u>and efficiently</u>.

1. People can develop post-traumatic stress disorder (PTSD). They develop it after experiencing a dangerous situation. They will also have felt fear for their survival.
2. The disorder can be triggered by a wide variety of events. Combat is a typical cause. Similarly, natural disasters can result in PTSD. Some people experience PTSD after a hostage situation.
3. PTSD can occur immediately after the stressful incident. Or it may not appear until many years later.
4. Sometimes people with PTSD will act irrationally. Moreover, they often become angry.
5. Other symptoms include dreaming that one is reliving the experience. They include hallucinating that one is back in the terrifying place. In another symptom one imagines that strangers are actually one's former torturers.

EXERCISE 4
Revising: Parallelism
Revise the following paragraph to create parallelism wherever it is required for grammar or for coherence. (You can download a double-spaced, editable version of this exercise from this book's Web site: see the box on p. 428.)

//
25

    The great white shark has an undeserved bad reputation. Many people consider the great white not only swift and powerful but also to be a cunning and cruel predator on humans. However, scientists claim that the great white attacks humans not by choice but as a result of chance. To a shark, our behavior in the water is similar to that of porpoises, seals, and sea lions—the shark's favorite foods. These sea mammals are both agile enough and can move fast enough to evade the shark. Thus the shark must attack with swiftness and noiselessly to surprise the prey and giving it little chance to escape. Humans become the shark's victims not because the shark has any preference or hatred of humans but because humans can neither outswim nor can they outmaneuver the shark. If the fish were truly a cruel human-eater, it would prolong the terror of its attacks, perhaps by circling or bumping into its intended victims before they were attacked.

Note See page 444 for an exercise involving parallelism along with other techniques for effective sentences.

CHAPTER 26

Achieving Variety

In a paragraph or an essay, each sentence stands in relation to those before and after it. To make sentences work together effectively, you need to vary their length, structure, and word order to reflect the importance and complexity of ideas. Variety sometimes takes care of itself, but you can practice established techniques for achieving varied sentences:

Ways to achieve variety among sentences

- Vary the length and structure of sentences so that important ideas stand out (p. 436).
- Vary the beginnings of sentences with modifiers, transitional words and expressions, and occasional expletive constructions (p. 438).
- Occasionally, invert the normal order of subject, verb, and object or complement (p. 441).
- Occasionally, use a command, question, or exclamation (p. 441).

A series of similar sentences will prove monotonous and ineffective, as this passage illustrates:

> Ulysses S. Grant and Robert E. Lee met on April 9, 1865. Their meeting place was the parlor of a modest house at Appomattox Court House, Virginia. They met to work out the terms for the surrender of Lee's Army of Northern Virginia. One great chapter of American life ended with their meeting, and another began. Grant and Lee were bringing the Civil War to its virtual finish. Other

http://www.ablongman.com/littlebrown
For added help with sentence variety, click on
➤ **Sentences**
  ➤ **Video tutorials** ➤ **Achieving variety**
  ➤ **Downloads** ➤ **Revising: Variety**
  ➤ **Web links** ➤ **Variety**

armies still had to surrender, and the fugitive Confederate government would struggle desperately and vainly. It would try to find some way to go on living with its chief support gone. Grant and Lee had signed the papers, however, and it was all over in effect.

These eight sentences are all between twelve and sixteen words long (counting initials and dates), they are about equally detailed, and they all begin with the subject. We get a sense of names, dates, and events but no immediate sense of how they relate or what is most important.

Now compare the preceding passage with the actual passage written by Bruce Catton. Here the four sentences range from eleven to fifty-five words, and only one sentence begins with its subject:

> When Ulysses S. Grant and Robert E. Lee met in the parlor of a modest house at Appomattox Court House, Virginia, on April 9, 1865, to work out the terms for the surrender of Lee's Army of Northern Virginia, a great chapter in American life came to a close, and a great new chapter began.

Suspenseful periodic sentence (p. 408) focuses attention on meeting. Details of place, time, and cause are in opening subordinate clause.

> These men were bringing the Civil War to its virtual finish.

Short sentence sums up.

> To be sure, other armies had yet to surrender, and for a few days the fugitive Confederate government would struggle desperately and vainly, trying to find some way to go on living now that its chief support was gone.

Cumulative sentence (p. 407) reflects lingering obstacles to peace.

> But in effect it was all over when Grant and Lee signed the papers.

Short final sentence indicates futility of further struggle.

> —BRUCE CATTON, "Grant and Lee"

The rest of this chapter suggests how you can vary your sentences for the kind of interest and clarity achieved by Catton.

Note Some grammar and style checkers will flag long sentences, and you can check for appropriate variety in a series of such sentences. But generally these programs cannot help you see where variety may be needed because they cannot recognize the relative importance and complexity of your ideas. To edit for variety, you need to listen to your sentences and determine whether they clarify your meaning.

var

26a

26a   Varying sentence length and structure

The sentences of a stylistically effective essay will vary most obviously in their length and the arrangement of main clauses and modifiers. The variation in length and structure makes writing both readable and clear.

1 ▪ Varying length

In most contemporary writing, sentences vary from about ten to about forty words, with an average of fifteen to twenty-five words.

If your sentences are all at one extreme or the other, your readers may have difficulty focusing on main ideas and seeing the relations among them:

- If most of your sentences contain thirty-five words or more, your main ideas may not stand out from the details that support them. Break some of the long sentences into shorter, simpler ones.
- If most of your sentences contain fewer than ten or fifteen words, all your ideas may seem equally important and the links between them may not be clear. Try combining them with coordination (p. 416) and subordination (p. 419) to show relationships and stress main ideas over supporting information.

2 ▪ Rewriting strings of brief and simple sentences

A series of brief and simple sentences is both monotonous and hard to understand because it forces the reader to sort out relations among ideas. If you find that you depend on brief, simple sentences, work to increase variety by combining some of them into longer units that emphasize and link important ideas while de-emphasizing incidental information. (See Chapter 24.)

The following examples show how a string of simple sentences can be revised into an effective piece of writing:

Monotonous	The moon is now drifting away from the earth. It moves away at the rate of about one inch a year. This movement is lengthening our days. They increase a thousandth of a second every century. Forty-seven of our present days will someday make up a month. We might eventually lose the moon altogether. Such great planetary movement rightly concerns astronomers, but it need not worry us. It will take 50 million years.
Revised	The moon is now drifting away from the earth <u>about one inch a year</u>. <u>At a thousandth of a second every century</u>, this movement is lengthening our days. Forty-seven of our present days will someday make up a month, <u>if we don't eventually lose the moon altogether</u>. Such great planetary movement rightly concerns astronomers, but it need not worry us. It will take 50 million years.

var
26a

In the revision, underlining indicates subordinate structures that were simple sentences in the original. With five sentences instead of the original eight, the revision emphasizes the moon's movement, our lengthening days, and the enormous span of time involved.

3 ■ Rewriting strings of compound sentences

Because compound sentences are usually just simple sentences linked with conjunctions, a series of them will be as weak as a series of brief, simple sentences, especially if the clauses of the compound sentences are all about the same length:

Monotonous	Physical illness may involve more than the body, for the mind may also be affected. Disorientation is common among sick people, but they are often unaware of it. They may reason abnormally, or they may behave immaturely.
Revised	Physical illness may involve the mind <u>as well as the body</u>. <u>Though often unaware of it</u>, sick people are commonly disoriented. They may reason abnormally <u>or behave immaturely</u>.

The first passage creates a seesaw effect. The revision, with some main clauses shortened or changed into modifiers (underlined), is both clearer and more emphatic. (See p. 417 for more on avoiding excessive coordination.)

EXERCISE 1
Revising: Varied sentence structures
Rewrite the following paragraph to increase variety so that important ideas receive greater emphasis than supporting information does. You will have to change some main clauses into modifiers and then combine and reposition the modifiers and the remaining main clauses.

Charlotte Perkins Gilman was a leading intellectual in the women's movement during the first decades of the twentieth century. She wrote *Women and Economics*. This book challenged Victorian assumptions about differences between the sexes, and it explored the economic roots of women's oppression. Gilman wrote little about gaining the vote for women, but many feminists were then preoccupied with this issue, and historians have since focused their analyses on this issue. As a result, Gilman's contribution to today's women's movement has often been overlooked.

var
26b

26b Varying sentence beginnings

An English sentence often begins with its subject, which generally captures old information from a preceding sentence (see p. 407):

The defendant's lawyer was determined to break the prosecution's witness. She relentlessly cross-examined the stubborn witness for a week.

However, an unbroken sequence of sentences beginning with the subject quickly becomes monotonous, as shown by the unvaried passage on Grant and Lee that opened this chapter (pp. 435–36). You can vary this subject-first pattern by adding modifiers or other elements before the subject.

Note The final arrangement of sentence elements should always depend on two concerns: the relation of a sentence to those preceding and following it and the emphasis required by your meaning.

Adverb modifiers

Adverbs modify verbs, adjectives, other adverbs, and whole clauses. They can often fall in a variety of spots in a sentence. Consider these different emphases:

For a week, the defendant's lawyer relentlessly cross-examined the stubborn witness.

Relentlessly, the defendant's lawyer cross-examined the stubborn witness for a week.

Relentlessly, for a week, the defendant's lawyer cross-examined the stubborn witness.

Notice that the last sentence, with both modifiers at the beginning, is periodic and thus highly emphatic (see p. 408).

CULTURE LANGUAGE In standard American English, placing certain adverb modifiers at the beginning of a sentence requires you to change the normal subject-verb order as well. The most common of these modifiers are negatives, including *seldom, rarely, in no case, not since,* and *not until.*

	adverb	subject	verb phrase
Faulty	Seldom	a witness	has held	the stand for so long.

	adverb	helping verb	subject	main verb
Revised	Seldom	has	a witness	held	the stand for so long.

var

26b

Adjective modifiers

Adjectives, modifying nouns and pronouns, may include participles and participial phrases, as in *flying geese* or *money well spent* (see pp. 253–55). These modifiers may sometimes fall at the beginning of a sentence to postpone the subject:

The witness was exhausted from his testimony, and he did not cooperate.

Exhausted from his testimony, the witness did not cooperate.

Coordinating conjunctions and transitional expressions

When the relation between two successive sentences demands, you may begin the second with a connecting word or phrase: a co-ordinating conjunction such as *and* or *but* (p. 265) or a transitional expression such as *first, for instance, however,* or *therefore* (p. 87).

> The witness had expected to be dismissed after his first long day of cross-examination. <u>But</u> he was not.

> The price of clothes has risen astronomically in recent years. <u>For example</u>, a cheap cotton shirt that once cost $6 now costs $25.

Occasional expletive constructions

An expletive construction—*it* or *there* plus a form of *be*—may occasionally be useful to delay and thus emphasize the subject of the sentence:

> His judgment seems questionable, not his desire.
> <u>It is</u> his judgment that seems questionable, not his desire.

However, expletive constructions are more likely to flatten writing by adding extra words. You should use them rarely, only when you can justify doing so. (See also p. 570.)

var

26b

EXERCISE 2
Revising: Varied sentence beginnings

Follow the instructions in parentheses to revise each group of sentences below: either create a single sentence that begins with an adverb or adjective modifier, or make one sentence begin with an appropriate connector.

> *Example:*
> The *Seabird* took first place. It moved quickly in the wind. (*One sentence with adjective modifier beginning <u>moving</u>.*)
> <u>Moving quickly in the wind</u>, the *Seabird* took first place.

1. Some people are champion procrastinators. They seldom complete their work on time. (*Two sentences with transitional expression.*)
2. Procrastinators may fear criticism. They may fear rejection. They will delay completing an assignment. (*One sentence with adverb modifier beginning <u>if</u>.*)
3. Procrastinators often desire to please a boss or a teacher. They fear failure so much that they cannot do the work. (*Two sentences with coordinating conjunction.*)
4. Procrastination seems a hopeless habit. It is conquerable. (*One sentence with adverb modifier beginning <u>although</u>.*)
5. Teachers or employers can be helpful. They can encourage procrastinators. They can give procrastinators the confidence to do good work on time. (*One sentence with adjective modifier beginning <u>helpfully encouraging</u>.*)

EXERCISE 3
Revising: Varied sentence beginnings

Revise the following paragraph to vary sentence beginnings by using each of the following at least once: an adverb modifier, an adjective modifier, a coordinating conjunction, and a transitional expression.

> Scientists in Egypt dug up 40-million-year-old fossil bones. They had evidence of primitive whales. The whale ancestors are called mesonychids. They were small, furry land mammals with four legs. These limbs were complete with kneecaps, ankles, and little toes. Gigantic modern whales have tiny hind legs inside their bodies and flippers instead of front legs. Scientists are certain that these two very different creatures share the same family tree.

26c   Inverting the normal word order

The word order of subject, verb, and object or complement is strongly fixed in English (see pp. 243–46). Thus an inverted sentence can be emphatic:

> Voters once had some faith in politicians, and they were fond of incumbents. But now all politicians, especially incumbents, voters seem to detest. [The object *all politicians* precedes the verb *detests*.]

Inverting the normal order of subject, verb, and complement can be useful in two successive sentences when the second expands on the first:

> Critics have not been kind to Presidents who have tried to apply the ways of private business to public affairs. Particularly explicit was the curt verdict of one critic of President Hoover: Mr. Hoover was never President of the United States; he was four years chairman of the board.   —Adapted from EMMET JOHN HUGHES, "The Presidency vs. Jimmy Carter"

var
26d

Inverted sentences used without need are artificial. Avoid descriptive sentences such as *Up came Larry and down went Cindy's spirits*.

26d   Mixing types of sentences

Most written sentences make statements. Occasionally, however, questions, commands, or exclamations may enhance variety.

Questions may set the direction of a paragraph, as in *What does a detective do?* or *How is the percentage of unemployed workers calculated?* More often, though, the questions used in exposition or argument do not require answers but simply emphasize ideas that readers can be expected to agree with. Such **rhetorical questions** are illustrated in the following passage:

> Another word that has ceased to have meaning due to overuse is *attractive*. *Attractive* has become verbal chaff. Who, by some stretch of language and imagination, cannot be described as attractive? And just what is it that attractive individuals are attracting?
>
> —Diane White

Commands occur frequently in an explanation of a process, particularly in directions, as this passage on freewriting illustrates:

> The idea is simply to write for ten minutes (later on, perhaps fifteen or twenty). Don't stop for anything. Go quickly, without rushing. Never stop to look back, to cross something out, to wonder how to spell something, to wonder what word or thought to use, or to think about what you are doing.   —Peter Elbow

Notice that the authors of these examples use questions and commands to achieve some special purpose. Variety occurs because a particular sentence type is effective for the context, not because the writer set out to achieve variety for its own sake.

EXERCISE 4
Writing varied sentences

Imagine that you are writing an essay on a transportation problem at your school. Practice varying sentences by composing a sentence or passage to serve each purpose listed below.

1. Write a question that could open the essay.
2. Write a command that could open the essay.
3. Write an exclamation that could open the essay.
4. For the body of the essay, write an appropriately varied paragraph of at least five sentences, including at least one short and one long sentence beginning with the subject; at least one sentence beginning with an adverb modifier; at least one sentence beginning with a coordinating conjunction or transitional expression; and one rhetorical question or command.

EXERCISE 5
Analyzing variety

Examine the following paragraph for sentence variety. By analyzing your own response to each sentence, try to explain why the author wrote each short or long sentence, each cumulative or periodic sentence, each sentence beginning with its subject or beginning some other way, and each question.

> That night in my rented room, while letting the hot water run over my can of pork and beans in the sink, I opened [H. L. Mencken's] *A Book of Prefaces* and began to read. I was jarred and shocked by the style, the clear, clean, sweeping sentences. Why did

var
26d

he write like that? And how did one write like that? I pictured the man as a raging demon, slashing with his pen, consumed with hate, denouncing everything American, extolling everything European or German, laughing at the weaknesses of people, mocking God, authority. What was this? I stood up, trying to realize what reality lay behind the meaning of the words. Yes, this man was fighting, fighting with words. He was using words as a weapon, using them as one would use a club. Could words be weapons? Well, yes, for here they were. Then, maybe, perhaps, I could use them as a weapon? No. It frightened me. I read on and what amazed me was not what he said, but how on earth anybody had the courage to say it.

—RICHARD WRIGHT, *Black Boy*

EXERCISE 6
Revising: Variety

The following paragraph consists entirely of simple sentences that begin with their subjects. As appropriate, use the techniques discussed in this chapter to vary sentences. Your goal is to make the paragraph more readable and make its important ideas stand out clearly. You will have to delete, add, change, and rearrange words. (You can download a double-spaced, editable version of this exercise from this book's Web site: see the box on p. 435.)

The Italian volcano Vesuvius had been dormant for many years. It then exploded on August 24 in the year AD 79. The ash, pumice, and mud from the volcano buried two busy towns. Herculaneum is one. The more famous is Pompeii. Both towns lay undiscovered for many centuries. Herculaneum and Pompeii were discovered in 1709 and 1748, respectively. The excavation of Pompeii was the more systematic. It was the occasion for initiating modern methods of conservation and restoration. Herculaneum was simply looted of its most valuable finds. It was then left to disintegrate. Pompeii appears much as it did before the eruption. A luxurious house opens onto a lush central garden. An election poster decorates a wall. A dining table is set for breakfast.

var
26

Note See the next page for an exercise involving variety along with parallelism and other techniques for effective sentences.

EXERCISE ON CHAPTERS 23–26
Revising: Effective sentences

Revise the paragraphs below to emphasize main ideas, de-emphasize supporting information, and achieve a pleasing, clear variety in sentences. As appropriate, employ the techniques discussed in Chapters 23–26, such as using subjects and verbs appropriately, subordinating and coordinating, creating parallelism, and varying sentence beginnings. Edit the finished product for punctuation. (To download a double-spaced, editable version of this exercise, go to *http://www.ablongman.com/littlebrown* and click on Sentences > Downloads > Revising: Effective sentences.)

Modern Americans owe many debts to Native Americans. Several pleasures are among the debts. Native Americans originated two fine junk foods. They discovered popcorn. Potato chips were also one of their contributions.

The introduction of popcorn to the European settlers came from Native Americans. Massasoit provided popcorn at the first Thanksgiving feast. The Aztecs offered popcorn to the Spanish explorer Hernando Cortés. The Aztecs wore popcorn necklaces. So did the natives of the West Indies. There were three ways that the Native Americans popped the corn. First, they roasted an ear over fire. The ear was skewered on a stick. They ate only some of the popcorn. They ate the corn that fell outside the flames. Second, they scraped the corn off the cob. The kernels would be thrown into the fire. Of course, the fire had to be low. Then the popped kernels that did not fall into the fire were eaten. The third method was the most sophisticated. It involved a shallow pottery vessel. It contained sand. The vessel was heated. The sand soon got hot. Corn kernels were stirred in. They popped to the surface of the sand and were eaten.

A Native American chef was responsible for devising the crunchy potato chip. His name was George Crum. In 1853 Crum was cooking at Moon Lake Lodge. The lodge was in Saratoga Springs, New York. Complaints were sent in by a customer. The man thought Crum's french-fried potatoes were too thick. Crum tried a thinner batch. These were also unsuitable. Crum became frustrated. He deliberately made the potatoes thin and crisp. They could not be cut with a knife and fork. Crum's joke backfired. The customer raved about the potato chips. The chips were named Saratoga Chips. Soon they appeared on the lodge's menu. They also appeared throughout New England. Crum later opened his own restaurant. Of course, he offered potato chips.

Now all Americans munch popcorn in movies. They crunch potato chips at parties. They gorge on both when alone and bored. They can be grateful to Native Americans for these guilty pleasures.

eff

Punctuation

Commas, semicolons, colons, dashes, parentheses

(For explanations, consult the pages in parentheses.)

Sentences with two main clauses

The bus stopped, but no one got off. (p. 455)
The bus stopped; no one got off. (p. 478)
The bus stopped; however, no one got off. (p. 480)
The mechanic replaced the battery, the distributor cap, and the starter;
    but still the car would not start. (p. 482)
Her duty was clear: she had to locate the problem. (p. 503)

Introductory elements

Modifiers (p. 457)
After the argument was over, we laughed at ourselves.
Racing over the plain, the gazelle escaped the lion.
To dance in the contest, he had to tape his knee.
Suddenly, the door flew open.
With 125 passengers aboard, the plane was half full.
In 1983 he won the Nobel Prize.

Absolute phrases (p. 464)
Its wing broken, the bird hopped around on the ground.

Interrupting and concluding elements

Nonessential modifiers (p. 459)
Jim's car, which barely runs, has been impounded.
We consulted the dean, who had promised to help us.
The boy, like his sister, wants to be a pilot.
They moved across the desert, shielding their eyes from the sun.
The men do not speak to each other, although they share a car.

Nonessential appositives
Bergen's only daughter, Candice, became an actress. (p. 461)
The residents of three counties—Suffolk, Springfield, and Morrison—
    were urged to evacuate. (p. 506)
Father demanded one promise: that we not lie to him. (p. 504)

Essential modifiers (p. 461)
The car that hit mine was uninsured.
We consulted a teacher who had promised to help us.
The boy in the black hat is my cousin.
They were surprised to find the desert teeming with life.
The men do not speak to each other because they are feuding.

Essential appositives (p. 461)

Shaw's play *Saint Joan* was performed last year.
Their sons Tony, William, and Steve all chose military careers, leaving only
  Joe to run the family business.

Transitional or parenthetical expressions

We suspect, however, that he will not come. (p. 461)
Jan is respected by many people—including me. (p. 507)
George Balanchine (1904–83) was a brilliant choreographer of classical
  ballet. (p. 508)

Absolute phrases (p. 464)

The bird, its wing broken, hopped about on the ground.
The bird hopped about on the ground, its wing broken.

Phrases expressing contrast (p. 464)

The humidity, not just the heat, gives me headaches.
My headaches are caused by the humidity, not just the heat.

Concluding summaries and explanations

The movie opened to bad notices: the characters were judged shallow
  and unrealistic. (p. 504)
We dined on gumbo and jambalaya—a Cajun feast. (p. 507)

Items in a series

Three or more items

Chimpanzees, gorillas, orangutans, and gibbons are all apes. (p. 465)
The cities singled out for praise were Birmingham, Alabama; Lincoln,
  Nebraska; Austin, Texas; and Troy, New York. (p. 482)

Two or more adjectives before a noun (p. 465)

Dingy, smelly clothes decorated their room.
The luncheon consisted of one tiny watercress sandwich.

Introductory series (p. 507)

Appropriateness, accuracy, and necessity—these criteria should govern
  your selection of words.

Concluding series

Every word should be appropriate, accurate, and necessary. (p. 474)
Every word should meet three criteria: appropriateness, accuracy, and
  necessity. (p. 504)
Pay attention to your words—to their appropriateness, their accuracy,
  and their necessity. (p. 507)

p

CHAPTER 27

End Punctuation

End punctuation marks—the period, the question mark, and the exclamation point—signal the ends of sentences.

Note Do not rely on a grammar and style checker to identify missing or misused end punctuation. Although a checker may flag missing question marks after direct questions or incorrect combinations of marks (such as a question mark and a period at the end of a sentence), it cannot do much else.

THE PERIOD

27a Use a period to end a statement, mild command, or indirect question.

Statements
These are exciting and trying times.
The airline went bankrupt.

Mild commands
Please do not smoke.
Think of the possibilities.

If you are unsure whether to use an exclamation point or a period after a command, use a period. The exclamation point should be used only rarely (see p. 451).

An **indirect question** reports what someone has asked but not in the form or exact words of the original.

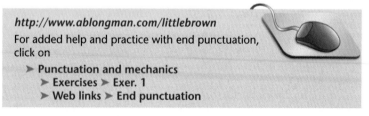

http://www.ablongman.com/littlebrown
For added help and practice with end punctuation, click on
➤ Punctuation and mechanics
  ➤ Exercises ➤ Exer. 1
  ➤ Web links ➤ End punctuation

Indirect questions

Students sometimes wonder whether their teachers read the papers they write.

Abused children eventually stop asking why they are being punished.

CULTURE LANGUAGE In standard American English, an indirect question uses the wording and subject-verb order of a statement: *The reporter asked why the negotiations failed*, not *why did the negotiations fail*.

27b Use periods with some abbreviations.

Use periods with abbreviations that consist of or end in small letters. Otherwise, omit periods from abbreviations.

Dr.	Mr., Mrs.	e.g.	Feb.	ft.
St.	Ms.	i.e.	p.	a.m., p.m.
PhD	BC, AD	USA	IBM	JFK
BA	AM, PM	US	USMC	AIDS

Note When a sentence ends in an abbreviation with a period, don't add a second period: *My first class is at 8 a.m.*

See also pages 530–33 on uses of abbreviations in writing.

EXERCISE 1
Revising: Periods

Revise the following sentences so that periods are used correctly.

> *Example:*
> Several times I wrote to ask when my subscription ended?
> Several times I wrote to ask when my subscription ended.

1. The instructor asked when Plato wrote *The Republic*?
2. Give the date within one century
3. The exact date is not known, but it is estimated at 370 BC
4. Dr Arn will lecture on Plato at 7:30 p.m..
5. The area of the lecture hall is only 1600 sq ft

THE QUESTION MARK

?
27c

27c Use a question mark after a direct question.

Direct questions

What is the difference between these two people?
Will economists ever really understand the economy?

After an indirect question, use a period: *The senator asked why the bill had passed.* (See pp. 448–49.)

Questions in a series are each followed by a question mark:

The officer asked how many times the suspect had been arrested. Three times**?** Four times**?** More than that**?**

The use of capital letters for questions in a series is optional (see p. 519).

Note Question marks are never combined with other question marks, exclamation points, periods, or commas:

Faulty   "What is the point?," readers ask.
Revised   "What is the point**?**" readers ask.

27d   Use a question mark within parentheses to indicate doubt about the correctness of a number or date.

The Greek philosopher Socrates was born in 470 (**?**) BC and died in 399 BC from drinking poison after having been condemned to death.

Note Don't use a question mark within parentheses to express sarcasm or irony. Express these attitudes through sentence structure and word choice. (See Chapters 23 and 39.)

Faulty   Stern's friendliness (?) bothered Crane.
Revised   Stern's <u>insincerity</u> bothered Crane.

EXERCISE 2
Revising: Question marks
Revise the following sentences so that question marks (along with other punctuation marks) are used correctly.

Example:
"When will it end?," cried the man dressed in rags.
"When will it end**?**" cried the man dressed in rags.

1. In Homer's *Odyssey*, Odysseus took seven years to travel from Troy to Ithaca. Or was it eight years. Or more?
2. Odysseus must have wondered whether he would ever make it home?
3. "What man are you and whence?," asks Odysseus's wife, Penelope.
4. Why does Penelope ask, "Where is your city? Your family?"?
5. Penelope does not recognize Odysseus and asks who this stranger is?

?
27d

THE EXCLAMATION POINT

27e Use an exclamation point after an emphatic statement, interjection, or command.

No! We must not lose this election!
Come here immediately!

Follow mild interjections and commands with commas or periods, as appropriate:

No, the response was not terrific.
To prolong your car's life, change its oil regularly.

Note Exclamation points are never combined with other exclamation points, question marks, periods, or commas:

Faulty   "This will not be endured!," he roared.
Revised   "This will not be endured!" he roared.

27f Use exclamation points sparingly.

Don't express sarcasm, irony, or amazement with the exclamation point. Rely on sentence structure and word choice to express these attitudes. (See Chapters 23 and 39.)

Faulty   After traveling 4.4 billion miles through space, *Voyager 2* was off-target by 21 miles (!).
Revised   After traveling 4.4 billion miles through space, *Voyager 2* was off-target by a mere 21 miles.

Relying on the exclamation point for emphasis is like crying wolf: the mark loses its power to impress the reader. Frequent exclamation points can also make writing sound overemotional. In the following passage, the writer could have conveyed ideas more effectively by punctuating sentences with periods:

Our city government is a mess! After just six months in office, the mayor has had to fire four city officials! In the same period the city councilors have done nothing but argue! And city services decline with each passing day!

!
27f

EXERCISE 3
Revising: Exclamation points
Revise the following sentences so that exclamation points (along with other punctuation marks) are used correctly. If a sentence is punctuated correctly as given, circle the number preceding it.

Example:
"Well, now!," he said loudly.
"Well, now!" he said loudly.

1. As the firefighters moved their equipment into place, the police shouted, "Move back!".
2. A child's cries could be heard from above: "Help me. Help."
3. When the child was rescued, the crowd called "Hooray."
4. The rescue was the most exciting event of the day!
5. Let me tell you about it.

EXERCISE 4
Revising: End punctuation

Insert appropriate punctuation (periods, question marks, or exclamation points) where needed in the following paragraph.

When visitors first arrive in Hawaii, they often encounter an unexpected language barrier Standard English is the language of business and government, but many of the people speak Pidgin English Instead of an excited "Aloha" the visitors may be greeted with an excited Pidgin "Howzit" or asked if they know "how fo' find one good hotel" Many Hawaiians question whether Pidgin will hold children back because it prevents communication with the *haoles,* or Caucasians, who run businesses Yet many others feel that Pidgin is a last defense of ethnic diversity on the islands To those who want to make standard English the official language of the state, these Hawaiians may respond, "Just 'cause I speak Pidgin no mean I dumb" They may ask, "Why you no listen" or, in standard English, "Why don't you listen"

Note See page 516 for a punctuation exercise combining periods with other marks of punctuation.

!
27f

CHAPTER 28

The Comma

Commas usually function within sentences to separate elements (see the box on the next page). Omitting needed commas or inserting needless ones can confuse the reader:

Comma needed	Though very tall Abraham Lincoln was not an overbearing man.
Revised	Though very tall, Abraham Lincoln was not an overbearing man.
Unneeded commas	The hectic pace of Beirut, broke suddenly into frightening chaos when the city became, the focus of civil war.
Revised	The hectic pace of Beirut broke suddenly into frightening chaos when the city became the focus of civil war.

Note Grammar and style checkers will ignore many comma errors. For example, a checker failed to catch the missing commas in *The boat ran aground and we were stranded* and in *We cooked lasagna spinach and apple pie.* At the same time the checker overlooked the misused commas in *The trip was short but, the weather was perfect* and *The travelers were tempted by, the many shops, and varied restaurants.* Revise any errors that your checker does catch, but you'll have to proofread your work on your own to find and correct most errors.

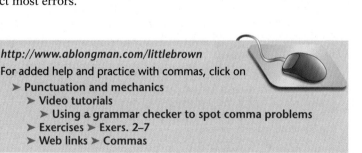

http://www.ablongman.com/littlebrown
For added help and practice with commas, click on
➤ **Punctuation and mechanics**
   ➤ **Video tutorials**
      ➤ **Using a grammar checker to spot comma problems**
   ➤ **Exercises** ➤ **Exers. 2–7**
   ➤ **Web links** ➤ **Commas**

453

Principal uses of the comma

- **Separate main clauses linked by a coordinating conjunction** (facing page):

The building is finished, but it has no tenants.

- **Set off most introductory elements** (p. 457):

Unfortunately, the only tenant pulled out.

- **Set off nonessential elements** (p. 459):

Main clause , nonessential element .

The empty building symbolizes a weak local economy, which affects everyone.

Beginning of main clause , nonessential element , end of main clause .

The primary cause, the decline of local industry, is not news.

- **Separate items in a series** (p. 465):

The city needs healthier businesses, new schools, and improved housing.

- **Separate coordinate adjectives** (p. 465):

... first adjective , second adjective word modified ...

A tall, sleek skyscraper is not needed.

Other uses of the comma:

Set off absolute phrases (p. 464).
Set off phrases expressing contrast (p. 464).
Separate parts of dates, addresses, long numbers (p. 467).
Separate quotations and signal phrases (p. 468).
Prevent misreading (p. 470).

See also page 471 for when *not* to use the comma.

28

28a   Use a comma before *and, but,* or another coordinating conjunction linking main clauses.

The coordinating conjunctions are *and, but, or, nor, for, so,* and *yet.* When these link words or phrases, do not use a comma: *Dugain plays and sings Irish and English folk songs.* However, *do* use a comma when a coordinating conjunction joins main clauses. A **main clause** has a subject and a predicate (but no subordinating word at the beginning) and makes a complete statement (see p. 258).

> Caffeine can keep coffee drinkers alert, and it may elevate their mood.

> Caffeine was once thought to be safe, but now researchers warn of harmful effects.

> Coffee drinkers may suffer sleeplessness, for the drug acts as a stimulant to the nervous system.

Note Do not add a comma *after* a coordinating conjunction between main clauses (see also pp. 472–73):

| **Not** | Caffeine increases the heart rate, and, it constricts blood vessels. |
| **But** | Caffeine increases the heart rate, and it constricts blood vessels. |

Exceptions When the main clauses in a sentence are very long or grammatically complicated, or when they contain internal punctuation, a semicolon before the coordinating conjunction will clarify the division between clauses (see p. 482):

> Caffeine may increase alertness, elevate mood, and provide energy; but it may also cause irritability, anxiety, stomach pains, and other ills.

When main clauses are very short and closely related in meaning, you may omit the comma between them as long as the resulting sentence is clear:

> Caffeine helps but it also hurts.

If you are in doubt about whether to use a comma in such a sentence, use it. It will always be correct.

∧
28a

EXERCISE 1
Punctuating linked main clauses

Insert a comma before each coordinating conjunction that links main clauses in the following sentences.

Example:

I would have attended the concert and the reception but I had to baby-sit for my niece.

I would have attended the concert and the reception**,** but I had to baby-sit for my niece.

1. Parents once automatically gave their children the father's surname but some no longer do.
2. Instead, they bestow the mother's name for they believe that the mother's importance should be recognized.
3. The child's surname may be just the mother's or it may link the mother's and the father's with a hyphen.
4. Sometimes the first and third children will have the mother's surname and the second child will have the father's.
5. Occasionally the mother and father combine parts of their names and a new hybrid surname is born.

EXERCISE 2
Sentence combining: Linked main clauses

Combine each group of sentences below into one sentence that contains only two main clauses connected by the coordinating conjunction in parentheses. Separate the main clauses with a comma. You will have to add, delete, and rearrange words.

Example:

The circus had come to town. The children wanted to see it. Their parents wanted to see it. (*and*)

The circus had come to town**,** and the children and their parents wanted to see it.

1. Parents were once legally required to bestow the father's surname on their children. These laws have been contested in court. They have been found invalid. (*but*)
2. Parents may now give their children any surname they choose. The arguments for bestowing the mother's surname are often strong. They are often convincing. (*and*)
3. Critics sometimes question the effects of unusual surnames on children. They wonder how confusing the new surnames will be. They wonder how fleeting the surnames will be. (*or*)
4. Children with surnames different from their parents' may suffer embarrassment. They may suffer identity problems. Giving children their father's surname is still very much the norm. (*for*)
5. Hyphenated names are awkward. They are also difficult to pass on. Some observers think they will die out in the next generation. Or they may die out before. (*so*)

28a

28b Use a comma to set off most introductory elements.

An introductory element modifies a word or words in the main clause that follows. These elements are usually set off from the rest of the sentence with a comma:

Subordinate clause (p. 258)

<u>Even when identical twins are raised apart,</u> they grow up very like each other.

<u>Because they are similar,</u> such twins interest scientists.

Verbal or verbal phrase (p. 253)

<u>Explaining the similarity,</u> some researchers claim that one's genes are one's destiny.

<u>Concerned,</u> other researchers deny the claim.

Prepositional phrase (p. 250)

<u>In a debate that has lasted centuries,</u> scientists use identical twins to argue for or against genetic destiny.

Transitional or parenthetical expression (p. 87)

<u>Of course,</u> scientists can now look directly at the genes themselves.

The comma may be omitted after short introductory elements if its omission does not create confusion. (If you are in doubt, however, the comma is always correct.)

Clear	<u>In a hundred years</u> genetics may no longer be a mystery.
Confusing	Despite intensive research scientists still have more questions than answers.
Clear	Despite intensive research, scientists still have more questions than answers.

Note Take care to distinguish *-ing* words used as modifiers from *-ing* words used as subjects, as shown in the following examples. The former almost always take a comma; the latter never do.

⌃
28b

http://www.ablongman.com/littlebrown

For added help and practice with commas and introductory elements, click on
➤ **Punctuation and mechanics**
  ➤ **Exercises** ➤ **Exer. 3**
  ➤ **Web links** ➤ **Commas**

```
  ┌────── modifier ──────┐   subject    verb
```
Studying identical twins, geneticists learn about inheritance.
```
  ┌────── subject ──────┐  verb
```
Studying identical twins helps geneticists learn about inheritance.

EXERCISE 3
Punctuating introductory elements

Insert commas where needed after introductory elements in the following sentences. If a sentence is punctuated correctly as given, circle the number preceding it.

> *Example:*
> After the new library opened the old one became a student union.
> After the new library opened, the old one became a student union.

1. Moving in a fluid mass is typical of flocks of birds and schools of fish.
2. Because it is sudden and apparently well coordinated the movement of flocks and schools has seemed to be directed by a leader.
3. However new studies have discovered that flocks and schools are leaderless.
4. When each bird or fish senses a predator it follows individual rules for fleeing.
5. Multiplied over hundreds of individuals these responses look as if they have been choreographed.

EXERCISE 4
Sentence combining: Introductory elements

Combine each pair of sentences below into one sentence that begins with an introductory phrase or clause as specified in parentheses. Follow the introductory element with a comma. You will have to add, delete, change, and rearrange words.

> *Example:*
> The girl was humming to herself. She walked upstairs. (*Phrase beginning Humming.*)
> Humming to herself, the girl walked upstairs.

1. Scientists have made an effort to explain the mysteries of flocks and schools. They have proposed bizarre magnetic fields and telepathy. (*Phrase beginning In.*)
2. Scientists developed computer models. They have abandoned earlier explanations. (*Clause beginning Since.*)
3. The movement of a flock or school starts with each individual. It is rapidly and perhaps automatically coordinated among individuals. (*Phrase beginning Starting.*)
4. One zoologist observes that human beings seek coherent patterns. He suggests that investigators saw purpose in the movement of flocks and schools where none existed. (*Phrase beginning Observing.*)

28b

5. One may want to study the movement of flocks or schools.
Then one must abandon a search for purpose or design. (*Phrase
beginning To.*)

28c   Use a comma or commas to set off nonessential elements.

Commas around part of a sentence often signal that the element is not essential to the meaning of the sentence:

Nonessential element

The company, which is located in Oklahoma, has a good reputation.

This **nonessential element** may modify or rename the word it refers to (*company* in the example), but it does not limit the word to a particular individual or group. (Because it does not restrict meaning, a nonessential element is also called a **nonrestrictive element**.) Nonessential elements are *not* essential, but punctuation *is*.

In contrast, an **essential** (or **restrictive**) element *does* limit the word it refers to:

Essential element

The company rewards employees who work hard.

In this example the underlined essential element cannot be omitted without leaving the meaning of *employees* too general. Because it is essential, such an element is *not* set off with commas. The element *is* essential, but punctuation is *not*.

Meaning and context

The same element in the same sentence may be essential or nonessential depending on your intended meaning and the context in which the sentence appears. For example, look at the second sentence in each of the following passages:

Essential

Not all the bands were equally well received, however. The band playing old music held the audience's attention. The other groups created much less excitement. [*Playing old music* identifies a particular band.]

28c

http://www.ablongman.com/littlebrown

For added help and practice with commas and nonessential elements, click on
➤ **Punctuation and mechanics**
  ➤ **Exercises** ➤ **Exer. 4**
  ➤ **Web links** ➤ **Commas**

A test for essential and nonessential elements

1. **Identify the element.**

   Hai Nguyen <u>who emigrated from Vietnam</u> lives in Denver.
   Those <u>who emigrated with him</u> live elsewhere.

2. **Remove the element. Does the fundamental meaning of the sentence change?**

   Hai Nguyen lives in Denver. **No.**
   Those live elsewhere. **Yes.** [Who are *Those?*]

3. **If *no,* the element is *nonessential* and should be set off with punctuation.**

   Hai Nguyen, <u>who emigrated from Vietnam,</u> lives in Denver.

   If *yes,* the element is *essential* and should *not* be set off with punctuation.

   Those <u>who emigrated with him</u> live elsewhere.

Nonessential

A new band called Fats made its debut on Saturday night. The band, <u>playing old music,</u> held the audience's attention. If this performance is typical, the group has a bright future. [*Playing old music* adds information about a band already named.]

Punctuation of interrupting nonessential elements

When a nonessential element falls in the middle of a sentence, be sure to set it off with a pair of commas, one *before* and one *after* the element. Dashes or parentheses may also set off nonessential elements (see pp. 506 and 508).

1 ▪ Use a comma or commas to set off nonessential clauses and phrases.

Clauses and phrases serving as adjectives and adverbs may be either nonessential or essential. In the following examples the underlined clauses and phrases are nonessential: they could be omitted without changing the meaning of the words they modify.

28c

Nonessential

Elizabeth Blackwell was the first woman to graduate from an American medical school, <u>in 1849.</u>

She was a medical pioneer, <u>helping to found the first medical college for women.</u>

She taught at the school, <u>which was affiliated with the New York Infirmary.</u>

Blackwell, <u>who published books and papers on medicine,</u> practiced pediatrics and gynecology.

She moved to England in 1869, when she was forty-eight.

Note Most adverb clauses are essential because they describe conditions necessary to the main clause. They are set off by a comma only when they introduce sentences (see p. 457) and when they are truly nonessential, adding incidental information (as in the example above) or expressing a contrast beginning *although, even though, though, whereas,* and the like.

In the following sentences, the underlined elements limit the meaning of the words they modify. Removing the elements would leave the meaning too general.

Essential

The history of aspirin began with the ancient Greeks.

Physicians who sought to relieve their patients' pains recommended chewing willow bark.

Willow bark contains a chemical that is similar to aspirin.

Note Whereas both nonessential and essential clauses may begin with *which*, only essential clauses begin with *that*. Some writers prefer *that* exclusively for essential clauses and *which* exclusively for nonessential clauses. See the Glossary of Usage, page 929, for advice on the use of *that* and *which*.

2 ■ Use a comma or commas to set off nonessential appositives.

An **appositive** is a noun or noun substitute that renames another noun just before it. (See p. 263.) Many appositives are nonessential; thus they are set off, usually with commas:

Nonessential

Toni Morrison's fifth novel, *Beloved,* won the Pulitzer Prize in 1988.

Morrison, a native of Ohio, won the Nobel Prize in 1993.

Take care *not* to set off essential appositives; like other essential elements, they limit or define the word to which they refer.

Essential

Morrison's novel *The Bluest Eye* is about an African American girl who longs for blue eyes.

The critic Michiko Kakutani says that Morrison's work "stands radiantly on its own as an American epic."

28c

3 ■ Use a comma or commas to set off transitional or parenthetical expressions.

Transitional expressions

Transitional expressions form links between ideas. They include conjunctive adverbs such as *however* and *moreover* as well as other words or phrases such as *for example* and *of course.* (See p. 87 for a list of transitional words and phrases.) Transitional expressions are nonessential, so set them off with a comma or commas:

> American workers, for example, receive fewer holidays than European workers do.

When a transitional expression links main clauses, precede it with a semicolon and follow it with a comma. (See p. 480.)

> European workers often have long paid vacations; indeed, they may receive a full month.

Note The conjunctions *and, but,* and *yet* are sometimes used as transitional expressions but are not followed by commas (see p. 472). Nor are commas required after some transitional expressions that we read without pauses, such as *also, hence, next, now,* and *thus.* A few transitional expressions, notably *therefore* and *instead,* do not need commas when they fall inside or at the ends of clauses.

> American workers thus put in more work days. But the days themselves may be shorter.

Parenthetical expressions

Parenthetical expressions provide comments, explanations, digressions, or other supplementary information not essential to meaning—for example, *fortunately, unfortunately, all things considered, to be frank, in other words.* Set parenthetical expressions off with commas:

> Few people would know, or even guess, the most celebrated holiday on earth.
> That holiday is, surprisingly, New Year's Day.

(Dashes and parentheses may also set off parenthetical expressions. See pp. 507 and 508, respectively.)

28c

4 ■ Use a comma or commas to set off *yes* and *no,* tag questions, words of direct address, and mild interjections.

Yes and *no*
Yes, the editorial did have a point.
No, that can never be.

Tag questions
Jones should be allowed to vote, should he not?
They don't stop to consider others, do they?

Direct address
Cody, please bring me the newspaper.
With all due respect, sir, I will not do that.

Mild interjections

Well, you will never know who did it.
Oh, they forgot all about the baby.

(You may want to use an exclamation point to set off a forceful interjection. See p. 451.)

EXERCISE 5
Punctuating essential and nonessential elements

Insert commas in the following sentences to set off nonessential elements, and delete any commas that incorrectly set off essential elements. If a sentence is correct as given, circle the number preceding it.

Example:

Our language has adopted the words, *garage* and *fanfare,* from the French.

Our language has adopted the words *garage* and *fanfare* from the French.

1. Italians insist that Marco Polo the thirteenth-century explorer did not import pasta from China.
2. Pasta which consists of flour and water and often egg existed in Italy long before Marco Polo left for his travels.
3. A historian who studied pasta says that it originated in the Middle East in the fifth century.
4. Most Italians dispute this account although their evidence is shaky.
5. Wherever pasta originated, the Italians are now the undisputed masters, in making and cooking it.
6. Marcella Hazan, who has written several books on Italian cooking, insists that homemade and hand-rolled pasta is the best.
7. Most cooks must buy dried pasta lacking the time to make their own.
8. The finest pasta is made from semolina, a flour from hard durum wheat.
9. Pasta manufacturers choose hard durum wheat, because it makes firmer cooked pasta than common wheat does.
10. Pasta, made from common wheat, tends to get soggy in boiling water.

28c

EXERCISE 6
Sentence combining: Essential and nonessential elements

Combine each pair of sentences below into one sentence that uses the element described in parentheses. Insert commas as appropriate. You will have to add, delete, change, and rearrange words. Some items have more than one possible answer.

Example:

Mr. Ward's oldest sister helped keep him alive. She was a nurse in the hospital. (*Nonessential clause beginning who.*)

Mr. Ward's oldest sister, who was a nurse in the hospital, helped keep him alive.

1. American colonists first imported pasta from the English. The English had discovered it as tourists in Italy. (*Nonessential clause beginning who.*)
2. The English returned from their grand tours of Italy. They were called *macaronis* because of their fancy airs. (*Essential phrase beginning returning.*)
3. A hair style was also called *macaroni*. It had elaborate curls. (*Essential phrase beginning with.*)
4. The song "Yankee Doodle" refers to this hairdo. It reports that Yankee Doodle "stuck a feather in his cap and called it macaroni." (*Essential clause beginning when.*)
5. The song was actually intended to poke fun at unrefined American colonists. It was a creation of the English. (*Nonessential appositive beginning a creation.*)

28d Use a comma or commas to set off absolute phrases.

An **absolute phrase** modifies a whole main clause rather than any word in the clause, and it usually consists of at least a participle (such as *done* or *having torn*) and its subject (a noun or pronoun). (See p. 257.) Absolute phrases can occur at almost any point in the sentence, and they are always set off by a comma or commas:

Household recycling having succeeded, the city now wants to extend the program to businesses.

Many businesses, their profits already squeezed, resist recycling.

28e Use a comma or commas to set off phrases expressing contrast.

The essay needs less wit, more pith.
The substance, not the style, is important.
Substance, unlike style, cannot be faked.

Note Writers often omit commas around contrasting phrases beginning with *but: A full but hazy moon shone down.*

28e

EXERCISE 7
Punctuating absolute phrases and phrases of contrast
Insert commas in the following sentences to set off absolute phrases and phrases of contrast.

Example:
The recording contract was canceled the band having broken up.
The recording contract was canceled, the band having broken up.

1. Prices having risen rapidly the government debated a price freeze.
2. A price freeze unlike a rise in interest rates seemed a sure solution.
3. The President would have to persuade businesses to accept a price freeze his methods depending on their resistance.
4. No doubt the President his advisers having urged it would first try a patriotic appeal.
5. The President not his advisers insisted on negotiations with businesses.

28f   Use commas between items in a series and between coordinate adjectives.

1 ▪ Use commas between words, phrases, or clauses forming a series.

Place commas between all elements of a **series**—that is, three or more items of equal importance:

> Anna Spingle married at the age of seventeen, had three children by twenty-one, and divorced at twenty-two.
>
> She worked as a cook, a baby-sitter, and a crossing guard.

Some writers omit the comma before the coordinating conjunction in a series (*Breakfast consisted of coffee, eggs and kippers*). But the final comma is never wrong, and it always helps the reader see the last two items as separate:

Confusing	Spingle's new job involves typing, filing and answering correspondence.
Clear	Spingle's new job involves typing, filing, and answering correspondence.

Exception When items in a series are long and grammatically complicated, they may be separated by semicolons. When the items contain commas, they must be separated by semicolons. (See p. 482.)

2 ▪ Use commas between two or more adjectives that equally modify the same word.

When two or more adjectives modify the same word equally, they are said to be **coordinate**. The adjectives may be separated either by *and* or by a comma, as in the following examples.

28f

---

http://www.ablongman.com/littlebrown

For added practice with commas in series and between coordinate adjectives, click on

➤ **Punctuation and mechanics** ➤ **Exercises** ➤ **Exer. 5**

Punctuating two or more adjectives

1. **Identify the adjectives.**

   She was a faithful sincere friend.
   They are dedicated medical students.

2. **Can the adjectives be reversed without changing meaning?**

   She was a sincere faithful friend. *Yes.*
   They are medical dedicated students. *No.*

3. **Can the word *and* be inserted between the adjectives without changing meaning?**

   She was a faithful and sincere friend. *Yes.*
   They are dedicated and medical students. *No.*

4. **If *yes* to both questions, the adjectives *are* coordinate and *should* be separated by a comma.**

   She was a faithful, sincere friend.

   If *no* to both questions, the adjectives are *not* coordinate and should *not* be separated by a comma.

   They are dedicated medical students.

Spingle's scratched and dented car is an eyesore, but it gets her to work.
She has dreams of a sleek, shiny car.

Adjectives are not coordinate—and should *not* be separated by commas—when the one nearer the noun is more closely related to the noun in meaning. In each of the next examples, the second adjective and the noun form a unit that is modified by the first adjective:

Spingle's children work at various odd jobs.
They all expect to go to a nearby community college.

See the box above for a test to use in punctuating adjectives.
   Note Numbers are not coordinate with other adjectives:

Faulty	Spingle has three, teenaged children.
Revised	Spingle has three teenaged children.

Do not use a comma between the final adjective and the noun:

Faulty	The children hope to avoid their mother's hard, poor, life.
Revised	The children hope to avoid their mother's hard, poor life.

28f

EXERCISE 8
Punctuating series and coordinate adjectives
Insert commas in the following sentences to separate coordinate adjectives or elements in series. Circle the number preceding each sentence whose punctuation is already correct.

Example:
Quiet by day, the club became a noisy smoky dive at night.
Quiet by day, the club became a noisy, smoky dive at night.

1. Shoes with high heels originated to protect feet from the mud garbage and animal waste in the streets.
2. The first known high heels worn strictly for fashion appeared in the sixteenth century.
3. The heels were worn by men and made of colorful silk brocades soft suedes or smooth leathers.
4. High-heeled shoes received a boost when the short powerful King Louis XIV of France began wearing them.
5. Eventually only wealthy fashionable French women wore high heels.

28g Use commas according to convention in dates, addresses, place names, and long numbers.

Use commas to separate most parts of dates, addresses, and place names: *June 20, 1950; 24 Fifth Avenue, Suite 601; Cairo, Illinois.* Within a sentence, any element preceded by a comma should be followed by a comma as well, as in the examples below:

Dates
July 4, 1776, is the date the Declaration of Independence was signed.

The bombing of Pearl Harbor on Sunday, December 7, 1941, prompted American entry into World War II.

Do not use commas between the parts of a date in inverted order: *Their anniversary on 15 December 1999 was their fiftieth.* You need not use commas in dates consisting of a month or season and a year: *For the United States the war began in December 1941 and ended in August 1945.*

Addresses and place names
Columbus, Ohio, is the state capital and the location of Ohio State University.

The population of Garden City, Long Island, New York, is 30,000.

Use the address 220 Cornell Road, Woodside, California 94062, for all correspondence.

As illustrated above, do not use a comma between a state and a zip code.

Long numbers
Use the comma to separate the figures in long numbers into groups of three, counting from the right. With numbers of four digits, the comma is optional.

A kilometer is 3,281 feet [*or* 3281 feet].

The new assembly plant cost $7,525,000 to design and build.

CULTURE LANGUAGE Usage in American English differs from that in some other languages and dialects, which use a period, not a comma, to separate the figures in long numbers.

EXERCISE 9
Punctuating dates, addresses, place names, numbers
Insert commas as needed in the following sentences.

> *Example:*
> The house cost $27000 fifteen years ago.
> The house cost $27,000 fifteen years ago.

1. The festival will hold a benefit dinner and performance on March 10 2005 in Asheville.
2. The organizers hope to raise more than $100000 from donations and ticket sales.
3. Performers are expected from as far away as Milan Italy and Kyoto Japan.
4. All inquiries sent to Mozart Festival PO Box 725 Asheville North Carolina 28803 will receive a quick response.
5. The deadline for ordering tickets by mail is Monday December 3 2004.

28h Use commas with quotations according to standard practice.

The words *he said, she writes,* and so on identify the source of a quotation. These **signal phrases** may come before, after, or in the middle of the quotation. A signal phrase must always be separated from the quotation by punctuation, usually a comma or commas. (See pp. 495–96 for a summary of this and other conventions regarding quotations.)

1 ■ Ordinarily, use a comma with a signal phrase before or after a quotation.

Eleanor Roosevelt said, "You must do the thing you think you cannot do."

---

http://www.ablongman.com/littlebrown
For added practice with commas and quotations, click on
➤ **Punctuation and mechanics**
  ➤ **Exercises** ➤ **Exer. 6**
  ➤ **Web links** ➤ **Commas**

"Knowledge is power," writes Francis Bacon.

Exceptions Do not use a comma when a signal phrase follows a quotation ending in an exclamation point or a question mark:

> "Claude!" Mrs. Harrison called.
> "Why must I come home?" he asked.

Do not use commas with a quotation introduced by *that* or with a quotation that is integrated into your sentence structure:

> James Baldwin insists that "one must never, in one's life, accept . . . injustices as commonplace."
>
> Baldwin thought that the violence of a riot "had been devised as a corrective" to his own violence.

Use a colon instead of a comma between a signal phrase and a quotation when the signal phrase is actually a complete sentence and the quotation is very formal or longer than a sentence.

> The Bill of Rights is unambiguous: "Congress shall make no law respecting an establishment of religion, or prohibiting the free exercise thereof."

2 ■ With an interrupted quotation, precede the signal phrase with a comma and follow it with the punctuation required by the quotation.

Quotation

"The shore has a dual nature, changing with the swing of the tides."

Signal phrase

"The shore has a dual nature," observes Rachel Carson, "changing with the swing of the tides." [The signal phrase interrupts the quotation at a comma and thus ends with a comma.]

Quotation

"However mean your life is, meet it and live it; do not shun it and call it hard names."

Signal phrase

"However mean your life is, meet it and live it," Thoreau advises in *Walden*; "do not shun it and call it hard names." [The signal phrase interrupts the quotation at a semicolon and thus ends with a semicolon.]

Quotation

"This is the faith with which I return to the South. With this new faith we will be able to hew out of the mountain of despair a stone of hope."

Signal phrase

"This is the faith with which I return to the South," Martin Luther King, Jr., proclaimed. "With this new faith we will be able to hew

28h

out of the mountain of despair a stone of hope." [The signal phrase interrupts the quotation at the end of a sentence and thus ends with a period.]

Note Using a comma instead of a semicolon or a period after the Thoreau and King signal phrases would result in the error called a comma splice: two main clauses separated only by a comma. (See pp. 357–61.)

3 ▪ Place commas that follow quotations within quotation marks.

"Death is not the greatest loss in life," claims Norman Cousins.

"The greatest loss," Cousins says, "is what dies inside us while we live."

EXERCISE 10
Punctuating quotations

Insert commas or semicolons in the following sentences to correct punctuation with quotations. Circle the number preceding any sentence whose punctuation is already correct.

Example:
The shoplifter declared "I didn't steal anything."
The shoplifter declared, "I didn't steal anything."

1. The writer and writing teacher Peter Elbow proposes an "open-ended writing process" that "can change you, not just your words."
2. "I think of the open-ended writing process as a voyage in two stages" Elbow says.
3. "The sea voyage is a process of divergence, branching, proliferation, and confusion" Elbow continues "the coming to land is a process of convergence, pruning, centralizing, and clarifying."
4. "Keep up one session of writing long enough to get loosened up and tired" advises Elbow "long enough in fact to make a bit of a voyage."
5. "In coming to new land" Elbow says "you develop a new conception of what you are writing about."

28i Use commas to prevent misreading.

In some sentences words may run together in unintended and confusing ways unless a comma separates them:

| Confusing | Soon after the business closed its doors. |
| Clear | Soon after, the business closed its doors. |

Always check whether a comma added to prevent misreading might cause some other confusion or error. In the first example below, the comma prevents *pasta* and *places* from running into each other as *pasta places*, but it separates the subject (*historian*) and the verb (*places*). The revision solves both problems.

Faulty   A historian who studied pasta, places its origin in the Middle East.

Revised   A historian who studied pasta <u>says that it originated</u> in the Middle East.

EXERCISE 11
Punctuating to prevent misreading
Insert commas in the following sentences to prevent misreading.

> *Example:*
> To Laura Ann symbolized decadence.
> To Laura, Ann symbolized decadence.

1. Though happy people still have moments of self-doubt.
2. In research subjects have reported themselves to be generally happy people.
3. Yet those who have described sufferings as well as joys.
4. Of fifty eight subjects reported bouts of serious depression.
5. For half the preceding year had included at least one personal crisis.

28j   Use commas only where required.

Commas can make sentences choppy and even confusing if they are used more often than needed. The main misuses of commas are summarized in the box on page 473.

1 ■ Delete any comma after a subject or a verb.

Commas interrupt the movement from subject to verb to object or complement, as in the following faulty examples.

no ↗
28j

---

http://www.ablongman.com/littlebrown
For added help and practice with avoiding misused commas, click on
  ➤ Punctuation and mechanics
    ➤ Exercises ➤ Exer. 7
    ➤ Web links ➤ Commas

Faulty	The returning soldiers, received a warmer welcome than they expected. [Separation of subject and verb.]
Revised	The returning soldiers received a warmer welcome than they expected.

Faulty	They had chosen, to fight for their country. [Separation of verb *chosen* and object *to fight*.]
Revised	They had chosen to fight for their country.

Exception Use commas between subject, verb, and object or complement only when other words between these elements require punctuation:

Americans, who are preoccupied with other sports, have only recently developed an interest in professional soccer. [Commas set off a nonessential clause.]

2 ■ Delete any comma that separates a pair of words, phrases, or subordinate clauses joined by a coordinating conjunction.

When linking elements with *and, or,* or another coordinating conjunction, do not use a comma unless the elements are main clauses (see p. 455):

Faulty	Banks could, and should help older people manage their money. [Compound helping verb.]
Revised	Banks could and should help older people manage their money.

Faulty	Older people need special assistance because they live on fixed incomes, and because they are not familiar with new accounts, and rates. [Compound subordinate clauses *because . . . because* and compound object of preposition *with*.]
Revised	Older people need special assistance because they live on fixed incomes and because they are not familiar with new accounts and rates.

Faulty	Banks, and community groups can assist the elderly, and eliminate the confusion they often feel. [Compound subject and compound predicate.]
Revised	Banks and community groups can assist the elderly and eliminate the confusion they often feel.

no ⌃
28j

3 ■ Delete any comma after a conjunction.

The coordinating conjunctions (*and, but,* and so on) and the subordinating conjunctions (*although, because,* and so on) are not followed by commas:

Principal misuses of the comma

- **Don't use a comma after a subject or verb:**

  Faulty   Anyone with breathing problems, should not exercise during smog alerts.

  Revised   Anyone with breathing problems should not exercise during smog alerts.

- **Don't separate a pair of words, phrases, or subordinate clauses joined by *and, or,* or *nor:***

  Faulty   Asthmatics are affected by ozone, and sulfur oxides.

  Revised   Asthmatics are affected by ozone and sulfur oxides.

- **Don't use a comma after *and, but, although, because,* or another conjunction:**

  Faulty   Smog is dangerous and, sometimes even fatal.

  Revised   Smog is dangerous and sometimes even fatal.

- **Don't set off essential elements:**

  Faulty   Even people, who are healthy, should be careful.

  Revised   Even people who are healthy should be careful.

- **Don't set off a series:**

  Faulty   Cars, factories, and even bakeries, contribute to smog.

  Revised   Cars, factories, and even bakeries contribute to smog.

- **Don't set off an indirect quotation or a single word that is an essential appositive:**

  Faulty   Experts say, that the pollutant, ozone, is especially damaging.

  Revised   Experts say that the pollutant ozone is especially damaging.

Faulty   Parents of adolescents notice increased conflict at pu-
berty, and, they complain of bickering.

Revised   Parents of adolescents notice increased conflict at pu-
berty, and they complain of bickering.

Faulty   Although, other primates leave the family at adolescence,
humans do not.

Revised   Although other primates leave the family at adolescence,
humans do not.

no ⌃
28j

4 ▪ Delete any commas that set off essential elements.

Commas do not set off an essential element, which limits the meaning of the word to which it refers (see p. 459):

Faulty	Hawthorne's work, *The Scarlet Letter,* was the first major American novel. [The title is essential to distinguish the novel from the rest of Hawthorne's work.]
Revised	Hawthorne's work *The Scarlet Letter* was the first major American novel.

Faulty	The symbols, that Hawthorne uses, have influenced other novelists. [The clause identifies which symbols have been influential.]
Revised	The symbols that Hawthorne uses have influenced other novelists.

5 ▪ Delete any comma before or after a series unless a rule requires it.

Commas separate the items *within* a series (p. 465) but do not separate the series from the rest of the sentence:

Faulty	The skills of, hunting, herding, and agriculture, sustained the Native Americans.
Revised	The skills of hunting, herding, and agriculture sustained the Native Americans.

In the following sentence the commas before and after the series are appropriate because the series is a nonessential appositive (see p. 461):

The four major television networks, ABC, CBS, Fox, and NBC, face fierce competition from the cable networks.

However, many writers prefer to use dashes rather than commas to set off series functioning as appositives (see p. 506).

6 ▪ Delete any comma setting off an indirect quotation or a single word that is an essential appositive.

Indirect quotation

Faulty	The report concluded, that dieting could be more dangerous than overeating.
Revised	The report concluded that dieting could be more dangerous than overeating.

Quoted or italicized word

A quoted or italicized word is an essential appositive when it limits the word it refers to (see p. 461). Do not use commas around an essential appositive:

Faulty	James Joyce's story, "Araby," was assigned last year. [The commas imply wrongly that Joyce wrote only one story.]
Revised	James Joyce's story "Araby" was assigned last year.

Faulty   The word, *open,* can be either a verb or an adjective.

Revised   The word *open* can be either a verb or an adjective.

The following sentence requires commas because the quoted title is a nonessential appositive:

Her only poem about death, "Mourning," was printed in *The New Yorker.*

EXERCISE 12
Revising: Needless or misused commas

Revise the following sentences to eliminate needless or misused commas. Circle the number preceding each sentence that is already punctuated correctly.

> *Example:*
>
> The portrait of the founder, that hung in the dining hall, was stolen by pranksters.
>
> The portrait of the founder that hung in the dining hall was stolen by pranksters.

1. Nearly 32 million US residents, speak a first language other than English.
2. After English the languages most commonly spoken in the United States are, Spanish, French, and German.
3. Almost 75 percent of the people, who speak foreign languages, used the words, "good" or "very good," when judging their proficiency in English.
4. Recent immigrants, especially those speaking Spanish, Chinese, and Korean, tended to judge their English more harshly.
5. The states with the highest proportion of foreign language speakers, are New Mexico, and California.

EXERCISE 13
Revising: Commas

Insert commas in the following paragraphs wherever they are needed, and eliminate any misused or needless commas.

Ellis Island New York reopened for business in 1990 but now the customers are tourists not immigrants. This spot which lies in New York Harbor was the first American soil seen, or touched by many of the nation's immigrants. Though other places also served as ports of entry for foreigners none has the symbolic power of, Ellis Island. Between its opening in 1892 and its closing in 1954, over 20 million people about two-thirds of all immigrants were detained there before taking up their new lives in the United States. Ellis Island processed over 2000 newcomers a day when immigration was at its peak between 1900 and 1920.

As the end of a long voyage and the introduction to the New World Ellis Island must have left something to be desired. The "huddled masses" as the Statue of Liberty calls them indeed were

no ⋀

28j

huddled. New arrivals were herded about kept standing in lines for hours or days yelled at and abused. Assigned numbers they submitted their bodies to the pokings and proddings of the silent nurses and doctors, who were charged with ferreting out the slightest sign of sickness, disability or insanity. That test having been passed the immigrants faced interrogation by an official through an interpreter. Those, with names deemed inconveniently long or difficult to pronounce, often found themselves permanently labeled with abbreviations, of their names, or with the names, of their hometowns. But, millions survived the examination humiliation and confusion, to take the last short boat ride to New York City. For many of them and especially for their descendants Ellis Island eventually became not a nightmare but the place where life began.

Note See page 516 for a punctuation exercise combining commas with other marks of punctuation.

CHAPTER 29

The Semicolon

The semicolon separates equal and balanced sentence elements, usually main clauses (below through p. 480), sometimes items in series (p. 482).

Note A grammar and style checker can spot a few errors in the use of semicolons. For example, a checker suggested using a semicolon after *perfect* in *The set was perfect, the director had planned every detail,* thus correcting a comma splice. But it missed the incorrect semicolon in *The set was perfect; deserted streets, dark houses, and gloomy mist* (a colon would be correct; see p. 484). Instead of relying on a checker, find semicolon errors by proofreading on your own.

29a Use a semicolon between main clauses not joined by *and, but,* or another coordinating conjunction.

Main clauses contain a subject and a predicate and do not begin with a subordinating word (see p. 258). When you join two main clauses in a sentence, you have two primary options for separating them:

- Insert a comma and a coordinating conjunction: *and, but, or, nor, for, so, yet.* (See p. 455.)

The drug does little to relieve symptoms, and it can have side effects.

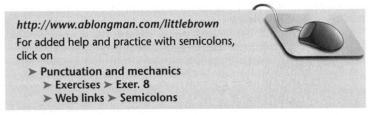

http://www.ablongman.com/littlebrown
For added help and practice with semicolons, click on
➤ **Punctuation and mechanics**
  ➤ **Exercises** ➤ **Exer. 8**
  ➤ **Web links** ➤ **Semicolons**

■ Insert a semicolon:

The side effects are not minor; some leave the patient quite ill.

Note If you do not link main clauses with a coordinating conjunction and you separate them only with a comma or with no punctuation at all, you will produce a comma splice or a fused sentence. (See Chapter 18.)

Exception Writers sometimes use a comma instead of a semicolon between very short and closely parallel main clauses:

The poor live, the rich just exist.

But a semicolon is safer, and it is always correct.

EXERCISE 1
Punctuating between main clauses
Insert semicolons to separate main clauses in the following sentences.

Example:
One man at the auction bid prudently another spent his bank account.
One man at the auction bid prudently; another spent his bank account.

1. More and more musicians are playing computerized instruments more and more listeners are worrying about the future of acoustic instruments.
2. The computer is not the first new technology in music the pipe organ and saxophone were also technological breakthroughs in their day.
3. Musicians have always experimented with new technology audiences have always resisted the experiments.
4. Most computer musicians are not merely following the latest fad they are discovering new sounds and new ways to manipulate sound.
5. Few musicians have abandoned acoustic instruments most value acoustic sounds as much as electronic sounds.

EXERCISE 2
Sentence combining: Related main clauses
Combine each set of three sentences below into one sentence containing only two main clauses, and insert a semicolon between the clauses. You will have to add, delete, change, and rearrange words. Most items have more than one possible answer.

Example:
The painter Andrew Wyeth is widely admired. He is not universally admired. Some critics view his work as sentimental.

;

29a

Distinguishing the comma, the semicolon, and the colon

The *comma* chiefly separates both equal and unequal sentence elements.

- It separates main clauses when they are linked by a coordinating conjunction (p. 455):

  An airline once tried to boost sales by advertising the tense alertness of its crews, but nervous fliers did not want to hear about pilots' sweaty palms.

- It separates subordinate information that is part of or attached to a main clause, such as an introductory element or a nonessential modifier (pp. 457, 459):

  Although the airline campaign failed, many advertising agencies, including some clever ones, copied its underlying message.

The *semicolon* chiefly separates equal and balanced sentence elements. Often the first clause creates an expectation, and the second clause fulfills the expectation.

- It separates complementary main clauses that are *not* linked by a coordinating conjunction (facing page):

  The airline campaign had highlighted only half the story; the other half was buried in the copy.

- It separates complementary main clauses that are related by a conjunctive adverb or other transitional expression (next page):

  The campaign should not have stressed the pilots' insecurity; instead, the campaign should have stressed the improved performance resulting from that insecurity.

The *colon* chiefly separates unequal sentence elements.

- It separates a main clause from a following explanation or summary, which may or may not be a main clause (pp. 503–04):

  Many successful advertising campaigns have used this message: the anxious seller is harder working and smarter than the competitor.

29a

;

The painter Andrew Wyeth is widely but not universally admired; some critics view his work as sentimental.

1. Electronic instruments are prevalent in jazz. They are also prevalent in rock music. They are less common in classical music.
2. Jazz and rock change rapidly. They nourish experimentation. They nourish improvisation.

3. Traditional classical music does not change. Its notes and in-
strumentation were established by a composer. The composer
was writing decades or centuries ago.
4. Contemporary classical music not only can draw on tradition.
It also can respond to innovations. These are innovations such
as jazz rhythms and electronic sounds.
5. Much contemporary electronic music is more than just one
type of music. It is more than just jazz, rock, or classical. It is a
fusion of all three.

29b Use a semicolon between main clauses related by *however, for example,* and so on.

Two kinds of words can relate main clauses: **conjunctive adverbs,** such as *consequently, hence, however, indeed,* and *thus* (see p.
267), and other **transitional expressions,** such as *even so, for example,* and *of course* (see pp. 86–88). When either of these connects two
main clauses, the clauses should be separated by a semicolon:

> An American immigrant, Levi Strauss, invented blue jeans in the
> 1860s; eventually, his product clothed working men throughout
> the West.

The position of the semicolon between main clauses never
changes, but the conjunctive adverb or transitional expression may
move around within a clause. The adverb or expression is usually
set off with a comma or commas (see pp. 461–62):

> Blue jeans have become fashionable all over the world; however,
> the American originators still wear more jeans than anyone else.

> Blue jeans have become fashionable all over the world; the Ameri-
> can originators, however, still wear more jeans than anyone else.

Its mobility distinguishes a conjunctive adverb or transitional expression from other connecting words, such as coordinating and
subordinating conjunctions. See page 268 on this distinction.

Note If you use a comma or no punctuation at all between
main clauses connected by a conjunctive adverb or transitional
expression, you will produce a comma splice or a fused sentence.
(See Chapter 18.)

;

29b

EXERCISE 3
**Punctuating main clauses related by conjunctive adverbs or
transitional expressions**

Insert a semicolon in each of the following sentences to separate
main clauses related by a conjunctive adverb or transitional expression. Also insert a comma or commas where needed to set off the
adverb or expression.

Example:

He knew that tickets for the concert would be scarce therefore he arrived at the box office hours before it opened.

He knew that tickets for the concert would be scarce; therefore, he arrived at the box office hours before it opened.

1. Music is a form of communication like language the basic elements however are not letters but notes.
2. Computers can process any information that can be represented numerically as a result they can process musical information.
3. A computer's ability to process music depends on what software it can run it must moreover be connected to a system that converts electrical vibration into sound.
4. Computers and their sound systems can produce many different sounds indeed the number of possible sounds is infinite.
5. The powerful music computers are very expensive therefore they are used only by professional musicians.

EXERCISE 4
Sentence combining: Main clauses related by conjunctive adverbs or transitional expressions

Combine each set of three sentences below into one sentence containing only two main clauses. Connect the clauses with the conjunctive adverb or transitional expression in parentheses, and separate them with a semicolon. (Be sure the adverbs and expressions are punctuated appropriately.) You will have to add, delete, change, and rearrange words. Each item has more than one possible answer.

Example:

The Albanians censored their news. We got little news from them. And what we got was unreliable. (*therefore*)

The Albanians censored their news; therefore, the little news we got from them was unreliable.

1. Most music computers are too expensive for the average consumer. Digital keyboard instruments can be inexpensive. They are widely available. (*however*)
2. Inside the keyboard is a small computer. The computer controls a sound synthesizer. The instrument can both process and produce music. (*consequently*)
3. The person playing the keyboard presses keys or manipulates other controls. The computer and synthesizer convert these signals. The signals are converted into vibrations and sounds. (*immediately*)
4. The inexpensive keyboards can perform only a few functions. To the novice computer musician, the range is exciting. The range includes drum rhythms and simulated instruments. (*still*)

;
29b

5. Would-be musicians can orchestrate whole songs. They start from just the melody lines. They need never again play "Chopsticks." (*thus*)

29c Use a semicolon to separate main clauses if they are complicated or contain commas, even with a coordinating conjunction.

We normally use a comma with a coordinating conjunction such as *and* or *but* between main clauses (see p. 455). But a semicolon makes a sentence easier to read when the main clauses contain commas or are grammatically complicated:

> By a conscious effort of the mind, we can stand aloof from actions and their consequences; and all things, good and bad, go by us like a torrent. —HENRY DAVID THOREAU

> I doubt if the texture of Southern life is any more grotesque than that of the rest of the nation, but it does seem evident that the Southern writer is particularly adept at recognizing the grotesque; and to recognize the grotesque, you have to have some notion of what is not grotesque and why. —FLANNERY O'CONNOR

29d Use semicolons to separate items in a series if they are long or contain commas.

We normally use commas to separate items in a series (see p. 465). But when the items are long or internally punctuated, semicolons help readers identify the items:

> The custody case involved Amy Dalton, the child; Ellen and Mark Dalton, the parents; and Ruth and Hal Blum, the grandparents.

> One may even reasonably advance the claim that the sort of communication that really counts, and is therefore embodied into permanent records, is primarily written; that "words fly away, but written messages endure," as the Latin saying put it two thousand years ago; and that there is no basic significance to at least fifty per cent of the oral interchange that goes on among all sorts of persons, high and low. —MARIO PEI

;
29d

EXERCISE 5
Punctuating long main clauses and series items
Substitute semicolons for commas in the following sentences to separate main clauses or series items that are long or contain commas.

Example:

After graduation he debated whether to settle in San Francisco, which was temperate but far from his parents, New York City, which was exciting but expensive, or Atlanta, which was close to home but already familiar.

After graduation he debated whether to settle in San Francisco, which was temperate but far from his parents; New York City, which was exciting but expensive; or Atlanta, which was close to home but already familiar.

1. The Indian subcontinent is separated from the rest of the world by clear barriers: the Bay of Bengal and the Arabian Sea to the east and west, respectively, the Indian Ocean to the south, and 1600 miles of mountain ranges to the north.
2. In the north of India are the world's highest mountains, the Himalayas, and farther south are fertile farmlands, unpopulated deserts, and rain forests.
3. India is a nation of ethnic and linguistic diversity, with numerous religions, including Hinduism, Islam, and Christianity, with distinct castes and ethnic groups, and with sixteen languages, including the official Hindi and the "associate official" English.
4. Between the seventeenth and nineteenth centuries, the British colonized most of India, taking control of government, the bureaucracy, and industry, and they assumed a social position above all Indians.
5. During British rule the Indians' own unresolved differences and their frustrations with the British erupted in violent incidents such as the Sepoy Mutiny, which began on February 26, 1857, and lasted two years, the Amritsar Massacre on April 13, 1919, and violence between Hindus and Muslims during World War II that resulted in the separation of Pakistan from India.

29e   Use the semicolon only where required.

Semicolons do not separate unequal sentence elements and should not be overused.

1 ■ Delete or replace any semicolon that separates a subordinate clause or a phrase from a main clause.

The semicolon does not separate subordinate clauses from main clauses or phrases from main clauses:

Faulty	Pygmies are in danger of extinction; because of encroaching development.
Revised	Pygmies are in danger of extinction because of encroaching development.
Faulty	According to African authorities; only about 35,000 Pygmies exist today.
Revised	According to African authorities, only about 35,000 Pygmies exist today.

;
29e

Note Many readers regard a phrase or subordinate clause set off with a semicolon as a kind of sentence fragment. (See Chapter 17.)

2 ▪ Delete or replace any semicolon that introduces a series or explanation.

Colons and dashes, not semicolons, introduce series, explanations, and so forth. (See p. 504.)

> Faulty   Teachers have heard all sorts of reasons why students do poorly; <u>psychological problems, family illness, too much work, too little time.</u>
>
> Revised   Teachers have heard all sorts of reasons why students do poorly**:** psychological problems, family illness, too much work, too little time.
>
> Revised   Teachers have heard all sorts of reasons why students do poorly—psychological problems, family illness, too much work, too little time.

3 ▪ Use the semicolon sparingly.

Use the semicolon only occasionally. Many semicolons in a passage, even when they are required by rule, often indicate repetitive sentence structure. To revise a passage with too many semicolons, you'll need to restructure your sentences, not just remove the semicolons. (See Chapter 26 for tips on varying sentences.)

> Semicolon overused
>
> The Make-a-Wish Foundation helps sick children; it grants the wishes of children who are terminally ill. The foundation learns of a child's wish; the information usually comes from parents, friends, or hospital staff; the wish may be for a special toy, perhaps, or a visit to Disneyland. The foundation grants some wishes with its own funds; for other wishes it appeals to those who have what the child desires.

> Revised
>
> The Make-a-Wish Foundation grants the wishes of children who are terminally ill. From parents, friends, or hospital staff, the foundation learns of a child's wish for a special toy, perhaps, or a visit to Disneyland. It grants some wishes with its own funds; for other wishes it appeals to those who have what the child desires.

;
29e

EXERCISE 6
Revising: Misused or overused semicolons
Revise the following sentences to eliminate misused or overused semicolons, substituting other punctuation as appropriate.

Example:

The doctor gave everyone the same advice; get exercise.
The doctor gave everyone the same advice: get exercise.

1. The main religion in India is Hinduism; a way of life as well as a theology and philosophy.
2. Unlike Christianity and Judaism; Hinduism is a polytheistic religion; with deities numbering in the hundreds.
3. Hinduism is unlike many other religions; it allows its creeds and practices to vary widely from place to place and person to person. Other religions have churches; Hinduism does not. Other religions have principal prophets and holy books; Hinduism does not. Other religions center on specially trained priests or other leaders; Hinduism promotes the individual as his or her own priest.
4. In Hindu belief there are four types of people; reflective, emotional, active, and experimental.
5. Each type of person has a different technique for realizing the true, immortal self; which has infinite existence, infinite knowledge, and infinite joy.

EXERCISE 7
Revising: Semicolons

Insert semicolons in the following paragraph wherever they are needed. Eliminate any misused or needless semicolons, substituting other punctuation as appropriate.

The set, sounds, and actors in the movie captured the essence of horror films. The set was ideal; dark, deserted streets, trees dipping their branches over the sidewalks, mist hugging the ground and creeping up to meet the trees, looming shadows of unlighted, turreted houses. The sounds, too, were appropriate, especially terrifying was the hard, hollow sound of footsteps echoing throughout the film. But the best feature of the movie was its actors; all of them tall, pale, and thin to the point of emaciation. With one exception, they were dressed uniformly in gray and had gray hair. The exception was an actress who dressed only in black; as if to set off her pale yellow, nearly white, long hair; the only color in the film. The glinting black eyes of another actor stole almost every scene, indeed, they were the source of all the film's mischief.

Note See page 516 for a punctuation exercise combining semicolons with other marks of punctuation.

;
29e

CHAPTER 30

The Apostrophe

Unlike other punctuation marks, which separate words, the apostrophe (') appears as *part* of a word to indicate possession or the omission of one or more letters.

Note Grammar and style checkers have mixed results in recognizing apostrophe errors. For instance, most flag missing apostrophes in contractions (as in *isnt*), but many cannot distinguish between *its* and *it's*, *their* and *they're*, *your* and *you're*, *whose* and *who's*. The checkers can identify some apostrophe errors in possessives but will overlook others and may flag correct plurals. Instead of relying on your checker, try using your word processor's Search or Find function to hunt for all words you have ended in *-s*. Then check them to ensure that they correctly omit or include apostrophes and that needed apostrophes are correctly positioned.

30a Use the apostrophe to indicate the possessive case for nouns and indefinite pronouns.

In English the **possessive case** shows ownership or possession of one person or thing by another. Possession may be shown with an *of* phrase (*the hair of the dog*); or it may be shown with the addition of an apostrophe and, usually, an *-s* (*the dog's hair*).

Note Apostrophes are easy to misuse. For safety's sake, check your drafts with two aims:

- Make sure that every word ending in *-s* neither omits a needed apostrophe nor adds an unneeded one.

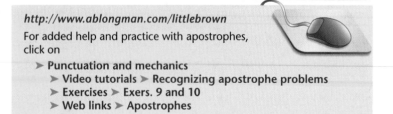

http://www.ablongman.com/littlebrown
For added help and practice with apostrophes, click on
➤ **Punctuation and mechanics**
　➤ **Video tutorials** ➤ **Recognizing apostrophe problems**
　➤ **Exercises** ➤ **Exers. 9 and 10**
　➤ **Web links** ➤ **Apostrophes**

- Remember that the apostrophe or apostrophe-plus-*s* is an *addition*. Before this addition, always spell the name of the owner or owners without dropping or adding letters: *girls* becomes *girls'*, not *girl's*.

Uses and misuses of the apostrophe

Uses of the apostrophe

- **Use an apostrophe to form the possessives of nouns and indefinite pronouns** (opposite).

Singular	Plural
Ms. Park's	the Parks'
lawyer's	lawyers'
everyone's	two weeks'

- **Use an apostrophe to form contractions** (p. 491).

it's a girl	shouldn't
you're	won't

- **The apostrophe is optional for plurals of abbreviations, dates, and words or characters named as words** (p. 492).

MAs or MA's	Cs or C's
1960s or 1960's	ifs or if's

Misuses of the apostrophe

- **Do not use an apostrophe plus -s to form the possessives of plural nouns ending in -s** (p. 488). Instead, use an apostrophe alone after the -s that forms the plural.

Not	But
the Kim's car	the Kims' car
boy's fathers	boys' fathers
babie's care	babies' care

- **Do not use an apostrophe to form plurals of nouns** (p. 489).

Not	But
book's are	books are
the Freed's	the Freeds

- **Do not use an apostrophe with verbs ending in -s** (p. 490).

Not	But
swim's	swims

- **Do not use an apostrophe to form the possessives of personal pronouns** (p. 490).

Not	But
it's toes	its toes
your's	yours

30a

1 ■ Add -'s to singular nouns and indefinite pronouns.

> Bill Boughton**'s** skillful card tricks amaze children.
> Anyone**'s** eyes would widen. [Indefinite pronoun.]
> Most tricks will pique an adult**'s** curiosity, too.

Add -'s as well to singular nouns that end in -s:

> Henry James**'s** novels reward the patient reader.
> Los Angeles**'s** weather is mostly warm.
> The business**'s** customers filed suit.

Exception We often do not pronounce the possessive -s of a few singular nouns ending in an *s* or *z* sound: names with more than one *s* sound (*Moses*), names that sound like plurals (*Rivers, Bridges*), and nouns followed by a word beginning in *s*. In these cases, many writers add only the apostrophe to show possession.

> Moses**'** mother concealed him in the bulrushes.
> Joan Rivers**'** jokes offend many people.
> For conscience**'** sake she confessed her lie.

However, usage varies widely, and the final -s is not wrong with words like these (*Moses***'s**, *Rivers***'s**, *conscience***'s**).

2 ■ Add -'s to plural nouns *not* ending in -s.

> The bill establishes children**'s** rights.
> Publicity grabbed the media**'s** attention.

3 ■ Add only an apostrophe to plural nouns ending in -s.

> Workers**'** incomes have not risen much over the past decade.
> Many students benefit from several years**'** work after high school.
> The Jameses**'** talents are extraordinary.

Note the difference in the possessives of singular and plural words ending in -s. The singular form usually takes -s: *James***'s**. The plural takes only the apostrophe: *Jameses***'**.

4 ■ Add -'s only to the last word of compound words or word groups.

> The council president**'s** address was a bore.
> The brother-in-law**'s** business failed.
> Taxes are always somebody else**'s** fault.

5 ■ With two or more words, add -'s to one or both depending on meaning.

Individual possession

> Zimbale**'s** and Mason**'s** comedy techniques are similar. [Each comedian has his own technique.]

30a

Joint possession

The child recovered despite her mother and father**'s** neglect. [The mother and father were jointly neglectful.]

EXERCISE 1
Forming possessives

Form the possessive case of each word or word group in brackets.

> *Example:*
> The [men] blood pressures were higher than the [women].
> The men**'s** blood pressures were higher than the women**'s**.

1. In the myths of the ancient Greeks, the [goddesses] roles vary widely.
2. [Demeter] responsibility is the fruitfulness of the earth.
3. [Athena] role is to guard the city of Athens.
4. [Artemis] function is to care for wild animals and small children.
5. [Athena and Artemis] father, Zeus, is the king of the gods.
6. Even a single [goddess] responsibilities are often varied.
7. Over several [centuries] time, Athena changes from a [mariner] goddess to the patron of crafts.
8. Athena is also concerned with fertility and with [children] well-being, since [Athens] strength depended on a large and healthy population.
9. Athena often changes into [birds] forms.
10. In [Homer] *Odyssey* she assumes a [sea eagle] form.
11. In ancient Athens the myths of Athena were part of [everyone] knowledge and life.
12. A cherished myth tells how Athena fights to retain possession of her [people] land when the god Poseidon wants it.
13. [Athena and Poseidon] skills are different, and each promises a special gift to the Athenians.
14. At the [contest] conclusion, Poseidon has given water and Athena has given an olive tree, for sustenance.
15. The other gods decide that the [Athenians] lives depend more on Athena than on Poseidon.

30b Delete or replace any apostrophe in a plural noun, a singular verb, or a possessive personal pronoun.

Not all words ending in -*s* take an apostrophe. Three kinds of words are especially likely to attract unneeded apostrophes.

Plural nouns

The plurals of nouns are generally formed by adding -*s* or -*es* (*boys, Smiths, families, Joneses*). Don't mistakenly add an apostrophe to form the plural:

| Faulty | The unleashed dog's began traveling in a pack. |
| Revised | The unleashed dogs began traveling in a pack. |

| Faulty | The Jones' and Bass' were feuding. |
| Revised | The Joneses and Basses were feuding. |

Singular verbs

Do not add an apostrophe to present-tense verbs used with *he, she, it,* and other third-person singular subjects. These verbs always end in *-s* but *never* with an apostrophe:

| Faulty | The subway break's down less often now. |
| Revised | The subway breaks down less often now. |

| Faulty | It run's more reliably. |
| Revised | It runs more reliably. |

Possessive personal pronouns

His, hers, its, ours, yours, theirs, and *whose* are possessive forms of the pronouns *he, she, it, we, you, they,* and *who.* They do not take apostrophes:

| Faulty | The credit is her's not their's. |
| Revised | The credit is hers, not theirs. |

The personal pronouns are often confused with contractions, such as *it's, you're,* and *who's.* See opposite.

EXERCISE 2
Distinguishing between plurals and possessives
Supply the appropriate form—possessive or plural—of each word given in brackets. Some answers require apostrophes, and some do not.

Example:
A dozen Hawaiian [shirt], each with [it] own loud design, hung in the window.
A dozen Hawaiian shirts, each with its own loud design, hung in the window.

1. Demeter may be the oldest of the Greek [god], older than Zeus.
2. Many prehistoric [culture] had earth [goddess] like Demeter.
3. In myth she is the earth mother, which means that the responsibility for the fertility of both [animal] and [plant] is [she].
4. The [goddess] festival came at harvest time, with [it] celebration of bounty.
5. The [people] [prayer] to Demeter thanked her for grain and other [gift].

30b

30c   Use an apostrophe to indicate the omission in a standard contraction.

it is, it has	it's	let us	let's
he is	he's	does not	doesn't
she is	she's	were not	weren't
they are	they're	class of 2006	class of '06
you are	you're	of the clock	o'clock
who is, who has	who's	madam	ma'am

Contractions are common in speech and in informal writing. They may also be used to relax style in more formal kinds of writing, as they are in this handbook. But be aware that many people disapprove of contractions in any kind of formal writing.

Note Contractions are easily confused with the possessive personal pronouns:

Contraction	Possessive pronoun
it's	its
they're	their
you're	your
who's	whose

Faulty   Legislators know <u>their</u> going to have to cut the budget to eliminate <u>it's</u> deficit.

Revised   Legislators know the**y're** going to have to cut the budget to eliminate <u>its</u> deficit.

If you tend to confuse these forms, search for both spellings throughout your drafts. Then test for correctness:

- Do you intend the word to contain the sentence verb *is, are,* or *has,* as in *It is a shame, It has happened, They are to blame, You are right, Who is coming? Who has responded?* Then use an apostrophe: *it's, they're, you're, who's.*
- Do you intend the word to indicate possession, as in *Its tail was wagging, Their car broke down, Your eyes are blue, Whose book is that?* Then don't use an apostrophe.

EXERCISE 3
Forming contractions

Form contractions from each set of words on the next page. Use each contraction in a complete sentence.

30c

http://www.ablongman.com/littlebrown

For added practice distinguishing between possessive pronouns and contractions, click on

➤ **Punctuation and mechanics** ➤ **Exercises** ➤ **Exer. 10**

Example:

we are: we're
We're open to ideas.

1. she would
2. could not
3. they are
4. he is
5. do not
6. she will
7. hurricane of 1962
8. is not
9. it is
10. will not

EXERCISE 4
Revising: Contractions and personal pronouns

Revise the following sentences to correct mistakes in the use of contractions and personal pronouns. Circle the number preceding any sentence that is already correct.

Example:

The agencies give they're employees their birthdays off.
The agencies give **their** employees their birthdays off.

1. In Greek myth the goddess Demeter has a special fondness for Eleusis, near Athens, and it's people.
2. She finds rest among the people and is touched by their kindness.
3. Demeter rewards the Eleusians with the secret for making they're land fruitful.
4. The Eleusians begin a cult in honor of Demeter, whose worshiped in secret ceremonies.
5. Its unknown what happened in the ceremonies, for no participant ever revealed their rituals.

30d Increasingly, the apostrophe does not mark plural abbreviations, dates, and words or characters named as words.

30d

You'll sometimes see apostrophes used to form the plurals of abbreviations (*BA's*), dates (*1900's*), and words or characters named as words (*but's*). However, most current style guides do not recommend the apostrophe in these cases.

BAs   PhDs
1990s   2000s

The sentence has too many <u>but</u>s [or *but*s].
Two <u>3</u>s [or *3*s] end the zip code.

Note Underline or italicize a word or character named as a word (see p. 527), but not the added *-s*.

EXERCISE 5
Revising: Apostrophes

In the following paragraph correct any mistakes in the use of the apostrophe or any confusion between contractions and possessive personal pronouns.

Landlocked Chad is among the worlds most troubled countries. The people's of Chad are poor: they're average per capita income equals $1000 a year. Just over 30 percent of Chads population is literate, and every five hundred people must share only two teacher's. The natural resources of the nation have never been plentiful, and now, as it's slowly being absorbed into the growing Sahara Desert, even water is scarce. Chads political conflicts go back to the nineteenth century, when the French colonized the land by brutally subduing it's people. The rule of the French—who's inept government of the colony did nothing to ease tensions among racial, tribal, and religious group's—ended with independence in 1960. But since then the Chadians experience has been one of civil war and oppression, and their also threatened with invasions from they're neighbors.

Note See page 516 for a punctuation exercise involving apostrophes along with other marks of punctuation.

30

CHAPTER 31

Quotation Marks

Quotation marks—either double (" ") or single (' ')—mainly enclose direct quotations from speech and from writing. The chart on the next two pages summarizes this use and the combination of quotation marks with commas, ellipsis marks, and other punctuation. Additional issues with quotations are discussed elsewhere in this book:

- Quoting sources versus paraphrasing or summarizing them (pp. 667–72).
- Integrating quotations into your text (pp. 674–79).
- Avoiding plagiarism when quoting (pp. 680–88).
- Formatting long prose quotations and poetry quotations in MLA style (pp. 738–39), Chicago style (pp. 821–30), and APA style (pp. 858–59).

Note Always use quotation marks in pairs, one at the beginning of a quotation and one at the end. Some grammar and style checkers will help you use quotation marks in pairs by flagging a lone mark. Most checkers can also be set to ignore other punctuation with quotations or to look for punctuation inside or outside quotation marks. If you set your checker to expect punctuation inside quotation marks, it may still fail to detect some errors. For example, a checker flagged *She said, "I must go".* (the period should fall inside the quotation mark), but it missed *Who said, "I am here?"* (the question mark should fall outside the quotation mark). Proofread carefully to catch errors in punctuating quotations that a checker cannot recognize.

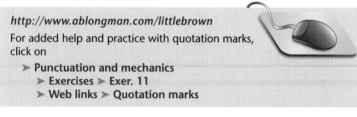

http://www.ablongman.com/littlebrown
For added help and practice with quotation marks, click on
➤ **Punctuation and mechanics**
 ➤ **Exercises** ➤ **Exer. 11**
 ➤ **Web links** ➤ **Quotation marks**

Handling quotations from speech or writing

(For explanations, consult the pages in parentheses.)

Direct and indirect quotation

Direct quotation (p. 496)

According to Lewis Thomas, "We are, perhaps uniquely among the earth's creatures, the worrying animal. We worry away our lives."

Quotation within quotation (p. 497)

Quoting a phrase by Lewis Thomas, the author adds, "We are 'the worrying animal.'"

Indirect quotation (p. 497)

Lewis Thomas says that human beings are unique among animals in their worrying.

Quotation marks with other punctuation marks

Commas and periods (p. 500)

Human beings are the "worrying animal," says Thomas.
Thomas calls human beings "the worrying animal."

Semicolons and colons (p. 501)

Machiavelli says that "the majority of men live content"; in contrast, Thomas calls us "the worrying animal."
Thomas believes that we are "the worrying animal": we spend our lives afraid and restless.

Question marks, exclamation points, dashes (p. 501)

When part of your own sentence:

Who said that human beings are "the worrying animal"?
Imagine saying that we human beings "worry away our lives"!
Thomas's phrase—"the worrying animal"—seems too narrow.

When part of the original quotation:

"Will you discuss this with me?" she asked.
"I demand that you discuss this with me!" she yelled.
"Please, won't you—" She paused.

Altering quotations

Brackets for additions (p. 510)

"We [human beings] worry away our lives," says Thomas.

Brackets for altered capitalization (p. 519)

"[T]he worrying animal" is what Thomas calls us. He says that "[w]e worry away our lives."

(continued)

" "

31

Handling quotations from speech or writing
(continued)

Ellipsis marks for omissions (p. 511)
"We are ... the worrying animal," says Thomas.
Worrying places us "uniquely among the earth's creatures. ... We worry away our lives."

Punctuating signal phrases with quotations
Introductory signal phrase (p. 468)
He says, "We worry away our lives."
An answer is in these words by Lewis Thomas: "We are, perhaps uniquely among the earth's creatures, the worrying animal."
Thomas says that "the worrying animal" is afraid and restless.

Concluding signal phrase (p. 468)
We are "the worrying animal," says Thomas.
"Who says?" she demanded.
"I do!" he shouted.

Interrupting signal phrase (p. 469)
"We are," says Thomas, "perhaps uniquely among the earth's creatures, the worrying animal."
"I do not like the idea," she said; "however, I agree with it."
Human beings are "the worrying animal," says Thomas. "We worry away our lives."

See also:
Special kinds of quoted material
Dialog (p. 498)
Poetry (p. 739)
Long prose passages (MLA style, p. 738; Chicago style, p. 829; APA style, p. 858)

Using quotations in your own text
Quotations versus paraphrases and summaries (p. 667)
Introducing quotations in your text (p. 674)
Avoiding plagiarism when quoting (p. 680)
Citing sources for quotations (p. 688)

" "

31a

31a Use double quotation marks to enclose direct quotations.

Direct quotations report what someone has said or written in the exact words of the original. Always enclose direct quotations in quotation marks:

"Fortunately," said the psychoanalyst Karen Horney, "analysis is not the only way to resolve inner conflicts. Life itself still remains a very effective therapist."

Indirect quotations report what has been said or written, but not in the exact words of the person being quoted. Indirect quotations are *not* enclosed in quotation marks:

The psychoanalyst Karen Horney remarked that analysis was not the only solution to inner conflicts, for life was a good therapist.

Indirect quotation often involves a change in the tense of verbs, as in the example here. See pages 309–10.

31b Use single quotation marks to enclose a quotation within a quotation.

When you quote a writer or speaker, use double quotation marks. When the material you quote contains yet another quotation, distinguish the two by enclosing the second one in single quotation marks:

"In formulating any philosophy," Woody Allen writes, "the first consideration must always be: What can we know? Descartes hinted at the problem when he wrote, 'My mind can never know my body, although it has become quite friendly with my leg.'"

Notice that two different quotation marks appear at the end of the sentence—one single (to finish the interior quotation) and one double (to finish the main quotation).

EXERCISE 1
Using double and single quotation marks
Insert double and single quotation marks as needed in the following sentences. Circle the number preceding any sentence that is already correct.

Example:
The purpose of this book, explains the preface, is to examine the meaning of the expression Dance is poetry.
"The purpose of this book," explains the preface, "is to examine the meaning of the expression 'Dance is poetry.'"

1. Why, the lecturer asked, do we say Bless you! or something else when people sneeze but not acknowledge coughs, hiccups, and other eruptions?
2. She said that sneezes have always been regarded differently.
3. Sneezes feel more uncontrollable than some other eruptions, she said.
4. Unlike coughs and hiccups, she explained, sneezes feel as if they come from inside the head.

" "

31b

5. She concluded, People thus wish to recognize a sneeze, if only with a Gosh.

31c   Set off quotations of dialog according to standard practice.

When quoting conversations, begin a new paragraph for each speaker:

> "What shall I call you? Your name?" Andrews whispered rapidly, as with a high squeak the latch of the door rose.
> "Elizabeth," she said. "Elizabeth."
> —GRAHAM GREENE, *The Man Within*

Note When you quote a single speaker for more than one paragraph, put quotation marks at the beginning of each paragraph but at the end of only the last paragraph. The absence of quotation marks at the end of each paragraph but the last tells readers that the speech is continuing.

31d   Put quotation marks around the titles of works that are parts of other works.

Use quotation marks to enclose the titles of works that are published or released within larger works: see the box opposite. As in the second article title in the box, use single quotation marks for a quotation within a quoted title, and enclose all punctuation in the title within the quotation marks.

Use underlining or italics for all other titles, such as books, plays, periodicals, and movies. (See p. 526.)

Note Some academic disciplines do not require quotation marks for titles within source citations. See pages 842–56 (APA style) and 871–78 (CSE style).

EXERCISE 2
Quoting titles

Insert quotation marks as needed for titles and words in the following sentences. If quotation marks should be used instead of underlining, insert them.

> *Example:*
> She published an article titled Marriage in Grace Paley's An Interest in Life.
> She published an article titled "Marriage in Grace Paley's 'An Interest in Life.'"

1. In Chapter 8, titled How to Be Interesting, the author explains the art of conversation.
2. The Beatles' song Let It Be reminds Martin of his uncle.

Titles to be enclosed in quotation marks

Other titles should be underlined or italicized. (See p. 526.)

Songs

"Lucy in the Sky with
  Diamonds"
"America the Beautiful"

Short poems

"Stopping by Woods on a
  Snowy Evening"
"Sunday Morning"

Articles in periodicals

"Comedy and Tragedy Trans-
  posed"
"Does 'Scaring' Work?"

Essays

"Politics and the English Language"
"Joey: A 'Mechanical Boy'"

Short stories

"The Battler"
"The Gift of the Magi"

**Page or document on a
Web site**

"Readers' Page" (on site
  Friends of Prufrock)

**Episodes of television and
radio programs**

"The Mexican Connection" (on
  60 Minutes)
"Cooking with Clams" (on Eating
  In)

Subdivisions of books

"Voyage to the Houyhnhnms"
  (Part IV of Gulliver's Travels)
"The Mast Head" (Chapter 35 of
  Moby-Dick)

---

3. The article that appeared in <u>Mental Health</u> was titled <u>Children of Divorce Ask, "Why?"</u>
4. In the encyclopedia the discussion under Modern Art fills less than a column.
5. One prizewinning essay, <u>Cowgirls on Wall Street</u>, first appeared in <u>Entrepreneur</u> magazine.

31e Quotation marks may be used to enclose words used in a special sense.

On movie sets movable "wild walls" make a one-walled room seem four-walled on film.

Writers often put quotation marks around a word they are using with irony—that is, with a different or even opposite meaning than usual:

> With all the "compassion" it could muster, the agency turned away two-thirds of those seeking help.   —JOAN SIMONSON

Readers quickly tire of such irony, though, so use it sparingly. Prefer language that expresses your meaning exactly. (See Chapter 39.)

Note For words you are defining, use underlining or italics. (See p. 527.)

" "

31e

31f Use quotation marks only where they are required.

Don't use quotation marks in the titles of your papers unless they contain or are themselves direct quotations:

Not	"The Death Wish in One Poem by Robert Frost"
But	The Death Wish in One Poem by Robert Frost
Or	The Death Wish in "Stopping by Woods on a Snowy Evening"

Don't use quotation marks to enclose common nicknames or technical terms that are not being defined:

Not	As President, "Jimmy" Carter preferred to use his nickname.
But	As President, Jimmy Carter preferred to use his nickname.

Not	"Mitosis" in a cell is fascinating to watch.
But	Mitosis in a cell is fascinating to watch.

Don't use quotation marks in an attempt to justify or apologize for slang and trite expressions that are inappropriate to your writing. If slang is appropriate, use it without quotation marks.

Not	We should support the President in his "hour of need" rather than "wimp out" on him.
But	We should give the President the support he needs rather than turn away like cowards.

(See pp. 544 and 562 for more on slang and trite expressions.)

31g Place other marks of punctuation inside or outside quotation marks according to standard practice.

The position of another punctuation mark inside or outside a closing quotation mark depends on what the other mark is and whether it appears in the quotation.

" "

31g

1 ■ Place commas and periods inside quotation marks.

Commas or periods fall *inside* closing quotation marks, even when (as in the third example) single and double quotation marks are combined:

Swift uses irony in his essay "A Modest Proposal."

Many first-time readers are shocked to see infants described as "delicious."

"'A Modest Proposal,'" writes one critic, "is so outrageous that it cannot be believed."

(See pp. 468–70 for the use of commas, as in the preceding example, to separate a quotation from a signal phrase such as *writes one critic.*)

Exception When a parenthetical source citation immediately follows a quotation, place any period or comma *after* the citation:

> One critic calls the essay "outrageous" (Olms 26).
>
> Partly because of "the cool calculation of its delivery" (Olms 27), Swift's satire still chills a modern reader.

See page 706 for more on placing parenthetical citations.

2 ■ Place colons and semicolons outside quotation marks.

> Some years ago the slogan in elementary education was "learning by playing"; now educators are concerned with basic skills.
>
> We all know what is meant by "inflation": more money buys less.

3 ■ Place dashes, question marks, and exclamation points inside quotation marks only if they belong to the quotation.

When a dash, question mark, or exclamation point is part of the quotation, put it *inside* quotation marks. Don't use any other punctuation such as a period or comma:

> "But must you—" Marcia hesitated, afraid of the answer.
>
> "Go away!" I yelled.
>
> Did you say, "Who is she?" [When both your sentence and the quotation would end in a question mark or exclamation point, use only the mark in the quotation.]

When a dash, question mark, or exclamation point applies only to the larger sentence, not to the quotation, place it *outside* quotation marks—again, with no other punctuation:

> One evocative line in English poetry—"After many a summer dies the swan"—comes from Alfred, Lord Tennyson.
>
> Who said, "Now cracks a noble heart"?
>
> The woman called me "stupid"!

" "

31g

EXERCISE 3
Revising: Quotation marks
The underlined words in the following sentences are titles or direct quotations. Remove underlining where appropriate, and insert quotation marks. Be sure that other marks of punctuation are correctly placed inside or outside the quotation marks.

> *Example:*
> The award-winning essay is <u>Science and Values</u>.
> The award-winning essay is "Science and Values."

1. In the title essay of her book <u>The Death of the Moth and Other Essays</u>, Virginia Woolf describes the last moments of a <u>frail and diminutive body</u>.
2. An insect's death may seem insignificant, but the moth is, in Woolf's words, <u>life, a pure bead</u>.
3. The moth's struggle against death, <u>indifferent, impersonal</u>, is heroic.
4. Where else but in such a bit of life could one see a protest so <u>superb</u>?
5. At the end Woolf sees the moth lying <u>most decently and uncomplainingly composed</u>; in death it finds dignity.

EXERCISE 4
Revising: Quotation marks

Insert quotation marks as needed in the following paragraph.

In one class we talked about a passage from I Have a Dream, the speech delivered by Martin Luther King, Jr., on the steps of the Lincoln Memorial on August 28, 1963:

> When the architects of our republic wrote the magnificent words of the Constitution and the Declaration of Independence, they were signing a promissory note to which every American was to fall heir. This note was a promise that all men would be guaranteed the unalienable rights of life, liberty, and the pursuit of happiness.

What did Dr. King mean by this statement? the teacher asked. Perhaps we should define promissory note first. Then she explained that a person who signs such a note agrees to pay a specific sum of money on a particular date or on demand by the holder of the note. One student suggested, Maybe Dr. King meant that the writers of the Constitution and Declaration promised that all people in America should be equal. He and over 200,000 people had gathered in Washington, DC, added another student. Maybe their purpose was to demand payment, to demand those rights for African Americans. The whole discussion was an eye opener for those of us (including me) who had never considered that those documents make promises that we should expect our country to fulfill.

Note See page 516 for a punctuation exercise involving quotation marks along with other marks of punctuation.

" "

31

CHAPTER 32

Other Punctuation Marks

This chapter covers the colon (below), the dash (p. 506), parentheses (p. 508), brackets (p. 510), the ellipsis mark (p. 511), and the slash (p. 514).

Note Many grammar and style checkers will flag a lone parenthesis or bracket so that you can match it with another parenthesis or bracket. But most checkers cannot recognize other misuses of the marks covered here and instead simply ignore the marks. You'll need to proofread your work carefully for errors.

THE COLON

32a Use the colon to introduce and to separate.

The colon is mainly a mark of introduction: it signals that the words following will explain or amplify. The colon also has several conventional uses, such as in expressions of time.

In its main use as an introducer, a colon is *always* preceded by a complete **main clause**—one containing a subject and a predicate and not starting with a subordinating word (see p. 258 for more on main clauses). A colon may or may not be followed by a main clause. This is one way the colon differs from the semicolon (see the box on the next page). The colon is interchangeable with the dash, though the dash is more informal and more abrupt (see p. 507).

Note Don't use a colon more than once in a sentence. The sentence should end with the element introduced by the colon.

---

http://www.ablongman.com/littlebrown
For added help and practice with the colon, the dash, parentheses, brackets, the ellipsis mark, and the slash, click on
  ➤ Punctuation and mechanics
    ➤ Exercises ➤ Exers. 12 and 13
    ➤ Web links ➤ Other punctuation marks

Distinguishing the colon and the semicolon

- **The *colon* is a mark of introduction that separates elements of *unequal* importance,** such as statements and explanations or introductions and quotations. The first element must be a complete main clause; the second element need not be. (See p. 503.)

  The business school caters to working students: it offers special evening courses in business writing, finance, and management.

  The school has one goal: to train students to be responsible, competent businesspeople.

- **The *semicolon* separates elements of *equal* importance,** almost always complete main clauses. (See p. 477.)

  Few enrolling students know exactly what they want from the school; most hope generally for a managerial career.

1 ■ **Use a colon to introduce a concluding explanation, series, appositive, or long or formal quotation.**

Depending on your preference, a complete sentence *after* the colon may begin with a capital letter or a small letter. Just be consistent throughout an essay.

Explanation
Soul food is a varied cuisine: it includes spicy gumbos, black-eyed peas, and collard greens.
Soul food has a deceptively simple definition: African American ethnic cooking.

Sometimes a concluding explanation is preceded by *the following* or *as follows* and a colon:

A more precise definition might be the following: ingredients, cooking methods, and dishes originating in Africa, brought to the New World by black slaves, and modified or supplemented in the Caribbean and the American South.

Series (p. 465)
At least three soul food dishes are familiar to most Americans: fried chicken, barbecued spareribs, and sweet potato pie.

Appositive (p. 263)
Soul food has one disadvantage: fat.

Certain expressions commonly introduce appositives, such as *namely* and *that is.* These expressions should *follow* the colon: *Soul food has one disadvantage: namely, fat.*

32a

Long or formal quotation

The comma generally separates a signal phrase from a quotation (see p. 468). But when you introduce a long or formal quotation with a complete sentence, use a colon instead:

> One soul food chef has a solution: "Soul food doesn't have to be greasy to taste good. Instead of using ham hocks to flavor beans, I use smoked turkey wings. The soulful, smoky taste remains, but without all the fat of pork."

2 ▪ Use a colon to separate titles and subtitles and the subdivisions of time.

Titles and subtitles	Time
Charles Dickens: An Introduction to His Novels	1:30 AM
Eros and Civilization: An Inquiry into Freud	12:26 PM

3 ▪ Use the colon only where required.

Use the colon only at the *end* of a main clause. Do not use it directly after a verb or preposition.

Not   Two critically acclaimed movies directed by Steven Spielberg are: *Schindler's List* and *Saving Private Ryan*.

But   Two critically acclaimed movies directed by Steven Spielberg are *Schindler's List* and *Saving Private Ryan*.

Not   Shakespeare possessed the qualities of a Renaissance thinker, such as: humanism and a deep interest in classical Greek and Roman literature.

But   Shakespeare possessed the qualities of a Renaissance thinker, such as humanism and a deep interest in classical Greek and Roman literature.

EXERCISE 1
Revising: Colons

Insert colons as needed in the following sentences, or delete colons that are misused.

> *Example:*
> Mix the ingredients as follows sift the flour and salt together, add the milk, and slowly beat in the egg yolk.
> Mix the ingredients as follows: sift the flour and salt together, add the milk, and slowly beat in the egg yolk.

1. In remote areas of many developing countries, simple signs mark human habitation a dirt path, a few huts, smoke from a campfire.
2. In the built-up sections of industrialized countries, nature is all but obliterated by signs of human life, such as: houses, factories, skyscrapers, and highways.

:
32a

3. The spectacle makes many question the words of Ecclesiastes 1.4 "One generation passeth away, and another cometh; but the earth abideth forever."
4. Yet many scientists see the future differently they hold that human beings have all the technology necessary to clean up the earth and restore the cycles of nature.
5. All that is needed is: a change in the attitudes of those who use technology.

THE DASH

32b Use a dash or dashes to indicate sudden changes in tone or thought and to set off some sentence elements.

The dash is mainly a mark of interruption: it signals an insertion or break.

Note In your papers, form a dash with two hyphens (--), or use the character called an em dash on your word processor. Do not add extra space around or between the hyphens or around the em dash.

1 ■ **Use a dash or dashes to indicate shifts and hesitations.**

Shift in tone

The novel—if one can call it that—appeared in 1994.

Unfinished thought

If the book had a plot—but a plot would be conventional.

Hesitation in dialog

"I was worried you might think I had stayed away because I was influenced by—" He stopped and lowered his eyes.

Astonished, Howe said, "Influenced by what?"

"Well, by—" Blackburn hesitated and for an answer pointed to the table. —LIONEL TRILLING

32b

2 ■ **Use a dash or dashes to emphasize nonessential elements.**

Dashes may be used in place of commas or parentheses to set off and emphasize nonessential elements. (See the box on the facing page.) Dashes are especially useful when these elements are internally punctuated. Be sure to use a pair of dashes when the element interrupts a main clause.

Appositive (p. 263)

The qualities Monet painted—bright sunlight, rich shadows, deep colors—abounded near the rivers and gardens he used as subjects.

Distinguishing dashes, commas, and parentheses

Dashes, commas, and parentheses may all set off nonessential elements.

- *Dashes* **give the information the greatest emphasis** (facing page):

  Many students—including some employed by the college—disapprove of the new work rules.

- *Commas* **are less emphatic** (p. 459):

  Many students, including some employed by the college, disapprove of the new work rules.

- *Parentheses* **are the least emphatic,** signaling that the information is just worth a mention (next page):

  Many students (including some employed by the college) disapprove of the new work rules.

Modifier

Though they are close together—separated by only a few blocks—the two neighborhoods could be in different countries.

Parenthetical expression (next page)

At any given time there exists an inventory of undiscovered embezzlement in—or more precisely not in—the country's businesses and banks. —JOHN KENNETH GALBRAITH

3 ■ Use a dash to set off introductory series and concluding series and explanations.

Introductory series

Shortness of breath, skin discoloration or the sudden appearance of moles, persistent indigestion, the presence of small lumps—all these may signify cancer.

A dash sets off concluding series and explanations more informally and more abruptly than a colon does (see p. 504):

Concluding series

The patient undergoes a battery of tests—CAT scan, bronchoscopy, perhaps even biopsy.

32b

Concluding explanation

Many patients are disturbed by the CAT scan—by the need to keep still for long periods in an exceedingly small space.

4 ■ Use the dash only where needed.

Don't use the dash when commas, semicolons, and periods are more appropriate. And don't use too many dashes. They can create a jumpy or breathy quality in writing.

Not   In all his life—eighty-seven years—my great-grandfather
       never allowed his picture to be taken—not even once. He
       claimed the "black box"—the camera—would steal his soul.

But   In all his eighty-seven years my great-grandfather did not
       allow his picture to be taken even once. He claimed the
       "black box"—the camera—would steal his soul.

EXERCISE 2
Revising: Dashes
Insert dashes as needed in the following sentences.

Example:
What would we do if someone like Adolf Hitler that monster
appeared among us?

What would we do if someone like Adolf Hitler—that monster—appeared among us?

1. The movie-theater business is undergoing dramatic changes
   changes that may affect what movies are made and shown.
2. The closing of independent theaters, the control of theaters by
   fewer and fewer owners, and the increasing ownership of theaters by movie studios and distributors these changes may reduce the availability of noncommercial films.
3. Yet at the same time the number of movie screens is increasing
   primarily in multiscreen complexes so that smaller films may
   find more outlets.
4. The number of active movie screens that is, screens showing
   films or booked to do so is higher now than at any time since
   World War II.
5. The biggest theater complexes seem to be something else as
   well art galleries, amusement arcades, restaurants, spectacles.

PARENTHESES

( )
32c

32c   Use parentheses to enclose parenthetical expressions and labels for lists within sentences.

Parentheses *always* come in pairs: one before and one after the
punctuated material.

1 ▪ Use parentheses to enclose parenthetical expressions.

Parenthetical expressions include explanations, digressions, and
examples that may be helpful or interesting but are not essential to
meaning. They are emphasized least when set off with a pair of
parentheses instead of commas or dashes. (See the box on p. 507.)

The population of Philadelphia (now about 1.5 million) has declined since 1950.

Ariel (published in 1965) contains Sylvia Plath's last poems.

Note Don't put a comma before a parenthetical expression enclosed in parentheses:

> **Not** Philadelphia's population compares with Houston's, (just over 1.6 million).
>
> **But** Philadelphia's population compares with Houston's (just over 1.6 million).

A comma, semicolon, or period falling after a parenthetical expression should be placed *outside* the closing parenthesis:

> Philadelphia has a larger African American population (nearly 40 percent), while Houston has a larger Latino population (nearly 28 percent).

When it falls between other complete sentences, a complete sentence enclosed in parentheses has a capital letter and end punctuation:

> In general, coaches will tell you that scouts are just guys who can't coach. (But then, so are brain surgeons.)   —ROY BLOUNT

2 ▪ Use parentheses to enclose labels for lists within sentences.

> Outside the Middle East, the countries with the largest oil reserves are (1) Venezuela (63 billion barrels), (2) Russia (57 billion barrels), and (3) Mexico (51 billion barrels).

When you set a list off from your text, do not enclose such labels in parentheses.

EXERCISE 3
Revising: Parentheses
Insert parentheses as needed in the following sentences.

> *Example:*
> Students can find good-quality, inexpensive furniture for example, desks, tables, chairs, sofas, even beds in junk stores.
> Students can find good-quality, inexpensive furniture (for example, desks, tables, chairs, sofas, even beds) in junk stores.

1. Many of those involved in the movie business agree that multi-screen complexes are good for two reasons: 1 they cut the costs of exhibitors, and 2 they offer more choices to audiences.
2. Those who produce and distribute films and not just the big studios argue that the multiscreen theaters give exhibitors too much power.

( )
32c

3. The major studios are buying movie theaters to gain control over important parts of the distribution process what gets shown and for how much money.
4. For twelve years 1938–50 the federal government forced the studios to sell all their movie theaters.
5. But because they now have more competition television and videocassette recorders, the studios are permitted to own theaters.

BRACKETS

32d Use brackets within quotations to indicate your own comments or changes.

Brackets have specialized uses in mathematical equations, but their main use for all kinds of writing is to indicate that you have altered a quotation. If you need to explain, clarify, or correct the words of the writer you quote, place your additions in a pair of brackets:

> "That Texaco station [just outside Chicago] is one of the busiest in the nation," said a company spokesperson.

Use brackets if you need to alter the capitalization of a quotation so that it will fit into your sentence. (See also p. 519.)

> "[O]ne of the busiest in the nation" is how a company spokesperson described the station.

You may also use a bracketed word or words to substitute for parts of a quotation that would otherwise be unclear. In the sentence below, the bracketed word substitutes for *they* in the original:

> "Despite considerable achievements in other areas, [humans] still cannot control the weather and probably will never be able to do so."

Some instructors prefer the use of brackets around ellipsis marks that indicate omissions from quotations. See opposite.

The word *sic* (Latin for "in this manner") in brackets indicates that an error in the quotation appeared in the original and was not made by you. When following MLA style, do not underline or italicize *sic* in brackets. Most other styles—including Chicago, APA, and CSE—do italicize *sic*.

> According to the newspaper report, "The car slammed thru [sic] the railing and into oncoming traffic."

Don't use *sic* to make fun of a writer or to note errors in a passage that is clearly nonstandard or illiterate.

[ ]
32d

THE ELLIPSIS MARK

32e Use the ellipsis mark to indicate omissions from quotations and pauses in speech.

The **ellipsis mark** consists of three spaced periods (. . .). It usually indicates an omission from a quotation, although it may also show an interruption in dialog.

Note Some instructors prefer that brackets surround any ellipsis mark that is added to a quotation:

"Natural ecosystems [. . .] maintain the world [. . .]."

Ask your instructor for his or her preference.

1 ▪ The ellipsis mark substitutes for omissions from quotations.

When you omit a part of a quotation, show the omission with an ellipsis mark. All the following examples quote from the passage below about environmentalism.

Original quotation

"At the heart of the environmentalist world view is the conviction that human physical and spiritual health depends on sustaining the planet in a relatively unaltered state. Earth is our home in the full, genetic sense, where humanity and its ancestors existed for all the millions of years of their evolution. Natural ecosystems—forests, coral reefs, marine blue waters—maintain the world exactly as we would wish it to be maintained. When we debase the global environment and extinguish the variety of life, we are dismantling a support system that is too complex to understand, let alone replace, in the foreseeable future."

—Edward O. Wilson, "Is Humanity Suicidal?"

1. Omission of the middle of a sentence

"Natural ecosystems . . . maintain the world exactly as we would wish it to be maintained."

2. Omission of the end of a sentence, without source citation

"Earth is our home. . . ." [The sentence period, closed up to the last word, precedes the ellipsis mark.]

. . .

32e

http://www.ablongman.com/littlebrown
For added help and practice with the ellipsis mark, click on
➤ **Punctuation and mechanics**
  ➤ **Exercises** ➤ **Exer. 13**
  ➤ **Web links** ➤ **Other punctuation marks**

3. Omission of the end of a sentence, with source citation

"Earth is our home . . ." (Wilson 27). [The sentence period follows the source citation.]

4. Omission of parts of two or more sentences

Wilson writes, "At the heart of the environmentalist world view is the conviction that human physical and spiritual health depends on sustaining the planet . . . where humanity and its ancestors existed for all the millions of years of their evolution."

5. Omission of one or more sentences

As Wilson puts it, "At the heart of the environmentalist world view is the conviction that human physical and spiritual health depends on sustaining the planet in a relatively unaltered state. . . . When we debase the global environment and extinguish the variety of life, we are dismantling a support system that is too complex to understand, let alone replace, in the foreseeable future."

6. Omission from the middle of a sentence through the end of another sentence

"Earth is our home. . . . When we debase the global environment and extinguish the variety of life, we are dismantling a support system that is too complex to understand, let alone replace, in the foreseeable future."

7. Omission of the beginning of a sentence, leaving a complete sentence

a. Bracketed capital letter

"[H]uman physical and spiritual health," Wilson writes, "depends on sustaining the planet in a relatively unaltered state." [No ellipsis mark is needed because the brackets around the *H* indicate that the letter was not capitalized originally and thus that the beginning of the sentence has been omitted.]

b. Small letter

According to Wilson, "human physical and spiritual health depends on sustaining the planet in a relatively unaltered state." [No ellipsis mark is needed because the small *h* indicates that the beginning of the sentence has been omitted.]

c. Capital letter from the original

Hami comments, ". . . Wilson argues eloquently for the environmentalist world view." [An ellipsis mark is needed because the quoted part of the sentence begins with a capital letter and it is not clear that the beginning of the original sentence has been omitted.]

8. Use of a word or phrase

Wilson describes the earth as "our home." [No ellipsis mark needed.]

Note the following features of the examples:

· · ·
32e

- Use an ellipsis mark when it is not otherwise clear that you have left out material from the source, as when you omit one or more sentences (examples 5 and 6) or when the words you quote form a complete sentence that is different in the original (examples 1–4 and 7c).
- You don't need an ellipsis mark when it is obvious that you have omitted something, such as when capitalization indicates omission (examples 7a and 7b) or when a phrase clearly comes from a larger sentence (example 8).
- After a grammatically complete sentence, an ellipsis mark follows the sentence period (examples 2, 5, and 6) *except* when a parenthetical source citation follows the quotation (example 3). Then the sentence period falls after the citation.

If you omit one or more lines of poetry or paragraphs of prose from a quotation, use a separate line of ellipsis marks across the full width of the quotation to show the omission:

> In "Song: Love Armed" from 1676, Aphra Behn contrasts two
>
> lovers' experiences of a romance:
>
> > Love in fantastic triumph sate,
> >
> > Whilst bleeding hearts around him flowed,
> >
> > . . . .
> >
> > But my poor heart alone is harmed,
> >
> > Whilst thine the victor is, and free. (lines 1-2, 15-16)

(See p. 738 for the format of displayed quotations like this one. And see p. 705 on the source-citation form illustrated here.)

2 ▪ The ellipsis mark indicates pauses or unfinished statements.

When writing dialog or when writing informally (not in academic writing), you can show hesitation or interruption with an ellipsis mark instead of a dash (p. 506).

"I wish ..." His voice trailed off.

32e

EXERCISE 4
Using ellipsis marks
Use ellipsis marks and any other needed punctuation to follow the numbered instructions for quoting from the following paragraph.

Women in the sixteenth and seventeenth centuries were educated in the home and, in some cases, in boarding schools. Men were educated at home, in grammar schools, and at the universities. The universities were closed to female students. For women, "learning the Bible," as Elizabeth Joceline puts it, was an impetus to learning to read. To be able to read the Bible in the vernacular was a liberating experience that freed the reader from hearing only the set passages read in the church and interpreted by the church. A Protestant woman was expected to read the scriptures daily, to meditate on them, and to memorize portions of them. In addition, a woman was expected to instruct her entire household in "learning the Bible" by holding instructional and devotional times each day for all household members, including the servants.

—CHARLOTTE F. OTTEN, *English Women's Voices, 1540–1700*

1. Quote the fifth sentence, but omit everything from *that freed the reader* to the end.
2. Quote the fifth sentence, but omit the words *was a liberating experience that.*
3. Quote the first and sixth sentences.

THE SLASH

32f Use the slash between options, between lines of poetry that are run in to the text, and in electronic addresses.

Option

I don't know why some teachers oppose pass/fail courses.

When used between options, the slash is not surrounded by extra space.

Note The options *and/or* and *he/she* should be avoided. (See the Glossary of Usage, pp. 916 and 922.)

Poetry

Many readers have sensed a reluctant turn away from death in Frost's lines "The woods are lovely, dark and deep, / But I have promises to keep" (13–14).

When separating lines of poetry in this way, leave a space before and after the slash. (See p. 738 for more on quoting poetry.)

/
32f

Electronic addresses

http://www.stanford.edu/depts/spc/spc.html

See pages 653–54 for more on electronic addresses.

EXERCISE 5
Revising: Colons, dashes, parentheses, brackets, ellipsis marks, slashes

Insert colons, dashes, parentheses, brackets, ellipsis marks, or slashes as needed in the following paragraph. When different marks would be appropriate in the same place, be able to defend the choice you make.

"Let all the learned say what they can, 'Tis ready money makes the man." These two lines of poetry by the Englishman William Somerville 1645–1742 may apply to a current American economic problem. Non-American investors with "ready money" pour some of it as much as $1.3 trillion in recent years into the United States. The investments of foreigners are varied stocks and bonds, savings deposits, service companies, factories, art works, even the campaigns of political candidates. Proponents of foreign investment argue that it revives industry, strengthens the economy, creates jobs more than 3 million, they say, and encourages free trade among nations. Opponents discuss the risks of heavy foreign investment it makes the American economy vulnerable to outsiders, sucks profits from the country, and gives foreigners an influence in governmental decision making. On both sides, it seems, "the learned say 'Tis ready money makes the man or country." The question is, whose money?

Note See the next page for a punctuation exercise combining colons, dashes, and parentheses with other marks of punctuation, such as commas and semicolons.

32

EXERCISE ON CHAPTERS 27–32
Revising: Punctuation

The following paragraphs are unpunctuated except for end-of-sentence periods. Insert periods, commas, semicolons, apostrophes, quotation marks, colons, dashes, or parentheses where they are required. When different marks would be appropriate in the same place, be able to defend the choice you make. (To download a double-spaced, editable version of this exercise, go to *http://www.ablongman.com/littlebrown* and click on Punctuation and mechanics > Downloads > Revising: Punctuation.)

Brewed coffee is the most widely consumed beverage in the world. The trade in coffee beans alone amounts to well over $6000000000 a year and the total volume of beans traded exceeds 4250000 tons a year. Its believed that the beverage was introduced into Arabia in the fifteenth century AD probably by Ethiopians. By the middle or late sixteenth century the Arabs had introduced the beverage to the Europeans who at first resisted it because of its strong flavor and effect as a mild stimulant. The French Italians and other Europeans incorporated coffee into their diets by the seventeenth century the English however preferred tea which they were then importing from India. Since America was colonized primarily by the English Americans also preferred tea. Only after the Boston Tea Party 1773 did Americans begin drinking coffee in large quantities. Now though the US is one of the top coffee-consuming countries consumption having been spurred on by familiar advertising claims Good till the last drop Rich hearty aroma Always rich never bitter.

Produced from the fruit of an evergreen tree coffee is grown primarily in Latin America southern Asia and Africa. Coffee trees require a hot climate high humidity rich soil with good drainage and partial shade consequently they thrive on the east or west slopes of tropical volcanic mountains where the soil is laced with potash and drains easily. The coffee beans actually seeds grow inside bright red berries. The berries are picked by hand and the beans are extracted by machine leaving a pulpy fruit residue that can be used for fertilizer. The beans are usually roasted in ovens a chemical process that releases the beans essential oil caffeol which gives coffee its distinctive aroma. Over a hundred different varieties of beans are produced in the world each with a different flavor attributable to three factors the species of plant *Coffea arabica* and *Coffea robusta* are the most common and the soil and climate where the variety was grown.

PART VIII

Mechanics

CHAPTER 33

Capitals

The conventions for using capital letters change often, but the following pages and a recent dictionary can help you decide whether to capitalize a particular word. The social, natural, and applied sciences require specialized capitalization for terminology, such as *Conditions A and B* or *Escherichia coli*. Consult one of the style guides listed on pages 838 (social sciences) and 869 (natural and applied sciences) for the requirements of particular disciplines.

 Note A grammar and style checker will flag overused capital letters and missing capitals at the beginnings of sentences. It will also spot missing capitals at the beginnings of proper nouns and adjectives—*if* the nouns and adjectives are in the checker's dictionary. For example, a checker caught *christianity* and *europe* but not *china* (for the country) or *Stephen king*. You'll need to proofread for capital letters on your own as well.

CULTURE LANGUAGE Conventions of capitalization vary from language to language. English, for instance, is the only language to capitalize the first-person singular pronoun (*I*), and its practice of capitalizing proper nouns but not most common nouns also distinguishes it from some other languages.

33a Capitalize the first word of every sentence.

Every writer should own a good dictionary.
Will inflation be curbed?
Watch out!

http://www.ablongman.com/littlebrown
For added help and practice with capital letters, click on
➤ **Punctuation and mechanics**
  ➤ **Exercises** ➤ **Exer. 14**
  ➤ **Web links** ➤ **Capitals**

When quoting other writers, you must reproduce the capital letters beginning their sentences or indicate that you have altered the source. Whenever possible, integrate the quotation into your own sentence so that its capitalization coincides with yours:

> "Psychotherapists often overlook the benefits of self-deception," the author argues.

> The author argues that "the benefits of self-deception" are not always recognized by psychotherapists.

If you need to alter the capitalization in the source, indicate the change with brackets (see p. 510):

> "[T]he benefits of self-deception" are not always recognized by psychotherapists, the author argues.

> The author argues that "[p]sychotherapists often overlook the benefits of self-deception."

Note Capitalization of questions in a series is optional. Both examples below are correct:

> Is the population a hundred? Two hundred? More?
> Is the population a hundred? two hundred? more?

Also optional is capitalization of the first word in a complete sentence after a colon (see p. 504).

33b   Capitalize most words in titles and subtitles of works.

Within your text, capitalize all the words in a title *except* the following: articles (*a, an, the*), *to* in infinitives, and connecting words (prepositions and coordinating and subordinating conjunctions) of fewer than five letters. Capitalize even these short words when they are the first or last word in a title or when they fall after a colon or semicolon.

The Sound and the Fury	*Management: A New Theory*
"Courtship Through the Ages"	"Once More to the Lake"
A Diamond Is Forever	*An End to Live For*
"Knowing Whom to Ask"	"Power: How to Get It"
Learning from Las Vegas	*File Under Architecture*
"The Truth About AIDS"	*Only when I Laugh*

Always capitalize the prefix or first word in a hyphenated word within a title. Capitalize the second word only if it is a noun or an adjective or is as important as the first word.

"Applying Stage Make-up"	*Through the Looking-Glass*
The Pre-Raphaelites	

cap
33b

Note The style guides of the academic disciplines have their own rules for capitals in titles. For instance, MLA style for English and some other humanities capitalizes all subordinating conjunctions but no prepositions. In addition, APA style for the social sciences and CSE style for the sciences capitalize only the first word and proper names in book and article titles within source citations. See pages 842–56 (APA) and 871–78 (CSE).

33c | **Always capitalize the pronoun *I* and the interjection *O*. Capitalize *oh* only when it begins a sentence.**

I love to stay up at night, but, oh, I hate to get up in the morning.
He who thinks himself wise, O heavens, is a great fool.

—VOLTAIRE

33d | **Capitalize proper nouns, proper adjectives, and words used as essential parts of proper nouns.**

Proper nouns name specific persons, places, and things: *Shakespeare, California, World War I*. **Proper adjectives** are formed from some proper nouns: *Shakespearean, Californian*.

1 ▪ Capitalize proper nouns and proper adjectives.

Capitalize all proper nouns and proper adjectives but not the articles (*a, an, the*) that precede them.

Proper nouns and adjectives to be capitalized

Specific persons and things

Stephen King	the Leaning Tower of Pisa
Napoleon Bonaparte	Boulder Dam
Doris Lessing	the Empire State Building

Specific places and geographical regions

New York City	the Mediterranean Sea
China	Lake Victoria
Europe	the Northeast, the South
North America	the Rocky Mountains

But: northeast of the city, going south

Days of the week, months, holidays

Monday	Yom Kippur
May	Christmas
Thanksgiving	Columbus Day

Historical events, documents, periods, movements

World War II	the Middle Ages
the Vietnam War	the Age of Reason
the Boston Tea Party	the Renaissance
the Treaty of Ghent	the Great Depression
the Constitution	the Romantic Movement
the Bill of Rights	the Cultural Revolution

Government offices or departments and institutions

House of Representatives	Polk Municipal Court
Department of Defense	Warren County Hospital
Appropriations Committee	Northeast High School

Political, social, athletic, and other organizations and associations and their members

Democratic Party, Democrats	Rotary Club, Rotarians
Sierra Club	League of Women Voters
Girl Scouts of America, Scout	Boston Celtics
B'nai B'rith	Chicago Symphony Orchestra

Races, nationalities, and their languages

Native American	Germans
African American	Swahili
Caucasian	Italian

But: blacks, whites

Religions and their followers

Christianity, Christians	Judaism, Orthodox Jews
Protestantism, Protestants	Hinduism, Hindus
Catholicism, Catholics	Islam, Muslims

Religious terms for the sacred

God	Buddha
Allah	the Bible [*but* biblical]
Christ	the Koran, the Qur'an

Note Pronouns referring to God are often capitalized in religious texts. In your writing follow your own preference in capitalizing the pronouns (*God . . . He*) or using small letters (*God . . . he*).

2 ▪ Capitalize common nouns used as essential parts of proper nouns.

Common nouns name general classes of persons, places, or things, and they generally are not capitalized. However, capitalize the common nouns *street, avenue, park, river, ocean, lake, company, college, county,* and *memorial* when they are part of proper nouns naming specific places or institutions:

Main Street	Lake Superior
Central Park	Ford Motor Company

cap

33d

Mississippi River   Madison College
Pacific Ocean   George Washington Memorial

3 ■ Capitalize trade names.

Trade names identify individual brands of certain products. When a trade name loses its association with a brand and comes to refer to a product in general, it is not capitalized. Refer to a dictionary for current usage when you are in doubt about a name.

Scotch tape   Xerox
Chevrolet   Bunsen burner
But: nylon, thermos

33e   Capitalize most titles of persons only when they precede proper names.

Professor Otto Osborne   Otto Osborne, a professor of English
Doctor Jane Covington   Jane Covington, a medical doctor
Governor Ella Moore   Ella Moore, the governor

Not   The Senator supported the bill.
But   The senator supported the bill.
Or   Senator Carmine supported the bill.

Exception Many writers capitalize a title denoting very high rank even when it follows a proper name or is used alone:

Lyndon Johnson, past President of the United States
the Chief Justice of the United States

33f   Capitalize only when required.

In general, modern writers capitalize fewer words than earlier writers did. Capitalize only when a rule says you must, and especially avoid miscapitalizing in the following situations.

1 ■ Use small letters for common nouns replacing proper nouns.

Not   I am determined to take an Economics course before I graduate from College.
But   I am determined to take an economics course before I graduate from college.
Or   I am determined to take Economics 101 before I graduate from Madison College.

cap
33f

2 ■ Capitalize compass directions only when they refer to specific geographical areas.

The storm blew in from the <u>northeast</u> and then veered <u>south</u> along the coast. [Here *northeast* and *south* refer to general directions.]

Students from the <u>South</u> have trouble adjusting to the <u>Northeast's</u> bitter winters. [Here *South* and *Northeast* refer to specific regions.]

3 ■ Use small letters for the names of seasons or the names of academic years or terms.

spring	autumn	senior year
summer	fall quarter	winter term

4 ■ Capitalize the names of relationships only when they form part of or substitute for proper names.

my mother	the father of my friend
my uncle John	John's brother

I remember how <u>Father</u> scolded us.

<u>Aunt</u> Annie, <u>Uncle</u> Jake, and <u>Uncle</u> Irvin died within two months of each other.

5 ■ Use capitals according to convention in online communication.

Although common in electronic mail and other online communication, messages written in all-capital letters or with no capital letters are difficult to read. Further, messages in all-capital letters may be taken as overly insistent, even rude (see also p. 195). Use capital letters according to rules 33a–33f in all your online communication.

EXERCISE
Revising: Capitals
Capitalize words as necessary in the following sentences, or substitute small letters for unnecessary capitals. Consult a dictionary if you are in doubt. If the capitalization in a sentence is already correct, circle the number preceding the sentence.

> *Example:*
> The first book on the reading list is mark twain's *a connecticut yankee in king arthur's court.*
> The first book on the reading list is Mark Twain's *A Connecticut Yankee in King Arthur's Court.*

1. San Antonio, texas, is a thriving city in the southwest.
2. The city has always offered much to tourists interested in the roots of spanish settlement of the new world.

cap
33f

3. The alamo is one of five Catholic Missions built by Priests to convert native americans and to maintain spain's claims in the area.

4. But the alamo is more famous for being the site of an 1836 battle that helped to create the republic of Texas.

5. Many of the nearby Streets, such as Crockett street, are named for men who gave their lives in that Battle.

6. The Hemisfair plaza and the San Antonio river link new tourist and convention facilities developed during mayor Cisneros's terms.

7. Restaurants, Hotels, and shops line the River. the haunting melodies of "Una paloma blanca" and "malagueña" lure passing tourists into Casa rio and other excellent mexican restaurants.

8. The university of Texas at San Antonio has expanded, and a Medical Center has been developed in the Northwest part of the city.

9. Sea World, on the west side of San Antonio, entertains grandparents, fathers and mothers, and children with the antics of dolphins and seals.

10. The City has attracted high-tech industry, creating a corridor of economic growth between san antonio and austin and contributing to the texas economy.

Note See page 540 for an exercise involving capitals along with underlining or italics and other mechanics.

cap

33

CHAPTER 34

Underlining or Italics

Underlining and *italic type* indicate the same thing: the word or words are being distinguished or emphasized. If you underline two or more words in a row, underline the space between the words, too: Criminal Statistics: Misuses of Numbers.

Note A grammar and style checker cannot recognize problems with underlining or italics. Check your work to ensure that you have used highlighting appropriately.

34a Use underlining or italics consistently and appropriately for your writing situation.

Word processors have made italic type possible in papers and other documents, and it is now used almost universally in business and academic writing. Still, some academic style guides, notably the *MLA Handbook*, continue to prefer underlining, especially in source citations. Ask your instructor for his or her own preference. (We use underlining for the examples in this chapter because it is easier to see than italics.)

Depending on your instructor's preference, use either italics or underlining consistently throughout a document. For instance, if you are writing an English paper and following MLA style for underlining in source citations, use underlining in the body of your paper as well.

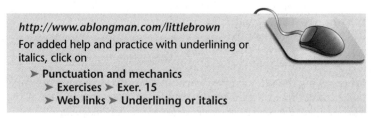

http://www.ablongman.com/littlebrown
For added help and practice with underlining or italics, click on
➤ **Punctuation and mechanics**
　➤ **Exercises** ➤ **Exer. 15**
　➤ **Web links** ➤ **Underlining or italics**

34b Underline or italicize the titles of works that appear independently.

Within your text, underline or italicize the titles of works, such as books and periodicals, that are published, released, or produced separately from other works (see the box below). Use quotation marks for all other titles, such as short stories and articles in periodicals. (See pp. 498–99.)

Titles to be underlined or italicized

Other titles should be placed in quotation marks. (See pp. 498–99.)

Books	**Television and radio programs**
War and Peace	All Things Considered
Psychology: An Introduction	NBC Sports Hour
Plays	**Long poems**
Hamlet	Beowulf
The Phantom of the Opera	Paradise Lost
Computer software	**Periodicals**
Microsoft Internet Explorer	Time
Acrobat Reader	Boston Globe
Web sites	Yale Law Review
Google	**Published speeches**
Friends of Prufrock	Lincoln's Gettysburg Address
Pamphlets	Pericles's Funeral Oration
The Truth About Alcoholism	**Movies and videotapes**
Plants of the Desert	Schindler's List
Long musical works	How to Relax
Tchaikovsky's Swan Lake	**Works of visual art**
The Beatles' Revolver	Michelangelo's David
But: Symphony in C	Picasso's Guernica

Note Underline or italicize marks of punctuation only when they are part of the title: *Did you read Catch-22?* (not *Catch-22?*). In titles of newspapers underline or italicize the name of the city only when it is part of the title:

New York Times   Manchester Guardian

When giving the title of a periodical in your text, you need not capitalize, underline, or italicize the article *the,* even if it is part of the title: *She has the New York Times delivered to her in Japan.*

Exceptions Legal documents, the Bible, the Koran, and their parts are generally not underlined or italicized:

Not   They registered their <u>deed</u>.
But   They registered their deed.

Not   We studied the <u>Book of Revelation</u> in the <u>Bible</u>.
But   We studied the Book of Revelation in the Bible.

Many sciences do not use underlining or italics for some or all titles within source citations. (See pp. 871–78 on CSE style.)

34c   Underline or italicize the names of ships, aircraft, spacecraft, and trains.

<u>Queen Elizabeth 2</u>   <u>Challenger</u>   <u>Orient Express</u>
<u>Spirit of St. Louis</u>   <u>Apollo XI</u>   <u>Montrealer</u>

34d   Underline or italicize foreign words and phrases that have not been absorbed into English.

English has adopted many foreign words and phrases—such as the French expression "bon voyage"—and these need not be underlined or italicized. A foreign phrase should be underlined or italicized when it has not been absorbed into our language. A dictionary will say whether a phrase is still considered foreign to English.

The scientific name for the brown trout is <u>Salmo trutta</u>. [The Latin scientific names for plants and animals are always underlined or italicized.]

What a life he led! He was a true <u>bon vivant</u>.

The Latin <u>De gustibus non est disputandum</u> translates roughly as "There's no accounting for taste."

34e   Underline or italicize words or characters named as words.

Use underlining or italics to indicate that you are citing a character or word as a word rather than using it for its meaning. Words you are defining fall under this convention:

The word <u>syzygy</u> refers to a straight line formed by three celestial bodies, as in the alignment of the earth, sun, and moon.

Some people say <u>th</u>, as in <u>thought</u>, with a faint <u>s</u> or <u>f</u> sound.

Carved into the column, twenty feet up, was a mysterious <u>7</u>.

und
34e

34f   Occasionally, underlining or italics may be used for emphasis.

Underlining or italics can stress an important word or phrase, especially in reporting how someone said something:

"Why on earth would _you_ do that?" she cried.

But use such emphasis very rarely. Excessive underlining or italics will make your writing sound immature or hysterical:

The settlers had _no_ firewood and _no_ food. Many of them _starved_ or _froze_ to death that first winter.

34g   In online communication, use alternatives for underlining or italics.

Electronic mail and other forms of online communication sometimes do not allow underlining or italics for the purposes described in this chapter. The program may not be able to produce the highlighting or may reserve it for a special function. (On World Wide Web sites, for instance, underlining indicates a link to another site.)

To distinguish elements that usually require underlining or italics, type an underscore before and after the element: _Measurements coincide with those in _Joule's Handbook_._ You can also emphasize words with asterisks: _I *will not* be able to attend._

Avoid using all-capital letters for emphasis. (See also p. 523.)

EXERCISE
Revising: Underlining or italics
Underline or italicize words and phrases as needed in the following sentences, or circle any words or phrases that are underlined unnecessarily. Note that some highlighting is correct as given.

Example:
Of Hitchcock's movies, Psycho is the scariest.
Of Hitchcock's movies, _Psycho_ is the scariest.

1. Of the many Vietnam veterans who are writers, Oliver Stone is perhaps the most famous for writing and directing the films Platoon and Born on the Fourth of July.
2. Tim O'Brien has written short stories for Esquire, GQ, and Massachusetts Review.
3. Going After Cacciato is O'Brien's dreamlike novel about the horrors of combat.
4. The word Vietnam is technically two words (Viet and Nam), but most American writers spell it as one word.

und
34g

5. American writers use words or phrases borrowed from Vietnamese, such as di di mau ("go quickly") or dinky dau ("crazy").

6. Philip Caputo's <u>gripping</u> account of his service in Vietnam appears in the book A Rumor of War.

7. Caputo's book was made into a television movie, also titled <u>A Rumor of War</u>.

8. <u>David Rabe's</u> plays—including The Basic Training of Pavlo Hummel, Streamers, and Sticks and Bones—depict the effects of the war <u>not only</u> on the soldiers <u>but</u> on their families.

9. Called the <u>poet laureate of the Vietnam war</u>, Steve Mason has published two collections of poems: Johnny's Song and Warrior for Peace.

10. The Washington Post published <u>rave</u> reviews of Veteran's Day, an autobiography by Rod Kane.

Note See page 540 for an exercise involving underlining or italics along with capitals and other mechanics.

und

34

CHAPTER 35

Abbreviations

The following guidelines on abbreviations pertain to the text of a nontechnical document. All academic disciplines use abbreviations in source citations, and much technical writing, such as in the sciences and engineering, uses many abbreviations in the document text. For the requirements of the discipline you are writing in, consult one of the style guides listed on pages 818 (humanities), 838 (social sciences), and 869 (natural and applied sciences).

Usage varies, but writers increasingly omit periods from abbreviations that consist of or end in capital letters: *US, BA, USMC, PhD.* See page 449 on punctuating abbreviations.

Note A grammar and style checker may flag some abbreviations, such as *ft.* (for *foot*) and *st.* (for *street*). A spelling checker will flag abbreviations it does not recognize. But neither checker can tell you whether an abbreviation is appropriate for your writing situation or will be clear to your readers.

Abbreviations for nontechnical writing

- Titles before or after proper names: *Dr. Jorge Rodriguez; Jorge Rodriguez, PhD.*
- Familiar abbreviations and acronyms: *USA, AIDS.*
- *BC, AD, AM, PM, no.,* and *$* with dates and numbers.
- *I.e., e.g.,* and other Latin abbreviations within parentheses and in source citations.
- *Inc., Bros., Co.,* and *&* with names of business firms.

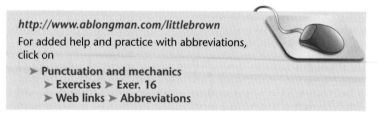

http://www.ablongman.com/littlebrown
For added help and practice with abbreviations, click on
➤ **Punctuation and mechanics**
  ➤ **Exercises** ➤ **Exer. 16**
  ➤ **Web links** ➤ **Abbreviations**

35a Use standard abbreviations for titles immediately before and after proper names.

Before the name

Dr. James Hsu
Mr., Mrs., Ms., Hon., St.,
Rev., Msgr., Gen.

After the name

James Hsu, MD
DDS, DVM, PhD, EdD,
OSB, SJ, Sr., Jr.

Use abbreviations such as *Rev., Hon., Prof., Rep., Sen., Dr.,* and *St.* (for *Saint*) only if they appear with a proper name. Spell them out in the absence of a proper name:

Not   We learned to trust the Dr.
But   We learned to trust the doctor.
Or   We learned to trust Dr. Kaplan.

The abbreviations for academic degrees—*PhD, MA, BA,* and the like—may be used without a proper name: *My brother took seven years to get his PhD. It will probably take me just as long to earn my BA.*

35b Familiar abbreviations and acronyms are acceptable in most writing.

An **acronym** is an abbreviation that spells a pronounceable word, such as WHO, NATO, and AIDS. These and other abbreviations using initials are acceptable in most writing as long as they are familiar. Abbreviations of two or more words written in all capital letters may be written without periods (see p. 449):

Institutions   LSU, UCLA, TCU
Organizations   CIA, FBI, YMCA, AFL-CIO
Corporations   IBM, CBS, ITT
People   JFK, LBJ, FDR
Countries   US, USA

Note If a name or term (such as *operating room*) appears often in a piece of writing, then its abbreviation (*OR*) can cut down on extra words. Spell out the full term at its first appearance, give its abbreviation in parentheses, and use the abbreviation from then on.

35c Use *BC, AD, AM, PM, no.,* and *$* only with specific dates and numbers.

44 BC	8:05 PM (*or* p.m.)	no. 36 (*or* No. 36)
AD 1492	11:26 AM (*or* a.m.)	$7.41

ab
35c

Not   Hospital routine is easier to follow in the <u>AM</u> than in the <u>PM</u>.

But   Hospital routine is easier to follow in the <u>morning</u> than in the <u>afternoon or evening</u>.

Note The abbreviation BC ("before Christ") always follows a date, whereas AD (*anno Domini*, Latin for "in the year of the Lord") precedes a date. Increasingly, these abbreviations are being replaced by BCE ("before the common era") and CE ("common era"), respectively. Both follow the date: *44 BCE, 1492 CE.*

35d Generally, reserve Latin abbreviations for source citations and comments in parentheses.

i.e.   *id est:* that is
cf.   *confer:* compare
e.g.   *exempli gratia:* for example
et al.   *et alii:* and others
etc.   *et cetera:* and so forth
NB   *nota bene:* note well

He said he would be gone a fortnight (i.e., two weeks).
Trees, too, are susceptible to disease (e.g., Dutch elm disease).
Bloom et al., editors, *Anthology of Light Verse*

(Note that these abbreviations are generally not italicized or underlined.)

Some writers avoid these abbreviations in formal writing, even within parentheses:

Informal

The cabs of some modern farm machines (<u>e.g.</u>, combines) look like airplane cockpits.

Formal

The cabs of some modern farm machines (<u>for example</u>, combines) look like airplane cockpits.

35e Use *Inc., Bros., Co.,* or & (for *and*) only in official names of business firms.

Not   The Santini <u>bros.</u> operate a large moving firm in New York City.

But   The Santini <u>brothers</u> operate a large moving firm in New York City.

Or   Santini <u>Bros.</u> is a large moving firm in New York City.

Not   We read about the Hardy Boys <u>&</u> Nancy Drew.

But   We read about the Hardy Boys <u>and</u> Nancy Drew.

35f Generally spell out units of measurement and names of places, calendar designations, people, and courses.

In most academic, general, and business writing, certain words should always be spelled out. (In source citations and technical writing, however, these words are more often abbreviated.)

Units of measurement

The dog is thirty inches [not in.] high.
The building is 150 feet [not ft.] tall.

Exception Long phrases such as *miles per hour* (*m.p.h.*) or *cycles per second* (*c.p.s.*) are usually abbreviated, with or without periods: *The speed limit on that road was once 75 m.p.h.* [or *mph*].

Geographical names

The publisher is in Massachusetts [not Mass. or MA].
He came from Auckland, New Zealand [not NZ].
She lived on Morrissey Boulevard [not Blvd.].

Exceptions The United States is often referred to as the USA or the US. In writing of the US capital, we use the abbreviation DC for District of Columbia when it follows the city's name: Washington, DC.

Names of days, months, and holidays

The truce was signed on Tuesday [not Tues.], April [not Apr.] 16.
The Christmas [not Xmas] holidays are uneventful.

Names of people

Virginia [not Va.] Woolf was British.
Robert [not Robt.] Frost wrote accessible poems.

Courses of instruction

I'm majoring in political science [not poli. sci.].
Economics [not Econ.] is a difficult course.

EXERCISE
Revising: Abbreviations
Revise the following sentences as needed to correct inappropriate use of abbreviations for nontechnical writing. Circle the number preceding any sentence in which abbreviations are appropriate as written.

Example:
One prof. lectured for five hrs.
One professor lectured for five hours.

1. In the Sept. 17, 1993, issue of *Science* magazine, Virgil L. Sharpton discusses a theory that could help explain the extinction of dinosaurs.

2. About 65 mill. yrs. ago, a comet or asteroid crashed into the earth.

3. The result was a huge crater about 10 km. (6.2 mi.) deep in the Gulf of Mex.

4. Sharpton's new measurements suggest that the crater is 50 pct. larger than scientists previously believed.

5. Indeed, 20-yr.-old drilling cores reveal that the crater is about 186 mi. wide, roughly the size of Conn.

6. The space object was traveling more than 100,000 m.p.h. and hit earth with the impact of 100 to 300 million megatons of TNT.

7. On impact, 200,000 cubic km. of rock and soil were vaporized or thrown into the air.

8. That's the equivalent of 2.34 bill. cubic ft. of matter.

9. The impact would have created 400-ft. tidal waves across the Atl. Ocean, temps. higher than 20,000 degs., and powerful earthquakes.

10. Sharpton theorizes that the dust, vapor, and smoke from this impact blocked the sun's rays for mos., cooled the earth, and thus resulted in the death of the dinosaurs.

Note See page 540 for an exercise involving abbreviations along with capitals and other mechanics.

CHAPTER 36

Numbers

This chapter addresses the use of numbers (numerals versus words) in the text of a document. All disciplines use many more numerals in source citations.

Note Grammar and style checkers will flag numerals beginning sentences and can be customized to ignore or to look for numerals. But they can't tell you whether numerals or spelled-out numbers are appropriate for your writing situation.

36a Use numerals according to standard practice in the field you are writing in.

Always use numerals for numbers that require more than two words to spell out:

The leap year has 366 days.
The population of Minot, North Dakota, is about 32,800.

In nontechnical academic writing, spell out numbers of one or two words:

Twelve nations signed the treaty.
The ball game drew forty-two thousand people. [A hyphenated number may be considered one word.]

In much business writing, use numerals for all numbers over ten (*five reasons, 11 participants*). In technical academic and business writing, such as in science and engineering, use numerals for all numbers over ten, and use numerals for zero through nine when they refer to exact measurements (*2 liters, 1 hour*). (Consult one of the style guides listed on pp. 838 and 869 for more details.)

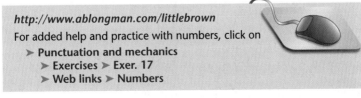

http://www.ablongman.com/littlebrown
For added help and practice with numbers, click on
➤ Punctuation and mechanics
   ➤ Exercises ➤ Exer. 17
   ➤ Web links ➤ Numbers

535

Note Use a combination of numerals and words for round numbers over a million: *26 million, 2.45 billion*. And use either all numerals or all words when several numbers appear together in a passage, even if convention would require a mixture:

Inconsistent	The satellite Galatea is about <u>twenty-six thousand</u> miles from Neptune. It is <u>110</u> miles in diameter and orbits Neptune in just over <u>ten</u> hours.
Revised	The satellite Galatea is about <u>26,000</u> miles from Neptune. It is <u>110</u> miles in diameter and orbits Neptune in just over <u>10</u> hours.

CULTURE LANGUAGE In American English a comma separates the numerals in long numbers (*26,000*), and a period functions as a decimal point (*2.06*).

36b Use numerals according to convention for dates, addresses, and other information.

Even when a number requires one or two words to spell out, we conventionally use numerals in the following situations:

Days and years

June 18, 2000   AD 12   456 BC   1999

Exception The day of a month may be expressed in words when it is not followed by a year (*June fifth; October first*).

Pages, chapters, volumes, acts, scenes, lines	**Decimals, percentages, and fractions**
Chapter 9, page 123	22.5
Hamlet, act 5, scene 3, lines 35–40	48% (*or* 48 percent)
	3½

Addresses	**Scores and statistics**
RD 2	21 to 7
419 Stonewall Street	a mean of 26
Washington, DC 20036	a ratio of 8 to 1

Exact amounts of money	**The time of day**
$4.50	9:00 AM
$3.5 million (*or* $3,500,000)	2:30 PM

Exceptions Round dollar or cent amounts of only a few words may be expressed in words: *seventeen dollars; fifteen hundred dollars; sixty cents*. When the word *o'clock* is used for the time of day, also express the number in words: *two o'clock* (not *2 o'clock*).

36c Always spell out numbers that begin sentences.

For clarity, spell out any number that begins a sentence. If the number requires more than two words, reword the sentence so that the number falls later and can be expressed as a numeral:

Not   3.5 billion people live in Asia.
But   The population of Asia is 3.5 billion.

EXERCISE
Revising: Numbers
Revise the following sentences so that numbers are used appropriately for nontechnical writing. Circle the number preceding any sentence in which numbers are already used appropriately.

> *Example:*
> Carol paid two hundred five dollars for used scuba gear.
> Carol paid $205 for used scuba gear.

1. The planet Saturn is nine hundred million miles, or nearly one billion five hundred million kilometers, from the sun.
2. A year on Saturn equals almost thirty of our years.
3. Thus, Saturn orbits the sun only two and four-tenths times during the average human life span.
4. It travels in its orbit at about twenty-one thousand six hundred miles per hour.
5. 15 to 20 times denser than Earth's core, Saturn's core measures 17,000 miles across.
6. The temperature at Saturn's cloud tops is minus one hundred seventy degrees Fahrenheit.
7. In nineteen hundred thirty-three, astronomers found on Saturn's surface a huge white spot 2 times the size of Earth and 7 times the size of Mercury.
8. Saturn's famous rings reflect almost seventy percent of the sunlight that approaches the planet.
9. The ring system is almost forty thousand miles wide, beginning 8800 miles from the planet's visible surface and ending forty-seven thousand miles from that surface.
10. Saturn generates about one hundred thirty trillion kilowatts of electricity.

Note See page 540 for an exercise involving numbers along with abbreviations and other mechanics.

num
36c

CHAPTER 37

Word Division

To avoid occasional short lines in your documents, you'll probably want to divide some words between the end of one line and the beginning of the next. You can set your word processor to divide words automatically at appropriate breaks (from the Tools menu, select Language and then Hyphenation). To divide words manually, follow these guidelines:

- Divide words only between syllables. Do not divide one-syllable words, such as *dropped* or *straight*. Consult a dictionary if you're not sure of syllable breaks.
- Put a hyphen at the end of the first line, never at the beginning of the second line.

Not all syllable breaks are appropriate for word division. Use the following rules to decide when and how to divide words.

37a Leave at least two letters at the end of a line and at least three letters at the beginning of a line.

Faulty   A newspaper or television editorial for or a-
         gainst a candidate can sway an election. A vot-
         er may have no other information to draw on.

Revised A newspaper or television editorial for or
         against a candidate can sway an election. A
         voter may have no other information to draw on.

37b Divide a hyphenated word only at the hyphen.

Faulty   If you want to have friends, be good-na-
         tured.

Revised If you want to have friends, be good-
         natured.

538

37c Do not divide words in electronic addresses.

If you must break an electronic address—for instance, in a source citation—do so only after a slash (MLA style) or after a slash or a period (APA style). Do not hyphenate, because readers may perceive any added hyphen as part of the address.

Not   http://www.library.miami.edu/staff/lmc/soc-
            race.html

But   http://www.library.miami.edu/staff/lmc/
            socrace.html

37d Make sure a word division will not confuse readers.

Some word divisions may momentarily confuse readers because the first or second part by itself forms a pronounceable (or unpronounceable) unit that does not fit with the whole—for example, *poi-gnant, read-dress, her-oism, in-dict.* Avoid word divisions like these.

EXERCISE
Revising: Word division
Revise the following sentences to improve inappropriate word divisions. Consult a dictionary if necessary. Circle the number preceding any sentence in which word division is already appropriate.

Example:
Samuel Johnson, the British essayist and poet, compiled the first English dictionary.
Samuel Johnson, the British essayist and
poet, compiled the first English dictionary.

1. Johnson read books about a wide range of subjects.
2. As a result he was probably the most well-edu-
cated man in England.
3. When he saw a new use for a word, he marked the passage for his secretary to copy.
4. The words were arranged alphabetically in large ledger books, with e-
nough room between words for definitions.
5. For each word the definitions were organized with specialized uses last.

Note See the next page for an exercise involving word division along with capitals and other mechanics.

div
37d

EXERCISE 33–37
Revising: Mechanics

Revise the paragraphs below to correct any errors in the use of capital letters, underlining or italics, abbreviations, numbers, and word division. (For abbreviations and numbers follow standard practice for nontechnical writing.) Consult a dictionary as needed. (To download a double-spaced, editable version of this exercise, go to *http://www.ablongman.com/littlebrown* and click on Punctuation and mechanics > Downloads > Revising: Mechanics.)

According to many sources—e.g., the Cambridge Ancient History and Gardiner's Egypt of the Pharaohs—the ancient egyptians devoted much attention to making Life more convenient and pleasurable for themselves.

Our word pharaoh for the ancient egyptian rulers comes from the egyptian word pr'o, meaning "great house." Indeed, the egyptians placed great emphasis on family residences, adding small bedrms. as early as 3500 yrs. By 3000 b.c., the egyptians made ice through evaporation of water at night and then used it to cool their homes. About the same time they used fans made of palm fronds or papyrus to cool themselves in the day. To light their homes, the egyptians abandoned the animal-fat lamps Humans had used for 50 thousand yrs. Instead, around 1300 b.c. the people of Egt. devised the 1st oil lamps.

egyptians found great pleasure in playing games. Four thousand three hundred yrs. ago or so they created one of the oldest board games known. the game involved racing ivory or stone pieces across a papyrus playing board. By three thousand b.c., egyptian children played marbles with semiprecious stones, some of which have been found in gravesites at nagada, EG. Around one thousand three hundred sixty b.c., small children played with clay rattles covered in silk and shaped like animals.

To play the game of love, egyptian men and women experimented with cosmetics applied to skin and eyelids. kohl, history's first eyeliner, was used by both sexes to ward off evil. 5000 yrs. ago egyptians wore wigs made of vegetable fibers or human hair. In 9 hundred b.c., queen Isimkheb wore a wig so heavy that she needed assistance in walking. To adjust their make-up and wigs, egyptians adapted the simple metal mirrors devised by the sumerians in the bronze age, ornamenting them with carved handles of ivory, gold, or wood. Feeling that only those who smelled sweet could be attractive, the egyptians made deodorants from perfumed oils, e.g., cinnamon and citrus.

mech

PART IX

Effective Words

CHAPTER 38

Using Appropriate Language

Appropriate language suits your writing situation—your subject, purpose, and audience. Like everyone, you vary your words depending on the context in which you are speaking and writing. Look, for example, at the underlined words in these two sentences:

> Some patients decide to <u>bag</u> counseling because their <u>shrinks</u> seem <u>strung out</u>.

> Some patients decide to <u>abandon</u> counseling because their <u>therapists</u> seem <u>disturbed</u>.

The first sentence might be addressed to friends in casual conversation. The second is more suitable for an academic audience.

The more formal language of the second example is typical of **standard American English.** This is the dialect of English normally expected and used in school, business, government, the professions, and the communications media. (For more on its role in academic writing, see pp. 17–18.)

The vocabulary of standard American English is huge, allowing expression of an infinite range of ideas and feelings; but it does exclude words that only some groups of people use, understand, or find inoffensive. Some of those more limited vocabularies should be avoided altogether; others should be used cautiously and in special situations, as when aiming for a special effect with an audience you know will appreciate it. Whenever you doubt a word's status, consult a dictionary (see p. 578).

 Note Many grammar and style checkers can be set to flag potentially inappropriate words, such as nonstandard dialect, slang, colloquialisms, and gender-specific terms (*manmade, mailman*). How-

---

http://www.ablongman.com/littlebrown
For added help and practice with appropriate language, click on
➤ **Effective words**
  ➤ **Video tutorials** ➤ **Using appropriate language**
  ➤ **Exercises** ➤ **Exers. 1 and 2**
  ➤ **Web links** ➤ **Using appropriate language**

Language in academic and business writing

Always appropriate
Standard American English

Sometimes appropriate

Regional words and expressions	Neologisms
Slang	Technical language
Colloquial language	Euphemisms

Rarely or never appropriate

Nonstandard dialect	Pretentious writing
Archaic and obsolete words	Biased language: sexist, racist,
Double talk	ethnocentric, etc.

ever, the checker can flag only words listed in its dictionary of questionable words. For example, a checker flagged *businessman* as potentially sexist in *A successful businessman puts clients first,* but the checker did not flag *his* in *A successful businessperson listens to his clients.* If you use a checker to review your language, you'll need to determine whether a flagged word is or is not appropriate for your writing situation, and you'll still need to hunt for possibly inappropriate words on your own.

38a   Revising nonstandard dialect   CULTURE LANGUAGE

Like many countries, the United States consists of scores of regional, social, or ethnic groups with their own distinct dialects, or versions of English. Standard American English is one of these dialects, and so are Black English, Appalachian English, Creole, and the English of coastal Maine. All the dialects of English share many features, but each also has its own vocabulary, pronunciation, and grammar.

If you speak a dialect of English besides standard American English, be careful about using your dialect in situations where standard English is the norm, such as in academic or business writing. Dialects are not wrong in themselves, but forms imported from

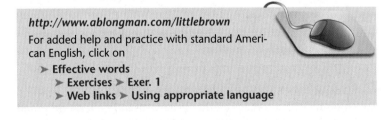

http://www.ablongman.com/littlebrown
For added help and practice with standard American English, click on
➤ **Effective words**
　➤ **Exercises** ➤ **Exer. 1**
　➤ **Web links** ➤ **Using appropriate language**

one dialect into another may still be perceived as unclear or incorrect. When you know standard English is expected in your writing, edit to eliminate expressions in your dialect that you know (or have been told) differ from standard English. These expressions may include *theirselves, hisn, them books,* and others labeled "nonstandard" by a dictionary. They may also include verb forms, as discussed on pages 286–97. For help identifying and editing nonstandard language, see "Guide to 🔲 **CULTURE LANGUAGE** ↘ Topics" inside the back cover of this book.

Your participation in the community of standard English does not require you to abandon your own dialect. You may want to use it in writing you do for yourself, such as journals, notes, and drafts, which should be composed as freely as possible. You may want to quote it in an academic paper, as when analyzing or reporting conversation in dialect. And, of course, you will want to use it with others who speak it.

38b   Using regionalisms only when appropriate

Regionalisms are expressions or pronunciations peculiar to a particular area. Southerners may say they *reckon,* meaning "think" or "suppose." People in Maine invite their Boston friends to come *down* rather than *up* (north) to visit. New Yorkers stand *on* rather than *in* line for a movie.

Regional expressions are appropriate in writing addressed to local readers and may lend realism to regional description, but they should be avoided in writing intended for a general audience.

38c   Using slang only when appropriate

All groups of people—from musicians and computer scientists to vegetarians and golfers—create novel and colorful expressions called slang. The following quotation, for instance, is from an essay on the slang of "skaters" (skateboarders):

> Curtis slashed ultra-punk crunchers on his longboard, while the Rube-man flailed his usual Gumbyness on tweaked frontsides and lofty fakie ollies.   —MILES ORKIN, "Mucho Slingage by the Pool"

"Slang," Orkin goes on to say, "is a convenient, creative, mildly poetic, cohesive agent in many subcultures." It reflects the experiences of a group and binds its members.

Some slang gives new meaning to old words, such as *bad* for "good." Some slang comes from other languages, such as *chow* (food) from the Chinese *chao,* "to stir or fry." The slang of a particular group may also spread to other groups, as *put on ice, funky,* and *dis* have spread beyond their African American origins.

Among those who understand it, slang may be vivid and forceful. It often occurs in dialog, and an occasional slang expression can enliven an informal essay. Some slang, such as *dropout* (*She was a high school dropout*), has proved so useful that it has passed into the general vocabulary.

But most slang is too flippant and imprecise for effective communication, and it is generally inappropriate for college or business writing. Notice the gain in seriousness and precision achieved in the following revision:

Slang	Many students start out <u>pretty together</u> but then <u>get weird</u>.
Revised	Many students start out <u>with clear goals</u> but then <u>lose their direction</u>.

38d Using colloquial language only when appropriate

Colloquial language designates the words and expressions appropriate to everyday spoken language. Regardless of our backgrounds and how we live, we all try to *get along with* each other. We play with *kids, go crazy* for something, and in our worst moments try to *get back at* someone who has made us do the *dirty work*.

When you write informally, colloquial language may be appropriate to achieve the casual, relaxed effect of conversation. An occasional colloquial word dropped into otherwise more formal writing can also help you achieve a desired emphasis. But colloquial language does not provide the exactness needed in more formal college, business, and professional writing. In such writing you should generally avoid any words and expressions labeled "informal" or "colloquial" in your dictionary. Take special care to avoid **mixed diction,** a combination of standard and colloquial words:

Mixed diction	According to a Native American myth, the Great Creator <u>had a dog hanging around with him</u> when he created the earth.
Revised	According to a Native American myth, the Great Creator <u>was accompanied by a dog</u> when he created the earth.

38e Revising obsolete or archaic words and neologisms

Since our surroundings and our lives are constantly changing, some words pass out of use and others appear to fill new needs. **Obsolete** and **archaic** are dictionary labels for words or meanings of words that we never or rarely use but that appear in older documents and literature still read today. Obsolete words or meanings are no longer used at all—for example, *enwheel* ("to encircle") and *cote* ("to pass"). Archaic words or meanings occur now only in special contexts such as poetry—for example, *fast* ("near," as in *fast by the road*) and *belike* ("perhaps"). Both obsolete and archaic words are inappropriate in nonfiction writing for an academic audience.

Neologisms are words created (or coined) so recently that they have not come into established use. An example is *prequel* (made up of *pre-*, meaning "before," and the ending of *sequel*), a movie or book that takes the story of an existing movie or book back in time. Some neologisms do become accepted as part of our general vocabulary—*motel,* coined from *motor* and *hotel,* is an example. But most neologisms pass quickly from the language. Unless such words serve a special purpose in your writing and are sure to be understood by your readers, you should avoid them.

38f   Using technical words with care

All disciplines and professions rely on special words or give common words special meanings. Chemists speak of *esters* and *phosphatides,* geographers and mapmakers refer to *isobars* and *isotherms,* and literary critics write about *motifs* and *subtexts.* Such technical language allows specialists to communicate precisely and economically with other specialists who share their vocabulary. But without explanation these words are meaningless to nonspecialists. When you are writing for nonspecialists, avoid unnecessary technical terms and carefully define terms you must use.

38g   Revising indirect or pretentious writing

In most writing, small, plain, and direct words are preferable to big, showy, or evasive words. Avoid euphemisms, double talk, and pretentious writing.

A **euphemism** is a presumably inoffensive word that a writer or speaker substitutes for a word deemed potentially offensive or too blunt, such as *passed away* for "died." Euphemisms appear whenever a writer or speaker wants to bury the truth, as when a governor mentions the *negative growth* (meaning "decline") in her state. Use euphemisms only when you know that blunt, truthful words would needlessly hurt or offend members of your audience.

A kind of euphemism that deliberately evades the truth is **double talk** (also called **doublespeak** or **weasel words**): language intended to confuse or to be misunderstood. Today double talk is unfortunately common in politics and advertising—the *revenue enhancement* that is really a tax, the *biodegradable* bags that last decades. Double talk has no place in honest writing.

Euphemism and sometimes double talk seem to keep company with fancy writing. Any writing that is more elaborate than its subject requires will sound **pretentious**—that is, excessively showy. Choose your words for their exactness and economy. The big, ornate word may be tempting, but pass it up. Your readers will be grateful.

Pretentious	To perpetuate our endeavor of providing funds for our elderly citizens as we do at the present moment, we will face the exigency of enhanced contributions from all our citizens.
Revised	We cannot continue to fund Social Security and Medicare for the elderly unless we raise taxes.

38h Revising sexist and other biased language

Even when we do not mean it to, our language can reflect and perpetuate hurtful prejudices toward groups of people, especially racial, ethnic, religious, age, and sexual groups. Such biased language can be obvious—words such as *nigger, whitey, mick, kike, fag, dyke,* or *broad.* But it can also be subtle, generalizing about groups in ways that may be familiar but that are also inaccurate or unfair. For instance, people with physical disabilities are as varied a group as any other: the only thing they have in common is some form of impairment. To assume that people with disabilities share certain attitudes (shyness, helplessness, victimization, whatever) is to disregard the uniqueness of each person.

Biased language reflects poorly on the user, not on the person or persons whom it mischaracterizes or insults. Unbiased language does not submit to false generalizations. It treats people as individuals and labels groups as they wish to be labeled.

1 ■ Avoiding stereotypes of race, ethnicity, religion, age, and other characteristics

A **stereotype** is a generalization based on poor evidence, a kind of formula for understanding and judging people simply because of their membership in a group:

Men are uncommunicative.
Women are emotional.
Liberals want to raise taxes.
Conservatives are affluent.

http://www.ablongman.com/littlebrown
For help and practice with recognizing and avoiding biased language, click on
➤ **Effective words**
  ➤ **Exercises** ➤ **Exer. 2**
    ➤ **Web links** ➤ **Using appropriate language**

At best, stereotypes betray an uncritical writer, one who is not thinking beyond notions received from others. Worse, they betray a writer who does not mind hurting others, or even *wants* to hurt others.

In your writing, be alert for any general statements about people based on only one or a few characteristics. Be especially cautious about substituting such statements for the evidence you should be providing instead.

Stereotype	Elderly drivers should have their licenses limited to daytime driving. [Implies that all elderly people are poor night drivers.]
Revised	Drivers with impaired night vision should have their licenses limited to daytime driving.

Some stereotypes have become part of the language, but they are still potentially offensive.

Stereotype	The administrators are too blind to see the need for a new gymnasium.
Revised	The administrators do not understand the need for a new gymnasium.

2 ■ Avoiding sexist language

Among the most subtle and persistent biased language is that expressing narrow ideas about men's and women's roles, position, and value in society. This **sexist language** distinguishes needlessly between men and women in such matters as occupation, ability, behavior, temperament, and maturity. Like other stereotypes, it can wound or irritate readers, and it indicates the writer's thoughtlessness or unfairness. The following box suggests some ways of eliminating sexist language.

Eliminating sexist language

- **Avoid demeaning and patronizing language**—for instance, identifying women and men differently or trivializing either gender:

Sexist	Dr. Keith Kim and Lydia Hawkins wrote the article.
Revised	Dr. Keith Kim and Dr. Lydia Hawkins wrote the article.
Revised	Keith Kim and Lydia Hawkins wrote the article.

Sexist	Ladies are entering formerly male occupations.
Revised	Women are entering formerly male occupations.

- **Avoid occupational or social stereotypes**, assuming that a role or profession is exclusively male or female:

| Sexist | The considerate doctor commends a nurse when she provides his patients with good care. |
| Revised | The considerate doctor commends a nurse who provides good care for patients. |

- **Avoid referring needlessly to gender:**

| Sexist | Marie Curie, a woman chemist, discovered radium. |
| Revised | Marie Curie, a chemist, discovered radium. |

| Sexist | The patients were tended by a male nurse. |
| Revised | The patients were tended by a nurse. |

- **Avoid using *man* or words containing *man* to refer to all human beings.** Here are a few alternatives:

businessman	businessperson
chairman	chair, chairperson
congressman	representative in Congress, legislator
craftsman	craftsperson, artisan
layman	layperson
mankind	humankind, humanity, human beings, people
policeman	police officer
salesman	salesperson, sales representative

| Sexist | Man has not reached the limits of social justice. |
| Revised | Humankind [or Humanity] has not reached the limits of social justice. |

| Sexist | The furniture consists of manmade materials. |
| Revised | The furniture consists of synthetic materials. |

- **Avoid the generic *he*,** the male pronoun used to refer to both genders. (See also pp. 329–30.)

Sexist	The newborn child explores his world.
Revised	Newborn children explore their world. [Use the plural for the pronoun and the word it refers to.]
Revised	The newborn child explores the world. [Avoid the pronoun altogether.]
Revised	The newborn child explores his or her world. [Substitute male and female pronouns.]

Use the last option sparingly—only once in a group of sentences and only to stress the singular individual.

CULTURE LANGUAGE Forms of address vary widely from culture to culture. In some cultures, for instance, one shows respect by referring to all older women as if they were married, using the equivalent of the title *Mrs.* Usage in the United States is changing toward making no assumptions about marital status, rank, or other characteristics—for instance, using the title *Ms.* for a woman unless she is known to prefer *Mrs.* or *Miss.*

3 ■ Using appropriate labels

We often need to label groups: *swimmers, politicians, mothers, Christians, westerners, students.* But labels can be shorthand stereotypes when they generalize about groups of people on the basis of a single characteristic. They can also slight the person labeled and ignore the preferences of the group members themselves. Showing sensitivity when applying labels reveals you to be alert to readers' needs and concerns. Although sometimes dismissed as "political correctness," such sensitivity hurts no one and helps gain your readers' trust and respect.

- *Avoid labels that (intentionally or not) disparage the person or group you refer to.* A person with emotional problems is not a *mental patient.* A person with cancer is not a *cancer victim.* A person using a wheelchair is not *wheelchair-bound.*
- *Use names for racial, ethnic, and other groups that reflect the preferences of each group's members,* or at least many of them. Examples of current preferences include *African American* or *black, latino/latina* (for Americans and American immigrants of Spanish-speaking descent), and *disabled* (rather than *handicapped*). But labels change often. To learn how a group's members wish to be labeled, ask them directly, attend to usage in reputable periodicals, or check a recent dictionary.

A helpful reference for appropriate labels is *Guidelines for Bias-Free Writing,* by Marilyn Schwartz and the Task Force on Bias-Free Language of the Association of American University Presses.

EXERCISE
Revising: Appropriate words
Rewrite the following sentences as needed for standard American English. Consult a dictionary to determine whether particular words are appropriate and to find suitable substitutes.

> *Example:*
> If negotiators get hyper during contract discussions, they may mess up chances for a settlement.
> If negotiators <u>become excited or upset</u> during contract discussions, they may <u>harm</u> chances for a settlement.

1. Acquired immune deficiency syndrome (AIDS) is a major deal all over the world.
2. The disease gets around primarily by sexual intercourse, exchange of bodily fluids, shared needles, and blood transfusions.

3. Those who think the disease is limited to homos and druggies are quite mistaken.
4. Stats suggest that one in every five hundred college kids carries the virus.
5. A person with AIDS does not deserve to be subjected to exclusionary behavior or callousness on the part of his fellow citizens. Instead, he has the necessity for all the compassion, medical care, and financial assistance due those who are in the extremity of illness.
6. An AIDS victim often sees a team of doctors or a single doctor with a specialized practice.
7. The doctor may help his patients by obtaining social services for them as well as by providing medical care.
8. The AIDS sufferer who loses his job may need public assistance.
9. For someone who is very ill, a full-time nurse may be necessary. She can administer medications and make the sick person as comfortable as possible.
10. Some people with AIDS have insurance, but others lack the bread for premiums.

CHAPTER 39

Using Exact Language

To write clearly and effectively, you will want to find the words that fit your meaning exactly and convey your attitude precisely. If, like many people, you feel uncertain about words and their meanings, consult the chapters on using a dictionary (41) and improving your vocabulary (42).

Don't worry too much about choosing exact words while you are drafting an essay. If the right word doesn't come to you, leave a blank. Revision (p. 51) or editing (p. 58) is the stage to consider tone, specificity, and precision.

Note   A grammar and style checker can provide some help with inexact language. For instance, you can set it to flag commonly confused words (such as *continuous/continual*), misused prepositions in idioms (such as *accuse for* instead of *accuse of*), and clichés. But the checker can flag only words stored in its dictionary. It can't help you at all with inappropriate connotation, excessive abstraction, or other problems discussed in this chapter. You'll need to read your work carefully on your own.

39a   Using the right word for your meaning

Precisely expressing your meaning requires understanding both the denotations and the connotations of words. A word's **denotation** is the thing or idea it refers to, the meaning listed in the dictionary without reference to the emotional associations it may arouse in a reader. Using words according to their established deno-

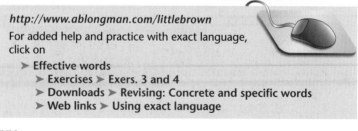

http://www.ablongman.com/littlebrown
For added help and practice with exact language, click on
➤ Effective words
  ➤ Exercises ➤ Exers. 3 and 4
  ➤ Downloads ➤ Revising: Concrete and specific words
  ➤ Web links ➤ Using exact language

tations is essential if readers are to grasp your meaning. Here are a few guidelines:

- Become acquainted with a dictionary. Consult it whenever you are unsure of a word's meaning.
- Distinguish between similar-sounding words that have widely different denotations:

    Inexact   Older people often suffer <u>infirmaries</u> [places for the sick].
    Exact   Older people often suffer <u>infirmities</u> [disabilities].

    Some words, called **homonyms** (from the Greek meaning "same name"), sound exactly alike but differ in meaning: for example, *principal/principle* or *rain/reign/rein*. (See pp. 590–91 for a list of commonly confused homonyms.)

- Distinguish between words with related but distinct denotations:

    Inexact   Television commercials <u>continuously</u> [unceasingly] interrupt programming.
    Exact   Television commercials <u>continually</u> [regularly] interrupt programming.

In addition to their emotion-free denotations, many words also carry associations with specific feelings. These **connotations** can shape readers' responses and are thus a powerful tool for writers. (At the same time they are a potential snare for readers. See p. 152.) Some connotations are personal: the word *dog,* for instance, may have negative connotations for the letter carrier who has been bitten three times. Usually, though, people agree about connotations. The following word pairs are just a few of many that have related denotations but very different connotations:

pride: sense of self-worth
vanity: excessive regard for oneself

firm: steady, unchanging, unyielding
stubborn: unreasonable, bullheaded

enthusiasm: excitement
mania: excessive interest or desire

http://www.ablongman.com/littlebrown
For added help and practice with denotation and connotation, click on
➤ **Effective words**
  ➤ **Exercises** ➤ **Exer. 3**
  ➤ **Web links** ➤ **Using exact language**

Understanding connotation is especially important in choosing among **synonyms,** words with approximately, but often not exactly, the same meanings. For instance, *cry* and *weep* both denote the shedding of tears, but *cry* more than *weep* connotes a sobbing sound accompanying the tears. *Sob* itself connotes broken, gasping crying, with tears, whereas *wail* connotes sustained sound, perhaps without tears.

Several resources can help you track down words with the exact connotations you want:

- A dictionary is essential. Many dictionaries list and distinguish among synonyms (see p. 588 for an example).
- A dictionary of synonyms lists and defines synonyms in groups (see p. 576 for a title).
- A thesaurus lists synonyms but does not distinguish among them (see p. 576 for a title).

Note Because a thesaurus lacks definitions, it can only suggest possibilities. You will still need a dictionary to discover the words' exact denotations and connotations. Most word processors include a thesaurus that makes it easy to look up synonyms and insert them into your documents. But with an electronic thesaurus, too, you must choose words carefully to ensure that they express your meaning exactly. (See p. 576 for more on electronic thesauruses.)

EXERCISE 1
Revising: Denotation
Revise any underlined word below that is not used according to its established denotation. Circle any word used correctly. Consult a dictionary if you are uncertain of a word's precise meaning.

Example:
Sam and Dave are going to Bermuda and Hauppauge, respect-fully, for spring vacation.
Sam and Dave are going to Bermuda and Hauppauge, respec-tively, for spring vacation.

1. Maxine Hong Kingston was rewarded many prizes for her first two books, *The Woman Warrior* and *China Men.*
2. Kingston sites her mother's tales about ancestors and ancient Chinese customs as the sources of these memoirs.
3. In her childhood Kingston was greatly effected by her mother's tale about a pregnant aunt who was ostracized by villagers.
4. The aunt gained avengeance by drowning herself in the village's water supply.
5. Kingston decided to make her nameless relative infamous by giving her immortality in *The Woman Warrior.*

EXERCISE 2
Considering the connotations of words

Fill the blank in each sentence below with the most appropriate word from the list in parentheses. Consult a dictionary to be sure of your choice.

Example:
Channel 5 _____ Oshu the winner before the polls closed. (*advertised, declared, broadcast, promulgated*)
Channel 5 <u>declared</u> Oshu the winner before the polls closed.

1. AIDS is a serious health _____. (*problem, worry, difficulty, plight*)
2. Once the virus has entered the blood system, it _____ T-cells. (*murders, destroys, slaughters, executes*)
3. The _____ of T-cells is to combat infections. (*ambition, function, aim, goal*)
4. Without enough T-cells, the body is nearly _____ against infections. (*defenseless, hopeless, desperate*)
5. To prevent exposure to the disease, one should be especially _____ in sexual relationships. (*chary, circumspect, cautious, calculating*)

39b   Balancing the abstract and concrete, the general and specific

To understand a subject as you understand it, your readers need ample guidance from your words. When you describe a building as *beautiful* and nothing more, you force readers to provide their own ideas of what makes a building beautiful. If readers bother (and they may not), they surely will not conjure up the image you had in mind. Use words to tell readers what you want them to know, that the beautiful building is *a sleek, silver skyscraper with blue-tinted windows,* for instance, or *a Victorian brick courthouse with tall, arched windows.*

Clear, exact writing balances abstract and general words, which outline ideas and objects, with concrete and specific words, which sharpen and solidify.

http://www.ablongman.com/littlebrown
For added help with concrete and specific language, click on
➤ **Effective words**
  ➤ **Downloads** ➤ **Revising: Concrete and specific words**
  ➤ **Web links** ➤ **Using exact language**

- **Abstract words** name qualities and ideas: *beauty, inflation, management, culture, liberal.* **Concrete words** name things we can know by our five senses of sight, hearing, touch, taste, and smell: *sleek, humming, brick, bitter, musty.*
- **General words** name classes or groups of things, such as *buildings, weather,* or *birds,* and include all the varieties of the class. **Specific words** limit a general class, such as *buildings,* by naming a variety, such as *skyscraper, Victorian courthouse,* or *hut.*

Note that *general* and *specific* are relative terms: the same word may be more general than some words but more specific than others.

General

weather	↑	bird
rain		parrot
downpour		cockatoo
sudden downpour	↓	my pet cockatoo Moyshe

Specific

Abstract and general words are useful in the broad statements that set the course for your writing:

The wild horse in America has a <u>romantic</u> history.

We must be <u>free</u> from <u>government interference</u> in our <u>affairs.</u>

<u>Relations</u> between the sexes today are only a <u>little</u> more <u>relaxed</u> than they were in the past.

But the sentences following these would have to develop the ideas with concrete and specific details. When your meaning calls for an abstract or general word, make sure you define it, explain it, and narrow it. Look at how concrete and specific information turns vague sentences into exact ones in the examples below:

| Vague | The size of his hands made his smallness real. [How big were his hands? How small was he?] |
| Exact | Not until I saw his delicate, doll-like hands did I realize that he stood a full head shorter than most other men. |

| Vague | The long flood caused a lot of awful destruction in the town. [How long did the flood last? What destruction did it cause? Why was the destruction awful?] |
| Exact | The flood waters, which rose swiftly and then stayed stubbornly high for days, killed at least six townspeople and made life a misery for the hundreds who had to evacuate their ruined homes and stores. |

If you write on a computer, you can use its Find function to help you find and revise abstract and general words that you tend to overuse. Examples of such words include *nice, interesting, things, very, good, a lot, a little,* and *some.*

EXERCISE 3
Revising: Concrete and specific words

Make the following paragraph vivid by expanding the sentences with appropriate details of your own choosing. Substitute concrete and specific words for the abstract and general ones that are underlined. (You can download a double-spaced, editable version of this exercise from this book's Web site: see the box on p. 555.)

    I remember <u>clearly</u> how <u>awful</u> I felt the first time I <u>attended</u> Mrs. Murphy's second-grade class. I had <u>recently</u> moved from a <u>small</u> town in Missouri to a <u>crowded</u> suburb of Chicago. My new school looked <u>big</u> from the outside and seemed <u>dark</u> inside as I <u>walked</u> down the <u>long</u> corridor toward the classroom. The class was <u>noisy</u> as I neared the door; but when I <u>entered</u>, <u>everyone</u> became <u>quiet</u> and <u>looked</u> at me. I felt <u>uncomfortable</u> and <u>wanted</u> a place to hide. However, in a <u>loud</u> voice Mrs. Murphy <u>directed</u> me to the front of the room to introduce myself.

EXERCISE 4
Using concrete and specific words

For each abstract or general word below, give at least two other words or phrases that illustrate increasing specificity or concreteness. Consult a dictionary as needed. Use the most specific or concrete word from each group in a sentence of your own.

    Example:
    awake, <u>watchful</u>, <u>vigilant</u>
    <u>Vigilant</u> guards patrol the buldings.

1. fabric	6. green	11. teacher
2. delicious	7. walk (*verb*)	12. nice
3. car	8. flower	13. virtue
4. narrow-minded	9. serious	14. angry
5. reach (*verb*)	10. pretty	15. crime

39c   Using idioms

    Idioms are expressions in any language whose meanings cannot be determined simply from the words in them or whose component words cannot be predicted by any rule of grammar; often, they

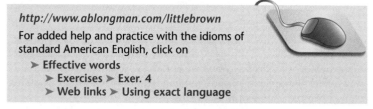

http://www.ablongman.com/littlebrown
For added help and practice with the idioms of standard American English, click on
➤ **Effective words**
    ➤ **Exercises** ➤ **Exer. 4**
    ➤ **Web links** ➤ **Using exact language**

violate conventional grammar. Examples of English idioms include *put up with, plug away at,* and *make off with.*

Idiomatic combinations of verbs or adjectives and prepositions can be confusing for both native and nonnative speakers of English. A number of these pairings are listed in the box below.

Idioms with prepositions

abide by a rule
abide in a place or state

accords with
according to

accuse of a crime

adapt from a source
adapt to a situation

afraid of

agree on a plan
agree to a proposal
agree with a person

angry with

aware of

based on

capable of

certain of

charge for a purchase
charge with a crime

concur in an opinion
concur with a person

contend for a principle
contend with a person

dependent on

differ about or over a question
differ from in some quality
differ with a person

disappointed by or in a person
disappointed in or with a thing

familiar with

identical with or to

impatient at her conduct
impatient of restraint
impatient for a raise
impatient with a person

independent of

infer from

inferior to

involved in a task
involved with a person

oblivious of or to one's surroundings
oblivious of something forgotten

occupied by a person
occupied in study
occupied with a thing

opposed to

part from a person
part with a possession

prior to

proud of

related to

rewarded by the judge
rewarded for something done
rewarded with a gift

similar to

superior to

wait at a place
wait for a train, a person
wait on a customer

CULTURE **LANGUAGE** If you are learning standard American English, you are justified in stumbling over its prepositions: their meanings can shift depending on context, and they have many idiomatic uses. In mastering the prepositions of standard English, you probably can't avoid memorization. But you can help yourself by memorizing related groups, such as the following.

At, in, or on in expressions of time

- Use *at* before actual clock time: <u>at</u> 8:30.
- Use <u>in</u> before a month, year, century, or period: <u>in</u> April, <u>in</u> 2007, <u>in</u> the twenty-first century, <u>in</u> the next month.
- Use <u>on</u> before a day or date: <u>on</u> Tuesday, <u>on</u> August 3, <u>on</u> Labor Day.

At, in, or on in expressions of place

- Use *at* before a specific place or address: <u>at</u> the school, <u>at</u> 511 Iris Street.
- Use *in* before a place with limits or before a city, state, country, or continent: <u>in</u> the house, <u>in</u> a box, <u>in</u> Oklahoma City, <u>in</u> China, <u>in</u> Asia.
- Use *on* to mean "supported by" or "touching the surface of": <u>on</u> the table, <u>on</u> Iris Street, <u>on</u> page 150.

For or since in expressions of time

- Use *for* before a period of time: <u>for</u> an hour, <u>for</u> two years.
- Use *since* before a specific point in time: <u>since</u> 1999, <u>since</u> Friday.

A dictionary of English as a second language is the best source for the meanings of prepositions; see the recommendations on page 574. In addition, some references focus on prepositions. See, for instance, volume 1 (*Verbs with Prepositions and Particles*) of the *Oxford Dictionary of Current Idiomatic English*.

EXERCISE 5
Using prepositions in idioms

Insert the preposition that correctly completes each idiom in the following sentences. Consult the box on the previous page or a dictionary as needed.

Example:

I disagree _____ many feminists who say women should not be homemakers.

I disagree <u>with</u> many feminists who say women should not be homemakers.

1. As Mark and Lana waited _____ the justice of the peace, they seemed oblivious _____ the other people in the lobby.
2. But Mark inferred _____ Lana's glance at a handsome man that she was no longer occupied _____ him alone.
3. Angry _____ Lana, Mark charged her _____ not loving him enough to get married.
4. Impatient _____ Mark's childish behavior, Lana disagreed _____ his interpretation of her glance.
5. They decided that if they could differ so violently _____ a minor incident, they should part _____ each other.

39d   Using figurative language

Figurative language (or a **figure of speech**) departs from the literal meanings (the denotations) of words, usually by comparing very different ideas or objects:

Literal	As I try to write, I can think of nothing to say.
Figurative	As I try to write, <u>my mind is a slab of black slate</u>.

Imaginatively and carefully used, figurative language can capture meaning more precisely and feelingly than literal language.

Figurative language is commonplace in speech. Having *slept like a log*, you may get up to find it *raining cats and dogs*. But the rapid exchange of speech leaves little time for inventiveness, and most figures of daily conversation, like those above, are worn and hackneyed. Writing gives you time to reject the tired figure and to search out fresh, concrete words and phrases.

The two most common figures of speech are the simile and the metaphor. Both compare two things of different classes, often one abstract and the other concrete. A **simile** makes the comparison explicit and usually begins with *like* or *as:*

> Whenever we grow, we tend to feel it, <u>as</u> a young seed must feel the weight and inertia of the earth when it seeks to break out of its shell on its way to becoming a plant.   —ALICE WALKER

> To hold America in one's thoughts is <u>like</u> holding a love letter in one's hand—it has so special a meaning.   —E. B. WHITE

Instead of stating a comparison, a **metaphor** implies it, omitting such words as *like* or *as:*

> I cannot and will not cut my conscience to fit this year's fashions.
> —LILLIAN HELLMAN

> A school is a hopper into which children are heaved while they are young and tender; therein they are pressed into certain standard shapes and covered from head to heels with official rubber stamps.
> —H. L. MENCKEN

Two other figures of speech are personification and hyperbole. **Personification** treats ideas and objects as if they were human:

> The economy consumes my money and gives me little in return.

> I could hear the whisper of snowflakes, nudging each other as they fell.

Hyperbole deliberately exaggerates:

> She appeared in a mile of billowing chiffon, flashing a rhinestone as big as an ostrich egg.

He yelled so loud that his voice carried to the next county.

To be successful, figurative language must be fresh and unstrained, calling attention not to itself but to the writer's meaning. One kind of figurative language gone wrong is the **mixed metaphor,** in which the writer combines two or more incompatible figures. Since metaphors often generate visual images in the reader's mind, a mixed metaphor can be laughable:

Mixed   Various thorny problems that we try to sweep under the rug continue to bob up all the same.

To revise a mixed metaphor, follow through consistently with just one image:

Improved   Various thorny problems that we try to weed out continue to thrive all the same.

EXERCISE 6
Analyzing figurative language
Identify each figure of speech in the following sentences as a simile or a metaphor, and analyze how it adds to the writer's meaning.

1. A distant airplane, a delta wing out of nightmare, made a gliding shadow on the creek's bottom that looked like a stingray crossing upstream.   —ANNIE DILLARD
2. Her roots ran deep into the earth, and from those roots she drew strength enough to hold still against all the forces of chance and disorder.   —N. SCOTT MOMADAY
3. As a member of the winning team (the graduating class of 1940) I had outdistanced unpleasant sensations by miles. I was headed for the freedom of open fields.   —MAYA ANGELOU
4. All artists quiver under the lash of adverse criticism.
          —CATHERINE DRINKER BOWEN
5. Every writer, in a roomful of writers, wants to be the best, and the judge, or umpire, or referee is soon overwhelmed and shouted down like a chickadee trying to take charge of a caucus of crows.   —JAMES THURBER

EXERCISE 7
Using figurative language
Invent appropriate figurative language of your own (simile, metaphor, hyperbole, or personification) to describe each scene or quality below, and use the figure in a sentence.

Example:
The attraction of a lake on a hot day
The small waves <u>like fingers beckoned</u> us irresistibly.

1. The sound of a kindergarten classroom
2. People waiting in line to buy tickets to a rock concert

3. The politeness of strangers meeting for the first time
4. A streetlight seen through dense fog
5. The effect of watching television for ten hours straight

39e Using fresh, not trite, expressions

Trite expressions, or **clichés,** are phrases so old and so often repeated that they have become stale. They include the following:

acid test	ladder of success
add insult to injury	moving experience
better late than never	needle in a haystack
beyond the shadow of a doubt	nose to the grindstone
brought back to reality	nutty as a fruitcake
cold, hard facts	point with pride
cool as a cucumber	ripe old age
cool, calm, and collected	sadder but wiser
crushing blow	shoulder the burden
dyed in the wool	smart as a whip
easier said than done	sneaking suspicion
face the music	sober as a judge
flat as a pancake	stand in awe
gentle as a lamb	strong as an ox
green with envy	thin as a rail
hard as a rock	tired but happy
heavy as lead	tried and true
hit the nail on the head	untimely death
hour of need	wise as an owl

Besides these old phrases, stale writing may also depend on fashionable words that are losing their effect: for instance, *lifestyle, enhance, excellent, fantastic,* and *caring.*

Many of these expressions were once fresh and forceful, but constant use has dulled them. They, in turn, will dull your writing by suggesting that you have not thought about what you are saying and have resorted to the easiest phrase.

Clichés may slide into your drafts while you are trying to express your meaning. In editing, then, be wary of any expression you have heard or used before. Substitute fresh words of your own or restate the idea in plain language.

Trite   A healthful <u>lifestyle enhances</u> your ability to <u>go for the</u> <u>gold</u>, allows <u>you to enjoy life to the fullest</u>, and helps you live <u>to a ripe old age</u>.

Revised   Living <u>healthfully</u> helps you <u>perform well</u>, enjoy life <u>thoroughly</u>, and <u>live long</u>.

EXERCISE 8
Revising: Trite expressions

Revise the following sentences to eliminate trite expressions.

Example:

The basketball team had almost seized victory, but it faced the test of truth in the last quarter of the game.

The basketball team <u>seemed about to win</u>, but the <u>real test</u> came in the last quarter of the game.

1. The disastrous consequences of the war have shaken the small nation to its roots.
2. Prices for food have shot sky high, and citizens have sneaking suspicions that others are making a killing on the black market.
3. Medical supplies are so few and far between that even civilians who are as sick as dogs cannot get treatment.
4. With most men fighting or injured or killed, women have had to bite the bullet and bear the men's burden in farming and manufacturing.
5. Last but not least, the war's heavy drain on the nation's pocket-book has left the economy in a shambles.

CHAPTER 40

Writing Concisely

Concise writing makes every word count. Conciseness is not the same as mere brevity: detail and originality should not be cut along with needless words. Rather, the length of an expression should be appropriate to the thought.

You may find yourself writing wordily when you are unsure of your subject or when your thoughts are tangled. It's fine, even necessary, to stumble and grope while drafting. But you should straighten out your ideas and eliminate wordiness during revision and editing.

 Note Any grammar and style checker will identify at least some wordy structures, such as repeated words, weak verbs, passive voice, and *there is* and *it is* constructions. But a checker can't identify all potentially wordy structures, nor can it tell you whether a structure is appropriate for your ideas. In short, a checker can't substitute for your own careful reading and editing.

CULTURE LANGUAGE As you'll see in the examples that follow, wordiness is not a problem of incorrect grammar. A sentence may be perfectly grammatical but still contain unneeded words that interfere with your idea.

40a Focusing on the subject and verb

Using the subjects and verbs of your sentences for the key actors and actions will reduce words and emphasize important ideas. (See pp. 404–06 for more on this topic.)

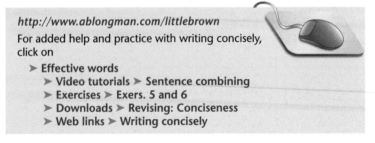

http://www.ablongman.com/littlebrown
For added help and practice with writing concisely, click on
➤ **Effective words**
  ➤ Video tutorials ➤ Sentence combining
  ➤ Exercises ➤ Exers. 5 and 6
  ➤ Downloads ➤ Revising: Conciseness
  ➤ Web links ➤ Writing concisely

Ways to achieve conciseness

Wordy (87 words)

The highly pressured <u>nature</u> of critical-care nursing <u>is due to the fact that</u> the patients have life-threatening illnesses. Critical-care nurses must have possession of steady nerves to care for patients who are critically ill and very sick. The nurses must also have possession of interpersonal skills. They must also have medical skills. It is considered by most health-care professionals that these nurses are essential if there is to be improvement of patients who are now in critical care from that status to the status of intermediate care.

Focus on subject and verb, and cut or shorten empty words and phrases.

Avoid nouns made from verbs.

Cut unneeded repetition.

Combine sentences.

Change passive voice to active voice.

Eliminate *there is* constructions.

Cut unneeded repetition, and reduce clauses and phrases.

Concise (37 words)

Critical-care nursing is highly pressured because the patients have life-threatening illnesses. Critical-care nurses must possess steady nerves and interpersonal and medical skills. Most health-care professionals consider these nurses essential if patients are to improve to intermediate care.

Wordy	The <u>reason</u> why most of the country shifts to daylight savings <u>time</u> <u>is</u> that winter days are much shorter than summer days.
Concise	Most of the <u>country</u> <u>shifts</u> to daylight savings time because winter <u>days</u> are much shorter than summer days.

Focusing on subjects and verbs will also help you avoid several other causes of wordiness (also discussed further on pages 404–06):

Nouns made from verbs

Wordy	The <u>occurrence</u> of the winter solstice, the shortest day of the year, <u>is</u> an event occurring about December 22.
Concise	The winter <u>solstice</u>, the shortest day of the year, <u>occurs</u> about December 22.

http://www.ablongman.com/littlebrown

For added practice focusing on the subject and verb, click on

➤ **Sentences** ➤ **Exercises** ➤ **Exer. 52**

w

40b

Weak verbs

Wordy   The earth's axis has a tilt as the planet is in orbit around
         the sun so that the northern and southern hemispheres
         are alternately in alignment toward the sun.

Concise The earth's axis tilts as the planet orbits around the sun
         so that the northern and southern hemispheres alter-
         nately align toward the sun.

Passive voice

Wordy   During its winter the northern hemisphere is tilted far-
         thest away from the sun, so the nights are made longer
         and the days are made shorter.

Concise During its winter the northern hemisphere tilts away from
         the sun, making the nights longer and the days shorter.

See also page 315 on changing the passive voice to the active
voice, as in the example above.

40b Cutting or shortening empty words and phrases

Empty words and phrases walk in place, gaining little or nothing in meaning. Shorten them to their essential meaning, or cut
them entirely. Your writing will move faster and work harder.

Many empty phrases can be cut entirely:

all things considered	in a manner of speaking
as far as I'm concerned	in my opinion
for all intents and purposes	last but not least
for the most part	more or less

Wordy   As far as I am concerned, discrimination against women
          continues to exist in medicine for all intents and pur-
          poses.

Revised   Discrimination against women continues in medicine.

Other empty words can be cut along with some of the words around
them:

angle	character	kind	situation
area	element	manner	thing
aspect	factor	nature	type
case	field		

Wordy		The <u>type</u> of large expenditures on advertising that manufacturers must make is a very important <u>aspect</u> of the cost of detergents.
Concise		Manufacturers' large advertising expenditures increase the cost of detergents.

Still other empty phrases can be reduced from several words to a single word:

For	Substitute
at all times	always
at the present time	now
at this point in time	now
in the nature of	like
for the purpose of	for
in order to	to
until such time as	until
for the reason that	because
due to the fact that	because
because of the fact that	because
by virtue of the fact that	because
in the event that	if
by means of	by
in the final analysis	finally

Wordy		<u>At this point in time</u>, the software is expensive <u>due to the fact that</u> it has no competition.
Revised		The software is expensive <u>now</u> <u>because</u> it has no competition.

EXERCISE 1
Revising: Subjects and verbs; empty words and phrases
Revise the following sentences to achieve conciseness by focusing on subjects and verbs and by cutting or reducing empty words and phrases. (See p. 406 for an additional exercise in focusing on subjects and verbs.)

Example:

I made college my destination because of many factors, but most of all because of the fact that I want a career in medicine.

I <u>came</u> to college <u>mainly because</u> I want a career in medicine.

1. *Gerrymandering* refers to a situation in which the lines of a voting district are redrawn so that a particular party or ethnic group has benefits.
2. The name is a reference to the fact that Elbridge Gerry, the governor of Massachusetts in 1812, redrew voting districts in Essex County.
3. On the map one new district was seen to resemble something in the nature of a salamander.

4. Upon seeing the map, a man who was for all intents and purposes a critic of Governor Gerry's administration cried out, "Gerrymander!"
5. At the present time, changes may be made in the character of a district's voting pattern by a political group by gerrymandering to achieve the exclusion of rival groups' supporters.

40c   Cutting unnecessary repetition

Planned repetition and restatement can make writing more coherent (p. 84) or emphatic (p. 411). But unnecessary repetition weakens sentences:

Wordy	Many unskilled workers <u>without training in a particular job</u> are unemployed <u>and do not have any work</u>.
Concise	Many unskilled workers are unemployed.

The use of one word two different ways within a sentence is confusing:

Confusing	Preschool instructors play a <u>role</u> in the child's understanding of male and female <u>roles</u>.
Clear	Preschool instructors contribute to the child's understanding of male and female roles.

The simplest kind of useless repetition is the phrase that says the same thing twice. In the following examples, the unneeded words are underlined:

biography <u>of his life</u>	habitual <u>custom</u>
circle <u>around</u>	important [basic] <u>essentials</u>
consensus <u>of opinion</u>	large <u>in size</u>
continue <u>on</u>	puzzling <u>in nature</u>
cooperate <u>together</u>	repeat <u>again</u>
few <u>in number</u>	return <u>again</u>
final <u>completion</u>	revert <u>back</u>
frank <u>and honest</u> exchange	square [round] <u>in shape</u>
the future <u>to come</u>	surrounding <u>circumstances</u>

CULTURE LANGUAGE ❧ Phrases like those above are redundant because the main word already implies the underlined word or words. The repetition is not emphatic but tedious. A dictionary will tell you what meanings a word implies. *Assassinate,* for instance, means "murder someone well known," so the following sentence is redundant: *Julius Caesar was <u>assassinated and killed</u>.*

EXERCISE 2
Revising: Unnecessary repetition
Revise the following sentences to achieve conciseness. Concentrate on eliminating repetition and redundancy.

Example:

Because the circumstances surrounding the cancellation of classes were murky and unclear, the editor of the student newspaper assigned a staff reporter to investigate and file a report on the circumstances.

Because the circumstances leading to the cancellation of classes were unclear, the editor of the student newspaper assigned a staffer to investigate and report the story.

1. Some Vietnam veterans coming back to the United States after their tours of duty in Vietnam had problems readjusting again to life in America.
2. Afflicted with post-traumatic stress disorder, a psychological disorder that sometimes arises after a trauma, some veterans had psychological problems that caused them to have trouble holding jobs and maintaining relationships.
3. Some who used to use drugs in Vietnam could not break their drug habits after they returned back to the United States.
4. The few veterans who committed crimes and violent acts gained so much notoriety and fame that many Americans thought all veterans were crazy, insane maniacs.
5. As a result of such stereotyping of Vietnam-era veterans, veterans are included into the same antidiscrimination laws that protect other victims of discrimination.

40d Reducing clauses to phrases, phrases to single words

Modifiers—subordinate clauses, phrases, and single words—can be expanded or contracted depending on the emphasis you want to achieve. (See pp. 249–64 on phrases and clauses and 419–22 on working with modifiers.) When editing your sentences, consider whether any modifiers can be reduced without loss of emphasis or clarity:

Wordy   The Channel Tunnel, which runs between Britain and France, bores through a bed of solid chalk that is twenty-three miles across.

Concise   The Channel Tunnel between Britain and France bores through twenty-three miles of solid chalk.

40e Eliminating *there is* and *it is* constructions

You can postpone the sentence subject with the words *there is* (*there are, there was, there were*) and *it is* (*it was*). (See p. 271.) These constructions can be useful to emphasize the subject (as when introducing it for the first time) or to indicate a change in direction.

But often they just add words and create limp substitutes for more vigorous sentences:

> Wordy   There were delays and cost overruns that plagued construction of the Channel Tunnel. It is the expectation of investors to earn profits at last, now that there are trains passing daily through the tunnel.
>
> Concise   Delays and cost overruns plagued construction of the Channel Tunnel. Investors expect to earn profits at last, now that trains pass daily through the tunnel.

40f Combining sentences

Often the information in two or more sentences can be combined into one tight sentence:

> Wordy   An unexpected problem with the Channel Tunnel is stowaways. The stowaways are mostly illegal immigrants. They are trying to smuggle themselves into England. They cling to train roofs and undercarriages.
>
> Concise   An unexpected problem with the Channel Tunnel is stowaways, mostly illegal immigrants who are trying to smuggle themselves into England by clinging to train roofs and undercarriages.

A number of exercises in this handbook give you practice in sentence combining. For a list, see "Sentence combining" in the Index.

40g Rewriting jargon

Jargon can refer to the special vocabulary of any discipline or profession (see p. 546). But it has also come to describe vague, inflated language that is overcomplicated, even incomprehensible. When it comes from government or business, we call it *bureaucratese*. It sounds almost as if the writer deliberately ignored every suggestion for clear, concise writing:

> Jargon   The necessity for individuals to become separate entities in their own right may impel children to engage

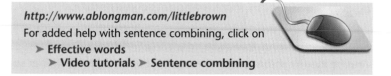

http://www.ablongman.com/littlebrown
For added help with sentence combining, click on
➤ **Effective words**
  ➤ **Video tutorials** ➤ **Sentence combining**

in open rebelliousness against parental authority or against sibling influence, with resultant bewilderment of those being rebelled against.

w

40g

Translation   Children's natural desire to become themselves may make them rebel against bewildered parents or siblings.

Jargon   The weekly social gatherings stimulate networking among members of management from various divisions, with the aim of developing contacts and maximizing the flow of creative information.

Translation   The weekly parties give managers from different divisions a chance to meet and to share ideas.

EXERCISE 3
Revising: Conciseness

Rewrite each passage below into a single concise sentence, using the techniques described in this chapter.

> *Example:*
> He was taking some exercise in the park. Then several thugs were suddenly ahead in his path.
>
> He was exercising [or jogging or strolling] in the park when several thugs suddenly loomed in his path.

1. Chewing gum was originally introduced to the United States by Antonio López de Santa Anna. He was the Mexican general.
2. After he had been defeated by the Texans in 1845, the general, who was exiled, made the choice to settle in New York.
3. A piece of chicle had been stashed by the general in his baggage. Chicle is the dried milky sap of the Mexican sapodilla tree.
4. There was more of this resin brought into the country by Santa Anna's friend Thomas Adams. Adams had a plan to make rubber.
5. The plan failed. Then the occasion arose for Adams to get a much more successful idea on the basis of the use to which the resin was put by General Santa Anna. That is, Adams decided to make a gum that could be chewed.

EXERCISE 4
Revising: Conciseness

Make the following passage as concise as possible. Be merciless. (You can download a double-spaced, editable version of this exercise from this book's Web site: see the box on p. 564.)

At the end of a lengthy line of reasoning, he came to the conclusion that the situation with carcinogens [cancer-causing substances] should be regarded as similar to the situation with the automobile. Instead of giving in to an irrational fear of cancer, we should consider all aspects of the problem in a balanced and dispassionate frame of mind, making a total of the benefits received from potential carcinogens (plastics, pesticides, and other similar products) and measuring said total against the damage done by such products. This is the nature of most discussions about the automobile. Instead of responding irrationally to the visual, aural, and air pollution caused by automobiles, we have decided to live with them (while simultaneously working to improve on them) for the benefits brought to society as a whole.

CHAPTER 41

Using Dictionaries

A dictionary can answer most of the questions about words you may ask. This chapter will show you how to choose a dictionary that suits your purpose and how to read a dictionary without difficulty.

41a Choosing a dictionary

1 ■ Abridged dictionaries

Abridged dictionaries are the most practical for everyday use. Often called desk dictionaries because of their convenient size, they usually list 150,000 to 200,000 words and concentrate on fairly common words and meanings.

Most of the dictionaries listed here are available both in print and on CD-ROM, and some are available online (see the box below). Your word processor may include a dictionary that you can customize with words or meanings it does not cover. With an electronic dictionary, as with a print dictionary, you can look up words as you write, checking spellings, meanings, synonyms, and other information.

> *The American Heritage College Dictionary.* This dictionary usually lists each word's most common meanings first. It is a more prescriptive dictionary than some of the others listed here, liberally applying usage labels (*slang, informal,* and so on) and including hundreds of usage notes.
>
> *Merriam-Webster's Collegiate Dictionary.* Based on the unabridged *Webster's Third New International* (see p. 575), this dictionary is more descriptive than prescriptive, emphasizing how the lan-

http://www.ablongman.com/littlebrown
For links to online dictionaries and other language resources, click on
➤ **Effective words** ➤ **Web links** ➤ **Dictionaries**

guage is actually used. Thus it applies usage labels less frequently than do some other dictionaries. It also emphasizes word histories, arranging meanings in order of their appearance in the language.

The Random House Webster's College Dictionary. Based on the unabridged *Random House Dictionary* (see below), this dictionary lists each word's most common meanings first. The dictionary avoids sexist language in definitions and explanations, and its usage notes indicate words or meanings considered offensive or disparaging to groups such as women and minorities. Appendixes include guidelines for avoiding sexist language.

Webster's New World Dictionary. This dictionary arranges meanings in order of their appearance in the language. Usage labels (*colloquial*, *slang*, and so on) are applied liberally, and words and phrases of American origin are starred.

CULTURE LANGUAGE If English is not your first language, you probably should have a dictionary prepared especially for ESL students in addition to one of the dictionaries listed above. The dictionaries listed below give much more information on such matters as count versus noncount nouns, prepositions with verbs and adjectives, and other concerns of ESL students.

COBUILD English Language Dictionary.

Longman Dictionary of Contemporary English. Longman Dictionary of American English is the American abridgment.

Oxford Advanced Learner's Dictionary. Oxford ESL Dictionary is the American edition.

2 ▪ Unabridged dictionaries

Unabridged dictionaries are the most scholarly and comprehensive of all dictionaries, sometimes consisting of many volumes. They emphasize the history of words and the variety of their uses. An unabridged dictionary is useful when you are studying a word in depth, reading or writing about the literature of another century, or looking for a quotation containing a particular word. The following unabridged dictionaries are available at most libraries.

The Oxford English Dictionary, 20 volumes. This is the greatest dictionary of the English language, defining over half a million words. Its entries illustrate the changes in a word's spelling, pronunciation, and meaning with quotations from writers of every century. Some entries span pages. The dictionary focuses on British words and meanings but includes American words and meanings.

The Random House Dictionary of the English Language. This dictionary is smaller (and less expensive) than many unabridged dictionaries. Its entries and definitions are especially up to date, and it includes hundreds of usage notes. Among its appendixes are short dictionaries of French, Spanish, Italian, and German.

Webster's Third New International Dictionary of the English Language. This dictionary attempts to record our language more as it *is* used than as it *should be* used. Therefore, usage labels (such as *slang*) are minimal. The dictionary gives meanings in order of their appearance in the language and provides most acceptable spellings and pronunciations. Plentiful illustrative quotations show variations in the uses of words.

3 ■ Special dictionaries

Special dictionaries limit their attention to a single class of word (for example, slang, engineering terms, abbreviations), to a single kind of information (synonyms, usage, word origins), or to a specific subject (African American culture, biography, history). (See Chapters 52–55 for lists of subject dictionaries in various academic disciplines.)

For guidance on English usage

Usage guides provide help with commonly confused and misused words, phrases, idioms, and other matters:

Follett, Wilson. *Modern American Usage.* Edited by Jacques Barzun.
Morris, William, and Mary Morris. *Harper Dictionary of Contemporary Usage.*
The New Fowler's Modern English Usage. Edited by R. W. Burchfield.

CULTURE LANGUAGE *Practical English Usage,* by Michael Swan, is a usage guide prepared especially for nonnative speakers of English.

For the origins of words

Dictionaries of etymology, or word history, explain how words have evolved:

Oxford Dictionary of English Etymology. Edited by Charles T. Onions et al.
Partridge, Eric. *Origins: A Short Etymological Dictionary of Modern English.*

For information on slang

Dictionaries of slang explain the histories and meanings of conversational expressions. They can make entertaining reading.

Green, Jonathan. *Cassell's Dictionary of Slang.*
Partridge, Eric. *A Concise Dictionary of Slang and Unconventional English.* Edited by Paul Beale.

Wentworth, Harold, and Stuart Berg Flexner. *Dictionary of American Slang.*

For information about synonyms

A thesaurus like *Roget's* provides extensive lists of words with related meanings. A dictionary of synonyms like *Webster's* contains discussions and illustrations of shades of meaning.

Roget's International Thesaurus. Revised by Robert L. Chapman.

Webster's New Dictionary of Synonyms.

Many electronic dictionaries include a thesaurus as well, and some thesauruses are available independently on CD-ROM or on-line. (This book's Web site provides links: see the box on p. 573.) With the thesaurus on your word processor, you can easily find synonyms and insert them into your documents. Take care with any thesaurus, ensuring that you know the meaning of a synonym before you use it.

41b Working with a dictionary's contents

Dictionaries use abbreviations and symbols to squeeze a lot of information into a relatively small book. This system of condensed information may at first seem difficult to read. But all dictionaries include in their opening pages detailed information on the arrangement of entries, pronunciation symbols, and abbreviations. And the format is quite similar from one dictionary to another, so becoming familiar with the abbreviations and symbols in one dictionary makes reading any dictionary an easy routine.

Here is a fairly typical entry, from *Merriam-Webster's Collegiate Dictionary.* The labeled parts are discussed on the pages that follow.

Spelling and word division — Pronunciation — Etymology — Meanings — Quotation and source — Idioms — Grammatical functions and forms — Label — Synonym

reck•on \'re-kən\ *vb* **reck•oned; reck•on•ing** \'re-kə-niŋ, 'rek-niŋ\ [ME *rekenen, fr.* OE *-recenian* (as in *gerecenian* to narrate); akin to OE *reccan*] *vt* (13c) **1 a :** COUNT ⟨~ the days till Christmas⟩ **b :** ESTIMATE, COMPUTE ⟨~ the height of a building⟩ **c :** to determine by reference to a fixed basis ⟨the existence of the U.S. is ~*ed* from the Declaration of Independence⟩ **2 :** to regard or think of as: CONSIDER **3** *chiefly dial* : THINK, SUPPOSE ⟨I ~ I've outlived my time —Ellen Glasgow⟩ ~ *vi* **1 :** to settle accounts **2 :** to make a calculation **3 a :** JUDGE **b** *chiefly dial* : SUPPOSE, THINK **4 :** to accept something as certain : place reliance ⟨I ~ on your promise to help⟩ — **reckon with** to take into consideration — **reckon without :** to fail to consider : IGNORE

41b

Spelling and word division

The small initial letters for *reckon* indicate that it is not normally capitalized. (In contrast, *Franklin stove* is capitalized in *Merriam-Webster's* because *Franklin* is a proper noun.)

The centered period in **reck·on** shows the division into syllables. If you are breaking a word at the end of a line, follow the dictionary's division of the word into syllables. For a hyphenated compound word, such as *cross-question,* a dictionary shows the hyphen as part of the spelling: **cross-ques·tion.**

Dictionaries provide any acceptable variant spellings of a word at the beginning of an entry. For the word *dexterous, Merriam-Webster's* has "**dex·ter·ous** or **dex·trous.**"

Pronunciation

In *Merriam-Webster's* the pronunciation appears in reversed slashes (\\). The stressed syllable is preceded by an accent mark (**'re-kən**).

Dictionaries use symbols to indicate how to pronounce a word because the alphabet itself does not record all the sounds in the language. (Listen, for example, to the different sounds of *a* in only three words: *far, make,* and *answer.*) Most dictionaries provide a key to the pronunciation symbols at the foot of each page or every two facing pages.

Grammatical functions and forms

Dictionaries give helpful information about a word's functions and forms. The *Merriam-Webster's* entry for *reckon* shows the word to be a verb (*vb*), with the past tense and past participle *reckoned* and the present participle *reckoning,* and with both transitive (*vt*) and intransitive (*vi*) meanings. (For the definitions of these terms, see pp. 284 and 243–44.)

Most dictionaries provide not only the principal forms of regular and irregular verbs but also the plural forms of irregular nouns and the *-er* and *-est* forms of adjectives and adverbs. An adjective or adverb without *-er* and *-est* forms in the dictionary requires the addition of *more* and *most* to show comparison (see p. 336).

Etymology

Dictionaries provide the **etymology** of a word (its history) to indicate its origin and the evolution of its meanings and forms. The dictionary can compress much information about a word into a small space through symbols, abbreviations, and different type fonts. An explanation of these systems appears in the dictionary's opening pages. *Merriam-Webster's* traces *reckon* back most recently to Middle English (ME) and then further back to Old English (OE).

The notation "(13c)" before the first definition indicates that the first recorded use of *reckon* to mean "count" occurred in the thirteenth century. When seeking the etymology of a word, be sure to read the entire history, not just the most recent event.

Meanings

Dictionaries divide the general meaning of a word into particular meanings on the basis of how the word is or has been actually used. They arrange a word's meanings differently, either in order of their appearance in the language, earliest first, or in order of their frequency of use, most common first. (*Merriam-Webster's* follows the former practice.) To learn your dictionary's arrangement, consult its opening pages. Then read through a word's entire entry before settling on the meaning that fits the context of what you're reading or writing.

The *Merriam-Webster's* entry for *reckon* ends with two uses of the word in idiomatic expressions (*reckon with* and *reckon without*). These phrases are defined because, as with all idioms, their meanings cannot be inferred simply from the words they consist of (see pp. 557–58).

Labels

Dictionaries apply labels to words or to particular meanings that have a special status or use.

Style labels restrict a word or one of its meanings to a particular level of usage:

- *Slang:* words or meanings inappropriate in writing except for a special effect, such as *crumb* for "a worthless or despicable person."
- *Informal* or *colloquial:* words or meanings appropriate for informal writing but not formal writing, such as *great* to mean "very good," as in *a great movie.*
- *Nonstandard* or *substandard:* words or meanings inappropriate for standard American English, such as *ain't.*
- *Vulgar* or *vulgar slang:* words or meanings considered offensive in speech and writing, such as profanity.
- *Poetic* or *literary:* words or meanings used only in poetry or the most formal writing, such as *eve* for *evening* and *o'er* for *over.*

Subject labels tell us that a word or one of its meanings has a special use in a discipline or profession. In its entry for *relaxation,* for instance, *American Heritage* presents specialized meanings with the subject labels *physiology, physics,* and *mathematics.*

Region labels indicate that a particular spelling, pronunciation, or meaning of a word is not national but limited to an area. A regional difference may be indicated by the label *dialect. Merriam-*

Webster's labels as dialect (*dial*) the uses of *reckon* to mean "suppose" or "think" (as in *I reckon I'll do that*). More specific region labels may designate areas of the United States or other countries.

Time labels indicate words or their meanings that the language, in evolving, has discarded. *Obsolete* designates words or meanings that are no longer used; *archaic* designates words or meanings that are out of date but used occasionally.

See pages 542–50 for further discussion of levels of usage and their appropriateness in your writing.

Synonyms

Synonyms are words whose meanings are approximately the same, such as *small* and *little*. *Merriam-Webster's* defines *reckon* with some words in small capital letters (COUNT, ESTIMATE, CONSIDER, and so on). These are both synonyms and cross-references, in that each word may be looked up in its alphabetical place. Some dictionaries devote separate paragraphs to words with many synonyms. (See p. 588 for a discussion of how to use the synonyms provided by a dictionary to increase your vocabulary.)

Illustrative quotations

Dictionaries are made by collecting quotations showing actual uses of words in all kinds of speech and writing. Some of these quotations, or others that the dictionary makers invent, may appear in the dictionary's entries as illustrations of how a word may be used. Five such quotations illustrate uses of *reckon* in the *Merriam-Webster's* entry (in these quotations, ~ stands for the word being illustrated).

Unabridged dictionaries usually provide many such quotations, not only to illustrate a word's current uses but also to show the changes in its meanings over time. Abridged dictionaries use quotations more selectively: to illustrate an unusual meaning of the word, to help distinguish between two closely related meanings of the same word, or to show the differences between synonyms.

EXERCISE
Using a dictionary

Consult your dictionary on five of the following words. First find out whether your dictionary lists the oldest or the most common meanings first in its entries. Then, for each word, write down (*a*) the division into syllables, (*b*) the pronunciation, (*c*) the grammatical functions and forms, (*d*) the etymology, (*e*) each meaning, and (*f*) any special uses indicated by labels. Finally, use the word in at least two sentences of your own.

1. depreciation	4. manifest	7. potlatch	10. toxic
2. secretary	5. assassin	8. plain (*adj.*)	11. steal
3. grammar	6. astrology	9. ceremony	12. obelisk

CHAPTER 42

Improving Your Vocabulary

A precise and versatile vocabulary will help you communicate effectively in speech and writing. To a great extent, you can improve your vocabulary by frequent and inquisitive reading, by troubling to notice and learn the interesting or unfamiliar words used by other writers.

This chapter has a twofold purpose: to provide a sense of the potential of English by acquainting you with its history and range of words; and to help you increase the range, versatility, and precision of your own vocabulary.

CULTURE LANGUAGE For nonnative speakers of English, learning the language means not only mastering its words (which this chapter can help with) but also becoming comfortable with its many idioms and other common expressions. For help, consult the ESL preposition guide listed on page 559, the ESL dictionaries listed on page 574, or a reference such as *English Idioms,* by Jennifer Seidl and W. McMordie.

42a Understanding the sources of English

English has over 500,000 words, probably more than any other language. This exceptional vocabulary and the power and range of expression that accompany it derive from its special mix of word sources. Unlike many other languages, English has borrowed a large number of words.

How English drew on its several sources and acquired its large vocabulary is the story of historical changes. The ancestor of English, Indo-European, was spoken (but not written) perhaps as far back as 5000 BC, and it eventually spread to cover the area from

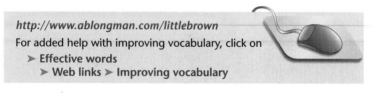

http://www.ablongman.com/littlebrown
For added help with improving vocabulary, click on
➤ Effective words
➤ Web links ➤ Improving vocabulary

Modern English evolved in the fourteenth and fifteenth centuries as the language's sound and spellings changed. This was the time of the Renaissance in Europe. Ancient Latin and Greek art, learning, and literature were revived, first in Italy and then throughout the continent. English vocabulary expanded rapidly, not only with more Latin and many Greek words (such as *democracy* and *physics*) but also with words from Italian and French. Advances in printing, beginning in the fifteenth century, made publications widely available to an increasingly literate audience. Modern American English is four centuries and an ocean removed from the Modern English of sixteenth-century England, but the two are fundamentally the same. The differences and the similarities are evident in this passage from the King James Bible, published in 1611:

> And the Lord God commanded the man, saying, Of euery tree of the garden thou mayest freely eate. But of the tree of the knowledge of good and euill, thou shalt not eate of it: for in the day that thou eatest thereof, thou shalt surely die.

42b   Learning the composition of words

Words can often be divided into meaningful parts. A *handbook,* for instance, is a book you keep at hand (for reference). A *shepherd* herds sheep (or other animals). Knowing what the parts of a word mean by themselves, as you do here, can often help you infer approximately what they mean when combined.

The following explanations of roots, prefixes, and suffixes provide information that can open up the meanings of words whose parts may not be familiar or easy to see. For more information, refer to a dictionary's etymologies, which provide the histories of words (see pp. 577–78).

1 ■ Learning roots

A **root** is the unchanging component of words related in origin and usually in meaning. Both *illiterate* ("unable to read and write") and *literal* ("sticking to the facts or to the first and most obvious meaning of an idea") share the root *liter,* derived from *littera,* a Latin word meaning "letter." A person who cannot understand the letters that make up writing is *illiterate.* A person who wants to understand the primary meaning of the letters (the words) in a contract is seeking the *literal* meaning of that contract.

At least half the words in English come from Latin and Greek. The following list includes some common Latin and Greek roots, their meanings, and examples of English words containing them:

present-day India west to present-day Ireland. In what is n
land, an Indo-European offshoot called Celtic was spoke
sively until the fifth century AD. But over the next few cent
vaders from the European continent, speaking a dialect of Ge
another Indo-European language, overran the native Brito
Germanic dialect became the original source of English.

Old English, spoken from the eighth to the twelfth ce
was a rugged, guttural language. It used a slightly different a
from the modern one (including the characters ð and þ
which has been transcribed in the sample below. The sampl
the opening lines of the Lord's Prayer: "Our Father, who
heaven, hallowed be thy name. Thy kingdom come. Thy will k
on earth as it is in heaven."

> Fæder ure thu the eart on heofonum, si thin nama gehalgod
> cume thin rice. Gewurthe thin willa on eorthan swa swa ⟨
> fonum.

Many English nouns—such as *stone*, *word*, *gift*, and *foot*–
from Old English. So do most pronouns, prepositions, and co
tions, some (such as *he*, *under*, and *to*) without any change in
ing. Other Germanic tribes, using a similar dialect but settli
the European continent instead of in England, fostered two
languages, Dutch and German. As a result, Dutch, German
English are related languages with some similar traits.

In 1066 the Normans from northern France invaded En
They made Norman French the language of law, literature, an
ruling class in England. As a result, English acquired many Fi
words, including many military and governmental words su
authority, *mayor*, *crime*, *army*, and *guard*. The common English
ple kept English alive during the Norman occupation, but
adopted many French words intact (*air*, *point*, *place*, *age*). Ev
ally, the French influence caused the language to shift from O
Middle English, which lasted from the twelfth through the fifte
centuries. During this time a great many Latin words also ent
English, for Latin formed the background of Norman French
was the language of the Church and of scholars. English words
entered Middle English directly from Latin or from Latin thro
French include *language*, *luminous*, *memory*, *liberal*, and *sober*.

Middle English, as the following passage from Geoffrey Ch
cer's *Canterbury Tales* shows, was much closer to the modern l
guage than to Old English:

> A clerk there was of Oxenford also,
> That unto logyk hadde longe ygo.
> As leene was his hors as is a rake,
> And he nas nat right fat, I undertake,
> But looked holwe, and therto sobrely.

Root (source)	Meaning	English words
aster, astr (G)	star	astronomy, astrology
audi (L)	to hear	audible, audience
bene (L)	good, well	benefit, benevolent
bio (G)	life	biology, autobiography
dic, dict (L)	to speak	dictator, dictionary
fer (L)	to carry	transfer, referral
fix (L)	to fasten	fix, suffix, prefix
geo (G)	earth	geography, geology
graph (G)	to write	geography, photography
jur, jus (L)	law	jury, justice
log, logue (G)	word, thought, speech	astrology, biology, neologism
meter, metr (G)	measure	metric, thermometer
op, oper (L)	work	operation, operator
path (G)	feeling	pathetic, sympathy
phil (G)	love	philosophy, Anglophile
phys (G)	body, nature	physical, physics
scrib, script (L)	to write	scribble, manuscript
tele (G)	far off	telephone, television
ter, terr (L)	earth	territory, extraterrestrial
vac (L)	empty	vacant, vacuum, evacuate
vid, vis (L)	to see	video, vision, television

42b

EXERCISE 1
Learning roots

Define the following underlined words, using the list of roots above and any clues given by the rest of the sentence. Check the accuracy of your meanings in a dictionary.

1. After guiding me through college, my <u>benefactor</u> will help me start a career.
2. Always afraid of leading a <u>vacuous</u> life, the heiress immersed herself in volunteer work.
3. The posters <u>affixed</u> to the construction wall advertised a pornographic movie.
4. After his <u>auditory</u> nerve was damaged, he had trouble catching people's words.
5. The child <u>empathized</u> so completely with his mother that he felt pain when she broke her arm.

2 ■ Learning prefixes

Prefixes are standard syllables fastened to the front of a word to modify its meaning. For example, the word *prehistory* combines the word *history*, meaning "based on a written record explaining past events," and the prefix *pre-*, meaning "before." *Prehistory* means "before a written record explaining past events," or before events were recorded.

42b

The following lists group prefixes according to sense. When prefixes have very different spellings but the same meaning, they usually derive from different languages, most often Latin and Greek.

Prefixes showing quantity

Meaning	Prefixes in English words
half	semiannual; hemisphere
one	unicycle; monarch, monorail
two	binary, bimonthly; dilemma, dichotomy
three	triangle, trilogy
four	quadrangle, quartet
five	quintet; pentagon
six	sextuplets; hexameter
seven	septuagenarian; heptarchy
eight	octave, octopus
nine	nonagenarian
ten	decade, decathlon
hundred	century; hectoliter
thousand	millimeter; kilocycle

Prefixes showing negation

Meaning	Prefixes in English words
without, no, not	asexual; illegal, immoral, invalid, irreverent; unskilled
not, absence of, opposing, against	nonbreakable; antacid, antipathy; contradict
opposite to, complement to	counterclockwise, counterweight
do the opposite of, remove, reduce	dehorn, devitalize, devalue
do the opposite of, deprive of	disestablish, disarm
wrongly, bad	misjudge, misdeed

Prefixes showing time

Meaning	Prefixes in English words
before	antecedent; forecast; precede; prologue
after	postwar
again	rewrite

Prefixes showing direction or position

Meaning	Prefixes in English words
above, over	supervise
across, over	transport
below, under	infrasonic; subterranean; hypodermic
in front of	proceed; prefix
behind	recede

into	injection, immerse; encourage, empower
around	circumference; perimeter
with	coexist, colloquial, communicate, consequence, correspond; sympathy, synchronize

42b

EXERCISE 2
Learning prefixes

Provide meanings for the following underlined words, using the lists of prefixes and any clues given by the rest of the sentence. Check the accuracy of your meanings in a dictionary.

1. In the twenty-first century some of our oldest cities will celebrate their quadricentennials.
2. Most poems called sonnets consist of fourteen lines divided into an octave and a sestet.
3. When the Congress seemed ready to cut Social Security benefits again, some representatives proposed the countermeasure of increasing Medicare payments.
4. By increasing Medicare payments, the representatives hoped to forestall the inevitable financial squeeze on the elderly.
5. Ferdinand Magellan, a Portuguese sailor, commanded the first expedition to circumnavigate the globe.

3 ■ Learning suffixes

Suffixes are standard syllables fastened to the end of a word to modify its meaning and usually its part of speech. The word *popular* is an adjective. With different suffixes, it becomes a different adjective, an adverb, two different verbs, and a noun:

Adjective	popular populous	Adverb	popularly
Verb	populate popularize	Noun	population

Many words change suffixes in the same way. In fact, suffixes help us recognize what parts of speech many words are, as the following examples show:

Noun suffixes

misery	miner	internship	randomness
reference	basement	presidency	brotherhood
relevance	nationalist	discussion	kingdom
operator	nationalism	agitation	

Verb suffixes

harden	purify
nationalize	agitate

42c

Adjective suffixes

miser<u>able</u>	presiden<u>tial</u>	wonder<u>ful</u>	use<u>less</u>
ed<u>ible</u>	gigan<u>tic</u>	fib<u>rous</u>	self<u>ish</u>
nat<u>ional</u>	friend<u>ly</u>	adop<u>tive</u>	flatu<u>lent</u>

The only suffix regularly applied to adverbs is *-ly: openly, selfishly, essentially.*

Note Inflectional endings—such as the plural *-s,* the past tense *-ed,* and the comparative *-er* or *-est*—appear at the ends of words but do not change a word's grammatical function.

> **EXERCISE 3**
> **Learning suffixes**
> Identify the part of speech of each word below, and then change it to the part or parts of speech in parentheses by deleting, adding, or changing a suffix. Use the given word and each created word in a sentence. Check a dictionary, if necessary, to be sure suffixes and spellings are correct.
>
> 1. magic (*adjective*)
> 2. durable (*noun; adverb*)
> 3. refrigerator (*verb*)
> 4. self-critical (*noun*)
> 5. differ (*noun; adjective*)
> 6. equal (*noun; adverb*)
> 7. conversion (*verb; adjective*)
> 8. strictly (*adjective; noun*)
> 9. assist (*noun*)
> 10. qualification (*verb; adjective*)

42c Learning to use new words

You can learn a new word not only by understanding its composition but also by examining the context in which it appears and by looking it up in a dictionary—both ways to increase your vocabulary by multiplying and varying your experience with language.

1 ▪ Examining context

Often, you can guess the meaning of an unfamiliar word by looking at the familiar words around it. This technique is helpful when you don't want to interrupt your reading to look up every unfamiliar word. (When you've finished reading, though, check your guesses in your dictionary.)

Parallelism (Chapter 25) shows you which ideas line up or go together and can often suggest the meaning of a new word. Watch for parallel ideas in the following sentence:

> The kittens see their mother hunt and kill, and they in turn take up <u>predatory</u> behavior.

Context clues suggest the meaning of *predatory:* parallel construction (*kittens see . . . and they . . . take up*); the tip-off phrase *in turn;* and the suggested idea of imitation (kittens watching their mother and taking up her behavior). These clues lead to the correct conclusion that predatory behavior consists of hunting and killing.

The phrase *is called* or the word *is* often signals a definition:

> The point where the light rays come together <u>is called</u> the *focus* of the lens.

Sometimes definitions are enclosed in parentheses or set off by punctuation:

> In early childhood these tendencies lead to the development of *schemes* (<u>organized patterns of behavior</u>).

> Many Chinese practice *Tai Chi,* <u>an ancient method of self-defense</u> performed as exercise in slow, graceful motions.

Noticing examples can also help you infer the meaning of a word. The expressions *such as, for example, for instance, to illustrate,* and *including* often precede examples:

> Society often has difficulty understanding nonconformists <u>such as</u> criminals, inventors, artists, saints, and political protesters.

The examples of people who go beyond the average or beyond the rules suggest that *nonconformists* do not adapt themselves to the usual standards and customs of society.

Sometimes an example that reveals the meaning of an unfamiliar word is not announced by a phrase:

> During the first weeks of rehabilitation, Smith exercised as best he could, took his medicine daily, and thought constantly about the physical condition he once possessed.

Guessing the meaning of *rehabilitation* requires considering what occurred during it: exercising, taking medicine, and thinking about past physical condition. Putting these examples together suggests that *rehabilitation* is returning to a healthy condition, which is one of its meanings.

EXERCISE 4
Examining context
Use context to determine the meanings of the underlined words below. Check the accuracy of your guess by consulting a dictionary.

1. Like America, Michael [Corleone, in *The Godfather*] began as a clean, brilliant young man endowed with incredible resources and believing in a humanistic idealism. Like America, Michael was an innocent who had tried to correct the ills and injustices of his <u>progenitors</u>. —Francis Ford Coppola

2. A <u>photograph</u> passes for <u>incontrovertible</u> proof that a given thing happened. The picture may distort; but there is always a presumption that something exists, or did exist, which is like what's in the picture. —Susan Sontag

3. It is not easy to describe or to account for our own culture's particular predilection for butter—a loyalty so fierce and so unreasoning that it is called, by those opposed to it, the "butter mystique." —MARGARET VISSER

4. "And this, too, shall pass away." How much [this sentence] expresses! How chastening in the hour of pride! How consoling in the depths of affliction! —ABRAHAM LINCOLN

5. In a community where public services have failed to keep abreast of private consumption, . . . in an atmosphere of private opulence and public squalor, the private goods have full sway. —JOHN KENNETH GALBRAITH

2 ■ Using a dictionary

A dictionary is a quick reference for the meanings of words (see p. 573). It can give the precise meaning of a word whose general meaning you have guessed by examining the word's context. It can also help you fix the word in your memory by showing its spelling, pronunciation, synonyms, and other features.

Although a dictionary of synonyms is the best source for the precise meanings of similar words (see p. 576), an abridged dictionary will supply much information about synonyms. The following paragraph comes after the main entry for the word *decrease* in *The American Heritage College Dictionary*. By drawing on this information as you edit, you can substitute a more precise word for *decrease* when your meaning calls for one.

> **Syns:** *decrease, lessen, reduce, dwindle, abate, diminish, subside.* These verbs mean to become or cause to become smaller or less. *Decrease* and *lessen* refer to steady or gradual diminution: *Lack of success decreases confidence. His appetite lessens as his illness progresses. Reduce* emphasizes bringing down in size, degree, or intensity: *The workers reduced their wage demands. Dwindle* suggests decreasing bit by bit to a vanishing point: *Their savings dwindled away. Abate* stresses a decrease in amount or intensity and suggests a reduction of excess: *Toward evening the fire began to abate. Diminish* implies taking away or removal: *The warden's authority diminished after the revolt. Subside* implies a falling away to a more normal level: *Our wild enthusiasm did not subside.*

EXERCISE 5
Using the dictionary

Consulting the dictionary entry above (and another dictionary if necessary), write five sentences that make precise use of *decrease* and four of its synonyms.

CHAPTER 43

Spelling and the Hyphen

English spelling is difficult, even for some very experienced and competent writers. You can train yourself to spell better, and this chapter will help you. But you can also improve instantly by acquiring three habits:

- Carefully proofread all of your writing.
- Be suspicious of your spellings.
- Check a dictionary *every time* you doubt a spelling.

Note A word processor's spelling checker can help you find and track spelling errors in your papers. But its usefulness is limited, mainly because it can't spot the common error of confusing words with similar spellings, such as *their/they're/there* and *principal/principle*. A grammar and style checker may flag such words, but only the ones listed in its dictionary, and you still must select the correct spelling. Proofread your papers yourself to catch spelling errors. See pages 186–89 for more on spelling checkers and grammar/style checkers.

43a Recognizing typical spelling problems

Spelling well involves recognizing situations that commonly lead to misspelling: pronunciation can mislead you in several ways; different forms of the same word may have different spellings; and some words have more than one acceptable spelling.

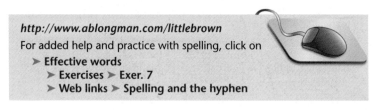

http://www.ablongman.com/littlebrown
For added help and practice with spelling, click on
➤ **Effective words**
  ➤ **Exercises** ➤ **Exer. 7**
  ➤ **Web links** ➤ **Spelling and the hyphen**

1 ■ Being wary of pronunciation

In English, unlike some other languages, pronunciation of words is an unreliable guide to their spelling. The same letter or combination of letters may have different sounds in different words. (Say aloud these different ways of pronouncing the letters *ough: tough, dough, cough, through, bough.*) In addition, some words contain letters that are not pronounced clearly or at all, such as the *ed* in *asked,* the silent *e* in *swipe,* or the unpronounced *gh* in *tight.*

Pronunciation is a particularly unreliable guide in spelling **homonyms,** words pronounced the same though they have different spellings and meanings: *great/grate, to/too/two.* Some commonly confused homonyms and near-homonyms, such as *accept/except,* are listed below. (See p. 598 for tips on how to use spelling lists.)

Words commonly confused

accept (to receive)
except (other than)

affect (to have an influence on)
effect (result)

all ready (prepared)
already (by this time)

allude (to refer to indirectly)
elude (to avoid)

allusion (indirect reference)
illusion (erroneous belief or
  perception)

ascent (a movement up)
assent (agreement)

bare (unclothed)
bear (to carry, or an animal)

board (a plane of wood)
bored (uninterested)

born (brought into life)
borne (carried)

brake (stop)
break (smash)

buy (purchase)
by (next to)

capital (the seat of a government)
capitol (the building where a
  legislature meets)

cite (to quote an authority)
sight (the ability to see)
site (a place)

desert (to abandon)
dessert (after-dinner course)

discreet (reserved, respectful)
discrete (individual or distinct)

elicit (to bring out)
illicit (illegal)

eminent (well known)
imminent (soon to happen)

fair (average, or lovely)
fare (a fee for transportation)

forth (forward)
fourth (after *third*)

gorilla (a large primate)
guerrilla (a kind of soldier)

hear (to perceive by ear)
here (in this place)

heard (past tense of *hear*)
herd (a group of animals)

hole (an opening)
whole (complete)

its (possessive of *it*)
it's (contraction of *it is* or *it has*)

lead (heavy metal)
led (past tense of *lead*)

lessen (to make less)
lesson (something learned)

meat (flesh)
meet (encounter)

no (the opposite of *yes*)
know (to be certain)

passed (past tense of *pass*)
past (after, or a time gone by)

patience (forbearance)
patients (persons under medical care)

peace (the absence of war)
piece (a portion of something)

persecute (to oppress, to harass)
prosecute (to pursue, to take legal action against)

plain (clear)
plane (a carpenter's tool, or an airborne vehicle)

presence (the state of being at hand)
presents (gifts)

principal (most important, or the head of a school)
principle (a basic truth or law)

rain (precipitation)
reign (to rule)
rein (a strap for controlling an animal)

raise (to build up)
raze (to tear down)

right (correct)
rite (a religious ceremony)
write (to make letters)

road (a surface for driving)
rode (past tense of *ride*)

scene (where an action occurs)
seen (past participle of *see*)

seam (junction)
seem (appear)

stationary (unmoving)
stationery (writing paper)

straight (unbending)
strait (a water passageway)

their (possessive of *they*)
there (opposite of *here*)
they're (contraction of *they are*)

to (toward)
too (also)
two (following *one*)

waist (the middle of the body)
waste (discarded material)

weak (not strong)
week (Sunday through Saturday)

weather (climate)
whether (*if*, or introducing a choice)

which (one of a group)
witch (a sorcerer)

who's (contraction of *who is* or *who has*)
whose (possessive of *who*)

your (possessive of *you*)
you're (contraction of *you are*)

---

2 ■ Distinguishing between different forms of the same word

Spelling problems may occur when the noun form and the verb form of the same word are spelled differently. For example:

Verb	Noun	Verb	Noun
advise	advice	enter	entrance
describe	description	marry	marriage
speak	speech	omit	omission

Sometimes the noun and the adjective forms of the same word differ:

Noun	Adjective	Noun	Adjective
comedy	comic	height	high
courtesy	courteous	Britain	British
generosity	generous		

The principal parts of irregular verbs are usually spelled differently:

begin, began, begun	know, knew, known
break, broke, broken	ring, rang, rung

Irregular nouns change spelling from singular to plural:

child, children	shelf, shelves
goose, geese	tooth, teeth
mouse, mice	woman, women

Notice, too, that the stem of a word may change its spelling in different forms:

four, forty	thief, theft

3 ■ Using preferred spellings   CULTURE LANGUAGE

Many words have variant spellings as well as preferred spellings. Often the variant spellings listed in an American dictionary are British spellings.

American	British
color, humor	colour, humour
theater, center	theatre, centre
canceled, traveled	cancelled, travelled
judgment	judgement
realize	realise

43b Following spelling rules

Misspelling is often a matter of misspelling a syllable rather than the whole word. The following general rules focus on troublesome syllables, with notes for the occasional exceptions.

1 ■ Distinguishing between *ie* and *ei*

Words like *believe* and *receive* sound alike in the second syllable, but the syllable is spelled differently. Use the familiar jingle to distinguish between *ie* and *ei:*

I before *e*, except after *c*, or when pronounced "ay" as in *neighbor* and *weigh*.

i before *e*	believe	bier	hygiene
	grief	thief	friend
ei after *c*	ceiling	conceive	perceive
	receive	deceit	conceit
ei sounded	neighbor	weight	eight
as "ay"	sleigh	freight	vein

Exceptions In some words an *ei* combination neither follows *c* nor is pronounced "ay." These words include *either, neither, foreign, forfeit, height, leisure, weird, seize,* and *seizure.* This sentence might help you remember some of them: *The weird foreigner neither seizes leisure nor forfeits height.*

EXERCISE 1
Distinguishing between *ie* and *ei*

Insert *ie* or *ei* in the words below. Check doubtful spellings in a dictionary.

1. br__f	5. for__gn	9. l__surely	13. h__ght
2. dec__ve	6. pr__st	10. ach__ve	14. fr__ght
3. rec__pt	7. gr__vance	11. pat__nce	15. f__nt
4. s__ze	8. f__nd	12. p__rce	16. s__ve

2 ■ Keeping or dropping a final *e*

Many words end with an unpronounced or silent *e: move, brave, late, rinse.* Drop the final *e* when adding an ending that begins with a vowel:

advise + able = advisable	surprise + ing = surprising
force + ible = forcible	guide + ance = guidance

Keep the final, silent *e* if the ending begins with a consonant:

battle + ment = battlement	care + ful = careful
accurate + ly = accurately	like + ness = likeness

Exceptions The silent *e* is sometimes retained before an ending beginning with a vowel. It is kept when *dye* becomes *dyeing,* to avoid confusion with *dying.* It is kept to prevent mispronunciation of words like *shoeing* (not *shoing*) and *mileage* (not *milage*). And the final *e* is often retained after a soft *c* or *g,* to keep the sound of the consonant soft rather than hard:

courageous	changeable	noticeable
outrageous	manageable	embraceable

The silent *e* is also sometimes *dropped* before an ending beginning with a consonant, when the *e* is preceded by another vowel:

argue + ment = argument
due + ly = duly
true + ly = truly

EXERCISE 2
Keeping or dropping a final *e*

Combine the following words and endings, keeping or dropping a final *e* as necessary to make correctly spelled words. Check doubtful spellings in a dictionary.

1. malice + ious	4. retire + ment	7. note + able
2. love + able	5. sue + ing	8. battle + ing
3. service + able	6. virtue + ous	9. suspense + ion

---

3 ▪ Keeping or dropping a final *y*

Words ending in *y* often change their spelling when an ending is added to them. Change the final *y* to an *i* when it follows a consonant:

beauty, beauties	worry, worried	supply, supplies
folly, follies	merry, merrier	deputy, deputize

But keep the *y* when it follows a vowel, when the ending is *-ing*, or when it ends a proper name:

day, days	cry, crying	May, Mays
obey, obeyed	study, studying	Minsky, Minskys

EXERCISE 3
Keeping or dropping a final *y*

Combine the following words and endings, changing or keeping a final *y* as necessary to make correctly spelled words. Check doubtful spellings in a dictionary.

1. imply + s	4. delay + ing	7. solidify + s
2. messy + er	5. defy + ance	8. Murphy + s
3. apply + ing	6. say + s	9. supply + ed

---

4 ▪ Doubling consonants

Whether to double a word's final consonant depends first on the number of syllables in the word. In one-syllable words, double the final consonant when a single vowel precedes the final consonant. Otherwise, don't double the consonant.

slap, slapping	pair, paired
tip, tipping	park, parking

In words of more than one syllable, double the final consonant when a single vowel precedes the final consonant *and* the consonant ends a stressed syllable once the ending is added. Otherwise, don't double the consonant.

refer, referring	refer, reference
begin, beginning	relent, relented
occur, occurrence	despair, despairing

EXERCISE 4
Doubling consonants
Combine the following words and endings, doubling final consonants as necessary to make correctly spelled words. Check doubtful spellings in a dictionary.

1. repair + ing	4. shop + ed	7. drip + ing
2. admit + ance	5. conceal + ed	8. declaim + ed
3. benefit + ed	6. allot + ed	9. parallel + ing

5 ■ Attaching prefixes

Adding a prefix such as *dis, mis,* and *un* does not change the spelling of a word. When adding a prefix, do not drop a letter from or add a letter to the original word:

uneasy	anti-intellectual	defuse	misstate
unnecessary	disappoint	de-emphasize	misspell
antifreeze	dissatisfied	misinform	

(See also p. 603 for when to use hyphens with prefixes: *prehistory* versus *ex-student.*)

6 ■ Forming plurals

Nouns

Most nouns form plurals by adding *s* to the singular form:

boy, boys	table, tables
carnival, carnivals	Murphy, Murphys

Some nouns ending in *f* or *fe* form the plural by changing the ending to *ve* before adding *s:*

leaf, leaves	wife, wives
life, lives	yourself, yourselves

Singular nouns ending in *s, sh, ch,* or *x* form the plural by adding *es:*

kiss, kisses	church, churches
wish, wishes	Jones, Joneses

(Notice that verbs ending in *s*, *sh*, *ch*, or *x* form the third-person singular in the same way. *Taxes* and *lurches* are examples.)

Nouns ending in *o* preceded by a vowel usually form the plural by adding *s:*

ratio, ratios   zoo, zoos

Nouns ending in *o* preceded by a consonant usually form the plural by adding *es:*

hero, heroes   tomato, tomatoes

Exceptions Some very common nouns form irregular plurals:

child, children   man, men
mouse, mice   woman, women

Some English nouns that were originally Italian, Greek, Latin, or French form the plural according to their original language:

analysis, analyses   datum, data
basis, bases   medium, media
beau, beaux   phenomenon, phenomena
crisis, crises   piano, pianos
criterion, criteria   thesis, theses

A few such nouns may form irregular or regular plurals: for instance, *index, indices, indexes*; *curriculum, curricula, curriculums*. The regular plural is more contemporary.

⟨ CULTURE LANGUAGE ⟩ Noncount nouns do not form plurals, either regularly (with an added *s*) or irregularly. Examples of noncount nouns include *equipment, courage,* and *wealth*. (See p. 341.)

Compound nouns

Form plurals of compound nouns in one of two ways. Add *s* to the last word when the component words are roughly equal in importance, whether or not they are hyphenated:

city-states   breakthroughs
painter-sculptors   bucket seats

Add *s* to a noun combined with other parts of speech:

fathers-in-law   passersby

Note, however, that most modern dictionaries give the plural of *spoonful* as *spoonfuls*.

EXERCISE 5
Forming plurals
Make correct plurals of the following singular words. Check doubtful spellings in a dictionary.

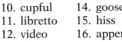

1. pile
2. donkey
3. beach
4. summary

5. mile per hour
6. box
7. switch
8. sister-in-law

9. Bales
10. cupful
11. libretto
12. video

13. thief
14. goose
15. hiss
16. appendix

43c Developing spelling skills

The techniques discussed below can help you improve your spelling. In addition, do not overrely on your computer's spelling checker (see pp. 186–88).

1 ■ Editing and proofreading carefully

If spelling is a problem for you, give it high priority while editing your writing (p. 58) and again while proofreading, your last chance to catch misspelled words (p. 62). Reading a draft backward, word by word, can help you spot mistakes such as switched or omitted letters in words you know. Because the procedure forces you to consider each word in isolation, it can also highlight spellings you may be less sure of. A sense of uncertainty is crucial in spotting and correcting spelling errors, even for good spellers who make relatively few errors. Listen to your own uncertainty, and let it lead you to the dictionary.

2 ■ Using a dictionary

How can you look up a word you can't spell? Start by guessing at the spelling and looking up your guess. If that doesn't work, pronounce the word aloud to come up with other possible spellings, and look them up. Unless the word is too specialized to be included in your dictionary, trial and error will eventually pay off.

If you're using a spelling checker, it may do the guessing for you by providing several choices for misspelled words. But you may still need to check a dictionary to verify your choice.

3 ■ Pronouncing carefully

Careful pronunciation is not always a reliable guide to spelling, (see p. 590), but it can keep you from misspelling words that are often mispronounced. For example:

athletics (*not* atheletics)
disastrous (*not* disasterous)
environment (*not* envirnment)
frustrate (*not* fustrate)
government (*not* goverment)

height (*not* heighth)
history (*not* histry)
irrelevant (*not* irrevelant)
laboratory (*not* labratory)
library (*not* libary)

lightning (*not* lightening)	recognize (*not* reconize)
mischievous (*not* mischievious)	representative (*not* representive)
nuclear (*not* nucular)	strictly (*not* stricly)

4 ■ Tracking and analyzing your errors

Keep a list of the words marked "misspelled" or "spelling" or "sp" in your papers. This list will contain hints about your particular spelling problems, such as that you tend to confuse *affect* and *effect* or to form plurals incorrectly. (If you need help analyzing the list, consult your writing instructor.) The list will also provide a personalized study guide, a focus for your efforts to spell better.

5 ■ Using mnemonics

Mnemonics (pronounced with an initial *n* sound) are techniques for assisting your memory. The *er* in *letter* and *paper* can remind you that *stationery* (meaning "writing paper") has an *er* near the end; *stationary* with an *a* means "standing in place." Or the word *dome* with its long *o* sound can remind you that the building in which the legislature meets is spelled *capitol*, with an *o*. The *capital* city is spelled with *al* like *Albany*, the capital of New York. If you identify the words you have trouble spelling, you can think of your own mnemonics, which may work better for you than someone else's.

6 ■ Studying spelling lists

Learning to spell commonly misspelled words will reduce your spelling errors. For general improvement, work with the following list of commonly misspelled words. Study only six or seven words at a time. If you are unsure of the meaning of a word, look it up in a dictionary and try using it in a sentence. Pronounce the word out loud, syllable by syllable, and write the word out. (The list of similar-sounding words on pp. 590–91 should be considered an extension of the one below.)

absence	acquire	all together
abundance	across	allegiance
acceptable	actually	almost
accessible	address	a lot
accidentally	admission	already
accommodate	adolescent	although
accomplish	advice	altogether
accumulate	advising	amateur
accuracy	against	among
accustomed	aggravate	amount
achieve	aggressive	analysis
acknowledge	all right	analyze

angel
annual
answer
apology
apparent
appearance
appetite
appreciate
appropriate
approximately
argument
arrest
ascend
assassinate
assimilation
assistance
associate
atheist
athlete
attendance
audience
average

bargain
basically
because
beginning
belief
believe
beneficial
benefited
boundary
breath
Britain
bureaucracy
business

calculator
calendar
caricature
carrying
cede
ceiling
cello
cemetery
certain
changeable
changing
characteristic
chief

chocolate
choose
chose
climbed
coarse
column
coming
commercial
commitment
committed
committee
competent
competition
complement
compliment
conceive
concentrate
concert
condemn
conquer
conscience
conscious
consistency
consistent
continuous
controlled
controversial
convenience
convenient
coolly
course
courteous
criticism
criticize
crowd
cruelty
curiosity
curious
curriculum

deceive
deception
decide
decision
deductible
definitely
degree
dependent
descend
descendant

describe
description
desirable
despair
desperate
destroy
determine
develop
device
devise
dictionary
difference
dining
disagree
disappear
disappoint
disapprove
disastrous
discipline
discriminate
discussion
disease
disgusted
dissatisfied
distinction
divide
divine
division
doctor
drawer

easily
ecstasy
efficiency
efficient
eighth
either
eligible
embarrass
emphasize
empty
enemy
entirely
entrepreneur
environment
equipped
especially
essential
every
exaggerate

exceed
excellent
exercise
exhaust
exhilarate
existence
expense
experience
experiment
explanation
extremely

familiar
fascinate
favorite
February
fiery
finally
forcibly
foreign
foresee
forty
forward
friend
frightening
fulfill

gauge
generally
ghost
government
grammar
grief
guarantee
guard
guidance

happily
harass
height
heroes
hideous
humorous
hungry
hurriedly
hurrying
hypocrisy
hypocrite

ideally
illogical

imaginary
imagine
imitation
immediately
immigrant
incidentally
incredible
independence
independent
individually
inevitably
influential
initiate
innocuous
inoculate
insistent
integrate
intelligence
interest
interference
interpret
irrelevant
irresistible
irritable
island

jealousy
judgment

kindergarten
knowledge

laboratory
leisure
length
library
license
lieutenant
lightning
likelihood
literally
livelihood
loneliness
loose
lose
luxury
lying

magazine
maintenance
manageable

marriage
mathematics
meant
medicine
miniature
minor
minutes
mirror
mischievous
missile
misspelled
morale
morals
mortgage
mournful
muscle
mysterious

naturally
necessary
neighbor
neither
nickel
niece
ninety
ninth
noticeable
nuclear
nuisance
numerous

obstacle
occasion
occasionally
occur
occurrence
official
omission
omit
omitted
opinion
opponent
opportunity
opposite
ordinary
originally

paid
panicky
paralleled
parliament

particularly
peaceable
peculiar
pedal
perceive
perception
performance
permanent
permissible
persistence
personnel
perspiration
persuade
persuasion
physical
physiology
physique
pitiful
planning
playwright
pleasant
poison
politician
pollute
possession
possibly
practically
practice
prairie
precede
preference
preferred
prejudice
preparation
prevalent
primitive
privilege
probably
procedure
proceed
process
professor
prominent
pronunciation
psychology
purpose
pursue
pursuit

quandary
quantity

quarter
questionnaire
quiet
quizzes

realistically
realize
really
rebel
rebelled
recede
receipt
receive
recognize
recommend
reference
referred
relief
relieve
religious
remembrance
reminisce
renown
repetition
representative
resemblance
resistance
restaurant
rhyme
rhythm
ridiculous
roommate

sacrifice
sacrilegious
safety
satellite
scarcity
schedule
science
secretary
seize
separate
sergeant
several
sheriff
shining
shoulder
siege
significance
similar

sincerely
sophomore
source
speak
specimen
speech
sponsor
strategy
strength
strenuous
stretch
strict
strictly
studying
succeed
successful
sufficient
summary
superintendent
supersede
suppress
surely
surprise
suspicious

teammate
technical
technique
temperature
tendency
than
then
thorough
though
throughout
together
tomatoes
tomorrow
tragedy
transferred
truly
twelfth
tyranny

unanimous
unconscious
undoubtedly
unnecessary
until
usable
usually

vacuum	weather	woman
vegetable	Wednesday	women
vengeance	weird	writing
vicious	wherever	
villain	whether	yacht
visible	wholly	

43d   Using the hyphen to form compound words

The hyphen (-) is a mark of punctuation used either to divide a word or to form a compound word. Always use a hyphen to divide a word at the end of a line and continue it on the next line, as explained in Chapter 37 on word division. Using a hyphen to form compound words is somewhat more complicated.

Compound words express a combination of ideas. They may be written as a single word (*breakthrough*), as two words (*decision making*), or as a hyphenated word (*cave-in*). Sometimes compound words with the same element are spelled differently—for example, *cross-reference*, *cross section*, and *crosswalk*. Several generalizations can be made about using the hyphen for compound words. But if you doubt the spelling of a compound word, consult a dictionary.

1 ■ Forming compound adjectives

When two or more words serve together as a single modifier before a noun, a hyphen or hyphens form the modifying words clearly into a unit:

> She is a well-known actor.
> The conclusions are based on out-of-date statistics.
> Some Spanish-speaking students work as translators.

When the same compound adjectives follow the noun, hyphens are unnecessary and are usually left out.

> The actor is well known.
> The statistics were out of date.
> Many students are Spanish speaking.

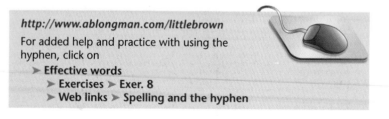

http://www.ablongman.com/littlebrown
For added help and practice with using the hyphen, click on
➤ Effective words
   ➤ Exercises ➤ Exer. 8
   ➤ Web links ➤ Spelling and the hyphen

Hyphens are also unnecessary in compound modifiers containing an *-ly* adverb, even when these fall before the noun: *clearly-defined terms; swiftly-moving train.*

When part of a compound adjective appears only once in two or more parallel compound adjectives, hyphens indicate which words the reader should mentally join with the missing part:

School-age children should have eight- or nine-o'clock bedtimes.

2 ▪ Writing fractions and compound numbers

Hyphens join the numerator and denominator of fractions and the parts of the whole numbers twenty-one to ninety-nine:

three-fourths	twenty-four
one-half	eighty-seven

3 ▪ Forming coined compounds

Writers sometimes create (coin) temporary compounds and join the words with hyphens:

Muhammad Ali gave his opponent a come-and-get-me look.

4 ▪ Attaching some prefixes and suffixes

Do not use hyphens with prefixes except as follows:

- With the prefixes *self-*, *all-*, and *ex-*: *self-control, all-inclusive, ex-student.*
- With a prefix before a capitalized word: *un-American.*
- With a capital letter before a word: *T-shirt.*
- To prevent misreading: *de-emphasize, anti-intellectual.*

The only suffix that regularly requires a hyphen is *-elect*, as in *president-elect.*

5 ▪ Eliminating confusion

If you wrote the sentence *Doonesbury is a comic strip character,* the reader might stumble briefly over your meaning. Is Doonesbury a character in a comic strip or a comic (funny) character who strips? A hyphen would prevent any possible confusion: *Doonesbury is a comic-strip character.*

Adding prefixes to words can sometimes create ambiguity. *Recreation* (*creation* with the prefix *re-*) could mean either "a new creation" or "diverting, pleasurable activity." The use of a hyphen, *re-creation,* limits the word to the first meaning. Without a hyphen the word suggests the second meaning.

sp

43d

EXERCISE 6

Using hyphens in compound words

Insert hyphens as needed in the following compounds. Circle all compounds that are correct as given. Consult a dictionary as needed.

1. reimburse
2. deescalate
3. forty odd soldiers
4. little known bar
5. seven eighths
6. seventy eight
7. happy go lucky
8. preexisting
9. senator elect
10. postwar
11. two and six person cars
12. ex songwriter
13. V shaped
14. reeducate

PART X

Research Writing

CHAPTER 44

Planning a Research Project

If you've ever watched a TV or movie detective pursue a culprit, you know that research can be exciting. When an investigator has a goal in sight, the seemingly mundane work of digging through files, interviewing witnesses, and piecing together clues becomes a concentrated and enthusiastic search.

This same excitement can be yours as you conduct research in school. Honest and inquisitive research writing does demand close attention to details, but the work will not be tedious if you see the details as steadily contributing to discoveries about yourself and the world around you. As you consider what others have to say about your subject and build on that to create new knowledge, you will become an expert in your own right. You will have a significant, in-depth understanding of a subject you care about, and you will communicate that understanding to others.

Through research writing, you will also learn skills that will help you in school, in work, and in life:

- Using the library and the Internet for research
- Analyzing and evaluating others' work
- Drawing on others' work to form, support, and extend your own opinions
- Documenting your sources

Your investigation will be influenced by whether you are expected mainly to report, to interpret, or to analyze sources.

- In **reporting,** you survey, organize, and objectively present the available evidence about a topic.

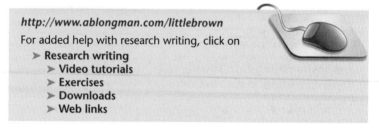

http://www.ablongman.com/littlebrown
For added help with research writing, click on
➤ **Research writing**
  ➤ **Video tutorials**
  ➤ **Exercises**
  ➤ **Downloads**
  ➤ **Web links**

- In **interpreting,** you examine a range of views on a topic in order to answer a question with your own conclusions.
- In **analyzing,** you attempt to solve a problem or answer a question through critical thinking about texts such as scholarly or literary works. (In this context, *analysis* stands for the entire process of critical reading and writing. See pp. 124–32.)

Throughout Chapters 44–48, we will follow the development of research papers by two students, Edward Begay and Vanessa Haley. Begay's work, emphasizing interpretation, receives somewhat more attention; Haley's work, emphasizing analysis, enters the discussion whenever her process differed significantly from Begay's. Both students' final papers appear in Chapter 50.

44a

44a Starting out

With its diverse and overlapping activities, research writing demands more planning than other kinds of writing. A thoughtful plan and systematic procedures will help you anticipate your needs, schedule your time, and complete the work successfully.

1 ▪ Preparing a schedule

As soon as you receive an assignment for a research project, you can begin developing a strategy for completing it. The first step should be making a schedule that apportions the available time to the necessary work. A possible schedule appears on the next page. In it the research-writing process corresponds to the general writing process discussed in Chapters 1–3: planning or developing (steps 1–9), drafting (step 10), and revising and editing (step 11), plus the additional important stage of documenting the sources you use (steps 12–13). You can download the schedule from this book's Web site: see the box opposite. Use a duplicate to plan and time the specific steps of each research project you work on.

2 ▪ Keeping a research journal

To keep track of your activities and ideas during research, always carry index cards, a notebook, or a laptop computer to use as a research journal, a place to record your activities and ideas. (See

http://www.ablongman.com/littlebrown
For added help with keeping a research journal, click on
➤ **Research writing** ➤ **Web links** ➤ **Planning a research project**

44a

Scheduling steps in research writing

(See the pages in parentheses for discussion of the steps.)

Complete
by:

_____ 1. Setting a schedule and beginning a research journal
             (previous page)
_____ 2. Finding a researchable subject and question (opposite)
_____ 3. Developing a research strategy (p. 612)
_____ 4. Finding sources, both print and electronic (p. 621), and mak-
             ing a working bibliography (p. 615)

_____ 5. Evaluating and synthesizing sources (pp. 651, 660)
_____ 6. Mining and interacting with sources (p. 663), often using
             summary, paraphrase, and direct quotation (p. 667)
_____ 7. Taking steps to avoid plagiarism (p. 680)
_____ 8. Developing a thesis statement (p. 690)

_____ 9. Creating a structure (p. 691)
_____ 10. Drafting the paper (p. 695), integrating summaries, para-
             phrases, and direct quotations into your ideas (p. 674)

_____ 11. Revising and editing the paper (p. 696)
_____ 12. Citing sources in your text (p. 688)
_____ 13. Preparing the list of works cited (p. 688)
_____ 14. Preparing and proofreading the final manuscript (p. 698)

_____   Final paper due

Each segment marked off by a horizontal line will occupy _roughly_ one-
fourth of the total time. The most unpredictable segments are the first
two, so it's wise to get started early enough to accommodate the unexpected.

pp. 20 and 117 on journal keeping.) In the journal's dated entries,
you can keep a record of sources you consult, the leads you want
to pursue, any dead ends you reach, and, most important, your
thoughts about sources, leads, dead ends, new directions, relationships, and anything else that strikes you. You will probably find that
the very act of writing in your journal opens your mind and clarifies
your thinking, making your research increasingly productive and
rewarding.

Note The research journal is the place to track and develop
your own ideas. To avoid mixing up your thoughts and those of others, keep separate notes on what your sources actually say, using
one of the methods discussed on pages 665–67.

44b Finding a researchable subject and question

Before reading this section, you may want to review the suggestions given on pages 5–8 for finding and limiting an essay subject. Generally, the same procedure applies to writing any kind of research paper: begin with an assigned subject or one that interests you (perhaps one you've already written about without benefit of research), and then narrow the subject to manageable size by asking questions about it. However, selecting and limiting a subject for a research paper can present special opportunities and problems.

44b

1 ■ Choosing an appropriate subject

A subject for a research paper has four primary requirements, each with corresponding pitfalls:

1. Ample sources of information are available on the subject. Other researchers should have had a chance to produce evidence on the subject, weigh the evidence, and publish their conclusions. And the sources should be accessible.

   Avoid very recent subjects, such as a new medical discovery or a breaking story in today's newspaper.

2. The subject encourages research in the kinds and number of sources required by the assignment.

   Avoid (*a*) subjects that depend entirely on personal opinion and experience, such as the virtues of your hobby; and (*b*) subjects that require research in only one source, such as a straight factual biography or a how-to like "Making Lenses for Eyeglasses." (An exception to *b* is a paper in which you analyze a single work such as a novel or painting.)

3. The subject will lead you to an assessment of sources and to defensible conclusions. Even when a research paper is intended to persuade, the success of the argument will depend on the balanced presentation of all significant points of view.

   Avoid controversial subjects that rest entirely on belief or prejudice, such as when human life begins or why women (or men) are superior. Though these subjects may certainly be disputed,

http://www.ablongman.com/littlebrown
For added help finding a research subject, click on
➤ **Research writing**
  ➤ **Web links** ➤ **Planning a research project**

Checklist for a good research subject

1. **Published sources are ample:** the subject is not so recent that other researchers will still be discovering it.
2. **Sources are diverse:** the subject is neither wholly personal nor wholly factual.
3. **Sources can be assessed objectively:** the subject is not solely a matter of belief, dogma, or prejudice.
4. **Sources can be examined thoroughly** in the assigned time and length: the subject is not too broad.

44b

---

your own preconceptions could slant your research or conclusions. Further, your readers are unlikely to be swayed from their own beliefs.

4. The subject suits the length of paper assigned and the time given for research and writing.

Avoid broad subjects that have too many sources to survey adequately, such as a major event in history or the collected works of a poet.

2 ■ Posing a research question

Asking a question about your subject can give direction to your research by focusing your thinking on a particular approach. You can even begin asking questions before you find your specific subject, as a way of opening avenues you may not have considered.

The students Edward Begay and Vanessa Haley arrived at their research questions by slightly different paths. For a composition course, Begay's instructor assigned an interpretation with a persuasive purpose but left the selection of subject to the student. Begay had recently read several newspaper articles on a subject that intrigued him: what kind of future computers might bring. Taking this broad subject as his starting point, he used clustering (see p. 26) to pursue some implications. While generating the cluster diagram on the facing page, Begay found himself giving the most thought to the Internet. He posed questions until a cluster about access to the Internet led him to a question that seemed interesting and significant: "Will the poor be excluded from the Internet?"

In developing a topic and question for an analysis paper assigned in a composition course, Vanessa Haley followed a somewhat different procedure. Instead of starting with a general subject, as Begay did, Haley began by looking for an unresolved question, an interesting problem, or a disagreement among the experts in some field of study. She had recently been reading an anthology of writings on the environment, and she had been disturbed by how many

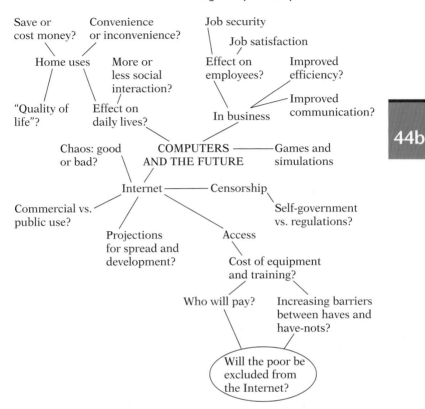

44b

naturalists and environmentalists view human beings not as part of "nature" but as something separate from it, usually as its destroyer. In her journal, Haley wrote this entry:

> Many writers see nature as a place for humans to retreat to, or a wonderful thing that humans are ruining. Humans aren't considered natural themselves—human civilization isn't considered natural. Human civ. is "anti-natural." Isn't such a separation unrealistic and damaging? We *are* natural. We're here to stay, and we're not going back to the Stone Age, so we'd better focus on the connections between "us" and "it" (nature) rather than just the differences. Dillard seems to do this—seems to connect human and natural worlds. People are neither better nor worse than nature but just bound up in it. "Nature is as careless as it is bountiful, and . . . with that extravagance goes a crushing waste that will one day include our own cheap lives" ("Fecundity").

At the end of this entry, Haley refers to and quotes the writer Annie Dillard, one of the authors represented in the anthology. Haley decided to explore Dillard's views further by reading and analyzing more of her work. Haley's opening question for investigation, then, was "How does Annie Dillard see the place of humanity in nature?"

EXERCISE 1
Finding a topic and question
Choose three of the following subjects (or three subjects of your own), and narrow each one to at least one subject and question suitable for beginning work on a research paper. (This exercise can be the first step in a research paper project that continues through Chapters 44–48.)

1. Bilingual education
2. National security and civil rights
3. Distribution of music by conventional versus electronic means
4. Dance in America
5. The history of women's suffrage
6. Genetically modified foods
7. Immigrants in the United States
8. Space exploration
9. Business espionage
10. The effect of television on professional sports
11. Child abuse
12. African Americans and civil rights
13. Successes in cancer research
14. Computer piracy
15. The European exploration of North America before Columbus
16. Hazardous substances in the workplace
17. Television evangelism
18. Science fiction
19. Treatment or prevention of AIDS
20. Water pollution
21. Women writers
22. Campaign financing
23. Comic film actors
24. An unsolved crime
25. Alternative fuels
26. Male and female heroes in modern fiction
27. Computers and the privacy of the individual
28. Gothic or romance novels in the nineteenth and twenty-first centuries
29. The social responsibility of business
30. Stem-cell research

44c Developing a research strategy

Before you start looking for sources, consider what you already know about your subject and where you are likely to find information on it.

http://www.ablongman.com/littlebrown
For added help with developing a research strategy, click on
➤ **Research writing** ➤ **Web links** ➤ **Planning a research project**

1 ■ Tapping into your own knowledge

Discovering what you already know about your subject will guide you in discovering what you don't know. Take some time to spell out facts you have learned, opinions you have heard or read elsewhere, and of course your own opinions. Use one of the discovery techniques discussed in Chapter 2 to explore and develop your ideas: keeping a journal, observing your surroundings, freewriting, list making, clustering, asking the journalist's questions, using the patterns of development, or thinking critically.

When you've explored your thoughts, make a list of questions for which you don't have answers, whether factual (*What is the distribution of computers among affluent and poor schools?*) or more open-ended (*Are computers necessarily a positive force in education?*). These questions will give you clues about the sources you need to look for first.

44c

2 ■ Setting goals for sources

For many research projects, you'll want to consult a mix of sources, as described below. You may start by seeking the outlines of your topic—the range and depth of opinions about it—in reference works and articles in popular periodicals or through a Web search. Then, as you refine your views and your research question, you'll move on to more specialized sources, such as scholarly books and periodicals and your own interviews or surveys. (See pp. 626–49 for more on each kind of source.)

Library and Internet sources

The print and electronic sources available through your library—mainly reference works, periodicals, and books—have two big advantages over most of what you'll find on the Internet: they are cataloged and indexed for easy retrieval; and they are generally reliable, having been screened first by their publishers and then by the library's staff. In contrast, the Internet's retrieval systems are more difficult to use effectively, and Internet sources tend to be less reliable because most do not pass through any screening before being posted. (There are many exceptions, such as online scholarly journals and reference works. But these sources may be available through your library's Web site as well.)

Most instructors expect research writers to consult sources found in and through the library, including print sources. But most will accept Internet sources, too, if you have used them judiciously. Even with its disadvantages, the Internet can be a valuable resource for primary sources, current information, and a diversity of views. For guidelines on evaluating both library and Internet sources, see pages 651–59.

Primary and secondary sources

As much as possible, you should rely on **primary sources,** or firsthand accounts: historical documents (letters, speeches, and so on), eyewitness reports, works of literature, reports on experiments or surveys conducted by the writer, or your own interviews, experiments, observations, or correspondence.

In contrast, **secondary sources** report and analyze information drawn from other sources (often primary ones): a reporter's summary of a controversial issue, a historian's account of a battle, a critic's reading of a poem, a physicist's evaluation of several studies. Secondary sources may contain helpful summaries and interpretations that direct, support, and extend your own thinking. However, most research-writing assignments expect your ideas to go beyond those in such sources.

Scholarly and popular sources

The scholarship of acknowledged experts is essential for depth, authority, and specificity. Generally, your instructors will expect you to emphasize scholarly sources in your research. But the general-interest views and information of popular sources can help you apply more scholarly approaches to daily life.

- *Check the publisher.* Is it a scholarly journal (such as *Education Forum*) or a publisher of scholarly books (such as Harvard University Press), or is it a popular magazine (such as *Time* or *Newsweek*) or a publisher of popular books (such as Random House)?
- *Check the author.* Have you seen the name elsewhere, which might suggest that the author is an expert?
- *Check the title.* Is it technical, or does it use a general vocabulary?

- *Check the electronic address.* Addresses for Internet sources often include an abbreviation that tells you something about the source: *edu* means the source comes from an educational institution, *gov* from a government body, *org* from a nonprofit organization, *com* from a commercial organization such as a corporation. (See p. 654 for more on interpreting electronic addresses.)

Older and newer sources

Check the publication date. For most subjects a combination of older, established sources (such as books) and current sources (such as newspaper articles, interviews, or Web sites) will provide both background and up-to-date information. Only historical subjects or very current subjects like Edward Begay's (the Internet) require an emphasis on one extreme or another.

Impartial and biased sources

Seek a range of viewpoints. Sources that attempt to be impartial can offer trustworthy facts and an overview of your subject. Sources with clear biases can offer a diversity of opinion. Of course, to discover bias, you may have to read the source carefully (see p. 651); but even a bibliographical listing can be informative.

- *Check the author.* You may have heard of the author before as a respected researcher (thus more likely to be objective) or as a leading proponent of a certain view (less likely to be objective).
- *Check the title.* It may reveal something about point of view. (Consider these contrasting titles uncovered by Edward Begay: "Computer Literacy and Ideology" versus "The Process of Introducing Internet-Based Classroom Projects and the Role of School Librarians.")

Note Internet sources must be approached with particular care. See pages 653–59.

Sources with helpful features

Depending on your topic and how far along your research is, you may want to look for sources with features such as illustrations (which can clarify important concepts), bibliographies (which can direct you to other sources), and indexes (which can help you develop keywords for electronic searches; see pp. 623–26).

EXERCISE 2
Developing a research strategy
Following the suggestions on page 613, write what you already know about the topic you selected in Exercise 1 (p. 612), and then frame some questions for which you'll need to find answers. Also in writing, consider the kinds of sources you'll probably need to consult, using the categories given on the preceding pages.

44d Making a working bibliography

When you begin searching for sources, it may be tempting to pursue each possibility as you come across it. But that approach would prove inefficient and probably ineffective. Instead, you'll want to find out the full range of sources available and then decide on a good number to consult. For a paper of 1800 to 2500 words, try for ten to thirty promising titles as a start.

To keep track of where sources are and what they are, make a **working bibliography,** a file of books, articles, Web sites, and other possibilities. When you have a substantial file, you can decide which sources seem most promising and look them up first or, if necessary, order them through interlibrary loan.

Record the information for a source as soon as you think you may want to use it, following the guidelines opposite. Then you'll be able to find the source when you're ready to consult it, and you'll have the information needed to cite the source in your paper.

1 ▪ Tracking source information

You have several options for making a working bibliography:

- *Copy source information by hand on note cards* (usually 3" × 5"), one source to a card. With this system, you can record source information no matter where you are, as long as you have a pen or pencil, and you can easily add, delete, and rearrange sources. Some instructors require that a working bibliography be submitted on note cards.
- *Create the working bibliography on your word processor,* either typing the information yourself or downloading it from online indexes, catalogs, and other sources. You'll be able to sort sources by subject or by author and to copy bibliographic data into your paper when you prepare final source citations.
- *Combine the two systems:* print and cut up computer-generated source listings, and then paste or tape each source on a note card.

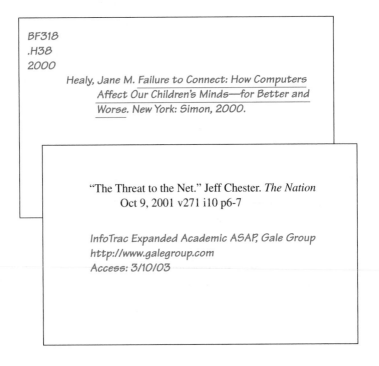

BF318
.H38
2000

Healy, Jane M. Failure to Connect: How Computers Affect Our Children's Minds—for Better and Worse. New York: Simon, 2000.

"The Threat to the Net." Jeff Chester. *The Nation* Oct 9, 2001 v271 i10 p6-7

InfoTrac Expanded Academic ASAP, Gale Group
http://www.galegroup.com
Access: 3/10/03

Whatever system you use, be sure to record all the information you will need. A downloaded listing, for instance, may look complete but lack the name of the database and other crucial information.

The two records on the facing page come from Edward Begay's working bibliography. The first, for a book, Begay handwrote on a note card. The second, for a magazine article, Begay downloaded from a subscription service, printed out, and then annotated with information he knew he would need.

44d

2 ■ Recording source information

When you turn in your paper, you will be expected to attach a list of the sources you have used. So that readers can check or follow up on your sources, your list must include all the information needed to find the sources, in a format readers can understand. The box below shows the information you should record for each type of

---

Information for a working bibliography

For books
Library call number
Name(s) of author(s), editor(s), translator(s), or others listed
Title and subtitle
Publication data:
  Place of publication
  Publisher's name
  Date of publication
Other important data, such as edition or volume number

For periodical articles
Name(s) of author(s)
Title and subtitle of article
Title of periodical
Publication data:
  Volume number and issue number (if any) in which article appears
  Date of issue
  Page numbers on which article appears

For electronic sources
Name(s) of author(s)
Title and subtitle
Publication data for books and articles (see above)

Date of release, online posting, or latest revision
Medium (online, CD-ROM, etc.)
Format of online source (Web site, Web page, e-mail, etc.)
Date you consulted the source
Complete electronic address (unless source was obtained through a subscription service and has no permanent address)
For source obtained through a subscription service:
  Name of database
  Name of service
  Electronic address of the service home page or search terms used to reach the source

For other sources
Name(s) of author(s) or others listed, such as a government department or a recording artist
Title of the work
Format, such as unpublished letter or live performance
Publication or production data:
  Publisher's or producer's name
  Date of publication, release, or production
  Identifying numbers (if any)

source so that you will not have to retrace your steps later. (You can download these lists from this book's Web site: see the box on p. 606. Copy the appropriate list for each source you're considering, and fill in the required information.)

Note Whenever possible, record source information in the correct format for the documentation style you will be using. Then you will be less likely to omit needed information or to confuse numbers, dates, and other data when it's time to write your citations. This book describes four styles: MLA (p. 700), Chicago (p. 818), APA (p. 838), and CSE (p. 869). For others, consult one of the guides listed on pages 838 and 869. (Begay's first card on p. 616 follows MLA style.)

44d

3 ■ Finding bibliographic information for online sources

Unlike that for printed materials, publication information for online sources can be difficult to find and make sense of. The screen shot opposite shows the beginning and end of a Web site's first page. Circled numbers refer to the following numbered explanations:

1. *The source's address, or URL, usually appears in the Address or Location field of the Web browser,* near the top of the screen. If the field does not appear, adjust the settings of the browser so that it displays the field.

2. *Use as the source title the title of the site or page you are consulting.* This information usually appears as a heading at the top of the page, but if not, it may also appear in the bar along the top of the browser window. When the page heading and the browser title differ, generally choose the browser title because it is the information used for search engines (see p. 640). However, if the browser title conveys no information—for instance, *Home Page*—then use the page heading.

3. *Publication information often appears at the bottom of each page.* Look here for (*a*) the name of the author or the sponsoring organization, (*b*) an address for reaching the sponsor or author directly, and (*c*) the publication date or the date of the last revision.

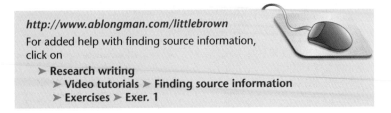

http://www.ablongman.com/littlebrown
For added help with finding source information, click on
➤ **Research writing**
  ➤ **Video tutorials** ➤ **Finding source information**
  ➤ **Exercises** ➤ **Exer. 1**

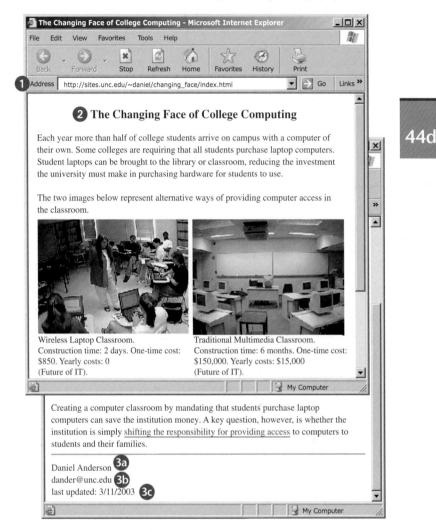

If the page you are reading does not list publication information, look for it on the site's home page. There may be a link to the home page, or you can find it by editing the address in the Address or Location field: working backward, delete the end of the address up to the last slash; then hit Enter. (For the address in the screen shot, you would delete *index.html*.) If that action doesn't take you to the home page, delete the end of the remaining address up to the preceding slash and hit Enter. Editing the address in this way, you'll eventually reach the home page.

When scouting a discussion list, Web forum, or newsgroup, save messages that may serve as sources, and keep track of when and where they were posted. You may be able to discover information about the author of a message from the list's archive or from an archive site such as *http://groups.google.com*. See pages 645–46 for more on these resources.

44d

EXERCISE 3
Compiling a working bibliography

Prepare a working bibliography of at least ten sources for a research paper on one of the following people or on someone of your own choosing. Begin by limiting the subject to a manageable size, posing a question about a particular characteristic or achievement of the person. Then consult reference works, periodical indexes, the library's catalog of books, and the Web. (See pp. 626–45 for more on these resources.) Record complete bibliographic information on note cards or on your computer.

1. Steven Jobs (a founder of Apple Computer), or another business entrepreneur
2. Sandra Day O'Connor, or another Supreme Court justice
3. Emily Dickinson, or another writer
4. Michael Jordan, or another sports figure
5. Isamu Noguchi, or another artist

CHAPTER 45

Finding Sources

Once you have discovered a subject and question for research, have developed a research strategy, and know how to make a working bibliography (all covered in the previous chapter), you're ready to find sources. This chapter discusses electronic searches and the kinds of sources, both print and electronic, that are available to you.

Note If you require sources that are not available from your own library, you may be able to obtain them from another library by mail, fax, or computer. Ask your librarian for help, and plan ahead: interlibrary loans can take a week or longer.

45a Searching electronically

As you conduct research, the World Wide Web will be your gateway to ideas and information. You will use the Web to find many of your library's extensive resources, such as books, periodicals, and reference works. And you may use the Web to reach non-library resources, such as a discussion among experts in a field, the publicity of a corporation, or the reports of a political or environmental group. Some of these resources are trustworthy; others are not. You need to be able to recognize both the type of source you're using and its likely validity.

Note Always begin your academic research on your library's Web site, not with a search engine such as *Google*. Although a direct Web search can be productive, you'll find a higher concentration of relevant and reliable sources through the library.

---

http://www.ablongman.com/littlebrown
For added help with finding sources, including searching electronically, click on
➤ Research writing
  ➤ Video tutorials ➤ Using keywords with a search engine
  ➤ Exercises ➤ Exer. 2
  ➤ Web links ➤ Finding sources

621

A tip for researchers

If you are unsure of how to use your library, either via the Web or at the library itself, consult a reference librarian. This person is very familiar with all the library's resources and with general and specialized research techniques. It is his or her job to help you and others with research. Even very experienced researchers often consult reference librarians.

45a

1 ■ Discovering what's available

Your search for electronic sources will be quicker and more productive if you take the time to find out what kinds of sources you have access to and how you can use them.

Kinds of electronic sources

Your school's library and the Web offer several kinds of electronic resources that are suitable for academic research. For more on searching these resources, see pages 630–45.

- ■ *The library's catalog of holdings* is a database that lists all the resources that the library owns or subscribes to: books, journals, magazines, newspapers, references works, and more. The catalog does not list the specific contents of resources—for instance, the chapters in a book or the articles in a journal. For that information, you locate a specific source on the library's shelves or consult one of the databases discussed below. The catalog may include not only your library's holdings but also those of other schools nearby or in your state.
- ■ *Online databases* include indexes, bibliographies, and other reference works. They are your main route to listings of specific journal articles and book chapters. For each listing, the databases usually provide detailed publication information and an abstract, or summary. They may also provide the full text of articles or chapters (see below). Your library subscribes to the databases and makes them available through its Web site. (You may also discover databases directly on the Web, but, again, the library is the more productive starting place.)
- ■ *Databases on CD-ROM*, or compact disk, include the same information as online databases, but they must be read at a library computer terminal. Increasingly, libraries are providing CD-ROM databases through their Web sites or are moving away from CD-ROMs in favor of online databases.
- ■ *Full-text resources* contain the entire contents of articles, book chapters, even whole books. Some of the library's online or CD-ROM databases provide access to the full text of listed sources.

In addition, the Web sites of many periodicals and organizations, such as government agencies, offer the full text of articles, reports, and other publications.

Locations of library resources

- *What library resources are available online?* You can probably reach your library from anywhere, at any time, via its Web site. The Web site most likely carries the library's catalog, and it may carry other databases and full-text resources as well. You'll need to visit the library itself for resources that aren't available online (see the note below).

- *Which periodical indexes, bibliographies, full-text resources, and other references are available electronically?* Many older references have not yet been converted to electronic form, so you may have to consult a printed index at the library for the back issues of a newspaper or journal. In addition, databases are expensive, so your library may purchase or subscribe to only some of them. What your library does not have may be available from another library or over the Web.

- *Are any of the library's books or collections not included in the online catalog?* Some libraries have not yet converted all their book records and collections to electronic format, so you may need to consult a bound or film catalog for some works.

Note You may be tempted to do all of your research online, skipping the resources that are available only at the library. But many of the best resources are on the library's shelves, and most instructors expect research papers to be built to some extent on these resources. When you spot promising sources while browsing the library's online databases, make records of them and look them up at the library.

Ways to record information

- *Can you save search results on your own hard drive or disk or e-mail them to yourself?* Most databases, including library catalogs, allow users to save copies of listings or even whole articles. You can rearrange and supplement source data for your working bibliography (see p. 616).

- *Can you print search results in the library?* Many libraries provide printers so that users can print catalog items, periodical listings, and other information.

2 ▪ Using keywords

Once you determine what resources are available, you should plan your search. Careful planning is essential: a too-casual search

45a

can miss helpful sources while returning hundreds, even thousands, of irrelevant sources.

Probably the most important element in planning a search is to develop **keywords**, or **descriptors**, that name your subject for databases and Web search engines.

Databases vs. the Web

To develop keywords it helps to understand what they do when you use them for a search. Most databases index sources by authors, titles, and publication years and also by subject headings found in each database's directory or thesaurus. Electronic databases can usually search among their listings and subjects for uses of your keywords, but they work more efficiently when you use their subject headings for keywords.

The Web has no overall directory that you can consult for keywords. Some Web search engines do categorize sites into subject directories, but they include only a small portion of the Web's offerings. Other search engines, so-called crawlers, seek your keywords in the titles, summaries, and texts of sites. Their performance depends on how well your keywords describe your subject and anticipate the words used in sources. If you describe your subject too broadly or describe it specifically but don't match the vocabulary in relevant sources, your search will turn up few relevant sources and probably many that aren't relevant.

Keyword refinement

Every database and search engine provides a system that you can use to refine your keywords for a productive search. The basic operations appear in the box opposite, but resources do differ. For instance, some assume that *AND* should link two or more keywords, while others provide options specifying "Must contain all the words," "May contain any of the words," and other equivalents for the operations in the box.

Trial and error

You will probably have to use trial and error in developing your keywords. Because different databases have different directories

45a

Ways to refine keywords

Most databases and search engines work with **Boolean operators,** terms or symbols that allow you to expand or limit your keywords and thus your search.

- Use *AND* or + to narrow the search by including only sources that use all the given words. The keywords *Internet AND access* request only the sources in the shaded area:

- Use *NOT* or – ("minus") to narrow the search by excluding irrelevant words. *Internet AND access NOT provider* excludes sources that use the word *provider.*

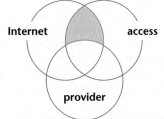

- Use *OR* to broaden the search by giving alternate keywords. *Internet OR cyberspace AND access* allows for sources that use a synonym for *Internet.*

- **Use parentheses or quotation marks to form search phrases.** For instance, *(Internet access)* requests the exact phrase, not the separate words. Only sources using *Internet access* would turn up.
- **Use *NEAR* to narrow the search** by requiring the keywords to be close to each other—for instance, *Internet NEAR education.* Depending on the resource you're using, the words could be directly next to each other or many words apart. Some resources use *WITHIN___* so that you can specify the exact number of words apart—for instance, *Internet WITHIN 10 education.*

(continued)

Ways to refine keywords
(continued)

■ **Use wild cards to permit different versions of the same word.** In *child**, for instance, the wild card * indicates that sources may include *child, children, childcare, childhood, childish, childlike,* and *childproof.* The example suggests that you have to consider all the variations allowed by a wild card and whether it opens up your search too much. If you seek only two or three from many variations, you may be better off using *OR: child OR children.* (Note that some systems use ?, :, or + for a wild card instead of *.)

■ **Be sure to spell your keywords correctly.** Some search tools will look for close matches or approximations, but correct spelling gives you the best chance of finding relevant sources.

---

and many search tools have no directory at all, you should count on occasionally running dry (turning up few or no sources) or hitting uncontrollable gushers (turning up hundreds or thousands of mostly irrelevant sources). But the process is not busywork—far from it. Besides leading you eventually to worthwhile sources, it can also teach you a great deal about your subject: how you can or should narrow it, how it is and is not described by others, what others consider interesting or debatable about it, and what the major arguments are.

Edward Begay's experiences illustrate the advantages of trial and error in devising keywords. When Begay tried the keywords *Internet AND access* on a Web search engine, he discovered that his words appeared in nearly 5.4 million sites. Yet the same keywords produced practically nothing on the database *Social Sciences Index.* From misses like these, Begay learned, among other things, that *access* to the Internet did not have the same meaning for him as for most users of the word, and he resolved to make his meaning clear if he used the word in his final paper.

45b   Finding reference works

Reference works, often available online or on CD-ROM, include encyclopedias, dictionaries, digests, bibliographies, indexes,

http://www.ablongman.com/littlebrown
For access to all types of online reference works, click on
➤ **Research writing** ➤ **Web links** ➤ **Finding sources**

Index to research sources

Reference works: helpful for summaries of topics and information for further research

45b

General books: literary works, nonfiction surveys, in-depth studies, and other materials, available for circulation

Periodicals: magazines, journals, and newspapers, containing detailed and current information

The World Wide Web: a network of computers providing access to libraries, publications, organizations, governments, and individuals

Other online sources:

Pamphlets and government publications: practical advice, raw data, reports, and other information *646*

Your own sources: interviews, surveys, and other primary sources you create *648*

---

atlases, and handbooks. Your research *must* go beyond reference works; indeed, many instructors discourage students from relying on such sources for ideas and information in final papers. But reference works can help you get started:

- They can help you decide whether your topic interests you and whether it meets the requirements for a research paper (p. 609).

- They can direct you to more detailed sources on your topic.
- They can help you refine keywords for electronic searches by giving you the terminology of the field you're researching.
- For an analysis paper, a specialized encyclopedia can identify the main debates in a field and the proponents of each side.

Edward Begay's use of reference works illustrates how helpful such sources can be as a starting point, even for a topic as current as the Internet. Begay first consulted *Bibliographic Guide to the History of Computing, Computers, and the Information Processing Industry* (to get some background on computers and the Internet) and *Encyclopedia of Sociology* (to explore the concept of equality in education).

The following lists give the types of reference works. Ask a reference librarian if you're unsure of where to start. The librarian can also advise you which sources are available through the library's Web site, in print or on CD-ROM at the library, or directly via the Web.

General encyclopedias

General encyclopedias give brief overviews and bibliographies. Covering all fields, they are convenient but very limited.

> *Academic American Encyclopedia*
> *Collier's Encyclopedia*
> *The Columbia Encyclopedia*
> *Encyclopedia Americana*
> *Encyclopedia International*
> *The New Encyclopaedia Britannica*
> *Random House Encyclopedia*

Specialized encyclopedias, dictionaries, bibliographies

A specialized encyclopedia, dictionary, or bibliography generally covers a single field or subject. These works will give you more detailed and more technical information than a general reference work will, and many of them (especially bibliographies) will direct you to particular books and articles on your subject. Note that many specialized references are available online or on CD-ROM as well as in print.

One general reference work providing information on sources in many fields is the *Essay and General Literature Index* (published since 1900 and now updated semiannually). It lists tens of thousands of articles and essays that appear in books (rather than periodicals) and that might not be listed elsewhere. For a list of specialized reference works in various disciplines, consult the lists elsewhere in this book:

- Literature (p. 796)
- Other humanities, including history, the arts, philosophy, and religion (p. 814)

- Social sciences, such as business and economics, criminal justice, education, and psychology (p. 838)
- Natural and applied sciences, such as biology, engineering, mathematics, and physics (p. 869)

Unabridged dictionaries and special dictionaries on language

Unabridged dictionaries are more comprehensive than college or abridged dictionaries. Special dictionaries give authoritative information on aspects of language. (See Chapter 41 for more on the kinds of dictionaries and how to use them.)

45b

Unabridged dictionaries

A Dictionary of American English on Historical Principles
The Oxford English Dictionary
The Random House Dictionary of the English Language
Webster's Third New International Dictionary of the English Language

Special dictionaries

Cassidy, Frederic G., et al., eds. *Dictionary of American Regional English.*
Chapman, Robert L., ed. *Roget's International Thesaurus.*
Follett, Wilson. *Modern American Usage.* Ed. Jacques Barzun.
Green, Jonathan. *The Cassell Dictionary of Slang.*
The New Fowler's Modern English Usage. Ed. R. W. Burchfield.
Onions, Charles T., et al., eds. *The Oxford Dictionary of English Etymology.*
Partridge, Eric. *A Dictionary of Slang and Unconventional English.* Ed. Paul Beale.
Partridge, Eric. *Origins: A Short Etymological Dictionary of Modern English.*
Webster's Dictionary of English Usage
Webster's New Dictionary of Synonyms
Wentworth, Harold, and Stuart Berg Flexner. *Dictionary of American Slang.*

Biographical reference works

If you want to learn about someone's life, achievements, credentials, or position, or if you want to learn the significance of a name you've come across, consult one of the reference works below.

American Men and Women of Science
Contemporary Authors
Current Biography
Dictionary of American Biography
Dictionary of American Negro Biography
Dictionary of Literary Biography
Dictionary of National Biography (British)
Dictionary of Scientific Biography
McGraw-Hill Encyclopedia of World Biography

Notable American Women, 1607–1950
Notable American Women: The Modern Period
Webster's New Biographical Dictionary
Who's Who in America
World Authors

Atlases and gazetteers

Atlases are bound collections of maps; gazetteers are geographical dictionaries.

Britannica Atlas
Cosmopolitan World Atlas
National Atlas of the United States of America
National Geographic Atlas of the World
Times Atlas of the World
Times Atlas of World History
Webster's New Geographical Dictionary

Almanacs and yearbooks

Both almanacs and yearbooks are annual compilations of facts. Yearbooks record information about the previous year in a country, field, or other subject. Almanacs give facts about a variety of fields.

Americana Annual
Britannica Book of the Year
Facts on File Yearbook
Information Please Almanac
US Bureau of the Census. *Statistical Abstract of the United States.*
World Almanac and Book of Facts

45c   Finding books

Books can provide background information, subject surveys, popular views of culture, statements of scholarly theory, research results—in short, a broad range of secondary and primary sources (see p. 614).

1 ■ Using the library catalog

Your library's catalog is probably stored on computer, so that you can search it either at a terminal in the library or via the library's Web site. Verify with a librarian that the electronic catalog includes all the available books (see p. 623).

http://www.ablongman.com/littlebrown
For added help with finding books and book reviews, click on
➤ **Research writing** ➤ **Web links** ➤ **Finding sources**

Through the Web, you also have access to the book catalogs of other libraries. You can search these catalogs as you do your own library's, and sometimes you can borrow books from another library in your area. Ask a librarian for assistance with remote searches and loans. And allow time for a book to be sent after your request.

All book catalogs contain similar information, though it may be organized differently from one library to the next. By far the most widely used format derives from the Library of Congress cataloging system and includes author, title, publisher, date of publication, description (number of pages, size, and other data), subject headings the book is listed under, and the library's call number (which directs you to the book's location in the stacks). See the next page for a complete book record showing all this information.

45c

2 ▪ Using a search strategy

Unless you seek a specific author or title, you'll want to find books with a subject or keyword search of the library's catalog. In a subject search, you start with headings found in *Library of Congress Subject Headings (LCSH)*, the massive directory under which the Library of Congress catalogs books. In a keyword search, you start with your own description of your subject as a way of locating appropriate *LCSH* headings.

The keyword approach is illustrated as part of Edward Begay's catalog search, shown below and on the next page. In his initial keyword search (screen 1), Begay used *Internet and access*. The search returned several books (screen 2), including a promising one titled *Social Consequences of Internet Use*. The complete record for this book (screen 3) showed that it was indexed under three *LCSH* subject headings: *Internet—Social aspects—United States; Digital divide —United States;* and *Telecommunication—Social aspects—United States.* Begay then used these headings to search the catalog further.

1. Initial keyword search of book catalog

45c

2. Search results

```
BRIEF RECORDS

1. Katz, James Everett. Social consequences of Internet use : access, involvement, and
   interaction / Cambridge, Mass. : MIT Press, c2002.

   | Location | Call Number     | Status         |
   | Polk     | HM851 .K38 2002 | c.1 Available  |

2. Access denied in the information age / New York : Palgrave, 2001.

   | Location | Call Number     | Status         |
   | Polk     | ZA4201 .A22 2001 | c.1 Available |

3. Cyberpath to development in Asia : issues and challenges / Westport, Conn. : Praeger,
   2002.

   | Location | Call Number        | Status         |
   | Polk     | HN655.2.I56 C93 2002 | c.1 Available |
```

3. Full record

```
FULL RECORD

Record #1
                                                    Title and subtitle
Title:        Social consequences of Internet use : access, involvement, and interaction / James
              E. Katz and Ronald E. Rice.
Author:       Katz, James Everett.                           Author
Publisher:    Cambridge, Mass. : MIT Press, c2002.           Publisher and date
Subject:      Internet--Social aspects--United States.
              Digital divide--United States.                 Subject headings
              Telecommunication--Social aspects--United States.  for book
Description:  xxiv, 460 p. : ill. ; 24 cm.
Notes:        Includes bibliographical references (p. [411]-438) and index.
Other Entry:  Rice, Ronald E.                                Coauthor
ISBN:         0262112698 (hc : alk. paper)
OCLC No:      49260842
                                                    Library call number
   | Location | Call Number     | Status         |
   | Polk     | HM851 .K38 2002 | c.1 Available  |
```

3 ▪ Using references to books

Two types of references can help you identify general books that have information about your topic: publishing bibliographies and digests. Publishing bibliographies tell whether a book is still in print, whether a paperback edition is available, what books were published on a certain topic in a certain year, and so on:

> *Books in Print.* Books indexed by author, title, and subject.
> *Cumulative Book Index*

You might, for example, want to know if the author of an encyclopedia article has published any relevant books since the date of the encyclopedia. You could look up the author's name in the latest *Books in Print* to find out.

If you want to evaluate a book's relevance to your topic before you search for it, a review index such as the following will direct you to published reviews of the book:

> *Book Review Digest.* Summarizes and indexes reviews of books.
> *Book Review Index*
> *Current Book Review Citations*

For specialized review indexes, see pages 836 (social sciences) and 867 (natural and applied sciences).

45d

45d Finding periodicals

Periodicals include newspapers, journals, and magazines. Newspapers, the easiest to recognize, are useful for detailed accounts of past and current events. Journals and magazines can be harder to distinguish, but their differences are important. Most college instructors expect students' research to rely more on journals than on magazines.

Journals	Magazines
Examples: *American Anthropologist, Journal of Black Studies, Journal of Chemical Education*	Examples: *The New Yorker, Time, Rolling Stone, People*
Articles are intended to advance knowledge in a particular field.	Articles are intended to express opinion, inform, or entertain.
Writers and readers are specialists in the field.	Writers may or may not be specialists in their subjects. Readers are members of the general public or a subgroup with a particular interest.

---

http://www.ablongman.com/littlebrown

For added help with finding and using periodicals, click on

➤ **Research writing** ➤ **Web links** ➤ **Finding sources**

45d

Journals

Articles always include source citations.

Appearance is bland, with black-only type, little or no decoration, and only illustrations that directly amplify the text, such as graphs.

Issues may appear quarterly or less often.

Issues may be paged separately (like a magazine) or may be paged sequentially throughout an annual volume, so that issue number 3 (the third issue of the year) could open on page 327. (The method of pagination affects source citations. See p. 719.)

Magazines

Articles rarely include source citations.

Appearance varies but is generally lively, with color, decoration (headings, sidebars, and other elements), and illustrations (drawings, photographs).

Issues may appear weekly, biweekly, or monthly.

Issues are paged separately, each beginning on page 1.

1 ▪ Using indexes to periodicals

How indexes work

Indexes provide information on the articles in journals, magazines, and newspapers. Often, these indexes include abstracts, or summaries, of the articles, and they may offer the full texts of the articles as well. Your library subscribes to periodical indexes and to large databases that include multiple indexes. (See pp. 637–38 for a list.) Depending on your library, you can consult the indexes through its Web site, on CD-ROMs, or in books.

Check the library's list of indexes to find the ones that seem most appropriate for your subject. (The library's Web site may include a search function to help you with this step.) Edward Begay, for instance, chose to avoid indexes of technical periodicals, such as *Applied Science and Technology Index* and *Computer Database*, because his subject was the social and economic effects of computers rather than the machines themselves. Instead, Begay chose databases such as *Sociofile*, for articles in sociology journals; *PsycLIT*, for articles in psychology journals; and *InfoTrac Expanded Academic*, for recent newspaper and magazine articles.

Searching electronic periodical indexes is discussed under electronic searches on pages 621–26. To recap, you'll need keywords reflecting the index's own terms for categorizing articles, found in the index's directory or thesaurus. You can consult the directory or use your own keywords to find equivalent terms in the directory. For instance, Edward Begay used his own keywords *Internet AND equality* to retrieve a list of possible sources from the database *EBSCOhost Academic Search* (screens 1 and 2, opposite). At the full record for one of these sources (screen 3, next page), Begay found several sub-ject headings under which the database lists the article. Using one of the headings, *Digital divide,* as his keywords, Begay was able to locate additional worthwhile articles.

Many databases allow you to limit your search to so-called peer-reviewed or refereed journals—that is, scholarly journals whose ar-ticles have been reviewed before publication by experts in the field and then revised by the author. (Begay's initial search of *EBSCOhost*

45d

1. Initial keyword search of periodical database

2. Partial search results

3. Full record with abstract

45d

EBSCOhost - Microsoft Internet Explorer

File   Edit   View   Favorites   Tools   Help

Back   Forward   Stop   Refresh   Home   Favorites   History   Print

Address http://web20.epnet.com/citation.asp?tb=1&_ug=dbs+1+In+en%2Dus+sid+B821E723%2DC577%2D42D5   Go   Links »

Title: *Internet* Connectedness and Inequality: Beyond the "Divide". ← Article title

Subject(s): INTERNET (Computer network); DIGITAL divide; INTERNET users ← Database subject headings

Source: Communication Research, Aug2001, Vol. 28 Issue 4, p507.29p, 10 charts, 4 graphs
  ↳ Journal title   ↳ Date

Author(s): Joo-Young Jung; Qiu, Jack Linchuan; Yong-Chan Kim ← Authors

Abstract: This article presents the *Internet* Connectedness Index (ICI), a measure for monitoring long-term inequalities in the quality of *Internet* connections among users, especially in terms of whether *Internet* connections will enhance the chances of people's upward mobility. This index is preferable to more established digital divide measures (e.g., gadgetry ownership or time online) for research on how the *Internet* is being incorporated into a world of structural inequalities. The ICI utilizes conventional time, history, and context measures, but goes beyond them to capture the scope and centrality of *Internet* incorporation into the everyday lives of diverse social groups. The validity and robustness of ICI vis-a-vis conventional ownership and time online measures are demonstrated in this article. In addition, the authors discuss theoretical, methodological, and policy implications based on the results. The analytical data are drawn from the Communication Technology and Community Program's Metamorphosis Project, an inquiry into the communication infrastructures of seven ethnically marked residential areas in Los Angeles. [ABSTRACT FROM AUTHOR] ← Abstract

AN: 5046216

ISSN: 0093-6502

Full Text Word Count: 9280

Database: Academic Search Elite ← Database

Done   Internet

4. Full text of article

EBSCOhost - Microsoft Internet Explorer

File   Edit   View   Favorites   Tools   Help

File   Forward   Stop   Refresh   Home   Favorites   History   Print

Address http://web20.epnet.com/citation.asp?tb=1&_ug=dbs+1+In+en%2Dus+sid+B821E723%2DC577%2D42D5   Go   Links »

Title: *INTERNET CONNECTIONS AND INEQUALITY: BEYOND THE "DIVIDE"* , By: Joo-Young Jung, Qiu, Jack Linchuan, Yong-Chan Kim, Communication Research, 00936502, Aug2001, Vol. 28, Issue 4

Database: *Academic Search Elite* ← Database   ↳ Article information

INTERNET CONNECTEDNESS AND INEQUALITY: BEYOND THE "DIVIDE"

Full text →

Contents

Limitations of Established Measures Employed in Research on the Digital Divide

Limitations of Dichotomous Conceptions and Measures of the Digital Divide

How is the digital divide in access to *Internet* technology different from the divide in owning a Mercedes Benz? Is the digital divide a problem? The debate about the size and shape of a digital divide in access to the *Internet* is contradictory, with one side claiming that the disparity is inevitable and will narrow in the process of increasing levels of adoption (Birdsell, Muzzio. Krane, & Cottreau, 1998; Nie & Erbring, 2000; Powell, 2001; Thierer, 2000), and the other side finding that various kinds of inequalities persist or may increase in the process of diffusion (Goslee, 1998; Lenhart, 2000; National Telecommunication and Information Administration [NTIA], 1999, 2000; Norris, 2001; Papadakis, 2000; UCLA *Internet* Report; 2000; Wilhelm, 2000). How the digital divide issue is perceived will surely lead to different diagnoses and prescriptions.

Done   Internet

Academic Search included this limitation, as shown in screen 1.) Limiting your search to peer-reviewed journals can help you navigate huge databases that might otherwise return scores of unusable articles from other kinds of periodicals.

Note As you follow leads in online indexes, it's easy to lose track of what database you're using. You'll need this information for any article you obtain online, so make sure you have it. If you print search records or e-mail them to yourself, the database information will appear on the record along with other bibliographic data (see screens 2–4).

The use of abstracts

The full article record in screen 3 shows a key feature of many databases' periodical listings: an abstract that summarizes the article. Describing research methods, conclusions, and other information, an abstract can tell you whether you want to pursue an article and thus save you time. However, the abstract cannot replace the actual article. If you want to use the work as a source, you must consult the full text, as described on the next page.

45d

Helpful databases

The list below includes databases to which academic libraries commonly subscribe. Some of these databases—for instance, *ProQuest Research Library* and *EBSCOhost Academic Search*—cover much the same material, so your library may subscribe to one or the other but not both.

Note More specific lists of indexes for academic disciplines appear later in this book: see pages 796 (literature), 815–16 (other humanities), 835–36 (social sciences), and 867 (natural and applied sciences).

> *EBSCOhost Academic Search.* A periodical index covering magazines and journals in the social sciences, sciences, arts, and humanities. Many articles are available full-text.
>
> *FirstSearch.* A Web interface to more than sixty databases, including *WorldCat, Books in Print, Dissertation Abstracts, Wilson Select, Article-First, Biography Index, Book Review Index, Education Abstracts, ERIC, Medline, PAIS,* and many more.
>
> *InfoTrac Expanded Academic.* The Gale Group's general periodical index covering the social sciences, sciences, arts, and humanities as well as national news periodicals. It includes full-text articles.
>
> *JSTOR.* Full-text articles from older volumes of several hundred journals in the sciences, social sciences, arts, humanities, and business.
>
> *LexisNexis Academic.* An index of news and business, legal, and reference information, with full-text articles. *LexisNexis* includes international, national, and regional newspapers, newsmagazines, and legal and business publications.
>
> *Nineteenth-Century Masterfile.* Perhaps the only electronic database for materials from the nineteenth century, including *Poole's Index to Periodical Literature* (1802–1906), W. T. Stead's *Index to Periodicals* (1890–1902), and indexes to books and journals.
>
> *ProQuest Research Library.* A periodical index covering the sciences, social sciences, arts, and humanities, including many full-text articles.

Wilson Databases. A collection of indexes, often provided in a package, including *Business Periodicals Index, Education Index, General Science Index, Humanities Index, Readers' Guide to Periodical Literature,* and *Social Sciences Index.*

While using databases like those above, you may want to consult a **citation index** to see what has been written *about* an article or book, as when one scholar comments on the work of another. The three main citation indexes are *Arts and Humanities Citation Index, Social Science Citation Index,* and *Science Citation Index.* All three are available on the database *ISI Web of Science,* which many libraries subscribe to.

45d

2 ■ Locating the articles in periodicals

Many article listings you find will include or link directly to the full text of the article, which you'll be able to read online and print or e-mail to yourself. (See p. 636, screen 4, for a full-text sample.) If the full text is not available online, you'll need to consult the periodical itself. Usually the article listing will also say whether the periodical is available in your library. If you don't see this information, then consult the library's list of periodicals (often called *serials*) either in the main catalog or in a separate catalog.

Your library probably holds recent issues of periodicals in the periodicals room. Back issues are usually stored elsewhere, in one of three forms: in bound volumes; on **microfilm,** a filmstrip showing pages side by side; or on **microfiche,** a sheet of film with pages arranged in rows and columns. Consulting periodicals stored on microfilm or microfiche requires using a special machine, or "reader," with which you locate the page and project it on a screen. (Some readers are also attached to coin-operated photocopiers.) Any member of the library's staff will show you how to operate the reader.

If the periodical you seek is not available in your library, you may be able to obtain the article by interlibrary loan. The article may arrive online, by mail, or by fax, and there may be a fee for the service. Even electronic loans can sometimes take a week or more, so place your order early.

Note Many periodicals are available both online and in print, and most documentation styles require you to specify which version you consulted. For scholarly journals, the two versions are likely to be identical in content though not in format: for instance, the online version may not include the print version's page breaks and numbers. (However, a full-text version in **PDF** format reproduces the actual pages of the print journal. To open PDF files, you may need to download a program called *Acrobat Reader.*) For newspapers and magazines, the two versions often differ more: for instance, the online version may be shorter or longer than the print version, may contain fewer illustrations, or may include links to other resources.

45e Finding sources on the Web

45e

As an academic researcher, you enter the World Wide Web in two ways: through your library's Web site, and through public search engines such as *Yahoo!* and *Google*. The library entrance, covered in the preceding sections, is your main path to the books and periodicals that, for most subjects, should make up most of your sources. The public entrance, discussed here, can lead to a wealth of information and ideas, but it also has a number of disadvantages:

- *The Web is a wide-open network.* Anyone with the right hardware and software can place information on the Internet, and even a carefully conceived search can turn up sources with widely varying reliability: journal articles, government documents, scholarly data, term papers written by high school students, sales pitches masked as objective reports, wild theories. You must be especially diligent about evaluating Internet sources (see p. 653).
- *The Web changes constantly.* No search engine can keep up with the Web's daily additions and deletions, and a source you find today may be different or gone tomorrow. Some sites are designed and labeled as archives: they do not change except with additions. But generally you should not put off consulting an online source that you think you may want to use. If it seems appropriate for your needs, take notes from it or (if the source allows) download it to your own computer. Be sure to record complete source information at the same time (see p. 617 for a list of what to record). Sometimes you can track down lost material at a site that documents Web history, such as *http://webdev.archive.org*, but don't count on it.
- *The Web provides limited information on the past.* Sources dating from before the 1980s or even more recently probably will not appear on the Web.
- *The Web is not all-inclusive.* Most books and many periodicals are available only in the library, not via the Web.

http://www.ablongman.com/littlebrown
For added help with searching the Web, click on
➤ **Research writing**
  ➤ **Video tutorials** ➤ **Using keywords with a search engine**
  ➤ **Exercises** ➤ **Exers. 2 and 3**
  ➤ **Web links** ➤ **Finding sources**

Clearly, the Web warrants cautious use. It should not be the only resource you work with.

1 ■ Using a search engine

To find sources on the Web, you use a **search engine** that catalogs Web sites in a series of directories and conducts keyword searches. Generally, use a directory when you haven't yet refined your topic or you want a general overview. Use keywords when you have refined your topic and you seek specific information.

45e

Current search engines

Dozens of search engines are available. The box below and on the facing page lists the currently most popular engines. (To reach any of them, enter its address in the Address or Location field of your Web browser.)

Web search engines

The features of search engines change often, and new ones appear constantly. For the latest on search engines, see the links collected by *Search Engine Watch* at *http://www.searchenginewatch.com/links.*

Directories that review sites
BUBL Link
   http://bubl.ac.uk/link
Internet Public Library
   http://www.ipl.org/div/subject
Internet Scout Project
   http://scout.wisc.edu/archives
Librarians' Index to the Internet
   http://lii.org

The most advanced and efficient engines
AlltheWeb
   http://www.alltheweb.com
One of the fastest and most comprehensive engines, *AlltheWeb* updates its database frequently so that it returns more of the Web's most recent sites. It allows searches for news, pictures, and audio and video files.

Google
   http://www.google.com
Also fast and comprehensive, *Google* ranks a site based not only on its content but also on the other sites that are linked to it, thus providing a measure of a site's usefulness. *Google* also allows searches for news, discussion groups, and images.

Other engines

AltaVista
   http://www.altavista.com
Ask Jeeves
   http://www.ask.com
Dogpile
   http://www.dogpile.com
Excite
   http://www.excite.com
Lycos
   http://www.lycos.com
MetaCrawler
   http://www.metacrawler.com
Yahoo!
   http://www.yahoo.com

45e

Note For a good range of reliable sources, try out more than a single search engine, perhaps as many as four or five. No search engine can catalog the entire Web—indeed, even the most powerful engine may not include half the sites available at any given time, and most engines include only a fifth or less. In addition, most search engines accept paid placements, giving higher billing to sites that pay a fee. These so-called sponsored links are usually marked as such, but they can compromise a search engine's method for arranging sites in response to your keywords.

A sample search engine

The screen shot below from the *Google* search engine shows the features common to most engines. The circled numbers are keyed to numbered comments following.

1. To search by keywords, type them into the Search field. (See pp. 623–26 on developing keywords.)
2. Click on listings for specific kinds of sources and information —for instance, images or postings to discussion groups.
3. Instead of searching by keywords, browse a subject directory to zero in on your general subject and perhaps your specific topic.
4. Click Advanced Search for more search options and for help using the search engine:

45e

Customize your search—for instance, select a date range, a language, or a number of results to see.

Learn how to limit or expand your keywords—for instance, whether and how to use *AND, NOT, OR,* and other operators.

Learn how to interpret the results of the search. When you perform a search using either keywords or a directory, the search engine generates a list of sites that match your search criteria. The matching sites, or **hits**, are listed in order of "relevance," which the search engine determines by criteria such as the number of times your keywords appear within a site or page, whether the terms appear in the title or the address, and (in *Google*'s case) which other sites have links to the site or page. If there are any special ways the search engine determines relevance, its Advanced Search or Help information will specify them.

Search records

Your Web browser includes functions that allow you to keep track of Web sources and your search:

- **Favorites** or **Bookmarks** save site addresses as links. Click one of these terms near the top of the browser screen to add a site you want to return to. A favorite or bookmark remains on file until you delete it.
- A browser's search history records the sites you visited over a certain period, such as a day, a week, or a month. (You can set the period from the browser's Tools menu.) After the period elapses, the history is deleted. If you forgot to bookmark a site, click History or Go to recover the site from the search history.

2 ■ Following a sample search

For his initial search of the Web, Edward Begay started with the keywords *Internet access* on the *Google* search engine. But the search returned nearly 5.4 *million* items, as shown in screen 1 opposite. Begay realized instantly that he needed to alter his search strategy. Scanning the first few screens of *Google*'s results, he noticed that most items had to do with commercial providers offering connection to the Internet. Clearly, the keywords *Internet access* were returning the wrong kinds of information.

Begay decided to try another approach and consult one of the reviewed subject directories listed on page 640. At the *Librarians'*

1. First *Google* results

45e

2. Reviewed subject directory

Index to the Internet (screen 2) he found broad categories such as *Science, Computers, & Technology* and *Society & Social Issues.* Clicking on the first category and then on *Internet,* he located a directory for *Statistics.* There he found links to sites presenting data about Internet users and reporting on Internet access in public schools. The reports covered access to computers, using terms such as *economic access to education* and *digital divide.*

45e   Begay then returned to *Google* with these new keywords. The keywords *Internet "economic access"* proved disappointing, returning dozens of irrelevant sites among the first fifty. But *Internet "economic access" education* was more successful, returning the results shown in screen 3 below. Though the total number of hits was still large, Begay could see four or five among the first ten that related directly to his topic. He added these sites to his Favorites list for later reference.

3. Second *Google* results

Begay wasn't finished. Knowing that no search engine catalogs every Web site, he decided to try his successful keywords at two other engines, *AlltheWeb* and *Dogpile.* The *AlltheWeb* search turned up an additional promising site among the first thirty. The *Dogpile*

search, which worked through multiple search engines, returned more than a thousand items, including many irrelevant ones but also (among the first thirty) one more possible source.

Begay's Web search illustrates the trial-and-error approach required to refine keywords so that they locate worthwhile sources. Almost any successful Web search will require similar persistence and patience.

45f Finding other online sources

Several online sources can put you directly in touch with experts and others whose ideas and information may inform your research. Because these sources, like Web sites, are unfiltered, you must always evaluate them carefully. (See pp. 658–59.)

1 ■ Using electronic mail

As a research tool, e-mail allows you to communicate with others who are interested in your topic. You may, for instance, carry on an e-mail conversation with a teacher at your school or with other students. Or you may interview an expert in another state to follow up on a scholarly article he or she published. (See pp. 195–96 on e-mail etiquette and p. 648 on conducting interviews.)

2 ■ Using discussion lists

A **discussion list** (sometimes called a **listserv** or just a **list**) uses e-mail to connect individuals who are interested in a common subject, often with a scholarly or technical focus. By sending a question to an appropriate list, you may be able to reach scores of people who know something about your topic. For an index of discussion lists, see *http://tile.net/lists* or *http://www.topica.com*.

When conducting research on a discussion list, follow the guidelines for e-mail etiquette on pages 195–96 as well as these:

- *Lurk for a while*—reading without posting messages. Make sure the discussion is relevant to your topic, and get a sense of how the group interacts.
- *Don't ask for information you can find elsewhere.* Most list members are glad to help with legitimate questions but resent mes-

---

http://www.ablongman.com/littlebrown

For added help with the online resources discussed here, click on

➤ **Research writing** ➤ **Web links** ➤ **Finding sources**

sages that rehash familiar debates or that ask them to do someone else's work.

- *Evaluate messages carefully.* Many list subscribers are passionate experts with fair-minded approaches to their topics, but almost anyone with an Internet connection can post a message to a list. See pages 658–59 on evaluating online sources.

45g

3 ■ Using Web forums and newsgroups

Web forums and newsgroups are more open and less scholarly than discussion lists, so their messages require even more diligent evaluation. **Web forums** allow participants to join a conversation simply by selecting a link on a Web page. For a directory of forums, see *http://www.delphiforums.com*. **Newsgroups** are organized under subject headings such as *soc* for social issues and *biz* for business. For a directory of newsgroups, see *http://groups.google.com*.

4 ■ Using synchronous communication

With e-mail and discussion groups, there's a delay between a message you send and any response you receive. But with **synchronous** (or simultaneous) **communication**, you and others can converse in real time, the way you talk on the phone. Synchronous programs include instant-messaging applications, Web courseware, Internet relay chat (IRC), and virtual environments called MOOs.

Synchronous communication can be used to conduct interviews or hold debates. Your instructor may ask you to use it for your coursework or research and will provide the software and instructions to get started. You can also find out more about synchronous communication at the Web site for this book: see the box on the preceding page.

45g Finding pamphlets and government publications

Organizations such as social-service groups, professional societies, and all branches of government publish booklets, compila-

---

http://www.ablongman.com/littlebrown

For added help with finding government publications, click on

➤ **Research writing** ➤ **Web links** ➤ **Finding sources**

tions of data, and other sources that usually cannot be retrieved through the library's book catalog or periodicals listings.

Pamphlets, bulletins, and other miscellaneous items are often stored in file drawers, called **vertical files.** To find out what is available in pamphlet form, consult the *Vertical File Index: A Subject and Title Index to Selected Pamphlet Materials.* If your library does not have the item you seek, the index tells you how to order it from its publisher. You'll need to allow extra time for such orders.

Government publications provide a vast array of data, public records, and other historical and contemporary information. For US government publications, by far the most numerous, consult the *Monthly Catalog of US Government Publications,* available online. Many federal, state, and local government agencies post important publications—legislation, reports, press releases—on their own Web sites. You can find lists of sites for various federal agencies by using the keywords *United States federal government* with any search engine. Edward Begay took this approach to find statistics from the Department of Commerce on computer use by people of various races (see the screen shot below).

45g

Besides what's available online, your library will have a large collection of printed government publications only if it is a depository library (that is, designated to receive such documents). If yours is not a depository library, a librarian may be able to help you obtain a needed publication from another library.

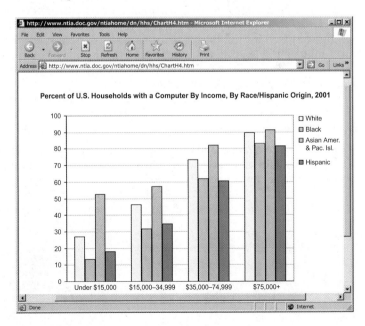

45h Generating your own sources

Many of the sources you consult for a research project—and most of the resources of the library—are likely to be secondary sources whose authors draw their information from other authors. However, academic writing will also require you to consult primary sources and to conduct primary research for information of your own. In many papers this primary research will be the sole basis for your writing, as when you analyze a poem or report on an experiment you conducted. In other papers you will be expected to use your research to support, extend, or refute the ideas of others.

Chapters 51–55 discuss the textual analyses, surveys, experiments, and other primary sources you may use in writing for various academic disciplines. One primary source not covered there is the personal interview with an expert in the topic you are researching. Because of the give-and-take of an interview, you can obtain answers to questions precisely geared to your topic, and you can follow up on points of confusion and unexpected leads. In addition, quotations and paraphrases from an interview can give your paper immediacy and authority. Edward Begay used just such an interview in his paper about the Internet (see p. 756).

You can conduct an interview in person, over the telephone, or online using electronic mail (see p. 645) or a form of synchronous communication (see p. 646). A personal interview is preferable if you can arrange it because you can see the person's expressions and gestures as well as hear his or her tone and words. But telephone and online interviews allow you to interview someone who resists a personal interview or who lives far away from you, while still retaining most advantages of interaction.

A few precautions will help you get the maximum information from an interview with the minimum disruption to the person you are interviewing:

- *Choose your subject carefully.* If you do not already know whom to consult for an interview, ask a teacher in the field or do some telephone or library research. Likely sources, depending on your topic, are those who have written about your topic or something closely related, officials in government, businesspeople,

http://www.ablongman.com/littlebrown
For added help with conducting interviews, click on
➤ **Research writing**
➤ **Web links** ➤ **Finding sources**

even a relative, if he or she is an expert in your topic because of experience, scholarship, or both.

- *Call or write for an appointment.* Tell the person exactly why you are calling, what you want to discuss, and how long you expect the interview to take. Be true to your word on all points.
- *Prepare a list of open-ended questions to ask*—perhaps ten or twelve for a one-hour interview. Plan on doing some research for these questions to discover background on the issues and your subject's published views on the issues.
- *Give your subject time to consider your questions.* Don't rush into silences with more questions.
- *Pay attention to your subject's answers* so that you can ask appropriate follow-up questions and pick up on unexpected but worthwhile points.
- *Take care in interpreting answers,* especially if you are online and thus can't depend on facial expressions, gestures, and tone of voice to convey the subject's attitudes. Ask for clarification when you need it.
- *Keep thorough notes.* Take notes during an in-person or telephone interview, or tape-record the interview, if you have the equipment and your subject agrees. For online interviews, save the discussion in a file of its own. (A synchronous discussion may require that you activate a "log" or "archive" function before you begin your interview in order to save it afterward.)
- *Verify quotations.* Before you quote your subject in your paper, check with him or her to ensure that the quotations are accurate.
- *Send a thank-you note immediately after the interview.* Promise your subject a copy of your finished paper, and send the paper promptly.

45h

EXERCISE 1
Using the library

To become familiar with the research sources available through your library, visit both the library and its Web site for answers to the following questions. (Ask a librarian for help whenever necessary.)

1. Which resources does the library include on its Web site? Which resources require a visit to the library?
2. Where are reference books stored in the library? How are they cataloged and arranged? Which ones are available through the Web site or on CD-ROM? Where and in what format(s) are (*a*) *Contemporary Authors,* (*b*) *Encyclopaedia Britannica,* and (*c*) *MLA International Bibliography of Books and Articles on the Modern Languages and Literatures*?

3. Where is the catalog of the library's periodicals? Where and in what format(s) does the library have the following periodicals: (*a*) the *New York Times*, (*b*) *Harper's* magazine, and (*c*) *Journal of Social Psychology*?

4. Where are the library's periodical indexes? Which ones are available through the Web site or on CD-ROM? Where and in what format(s) are (*a*) the *New York Times Index*, (*b*) *InfoTrac*, and (*c*) *Social Sciences Index*?

5. Does the book catalog cover all of the library's book holdings? If not, which books are not included, and where are they cataloged?

6. What are the library call numbers of the following books: (*a*) *The Power Broker*, by Robert Caro; (*b*) *Heart of Darkness*, by Joseph Conrad; and (*c*) *The Hero with a Thousand Faces*, by Joseph Campbell?

EXERCISE 2
Finding library sources

Locate at least six promising articles and books for the topic you began working on in the previous chapter (Exercise 1, p. 612, and Exercise 2, p. 615). Consider the sources "promising" if they seem directly to address your central research question. Following the guidelines on pages 615–18, make a working bibliography of the sources. Be sure to include all the information you will need to acknowledge the sources in your final paper.

EXERCISE 3
Finding Web sources

Use at least two Web search engines to locate six or seven promising sources for your research project. Begin by developing a list of keywords that can be used to query one of the search engines (see pp. 623–26). Check the Advanced Search or Help option of the engine if you need to narrow your search. Then try your refined keywords on the other search engine as well. How do the results differ? What keyword strategies worked best for finding relevant information?

CHAPTER 46

Working with Sources

The previous chapters helped you lay the groundwork for a research project. This chapter takes you into the most personal, most intensive, and most rewarding part of research writing: using the sources you've found to extend and support your own ideas, to make your topic your own. As before, the work of Edward Begay (on access to the Internet) and Vanessa Haley (on the work of Annie Dillard) will illustrate the activity and thought that go into research writing.

CULTURE LANGUAGE ➤ Making a topic your own requires thinking critically about sources and developing independent ideas. These goals may at first be uncomfortable if your native culture emphasizes understanding and respecting established authority more than questioning and enlarging it. This chapter offers guidance in working with sources so that you can become an expert in your own right and convincingly convey your expertise to others.

46a Evaluating sources

1 ■ Gaining an overview

Once you have a satisfactory working bibliography, you want to get a sense of your sources' usefulness and value.

- *Look first at sources that seem most likely to define your subject.* Edward Begay initially consulted a government report on computer use by different segments of society. Vanessa Haley

---

http://www.ablongman.com/littlebrown
For added help with evaluating sources, click on
➤ **Research writing**
  ➤ Video tutorials ➤ **Evaluating online sources**
  ➤ **Downloads**
    ➤ **Questions for evaluating sources**
    ➤ **Questions for evaluating Web sites**
    ➤ **Questions for evaluating online discussions**
  ➤ Exercises ➤ Exers. 3 and 4
  ➤ Web links ➤ **Working with sources**

turned first to a book by Annie Dillard, Haley's subject. (For a paper like Haley's that analyzes a writer's work, that work is always the starting point.)

- *Scan sources to gauge the kind and extent of their ideas and information.* Don't get bogged down collecting information at this point. Instead, ensure that your sources are appropriately detailed and cover the full range of your subject—that together they promise to help you answer your research question.

46a

2 ▪ Judging relevance and reliability

Not all the sources you find will prove worthwhile: some may be irrelevant to your topic, and others may be unreliable. Gauging the relevance and reliability of sources is the essential task of evaluating them. If you haven't already done so, read this book's Chapters 5 and 6 on critical reading. They provide a foundation for answering the questions in the box below. (You can download these questions from this book's Web site: see the box on p. 651. Make a copy for each source you're evaluating, and provide written answers between the questions.)

Questions for evaluating sources

For online sources, supplement these questions with those on pages 654 and 658.

Relevance

- **Does the source devote some attention to your subject?** Check whether the source focuses on your subject or covers it marginally, and compare the source's coverage to that in other sources.
- **Is the source appropriately specialized for your needs?** Check the source's treatment of a topic you know something about, to ensure that it is neither too superficial nor too technical.
- **Is the source up to date enough for your subject?** Check the publication date. If your subject is current, your sources should be, too.

Reliability

- **Where does the source come from?** It matters whether you found the source through your library or directly on the Internet. (If the latter, see pp. 653–59.) Check whether a library source is popular or scholarly. Scholarly sources, such as refereed journals and university press books, are generally deeper and more reliable.
- **Is the author an expert in the field?** The authors of scholarly publications tend to be experts. To verify expertise, check an author's credentials in a biography (if the source includes one), in a biographical reference (see p. 629), or by a keyword search of the Web. Look for the author's other publications and for his or her job and any affiliation, such as teacher at a university, researcher with a nonprofit organization, author of general-interest books, or writer for popular magazines.

- **What is the author's bias?** Every author has a point of view that influences the selection and interpretation of evidence. You may be able to learn about an author's bias from biographies, citation indexes (p. 638), and review indexes (p. 633). But also look at the source itself. How do the author's ideas relate to those in other sources? What areas does the author emphasize, ignore, or dismiss? When you're aware of sources' biases, you can attempt to balance them.
- **Is the source fair and reasonable?** Even a strongly biased work should present sound reasoning, adequate evidence, and a fair picture of opposing views—all in an objective, calm tone. The absence of any of these qualities should raise a warning flag.
- **Is the source well written?** A logical organization and clear, error-free sentences indicate a careful author.

46a

Note In evaluating sources, you need to consider how they came to you. The sources you find through the library, both print and online, have been previewed for you by their publishers and by the library's staff. They still require your critical reading, but you can have some confidence in the information they contain. With online sources you reach directly, however, you can't assume similar previewing, so your critical reading must be especially rigorous. Special tips for evaluating Web sites and postings to discussion groups appear below and on the following pages.

3 ▪ Evaluating a Web site

To a great extent, the same critical reading that helps you evaluate library sources will help you evaluate Web sites. But most Web sites have not undergone prior screening by editors and librarians. On your own, you must distinguish scholarship from corporate promotion, valid data from invented statistics, well-founded opinion from clever propaganda.

The following strategy can help you make such distinctions. (You can download the summary questions on the next page from this book's Web site: see the box on p. 651.) We'll apply the strategy to the Web site shown on page 655, *Global Warming Information Center*, which turned up in a search for views and data on global warming.

Check the electronic address.

Every file on the Web has a unique address called a **uniform resource locator,** or **URL.** In the screen shot on page 655, the URL (seen in the Address field) is *http://www.nationalcenter.org/Kyoto.html.* For purposes of evaluation, the most important part of any URL is the domain name—here, *nationalcenter.org*—which generally contains the name of the organization that sponsors the site

Questions for evaluating Web sites

Supplement these questions with those on pages 652–53.

- **What does the URL lead you to expect from the site?** Are those expectations fulfilled?
- **Who is the author or sponsor?** How credible is the person or group responsible for the site?
- **What is the purpose of the site?** What does the site's author or sponsor intend to achieve?
- **What does context tell you?** What do you already know about the site's subject that can inform your evaluation? What kinds of support or other information do the site's links provide?
- **What does presentation tell you?** Is the site's design well thought out and effective? Is the writing clear and error-free?
- **How worthwhile is the content?** Are the site's claims well supported by evidence? Is the evidence from reliable sources?

46a

(*nationalcenter*) and an abbreviation that describes the type of organization (*org*). *Org* designates a nonprofit organization. The other major abbreviations are *edu* (educational institution), *gov* (government body), *mil* (military), and *com* (commercial organization).

The domain abbreviation can inform your evaluation to some extent: a *com* site usually reflects the company's commercial purposes, an *edu* site usually supports and distributes scholarly pursuits, and an *org* site usually centers on the public interest. But the abbreviation should not unduly influence your evaluation. A *com* site may offer reliable data, an *edu* site may contain unfiltered student work, and an *org* site may promote a bigoted agenda.

Identify the author or sponsor.

A reputable site will list the author or group responsible for the site and will provide information or a link for contacting the author or group. If none of this information is provided, you should not use the source. If you have only the author or group name, you may be able to discover more in a biographical dictionary or through a keyword search. You should also look for mentions of the author or group in your other sources.

The Web site *Global Warming Information Center* names its sponsor right up front: the John P. McGovern M.D. Center for Environmental and Regulatory Affairs, which is part of the National Center for Public Policy Research (the *nationalcenter* of the site's domain name). The McGovern Center sounds like an organization involved in research about the environment, but discovering more about it proves difficult. The site includes no links to the McGovern Center, so locating it involves following links to the National Center. When finally reached, the McGovern Center home page links to an

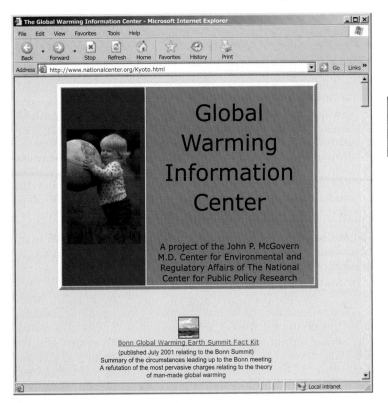

informative explanation of the center's mission and activities, as described below.

Gauge purpose.

A Web site's purpose determines what ideas and information it offers. Inferring that purpose tells you how to interpret what you see on the site. If a site is intended to sell a product or an opinion, it will likely emphasize favorable ideas and information while ignoring or even distorting what is unfavorable. In contrast, if a site is intended to build knowledge—for instance, a scholarly project or journal—it will likely acknowledge diverse views and evidence.

Determining the purpose of a site often requires looking beyond the first page and beneath the surface of words and images. The elements of the *Global Warming* site—the title, the green background, the photo of a child carrying a globe through a field of grass—suggest an environmentalist purpose of informing readers about the theory and consequences of rising earth temperatures caused by pollution. The site's purpose is actually different, though. Below the title box, a link to the "Bonn Global Warming Earth

Summit Fact Kit" promises "A refutation of the most pervasive charges relating to the theory of man-made global warming." The site appears, then, to reject the theory. A definite statement of the McGovern Center's purpose appears on another page:

> to help arm conservatives with the tools for the environmental policy debate it had been lacking, among them: 1) a forum for coordination and sharing of strategy and information; 2) numerous accounts of how environmental regulations work in practice; 3) explanations of the perspectives of various groups on environmental issues; 4) a marketing apparatus to help grassroots environmental activists, persons knowledgeable about environmental regulations and reputable economists and scientists gain greater access to the media; 5) a system for countering "junk science" when it appears, especially in the media.

The McGovern Center's *Global Warming* site seems intended to inform readers about the evidence against global warming in the interest of reducing or overturning environmental regulations.

Consider context.

Your evaluation of a Web site should be informed by considerations outside the site itself. Chief among these is your own knowledge: What do you already know about the site's subject and the prevailing views of it? Where does this site seem to fit into that picture? What can you learn from this site that you don't already know?

In addition, you can follow some of the site's links to see how they support, or don't support, the site's credibility. For instance, links to scholarly sources lend authority to a site—but *only if* the scholarly sources actually relate to and back up the site's claims.

Examining the *Global Warming* site, you might register the antiregulatory bias but also recognize that this view is a significant one in the debates over global warming. That is, the bias does not necessarily disqualify the site as a source on global warming. The question then is the reliability of its information: does it come from trustworthy, less biased sources? All the site's links lead to the McGovern Center's publications or to the parent organization, the National Center for Public Policy Research, which describes itself as a "communication and research foundation dedicated to providing free-market solutions to today's public policy programs." Because the links do not go outside the National Center, the question of reliability remains open, to be answered only by examining the *Global Warming* site further.

Look at presentation.

Considering both the look of a site and the way it's written can illuminate its intentions and reliability. Are the site's elements all functional and well integrated, or is the site cluttered with irrelevant material and graphics? Does the design reflect the apparent page maintains that "[t]here is no serious evidence that man-made global warming is taking place." It offers statistics to support this statement and in answer to the second question cites a professor at Massachusetts Institute of Technology and a report by the National Academy of Sciences. Footnote numbers key to a description of sources, which should include scholarly publications that explain the methods of gathering and interpreting the cited data, a scholarly article by the MIT scientist, and perhaps the NAS report. However, none of this appears in the fifteen footnotes, which cite an article by the scientist in the *Wall Street Journal,* other newspaper articles, and reports by the National Center and other conservative groups. A look at sources for the site's other publications indicates a similar source mix.

The public controversy on global warming reflects disagreement among scholars over whether the earth's temperatures are rising significantly, whether human-made pollution is an important cause, how serious the consequences may be, and how to solve the problem. However, the *Global Warming* site does not offer or refer to the scholarly research. As a result, the claims and evidence must be viewed suspiciously and probably rejected for use in a research paper. A usable source need not be less biased, but it must be more substantial.

4 ■ Evaluating online discussions

The contributions to online discussions require the same critical scrutiny as Web sites do. On an e-mail discussion list (p. 645), whose subscribers are likely to be professionals in the field, you will still find wrong or misleading data and skewed opinions. On more accessible Web forums and newsgroups (p. 646), messages are even more suspect. A reliable discussion-group message may provide very current information or eyewitness testimony, but it will not have the authority of a scholarly publication.

Use the following strategy for evaluating messages in online discussions. You can download the summary questions below from this book's Web site: see the box on page 651.

Questions for evaluating online discussions

Supplement these questions with those on pages 652–53.

- ■ **Who is the author?** How credible is the person writing?
- ■ **What is the context of the message?** What do the other messages in the discussion thread tell you about the reliability of this message?
- ■ **How worthwhile is the content?** Are the message's claims supported by evidence? Is the evidence from reliable sources? Is the tone moderate?
- ■ **How does the message compare with other sources?** Do the author's claims seem accurate given what you've seen in sources you know to be reliable?

---

purpose of the site, or does it undercut or conceal that pur[pose]
some way? Is the text clearly written, or is it difficult to unde[rstand]?
Is it error-free, or does it contain typos and grammatical err[ors]?

At first glance, as noted earlier, the *Global Warming* si[te]
a pro-environmentalist image that turns out not to coinci[de with]
its purpose. Otherwise, the site is cleanly designed, with [its]
elements laid out clearly. The text on other pages is stra[ight]-
ward and readable. Together, design and readability indicate [the]
sponsor takes its purpose seriously and has thought out its [presen]-
tation.

Analyze content.

With information about a site's author, purpose, and [bias,]
you're in a position to evaluate its content. Are the ideas [and in]-
formation slanted and, if so, in what direction? Are the vi[ews and]
data authoritative, or do you need to balance them—or ev[en reject]
them? These questions require close reading of both the te[xt and its]
sources.

The *Global Warming* site links to a wealth of informati[on on the]
issue it addresses, mostly reports and fact kits like the o[ne shown]
on the home page. The site also links to "Questions and [Answers]
on Global Warming," partly shown below. As might be exp[ected,]

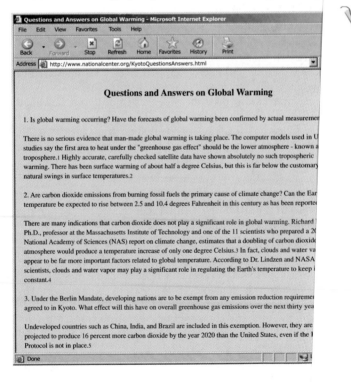

Identify the author.

As with a Web site, checking out the author of an online message can help you judge the reliability of the message. If the author uses a screen name, write directly to him or her requesting full name and credentials. Do not use the message as a source if the author fails to respond. Once you know an author's name, you may be able to obtain background information from a keyword search of the Web or a biographical dictionary.

46a

You can also obtain a sense of the interests and biases of an author by tracking down his or her other messages. For newsgroups, *Google*'s site (*http://groups.google.com*) allows you to find other messages by the author of any posting. For discussion lists or Web forums, use the groups' archives to locate an author's other messages.

Consider messages in context.

Messages are often more difficult to evaluate in isolation than in the context of the overall thread of conversation. By returning to the initial posting in the thread and reading forward, you can see how a message relates to other postings. Does the message respond fairly to others' views? Do others object to the message or confirm it?

Analyze content.

A reliable online message will offer evidence for claims and sources for evidence. If you don't see such supporting information, ask the author for it. (If the author does not respond, ignore the message.) Then verify the sources with your own research: are they reputable?

The tone of a message can also be a clue to its reliability. Online discussions are generally more rushed and heated than other kinds of dialog, but look askance at a message that's contemptuous, dismissive, or shrill.

Compare with other sources.

Always consider discussion-group messages in the context of other sources so that you can distinguish singular, untested views from more mainstream views that have been subject to verification.

Be wary of postings that reproduce periodical articles, reports, or other publications. Try to locate the original version of the publication to be sure it has been reproduced fully and accurately, not quoted selectively or distorted. If you can't locate the original version, then don't use the publication as a source.

EXERCISE 1
Evaluating a source

Imagine that you are researching a paper on the advertising techniques that are designed to persuade consumers to buy products. You have listed the following book in your working bibliography:

Vance Packard, *The Hidden Persuaders*, revised edition, 1981.

On your own or with your classmates (as your instructor wishes), obtain this book from a library and evaluate it as a source for your paper. Use the guidelines on pages 652–53.

EXERCISE 2
Evaluating Web sites

Find and evaluate three Web sites: a commercial site, such as Microsoft's or Apple's; a site for a nonprofit organization, such as the American Medical Association or Greenpeace; and the personal site of an individual. What do you know or can you infer about each site's sponsor or author? What seems to be the site's purpose or purposes? What do the site's links contribute? How effective is the site's design? How reliable do you judge the site's information to be? How do the three types of sites differ in these respects?

EXERCISE 3
Evaluating an online discussion

Using the *Google* site given on the previous page, locate a newsgroup on a subject that interests you. (If you already participate in an online discussion group, you can use it instead.) Pick one series of at least ten related messages on a single topic. Write a brief summary of each message (see pp. 123–24 on summarizing). Then analyze and synthesize the messages to develop a one- or two-paragraph evaluation of the discussion. Which messages seem reliable? Which don't? Why?

46b Synthesizing sources

When you begin to locate the differences and similarities among sources, you move into the most significant part of research writing: forging relationships for your own purpose. This **synthesis**, an essential step in critical reading (pp. 129–31), continues through the drafting and revision of a research paper. As you infer connections—say, between one writer's ideas and another's or between two works by the same author—you create new knowledge.

All kinds of connections may occur to you as you work with sources. Edward Begay, researching the potential accessibility of the Internet to both the affluent and the poor, found data in one source to support another source's assertions about a technological gap between private and public schools. He also uncovered a cen-

http://www.ablongman.com/littlebrown
For added help with synthesizing sources, click on
➤ **Research writing** ➤ **Web links** ➤ **Working with sources**

tral disagreement among sources over whether the Internet would prove a boon or an obstruction to education. Vanessa Haley, writing about Annie Dillard, sought and found similarities in Dillard's ideas about the place of humanity in nature, ideas expressed in varying contexts throughout Dillard's best-known book. Haley also discovered that her view of Dillard was partly supported by some of the critics she consulted but not supported by others. She knew she would have to take account of these divergent views in her paper.

46b

Your synthesis of sources will grow more detailed and sophisticated as you proceed through the research-writing process. Unless, like Vanessa Haley, you are analyzing primary sources such as the works of a writer, at first read your sources quickly and selectively to obtain an overview of your topic and a sense of how the sources approach it. Don't get bogged down in taking detailed notes, but *do* record your own ideas about sources in your research journal (pp. 607–08).

Respond to sources.

Write down what your sources make you think. Do you agree or disagree with the author? Do you find his or her views narrow, or do they open up new approaches for you? Is there anything in the source that you need to research further before you can understand it? Does the source prompt questions that you should keep in mind while reading other sources?

Connect sources.

When you notice a link between sources, jot it down. Do two sources differ in their theories or their interpretations of facts? Does one source illuminate another—perhaps commenting or clarifying or supplying additional data? Do two or more sources report studies that support a theory you've read about or an idea of your own?

Heed your own insights.

Apart from ideas prompted by your sources, you are sure to come up with independent thoughts: a conviction, a point of confusion that suddenly becomes clear, a question you haven't seen anyone else ask. These insights may occur at unexpected times, so it's good practice to keep a notebook handy to record them.

Use sources to support your own ideas.

As your research proceeds, the responses, connections, and insights you form through synthesis will lead you to answer your starting research question with a statement of your thesis (see p. 690). They will also lead you to the main ideas supporting your thesis—conclusions you have drawn from your synthesis of sources, forming the main divisions of your paper. When drafting the paper, make sure each paragraph focuses on an idea of your own, with the support for the idea coming from your sources. In this way, your paper will synthesize others' work into something wholly your own.

EXERCISE 4
Synthesizing sources

The following three passages address the same issue, the legalization of drugs. What similarities do you see in the authors' ideas? What differences? Write a paragraph of your own in which you use these authors' views as a point of departure for your own view about drug legalization.

Perhaps the most unfortunate victims of drug prohibition laws have been the residents of America's ghettos. These laws have proved largely futile in deterring ghetto-dwellers from becoming drug abusers, but they do account for much of what ghetto residents identify as the drug problem. Aggressive, gun-toting drug dealers often upset law-abiding residents far more than do addicts nodding out in doorways. Meanwhile other residents perceive the drug dealers as heroes and successful role models. They're symbols of success to children who see no other options. At the same time the increasingly harsh criminal penalties imposed on adult drug dealers have led drug traffickers to recruit juveniles. Where once children started dealing drugs only after they had been using them for a few years, today the sequence is often reversed. Many children start using drugs only after working for older drug dealers for a while. Legalization of drugs, like legalization of alcohol in the early 1930s, would drive the drug-dealing business off the streets and out of apartment buildings and into government-regulated, tax-paying stores. It also would force many of the gun-toting dealers out of the business and convert others into legitimate business-men.   —ETHAN A. NADELMANN, "Shooting Up"

Statistics argue against legalization. The University of Michigan conducts an annual survey of twelfth graders, asking the students about their drug consumption. In 1980, 50 percent of those polled said they had used marijuana in the past twelve months, whereas in 2002 only 37 percent had done so. Cocaine use was halved in the same period (12 percent to 6 percent). At the same time, twelve-month use of legally available drugs—alcohol and nicotine-containing cigarettes—remained fairly steady around 75 percent and 55 percent, respectively. The numbers of illegal drug users haven't declined nearly enough: those teenaged marijuana and cocaine users are still vulnerable to addiction and even death, and they threaten to infect their impressionable peers. But clearly the prohibition of illegal drugs has helped, while the legal status of alcohol and cigarettes has not made them less popular.
                  —SYLVIA RUNKLE, "The Case Against Legalization"

I have to laugh at the debate over what to do about the drug problem. Everyone is running around offering solutions—from making drug use a more serious criminal offense to legalizing it. But there isn't a real solution. I know that. I used and abused drugs, and people, and society, for two decades. Nothing worked to get me to stop all that behavior except just plain being sick and tired. Nothing. Not threats, not ten-plus years in prison, not anything that was said to me. I used until I got through. Period. And that's when you'll win the war. When all the dope fiends are done. Not a minute before. —MICHAEL W. POSEY, "I Did Drugs Until They Wore Me Out. Then I Stopped."

EXERCISE 5
Evaluating and synthesizing sources
Look up the sources in the working bibliography you made in Chapter 45, Exercise 2 (p. 650). Evaluate the sources for their relevance and reliability. If the sources seem unreliable or don't seem to give you what you need, expand your working bibliography and evaluate the new sources. In your research journal, write down your responses to sources, the connections you perceive among sources, and other original ideas that occur to you.

46c Mining and interacting with sources

When you have decided which sources to pursue, you may be ready to gather information, or you may want to step back and get your bearings. Your choice will depend mainly on how familiar you are with the main issues of your subject and whether you have formed a central idea about it.

■ *When you know what you're looking for, proceed with information gathering.* If you've formed a good idea of your thesis and a sense of the subjects you will cover, you'll have a framework in which to use sources.

■ *When you're uncertain of your direction, stop to draft a thesis statement and create an outline.* These steps (discussed on pp. 690–94) can help when you're attracted to several different theses or when you don't see how the various areas of your subject relate.

The following sections discuss a way of reading sources and methods of gathering and organizing information from sources.

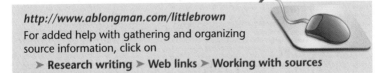

http://www.ablongman.com/littlebrown
For added help with gathering and organizing source information, click on
➤ **Research writing** ➤ **Web links** ➤ **Working with sources**

1 ■ Skimming and then reading

The most efficient method of reading secondary sources during research is **skimming**, reading quickly to look for pertinent information. (Primary sources usually need to be read more carefully, especially when they are the focus of your paper.) Follow these guidelines for skimming:

46c

- *Read with a specific question in mind,* not randomly in hopes of hitting something worthwhile.
- *Consult reference aids*—table of contents, menu, index, or headings—to find what you want.
- *Concentrate on headings and main ideas,* skipping material unrelated to the specific question you are researching.

When you find something relevant, read slowly and carefully to achieve a clear understanding of what the author is saying and to interpret and evaluate the material in the context of your own and others' opinions.

2 ■ Gathering and organizing information

Before you begin mining your sources, decide on categories into which your subject can be divided. (If you have previously outlined your preliminary ideas, use outline headings for these categories.) Edward Begay, for instance, divided his general subject of Internet access into these categories:

History of the Internet
Traditional vs. innovative models of education
Business use of the Internet
Differences between rich and poor schools
Training of Internet users
Costs of hooking up to the Internet
Internet and economic inequality
Role of librarians and teachers in Internet use
Role of businesses in Internet use

Headings for your categories will go at the top of each note to cue you about its content.

Researchers vary in their methods for working with sources, but all methods share the same goals:

- *Keep accurate records of what sources say.* Accuracy helps prevent misrepresentation and plagiarism.
- *Keep accurate records of how to find sources.* These records are essential for retracing steps and for citing sources in the final paper. (See pp. 615–20 on recording information in a working bibliography.)
- *Interact with sources.* Information gathering is not mechanical but critical, leading to an understanding of sources, the relationships among them, and their support for one's own ideas.

You can accomplish these goals by taking handwritten notes, typing notes into your computer, annotating photocopies or printouts of sources, or annotating downloaded documents. On any given project, you may use all the methods. Each has advantages and disadvantages.

Note Whichever method you use, take two steps with every note, photocopy, printout, or downloaded document:

46c

- *Key the material to your outline* so that you know where it belongs.
- *Record the source's complete publication information,* or use the author's name as a shorthand reference to a list where you keep complete publication information.

Handwritten notes

The traditional method of writing notes on 4″ × 6″ cards will prove useful when you come across a source with no computer or photocopier handy or when you need to record something brief. Handwritten notes can be risky, though. It's easy to introduce errors as you work from source to note card. And it's possible to copy source language and then later mistake and use it as your own, thus plagiarizing the source. Always take care to make accurate notes and to place big quotation marks around any passage you quote. Some researchers reduce the risk of plagiarism by summarizing or paraphrasing sources on notes instead of quoting them, as described on pages 667–70. Other researchers delay this step until drafting because it increases the risk of error.

Notes on computer

Taking notes on your computer can streamline the path of source to note to paper because you can import the notes into your draft as you write. Using word-processor files, you can label and sort notes much as you would on note cards. (The examples on pages 668–69 illustrate one way of labeling computer notes.)

Computer notes have the same disadvantages as handwritten notes: the risk of introducing errors and the risk of plagiarizing. As with handwritten notes, strive for accuracy, and use quotation marks for quotations.

Photocopies and printouts

Photocopying from print sources or printing out online sources each has distinct advantages for researchers:

- *Both methods are convenient,* particularly when sources must remain in the library (for instance, bound periodicals and reference works) or when you find sources online (for instance, full-text articles or trustworthy Web pages).
- *Both methods may be safer than handwritten or computer notes.*

Many researchers and teachers believe that photocopying or printing out sources reduces the risks of error and plagiarism. Each method requires manipulating source material only once, not twice, to use it in your paper. And with each method you see exactly what's quoted as you work the source material into your draft.

But photocopies and printouts have disadvantages, too:

46c

- *They can discourage interaction with sources* by substituting busy-work for thinking. You must read photocopied and printed-out sources as critically as you would any others. Highlight or annotate the relevant passages with underlining, circles, and marginal notes about their significance for your subject. (See the example below.)
- *Source records can get lost.* You must take special care to note the publication information for sources directly on a printout or photocopy. If you don't have this information for your final paper, you can't use the source.
- *Photocopies and printouts can encourage unselective quotation.* Drafting from a complete source rather than notes on the source, you may be tempted to import whole blocks rather than the bits that advance and support your ideas. See page 671 for guidelines on judicious use of quotations.

Internet and income inequality
Commerce Dept., *Falling* ... http://www.ntia.gov/ntiahome/
fttn00/Falling.htm#2.1

Figure I-9 presents some evidence that both income and education are independently associated with Internet access. Although the average Internet access rate for incomes of $75,000 and greater is 77.7%, it ranges from 82% for those with a college degree or more down to 51% for those with less than a high school education. Likewise, households with incomes between $15,000 and $34,999 had an average access rate of 28%, ranging from 46% for college or more down to 11% for less than high school. The same wide disparities occur within education categories. For example, among households in which the householder had some schooling beyond high school but not a college degree, home Internet access reached 76% in the over $75,000 income group but only 26% in the under $15,000 income group. Among households with incomes below $15,000 and less than a high school education, only 4% had Internet access at home.

greatest access = high educ. high income

least access = low educ. low income

Downloads

Researching online, you can usually download full-text articles, Web pages, discussion-group messages, and other materials into your word processor. If you also take notes on your word processor, you can organize much or all of your research on your computer. While drafting, you can import source information from one file into another.

These advantages of downloading are offset by clear disadvantages:

- *Directly importing source material creates a high risk of plagiarism.* You must keep clear boundaries between your own ideas and words and those of others—perhaps by using distinctive type fonts or colors. And make sure to record publication information as part of every downloaded document.
- *Downloading can discourage interaction with sources.* Even more than with photocopies and printouts, you must make an effort with downloads to analyze and synthesize sources. Many researchers print out downloaded sources and mark up paper copies. Alternatively, you can use your word processor's Comment and Highlight functions to annotate the electronic file or simply type your own comments into the source. (But use a different color or font!)

46d   Using summary, paraphrase, and quotation

As you take notes from sources or work source material into your draft, you can summarize, paraphrase, quote, or combine methods. The choice should depend on why you are using a source.

Note *Summaries, paraphrases, and quotations all require source citations. A summary or paraphrase without a source citation or a quotation without quotation marks is plagiarism.* (See pp. 680–88 for more on plagiarism.)

1 ■ Summarizing

When you **summarize**, you condense an extended idea or argument into a sentence or more in your own words. A full discussion of summary appears on pages 123–24, and you should read that section if you have not already done so.

Summary is most useful when you want to record the gist of an author's idea without the background or supporting evidence.

http://www.ablongman.com/littlebrown
For added help and practice with summary, paraphrase, and quotation, click on
➤ **Research writing**
    ➤ **Exercises** ➤ **Exers. 5–7**
    ➤ **Web links** ➤ **Working with sources**

Edward Begay summarized the following quotation from one of his sources—Max Frankel, "The Moon, This Time Around," *New York Times Magazine,* page 42:

> A recent Rand study, with research supported by the Markle Foundation, concluded that in the foreseeable future the free market is likely to deliver e-mail to only half of America. Without induced subsidies, perhaps from Internet access fees, the computer industry may never produce the inexpensive technologies that would enable television sets, telephones and computer games to bring e-mail into the home. Interim subsidies and technologies would also be needed if less-affluent citizens are to get their e-mail outside the home, in apartment lobbies, libraries and schools.

In the following one-sentence summary of this passage, Begay picks out the kernel of Frankel's idea and expresses it in his own words:

Internet and economic inequality

Frankel 42

Rand study says government direction and subsidy may be required to make e-mail technology universal and accessible to all.

2 ■ Paraphrasing

When you **paraphrase,** you follow much more closely the author's original presentation, but you still restate it in your own words. Paraphrase is most useful when you want to present or examine an author's line of reasoning but don't feel the original words merit direct quotation.

The note below shows how Begay might have paraphrased the passage by Frankel given above:

Internet and economic inequality

Frankel 42

If market forces prevail, according to Rand, e-mail may fail to reach many Americans. The government may have to underwrite the adaptation of household devices to e-mail, possibly by charging for use of the Internet. Similar measures will be required in the short term to make e-mail available to poorer people in public places.

Notice how the paraphrase differs from the Frankel passage in sentence structures and wording, except in the case of terms that lack synonyms such as *government* and *e-mail:*

46d

Frankel's words	Begay's paraphrase
A recent Rand study, with research supported by the Markle Foundation, concluded that in the foreseeable future the free market is likely to deliver e-mail to only half of America.	If market forces prevail, according to Rand, e-mail may fail to reach many Americans.
Without induced subsidies, perhaps from Internet access fees, the computer industry may never produce the inexpensive technologies that would enable television sets, telephones and computer games to bring e-mail into the home.	The government may have to underwrite the adaptation of household devices to e-mail, possibly by charging for use of the Internet.
Interim subsidies and technologies would also be needed if less-affluent citizens are to get their e-mail outside the home, in apartment lobbies, libraries and schools.	Similar measures will be required in the short term to make e-mail available to poorer people in public places.

Follow these guidelines when paraphrasing:

- *Read the material several times to be sure you understand it.*
- *Restate the main ideas in your own words and sentence structures.* You need not put down in new words the whole passage or all the details. Select what is pertinent and restate only that. If complete sentences seem too detailed or cumbersome, use phrases. Edward Begay might have written this more telegraphic paraphrase of the quotation by Frankel:

Internet and economic inequality

Frankel 42

From Rand: Mkt. forces may leave many Americans without e-mail. Thus govt. role: ensure compatible technology, underwrite adaptation of household devices, make e-mail available to poor in public places.

- *Be careful not to distort meaning.* Don't change the source's emphasis or omit connecting words, qualifiers, and other material whose absence will confuse you later or cause you to misrepresent the source. (See also p. 672.)

See pages 684–85 for examples of unacceptable (plagiarized) paraphrases.

CULTURE LANGUAGE ➤ If English is not your native language, you may have difficulty paraphrasing the ideas in sources because synonyms don't occur to you or you don't see how to restructure sentences. Before attempting a paraphrase, read the original passage several times. Then, instead of "translating" line by line, try to state the gist of the passage without looking at it. Check your effort against the original to be sure you have captured the source author's meaning and emphasis without using his or her words and sentence structures. If you need a synonym for a word, look it up in a dictionary.

46d

3 ▪ Quoting

Deciding when to quote

Your notes from sources may include many quotations, especially if you rely on photocopies, printouts, or downloads. Whether to use a quotation in your draft, instead of a summary or paraphrase, depends on whether the source is primary or secondary and on how important the exact words are:

- *Quote extensively when you are analyzing primary sources,* such as literary works and historical documents. The quotations will often be both the target of your analysis and the chief support for your ideas. You may need to quote many brief passages, integrated into your sentences, and then comment on the quotations to clarify your analysis and win readers' agreement with it. For examples, see Vanessa Haley's analysis of Annie Dillard's writing (p. 775) and the three literary analyses in Chapter 52 (pp. 802, 806, and 809).
- *Quote selectively when you are drawing on secondary sources.* Favor summaries and paraphrases over quotations, and put every quotation to each test in the box opposite. Most papers of ten or so pages should not need more than two or three quotations that are longer than a few lines each.

Transcribing quotations

When you quote a source, either in your notes or in your draft, take some precautions to avoid plagiarism or misrepresentaton of the source:

- *Copy the material carefully.* Take down the author's exact wording, spelling, capitalization, and punctuation.

Tests for direct quotations from secondary sources

The author's original satisfies one of these requirements:

- The language is unusually vivid, bold, or inventive.
- The quotation cannot be paraphrased without distortion or loss of meaning.
- The words themselves are at issue in your interpretation.
- The quotation represents and emphasizes a body of opinion or the view of an important expert.
- The quotation emphatically reinforces your own idea.
- The quotation is a graph, diagram, or table.

The quotation is as short as possible:

- It includes only material relevant to your point.
- It is edited to eliminate examples and other unneeded material. (For editing quotations, see the bulleted list below.)

46d

- *Proofread every direct quotation at least twice.*
- *Use quotation marks around the quotation* so that later you won't confuse it with a paraphrase or summary.
- *Use brackets* to add words for clarity or change the capitalization of letters (see pp. 510, 519).
- *Use ellipsis marks* to omit irrelevant words or sentences (see p. 511).

For a summary of all conventions regarding quotations, see the chart on pages 495–96.

The note below shows how Edward Begay might have quoted part of the passage from Frankel on page 668, using ellipsis marks and brackets to make the quotation more concise and specific.

Internet and economic inequality

Frankel 42

"A recent Rand study . . . concluded that . . . the free market is likely to deliver e-mail to only [the more affluent] half of America. Without induced subsidies, . . . the computer industry may never produce the inexpensive technologies that would enable television sets, telephones and computer games to bring e-mail into the home. Interim subsidies . . . would also be needed if less-affluent citizens [who lack home computers] are to get their e-mail outside the home, in apartment lobbies, libraries and schools."

4 ■ Combining quotation, summary, and paraphrase

Using quotation in combination with summary or paraphrase can help you shape the material to suit your purposes (although you must be careful not to distort the author's meaning). The note below shows how Edward Begay might have used a combination of quotation and paraphrase to record the statement by Frankel.

> Internet and economic inequality
>
> Frankel 42
>
> If market forces prevail, according to Rand, e-mail may fail to reach many Americans. The government may have to under-write the adaptation of household devices "to bring e-mail into the home." Similar measures will be required in the short term "if less-affluent citizens [who lack home computers] are to get their e-mail outside the home, in apartment lobbies, libraries and schools."

5 ■ Using sources accurately and fairly

In summarizing, paraphrasing, or quoting sources, you must represent the author's meaning exactly, without distorting it. In the following inaccurate summary the writer has stated a meaning exactly opposite that of the original. The original quotation, from the artist Henri Matisse, appears in Jack D. Flam, *Matisse on Art,* page 148.

Original	For the artist creation begins with vision. To see is itself a creative operation, requiring an effort. Everything that we see in our daily life is more or less distorted by acquired habits, and this is perhaps more evident in an age like ours when cinema posters and magazines present us every day with a flood of ready-made images which are to the eye what prejudices are to the mind.
Inaccurate summary	Matisse said that the artist can learn how to see creatively by looking at posters and magazines (qtd. in Flam 148).

The revision below combines summary and quotation to represent the author's meaning exactly:

Accurate summary	Matisse said that the artist must overcome visual "habits" and "prejudices," particularly those developed in response to popular cultural images (qtd. in Flam 148).

EXERCISE 6
Summarizing and paraphrasing

Prepare two source notes, one summarizing the entire paragraph below and the other paraphrasing the first four sentences (ending with the word *autonomy*). Use the note format illustrated in the preceding section, omitting only the subject heading.

46d

> Federal organization [of the United States] has made it possible for the different states to deal with the same problems in many different ways. One consequence of federalism, then, has been that people are treated differently, by law, from state to state. The great strength of this system is that differences from state to state in cultural preferences, moral standards, and levels of wealth can be accommodated. In contrast to a unitary system in which the central government makes all important decisions (as in France), federalism is a powerful arrangement for maximizing regional freedom and autonomy. The great weakness of our federal system, however, is that people in some states receive less than the best or the most advanced or the least expensive services and policies that government can offer. The federal dilemma does not invite easy solutions, for the costs and benefits of the arrangement have tended to balance out.
> —PETER K. EISINGER ET AL., *American Politics*, p. 44

EXERCISE 7
Combining summary, paraphrase, and direct quotation

Prepare a source note containing a combination of paraphrase or summary and direct quotation that states the major idea of the passage below. Use the note format illustrated in the preceding section, omitting only the heading.

> Most speakers unconsciously duel even during seemingly casual conversations, as can often be observed at social gatherings where they show less concern for exchanging information with other guests than for asserting their own dominance. Their verbal dueling often employs very subtle weapons like mumbling, a hostile act which defeats the listener's desire to understand what the speaker claims he is trying to say (but is really not saying because he is mumbling!). Or the verbal dueler may keep talking after someone has passed out of hearing range—which is often an aggressive challenge to the listener to return and acknowledge the dominance of the speaker. —PETER K. FARB, *Word Play*, p. 107

EXERCISE 8
Gathering information from sources

Continuing from Exercise 5 (p. 663), as the next step in preparing a research paper, gather and organize the information from your sources. Mark every note, photocopy, printout, and download with the source's publication information and a heading related to your paper. Annotate relevant passages of photocopies, printouts, and downloads. For handwritten or computer notes, use direct quotation, summary, or paraphrase as seems appropriate, being careful to avoid inaccuracy and plagiarism. (If you need help recognizing plagiarism, see Chapter 47.)

46e Integrating sources into your text

The evidence of others' information and opinions should *back up* your conclusions. You don't want to let your evidence overwhelm your own point of view and voice. The point of research writing is to investigate and go beyond sources, to interpret them and use them to support your own independent ideas.

Note Integrating quotations into your sentences involves punctuating signal phrases such as *he insists* (p. 468), using ellipsis marks for omissions (p. 511), and using brackets for additions and changes (p. 510). In addition, most disciplines offer specific guidelines for when to run quotations into your text and when to display them separately. See pages 738 (MLA style), 829 (Chicago style), and 858 (APA style).

1 ▪ Introducing borrowed material

When using a summary, paraphrase, or quotation, work to smooth the transition between your ideas and words and those of the source.

Note The examples in this and the next section use the MLA style of source documentation and also present-tense verbs (such as *disagrees*). For specific variations in documentation and verb tense within the academic disciplines, see pages 678–79.

Links between borrowed material and your own sentences

Readers will be distracted from your point if borrowed material does not fit into your sentence. In the passage below, the writer has not meshed the structures of her own and her source's sentences:

> Awkward One editor disagrees with this view and "a good reporter does not fail to separate opinions from facts" (Lyman 52).

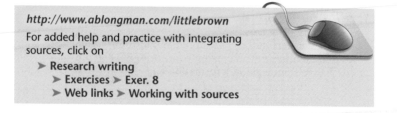

http://www.ablongman.com/littlebrown

For added help and practice with integrating sources, click on
  ➤ **Research writing**
    ➤ **Exercises** ➤ **Exer. 8**
    ➤ **Web links** ➤ **Working with sources**

In the following revision the writer adds words to integrate the quotation into her sentence:

> **Revised**   One editor disagrees with this view, <u>maintaining that</u> "a good reporter does not fail to separate opinions from facts" (Lyman 52).

Alterations of quotations

To mesh your own and your source's words, you may sometimes need to make a substitution or addition to the quotation, signaling your change with brackets:

46e

Words added

"The tabloids [of England] are a journalistic case study in bad reporting," claims Lyman (52).

Verb form changed

A bad reporter, Lyman implies, is one who "[fails] to separate opinions from facts" (52). [The bracketed verb replaces *fail* in the original.]

Capitalization changed

"[T]o separate opinions from facts" is a goal of good reporting (Lyman 52). [In the original, *to* is not capitalized.]

Noun supplied for pronoun

The reliability of a news organization "depends on [reporters'] trustworthiness," says Lyman (52). [The bracketed noun replaces *their* in the original.]

2 ■ Interpreting borrowed material

Even when it does not conflict with your own sentence structure, borrowed material will be ineffective if you merely dump it in readers' laps without explaining how you intend it to be understood. Reading the following passage, we must figure out for ourselves that the writer's sentence and the quotation state opposite points of view.

> **Dumped**   Many news editors and reporters maintain that it is impossible to keep personal opinions from influencing the selection and presentation of facts. "True, news reporters, like everyone else, form impressions of what they see and hear. However, a good reporter does not fail to separate opinions from facts" (Lyman 52).

In the revision the underlined additions tell us how to interpret the quotation:

> **Revised**   Many news editors and reporters maintain that it is impossible to keep personal opinions from influencing the selection and presentation of facts. <u>Yet not all au-</u>

thorities agree with this view. One editor grants that "news reporters, like everyone else, form impressions of what they see and hear." But, he insists, "a good reporter does not fail to separate opinions from facts" (Lyman 52).

Signal phrases

In the revised passage above, the words *One editor grants* and *he insists* are **signal phrases**: they tell readers who the source is and what to expect in the quotations that follow. Signal phrases usually contain (1) the source author's name (or a substitute for it, such as *One editor* and *he*) and (2) a verb that indicates the source author's attitude or approach to what he or she says. In the preceding example, *grants* implies concession and *insists* implies argument. The box below includes a list of verbs for signal phrases.

46e

Verbs for signal phrases

Use verbs that convey information about source authors' attitudes or approaches. In the sentence *Smith _____ that the flood might have been disastrous,* filling the blank with *observes, finds,* or *insists* would create different meanings.

Note Disciplines vary in the tenses of verbs within signal phrases. The verbs listed below are in the present tense, typical of writing in the humanities. But in the social and natural sciences, past or past perfect is more common. See pages 678–79.

Author is neutral	Author infers or suggests	Author argues	Author is uneasy or disparaging
comments	analyzes	claims	belittles
describes	asks	contends	bemoans
explains	assesses	defends	complains
illustrates	concludes	disagrees	condemns
notes	finds	holds	deplores
observes	predicts	insists	deprecates
points out	proposes	maintains	derides
records	reveals		laments
relates	shows	**Author agrees**	warns
reports	speculates	admits	
says	suggests	agrees	
sees	supposes	concedes	
thinks		concurs	
writes		grants	

Vary your signal phrases to suit your interpretation of borrowed material and also to keep readers' interest. A signal phrase may precede, interrupt, or follow the borrowed material:

Signal phrase precedes

Lyman insists that "a good reporter does not fail to separate opinions from facts" (52).

Signal phrase interrupts

"However," Lyman insists, "a good reporter does not fail to separate opinions from facts" (52).

Signal phrase follows

"[A] good reporter does not fail to separate opinions from facts," Lyman insists (52).

46e

Background information

You can add information to a signal phrase to inform readers why you are using a source. In most cases, provide the author's name in the text, especially if the author is an expert or if readers will recognize the name:

Author named

Harold Lyman grants that "news reporters, like everyone else, form impressions of what they see and hear." But, Lyman insists, "a good reporter does not fail to separate opinions from facts" (52).

If the source title contributes information about the author or the context of the quotation, you can provide it in the text:

Title given

Harold Lyman, in his book *The Conscience of the Journalist*, grants that "news reporters, like everyone else, form impressions of what they see and hear." But, Lyman insists, "a good reporter does not fail to separate opinions from facts" (52).

Finally, if the quoted author's background and experience reinforce or clarify the quotation, you can provide these credentials in the text:

Credentials given

Harold Lyman, a newspaper editor for more than forty years, grants that "news reporters, like everyone else, form impressions of what they see and hear." But, Lyman insists, "a good reporter does not fail to separate opinions from facts" (52).

You need not always name the author, source, or credentials in your text. In fact, such introductions may get in the way when you are simply establishing facts or weaving together facts and opinions from varied sources. In the following passage, the information is more important than the source, so the name of the source is confined to a parenthetical acknowledgment:

To end the abuses of the British, many colonists were urging three actions: forming a united front, seceding from Britain, and taking control of their own international relations (Wills 325–36).

3 ■ Following discipline styles for integrating sources

The preceding guidelines for introducing and interpreting borrowed material apply generally across academic disciplines, but there are differences in verb tenses and documentation style.

English and some other humanities

Writers in English, foreign languages, and related disciplines use MLA style for documenting sources (see Chapter 49) and generally use the present tense of verbs in signal phrases. In discussing sources other than works of literature, the present perfect tense is also sometimes appropriate:

> Lyman <u>insists</u> . . . [present].
> Lyman <u>has insisted</u> . . . [present perfect].

In discussing works of literature, use only the present tense to describe both the work of the author and the action in the work:

> Kate Chopin <u>builds</u> irony into every turn of "The Story of an Hour." For example, Mrs. Mallard, the central character, <u>finds</u> joy in the death of her husband, whom she <u>loves</u>, because she <u>anticipates</u> "the long procession of years that would belong to her absolutely" (23).

Avoid shifting tenses in writing about literature. You can, for instance, shorten quotations to avoid their past-tense verbs:

> **Shift**   Her freedom <u>elevates</u> her, so that "she <u>carried</u> herself unwittingly like a goddess of victory" (24).
>
> **No shift**   Her freedom <u>elevates</u> her, so that she <u>walks</u> "unwittingly like a goddess of victory" (24).

History and other humanities

Writers in history, art history, philosophy, and related disciplines generally use the present tense or present perfect tense of verbs in signal phrases:

> Lincoln persisted, as Haworth <u>has noted</u>, in "feeling that events controlled him."[3]
>
> What Miller <u>calls</u> Lincoln's "severe self-doubt"[6] undermined his effectiveness on at least two occasions.

The raised numbers after the quotations are part of the Chicago documentation style, used in history and other disciplines and discussed on pages 818–28.

Social and natural sciences

Writers in the sciences generally use a verb's present tense just for reporting the results of a study (*The data <u>suggest</u>* . . .). Otherwise, they use a verb's past tense or past perfect tense in a signal phrase, as when introducing an explanation, interpretation, or other commentary. (Thus when you are writing for the sciences, generally convert the list of signal-phrase verbs on p. 676 from the present to the past or past perfect tense.)

> Lin (1999) has suggested that preschooling may significantly affect children's academic performance through high school (pp. 22–23).
>
> In an exhaustive survey of the literature published between 1990 and 2000, Walker (2001) found "no proof, merely a weak correlation, linking place of residence and rate of illness" (p. 121).

46e

These passages conform to APA documentation style, discussed on pages 839–42. APA style, or one quite similar to it, is also used in sociology, education, nursing, biology, and many other sciences.

EXERCISE 9
Introducing and interpreting borrowed material
Drawing on the ideas in the following paragraph and using examples from your own observations and experiences, write a paragraph about anxiety. Integrate at least one direct quotation and one paraphrase from the following paragraph into your own sentences. In your paragraph identify the author by name and give his credentials: he is a professor of psychiatry and a practicing psychoanalyst.

> There are so many ways in which man is different from all the lower forms of animals, and almost all of them make us uniquely susceptible to feelings of anxiousness. Our imagination and reasoning powers facilitate anxiety; the anxious feeling is precipitated not by an absolute impending threat—such as the worry about an examination, a speech, travel—but rather by the symbolic and often unconscious representations. We do not have to be experiencing a potential danger. We can experience something related to it. We can recall, through our incredible memories, the original symbolic sense of vulnerability in childhood and suffer the feeling attached to that. We can even forget the original memory and still be stuck with the emotion—which is then compounded by its seemingly irrational quality at this time. It is not just the fear of death which pains us, but the anticipation of it; or the anniversary of a specific death; or a street, a hospital, a time of day, a color, a flower, a symbol associated with death.
>
> —WILLARD GAYLIN, "Feeling Anxious," p. 23

CHAPTER 47

Avoiding Plagiarism and Documenting Sources

Plagiarism (from a Latin word for "kidnapper") is the presentation of someone else's ideas or words as your own. Whether deliberate or accidental, plagiarism is a serious offense.

- *Deliberate* plagiarism:

    Copying or downloading a phrase, a sentence, or a longer passage from a source and passing it off as your own by omitting quotation marks and a source citation.

    Summarizing or paraphrasing someone else's ideas without acknowledging your debt in a source citation.

    Handing in as your own work a paper you have bought, copied off the Web, had a friend write, or accepted from another student.

- *Accidental* plagiarism:

    Forgetting to place quotation marks around another writer's words.

    Carelessly omitting a source citation for a paraphrase.

    Omitting a source citation for another's idea because you are unaware of the need to acknowledge the idea.

In most schools a code of academic honesty calls for severe consequences for deliberate or accidental plagiarism: a failing grade, suspension from school, or even expulsion.

The way to avoid plagiarism is to acknowledge your sources by documenting them. This chapter discusses plagiarism and the Internet (p. 682), shows how to distinguish what doesn't require acknowledgment from what does (pp. 682–85), covers issues particular

---

http://www.ablongman.com/littlebrown
For added help with avoiding plagiarism, click on
  ➤ **Research writing**
    ➤ **Video tutorials** ➤ Avoiding plagiarism
    ➤ **Exercises** ➤ Exer. 9
    ➤ **Downloads** ➤ Checklist for avoiding plagiarism
    ➤ **Web links** ➤ Avoiding plagiarism

to online sources (pp. 686–88), and provides an overview of source documentation (pp. 688–89).

◖ CULTURE LANGUAGE ◗ More than in many other cultures, teachers in the United States value students' original thinking and writing. In some other cultures, for instance, students may be encouraged to copy the words of scholars without acknowledgment, in order to demonstrate their mastery of or respect for the scholars' work. In the United States, however, the writing of an author is considered his or her property, and using that writing without a source citation is considered theft. When in doubt about the guidelines in this chapter, ask your instructor for advice.

Checklist for avoiding plagiarism

Type of source

Are you using

- your own independent material,
- common knowledge, or
- someone else's independent material?

You must acknowledge someone else's material.

Quotations

- Do all quotations exactly match their sources? Check them.
- Have you inserted quotation marks around quotations that are run into your text?
- Have you shown omissions with ellipsis marks and additions with brackets?
- Does every quotation have a source citation?

Paraphrases and summaries

- Have you used your own words and sentence structures for every paraphrase and summary? If not, use quotation marks around the original author's words.
- Does every paraphrase and summary have a source citation?

The Web

- Have you obtained any necessary permission to use someone else's material on your Web site?

Source citations

- Have you acknowledged every use of someone else's material in the place where you use it?
- Does your list of works cited include all the sources you have used?

You can download this checklist from this book's Web site: see the box opposite. Working with a copy of the list, question every use you make of someone else's material.

47a Committing and detecting plagiarism on the Internet

The Internet has made it easier to plagiarize than ever before, but it has also made plagiarism easier to catch.

Even honest students risk accidental plagiarism by downloading sources and importing portions into their drafts. Dishonest students may take advantage of the downloading process to steal others' work. They may also use the term-paper businesses on the Web, which offer both ready-made research and complete papers, usually for a fee. *Paying for research or a paper does not make it the buyer's work.* Anyone who submits someone else's work as his or her own is a plagiarist.

Students who plagiarize from the Internet both deprive themselves of an education in honest research and expose themselves to detection. Teachers can use search engines to find specific phrases or sentences anywhere on the Web, including among scholarly publications, all kinds of Web sites, and term-paper collections. They can search term-paper sites as easily as students can, looking for similarities with papers they've received. They can also use special detection software that compares students' work with other work anywhere on the Internet, seeking matches as short as a few words.

Some instructors suggest that their students use plagiarism-detection programs to verify that their own work does not include accidental plagiarism, at least not from the Internet. This book's Web site includes links to such programs: see the box on page 680.

47b Knowing what you need not acknowledge

Two kinds of information do not have to be acknowledged in source citations: your own independent material and common knowledge.

1 ▪ Using your independent material

Your own independent material includes your thoughts, observations from experience, compilations of facts, or experimental results, expressed in your words or format. For example, you might offer a conclusion about crowd behavior based on watching crowds at concerts or draw a diagram from information you gathered yourself. Though you generally should describe the basis for your conclusions so that readers can evaluate your thinking, you need not cite sources for them.

Note that someone else's ideas and facts are not yours, even when you express them entirely in your own words and sentence structures. The ideas and facts require acknowledgment.

2 ■ Using common knowledge

Common knowledge consists of the standard information of a field of study as well as folk literature and commonsense observations.

- *Standard information* includes the major facts of history, such as the dates during which Charlemagne ruled as emperor of Rome (800–14). It does *not* include interpretations of facts, such as a historian's opinion that Charlemagne was sometimes needlessly cruel in extending his power.
- *Folk literature,* such as the fairy tale "Snow White," is popularly known and cannot be traced to a particular writer. Literature traceable to a writer is *not* folk literature, even if it is very familiar.
- *A commonsense observation* is something most people know, such as that inflation is most troublesome for people with low and fixed incomes. An economist's idea about the effects of inflation on Chinese immigrants is *not* a commonsense observation.

As long as you express it in your own words and sentence structures, you may use common knowledge as your own.

The first time you come across an idea or a piece of information that you may want to use, record the publication information for the source. If in wider reading you repeatedly encounter the same idea or information without cited sources, then you may assume it's common knowledge. Don't take unnecessary risks, however: a source citation for common knowledge is not wrong.

47c ■ Knowing what you *must* acknowledge

You must always acknowledge other people's independent material—that is, any facts or ideas that are not common knowledge or your own. The source may be anything, including a book, an article, a movie, an interview, a microfilmed document, a Web page, a newsgroup posting, or an opinion expressed on the radio. You must acknowledge summaries or paraphrases of ideas or facts as well as quotations of the language and format in which ideas or facts appear: wording, sentence structures, arrangement, and special graphics (such as a diagram).

You need to acknowledge another's material no matter how you use it, how much of it you use, or how often you use it. Whether you are quoting a single important word, paraphrasing a single sentence, or summarizing three paragraphs, and whether you are using the source only once or a dozen times, you must acknowledge the original author every time. See pages 688–89 for how to acknowledge sources and pages 706–08 for where to place source citations in relation to cited material.

1 ■ Using copied language: Quotation marks and a source citation

Copied words and sentence structure

47c

The following example baldly plagiarizes the original quotation from Jessica Mitford's *Kind and Usual Punishment,* page 9. Without quotation marks or a source citation, the example matches Mitford's wording (underlined) and closely parallels her sentence structure:

Original	The character and mentality of the keepers may be of more importance in understanding prisons than the character and mentality of the kept.
Plagiarism	But the character of prison officials (the keepers) is more important in understanding prisons than the character of prisoners (the kept).

To avoid plagiarism, the writer can paraphrase and cite the source (see the facing page) or use Mitford's actual words *in quotation marks and with a source citation* (here, in MLA style):

Revision (quotation)	According to one critic of the penal system, "The character and mentality of the keepers may be of more importance in understanding prisons than the character and mentality of the kept" (Mitford 9).

Changed sentence structure but copied words

Even with a source citation and with a different sentence structure, the next example is still plagiarism because it uses some of Mitford's words (underlined) without quotation marks:

Plagiarism	According to one critic of the penal system, the psychology of the kept may say less about prisons than the psychology of the keepers (Mitford 9).
Revision (quotation)	According to one critic of the penal system, the psychology of "the kept" may say less about prisons than the psychology of "the keepers"(Mitford 9).

2 ■ Using a paraphrase or summary: Your own words and sentence structure and a source citation

Changed sentence structure but copied words

The following example changes the sentence structure of the original Mitford quotation above, but it still uses Mitford's words (underlined) without quotation marks and without a source citation:

Plagiarism   <u>In understanding prisons</u>, we might focus less on <u>the character and mentality of the kept</u> than on those <u>of the keepers</u>.

To avoid plagiarism, the writer can use quotation marks and cite the source (see the facing page) or *use his or her own words* and still *cite the source* (because the idea is Mitford's, not the writer's):

Revision   <u>Mitford</u> holds that we may be able to learn less
(paraphrase) about prisons from the psychology of prisoners than from the psychology of prison officials (<u>9</u>).

Revision   We may understand prisons better if we focus on
(paraphrase) the personalities and attitudes of the prison workers rather than those of the inmates (<u>Mitford 9</u>).

47c

Changed words but copied sentence structure

In the next example, the writer cites Mitford and does not use her words but still plagiarizes her sentence structure:

Plagiarism   One critic of the penal system maintains that <u>the psychology of prison officials may be more informative about prisons than the psychology of prisoners</u> (Mitford 9).

Revision   One critic of the penal system maintains that we
(paraphrase) may be able to learn less from the psychology of prisoners than from the psychology of prison officials (Mitford 9).

EXERCISE
Recognizing plagiarism

The numbered items below show various attempts to quote or paraphrase the following passage. Carefully compare each attempt with the original passage. Which attempts are plagiarized, inaccurate, or both, and which are acceptable? Why?

I would agree with the sociologists that psychiatric labeling is dangerous. Society can inflict terrible wounds by discrimination, and by confusing health with disease and disease with badness.
　　　　　　　　—George E. Vaillant, *Adaptation to Life*, p. 361

1. According to George Vaillant, society often inflicts wounds by using psychiatric labeling, confusing health, disease, and badness (361).
2. According to George Vaillant, "psychiatric labeling [such as 'homosexual' or 'schizophrenic'] is dangerous. Society can inflict terrible wounds by . . . confusing health with disease and disease with badness" (361).
3. According to George Vaillant, when psychiatric labeling discriminates between health and disease or between disease and badness, it can inflict wounds on those labeled (361).

4. Psychiatric labels can badly hurt those labeled, says George Vaillant, because they fail to distinguish among health, illness, and immorality (361).

5. Labels such as "homosexual" and "schizophrenic" can be hurtful when they fail to distinguish among health, illness, and immorality.

6. "I would agree with the sociologists that society can inflict terrible wounds by discrimination, and by confusing health with disease and disease with badness" (Vaillant 361).

47d

47d   Acknowledging online sources

Online sources are so accessible and so easy to download into your own documents that it may seem they are freely available, exempting you from the obligation to acknowledge them. They are not. Acknowledging online sources is somewhat trickier than acknowledging print sources, but no less essential. Further, if you are publishing your work online, you need to take account of sources' copyright restrictions as well.

Note Ask your instructor for advice whenever you are unsure about citing an online source or seeking permission to use copyrighted material.

1 ■ Acknowledging online sources in an unpublished project

When you use material from an online source in a print or online document to be distributed just to your class, your obligation to cite sources does not change: you must acknowledge someone else's independent material in whatever form you find it. With online sources, that obligation can present additional challenges:

■ *Record complete publication information each time you consult an online source.* Online sources may change from one day to the next or even disappear entirely. See page 617 for the information to record, such as the electronic address and the publication date. Without the proper information, you *may not* use the source.

■ *Acknowledge linked sites.* If you use not only a Web site but also one or more of its linked sites, you must acknowledge the linked sites as well. The fact that one person has used a second person's work does not release you from the responsibility to cite the second work.

■ *Seek the author's permission before using an e-mail message or a contribution to a discussion group.* (See p. 659 for advice on tracing online authors.) Obtaining permission advises the author that his or her ideas are about to be distributed more widely and lets the author verify that you have not misrepresented the ideas.

2 ■ Acknowledging print and online sources in a Web composition

When you use material from print or online sources in a composition for the Web, you must not only acknowledge your sources, as discussed above, but take the additional precaution of observing copyright restrictions. A Web site is a form of publication just as a book or magazine is and so involves the same responsibility to obtain reprint permission from copyright holders.

47d

The legal convention of **fair use** allows an author to quote a small portion of copyrighted material without obtaining the copyright holder's permission, as long as the author acknowledges the source. The online standards of fair use differ for print and online sources and are not fixed in either case. The guidelines below are conservative:

- *Print sources:* Quote without permission fewer than fifty words from an article or fewer than three hundred words from a book. You'll need the copyright holder's permission to use any longer quotation from an article or book; any quotation at all from a play, poem, or song; and any use of an entire work—such as a photograph, chart, or other illustration.
- *Online sources:* Quote without permission text that represents just a small portion of the whole—say, forty words out of three hundred. Follow the print guidelines above for plays, poems, songs, and illustrations, adding multimedia elements (audio or video clips) to the list of works that require reprint permission for any use.
- *Links:* You may need to seek permission to link your site to another one—for instance, if you rely on the linked site to provide substantial evidence for your claims or if you incorporate a linked site's multimedia element (an image or a sound or video clip) into your site.

Generally, you can find information about a site's copyright on the home page or at the bottoms of other pages: look for a notice using the symbol ©. Most worthwhile sites also provide information for contacting the author or sponsor. (See p. 619 for an illustration.)

---

http://www.ablongman.com/littlebrown
For added help with copyright and fair use,
click on
➤ **Research writing** ➤ **Web links** ➤ **Avoiding plagiarism**

If you don't find a copyright notice, you *cannot* assume that the work is unprotected by copyright. Only if the site explicitly says it is not copyrighted or is available for free use can you exceed fair use without permission.

Note Although most online sources are copyrighted, much valuable material is not: either the creator does not claim copyright, or the copyright has lapsed so that the work is in the public domain. The first category includes most government documents; the second includes most works by authors who have been dead at least fifty years. You do not need permission to reprint from such a source, but *you still must cite the source.*

47e Documenting sources

Every time you borrow the words, facts, or ideas of others, you must **document** the source—that is, supply a reference (or document) telling readers that you borrowed the material and where you borrowed it from.

Editors and teachers in most academic disciplines require special documentation formats (or styles) in their scholarly journals and in students' papers. All the styles use a citation in the text that serves two purposes: it signals that material is borrowed, and it refers readers to detailed information about the source so that they can locate both the source and the place in the source where the borrowed material appears. The detailed source information appears either in footnotes or at the end of the paper.

Aside from these essential similarities, the disciplines' documentation styles differ markedly in citation form, arrangement of source information, and other particulars. Each discipline's style reflects the needs of its practitioners for certain kinds of information presented in certain ways. For instance, the currency of a source is important in the social and natural sciences, where studies build on and correct each other; thus in-text citations in these disciplines usually include a source's date of publication. In the humanities, however, currency is less important, so in-text citations do not include date of publication.

The disciplines' documentation formats are described in style guides listed elsewhere in this book for the humanities (p. 818), the

http://www.ablongman.com/littlebrown

For added help with documenting sources, click on

➤ Research writing ➤ Web links ➤ Avoiding plagiarism
➤ Documentation in the disciplines

social sciences (p. 838), and the natural and applied sciences (p. 869). This book discusses and illustrates four common documentation styles:

- MLA style, used in English, foreign languages, and some other humanities (p. 700).
- Chicago style, used in history, art history, philosophy, religion, and some other humanities (p. 818).
- APA style, used in psychology and some other social sciences (p. 838).
- CSE style, used in the biological and some other sciences (p. 870).

47e

Ask your instructor which style you should use. If no style is required, use the guide that's most appropriate for the discipline in which you're writing. Do follow one system for citing sources—and one system only—so that you provide all the necessary information in a consistent format.

Note Bibliography software, such as *Bibliocite* and *Endnote,* can help you format your source citations in the style of your choice. Always ask your instructors if you may use such software for your papers. The programs prompt you for needed information (author's name, book title, and so on) and then arrange, capitalize, underline, and punctuate the information as required by the style. But no program can anticipate all the varieties of source information, nor can it substitute for your own care and attention in giving your sources complete acknowledgment using the required form.

CHAPTER 48

Writing the Paper

Writing a research paper begins when you seek a topic and continues as you evaluate and gather information from your sources. During research, you might even pause to draft paragraphs or sections that pull your sources together to support your ideas. At some point, though, you'll need to turn your attention to the whole paper—ensuring that it has a clear thesis (below), creating a structure (opposite), writing the complete draft (p. 695), revising and editing the paper (p. 696), and preparing the final draft (p. 698). To illustrate these stages, we continue to draw on Edward Begay's and Vanessa Haley's work.

Note This chapter complements and extends the detailed discussion of the writing situation and the writing process in Chapters 1–3, which also include many tips for using a word processor and more links to this book's Web site. If you haven't already done so, you may want to read Chapters 1–3 before this one.

48a Developing a thesis statement

Perhaps earlier in the research-writing process, but certainly once you have gathered information from your sources, you will want to express your central idea and perspective in a thesis statement of one or two sentences. (See pp. 31–35 if you need guidance on developing a thesis statement.) Drafting a thesis statement will help you see the overall picture and organize your notes.

Edward Begay's and Vanessa Haley's work on their research papers illustrates how a thesis statement evolves to become complete and specific. Before finishing his reading on access to the Internet, Begay wrote the following draft of a thesis statement.

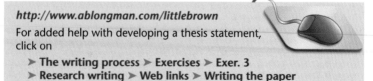

http://www.ablongman.com/littlebrown
For added help with developing a thesis statement, click on
➤ **The writing process** ➤ **Exercises** ➤ **Exer. 3**
➤ **Research writing** ➤ **Web links** ➤ **Writing the paper**

Tentative thesis statement

Because of the cost of hooking up to the Internet and training people to use it, the nation faces the possibility of a widening gap between rich and poor in information, skills, and income.

This statement captured Begay's preliminary idea that the Internet poses a threat to equality. But with further reading, Begay rethought this idea: many of his sources mentioned Internet access through public schools and libraries, and he began to focus on these institutions as a solution to the problem. The solution opened up new questions: how would schools and libraries have to change, and what would the change cost? With more reading, Begay revised his thesis statement:

48b

Revised thesis statement

To make Internet access universal, public libraries and schools must obtain the necessary resources from government and business both to go online and to offer enough computers for clients' use.

For Vanessa Haley, framing a thesis statement for her paper on Annie Dillard required drawing together (synthesizing) Dillard's ideas about humanity and nature into a single statement of Haley's own. The first draft merely conveyed Haley's interest in Dillard:

Tentative thesis statement

Unlike many other nature writers, Dillard does not reinforce the separation between humanity and nature.

Haley's revision stated her synthesis of Dillard's ideas:

Revised thesis statement

In her encounters with nature, Dillard probes a spiritual as well as a physical identity between human beings and nature that could help to heal the rift between them.

EXERCISE 1
Developing a thesis statement
Draft and revise a thesis statement for your developing research paper. Make sure the revised version specifically asserts your main idea.

48b Creating a structure

Before starting to draft your research paper, organize your ideas and information so that you know the main divisions of your paper, the order you'll cover them in, and the important supporting ideas for each division. The goal is to create a structure that presents your ideas in a sensible and persuasive sequence and that supports ideas at each level with enough explanation and evidence.

Consult the discussion of organization on pages 35–45 if you need help distinguishing general and specific information, arranging groups of information, or using a computer effectively for developing a structure.

1 ▪ Arranging ideas and support

Creating a structure for a research paper involves almost constant synthesis, the forging of relationships among ideas (see p. 660). As you arrange and rearrange source information and your own thoughts, you find connections among ideas and determine which are most important, which are merely supportive, and which are not relevant at all.

To build a structure, follow these guidelines:

- *Arrange your source information in categories* according to the subject headings you attached to each note, photocopy, or printout. Each category should correspond to a main section of your paper: a key idea of your own that supports the thesis along with the evidence for that idea.
- *Review your research journal.* Hunt for connections between sources, opinions of sources, and other thoughts that can help you organize your paper.
- *Look objectively at your categories.* If some are skimpy, with little information, consider whether you should drop the categories or conduct more research to fill them out. If most of your information falls into one or two categories, consider whether the categories are too broad and should be divided. (Does any of this rethinking affect your thesis statement? If so, revise it accordingly.)
- *Within each category, distinguish between the main idea and the supporting ideas and evidence.* Only the support should come from your sources. The main idea should be your own.

2 ▪ Using an outline

An outline can help you shape your research and also discover potential problems, such as inadequate support and overlapping or irrelevant ideas.

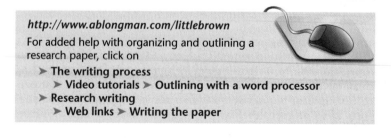

http://www.ablongman.com/littlebrown
For added help with organizing and outlining a research paper, click on
➤ **The writing process**
    ➤ **Video tutorials** ➤ **Outlining with a word processor**
➤ **Research writing**
    ➤ **Web links** ➤ **Writing the paper**

48b

Informal outline

For some research projects, you may find an **informal outline** sufficient: you list main points and supporting information in the order you expect to discuss them. Because of its informality, such an outline can help you try out different arrangements of material, even fairly early in the research process.

Edward Begay experimented with an informal outline while examining his sources, in order to see how his developing ideas might fit together:

48b

> History of the Internet
>   Packet-switching networks—UK, France
>   ARPANET—linked US Defense Dept., contractors, universities
>   Network of networks—UNIX, NSFNET, and onward
>
> Commercial vs. public use
>   1st users universities, libraries, govts.
>   Business sees commercial uses
>   PCs, modems increase home use
>
> Access to Internet
>   Tech. skills needed
>   Problems for equality, democracy
>   Expense of going online
>   Imp. of Internet to democratic society
>   Libraries & schools: sites for widespread access
>   Libraries & schools need to adapt, find money to go online

This informal outline helped Begay decide not to continue researching the history of the Internet or the conflicts between commercial and public use (the first two sections) because they seemed likely to overwhelm his central concern, equal access to the Internet (last section). Note that Begay did include an endnote in his paper referring to the history of the Internet (p. 768).

Formal outline

Unlike an informal outline, a **formal outline** arranges ideas tightly and in considerable detail, with close attention to hierarchy and phrasing. The example below shows the formal outline's format and schematic content:

> I. First main idea
>   A. First subordinate idea
>   1. First evidence for subordinate idea
>   a. First detail of evidence
>   b. Second detail of evidence
>   2. Second evidence for subordinate idea
>   B. Second subordinate idea
> II. Second main idea

In this model, levels of headings correspond to levels of importance or detail in the paper:

48b

- *Main ideas (Roman numerals) are the major divisions of the paper.* Each division addresses a principal part of your thesis statement and will probably take a number of paragraphs to develop.
- *Subordinate ideas (capital letters) are the building blocks.* These ideas are your own and will probably take a paragraph or two to develop. They may serve as the topic sentences of paragraphs.
- *Evidence (Arabic numerals) and its details (small letters) support each idea.* The evidence from one or more sources will occupy much of each body paragraph. (A fourth sublevel, if needed, is labeled with Arabic numerals enclosed in parentheses.)

Each level of the outline is indented farther than the level it supports. (Your word processor may be able to help you with labels and indentions. See p. 190.)

A formal outline can help you decide not only what your main ideas are and how you will arrange them but also how you will support them. Some of this information may not emerge until you are drafting, however, so remain open to revising the outline as you proceed. And consider using a formal outline as a revision tool as well, creating a map of your completed first draft to check and improve the structure (see p. 52).

To be an effective organizer for your thoughts, or an effective revision tool, a formal outline should be detailed and should adhere to several principles of logical arrangement, clarity, balance, and completeness. These are discussed in detail and illustrated on pages 39–41. Briefly:

- *The outline should indicate which ideas are primary and which are subordinate.* A long, undivided list of parallel items probably needs to be subdivided.
- *Parallel headings should represent ideas of equal importance and generality.* They should not overlap one another.
- *Single sublevels should be avoided.* They illogically imply that something is divided into only one part.

A formal outline is usually written either in phrases (a **topic outline**) or in sentences (a **sentence outline**). A complete topic outline is illustrated on pages 39–40. A complete sentence outline accompanies Edward Begay's research paper on pages 744–45. Either is suitable for a research paper, though a sentence outline, because it requires complete statements, conveys more information.

EXERCISE 2
Creating a structure

Continuing from Exercise 1 (p. 691), arrange your notes into a structure. As specified by your instructor, make an informal outline or a formal sentence or topic outline to guide the drafting of your paper.

48c   Drafting the paper

Beginning a draft of what will be a relatively long and complicated paper can be difficult, so it may help to remember that you do not have to proceed methodically from beginning to end. Here are some ideas for writing a draft:

Tips for drafting a research paper

- **Write a quick two- or three-paragraph summary of what the paper will be about.** This writing will get your juices flowing and give you a sense of direction. (Pretend you're writing to a friend if that will help loosen you up.) A version of the material you generate in this way may eventually prove useful for your paper's introduction or conclusion.
- **Start with the section of the paper you feel most confident about.** At first, skip any parts that scare you or give you undue trouble, even the introduction.
- **Work in chunks, one unit or principal idea at a time.** Fit the sections together only after you begin to see the draft take shape.
- **Center each section on an idea of your own.** Use source material to back up the idea.
- **Take great care in working with source material.** Integrate sources into your own ideas (p. 674), and do not plagiarize (p. 680).
- **Insert source citations into the draft as you quote, paraphrase, or summarize.** Use authors' names and page numbers.

---

1 ▪ Working section by section

In writing a first draft, remember that a primary reason for doing a research paper is learning how to interpret and evaluate the evidence in sources, draw your own conclusions from the evidence, and weave the two together in a way that establishes your expertise in your subject. The weaving will be easier if you view each principal idea of your paper (each Roman numeral of your outline) as a unit. Usually these principal ideas require a block of paragraphs to develop.

Compose the units of your paper as if each will stand alone (though of course you will pull the units together before your draft is complete).

---

http://www.ablongman.com/littlebrown
For added help with drafting, click on
➤ **Research writing**
  ➤ **Web links** ➤ **Writing the paper**

- *Begin each unit by stating the idea,* which should be a conclusion you have drawn from reading and responding to your sources.
- *Follow the statement with specific support from your sources:* facts and examples; summaries, paraphrases, or quotations of secondary sources; quotations of passages from primary sources with your analysis.
- *Present fairly any disagreements among experts.* Give the evidence that leads you to side with one expert or another.
- *Try to remain open to new interpretations or new arrangements of ideas that occur to you.*

Proceeding in this way will help you avoid a common trap of research writing: allowing your sources to control you, rather than vice versa. Make sure each unit of your paper centers on an idea of your own, not someone else's, and that your paragraphs are pointed toward demonstrating that idea, not merely presenting sources.

2 ▪ Tracking source citations

As you draft your paper, insert the source of each summary, paraphrase, and quotation in parentheses in the text—for instance, "(Frankel 42)" referring to page 42 in a work by Frankel. If you are conscientious about inserting these notes and carrying them through successive drafts, you will be less likely to plagiarize accidentally and you will have little difficulty documenting your sources in the final paper.

EXERCISE 3
Drafting your paper
Draft the research paper you have been developing in Chapters 44–47. Before beginning the draft, study your research journal and your source information. While drafting, follow your thesis statement and outline as closely as you need to, but stay open to new ideas, associations, and arrangements.

48d   Revising and editing the paper

When you have written a first draft, take a break for at least a day so that you can gain some objectivity about your work and read the draft critically when you begin to revise.

1 ▪ Revising

Always revise your draft first, editing sentences and words only when you're satisfied with the content and shape of the whole. For revision, begin with the advice and checklist on pages 51–55, and supplement with the checklist below. (You can download this check-list from this book's Web site: see the box at the bottom of the page. Copy the checklist for each research paper, answering the questions in writing.)

Checklist for revising a research paper

Thesis statement
How well does your thesis statement describe your subject and your per-spective as they emerged during drafting?

Structure
(Outlining your draft as suggested on p. 694 can help you see structure at a glance.)

How consistently does borrowed material illuminate and support—not lead and dominate—your own ideas? How well is the importance of ideas reflected in the emphasis they receive? Will the arrangement of ideas be clear to readers?

Evidence
Where might supporting evidence seem weak or irrelevant to readers?

Reasonableness and clarity
How reasonable will readers find your arguments? (See pp. 166–70.) Where do you need to define terms or concepts that readers may not know or may dispute?

48d

2 ■ Editing

When you complete your revision—and only then—you are ready to edit. If you do not compose on a computer, copy or retype the new draft if possible so that you have a clean copy to work on. If you do compose on a computer, you can edit directly on screen or print a clean copy. (Some writers find it easier to spot errors on pa-per than on screen.)

For editing, consult the advice and checklist on pages 58–61. Try to read the paper from the point of view of someone who has not spent hours planning and researching but instead has come

---

http://www.ablongman.com/littlebrown

For added help revising a research paper, click on
➤ **The writing process**
  ➤ **Video tutorials** ➤ **Revising with a word processor**
➤ **Research writing**
  ➤ **Downloads** ➤ **Checklist for revising a research paper**
  ➤ **Web links** ➤ **Writing the paper**

fresh to the paper. Look for lapses in sense, awkward passages, wordiness, poor transitions between ideas and evidence, unnecessary repetition, wrong or misspelled words, errors in grammar, punctuation, or mechanics—in short, anything that is likely to interfere with a reader's understanding of your meaning.

3 ■ Completing source citations

Before you prepare your final draft (next section), you must insert final source citations into your text and prepare the list of sources for the end of the paper. See pages 688–89 on documenting sources in various disciplines' styles.

> **EXERCISE 4**
> **Revising and editing your paper**
> Using the revision and editing checklists on pages 55 and 60 and the checklist and pointers here, revise and edit your research paper. Work to improve not only the presentation of ideas but also, if necessary, the ideas themselves. Make sure you have provided an in-text citation for every summary, paraphrase, and direct quotation of a source and that your list of sources is complete.

48e   Preparing and proofreading the final draft

Prepare the final draft of your paper when you have edited the text, added the source citations, and written the list of works cited. Most instructors expect research papers to be neatly typed with clear titling, double spacing, standard margins, and minimal handwritten corrections. Your instructor may have additional requirements, suggested by the discipline in which you are writing. This book explains four such document formats:

- In English, foreign languages, and some other humanities, use MLA format. See pages 709 and 736–39 for a description and illustrations, and see Chapter 50 for the sample research papers of Edward Begay and Vanessa Haley.
- In history, art history, religion, philosophy, and some other humanities, use Chicago format. See pages 819–20 and 828–30 for a description and illustrations.
- In psychology and other social sciences, use APA format. See pages 842–44 and 856–59 for a description and illustrations.
- In the natural and applied sciences, use CSE format. See pages 871–73 and 878–79 for a description and illustrations.

 In any discipline, you can use a word processor to present your ideas effectively and attractively with readable type fonts, headings, illustrations, and other elements. See Chapter 9 for ideas and examples.

Before you submit your paper, proofread it carefully for typographical errors, misspellings, and other slight errors. (See p. 67 for proofreading tips.) Unless the errors are very numerous (more than several on a page), you can correct them by whiting out or crossing out (neatly) and inserting the correction (neatly) in ink. Don't let the pressure of a deadline prevent you from proofreading, for even minor errors can impair clarity or annoy readers and thus negate some of the hard work you have put into your project.

48e

EXERCISE 5
Preparing and proofreading your final draft
Prepare the final draft of your research paper, following your instructor's requirements for document format. If your instructor does not specify a format, follow the MLA guidelines on pages 736–39. Proofread and correct the paper before submitting it.

CHAPTER 49

Using MLA Documentation and Format

English, foreign languages, and some other humanities use the documentation style and document format of the Modern Language Association, detailed in the *MLA Handbook for Writers of Research Papers,* 6th ed. (2003).

MLA documentation style employs brief parenthetical citations within the text that direct readers to a list of works cited at the end of the text. A parenthetical citation might look like this:

> Only one article mentions this discrepancy (Wolfe 62).

The name "Wolfe" directs readers to the article by Wolfe in the list of works cited, and the page number "62" specifies the page in the article on which the cited material appears.

This chapter describes MLA style: what to include in a parenthetical citation (below), where to place citations (p. 706), when to use footnotes or endnotes in addition to parenthetical citations (p. 708), how to create the list of works cited (p. 709), and how to format the entire paper (p. 736).

49a Using MLA in-text citations

1 ■ Writing parenthetical text citations

In-text citations of sources have two requirements:

- They must include just enough information for the reader to locate the appropriate source in your list of works cited.

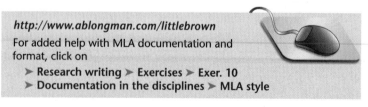

http://www.ablongman.com/littlebrown

For added help with MLA documentation and format, click on

➤ **Research writing** ➤ **Exercises** ➤ **Exer. 10**
➤ **Documentation in the disciplines** ➤ **MLA style**

■ They must include just enough information for the reader to locate the place in the source where the borrowed material appears.

For any kind of source, you can usually meet both these requirements by providing the author's last name and (if the source uses them) the page numbers where the material appears. The reader can find the source in your list of works cited and find the borrowed material in the source itself.

Note For most sources, you will provide the author's or authors' last names and a page reference. Do not include the title unless you are citing more than one work by exactly the same author(s) or the source has no listed author (models 8 and 9, p. 704). The examples below cite a book to which neither of these exceptions applies:

> Not One text discusses the "ethical dilemmas in public relations practice" (Wilcox, Ault, and Agee, <u>Public Relations</u> 125).
>
> Not One text discusses the "ethical dilemmas in public relations practice" (<u>Public Relations</u> 125).
>
> But One text discusses the "ethical dilemmas in public relations practice" (Wilcox, Ault, and Agee 125).

1. Author not named in your text

When you have not already named the author in your sentence, provide the author's last name and the page number(s), with no punctuation between them, in parentheses.

> One researcher concludes that "women impose a distinctive construction on moral problems, seeing moral dilemmas in terms of conflicting responsibilities" (Gilligan 105).

MLA parenthetical text citations

See models 5 and 6 (next page) for the forms to use when the source does not provide page numbers.

2. Author named in your text

If the author's name is already given with the material you're citing, you need not repeat it in the parenthetical citation. The citation gives just the page number(s).

> One researcher, Carol Gilligan, concludes that "women impose a
> distinctive construction on moral problems, seeing moral dilem-
> mas in terms of conflicting responsibilities" (105).

3. A work with two or three authors

If the source has two or three authors, give all their last names in the text or in the citation. Separate two authors' names with "and":

> As Frieden and Sagalyn observe, "The poor and the minorities
> were the leading victims of highway and renewal programs" (29).

> According to one study, "The poor and the minorities were the
> leading victims of highway and renewal programs" (Frieden and
> Sagalyn 29).

With three authors, add commas and also "and" before the final name:

> The text by Wilcox, Ault, and Agee discusses the "ethical dilemmas
> in public relations practice" (125).

> One text discusses the "ethical dilemmas in public relations prac-
> tice" (Wilcox, Ault, and Agee 125).

4. A work with more than three authors

If the source has more than three authors, you may list all their last names or use only the first author's name followed by "et al." (the abbreviation for the Latin *et alii,* "and others"). The choice depends on what you do in your list of works cited (see p. 712).

> It took the combined forces of the Americans, Europeans, and
> Japanese to break the rebel siege of Beijing in 1900 (Lopez et al.
> 362).

> It took the combined forces of the Americans, Europeans, and
> Japanese to break the rebel siege of Beijing in 1900 (Lopez, Blum,
> Cameron, and Barnes 362).

5. A work with numbered paragraphs or screens instead of pages

Some electronic sources number each paragraph or screen instead of each page. In citing passages in these sources, give the paragraph or screen number(s) and distinguish them from page numbers: after the author's name, put a comma, a space, and "par." (one paragraph), "pars." (more than one paragraph), "screen," or "screens."

> Twins reared apart report similar feelings (Palfrey, pars. 6-7).

6. An entire work or a work with no page or other reference numbers

When you cite an entire work rather than a part of it, you may omit any page or paragraph number. Try to work the author's name into your text, in which case you will not need a parenthetical citation. But remember that the source must appear in the list of works cited.

> Boyd deals with the need to acknowledge and come to terms with
>
> our fear of nuclear technology.

Use the same format when you cite a specific passage from a work with no page, paragraph, or other reference numbers, such as an online source.

If the author's name does not appear in your text, put it in a parenthetical citation.

> Almost 20 percent of commercial banks have been audited for the
>
> practice (Friis).

7. A multivolume work

If you consulted only one volume of a multivolume work, your list of works cited will indicate as much (see model 14 on p. 715), and you can treat the volume as any book.

If you consulted more than one volume of a multivolume work, give the appropriate volume in your text citation.

> After issuing the Emancipation Proclamation, Lincoln said, "What
>
> I did, I did after very full deliberations, and under a very heavy
>
> and solemn sense of responsibility" (5: 438).

The number 5 indicates the volume from which the quotation was taken; the number 438 indicates the page number in that volume. When the author's name appears in such a citation, place it before the volume number with no punctuation: (Lincoln 5: 438).

If you are referring generally to an entire volume of a multivolume work and are not citing specific page numbers, add the abbreviation "vol." before the volume number as in (vol. 5) or (Lincoln, vol. 5) (note the comma after the author's name). Then readers will not misinterpret the volume number as a page number.

8. A work by an author of two or more cited works

If your list of works cited includes two or more works by the same author, then your citation must tell the reader which of the author's works you are referring to. Give the title either in the text or in a parenthetical citation. In a parenthetical citation, give the full title only if it is brief; otherwise, shorten the title to the first one or two main words (excluding *A, An,* or *The*).

> At about age seven, children begin to use appropriate gestures
> with their stories (Gardner, Arts 144–45).

The title Arts is shortened from the full title of Gardner's book, *The Arts and Human Development* (see the works-cited entry for this book on p. 712).

9. An anonymous work

For a work with no named author or editor, use a full or short-ened version of the title, as explained above. In your list of works cited, you will alphabetize an anonymous work by the first main word of the title (see p. 714), so the first word of a shortened title should be the same. This citation refers to an unsigned article titled "The Right to Die."

> One article notes that a death-row inmate may demand his own ex-
> ecution to achieve a fleeting notoriety ("Right").

(A page number is omitted for this source because the article is no longer than a page. See the entry for the article on p. 720.)

If two or more anonymous works have the same title, distin-guish them with additional information in the text citation, such as the publication date, periodical title, or online site title.

10. A government publication or a work with a corporate author

If the author of the work is listed as a government body or a cor-poration, cite the work by that organization's name. If the name is long, work it into the text to avoid an intrusive parenthetical citation.

> A 2002 report by the Hawaii Department of Education predicts an
> increase in enrollments (6).

11. An indirect source

When you want to use a quotation that is already in quotation marks—indicating that the author you are reading is quoting someone else—try to find the original source and quote directly from it. If you can't find the original source, then your citation must indicate that your quotation of it is indirect. In the following citation, "qtd. in" ("quoted in") says that Davino was quoted by Boyd:

> George Davino maintains that "even small children have vivid
>
> ideas about nuclear energy" (qtd. in Boyd 22).

MLA
49a

The list of works cited then includes only Boyd (the work consulted), not Davino.

12. A literary work

Novels, plays, and poems are often available in many editions, so your instructor may ask you to provide information that will help readers find the passage you cite no matter what edition they consult.

For novels, the page number comes first, followed by a semicolon and then information on the appropriate part or chapter of the work.

> Toward the end of James's novel, Maggie suddenly feels "the thick
>
> breath of the definite--which was the intimate, the immediate, the
>
> familiar, as she hadn't had them for so long" (535; pt. 6, ch. 41).

For poems that are not divided into parts, you can omit the page number and supply the line number(s) for the quotation. To prevent confusion with page numbers, precede the numbers with "line" or "lines" in the first citation; then just use the numbers.

> In Shakespeare's Sonnet 73 the speaker identifies with the trees of
>
> late autumn, "Bare ruined choirs, where late the sweet birds sang"
>
> (line 4). "In me," Shakespeare writes, "thou seest the glowing of
>
> such fire / That on the ashes of his youth doth lie" (9-10).

See pages 806–07 for a sample paper on a poem.

For verse plays and poems that are divided into parts, omit a page number and cite the appropriate part—act (and scene, if any), canto, book, and so on—plus the line number(s). Use Arabic numerals for parts, including acts and scenes (3.4), unless your instructor specifies Roman numerals (III.iv).

> Later in <u>King Lear</u> Shakespeare has the disguised Edgar say, "The
>
> prince of darkness is a gentleman" (3.4.147).

See pages 809–11 for a sample paper on a verse play.

For prose plays, provide the page number followed by the act and scene, if any. See the reference to *Death of a Salesman* on page 708.

13. The Bible

When you cite passages of the Bible in parentheses, abbreviate the title of any book longer than four letters—for instance, "Gen." (Genesis), "1 Sam." (1 Samuel), "Ps." (Psalms), "Matt." (Matthew), "Rom." (Romans). Then give the chapter and verse(s) in Arabic numerals.

> According to the Bible, at Babel God "did . . . confound the lan-
> guage of all the earth" (Gen. 11.9).

14. An electronic source

Cite an electronic source as you would any other source: usually by author's name or, if there is no author, by title.

> Business forecasts for the fourth quarter tended to be optimistic
> (White 4).

This example cites a source with page numbers. For a source with paragraph or screen numbers or no numbering, see models 5 and 6 (p. 703).

15. Two or more works in the same citation

If you use a single parenthetical citation to refer to more than one work, separate the references with a semicolon.

> Two recent articles point out that a computer badly used can be
> less efficient than no computer at all (Gough and Hall 201;
> Richards 162).

Since long citations in the text can distract the reader, you may choose to cite several or more works in an endnote or footnote rather than in the text. See page 708.

2 ■ Positioning and punctuating parenthetical citations

Where to place citations

Position text citations to accomplish two goals:

- Make it clear exactly where your borrowing begins and ends.
- Keep the citation as unobtrusive as possible.

You can accomplish both goals by placing the parenthetical citation at the end of the sentence element containing the borrowed material. This sentence element may be a phrase or a clause, and it may begin, interrupt, or conclude the sentence. Usually, as in the following examples, the element ends with a punctuation mark.

The inflation rate might climb as high as 30 percent (Kim 164), an increase that could threaten the small nation's stability.

The inflation rate, which might climb as high as 30 percent (Kim 164), could threaten the small nation's stability.

The small nation's stability could be threatened by its inflation rate, which, one source predicts, might climb as high as 30 percent (Kim 164).

In the last example the addition of *one source predicts* clarifies that Kim is responsible only for the inflation-rate prediction, not for the statement about stability.

When your paraphrase or summary of a source runs longer than a sentence, clarify the boundaries by using the author's name in the first sentence and placing the parenthetical citation at the end of the last sentence.

Juliette Kim studied the effects of acutely high inflation in several South American and African countries since World War II. She discovered that a major change in government accompanied or followed the inflationary period in 56 percent of cases (22-23).

How to punctuate citations

For citations in your running text, generally place the parenthetical citation *before* any punctuation required by your sentence, as in the examples above. If the borrowed material is a quotation, place the citation *between* the closing quotation mark and the punctuation.

Spelling argues that during the 1970s American automobile manufacturers met consumer needs "as well as could be expected" (26), but not everyone agrees with him.

The exception is a quotation ending in a question mark or exclamation point. Then use the appropriate punctuation inside the closing quotation mark, and follow the quotation with the text citation and a period:

"Of what use is genius," Emerson asks, "if the organ . . . cannot find a focal distance within the actual horizon of human life?" ("Experience" 60). Mad genius is no genius.

When a citation appears at the end of a quotation set off from the text, place it one space *after* the punctuation ending the quotation. No additional punctuation is needed.

In Arthur Miller's <u>Death of a Salesman</u>, the most poignant defense of Willie Loman comes from his wife, Linda:

> He's not the finest character that ever lived. But he's a human being, and a terrible thing is happening to him. So attention must be paid. He's not to be allowed to fall into his grave like an old dog. Attention, attention must finally be paid to such a person. (56; act 1)

(This citation of a play includes the act number as well as the page number. See p. 705.)

See the two sample research papers starting on pages 742 and 775 for further examples of placing parenthetical references in relation to summaries, paraphrases, and quotations.

3 ■ Using footnotes or endnotes in special circumstances

Occasionally, you may want to use footnotes or endnotes in place of parenthetical citations. If you need to refer to several sources at once, listing them in a long parenthetical citation could be intrusive. In that case, signal the citation with a numeral raised above the appropriate line of text and write a note with the same numeral to cite the sources:

Text   At least five studies have confirmed these results.[1]

Note   [1] Abbott and Winger 266-68; Casner 27; Hoyenga 78-79; Marino 36; Tripp, Tripp, and Walk 179-83.

You may also use a footnote or endnote to comment on a source or provide information that does not fit easily in the text:

Text   So far, no one has confirmed these results.[2]

Note   [2] Manter reports spending a year trying to replicate the experiment, but he was never able to produce the high temperatures reported by the original experimenters (616).

In a note the raised numeral is indented five spaces or one-half inch and is followed by a space. If the note appears as a footnote, place it at the bottom of the page on which the citation appears, set it off from the text with quadruple spacing, and single-space the note itself. If the note appears as an endnote, place it in numerical order with the other endnotes on a page between the text and the list of works cited. Double-space all the endnotes. (See pp. 768–69 for examples of endnotes and the format to use in typing a page of endnotes.)

49b Preparing the MLA list of works cited

In the documentation style of the *MLA Handbook,* your in-text parenthetical citations (discussed in 46a) refer the reader to complete information on your sources in a list you title Works Cited and place at the end of your paper. The list should include all the sources you quoted, paraphrased, or summarized in your paper. (If your instructor asks you to include sources you examined but did not cite, title the list Works Consulted.)

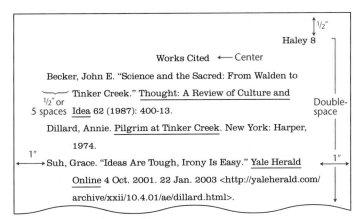

Follow this format for the list of works cited:

- Arrange your sources in alphabetical order by the last name of the author. If an author is not given in the source, alphabetize the source by the first main word of the title (excluding *A, An,* or *The*).
- Type the entire list double-spaced (both within and between entries).
- Indent the second and subsequent lines of each entry one-half inch or five spaces from the left.

For complete lists of works cited, see the papers by Edward Begay (p. 770) and Vanessa Haley (p. 780).

The box on the next two pages directs you to the MLA formats for works-cited entries. Use your best judgment in adapting the models to your particular sources. If you can't find a model that exactly matches a source you used, locate and follow the closest possible match. You will certainly need to combine formats—for instance, drawing on model 2 ("A book with two or three authors") and model 26 ("An article in a daily newspaper") for a newspaper article with two authors.

MLA works-cited models

1 ■ Listing books

The basic format for a book includes the following elements:

Gilligan, Carol. In a Different Voice: Psychological Theory and

Women's Development. Cambridge: Harvard UP, 1982.

① *Author.* Use the author's full name: last name first, followed by a comma, and then the first name and any middle name or initial. Omit any title or degree attached to the author's name, such as Dr. or PhD. End the name with a period and one space.

② *Title.* Give the full title, including any subtitle. Underline the title unless your instructor specifically calls for italics (see p. 525). Capitalize all important words (see pp. 519–20), separate the main title and the subtitle with a colon and one space, and end the title with a period and one space. For citing a part of a book, such as an essay or poem, see model 18 (pp. 716–17).

③ *Publication information.* You can usually find this information on the book's title page or on the back of the title page.

   ⓐ *The city of publication,* followed by a colon and one space. Use only the first city if the source lists more than one. If no place of publication is given, use the abbreviation "N.p." instead.

   ⓑ *The name of the publisher,* followed by a comma. Shorten most publishers' names, often to a single word: "Little" for Little, Brown, "Knopf" for Alfred A. Knopf. For university presses, use the abbreviations "U" and "P," as in the example. If the title page lists an imprint and a publisher—for instance, Vintage Books and Random House—give both names with a hyphen: "Vintage-Random." If no publisher is named, use the abbreviation "n.p." instead.

   ⓒ *The date of publication,* ending with a period. If no publication date is given, use the abbreviation "n.d." instead.

When citing a book that has no page numbers, add the abbreviation "N. pag." at the end of the entry. The abbreviation will explain why you don't cite page numbers in your in-text citations of the work.

Other information besides that listed above usually falls either between the author's name and the title or between the title and the publication information, as specified in the following models.

1. A book with one author

Gilligan, Carol. In a Different Voice: Psychological Theory and Women's Development. Cambridge: Harvard UP, 1982.

2. A book with two or three authors

Lifton, Robert Jay, and Greg Mitchell. Who Owns Death: Capital Punishment, the American Conscience, and the End of Executions. New York: Morrow, 2000.

Wilcox, Dennis L., Phillip H. Ault, and Warren K. Agee. Public Relations: Strategies and Tactics. 4th ed. New York: Harper, 1999.

Give the authors' names in the order provided on the title page. Reverse the first and last names of the first author *only,* not of any other authors. Separate two authors' names with a comma and "and"; separate three authors' names with commas and with "and" before the third name.

3. A book with more than three authors

Lopez, Robert S., Susan Blum, Susan Cameron, and William J. Barnes. Civilizations: Western and World. Boston: Little, 1995.

Lopez, Robert S., et al. Civilizations: Western and World. Boston: Little, 1995.

You may, but need not, give all authors' names if the work has more than three authors. If you choose not to give all names, provide the name of the first author only, and follow the name with a comma and the abbreviation "et al." (for the Latin *et alii,* meaning "and others").

4. Two or more works by the same author(s)

Gardner, Howard. The Arts and Human Development. New York: Wiley, 1973.

---. The Quest for Mind: Piaget, Lévi-Strauss, and the Structuralist Movement. New York: Knopf, 1973.

Give the author's name only in the first entry. For the second and any subsequent works by the same author, substitute three hyphens for the author's name, followed by a period. (If you are citing two or more works by the same editor, editors, or translator, follow the hyphens with a comma and "ed.," "eds.," or "trans." as appropriate. See models 5, 6, and 7.) Note that the three hyphens stand for *exactly* the same name or names. If the second Gardner source were by Gardner and somebody else, both names would have to be given in full.

Place an entry or entries using three hyphens immediately after the entry that names the author. Within the set of entries by the same author, arrange the sources alphabetically by the first main word of the title, as in the Gardner examples (<u>Arts</u>, then <u>Quest</u>).

5. A book with an editor

Holland, Merlin, and Rupert Hart-Davis, eds. <u>The Complete Letters</u>

of Oscar Wilde. New York: Holt, 2000.

Handle editors' names like authors' names (models 1–3), but add a comma and the abbreviation "ed." (one editor) or "eds." (two or more editors) after the last editor's name.

6. A book with an author and an editor

Mumford, Lewis. <u>The City in History</u>. Ed. Donald L. Miller. New

York: Pantheon, 1986.

When citing the work of the author, give his or her name first, and give the editor's name after the title, preceded by "Ed." (singular only, meaning "Edited by"). When citing the work of the editor, use model 5 for a book with an editor, and give the author's name after the title preceded by "By": Miller, Donald L., ed. <u>The City in History</u>. By Lewis Mumford.

7. A translation

Alighieri, Dante. <u>The Inferno</u>. Trans. John Ciardi. New York: NAL,

1971.

When citing the work of the author, give his or her name first, and give the translator's name after the title, preceded by "Trans." ("Translated by"). When citing the work of the translator, give his or her name first, followed by a comma and "trans."; then follow the title with "By" and the author's name: Ciardi, John, trans. <u>The Inferno</u>. By Dante Alighieri.

When a book you cite by author has a translator *and* an editor, give the translator's and editor's names in the order used on the book's title page. For a translated selection from an edited book, see model 18, page 716.

8. A book with a corporate author

Lorenz Research, Inc. <u>Research in Social Studies Teaching</u>. Baltimore: Arrow, 2000.

List the name of the corporation, institution, or other body as author.

9. An anonymous book

<u>The Dorling Kindersley World Reference Atlas</u>. London: Dorling, 2003.

List an anonymous book by its full title. Alphabetize the book by the title's first main word (here <u>Dorling</u>), omitting *A, An,* or *The.*

10. The Bible

The Bible. King James Version.

<u>The New English Bible</u>. London: Oxford UP and Cambridge UP, 1970.

When citing a standard version of the Bible (first example), do not underline the title or the name of the version, and you need not provide publication information. For an edition of the Bible (second example), underline the title and give full publication information.

11. A later edition

Bollinger, Dwight L. <u>Aspects of Language</u>. 2nd ed. New York: Harcourt, 1975.

For any edition after the first, place the edition number after the title. (If an editor's name follows the title, place the edition number after the name. See model 18.) Use the appropriate designation for editions that are named or dated rather than numbered—for instance, "Rev. ed." for "Revised edition."

12. A republished book

James, Henry. <u>The Golden Bowl</u>. 1904. London: Penguin, 1966.

Republished books include paperbound editions of books originally released in hard bindings and books reissued under new titles. Place the original date of publication (but not the place of publication or the publisher's name) after the title, and then provide the full publication information for the source you are using. If the book was originally published under a different title, add this title at the end of the entry and move the original publication date to follow the title—for example, Rpt. of <u>Thomas Hardy: A Life</u>. 1941.

MLA

49b

13. A book with a title in its title

Eco, Umberto. <u>Postscript to</u> The Name of the Rose. Trans. William

  Weaver. New York: Harcourt, 1983.

When a book's title contains another book title (as here: *The Name of the Rose*), do not underline the second title. When a book's title contains a quotation or the title of a work normally placed in quotation marks, keep the quotation marks and underline both titles: <u>Critical Response to Henry James's "Beast in the Jungle."</u> (Note that the underlining extends under the closing quotation mark.)

14. A work in more than one volume

Lincoln, Abraham. <u>The Collected Works of Abraham Lincoln</u>. Ed.

  Roy P. Basler. 8 vols. New Brunswick: Rutgers UP, 1953.

Lincoln, Abraham. <u>The Collected Works of Abraham Lincoln</u>. Ed.

  Roy P. Basler. Vol. 5. New Brunswick: Rutgers UP, 1953.

  8 vols.

If you use two or more volumes of a multivolume work, give the work's total number of volumes before the publication information ("8 vols." in the first example). Your text citation will indicate which volume you are citing (see pp. 703–04). If you use only one volume, give that volume number before the publication information ("Vol. 5" in the second example). You may add the total number of volumes to the end of the entry ("8 vols." in the second example).

If you cite a multivolume work published over a period of years, give the inclusive years as the publication date: for instance, Cambridge: Harvard UP, 1978-90.

15. A work in a series

Bergman, Ingmar. <u>The Seventh Seal</u>. Mod. Film Scripts Ser. 12.

  New York: Simon, 1968.

Place the name of the series (not quoted or underlined) just before the publication information. Abbreviate common words such as *modern* and *series*. Add any series number after the series title.

16. Published proceedings of a conference

<u>Watching Our Language: A Conference Sponsored by the Program</u>

  <u>in Architecture and Design Criticism</u>. 6-8 May 2002. New

  York: Parsons School of Design, 2002.

Whether in or after the title of the conference, supply information about who sponsored the conference, when it was held, and who published the proceedings. Treat a particular presentation at the conference like a selection from an anthology (model 18).

17. An anthology

Kennedy, X. J., and Dana Gioia, eds. <u>Literature: An Introduction</u>.

    8th ed. New York: Longman, 2001.

Cite an entire anthology only when citing the work of the editor or editors or when your instructor permits cross-referencing like that shown in model 19. Give the name of the editor or editors (followed by "ed." or "eds.") and then the title of the anthology.

18. A selection from an anthology

Singer, Isaac Bashevis. "Gimpel the Fool." Trans. Saul Bellow.

    <u>Literature: An Introduction</u>. Ed. X. J. Kennedy and Dana

    Gioia. 8th ed. New York: Longman, 2001. 98-109.

The essentials of this listing are these: author of selection; title of selection (in quotation marks); title of anthology (underlined); editors' names preceded by "Ed." (meaning "Edited by"); publication information for the anthology; and inclusive page numbers for the selection (without the abbreviation "pp."). In addition, this source requires a translator for the selection and an edition number for the anthology. If you wish, you may also supply the original date of publication for the work you are citing, after its title. See model 12 on page 714.

If the work you cite comes from a collection of works by one author and with no editor, use the following form:

Auden, W. H. "Family Ghosts." <u>The Collected Poetry of W. H.</u>

    <u>Auden</u>. New York: Random House, 1945. 132-33.

If the work you cite is a scholarly article that was previously printed elsewhere, provide the complete information for the earlier publication of the piece, followed by "Rpt. in" ("Reprinted in") and the information for the source in which you found the piece:

Molloy, Francis C. "The Suburban Vision in John O'Hara's Short

    Stories." <u>Critique: Studies in Modern Fiction</u> 25.2 (1984):

    101-13. Rpt. in <u>Short Story Criticism: Excerpts from Criti-</u>

    <u>cism of the Works of Short Fiction Writers</u>. Ed. David Segal.

    Vol. 15. Detroit: Gale, 1989. 287-92.

San Juan, E. "Theme Versus Imitation: D. H. Lawrence's 'The

    Rocking-Horse Winner.'" <u>D. H. Lawrence Review</u> 3 (1970):

    136-40. Rpt. in <u>From Fiction to Film: D. H. Lawrence's "The</u>

Rocking-Horse Winner." Ed. Gerald R. Barrett and Thomas

L. Erskine. Dickenson Literature and Film Ser. Encino: Dick-

enson, 1974. 70-74.

19. Two or more selections from the same anthology

Chopin, Kate. "The Storm." Kennedy and Gioia 113–17.

Kennedy, X. J., and Dana Gioia, eds. Literature: An Introduction.

8th ed. New York: Longman, 2001.

Paz, Octavio. "My Life with the Wave." Kennedy and Gioia

392–99.

MLA
49b

When you are citing more than one selection from the same source, your instructor may allow you to avoid repetition by giving the source in full (as in the Kennedy and Gioia entry) and then simply cross-referencing it in entries for the works you used. Thus, instead of full information for the Chopin and Paz works, give Kennedy and Gioia and the appropriate pages in that book. Note that each entry appears in its proper alphabetical place among other works cited.

20. An introduction, preface, foreword, or afterword

Donaldson, Norman. Introduction. The Claverings. By Anthony

Trollope. New York: Dover, 1977. vii-xv.

An introduction, foreword, or afterword is often written by someone other than the book's author. When citing such a piece, give its name without quotation marks or underlining. (But if the piece has a title of its own, provide it, in quotation marks, between the name of the author and the name of the piece.) Follow the title of the book with its author's name preceded by "By." Give the inclusive page numbers of the part you cite. (In the preceding example, the small Roman numerals indicate that the cited work is in the front matter of the book, before page 1.)

When the author of a preface or introduction is the same as the author of the book, give only the last name after the title:

Gould, Stephen Jay. Prologue. The Flamingo's Smile: Reflections in

Natural History. By Gould. New York: Norton, 1985. 13-20.

21. An article in a reference work

Mark, Herman F. "Polymers." The New Encyclopaedia Britannica:

Macropaedia. 15th ed. 1991.

"Reckon." Merriam-Webster's Collegiate Dictionary. 10th ed.

1995.

List an article in a reference work by its title (second example) unless the article is signed (first example). For works with entries arranged alphabetically, you need not include volume or page numbers. For well-known works like those listed on the previous page, you may also omit the editors' names and all publication information except any edition number and the year of publication. For works that are not well known, give full publication information:

> "Hungarians in America." <u>The Ethnic Almanac</u>. Ed. Stephanie
>
> Bernardo. New York: Doubleday, 1991. 109-11.

2 ■ Listing periodicals: Journals, magazines, and newspapers

The basic format for an article from a periodical includes the following information:

> ———①——— ————————②——————————— ┌─③a─
> Lever, Janet. "Sex Differences in the Games Children Play." <u>Social</u>
> ——③a—— ③b ③c   ③d
> <u>Problems</u> 23 (1976): 478-87.

① *Author.* Use the author's full name: last name first, followed by a comma, and then the first name and any middle name or initial. Omit any title or degree attached to the author's name on the source, such as Dr. or PhD. End the name with a period and one space.

② *Title of the article.* Give the full title, including any subtitle. Place the title in quotation marks, capitalize all important words in the title (see pp. 519–20), and end the title with a period (inside the final quotation mark) and one space.

③ *Publication information.*

    ⓐ *The title of the periodical,* underlined, followed by a space. Omit any *A, An,* or *The* from the beginning of the title.

    ⓑ *The volume and/or issue number* (in Arabic numerals), followed by a space. See the note following.

    ⓒ *The date of publication,* followed by a colon and a space. See the note following.

    ⓓ *The inclusive page numbers of the article* (without the abbreviation "pp."). For the second number in inclusive page numbers over 100, provide only as many digits as needed for clarity (usually two): 87–88, 100–01, 398–401, 1026–36, 1190–206. If the article does not run on consecutive pages, provide only the first page number followed by a plus sign: 16+. (See also model 26, p. 720.) See page 727 on electronic sources that lack page or other reference numbers.

Note The treatment of volume and issue numbers and publication dates varies depending on the kind of periodical being cited, as the models indicate. For the distinction between journals and magazines, see pages 633–34.

22. An article in a journal with continuous pagination throughout the annual volume

Lever, Janet. "Sex Differences in the Games Children Play." Social

Problems 23 (1976): 478-87.

Some journals number the pages of issues consecutively throughout a year, so that each issue after the first in a year begins numbering where the previous issue left off—say, at page 132 or 416. For this kind of journal, give the volume number after the title ("23" in the example above) and place the year of publication in parentheses. The page numbers will be enough to guide readers to the issue you used.

23. An article in a journal that pages issues separately or that numbers only issues, not volumes

Dacey, June. "Management Participation in Corporate Buy-Outs."

Management Perspectives 7.4 (1998): 20-31.

Some journals page each issue separately (starting each issue at page 1). For these journals, give the volume number, a period, and the issue number (as in "7.4" in the Dacey entry above). Then readers know which issue of the periodical to consult. When citing an article in a journal that numbers only issues, not annual volumes, treat the issue number as if it were a volume number, as in model 22.

24. An article in a monthly or bimonthly magazine

Garber, Marjorie. "Our Genius Problem." Atlantic Monthly Dec.

2002: 46-53.

Follow the magazine title with the month and the year of publication. (Abbreviate all months except May, June, and July.) Don't place the date in parentheses, and don't provide a volume or issue number.

25. An article in a weekly or biweekly magazine

Auletta, Ken. "The Media Mogul." New Yorker 27 Jan. 2003:

26-30.

Follow the magazine title with the day, the month (abbreviated), and the year of publication. (Abbreviate all months except May, June, and July.) Don't place the date in parentheses, and don't provide a volume or issue number.

26. An article in a daily newspaper

Kolata, Gina. "Kill All the Bacteria!" New York Times 7 Jan. 2001,

natl. ed.: B1+.

Give the name of the newspaper as it appears on the first page (but without *A*, *An*, or *The*). If the name of the city is not in the title of a local newspaper, add the city name in brackets after the title, without underlining: Gazette [Chicago]. Then follow model 25, with two differences: (1) If the newspaper lists an edition at the top of the first page, include that information after the date and a comma. (See "natl. ed." above.) (2) If the newspaper is divided into lettered or numbered sections, provide the section designation before the page number when the newspaper does the same (as in "B1+" above); otherwise, provide the section designation before the colon—for instance, "sec. 1: 1+." The plus sign here and with "B1+" in the model above indicates that the articles do not run on consecutive pages but start on page 1 or B1 and continue later.

27. An anonymous article

"The Right to Die." Time 11 Oct. 1976: 101.

For an article with no named author, begin the entry with the title of the article. In the list of works cited, alphabetize an anonymous source by the first main word of the title ("Right" in this model).

28. An editorial or letter to the editor

"Dualing Power Centers." Editorial. New York Times 14 Jan. 2001,

natl. ed.: A16.

Add the word "Editorial" or "Letter"—but without quotation marks—after the title if there is one or after the author's name, as follows:

Dowding, Michael. Letter. Economist 5-11 Jan. 1995: 4.

(The numbers "5-11" in this entry are the publication days of the periodical: the issue spans January 5 through 11.)

29. A review

Nelson, Cary. "Between Anonymity and Celebrity." Rev. of Anxious

Intellects: Academic Professionals, Public Intellectuals, and

Enlightenment Values, by John Michael. College English 64

(2002): 710-19.

"Rev." is an abbreviation for "Review." The name of the author of the work being reviewed follows the title of the work, a comma, and "by." If the review has no title of its own, then "Rev. of . . ." (without quotation marks) immediately follows the name of the reviewer.

30. An abstract of a dissertation or article

Steciw, Steven K. "Alterations to the Pessac Project of Le Cor-
busier." Diss. U of Cambridge, England, 1986. DAI 46
(1986): 565C.

For an abstract appearing in *Dissertation Abstracts* (*DA*) or *Dissertation Abstracts International* (*DAI*), give the author's name and the title, "Diss." (for "Dissertation"), the institution granting the author's degree, the date of the dissertation, and the publication information.

For an abstract of an article, first provide the publication information for the article itself, followed by the information for the abstract. If the abstract publisher lists abstracts by item rather than page number, add "item" before the number.

Lever, Janet. "Sex Differences in the Games Children Play." Social
Problems 23 (1976): 478-87. Psychological Abstracts 63
(1976): item 1431.

3 ■ Listing electronic sources

Electronic sources include those available on CD-ROM and those available online, either through your library's Web site or directly over the Internet. Like citations of print sources, citations of electronic sources require available information such as author, title, and date of publication. CD-ROMs require additional information such as vendor name (see models 31 and 32). Online sources require even more additional information, as shown in the sample below. If you need help with finding authors, titles, dates, and other features of online sources, see pages 618–20.

> ──①── ──②── ──③──
> Sagoff, Mark. "Do We Consume Too Much?" Environmental
> ──③──
> Challenges to Business. Ed. Joel Reichart and Patricia
> ──③──
> H. Werhane. Washington, DC: Soc. for Business Ethics,
> ──③── ──④a──
> 2000. 106-16. Olsson Center for Applied Ethics.
> ──④b── ──④c── ──⑤──
> 18 Feb. 2003. U of Virginia. 4 Mar. 2003 <http://
> ──⑥──
> www.ocae.virginia.edu/ruffin2/sagoff.html>.

① *Author.* Use the author's full name: last name first, followed by a comma, and then the first name and any middle name or initial. If you don't see the author's name at the top of the source, look at the end of the document page. If no author is listed, begin with the title.

② *Title.* Use quotation marks around the title of a periodical article, a part of a book, or an individual document or page on a site. Use underlining for the title of an entire site.

③ *Publication information for the print version, if any.* Many online sources also appear in print, though often in a different format and sometimes with different content. If the source gives information about a print version, provide it after the source title, following an appropriate model from the previous pages. The source here, a selection from an anthology, follows model 18 (p. 716): anthology title, editors' names, place of publication, publisher, date of publication, and inclusive page numbers for the selection.

④ *Publication information for the online version.*

   ⓐ *Title of the site,* underlined.
   ⓑ *Date of electronic publication or last update.* This date is important even if the source has a print version.
   ⓒ *Name of the organization or institution sponsoring the site.*

If the site has an editor or a version number, add that information immediately after the site title.

⑤ *Date of your access.* Since online sources can and often do change, providing the date you last consulted the source tells readers which version you consulted. Do not add a period or other punctuation between the access date and the electronic address.

⑥ *Electronic address, or URL,* enclosed in angle brackets (< >). Usually you'll find the URL in the Location or Address field near the top of your browser screen. To ensure that you get the complete and accurate URL, use Copy and Paste to copy it from the browser into a word-processing file or an e-mail to yourself. In your list of works cited, break a URL *only* after a slash. Do not hyphenate.

Note A URL does not always provide a usable route to a source. The URL may be too long to copy accurately or conveniently, it may be unique to a particular search, or it may be unique to a particular library. In such a case, you may provide the URL of the site's search page, from which the reader can locate your source by author or title, or you may provide the URL of the site's home page along with any keywords or sequence of links you used to reach the source. For a subscription service, you may give just the home page URL or omit the URL; see models 33 and 34.

Try to locate all the information required in the following models. However, if you search for and still cannot find some information, then give what you can find.

31. A source on a periodical CD-ROM database

Kolata, Gina. "Kill All the Bacteria!" New York Times 7 Jan. 2001,
natl. ed.: B1+. New York Times Ondisc. CD-ROM. UMI-
ProQuest. Mar. 2001.

Databases on CD-ROM are issued periodically—for instance, every six months or every year. The journals, newspapers, and other publications included in such a database are generally available in print as well, so your works-cited entry should give the information for both formats: ① Information for the print version, following models on pages 719–21. ② Title of the CD-ROM, underlined. ③ Medium, "CD-ROM," without quotation marks or underlining. ④ Name of the vendor (or distributor) of the CD-ROM. ⑤ Date of electronic publication.

32. A source on a nonperiodical CD-ROM

Shelley, Mary Wollstonecraft. Frankenstein. Classic Library.
CD-ROM. Alameda: Andromeda, 1993.

If you cite a single-issue CD-ROM, use this format: ① Author. ② Title. Underline titles of books or similarly long works. Use quotation marks for short works such as stories or chapters in books. ③ Title of the entire CD-ROM, if any, underlined. ④ Medium, "CD-ROM," without quotation marks or underlining. ⑤ CD-ROM's place of publication, publisher, and date of publication.

If the work you cite or the entire disk has a version or edition number, add it at the appropriate place, as shown in the model below:

"Sugar." Concise Columbia Encyclopedia. 3rd ed. Microsoft Bookshelf. CD-ROM. 2002-03 ed. Redmond: Microsoft, 2002.

This model also shows citation of a part of a work (in quotation marks) with no author.

33. A work from an online service to which your library subscribes

Netchaeva, Irina. "E-Government and E-Democracy." International Journal for Communication Studies 64 (2002):

—②—— ┌——③———————┐ ④ ┌——————⑤————
467-78. <u>Academic Search Elite</u>. EBSCOhost. Santa Clara U,
——⑤—— ┌——⑥—————┐ ┌——————⑦—————
Orradre Lib. 20 Dec. 2002 <http://www.epnet.com>.

Your library subscribes to a number of online services—such as EBSCOhost, ProQuest, and LexisNexis—that often provide access to the full text of articles in periodicals, reference works, and other sources. These services sometimes provide source URLs that you can use to direct your readers to the sources (see below). More often, however, the services provide URLs that readers can't follow because they are too long (extending even beyond the browser's Location or Address field), are temporary (generated for each search), or are unique to the subscribing library. In this case follow the model above, if possible, giving the following information: ① Author and title. ② Information for print publication of the source, if any, following the appropriate model for a book or article (pp. 712–21). ③ Name of the database, underlined. (The database is the specific index or other reference you consulted.) ④ Name of the service, not underlined. ⑤ Names of the subscribing institution and library. (Add city and state if necessary to identify the library location.) ⑥ Date of your access. ⑦ URL of the service's home page, if known, so that readers can locate information about the service. If you can't find this URL, you may end the entry with the date of your access.

If the service provides a usable URL for a source, follow one of models 38–46. For the Netchaeva example above (a journal article), you would use model 40.

34. A work from an online service to which you subscribe

┌——————————①——————————┐ ┌—②——
"China--Dragon Kings." <u>The Encyclopedia Mythica</u>. America
—②—┐ ┌——③———┐ ┌——————④——————
Online. 6 Jan. 2003. Path: Research and Learn; Encyclope-
——————————④——————————
dia; More Encyclopedias; Encyclopedia Mythica.

If you find a source through America Online, MSN, or another personal online service, you may not see a usable URL or any URL for the source. In that case, provide the path you used to get to the source, as in the example above: ① Title of source, in quotation marks, and title of larger work, underlined. ② Name of the service, neither underlined nor quoted. ③ Date of your access, followed by a period. ④ "Path:" (without quotation marks) and the sequence of topics required to reach the source, with the topics separated by semicolons.

If you used a keyword instead of a path to reach the source, give that information instead: Keyword: Chinese dragon kings.

If the online service provides a usable URL for the source, use one of models 38–46. For the source shown on the facing page (an article in an encyclopedia), you would use model 45 for an information database.

35. An entire online site (scholarly project, professional site, personal site, etc.)

A scholarly project or professional site:

Scots Teaching and Research Network. Ed. John Corbett.
2 Feb. 2002. U of Glasgow. 5 Mar. 2003 <http://
www.arts.gla.ac.uk/www/english/comet/starn/htm>.

When citing an academic site, include the following: ① Title of the site, underlined. ② Name of any editor(s) of the site, preceded by "Ed." ③ Date of publication or most recent update. ④ Name of any organization or institution that sponsors the site. ⑤ Date of your access. ⑥ URL.

A personal site:

Lederman, Leon. Topics in Modern Physics--Lederman.
28 Aug. 2002. 12 Dec. 2002 <http://www-ed.fnal.gov/
samplers/hsphys/people/lederman.html>.

Cite a personal site with this information: ① Author's name, if any. ② Title, if any, underlined. If the site has no title, describe it with a label such as Home page, without quotation marks or underlining. ③ Date of last revision. ④ Date of your access. ⑤ URL.

36. A short work from an online site

Barbour, John. "The Brus." Scots Teaching and Research
Network. Ed. John Corbett. 2 Feb. 2002. U of Glasgow.
5 Mar. 2003 <http://www.arts.gla.ac.uk/www/english/comet/
starn/poetry/brus/contents/htm>.

For a poem, an article, or another short work appearing on a site, give the following: ① Author's name. ② Title of the short work, in quotation marks. ③ Title, editor, and publication information for the entire site, as in model 35 above. ④ Date of your access. ⑤ URL for the short work.

37. The home page for a course

Anderson, Daniel. Business Communication. Course home page.

Jan.-June 2003. Dept. of English, U of North Carolina.

16 Feb. 2003 <http://sites.unc.edu/daniel/eng32/

index.html>.

For the home page of a course, provide this information: ① Instructor's name. ② Course title, without quotation marks or underlining. ③ The description Course home page, without quotation marks or underlining. ④ Inclusive dates of the course. ⑤ Names of the department and the school, separated by a comma. ⑥ Date of your access. ⑦ URL for the home page.

38. An online book

An entire book:

Austen, Jane. Emma. Ed. Ronald Blythe. Harmondsworth:

Penguin, 1972. Oxford Text Archive. 1994. Oxford U.

15 Dec. 2002 <http://ota.ox.ac.uk/pub/ota/public/english/

Austen/emma.1519>.

For a book published online, give the following information: ① Author and title. ② Name of any editor or translator. ③ Any publication information for the original print version of the book, following one of models 1–17 (pp. 712–16). ④ Title of the site, underlined. ⑤ Date of electronic publication. ⑥ Name of any sponsoring organization or institution. ⑦ Date of your access. ⑧ URL for the book. If the site has an editor, add the name after the site's title (see model 35, previous page).

A part of a book:

Conrad, Joseph. "A Familiar Preface." Modern Essays. Ed. Chris-

topher Morley. New York: Harcourt, 1921. Bartleby.com:

Great Books Online. Ed. Steven van Leeuwan. Nov. 2000.

16 Feb. 2003 <http://www.bartleby.com/237/8.html>.

For a part of a book published online, provide this information: ① Author of the part. ② Title of the part, in quotation marks. (Do not use quotation marks for Introduction, Foreword, or another standard part. See model 20, p. 717.) ③ Title of the book (underlined), editor of the book (if any), and publication information for the print version of the book. ④ Title of the site (underlined) and editor of the site (if any). ⑤ Date of electronic publication. ⑥ Date of your access. ⑦ URL for the part of the book. If the site as a whole has a sponsoring organization, give the name between the date of electronic publication and the date of your access (see the Austen model opposite).

39. An online government publication

United States. Dept. of Commerce. National Telecommunications
    and Information Admin. Falling through the Net:
    Toward Digital Inclusion. Oct. 2001. 1 Mar. 2003
    <http://www.ntia.doc.gov/ntiahome/fttn00/
    contents00.html>.

See page 732 for models of government publications in print. Provide the same information for online publications, and add facts of electronic publication. The model above includes the following: ① Names of government, department, and agency. ② Title of publication, underlined. ③ Date of publication. ④ Date of your access. ⑤ URL.

40. An article in an online journal

Palfrey, Andrew. "Choice of Mates in Identical Twins." Modern
    Psychology 4.1 (1996): 26-40. 25 Feb. 2003
    <http://www.liasu.edu/modpsy/palfrey4(1).htm>.

Give the following information for an online scholarly article that you reach directly: ① Author, article title, journal title, volume and any issue numbers, and publication date, as in model 22 or 23 on page 719. ② Page numbers in the journal or total number of pages, paragraphs, or sections, if any of these is given. Omit reference numbers if none are supplied. ③ Date of your access. ④ URL for the article.

For a journal article reached through a subscription service, see model 33 (pp. 723–24).

41. An online abstract

Palfrey, Andrew. "Choice of Mates in Identical Twins." Modern
    Psychology 4.1 (1996): 26-40. Abstract. 25 Feb. 2003
    <http://www.liasu.edu/modpsy/abstractpalfrey4(1).htm>.

Treat an online abstract like an online journal article (model 40), but add "Abstract" (without quotation marks or underlining) between the publication information and the date of your access.

42. An article in an online newspaper or on a newswire

Still, Lucia. "On the Battlefields of Business, Millions of Casual-①
ties." New York Times on the Web 3 Mar. 1999. 17 Aug. 2002 ②
<http://www.nytimes.com/specials/downsize/03down1.html>. ③

Provide the following information for an online newspaper article that you reach directly: ① Author, article title, newspaper title, and publication date as in model 26 (p. 720). Give section, page, or paragraph numbers if the newspaper does. ② Date of your access. ③ URL for the article.

Treat a newswire article similarly, substituting the title of the online wire service for the newspaper title (this article has no named author):

> "Film, Fashion Asked to Stop Glamorizing Smoking." Reuters
>
> 18 Feb. 2003. 28 Feb. 2003 <http://www.reuters.com/
>
> newsArticle.jhtml?type=industryNewsID2246811>.

See model 33 (pp. 723–24) when citing a newspaper or newswire article that you reached through a subscription service.

43. An article in an online magazine

Lewis, Ricki. "The Return of Thalidomide." Scientist 22 Jan. 2001: ①
5. 24 Jan. 2003 <http://www.the-scientist.com/yr2001/jan/ ② ③ ④
lewis_pl_010122.html>. ④

Provide the following information for an online magazine article that you reach directly: ① Author's name, article title, magazine title, and publication date, as in model 24 or 25 on page 719. ② Any page, paragraph, or other reference numbers. ③ Date of your access. ④ URL for the article.

See model 33 (pp. 723–24) when citing a magazine article that you reached through a subscription service.

44. An online review

Detwiler, Donald S., and Chu Shao-Kang. Rev. of Important ①
Documents of the Republic of China, ed. Tan Quon Chin. ①

Journal of Military History 56.4 (1992): 669-84. 16 Sept.

2002 <http://www.jstor.org/fcgi-bin/jstor/viewitem.fcg/

08993718/96p0008x>.

Cite an online review as follows: ① Author, any review title, "Rev. of" and the title of the reviewed book, author or editor of the reviewed book, and publication information—all as in model 29 (p. 720). ② Date of your access. ③ URL for the review.

See model 33 (pp. 723–24) when citing a review that you reached through a subscription service.

45. An article in an online information database

Pull, Jack L. "Wu-ti." Encyclopaedia Britannica Online.

Vers. 99.1. 2002. Encyclopaedia Britannica. 23 Dec. 2002

<http://www.eb.com:80>.

For an article in an information database, such as an encyclopedia, provide the following: ① Author's name, if any is given. ② Title of the article, in quotation marks. ③ Title of the database, underlined. ④ Version number, if any is given. ⑤ Date of electronic publication. ⑥ Name of sponsoring organization or publisher. ⑦ Date of your access. ⑧ URL for the article.

See models 33 and 34 (pp. 723–25) when citing an information database that you reached through a library or personal subscription service.

46. An online graphic, video, or audio source

In general, you can base citations of online visual or audio sources on models 55–58 and 63 (pp. 733–34, 735), adding information for the online source, particularly site title, date of your access, and URL. The following examples show a range of possibilities:

A work of art:

Pollock, Jackson. Shimmering Substance. 1946. Museum of

Modern Art, New York. WebMuseum. 12 Mar. 2003

<http://www.ibiblio.org/wm/paint/auth/Pollock/

pollock.shimmering.jpg>.

A map or other illustration:

Hamilton, Calvin J. "Components of Comets." Diagram. Space Art.

2001. 20 Dec. 2002 <wysisiwyg://94/http://spaceart.com/

solar/eng/comet.htm>.

A television or radio program:

> Terry Gross, host. <u>Fresh Air</u>. National Public Radio. 11 Feb. 2003.
>
> > 12 Feb. 2003 <http://discover.npr.org/freshair/
> >
> > day_fa.html?display=February/11/2003>.

A sound recording or clip:

> Reagan, Ronald W. State of the Union Address. 26 Jan. 1982.
>
> > <u>Vincent Voice Library</u>. Digital and Multimedia Center,
> >
> > U of Michigan. 6 May 2003 <http://www.lib.msu.edu/
> >
> > vincent/presidents/reagan.htm>.

A film or film clip:

> Stewart, Leslie J. <u>96 Ranch Rodeo and Barbecue</u>. 1951.
>
> > Library of Congress. 7 Jan. 2003 <http://
> >
> > memory.loc.gov/cgi-bin/query/ammem/
> >
> > ncr:@field(DocID+@lit(nv034))>.

47. Electronic mail

> ①   ②   ③
> Millon, Michele. "Re: Grief Therapy." E-mail to the author.
> ④
> 4 May 2003.

For e-mail, give the following: ① Writer's name. ② Title, if any, from the e-mail's subject heading, in quotation marks. ③ Description of the transmission, including to whom it was sent. ④ Date of posting.

48. A posting to an e-mail discussion list

> ①   ②
> Tourville, Michael. "European Currency Reform."
> ③   ④   ⑤
> Online posting. 6 Jan. 2003. International Finance
> ⑤   ⑥   ⑦
> Discussion List. 12 Jan. 2003 <http://www.weg.isu/
> ⑦
> finance-dl/archive/46732>.

Whenever possible, cite an archived version of a posting to an e-mail discussion list so that readers can find it without difficulty. Give this information for the posting: ① Author's name. ② Title, if any, from the e-mail's subject heading, in quotation marks. ③ On-line posting, without quotation marks or underlining. ④ Date of posting. ⑤ Name of the discussion list, without quotation marks or underlining. ⑥ Date of your access. ⑦ URL, if known, or e-mail address for the moderator or supervisor of the list.

49. A posting to a newsgroup or Web forum

A newsgroup:

Cramer, Sherry. "Recent Investment Practices in U.S. Business."
Online posting. 26 Mar. 2002. 3 Apr. 2002.
<news:biz.investment.current.2700>.

MLA
49b

For a posting to a newsgroup, give the following: ① Author's name. ② Title from the subject heading, in quotation marks. ③ Online posting, without quotation marks or underlining. ④ Date of posting. ⑤ Date of your access. ⑥ Group's name preceded by news:—both enclosed in angle brackets.

A Web forum:

Dente, Robert. "The Abandoned House." Online posting.
25 Jan. 2003. The Creative Process. 27 Jan. 2003
<http://forums/nytimes.com/webin/WebX?1418294@ea7>.

For a posting to a Web forum, provide this information: ① Author's name. ② Title, if any, in quotation marks. ③ Online posting, without quotation marks or underlining. ④ Date of posting. ⑤ Name of the forum, without quotation marks or underlining. ⑥ Date of your access. ⑦ URL.

50. A synchronous communication

Bruckman, Amy. MediaMOO Symposium: Virtual Worlds
for Business? 20 Jan. 2002. MediaMOO. 26 Feb. 2002
<http://www.co.gatech.edu/fac/Amy.Bruckman/MediaMOO/
cscw-symposium-02.html>.

Whenever possible, cite an archived version of a synchronous communication so that readers can find it without difficulty. Provide this information: ① Speaker's name. ② Description of the event, without quotation marks or underlining. ③ Date of the event. ④ Forum, without quotation marks or underlining. ⑤ Date of your access. ⑥ URL.

51. Computer software

Project Scheduler 9000. Vers. 5.1. Orlando: Scitor, 2003.

For software, provide the following: ① Title, underlined. ② Version number. ③ Publication information, including place of publication, publisher, and date. If the software has a listed author, give his or her name first in the entry. If you consulted or obtained the software online, replace the publication information with the date of your access and the URL, as in previous examples.

4 ▪ Listing other sources

52. A government publication

Board of Governors. US Federal Reserve System. <u>Federal Reserve
Bulletin</u> Aug. 2002: 20-21.

Hawaii. Dept. of Education. <u>Kauai District Schools, Profile
2000-01</u>. Honolulu: Hawaii Dept. of Education, 2002.

Stiller, Ann. <u>Historic Preservation and Tax Incentives</u>. US Dept. of
Interior. Washington: GPO, 1996.

United States. Cong. House. Committee on Ways and Means.
<u>Medicare Payment for Outpatient Occupational Therapy
Services</u>. 107th Cong., 1st sess. Washington: GPO, 2001.

If an author is not listed for a government publication, give the appropriate agency as author, as in the second and last examples. Provide information in the order illustrated, separating elements with a period and a space: the name of the government, the name of the agency (which may be abbreviated), and the title and publication information. For a congressional publication (last example), give the house and committee involved before the title, and give the number and session of Congress after the title. In the last two examples, "GPO" stands for the US Government Printing Office.

53. A pamphlet

<u>Medical Answers About AIDS</u>. New York: Gay Men's Health
Crisis, 2002.

Most pamphlets can be treated as books. In the example above, the pamphlet has no listed author, so the title comes first. If the pamphlet has an author, list his or her name first, followed by the title and publication information as given here.

54. An unpublished dissertation or thesis

Wilson, Stuart M. "John Stuart Mill as a Literary Critic." Diss.
U of Michigan, 1990.

The title is quoted rather than underlined. "Diss." stands for "Dissertation." "U of Michigan" is the institution that granted the author's degree.

55. A film or video recording

<u>Schindler's List</u>. Dir. Steven Spielberg. Perf. Liam Neeson and Ben
  Kingsley. Universal, 1993.

Start with the title of the work you are citing, unless you are citing the contribution of a particular individual (see the next model). Give additional information (writer, lead performers, and so on) as you judge appropriate. For a film, end with the distributor and date.

For a videocassette, filmstrip, or slide program, include the original release date (if any) and the medium (without underlining or quotation marks) before the distributor's name:

George Balanchine, chor. <u>Serenade</u>. Perf. San Francisco Ballet.
  Dir. Hilary Bean. 1981. Videocassette. PBS Video, 1987.

56. A sound recording

Springsteen, Bruce. "Empty Sky." <u>The Rising</u>. Columbia, 2002.

Brahms, Johannes. Piano concerto no. 2 in B-flat, op. 83. Perf.
  Artur Rubinstein. Cond. Eugene Ormandy. Philadelphia
  Orch. LP. RCA, 1972.

Begin with the name of the individual whose work you are citing. If you're citing a song or song lyrics, give the title in quotation marks. Then provide the title of the recording, underlining the title (first example) unless it identifies a composition by form, number, and key (second example). After the title, provide the names of any other artists it seems appropriate to mention, the manufacturer of the recording, and the date of release. If the medium is other than compact disk, provide it immediately before the manufacturer's name—for instance, LP (as in the second example) or Audiocassette.

57. A television or radio program

Kenyon, Jane, and Donald Hall. "A Life Together." <u>Bill Moyers'</u>
  <u>Journal</u>. PBS. WNET, New York. 17 Dec. 1998.

Start with a title unless you are citing the work of a person or persons. The example above begins with the participants' names, then the episode title (in quotation marks), then the program title (underlined). Finish the entry with the name of the network, the local station and city, and the date.

58. A musical composition or work of art

Fauré, Gabriel. Sonata for Violin and Piano no. 1 in A Major, op. 15.

Don't underline musical compositions, such as the one above, that are identified only by form, number, and key. Do underline titled operas, ballets, and compositions (Carmen, Sleeping Beauty).

For a work of art, underline the title and include the name and location of the owner. For a work you see only in a photograph, provide the complete publication information, too, as in the following model. Omit such information only if you examined the actual work.

Sargent, John Singer. Venetian Doorway. Metropolitan Museum of

Art, New York. Sargent Watercolors. By Donelson F. Hoopes.

New York: Watson, 1976. 31.

59. A performance

The English Only Restaurant. By Silvio Martinez Palau. Dir.

Susana Tubert. Puerto Rican Traveling Theater, New York.

27 July 2002.

Eddins, William, cond. Chicago Symphony Orch. Symphony Cen-

ter, Chicago. 22 Jan. 2003.

As with films and television programs, place the title first unless you are citing the work of an individual (second example). Provide additional information about participants after the title, as well as the theater, city, and date. Note that the orchestra name in the second example is neither quoted nor underlined.

60. A letter

Buttolph, Mrs. Laura E. Letter to Rev. and Mrs. C. C. Jones. 20

June 1857. In The Children of Pride: A True Story of Georgia

and the Civil War. Ed. Robert Manson Myers. New Haven:

Yale UP, 1972. 334-35.

List a published letter under the writer's name. Specify that the source is a letter and to whom it was addressed, and give the date on which it was written. Treat the remaining information like that for a selection from an anthology (model 18, p. 716). (See also p. 720 for the format of a letter to the editor of a periodical.)

For a letter in the collection of a library or archive, specify the writer, recipient, and date, as above, and give the name and location of the archive as well:

James, Jonathan E. Letter to his sister. 16 Apr. 1970. Jonathan E.

James Papers. South Dakota State Archive, Pierre.

For a letter you receive, give the name of the writer, note the fact that the letter was sent to you, and provide the date of the letter:

Packer, Ann E. Letter to the author. 15 June 2002.

Use the form above for personal e-mail as well, substituting "E-mail" for "Letter": E-mail to the author (see p. 730).

61. A lecture or address

Carlone, Dennis. "Architecture for the City of the Twenty-First

Century." Symposium on the City. Urban Issues Group.

Cambridge City Hall, Cambridge. 22 May 2002.

Give the speaker's name, the title (in quotation marks), the title of the meeting, the name of the sponsoring organization, the location of the lecture, and the date. If the lecture has no title, use Lecture, Address, or another description (not in quotation marks) instead.

Although the *MLA Handbook* does not provide a specific style for classroom lectures in your courses, you can adapt the preceding format for this purpose:

Ezzy, T. G. Class lecture on the realist novel. Dawson College. 20

Jan. 2003.

62. An interview

Graaf, Vera. Personal interview. 19 Dec. 2002.

Rumsfeld, Donald. Interview. <u>Frontline</u>. PBS. WGBH, Boston. 10

Oct. 2002.

Begin with the name of the person interviewed. For an interview you conducted, specify Personal interview or the medium (such as Telephone interview or E-mail interview)—without quotation marks or underlining—and then give the date. For an interview you read, heard, or saw, provide the title if any or Interview if there is no title, along with other bibliographic information and the date.

63. A map or other illustration

<u>Women in the Armed Forces</u>. Map. <u>Women in the World: An Inter-</u>

<u>national Atlas</u>. By Joni Seager and Ann Olson. New York:

Touchstone, 2003. 44-45.

List the illustration by its title (underlined). Provide a descriptive label (Map, Chart, Table), without underlining or quotation marks, and the publication information. If the creator of the illustration is credited in the source, put his or her name first in the entry, as with any author.

EXERCISE
Writing works-cited entries

Prepare works-cited entries from the following information. Follow the models of the *MLA Handbook* given in this chapter unless your instructor specifies a different style. For titles, use underlining (as here) unless your instructor requests italics. Arrange the finished entries in alphabetical order. (Do not number entries in a list of works cited.)

1. An article titled "Use of Third Parties to Collect State and Local Taxes on Internet Sales," appearing in The Pacific Business Journal, volume 5, issue 2, in 1999. The authors are Malai Zimmerman and Kent Hoover. The article appears on pages 45 through 48 of the journal.

2. A government publication you consulted on November 12, 2002, over the Internet. The author is the Advisory Commission on Electronic Commerce, an agency of the United States government. The title of the publication is Report to Congress. It was published in April 2000 and can be reached at http://www.ecommercecommission.org/report.htm.

3. A Web site with no listed author. The title is The Internet Tax Freedom Act Home Page, and the site is dated June 3, 2002. The address is http://cox.house.gov/nettax/frmain.htm. You consulted the site on November 2, 2002.

4. An article in the magazine Forbes, published December 17, 1999, on pages 56 through 58. The author is Anne Granfield. The title is "Taxing the Internet."

5. A book titled All's Fair in Internet Commerce, or Is It? by Sally G. Osborne. The book was published in 2002 by Random House in New York, New York.

6. An e-mail interview you conducted with Nora James on November 1, 2002.

7. An article titled "State and Local Sales/Use Tax Simplification," appearing on pages 67 through 80 of an anthology, The Sales Tax in the Twenty-First Century. The anthology is edited by Matthew N. Murray and William F. Fox. The article is by Wayne G. Eggert. The anthology was published in 2000 by Praeger in Westport, Connecticut.

49c Using MLA document format

The document format recommended by the *MLA Handbook* is fairly simple, with just a few elements. See also pages 203–12 for guidelines on type fonts, headings, lists, illustrations, and other features that are not specified in MLA style.

The illustrations on the facing page show the formats for the first page and a later page of a paper. For the format of the list of works cited, see page 709.

First page of paper

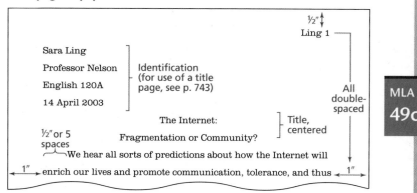

A later page of the paper

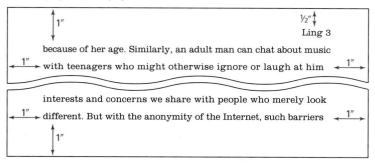

Margins

Use minimum one-inch margins on all sides of every page.

Spacing and indentions

Double-space throughout. Indent paragraphs one-half inch or five spaces. (See the next page for indention of poetry and long prose quotations.)

Paging

Begin numbering on the first page, and number consecutively through the end (including the list of works cited). Type Arabic numerals (1, 2, 3) in the upper right about one-half inch from the top. Place your last name before the page number in case the pages later become separated.

Identification and title

The *MLA Handbook* does not require a title page for a paper. If your instructor asks you to supply a title page, see the illustration and instructions on pages 742–43. Otherwise, follow the sample on the previous page, providing your name and the date, plus any other information requested by your instructor, on the first text page. Place this identification an inch from the top of the page, aligned with the left margin and double-spaced.

Double-space again, and center the title. Do not underline or boldface the title, set it in larger type, or place quotation marks around it. Capitalize the words in the title according to guidelines on pages 519–20. Double-space the lines of the title and between the title and the first line of text.

Poetry and long prose quotations

Treat a single line of poetry like any other quotation, running it into your text and enclosing it in quotation marks. You may run in two or three lines of poetry as well, separating the lines with a slash surrounded by space.

> An example of Robert Frost's incisiveness is in two lines from
>
> "Death of the Hired Man": "Home is the place where, when you
>
> have to go there / They have to take you in" (119-20).

Always set off quotations of more than three lines of poetry from your text. Use double spacing and a one-inch or ten-space indention. *Do not add quotation marks.*

> Emily Dickinson stripped ideas to their essence, as in this descrip-
>
> tion of "A narrow Fellow in the Grass," a snake:
>
>> I more than once at Noon
>>
>> Have passed, I thought, a Whip lash
>>
>> Unbraiding in the Sun
>>
>> When stopping to secure it
>>
>> It wrinkled, and was gone – (12-16)

Also set off prose quotations of five or more typed lines. *Do not add quotation marks.*

> In his 1967 study of the lives of unemployed black men, Elliot
>
> Liebow observes that "unskilled" construction work requires more
>
> experience and skill than is generally assumed:
>
>> A healthy, sturdy, active man of good intelligence re-
>>
>> quires from two to four weeks to break in on a con-
>>
>> struction job. . . . It frequently happens that his fore-
>>
>> man or the craftsman he services is not willing to wait
>>
>> that long for him to get into condition or to learn at a

> glance the difference in size between a rough 2 x 8 and
>
> a finished 2 x 10. (62)

Do not use a paragraph indention for a quotation of a single complete paragraph or a part of a paragraph. Use paragraph indentions only for a quotation of two or more complete paragraphs.

CHAPTER 50

Two Research Papers in MLA Style

The following pages show the research papers of Edward Begay and Vanessa Haley, whose work we followed in Chapters 44–48. (Begay's paper begins on p. 742, Haley's on p. 775.) Both students followed the style of the *MLA Handbook* for documenting sources and formatting their papers (Chapter 49). Accompanying both students' papers are comments on format, content, source citations, and other matters. The more extensive comments on Begay's paper are indexed below by *italic* page number and **boldface** comment number (in parentheses).

MLA
50

MLA
50

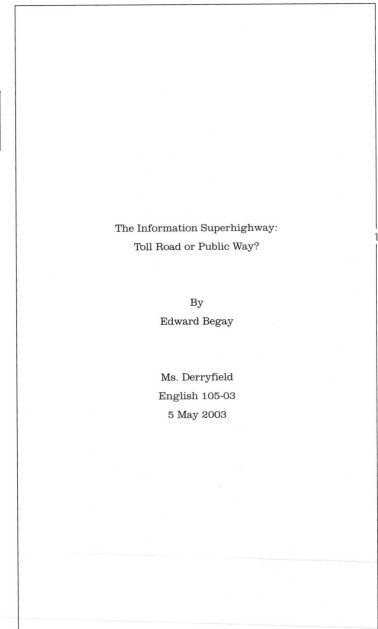

The Information Superhighway:

Toll Road or Public Way?

1

By

Edward Begay

Ms. Derryfield

English 105-03

5 May 2003

MLA
50

1. **Title page format.** A title page is not required by MLA style but may be required by your instructor. If so, or if you are required to submit an outline with your paper, prepare a title page as shown opposite: the title of the paper about a third of the way down the page; your name (preceded by "By") about an inch below the title; and, starting about an inch below your name, your instructor's name, the course number, and the date. Center all lines in the width of the page and separate them from each other with at least one line of space.

   If your instructor does not require a title page for your paper, follow MLA style: place your name, the identifying information, and the date on the first page of the paper. See Vanessa Haley's paper, page 755, for this format.

   Next two pages

2. **Outline format.** If your instructor asks you to include your final outline, place it between the title page and the text, as Begay does on the following pages. Number the pages with small Roman numerals (i, ii), and place your last name just before the page numbers in case the pages of your paper become separated. Place the heading Outline an inch from the top of the first page, and double-space under the heading.

3. **Outline content.** Begay includes his final thesis statement as part of his outline so that his instructor can see how the parts relate to the whole. Notice that each main division (numbered with Roman numerals) relates to the thesis statement and that all the subdivisions relate to their main division.

   Begay casts his final outline in full sentences. Some instructors request topic outlines, in which ideas appear in phrases instead of in sentences and do not end with periods. (See pp. 39–40 for this format.)

Outline

Thesis statement: To make Internet access universal, public libraries and schools must obtain the necessary resources from government and business both to go online and to offer enough computers for their clients' use.

    I. The "digital divide" is wide: poor people have much less access to computer technology than middle-class and affluent people do.

   II. Public libraries can provide Internet access to those who do not own computers, but they face several challenges.

      A. Those who have no access to computers at work or school take advantage of library computers for Internet access.

      B. Providing Internet access creates significant funding challenges for libraries.

      C. Commercialization of the Internet is a threat to libraries but may provide possibilities for funding.

        1. Businesses' spending on Internet infrastructure can benefit libraries.

        2. Businesses can subsidize library access to the Internet, as in the FCC's Universal Service Program.

  III. Schools must investigate the role of the Internet in education as well as ways to fund school connections.

      A. Although some experts question the value of technology in the classroom, evidence suggests that computers enhance learning.

Begay ii

1. Some critics say technology undermines
   education.
2. Some teachers say that technology fits in
   well with recent theories of education.
3. Students in schools across the country are
   using the Internet effectively.

B. Wealthy schools have far greater access to
   technology than poor ones.

   1. Wealthier school systems can fund Internet
      connections.
   2. Poorer systems lack funds for new tech-
      nology.
   3. In poorer systems, outdated computers and
      lack of Internet access lead to "drill and skill"
      use of computers.

IV. Libraries and schools must join with businesses
    and governments in seeking funds to go online and
    to train teachers and librarians to use technology.

    A. Local, state, and federal agencies must step up
       existing efforts to help put classrooms online
       and to train teachers.

    B. Businesses must also increase assistance to
       schools and libraries.

       1. High-technology companies can provide
          materials and training.
       2. Local businesses can form partnerships with
          schools.

Begay 1

The Information Superhighway:

Toll Road or Public Way?

4

The "information superhighway," referring to the great communication potential of the Internet, is now a familiar term, even among those who are not yet online. This mass of electronic connections has grown dramatically,[1] accompanied by constant predictions of how it will change our lives for the better. But the superhighway has a serious problem that receives less attention: its on-ramps--networked computers and the knowledge to operate them--are not accessible to everyone. Many observers see a real danger that the Internet may widen the gap between rich and poor in this country. According to an important study by the US Department of Commerce, "The widening gap between those with and without access to the Internet threatens our democratic society" (xii; emphasis added).

5

6

7

8

The concern expressed by the Department of Commerce study is fact-based: as discussed below, data from that study and others do show a wide gap in access to the Internet. The question, then, is how we can narrow or even close the gap to ensure that computer technology makes our society more equal rather than more unequal. In answer, most analysts look to public libraries and schools because these institutions are open to all. However, to make Internet access universal, public libraries and schools must obtain the necessary resources from government and business both to go online and to offer enough computers for their clients' use.

9

Statistics vary,[2] but all research agrees that people have much greater access to computer technology if they are middle class or affluent. Very comprehensive

10

4. **Title.** Begay's title plays on the image of the Internet as a highway to suggest his theme of accessibility. A more descriptive title, such as "Equality on the Internet," would also have been appropriate. **Paper format.** Because he provides a title page as requested by his instructor, Begay does not repeat his full name on the first page of text. For MLA style, which omits a title page, the following would appear in the upper left of this first page:

Edward Begay

Ms. Derryfield

English 105-03

5 May 2003

(See pp. 736–39 for more on MLA format and p. 775 for an example of a research paper without a title page.)

    Even with a title page, Begay centers his title an inch below the top edge of the first page, using no quotation marks or underlining. He provides his last name and the page number on the top right of every page, one-half inch below the top of the paper. The margins of the paper are one inch all around, and everything is double-spaced.

5. **Introduction.** Begay picks up the image of the superhighway from his title to lead into the problem of access. He delays presenting his thesis in order to establish some background about the risks of unequal access. The question at the beginning of the next paragraph sets up the thesis statement at the end of the paragraph.

6. **Using an endnote for supplementary information.** Begay just mentions the growth of the Internet. For readers interested in more, he provides a source in a note at the end of the paper (p. 768). He signals the note with the raised numeral 1.

7. **Citation of an anonymous work.** The government study Begay cites does not list an author, so he gives as its author the name of the sponsoring body.

8. **Citation when the author is named in your text.** Because Begay names the US Department of Commerce in his text, he gives only the page number xii in the parenthetical citation. **Adding emphasis to quotations.** Begay underlines important words in the quotation. He acknowledges this change inside the parenthetical citation with the words "emphasis added," separated by a semicolon from the page number.

9. **Thesis statement.** Begay's introduction has led up to this sentence, which asserts the idea that he will demonstrate in the paper.

10. **Relation to outline.** This paragraph begins part I of Begay's outline (see p. 744). **Using an endnote for supplementary information.** Here Begay inserts a reference to a note at the end of the paper in which he explains the difficulty of interpreting statistics about computers in schools.

Begay 2

data appear in the Department of Commerce study, which paints the unsettling picture shown in Table 1.

Table 1   11

Computers and Internet Use by Household Income

Household Income	Percentage of Households with Computers	Percentage of Persons Using the Internet
$5000-$9999	19.2	18.9
$15,000-$19,999	30.1	25.5
$35,000-$49,999	58.6	46.5
More than $75,000	86.3	70.1

Source: United States. Dept. of Commerce. National
    Telecommunications and Information Admin.
    Falling through the Net: Toward Digital Inclusion.
    Oct. 2001. 1 Mar. 2003 <http://www.ntia.doc.gov/
    ntiahome/fttn00/Falling.htm#25> 17, 43.

Public libraries have long provided free access to   12
information, and many see them as an essential component in broadening access to the Internet. A pamphlet
published by the American Library Association states
the role this way:

> [O]ur nation's libraries are uniquely posi-   13
> tioned to serve as the public's means of
> access to the information superhighway--a
> place where all people can tap into new tech-
> nology with the expert assistance of a librar-
> ian. (Equity 5)   14

11. **Use of a table.** Begay uses a table to present statistics from the Department of Commerce study so that the data are easy to compare and the differences are emphatic. **Table format.** Following MLA style, Begay double-spaces the entire table. **Citation of a source for a table.** Also following MLA style, Begay provides a source note indicating where he obtained the data in the table. The note includes complete information on the source even though Begay also cites the work fully in his list of works cited. The numbers following the electronic address at the end of the note are the pages where Begay found the table's data.

12. **Relation to outline.** This paragraph begins part II of Begay's outline. See page 744.

13. **Format of a long quotation.** This quotation exceeds four typed lines, so Begay sets it off from the text without quotation marks and with double spacing above and below. The quotation is double-spaced and is indented one inch from the left margin. **Editing a quotation with brackets.** By using brackets around the capital *O*, Begay indicates that he has omitted the beginning of the original sentence and changed the capitalization (see p. 519). No ellipsis mark is needed because the brackets already signal an omission (see p. 512).

14. **Citation with displayed quotation.** The parenthetical citation after the quotation falls *outside* the sentence period and is separated from the period by one space. **Citation of an anonymous source.** The source Begay cites does not name an author, so he uses the first main word of the full title, *Equity on the Information Superhighway: Problems and Possibilities.*

MLA

50

Most public libraries do have some level of Internet access to serve their patrons: 73.3 percent, according to the most comprehensive report available (Bertot and McClure 2). And the access specifically benefits those who need it most. The Department of Commerce data show that nearly 30 percent of unemployed adults and 20 percent of those "not in the workforce" take advantage of a public library's computers to use the Internet, whereas fewer than 6 percent of employed adults do so (54).

However, providing Internet access creates significant funding challenges for libraries. For example, almost 75 percent of public libraries have three or fewer computer terminals through which they can offer Internet access (Bertot and McClure 35). Clearly, with the length of time Internet searches can take (not to mention browsing the Internet), three terminals cannot serve many library patrons. Yet terminals are costly and require frequent upgrading.

Many librarians worry that not only cost but also the commercialization of the Internet will prevent libraries from keeping up with the Internet revolution. Early users of the Internet were primarily public institutions, but the network is now dominated by commercial interests. Market forces rather than public good often dictate Internet services and their cost. For example, telecommunication companies have merged in part to increase profits from online services. Although the mergers have often disappointed stockholders, they have had the desired effect of reducing choice and sustaining the costs to users. The focus on profit poses a threat to public users such as libraries and schools, altering the Internet environment (Equity 7).

15. **Citation when the author is not named in your text.** Because Begay has not used Bertot's and McClure's names in the text, he provides them in the parenthetical citation along with the page number.

16. **Revision of a draft.** In his first draft Begay sometimes strung his source information together without interpreting it. In revising he added comments of his own to introduce the information in the context of his ideas:

> ¶However, providing Internet access creates significant funding challenges for libraries. For example,

The Department of Commerce data show that nearly 30 percent of unemployed adults and 20 percent of those "not in the workforce" take advantage of a public library's computers to use the Internet, whereas fewer than 6 percent of employed adults do so (54).

Yet almost 75 percent of public libraries have three or fewer computer terminals through which they can offer Internet access (Bertot and McClure 35). *Clearly, with the length of time Internet searches can take (not to mention browsing the Internet), three terminals cannot serve many library patrons. Yet terminals are costly and require frequent upgrading.*

Begay 4

Could the profit quest possibly help libraries as well? Some observers believe it could, either through a kind of trickle-down effect or through business subsidies of libraries. The librarian Maurice Mitchell points out that businesses' spending on Internet research and development ultimately benefits all Internet users, including libraries, when businesses offer to wire libraries as a way to reach customers (par. 7). As long ago as 1996, Max Frankel, then a New York Times columnist, was arguing that businesses' spending should not be voluntary: "Rich companies should be charged fees for profitable private uses of the Internet . . . to subsidize the Net's penetration of every community" (42).

In fact, the US Federal Communications Commission does assess telecommunication providers to fund the Universal Service Program. Commonly called the E-Rate, the program allocates up to $2.25 billion annually to help both libraries and primary and secondary schools purchase telecommunication services. However, the fund is modest and does not cover training of staff or purchases of computers-- "the asphalt of the [information] highway," according to Larry Irving, a former assistant secretary of the US Department of Commerce. Given the transformation of our economy and culture caused by the Internet, $2.25 billion barely amounts to a token gesture.

As intense as they are, the debates over computers in libraries pale beside the debates over computers in schools. For the Internet to be truly democratic, the public schools must provide all students with

17. **Selecting supporting evidence.** Begay uses two sources in this paragraph to develop his point about possible library benefits from business activity, mixing a paraphrase from a professional librarian and a quotation from a newspaper columnist. The use of the authors' names to introduce the paraphrase and quotation clarifies who said what.

18. **Citation of a source using a paragraph number.** Begay uses "par." ("paragraph") to indicate that the source numbers paragraphs rather than pages. He cites paragraph 7. (See p. 703 for more on this form of citation.)

19. **Editing a quotation with an ellipsis mark.** Begay uses an ellipsis mark (three spaced periods) to show that he has omitted some of Frankel's words.

20. **Omission of parenthetical citations.** Begay does not provide parenthetical citations for the Federal Communications Commission report here or the Irving quotation later in this paragraph because he names the authors in his text and the sources have no page or other reference numbers.

21. **Adding to a quotation with brackets.** In case readers would misunderstand what kind of highway Irving was discussing, Begay adds a clarifying word to the quotation and surrounds the word with brackets to indicate that it did not appear in the original. (See p. 510.)

22. **Relation to outline.** With this paragraph Begay begins part III of his outline (see p. 744). **Transitional paragraph.** Begay devotes a whole paragraph to his shift in direction, briefly reflecting the ideas in the introduction, summing up the preceding section, and introducing his next point.

MLA
50

Begay 5

access to it. But the questions raised by technology in education are complex.

Before considering how all students can have equal access to the Internet, it is necessary to look at the effect of technology on schools and learning. Jane M. Healy, a noted educational psychologist and educator, questions children's use of computers in schools, arguing that "some of the most popular 'educational' software may . . . be damaging to creativity, attention, and motivation" (20). Another education expert, Harold Wenglinsky of the Educational Testing Service, found in a well-regarded 1998 study that fourth and eighth graders who used computers frequently in school actually did worse on tests than their peers who used computers less often (Does It Compute? 21). In a later article, Wenglinsky concludes that "the quantity of use matters far less than the quality of use." However, he says, high-quality computer work, involving critical thinking, is still rare in the schools ("In Search" 17).[3]

Many educators, however, see the introduction of technology as a welcome boost to newer education theories. Some theorists argue that the old "transmission" model of education, in which teachers transmit knowledge to passive students, will not prepare students to live and work in the information age (Conte 923-24). Instead, these theorists favor a model closer to cognitive psychology and constructivism, emphasizing active learning and "dealing with complex, real-world problems"--a model well served by computer networking (Conte 935-36).

23

24

25
26

27

28

29

30

23. **Integrating quotations.** Here and elsewhere, Begay establishes his source's credentials in a signal phrase and effectively integrates quotations into his own sentences. (See pp. 674–79.) **Omission of ellipsis marks.** Begay does not use an ellipsis mark at the beginning of the Healy quotation because the small *s* makes it clear that he omitted the opening of Healy's sentence. (See p. 512).

24. **Punctuation with a parenthetical citation.** The period that ends a sentence containing a quotation comes after the citation.

25. **Citation of two works by the same author.** Begay gives a brief version of Wenglinsky's title in the parenthetical citation here in order to distinguish this source from another one by Wenglinsky, cited at the end of the paragraph. (See p. 704.)

26. **Introducing and citing a discussion of one work.** By mentioning Wenglinsky's name at the beginning of these two sentences and giving the rest of the citation at the end, Begay indicates that everything in between comes from Wenglinsky. **Mixing quotation and paraphrase.** Begay quotes and paraphrases from Wenglinsky's article to give readers a good sense of the issue Wenglinsky raises.

27. **Punctuation with a quotation.** A period falls inside a closing quotation mark, as here.

28. **Introducing borrowed material.** Begay here begins paraphrasing and quoting Conte as an expert, so he should have named Conte in the text and identified him with his credentials. **Paraphrasing.** Begay paraphrases a quotation by Conte. His computer note follows:

> Traditional vs. innovative models of education
>
> Conte 923-24
>
> "[T]he traditional classroom, with its strong central authority and its emphasis on training students to take orders and perform narrow tasks, may have prepared students for work in 20th-century factories. But it can't impart the skills they need in the workplace of the 21st century, where there's a premium on workers who are flexible, creative, self-directed and able to solve problems collaboratively."

29. **Citation of a paraphrase.** Because he does not use Conte's name in the text, Begay correctly gives Conte's name in the citation.

30. **Defining terms.** Begay uses two terms here, *cognitive psychology* and *constructivism*, that he picked up from Conte and other sources. He should have defined the terms to avoid confusing readers.

MLA
50

In fact, many teachers see the Internet as the most powerful resource in education. Mary E. McArthur, a veteran teacher in Massachusetts, told me in an online interview that the Internet presents new possibilities for student learning:

> My students have a much better sense of the relevance of their education now that they're online. When we were studying ecology, for example, some students e-mailed a represen- tative of the EPA [Environmental Protection Agency] in Washington, asking questions and offering suggestions about a proposed local landfill, and received an immediate re- sponse. They took that response to the town's planning board when the landfill issue was discussed.

The Internet, according to McArthur, has made her stu- dents not only better learners but better citizens as well. And contrary to Healy's vision of uncreative, unmoti- vated students, McArthur told me that since her stu- dents began using technology, "conversation is con- stant. Students are talking online, to each other, and to me--questioning, criticizing, analyzing what they're learning."

McArthur's and her students' experiences are not unique: success stories about education on the Internet are common in popular and scholarly sources.[4] But many teachers and students are not discovering what they might accomplish with the Internet.

The statistics on public schools' access to the Internet are actually more positive than those for US households and individuals: according to the US

31. **Primary source: personal interview.** Begay tested his ideas by conducting an e-mail interview of a teacher in a public school. He uses both paraphrase and quotation from the interview, with the subject's permission.

32. **Adding words to quotations.** Begay spells out the full name of the EPA for readers who may not recognize the abbreviation, and he encloses his addition in brackets. (See p. 510.)

33. **Omission of parenthetical citation.** Begay does not use a parenthetical citation at the end of the quotation because the source (an interview) has no page or other reference numbers and the necessary information (McArthur's name) appears in the text before the quotation.

34. **Transitional paragraph.** This paragraph within the section on schools shifts the emphasis from the educational value of technology to its cost. **Summary of sources.** Rather than belabor the Internet success stories, Begay wraps up with a summary. **Using an endnote for citation of several sources.** Begay avoids a lengthy and obtrusive parenthetical citation by referring readers to endnote 4, which lists several sources (see p. 768).

MLA

50

Department of Education, 68 percent of low-income   35
schools now have Internet access. But a distinct "digital divide" still exists, for the same source shows that
94 percent of high-income schools have Internet access.
Low-income students are clearly less likely to have the
hands-on Internet experience that will prepare them
for the information age.

The Department of Education reveals another interesting difference between low- and high-income
schools as well. The poorer schools dominate the 35 percent of Internet-connected schools that have only a single room devoted to Internet use. In richer schools,
more than five such rooms are common. The Department of Education does not comment further, but this
difference spells an important difference in the access
each student has to the Internet. Even the student who
attends a wired school may not be receiving much instruction in Internet use or much time actually working online.

Not only is Internet access unavailable or restricted in many low-income schools, but the computer
equipment these schools have is often outdated. An example is La Entrada School in a poor section of Oak-
land, California (Richards). La Entrada is equipped with   36
used computers that are slow and have few of the
graphical interfaces needed to take advantage of the Internet, especially the Web. With such limited equipment,
students at La Entrada and other poor schools often
cannot match their more affluent peers in communicating with experts or with fellow students from other districts or countries. Nor can they gain quick access to
many of the resources, such as up-to-date specialized

35. **Synthesis of sources.** In this and the next paragraph, Begay integrates information from a source with his own conclusions about the significance of the data. **Citation of long source name in the text.** To avoid an awkwardly long parenthetical citation in this paragraph, Begay gives the name of the government body in his text. **Omission of parenthetical citation.** Because the online source cited in this paragraph and the next has no page or other reference numbers and Begay gives the author in his text, he does not supply parenthetical citations.

36. **Citation of an online newspaper article without page numbers.** Richards's article, which Begay found online, does not have any page or other reference numbers, so the citation includes only the author's name.

encyclopedias, that are available online. Rather than in-   37
teracting with others through their computers, these
students tend to use computers for "drill and skill"
work in reading and arithmetic: they "learn to do what
the computer tells them," according to Delia Neuman of
the University of Maryland (qtd. in Conte 931).   38

Students who do not have access to the Internet
may well find themselves left out of a society in which
computer skills will earn a worker 29 percent more
than another worker without such skills (Twist, par. 6).
And the nation's economy will suffer as well. Larry Irving, the former Commerce Department official, describes the risk:

> Almost 60 percent of jobs created today . . .
> require an understanding of information
> technology. Yet too many of our students are
> graduating from schools that don't give them
> the training they need for the jobs they need
> to hold.   39

The result, then, is a shortage of just the workers the
country needs.

The problem for schools like La Entrada is, of   40
course, money. Leaders in poor school districts are
aware of the importance of technology, but they are
also worried about leaking roofs, aging furniture,
and overcrowded classrooms. The money to buy the
equipment, make the connections, and train teachers
to use and maintain the networks is not easily found
even in middle-class school districts, much less in
poorer districts.

If libraries and schools are to provide widespread   41
access to the Internet, they must find ways not only to

37. **Combining paraphrase and quotation.** Begay had a long quotation by Neuman, but he did not want to devote quite so much space to the side issue of drill-and-skill teaching. Thus he paraphrased Neuman's idea and quoted only the most striking language. The entire quotation appears in the following note:

> Difference between rich & poor schools
>
> Conte 931
>
> From Delia Neuman, prof., U Maryland Coll. of Library & Information Services: "Economically disadvantaged students, who often use the computer for remediation and basic skills, learn to do what the computer tells them, while more affluent students, who use it to learn programming and tool application, learn to tell the computer what to do."

38. **Citation of an indirect source.** With the use of "qtd. in," Begay indicates correctly that he found the quotation by Neuman in the article by Conte. (Neuman is an indirect source; Conte is a direct source.) **Indirect sources.** Indirect sources (and "qtd. in") are appropriate only when the quoted material is not available to consult. But Begay's source, Conte, gave full bibliographic information on Neuman's original article and even an e-mail address for reaching Neuman. Instead of relying on the quotation in Conte, Begay should have gone directly to Neuman's article.

39. **Omission of a parenthetical citation.** Begay took this quotation from an online source lacking page or other reference numbers. Since the author is named in the text, no parenthetical citation is needed.

40. **Drawing conclusions.** Rather than leaving it to his readers to figure out the significance of the preceding paragraphs, Begay here wraps up his discussion of schools with his own conclusions about the costs of and thus the limits on technological change in education.

41. **Relation to outline.** With this paragraph Begay begins part IV of his outline (see p. 745). **Summary statement.** To introduce this final section of his paper, Begay begins this paragraph with a statement that pulls together libraries and schools and clearly distinguishes the educational from the financial responsiblities for broadening Internet access.

integrate technology into their programs but also to
pay the bills associated with going online. Adapting the
work of libraries and schools to the technological age is
the responsibility of the experts within those systems.
But finding the money to finance technological advances must involve more elements of society. It will be
necessary for government and business to play an active role in wiring libraries and schools, providing terminals, and training professionals to work with the
technology.

Governments are already encouraging cooperation. Officials in federal, state, and local governments
increasingly urge companies to work with schools to
achieve rapid educational access. Many states organize
annual NetDay campaigns designed to bring educators,
school boards, community volunteers, and corporations
together to wire schools (Irving; NetDay).

It is clear, however, that governments need to offer more than just encouragement. The E-Rate program of the Federal Communications Commission is a
start, but just a start. Divided among nearly 17,000
public libraries and 114,000 primary and secondary
schools (World Almanac 251, 253), the program's $2.25
billion comes to less than $20,000 per institution per
year. Because the fund does not cover hardware or
training, schools and libraries must still hustle for
these essential (and expensive) components of Internet
access. Stressing the importance of training, Jane M.
Healy notes that most school systems spend but a small
portion of their technology budgets to ensure that their
teachers know what to do with the technology (64). The
Department of Education reports that half the teachers

42. **Common knowledge.** In his reading, Begay saw many references to government encouragement of cooperation. Thus he treats the information as common knowledge and does not cite a source for it. (See p. 683 for further discussion of common knowledge.)

43. **Parenthetical citation of more than one work.** Begay discovered information about NetDay campaigns in two sources, so he cites both in parentheses, separating the two with a semicolon. Because both sources lack page or other reference numbers, the citations omit such numbers.

44. **Use of an almanac.** Begay consulted an almanac for the number of public libraries and primary and secondary schools so that he could calculate the average amount of aid under the E-Rate program. **Positioning of parenthetical citation.** Because Begay used the almanac only for the number of libraries and schools, not for the calculation, he places the parenthetical citation directly after the almanac data.

MLA

50

it surveyed had to acquire technology skills on their own time, with their own money. In schools and libraries, training staff, wiring, and purchasing equipment must be top priorities. Openly espousing technology is not enough of a role for governments: they must come through with the funds for these priorities if Internet access is to be truly democratic.

Business must also join in. Commercial enterprises have long recognized their responsibility to the larger community--for instance, supporting youth athletics and contributing to charities through the Chamber of Commerce. Now business needs to help put the community online. Some businesses are already working with schools and libraries to increase Internet access. For many years computer manufacturers such as IBM and Apple have donated new and used computers to schools. A guide to private funding for schools singles out the Bill and Melinda Gates Foundation (established by the Microsoft founder and his wife), which provides computers and Internet access to libraries with low-income patrons, and 3COM Corporation, which provides grants and consultants to help train teachers and students (Jordahl and Orwig 25).

For computer companies, cooperation with schools and libraries seems good business, paying off in free advertising, enhanced image, and potential sales. But almost every business has a vested interest in widespread access to technology. As Larry Irving notes, if today's students are not prepared for tomorrow's world, then businesses will suffer. That is one of the reasons why some noncomputer companies are working to help students become familiar with technology. In Seattle, for

45. **Common knowledge.** Begay already knew of manufacturers' programs to place computers in schools; in fact, he had used a donated IBM PC in high school. Thus he treats this information as common knowledge.

46. **Parenthetical citation of a source with two authors.** Begay gives both authors' last names, separating them with "and" and no punctuation.

Begay 11

example, three local banks assign employee mentors to public school students to help the students learn to use the Internet effectively for schoolwork (Jordahl and Orwig 24). And in Boston, Massachusetts, retail stores, insurance companies, and law firms have joined technology companies to provide computer training and equipment in the public libraries and schools, making the city one of the most Internet-connected in the nation (Pace 36).

Internet access is or soon will be "access to the central nervous system of our democracy," says Jeff Chester of the Center for Digital Democracy (6). Providing this access through libraries and schools is perhaps the only way to ensure that both poor and rich have equal access to job opportunities and can participate equally in our democratic processes and institutions. But the schools and libraries cannot do the job alone. They need the strong support of business and government to help make the information superhighway a truly public way.

47

47. **Conclusion.** In his final paragraph Begay summarizes the main points of his paper to remind readers of both the need for universal Internet access and the ways it can be funded. By referring to the image of the information superhighway from his title and introduction, Begay comes full circle and leaves his readers with a vivid impression of his idea.

MLA

50

Notes

[1] For more information on the history of the Internet, see Hardy.

[2] The US Department of Commerce study cited here is the most recent and most comprehensive available. Beyond this study, statistics on Internet use are difficult to compare and summarize because they often measure different variables. For example, one study may provide the number of households with Internet access, while another may provide the number of persons or the number of adults. In addition, with a subject this current the data are constantly changing. Nonetheless, all studies agree on the inequities between the affluent and the poor.

[3] For additional criticism of computers in education, see Goodson et al.

[4] See, for example, Conte, Jordahl and Orwig, and Pace.

48. **Format of notes.** The heading Notes is centered one inch from the top of the page. (The heading would be singular—Note—if Begay had only one note.) The notes begin two lines (one double space) below the heading. The notes themselves are double-spaced. The first line of each is indented one-half inch and is preceded by a raised number corresponding to the number used in the text. A space separates the number and the note.

49. **Endnotes for additional relevant information.** Begay uses endnotes for sources and information that are somewhat relevant to his thesis but not essential and that don't fit easily into the text. Note 1 refers interested readers to an online article on the history of the Internet. Note 2 provides information on Begay's difficulties interpreting statistics. Note 3 highlights a notable critique of computers in education. And note 4 cites several sources that would be obtrusive in a parenthetical citation. (See p. 708 for more on supplementary notes.)

50. **Citation of a source with more than three authors.** The Goodson citation indicates with "et al." ("and others") that Goodson was a coauthor with at least three others. See the works-cited entry for this source on the next page.

MLA

50

Begay 13

Works Cited 51

Bertot, John Carlo, and Charles R. McClure. The National Survey of US Public Library Outlet Internet
Connectivity: Final Report. American Library Association and US National Commission on Libraries and Information Science. Feb. 2001. 15
Mar. 2003 <http://www.ala.org/oitp/survey.html>.

Chester, Jeff. "The Threat to the Net." Nation 9 Oct. 52
2001: 6-7. Expanded Academic ASAP. InfoTrac.
Southeast State U, Polk Lib. 3 Mar. 2003 <http://
www.galegroup.com>.

Conte, Christopher. "Networking the Classroom." CQ 53
Researcher 5 (2001): 923-43.

Equity on the Information Superhighway: Problems 54
and Possibilities. Chicago: ALA, 2002.

Frankel, Max. "The Moon, This Time Around." New 55
York Times Magazine 5 May 1996: 40+. New York
Times Ondisc. CD-ROM. UMI-ProQuest. Nov. 1996.

Goodson, Ivor F., et al. "Computer Literacy as Ideology." 56
British Journal of Sociology of Education 17
(1999): 65-80.

Hardy, Henry Edward. "A Short History of the Net." 57
Ocean Home Page. 12 Mar. 2003 <http://
www.ocean.ic.net/doc/snethist.html>.

Healy, Jane M. Failure to Connect: How Computers 58
Affect Our Children's Minds--for Better and
Worse. New York: Simon, 2000.

Irving, Larry. Keynote address. American Library Assn. 59
Midwinter Meeting. Washington Convention
Center, Washington, DC. 14 Jan. 2001. American
Library Association. 8 Aug. 2001. 6 Mar. 2003
<http://www.ala.org/kranich/mw2001_prog.html>.

MLA
50

51. **Format of list of works cited.** The heading Works Cited is centered one inch from the top of the page. The first entry is typed two lines (one double space) below the heading, and the entire list is double-spaced. The first line of each entry begins at the left margin; subsequent lines of the same entry are indented one-half inch or five spaces. The entries are alphabetized by the last name of the first author or (for sources without authors) by the first main word of the title.

52. Entry for an **article from an online service to which the library subscribes** (see p. 723). Because the service does not provide usable URLs for articles—that is, URLs that readers can use to reach the articles directly—Begay instead gives the names of the database and service, the names of his school and library, and the URL for the home page of the service.

53. Entry for an **article in a journal with continuous pagination throughout an annual volume** (see p. 719).

54. Entry for a **pamphlet** (see p. 732). This entry also cites an **anonymous source** and so is listed and alphabetized by its title (see p. 714).

55. Entry for a **weekly magazine** (see p. 719) and a **source on CD-ROM that also appears in print** (see p. 723). The first date is the publication date of the article; the second is the publication date of the CD-ROM. This entry also illustrates an **article in which pagination is not consecutive.** The "+" indicates that the article does not continue on page 41 but farther back in the issue.

56. Entry for an **article with more than three authors.** A source with more than three authors may be listed with all authors' names or just with the first author's name followed by "et al." ("and others"). (See p. 712.) Begay had all the names in his working bibliography, but he opted not to use them. His parenthetical citation is consistent with this decision (p. 768).

57. Entry for a **personal online site** (see p. 725). In this case, Begay used a part of the site, so he provides the title of the part in quotation marks as well as the title of the site with underlining. For all his online sources, Begay provides a URL between angle brackets, as recommended in MLA style.

58. Entry for a **book with one author** (see p. 712).

59. Entry for a **lecture or address obtained online.** The *MLA Handbook* does not provide a model for this kind of source, so Begay improvised, using the model for a lecture or address (p. 735) and adding the title of the site (underlined), the date of electronic publication, the date of his access, and the URL.

Begay 14

Jordahl, Gregory, and Ann Orwig. "Getting Equipped   60
and Staying Equipped, Part 6: Finding the
Funds." Technology and Learning Apr. 2002:
20-26.

McArthur, Mary E. E-mail interview. 20 Mar. 2003.   61

Mitchell, Maurice. "Business Ventures in Libraries: Im-   62
plications for Patrons." Computers in Libraries
22.4 (2002): 16 pars. 21 Mar. 2003 <http://
netlib.nevada.edu/pub/lib/4621>.

NetDay. "About Us." NetDay. Jan. 2003. 21 Mar. 2003   63
<http://www.netday.org>.

Pace, Don. "Building the Digital Bridge in Boston."
Converge Dec. 2002: 35-37.

Richards, Greg. "Digital Divide on Site." San Jose Mer-   64
cury News 22 Nov. 2002, morning final ed. News-
Bank. Southeast State U, Polk Lib. 17 Mar. 2003
<http://www.newsbank.com>.

Twist, Kade. "Disparities along the Information Age   65
Career Path." Digital Divide Network. 2002.
Benton Foundation. 3 Mar. 2003 <http://
www.digitaldividenetwork.org/content/
index.cfm26>.

United States. Dept. of Commerce. National Telecom-   66
munications and Information Admin. Falling
through the Net: Toward Digital Inclusion.
Oct. 2001. 1 Mar. 2003 <http://www.ntia.doc.gov/
ntiahome/fttn00/contents00.html>.

---. Dept. of Education. National Center for Education   67
Statistics. Internet Access in Public Schools.
6 Oct. 2002. 12 Mar. 2003 <http://www.ed.gov/
nces/edstats>.

MLA
50

60. Entry for an **article in a monthly magazine** (see p. 719) and for a **source with two authors** (see p. 712).
61. Entry for a **personal interview by e-mail** (see p. 735).
62. Entry for an **article in an online journal.** Online and print journals have similar citation formats (see p. 727). Like some online journals, this one numbers paragraphs rather than pages, so Begay provides the total number of paragraphs where he would otherwise give the inclusive pages ("pars." is short for "paragraphs").
63. Entry for a **page on an organization's Web site.** MLA does not specifically cover an online site for this type of organization, so Begay adapted the format for a short work from an online site (p. 725). He provided all the information a reader would need to find the source, including the page title, site title, date of publication, date of his access, and URL of the page.
64. Entry for an **article from an online service to which the library subscribes.** See annotation 52 on page 771.
65. Entry for an **article from a foundation's Web site.** Begay found this article on the Web site of a nonprofit foundation. He treated the source as a short work from an outline site, making sure to include the specific URL for the article.
66. Entries for **online government publications.** This and the next two entries all cite government publications that Begay found online. Since none of the sources had a named author, Begay lists as author the government body responsible for the source: the government (United States), the department or agency, and (in the first two sources) the group within the department or agency. In each entry, the date of the source comes first, followed by the date Begay consulted the source. Each citation ends with the source's URL in angle brackets.
67. Entries for **additional sources by the same author.** Since the previous entry also lists the United States as author, Begay replaces those words in this and the next entry with three hyphens (see p. 712). He does not replace author information that is unique to each source.

MLA
50

Begay 15

---. Federal Communications Comm. <u>Universal Service
    Program</u>. 28 Sept. 2000. 6 Mar. 2003 <http://
    www.fcc.gov/Bureaus/Common_Carrier/
    Public_Notices/1998/da971374.html>.

Wenglinsky, Harold. <u>Does It Compute? The Relationship
    Between Educational Technology and Student
    Achievement</u>. Princeton: Educational Testing Ser-
    vice, 1998.

---. "In Search of the Workable." <u>Converge</u> Oct. 2002:
    16-17.

<u>The World Almanac and Book of Facts 2003</u>. Mahwah:
    World Almanac, 2002.

Haley 1

Vanessa Haley

Professor Moisan

English 101

24 March 2003

Format of heading and title when no title page is required (see also p. 737)

Annie Dillard's Healing Vision

It is almost a commonplace these days that human arrogance is destroying the environment. Environmentalists, naturalists, and now the man or woman on the street seem to agree: the long-held belief that human beings are separate from nature, destined to rise above its laws and conquer it, has been ruinous.

Introduction of environmental theme

Unfortunately, the defenders of nature tend to respond to this ruinous belief with harmful myths of their own: nature is pure and harmonious; humanity is corrupt and dangerous. Much writing about nature lacks a recognition that human beings and their civilization are as much a part of nature as trees and whales are, neither better nor worse. Yet without such a recognition, how can humans overcome the damaging sense of separation between themselves and the earth? How can humans develop realistic solutions to environmental problems that will work for humanity and the rest of nature?

Focus on issue to be resolved

One nature writer who seems to recognize the naturalness of humanity is Annie Dillard. In her best-known work, the Pulitzer Prize-winning Pilgrim at Tinker Creek, she is a solitary person encountering the natural world, and some critics fault her for turning her back on society. But in those encounters with nature, Dillard probes a spiritual as well as a physical identity between human beings and nature that could help to heal the rift between them.

Introduction of Dillard to resolve issue

Thesis statement

Haley 2

Dillard is not renowned for her sense of involvement with human society. Like Henry David Thoreau, with whom she is often compared, she retreats from rather than confronts human society. The critic Gary McIlroy points out that although Thoreau discusses society a great deal in Walden, he makes no attempt "to find a middle ground between it and his experiment in the woods" (113). Dillard has been similarly criticized. For instance, the writer Eudora Welty comments that

> Annie Dillard is the only person in her book, substantially the only one in her world; I recall no outside human speech coming to break the long soliloquy of the author. Speaking of the universe very often, she is yet self-surrounded and, beyond that, book-surrounded. Her own book might have taken in more of human life without losing a bit of the wonder she was after. (37)

It is true, as Welty says, that in Pilgrim Dillard seems detached from human society. However, she actually was always close to it at Tinker Creek. In a later book, Teaching a Stone to Talk, she says of the neighborhood, "This is, mind you, suburbia. It is a five-minute walk in three directions to rows of houses. . . . There's a 55 mph highway at one end of the pond, and a nesting pair of wood ducks at the other" (qtd. in Suh).

Rather than hiding from humanity, Dillard seems to be trying to understand it through nature. In Pilgrim she reports buying a goldfish, which she names Ellery Channing. She recalls once seeing through a microscope "red blood cells whip, one by one, through the capillaries" of yet another goldfish (124). Now watching

Acknowledgment of opposing critical view

First response to opposing view

Second response to opposing view

Ellery Channing, she sees the blood in his body as a bond between fish and human being: "Those red blood cells are coursing in Ellery's tail now, too, in just that way, and through his mouth and eyes as well, and through mine" (125). Gary McIlroy observes that this blood, "a symbol of the sanctity of life, is a common bond between Dillard and the fish, between animal and human life in general, and between Dillard and other people" (115).

For Dillard, the terror and unpredictability of death unify all life. The most sinister image in Pilgrim-- one that haunts Dillard--is that of the frog and the water bug. Dillard reports walking along an embankment scaring frogs into the water when one frog refused to budge. As Dillard leaned over to investigate, the frog "slowly crumpled and began to sag. The spirit vanished from his eyes as if snuffed. His skin emptied and dropped; his very skull seemed to collapse and settle like a kicked tent" (6). The frog was the victim of a water bug that injects poisons to "dissolve the victim's muscles and bones and organs" (6). Such events lead Dillard to wonder about a creator who would make all life "power and beauty, grace tangled in a rapture with violence" (8). Human beings no less than frogs and water bugs are implicated in this tangle.

Dillard is equally as disturbed by birth as by death. In a chapter of Pilgrim called "Fecundity," she focuses on the undeniable reproductive urge of entire species. Her attitude is far from sentimental:

> I don't know what it is about fecundity that
> so appalls. I suppose it is the teeming evi-
> dence that birth and growth, which we value,

MLA

50

Secondary source's analysis of Dillard

Combination of quotation and Haley's own analysis (next four paragraphs): interprets and synthesizes Dillard's ideas

Mixture of summary and quotation: provides context and keeps quotations trim

Discussion of physical identity of all creatures: death and birth

Comment on quotation: advises reader what to look for

MLA
50

> are ubiquitous and blind, that life itself is so
> astonishingly cheap, that nature is as care-
> less as it is bountiful, and that with extrava-
> gance goes a crushing waste that will one
> day include our own cheap lives. (160)

Long quotations, set off from the text: convey Dillard's voice as well as her ideas

The cheapness and brutality of life are problems
Dillard wrestles with, wondering which is "amiss": the
world, a "monster," or human beings, with their "excessive emotions" (177-78). No matter how hard she tries to
leave human society, Dillard has no choice but to "bring
human values to the creek" (179). The violent, seemingly pointless birth and death of all life are, spiritually,

Discussion of spiritual identity of all creatures

> two branches of the same creek, the creek
> that waters the world. . . . We could have
> planned things more mercifully, perhaps, but
> our plan would never get off the drawing
> board until we agreed to the very compromis-
> ing terms that are the only ones that being
> offers. (180)

For Dillard, accepting the monstrousness as well as the
beauty of "being" is the price all living things pay for
freedom.

Haley's interpretation of Dillard's ideas

In "The Waters of Separation," the final chapter of
Pilgrim, Dillard writes about a winged maple key, or
seed. At this point in the book, the critic Sandra Humble
Johnson notes, Dillard "has been humbled and emptied;
she can no longer apply effort to her search for meaning in a parasitic world" (4). It is the winter solstice--the
shortest day of the year. And then Dillard spies the
maple key descending to earth and germination. "It
rose, just before it would have touched a thistle, and
hovered pirouetting in one spot, then twirled on and

Resolution of Dillard's concerns

Haley 5

finally came to rest" (267). The key moved, says Dillard, "like a creature muscled and vigorous, or a creature spread thin to that other wind, the wind of the spirit . . . , a generous, unending breath" (268). Dillard vows to see the maple key in all of the earth and in herself. "If I am a maple key falling, at least I can twirl" (268).

According to the critic John Becker, "Annie Dillard does not walk out on ordinary life in order to bear witness against it"; instead, she uses the distance from other people "to make meaning out of the grotesque disjointedness of man and nature" (408). Gary McIlroy says, nonetheless, that Dillard "does not succeed in encompassing within her vision any but the most fragmentary consequences for society at large" (116). Possibly both are correct. In Pilgrim at Tinker Creek, Annie Dillard suggests a vision of identity among all living things that could inform modern humanity's efforts to thrive in harmony with its environment, but she does not make the leap to practicalities. Life, she says, "is a faint tracing on the surface of a mystery. . . . We must somehow take a wider view, look at the whole landscape, really see it, and describe what's going on here" (9). The description, and acting on it, may take generations. As we proceed, however, we may be guided by Dillard's efforts to mend the disjointedness, to see that human beings and maple keys alike twirl equally.

MLA
50

Conclusion: ties together divergent critical views, environmental theme, and Dillard's work

Works Cited

Becker, John E. "Science and the Sacred: From Walden
    to Tinker Creek." Thought: A Review of Culture
    and Idea 62 (1987): 400-13.

Dillard, Annie. Pilgrim at Tinker Creek. New York:
    Harper, 1974.

Johnson, Sandra Humble. The Space Between: Literary
    Epiphany in the Work of Annie Dillard. Kent:
    Kent State UP, 1992.

McIlroy, Gary. "Pilgrim at Tinker Creek and the Social
    Legacy of Walden." South Atlantic Quarterly 85.2
    (1986): 111-16.

Suh, Grace. "Ideas Are Tough, Irony Is Easy." Yale Her-
    ald Online 4 Oct. 2001. 22 Jan. 2003 <http://
    yaleherald.com/archive/xxii/10.4.01/ae/
    dillard.html>.

Welty, Eudora. Rev. of Pilgrim at Tinker Creek, by
    Annie Dillard. New York Times Book Review 24
    Mar. 1974: 36-37. New York Times Ondisc.
    CD-ROM. UMI-ProQuest. June 1994.

MLA
50

CHAPTER 51

Working with the Disciplines' Goals and Requirements

Writing in the academic disciplines you study in college does much more than simply demonstrate your competence. Writing is actually a way you learn concepts, focus ideas, analyze data, uncover assumptions, interpret patterns, and ask and answer questions.

Academic disciplines both resemble each other and differ in their methods and evidence, assignments, tools and language, and style for source citations and document format. This chapter introduces the goals and requirements common to any academic writing. Then the following chapters enlarge this information for various academic disciplines: literature (52), other humanities (53), the social sciences (54), and the natural and applied sciences (55). The chapters add three documentation styles to MLA style (p. 700): Chicago, APA, and CSE.

Note The chapters in this part build on earlier material: Chapters 1–3 on the writing process, Chapters 5–7 on critical thinking and argument, and Chapters 44–48 on research writing.

51a Using the disciplines' methods and evidence

The **methodology** of a discipline is the way its practitioners study their subjects—that is, how they proceed when investigating

http://www.ablongman.com/littlebrown
For added help with writing in the academic disciplines, click on
  ➤ Research writing ➤ Web links
    ➤ Writing in the disciplines
    ➤ General online resources
    ➤ Sources in literature and other humanities
    ➤ Sources in the social sciences
    ➤ Sources in the natural and applied sciences
  ➤ Documentation in the disciplines

the answers to questions. Methodology relates to the way practitioners analyze evidence and ideas (see pp. 125–27). For instance, a literary critic and a social historian would probably approach Shakespeare's *Hamlet* quite differently: the literary critic might study the play for a theme among its poetic images; the historian might examine the play's relation to Shakespeare's context, England at the turn of the seventeenth century.

Whatever their approach, academic writers do not compose entirely out of their personal experience. Rather, they combine the evidence of their experience with that appropriate to the discipline, drawing well-supported conclusions about their subjects. The evidence of the discipline comes from research like that described in Chapters 44–46—from primary or secondary sources.

Primary sources are firsthand or original accounts, such as historical documents, works of art, and reports on experiments that the writer has conducted. When you use primary sources, you conduct original research, generating your own evidence. You might use your analysis of a painting as evidence for an interpretation of the painting. You might use eyewitness reports on a historical event as the basis for explaining the causes of the event. Or you might use data from your own survey of students to support your conclusions about students' attitudes.

Many primary sources can be found in the library or through the library's Web site. But more prevalent among a library's offerings are **secondary sources,** books and articles written *about* primary sources. Much academic writing requires that you use such sources to spark, extend, or support your own ideas, as when you review the published opinions on your subject before contributing conclusions from your original research.

51b Understanding the disciplines' writing assignments

For most academic writing, your primary purpose will be either to explain something to your readers or to persuade them to accept your conclusions. To achieve your purpose, you will adapt your writing process to the writing situation, particularly to the kinds of evidence required by the assignment and to the kinds of thinking you are expected to do. Most assignments will contain key words that tell you what these expectations are—words such as *compare, define, analyze,* and *illustrate* that express customary ways of thinking about and organizing a vast range of subjects. Pages 92–101 and 886 explore these so-called patterns of development. You should be aware of them and alert to the wording in assignments that directs you to use them.

Guidelines for academic writers

- Become familiar with the methodology and the kinds of evidence for the discipline in which you are writing.
- Analyze the special demands of each assignment—the kind of research and sources you need. The questions you set out to answer, the assertions you wish to support, will govern how you choose your sources and evidence.
- Become familiar with the discipline's specialized tools and language.
- Use the discipline's style for source citations and document format.

51d

51c Using the disciplines' tools and language

When you write in an academic discipline, you use the scholarly tools of that discipline, particularly its periodical indexes. In addition, you may use the aids developed by practitioners of the discipline for efficiently and effectively approaching research, conducting it, and recording the findings. Many of these aids, such as a system for recording evidence from sources, are discussed in Chapters 44–46 and can be adapted to any discipline. Other aids are discussed in the following chapters.

Pay close attention to the texts assigned in a course and any materials given out in class, for these items may introduce you to valuable references and other research aids, and they will use the specialized language of the discipline. This specialized language allows practitioners to write to each other both efficiently and precisely. It also furthers certain concerns of the discipline, such as accuracy and objectivity. Scientists, for example, try to interpret their data objectively, so they avoid *undoubtedly, obviously,* and other words that slant conclusions. Some of the language conventions like this one are discussed in the following chapters. As you gain experience in a particular discipline, keep alert for such conventions and train yourself to follow them.

51d Following the disciplines' styles for source citations and document format

Most disciplines publish journals that require authors to use a certain style for source citations and a certain format for documents. In turn, most instructors in a discipline require the same of students writing papers for their courses.

When you cite your sources, you tell readers which ideas and information you borrowed and where they can find your sources. Thus source citations indicate how much knowledge you have and how broad and deep your research was. They also help you avoid **plagiarism,** the serious offense of presenting the words, ideas, and data of others as if they were your own. (See Chapter 47 on avoiding plagiarism.)

Document format includes such features as margins and the placement of the title. But it also extends to special elements of the manuscript, such as tables or an abstract, that may be required by the discipline.

Chapters 53–55 direct you to the style guides published by different disciplines and outline the requirements of the ones used most often. If your instructor does not require a particular style, use that of the Modern Language Association, which is described and illustrated at length in Chapter 49.

51d

CHAPTER 52

Reading and Writing About Literature

By Sylvan Barnet

Why read literature? Let's approach this question indirectly by asking why people *write* literature. A thousand years ago a Japanese writer, Lady Murasaki, offered an answer. Here is one of her characters talking about what motivates a writer:

> Again and again something in one's own life or in the life around one will seem so important that one cannot bear to let it pass into oblivion. There must never come a time, the writer feels, when people do not know about this.

When we read certain works—Murasaki's *The Tale of Genji* is one of them—we share this feeling; we are caught up in the writer's world, whether it is the Denmark of Shakespeare's *Hamlet* or the America of Toni Morrison's *Beloved*. We read literature because it gives us an experience that seems important, usually an experience that is both new and familiar. A common way of putting this is to say that reading broadens us and helps us understand our own experience.

52a Using the methods and evidence of literary analysis

When we read nonliterary writings, it may be enough to get the gist of the argument; in fact, we may have to peer through a good deal of wordiness to find the heart of the matter—say, three claims on behalf of capital punishment. But when we read a story, a poem,

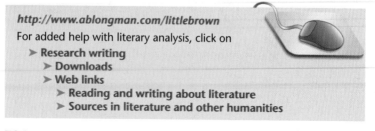

http://www.ablongman.com/littlebrown

For added help with literary analysis, click on
- ➤ **Research writing**
  - ➤ **Downloads**
  - ➤ **Web links**
    - ➤ **Reading and writing about literature**
    - ➤ **Sources in literature and other humanities**

or a play, we must pay extremely close attention to what might be called the feel of the words. For instance, the word *woods* in Robert Frost's "Stopping by Woods on a Snowy Evening" has a rural, folksy quality that *forest* doesn't have, and many such small distinctions contribute to the poem's effect.

Literary authors are concerned with presenting human experience concretely, with *showing* rather than *telling*. Consider the following proverb and an unmemorable paraphrase of it:

A rolling stone gathers no moss.

If a rock is always moving around, vegetation won't have a chance to grow on it.

The familiar original offers a small but complete world: hard (stone) and soft (moss), inorganic and organic, at rest and in motion. The original is also shapely: each noun (*stone, moss*) has one syllable, and each word of motion (*rolling, gathers*) has two syllables, with the accent on the first of the two. Such relationships unify the proverb into a pleasing whole that stays in our minds.

52a

1 ■ Reading a work of literature

Reading literature critically involves interacting with a text. The techniques complement those for critically reading any text, so if you haven't read Chapter 5 on such reading, you should do so. Responding critically is a matter not of making negative judgments but of analyzing the parts, interpreting their meanings, seeing how the parts relate, and evaluating significance or quality.

Previewing and responding

You can preview a literary text somewhat as you can preview any other text. You may gauge the length of the text to determine whether you can read it in one sitting, and you may read a biographical note to learn about the author. In a literary text, however, you won't find aids such as section headings or summaries that can make previewing other texts especially informative. You have to dive into the words themselves.

Do write while reading. If you own the book you are reading, don't hesitate to underline or highlight passages that especially interest you for one reason or another. Don't hesitate to annotate the margins, indicating your pleasures, displeasures, and uncertainties with remarks such as *Nice detail* or *Do we need this long description?* or *Not believable*. If you don't own the book, make these notes on separate sheets or on your computer.

An effective way to interact with a text is to keep a **reading journal**. A journal is not a diary in which you record your doings; instead, it is a place to develop and store your reflections on what you read, such as an answer to a question you may have posed in the margin of the text. You could make an entry in the form of a letter to the author or from one character to another. In many literature courses, students collaborate to develop their understanding of a literary work. In such a case, you may want to use your journal to reflect on what other students have said—for instance, why your opinion differs so much from someone else's.

You can keep a reading journal in a notebook or on your computer. Some readers prefer a two-column format like that illustrated on page 120, with summaries, paraphrases, and quotations from the text on the left and with their own responses to these passages on the right. Or you may prefer a less structured format like that illustrated on page 791.

52a   Reading a sample story

Here is a very short story by Kate Chopin (1851–1904). (The last name is pronounced in the French way, something like "show pan.") Following the story are a student's annotations and journal entry on the story.

Kate Chopin

The Story of an Hour

Knowing that Mrs. Mallard was afflicted with a heart trouble, great care was taken to break to her as gently as possible the news of her husband's death.

It was her sister Josephine who told her, in broken sentences, veiled hints that revealed in half concealing. Her husband's friend Richards was there, too, near her. It was he who had been in the newspaper office when intelligence of the railroad disaster was received, with Brently Mallard's name leading the list of "killed." He had only taken the time to assure himself of its truth by a second telegram, and had hastened to forestall any less careful, less tender friend in bearing the sad message.

She did not hear the story as many women have heard the same, with a paralyzed inability to accept its significance. She wept at once with sudden, wild abandonment, in her sister's arms. When the storm of grief had spent itself she went away to her room alone. She would have no one follow her.

There stood, facing the open window, a comfortable, roomy armchair. Into this she sank, pressed down by a physical exhaustion that haunted her body and seemed to reach into her soul.

She could see in the open square before her house the tops of trees that were all aquiver with the new spring life. The delicious breath of rain was in the air. In the street below a peddler was crying his wares. The notes of a distant song which some one was singing reached her faintly, and countless sparrows were twittering in the eaves.

There were patches of blue sky showing here and there through the clouds that had met and piled one above the other in the west facing her window.

She sat with her head thrown back upon the cushion of the chair quite motionless, except when a sob came up into her throat and shook her, as a child who has cried itself to sleep continues to sob in its dreams.

She was young, with a fair, calm face, whose lines bespoke repression and even a certain strength. But now there was a dull stare in her eyes, whose gaze was fixed away off yonder on one of those patches of blue sky. It was not a glance of reflection, but rather indicated a suspension of intelligent thought.

There was something coming to her and she was waiting for it, fearfully. What was it? She did not know; it was too subtle and elusive to name. But she felt it creeping out of the sky, reaching toward her through the sounds, the scents, the color that filled the air.

52a

Now her bosom rose and fell tumultuously. She was beginning to recognize this thing that was approaching to possess her, and she was striving to beat it back with her will—as powerless as her two white slender hands would have been.

When she abandoned herself a little whispered word escaped her slightly parted lips. She said it over and over under her breath: "Free, free, free!" The vacant stare and the look of terror that had followed it went from her eyes. They stayed keen and bright. Her pulses beat fast, and the coursing blood warmed and relaxed every inch of her body.

She did not stop to ask if it were not a monstrous joy that held her. A clear and exalted perception enabled her to dismiss the suggestion as trivial.

She knew that she would weep again when she saw the kind, tender hands folded in death; the face that had never looked save with love upon her, fixed and gray and dead. But she saw beyond that bitter moment a long procession of years to come that would belong to her absolutely. And she opened and spread her arms out to them in welcome.

There would be no one to live for her during those coming years; she would live for herself. There would be no powerful will bending her in the blind persistence with which men and women believe they have a right to impose a private will upon a fellow creature. A kind intention or a cruel intention made the act seem no less a crime as she looked upon it in that brief moment of illumination.

And yet she had loved him—sometimes. Often she had not. What did it matter! What could love, the unsolved mystery, count for in face of this possession of self-assertion which she suddenly recognized as the strongest impulse of her being.

"Free! Body and soul free!" she kept whispering.

Josephine was kneeling before the closed door with her lips to the keyhole, imploring for admission. "Louise, open the door! I beg; open the door—you will make yourself ill. What are you doing, Louise? For heaven's sake open the door."

"Go away. I am not making myself ill." No; she was drinking in the very elixir of life through that open window.

Her fancy was running riot along those days ahead of her. Spring days, and summer days, and all sorts of days that would be her own. She breathed a quick prayer that life might be long. It was only yesterday she had thought with a shudder that life might be long.

She arose at length and opened the door to her sister's importunities. There was a feverish triumph in her eyes, and she carried herself unwittingly like a goddess of Victory. She clasped her sister's waist and together they descended the stairs. Richards stood waiting for them at the bottom.

Some one was opening the front door with a latchkey. It was Brently Mallard who entered, a little travel-stained, composedly carrying his grip-sack and umbrella. He had been far from the scene of accident, and did not even know there had been one. He stood amazed at Josephine's piercing cry; at Richards' quick motion to screen him from the view of his wife.

But Richards was too late.

When the doctors came they said she had died of heart disease—of joy that kills.

Following a student's work

The analysis and writing of a student, Janet Vong, illustrate one approach to Chopin's story. Vong annotated the story while reading it. The first five paragraphs, with her notes, appear below:

Knowing that Mrs. Mallard was afflicted with a heart trouble, great care was taken to break to her as gently as possible the news of her husband's death.

"heart disease" at end of story

It was her sister Josephine who told her, in broken sentences, veiled hints that revealed in half concealing. Her husband's friend Richards was there, too, near her. It was he who had been in the newspaper office when intelligence of the railroad disaster was received, with Brently Mallard's name leading the list of "killed." He had only taken the time to assure himself of its truth by a second telegram, and had hastened to forestall any less careful, less tender friend in bearing the sad message.

Too hasty, it turns out

Would men have heard differently? Is au. sexist?

She did not hear the story as many women have heard the same, with a paralyzed inability to accept its significance. She wept at once with sudden, wild abandonment, in her sister's arms. When the storm of grief had spent itself she went away to her room alone. She would have no one follow her.

←old-fashioned style

There stood, facing the open window, a comfortable, roomy armchair. Into this she sank, pressed down by a physical exhaustion that haunted her body and seemed to reach into her soul.

> She could see in the open square before her \ *Notices*
> house the tops of trees that were all aquiver with ⎰ *spring: odd*
> the new spring life. The delicious breath of rain was ⎱ *in a story of*
> in the air. In the street below a peddler was crying / *death*
> his wares. The notes of a distant song which some
> one was singing reached her faintly, and countless
> sparrows were twittering in the eaves.

Writing in her journal, Vong posed questions about the story— critical points, curiosities about characters, possible implications:

> Title nothing special. What might be a better title?
> Could a woman who loved her husband be so heartless? *Is* she
>   heartless? *Did* she love him?
> What are (were) Louise's feelings about her husband?
> Did she want too much? *What* did she want?
> Could this story happen today? Feminist interpretation?
> Sister (Josephine)—a busybody?
> Tricky ending—but maybe it could be true.
> "And yet she had loved him—sometimes. Often she had not." Why
>   does one love someone "sometimes"?
> Irony: plot has reversal. Are characters ironic too?

Vong's journal entry illustrates brainstorming—the discovery technique of listing ideas (or questions) however they occur, without editing (see pp. 24–26). Another productive journal technique is focused freewriting—concentrating on a single issue (such as one of Vong's questions) and writing nonstop for a set amount of time, again without editing (p. 24).

52a

2 ■ Analyzing a work of literature

Like any discipline, the study of literature involves particular frameworks of analysis—particular ways of seeing literary works that help determine what parts the critical reader identifies and how he or she interprets them. For instance, some critics look at a literary work mainly as an artifact of the particular time and culture in which it was created, while other critics emphasize the work's effect on its readers.

This chapter emphasizes so-called formalist criticism, which focuses on a literary work primarily as something to be understood in itself. This critical framework engages the reader immediately in the work of literature, without requiring extensive historical or cultural background, and introduces the conventional elements of literature that all critical approaches discuss, even though they view the elements differently. The box on the next two pages lists these elements—plot, characters, setting, and so on—and offers questions about each one that can help you think constructively and imaginatively about what you read. (You can download these questions

Questions for a literary analysis

See later boxes for specific questions on fiction (p. 804), poetry (p. 805), and drama (p. 808).

Plot

The relationships and patterns of events. (Even a poem has a plot, such as a change in mood from bitterness to resignation.)

What actions happen?
What conflicts occur?
How do the events connect to each other and to the whole?

Characters

The people the author creates (including the narrator of a story or the speaker of a poem).

Who are the principal people in the work?
How do they interact?
What do their actions, words, and thoughts reveal about their personalities and the personalities of others?
Do the characters stay the same, or do they change? Why?

Point of view

The perspective or attitude of the speaker in a poem or the voice who tells a story. The point of view may be **first person** (a participant, using *I*) or **third person** (an outsider, using *he, she, it, they*). A first-person narrator may be a major or a minor character in the narrative and may be **reliable** or **unreliable** (unable to report events wholly or accurately). A third-person narrator may be **omniscient** (knows what goes on in all characters' minds), **limited** (knows what goes on in the mind of only one or two characters), or **objective** (knows only what is external to the characters).

Who is the narrator (or the speaker of a poem)?
How does the narrator's point of view affect the narrative?

Tone

The narrator's or speaker's attitude, perceived through the words (for instance, joyful, bitter, or confident).

What tone (or tones) do you hear? If there is a change, how do you account for it?
Is there an ironic contrast between the narrator's tone (for instance, confidence) and what you take to be the author's attitude (for instance, pity for human overconfidence)?

Imagery

Word pictures or details involving the senses (sight, sound, touch, smell, taste).

What images does the writer use? What senses do they draw on?
What patterns are evident in the images (for instance, religious or commercial images)?
What is the significance of the imagery?

52a

Symbolism

Concrete things standing for larger and more abstract ideas (for instance, the American flag may symbolize freedom, a tweeting bird may symbolize happiness, or a dead flower may symbolize mortality).

What symbols does the author use? What do they seem to signify?
How does the symbolism relate to the other elements of the work, such as character or theme?

Setting

The place where the action happens.

What does the locale contribute to the work?
Are scene shifts significant?

Form

The shape or structure of the work.

What *is* the form? (For example, a story might divide sharply in the middle, moving from happiness to sorrow.)
What parts of the work does the form emphasize, and why?

Theme

The central idea, a conception of human experience suggested by the work as a whole. Theme is neither plot (what happens) nor subject (such as mourning or marriage). Rather it is what the author says with that plot about that subject.

Can you state the theme in a sentence? For instance, you might state the following about Kate Chopin's "The Story of an Hour": *Happiness depends partly on freedom.*
Do certain words, passages of dialog or description, or situations seem to represent the theme most clearly?
How do the work's elements combine to develop the theme?

Appeal

The degree to which the work pleases you.

What do you especially like or dislike about the work?
Do you think your responses are unique, or would they be common to most readers? Why?

52a

---

from this book's Web site: see the box on p. 786. Copy the questions for each work you read, and answer the questions in writing.)

One significant attribute of a literary work is its *meaning,* or what we can interpret to be its meaning. Readers may well disagree over the persuasiveness of someone's argument, but they will rarely disagree over its meaning. With literature, however, disagreements over meaning occur all the time because (as we have seen) literature *shows* rather than *tells:* it gives us concrete images of imagined human experiences, but it usually does not say how we ought to understand the images.

Further, readers bring to their reading not only different critical views, as noted earlier, but also different personal experiences. To take an extreme case, a woman who has recently lost her husband may interpret "The Story of an Hour" differently from most other readers. Or a story that bores a reader at age fifteen may deeply move him at twenty-five. The words on the page remain the same, but their meaning changes.

In writing about literature, then, we can offer only our *interpretation* of meaning rather than *the* meaning. Still, most people agree that there are limits to interpretation: it must be supported by evidence that a reasonable reader finds at least plausible if not totally convincing. For instance, the student who says that in "The Story of an Hour" Mrs. Mallard does not die but merely falls into a deathlike trance goes beyond the permissible limits because the story offers no evidence for such an interpretation.

52b

3 ▪ Using evidence in writing about literature

The evidence for a literary analysis always comes from at least one primary source (the work or works being discussed) and may come from secondary sources (critical and historical works). (See p. 614 for more on primary and secondary sources.) For example, if you were writing about Chopin's "The Story of an Hour," the primary material would be the story itself, and the secondary material (if you used it) might be critical studies of Chopin.

The bulk of your evidence in writing about literature will usually be quotations from the work, although you will occasionally summarize or paraphrase as well (see pp. 667–70). When using quotations, keep in mind the criteria in the box on page 799.

Your instructor will probably tell you if you are expected to consult secondary sources for an assignment. They can help you understand a writer's work, but your primary concern should always be the work itself, not what critics A, B, and C say about it. In general, then, quote or summarize secondary material sparingly. And always cite your sources.

52b Understanding writing assignments in literature

A literature instructor may ask you to write one or more of the following types of papers. The first two are the most common.

- ▪ *A literary analysis paper:* give your ideas about a work of literature—your interpretation of its meaning, context, or representations based on specific words, passages, characters, and events. For guidelines on analyzing a work of literature, see pages 792–93. (For specific guidelines on analyzing fiction, poetry, and drama, see the boxes on pp. 804, 805, and 808, respectively.)

- A *literary research paper:* combine analysis of a literary work with research about the work and perhaps its author. A literary research paper draws on both primary and secondary sources. For example, you might respond to what scholars have written about the symbolism in a play by Tennessee Williams, or you might research medieval England as a way to understand the context of Chaucer's *Canterbury Tales.*
- A *personal response or reaction paper:* give your thoughts and feelings about a work of literature. For example, you might compare a novel's description of a city with your experience of the same city.
- A *book review:* give a summary of a book and a judgment about the book's value. In a review of a novel, for example, you might discuss whether the plot is interesting, the characters are believable, and the writing style is enjoyable. You might also compare the work to other works by the author.
- A *theater review:* give your reactions to and opinions about a theatrical performance. You might summarize the plot of the play, describe the characters, identify the prominent themes, evaluate the other elements (writing, performances, direction, stage setting), and make a recommendation to potential viewers.

52c

52c Using the tools and language of literary analysis

1 ■ Writing tools

The fundamental tool for writing about literature is reading critically. Asking analytical questions such as those on pages 792–93 can help you focus your ideas. In addition, keeping a reading journal can help you develop your thoughts. Keep careful, well-organized notes on any research materials. Finally, discuss the work with others who have read it. They may offer reactions and insights that will help you shape your own ideas.

2 ■ Language considerations

Use the present tense of verbs to describe both the action in a literary work (*Brently Mallard suddenly appears*) and the writing of an author (*Chopin briefly describes the view* or *In his essay he comments that . . .*). Use the past tense to describe events that actually occurred in the past (*Chopin was born in 1851*).

Some instructors discourage students from using the first-person *I* (as in *I felt sorry for the character*) in writing about literature. At least use *I* sparingly to avoid sounding egotistical. Rephrase sentences to avoid using *I* unnecessarily—for instance, *The character evokes the reader's sympathy.*

3 ▪ Research sources

In addition to these resources on literature, you may also want to consult some on other humanities (pp. 814–18).

Specialized encyclopedias, dictionaries, and bibliographies

> *Bibliographical Guide to the Study of the Literature of the U.S.A.*
> *Cambridge Bibliography of English Literature*
> *Cambridge Encyclopedia of Language*
> *Cambridge Guide to Literature in English*
> *Dictionary of Literary Biography*
> *Handbook to Literature*
> *Literary Criticism Index*
> *McGraw-Hill Encyclopedia of World Drama*
> *MLA International Bibliography of Books and Articles on the Modern Languages and Literatures*
> *New Princeton Encyclopedia of Poetry and Poetics*
> *Oxford Companion to American Literature*
> *Oxford Companion to the Theatre*
> *Schomburg Center Guide to Black Literature from the Eighteenth Century to the Present*

Periodical indexes

> *Humanities Index*
> *Literary Criticism Index*
> *MLA International Bibliography of Books and Articles on the Modern Languages and Literatures*

Abstracts and citation indexes

> *Abstracts of Folklore Studies*
> *Dissertation Abstracts International* (doctoral dissertations). Before 1969, the title was *Dissertation Abstracts.*
> *Humanities Index*

Book reviews

> *Book Review Digest*
> *Book Review Index*
> *Index to Book Reviews in the Humanities*

Web sources

For updates of these sources and addresses, see this book's Web site (box on p. 786).

52c

ALEX Catalog of Electronic Texts
  http://www.infomotions.com/alex
EServer.org
  http://eserver.org
Gale Group Literary Index
  http://www.galenet.com/servlet/LitIndex
Internet Public Library's Online Literary Criticism Collection
  http://www.ipl.org/div/litcrit
Key Sites on American Literature
  http://usinfo.state.gov/products/pubs/aol/amlitweb.htm
Literary Resources on the Net
  http://andromeda.rutgers.edu/~jlynch/Lit
Online Books Page
  http://digital.library.upenn.edu/books
Voice of the Shuttle Drama, Theater, and Performance Art Studies
  http://vos.ucsb.edu/browse.asp?id=782
Voice of the Shuttle Literature (in English)
  http://vos.ucsb.edu/browse.asp?id=3
Voice of the Shuttle Literatures (Other than English)
  http://vos.ucsb.edu/browse.asp?id=2719

52d   Citing sources and formatting documents in writing about literature

Unless your instructor specifies otherwise, use the style of the Modern Language Association (MLA), detailed in Chapter 49. In this style, parenthetical citations in the text of the paper refer to a list of works cited at the end. Sample papers illustrating this style appear in Chapter 50 as well as in this chapter.

Use MLA format for headings, margins, and other elements, as detailed on pages 736–39.

52e   Drafting and revising a literary analysis

The process for writing a literary analysis is similar to that for any other kind of essay: once you've done the reading and thought about it, you need to focus your ideas, gather evidence, draft, and revise.

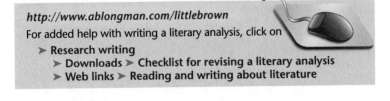

http://www.ablongman.com/littlebrown
For added help with writing a literary analysis, click on
  ➤ **Research writing**
    ➤ **Downloads** ➤ **Checklist for revising a literary analysis**
    ➤ **Web links** ➤ **Reading and writing about literature**

1 ■ Conceiving a thesis

After reading, rereading, and making notes, you probably will be able to formulate a tentative thesis statement—an assertion of your main point, your argument. (For more on thesis statements, see pp. 31–35.) Clear the air by glancing over your notes and by jotting down a few especially promising ideas—brief statements of what you think your key points may be and their main support. One approach is to seek patterns in the work, such as recurring words, phrases, images, events, symbols, or other elements. (Go back to the work, if necessary, to expand the patterns your notes reveal.) Such patterns can help you see themes both in the work itself and in your ideas about it.

Considering Kate Chopin's "The Story of an Hour," Janet Vong at first explored the idea that Mrs. Mallard, the main character, was unrealistic and thus unconvincing. (See Vong's journal entry on p. 791.) But the more Vong examined the story and her notes, the more she was impressed by a pattern of ironies, or reversals, that actually helped to make Mrs. Mallard believable. In her journal Vong explored the idea that the many small reversals paved the way for Mrs. Mallard's own reversal from grief to joy:

> title? "Ironies in an Hour" (?) "An Hour of Irony" (?) "Kate Chopin's Irony" (?)
> thesis: irony at end is prepared for
> chief irony: Mrs. M. dies just as she is beginning to enjoy life
> smaller ironies:
>   1. "sad message" brings her joy
>   2. Richards is "too late" at end
>   3. Richards is too early at start
>   4. "joy that kills"
>   5. death brings joy and life

From these notes Vong developed her thesis statement:

> The irony of the ending is believable partly because it is consistent with earlier ironies in the story.

This thesis statement asserts a specific idea that can be developed and convincingly argued with evidence from Chopin's story. A good thesis statement will neither assert a fact (*Mrs. Mallard dies soon after hearing that her husband has died*) nor overgeneralize (*The story is an insult to women*).

2 ■ Gathering evidence

In writing about literature, you use mainly evidence gathered from the work itself: quotations and sometimes paraphrases that support your ideas about the work. You can see examples of such

52e

Guidelines for using quotations in literary analysis

- **Use quotations to support your assertions, not to pad the paper.** Quote at length only when necessary to your argument.
- **Specify how each quotation relates to your idea.** Introduce the quotation—for example, *At the outset Chopin conveys the sort of person Richards is:* ". . ." Sometimes, comment after the quotation. (See pp. 674–79 for more on integrating quotations into your writing.)
- **Reproduce spelling, punctuation, capitalization, and all other features exactly as they appear in the source.** See p. 510 for the use of brackets when you need to add something to a quotation, and see p. 511 for the use of an ellipsis mark when you need to omit something from a quotation.
- **Document your sources.** (See p. 797.)

52e

quoting and paraphrasing in Janet Vong's final draft on pages 802–03. The box above offers guidelines for using quotations in literary analysis.

You may wonder how much you should summarize the plot of the work. A brief plot summary can be helpful to readers who are unfamiliar with the work. Sometimes plot elements place your ideas in the context of the work or remind readers where your quotations come from. Plot elements may even be used as evidence, as Vong uses the ironic ending of the Chopin story. But plot summary is not literary analysis, and summary alone is not sufficient evidence to support a thesis. Keep any plot summaries brief and to the point.

For a literary research paper, evidence will come from the work itself and from secondary sources such as scholarly works and critical appraisals. The thesis and principal ideas of the paper must still be your own, but you may supplement your reading of the work with the views of respected scholars or critics. Sometimes you may choose to build your own argument in part by disputing others' views. However you draw on secondary sources, remember that they must be clearly identified and documented, even when you use your own words.

Note You can find student essays on the Web that may lead you to other sources or may suggest ideas you hadn't considered. If you want to use another student's paper as a secondary source, you must evaluate it with special care because it will not have passed through a reviewing process, as an article in a scholarly journal does. (See pp. 653–59 on evaluating online sources.) You must also, of course, clearly identify and document the source: borrowing other students' ideas or words without credit is plagiarism. (See pp. 680–88.)

3 ■ Writing a draft

Drafting your essay is your opportunity to develop your thesis or to discover it if you haven't already. (See pp. 47–49 for tips on drafting.) The draft below was actually Janet Vong's second: she deleted some digressions from her first draft and added more evidence for her points. The numbers in parentheses refer to the pages from which she drew the quotations. (See pp. 700–06 on this form of documentation.) Ask your instructor whether you should always give such citations, especially for a short poem or story like Chopin's.

Ironies in an Hour

After we know how the story turns out, if we reread it we find irony at the very start, as is true of many other stories. Mrs. Mallard's friends assume, mistakenly, that Mrs. Mallard was deeply in love with her husband, Brently Mallard. They take great care to tell her gently of his death. The friends mean well, and in fact they do well. They bring her an hour of life, an hour of freedom. They think their news is sad. Mrs. Mallard at first expresses grief when she hears the news, but soon she finds joy in it. So Richards's "sad message" (12), though sad in Richards's eyes, is in fact a happy message.

Among the ironic details is the statement that when Mallard entered the house, Richards tried to conceal him from Mrs. Mallard, but "Richards was too late" (13). This is ironic because earlier Richards "hastened" (12) to bring his sad message; if he had at the start been "too late" (13), Brently Mallard would have arrived at home first, and Mrs. Mallard's life would not have ended an hour later but would simply have gone on as it had been. Yet another irony at the end of the story is the diagnosis of the doctors. The doctors say she died of "heart disease--of joy that kills" (13). In one sense the doctors are right: Mrs. Mallard has experienced a great joy. But of course the doctors totally misunderstand the joy that kills her.

The central irony resides not in the well-intentioned but ironic actions of Richards, or in the unconsciously ironic words of the doctors, but in her own life. She "sometimes" (13) loved her husband, but in a way she has been dead. Now, his apparent death brings her new life. This new life comes to her at the season of the year when "the tops of trees . . . were all aquiver with the new spring life" (12). But, ironically, her new life will last only an hour. She looks forward to "summer days" (13), but she will not see even the end of this spring day. Her years of marriage were ironic. They brought her a sort of living death instead of joy. Her new life is ironic, too. It grows out of her moment of grief for her supposedly dead husband, and her vision of a new life is cut short.

4 ■ Revising and editing

As in other writing, use at least two drafts to revise and edit, so that you can attend separately to the big structural issues and the smaller surface problems. See pages 55 and 60 for general revision and editing checklists. The additional checklist below can help you with a literary analysis. (You can download the checklist from this book's Web site: see the box on p. 797. Using a duplicate, write out answers for each paper you revise.)

Checklist for revising a literary analysis

- **Title:** Does the title of your essay give the title and author of the work you discuss and also an idea of your approach to the work?
- **Introduction:** Does the introductory paragraph name the author and the title so that readers know exactly what work you are discussing? (Avoid opening sentences such as "In this story. . . .") Does the introduction state and develop your thesis a bit so that readers know where they will be going?
- **Organization:** How effective is the organization? The essay should not dwindle or become anticlimactic; rather, it should build up.
- **Quotations:** What evidence does each quotation provide? Do quotations let readers hear the author's voice?
- **Analysis vs. summary:** Is the essay chiefly devoted to analysis, not to summary? Summarize the plot only briefly and only to further your own ideas. A summary is not an essay.
- **Verb tenses:** Have you used the present tense of verbs to describe both the author's work and the action in the work (for example, *Chopin shows* or *Mrs. Mallard dies*)?
- **Evaluation:** How well will readers understand your evaluation of the work and what it is based on? Your evaluation may be implied (as in Janet Vong's essay on "The Story of an Hour"), or it may be explicit. In either case, give the reasons for judging the work to be effective or not, worth reading or not. It is not enough to express your likes or dislikes; readers need the support of specific evidence from the work.
- **Are all your sources documented in MLA style?**

Janet Vong's final draft follows on the next page. The main changes are explained below and keyed by number to the draft.

1. Vong retitled the paper to incorporate the author and title of the work she was analyzing.

2. Vong added a new introduction to set up the paper. It names the story's author and title, introduces the story's overall irony, very briefly summarizes the story, and states Vong's thesis.
3. At many points, Vong added details and quotations to clarify the ironies in the story by emphasizing the reversals.
4. Vong added a new page for her work cited. (See p. 709 for the format of such a page.)

An essay on fiction (no secondary sources)

Janet Vong

Mr. Romano

English 102

February 20, 2003

52e

Ironies of Life in Kate Chopin's   1

"The Story of an Hour"

Kate Chopin's "The Story of an Hour"--which takes only a few   2
minutes to read--has an ironic ending: Mrs. Mallard dies just when
she is beginning to live. On first reading, the ending seems almost
too ironic for belief. On rereading the story, however, one sees that
the ending is believable partly because it is consistent with other
ironies in the story.

After we know how the story turns out, if we reread it we find
irony at the very start. Because Mrs. Mallard's friends and her sister
assume, mistakenly, that she was deeply in love with her husband,
Brently Mallard, they take great care to tell her gently of his death.
They mean well, and in fact they <u>do</u> well, bringing her an hour of life,
an hour of joyous freedom, but it is ironic that they think their news   3
is sad. True, Mrs. Mallard at first expresses grief when she hears the
news, but soon (unknown to the others) she finds joy. So Richards's
"sad message" (12), though sad in Richards's eyes, is in fact a happy
message.

Among the small but significant ironic details is the statement
near the end of the story that when Mallard entered the house,
Richards tried to conceal him from Mrs. Mallard, but "Richards was
too late" (13). Almost at the start of the story, in the second para-   3
graph, Richards "hastened" (12) to bring his sad news. But if
Richards had arrived "too late" at the start, Brently Mallard would
have arrived at home first, and Mrs. Mallard's life would not have
ended an hour later but would simply have gone on as it had been.

Yet another irony at the end of the story is the diagnosis of the doctors. They say she died of "heart disease--of joy that kills" (13). In one sense they are right: Mrs. Mallard has for the last hour experienced a great joy. But of course the doctors totally misunderstand the joy that kills her. It is not joy at seeing her husband alive, but her realization 3 that the great joy she experienced during the last hour is over.

All of these ironic details add richness to the story, but the central irony resides not in the well-intentioned but ironic actions of Richards, or in the unconsciously ironic words of the doctors, but in Mrs. Mallard's own life. She "sometimes" (13) loved her husband, but in a way she has been dead, a body subjected to her husband's will. Now, his apparent death brings her new life. Appropriately, this new 3 life comes to her at the season of the year when "the tops of trees . . . were all aquiver with the new spring life" (12). But, ironically, her new life will last only an hour. She is "Free, free, free" (12)--but only 3 until her husband walks through the doorway. She looks forward to "summer days" (13), but she will not see even the end of this spring day. If her years of marriage were ironic, bringing her a sort of living death instead of joy, her new life is ironic, too, not only because it grows out of her moment of grief for her supposedly dead husband, but also because her vision of "a long procession of years" (12) is cut 3 short within an hour on a spring day.

[New page.]

Work Cited   4

Chopin, Kate. "The Story of an Hour." Literature for Composition. Ed.
    Sylvan Barnet et al. 6th ed. New York: Longman, 2003. 12-13.

52f Writing about fiction, poetry, and drama

A work of literature falls into a category, or **genre**—fiction, poetry, or drama—depending on how it is structured. The different genres of literature require different approaches in writing.

1 ▪ Writing about fiction

The "Questions for a literary analysis" on pages 792–93 will help you think about any work of literature, including a story or novel, and find a topic to write on. The following questions provide additional prompts for thinking about fiction. (You can download these questions from this book's Web site: see the box at the bottom of the page.) For an example of writing about fiction, see Janet Vong's essay on the previous two pages.

Questions for analyzing fiction

- **What happens in the story?** For yourself, summarize the plot (the gist of the happenings). Think about what your summary *leaves out.*
- **Is the story told in chronological order, or are there flashbacks or flashforwards?** On rereading, what foreshadowing (hints of what is to come) do you detect?
- **What conflicts does the work include?**
- **How does the writer develop characters?** Is character revealed by explicit comment or through action? With which character(s) do you sympathize? Are the characters plausible? What motivates them? What do minor characters contribute to the work?
- **Who tells the story?** Is the narrator a character, or does the narrator stand entirely outside the characters' world? What does the narrator's point of view contribute to the story's theme? (On narrative points of view, see p. 792.)
- **What is the setting?** What do the time and place of the action contribute to the work?
- **Are certain characters, settings, or actions symbolic?** Do they stand for something in addition to themselves?
- **What is the theme?** That is, what does the work add up to? Does the theme reinforce your values, or does it challenge them?
- **Is the title informative?** Did its meaning change for you after you read the work?

2 ▪ Writing about poetry

Two types of essays on poetry are especially common. One is an analysis of some aspect of the poem in relation to the whole—for instance, the changes in the speaker's tone or the functions of meter and rhyme. The second is an **explication**, a line-by-line (sometimes almost word-by-word) reading that seeks to make explicit everything that is

http://www.ablongman.com/littlebrown
For added help with writing about fiction and poetry, click on
 ➤ **Research writing**
  ➤ **Downloads**
   ➤ **Questions for analyzing fiction**
   ➤ **Questions for analyzing poetry**
  ➤ **Web links**
   ➤ **Reading and writing about literature**

implicit in the poem. Thus an explication of the first line of Robert Frost's "Stopping by Woods on a Snowy Evening" (the line goes "Whose woods these are I think I know") might call attention to the tentativeness of the line ("I think I know") and to the fact that the words are not in the normal order ("I think I know whose woods these are"). These features might support the explanation that the poet is introducing—very quietly—a note of the *un*usual, in preparation for the experience that follows. Although one might conceivably explicate a long poem, the method is so detailed that in practice writers usually confine it to short poems or to short passages from long poems.

The "Questions for a literary analysis" on pages 792–93 will help you think about any work of literature, including a poem, and find a topic to write on. The questions below provide additional ways to think about poetry. (You can download these questions from this book's Web site: see the box at the bottom of the previous page.)

52f

Questions for analyzing poetry

- **What parts of the poem interest or puzzle you?** What words seem especially striking or unusual?
- **How can you describe the poem's *speaker* (sometimes called the *persona* or the *voice*)?** (The speaker may be very different from the author.) What tone or emotion do you detect—for instance, anger, affection, sarcasm? Does the tone change during the poem?
- **What is the structure of the poem?** Are there stanzas (groups of lines separated by space)? If so, how is the thought related to the stanzas?
- **What is the theme of the poem?** What is it about? Is the theme stated or implied?
- **What images do you find?** Look for evocations of sight, sound, taste, touch, or smell. Is there a surprising pattern of images—say, images of business in a poem about love? What does the poem suggest symbolically as well as literally? (Trust your responses. If you don't sense a symbolic overtone, move on. Don't hunt for symbols.)

An essay on poetry with secondary sources

The following sample paper on a short poem by Gwendolyn Brooks illustrates a literary analysis that draws not only on the poem itself but also on secondary sources—that is, critical works *about* the poem. In the opening paragraph, for instance, the writer uses brief quotations from two secondary sources to establish the problem, the topic that he will address. These quotations, like the two later quotations from secondary material, are used to make points, not to pad the essay.

Note In the paper, the parenthetical citations for Brooks's poem give line numbers of the poem, whereas the citations for the secondary sources give page numbers of the sources. See pages 705 and 701–02, respectively, for these two forms of citation.

Gwendolyn Brooks

The Bean Eaters

They eat beans mostly, this old yellow pair.
Dinner is a casual affair.
Plain chipware on a plain and creaking wood,
Tin flatware.

Two who are Mostly Good.   5
Two who have lived their day,
But keep on putting on their clothes
And putting things away.

And remembering . . .
Remembering, with tinklings and twinges,   10
As they lean over the beans in their rented back room that is
    full of beads and receipts and dolls and cloths, tobacco
    crumbs, vases and fringes.

52f

Kenneth Scheff

Professor MacGregor

English 101A

February 7, 2003

Marking Time Versus Enduring in

Gwendolyn Brooks's "The Bean Eaters"

Gwendolyn Brooks's poem "The Bean Eaters" runs only eleven
lines. It is written in plain language about very plain people. Yet its
meaning is ambiguous. One critic, George E. Kent, says the old couple
who eat beans "have had their day and exist now as time-markers"
(141). However, another reader, D. H. Melhem, perceives not so much
time marking as "endurance" in the old couple (123). Is this poem a despairing picture of old age or a more positive portrait?

"The Bean Eaters" describes an "old yellow pair" who "eat beans
mostly" (line 1) off "Plain chipware" (3) with "Tin flatware" (4) in "their
rented back room" (11). Clearly, they are poor. Their existence is accompanied not by friends or relatives--children or grandchildren are
not mentioned--but by memories and a few possessions (9-11). They are
"Mostly Good" (5), words Brooks capitalizes at the end of a line, perhaps to stress the old people's adherence to traditional values as well as
their lack of saintliness. They are unexceptional, whatever message
they have for readers.

The isolated routine of the couple's life is something Brooks
draws attention to with a separate stanza:

Two who are Mostly Good.

Two who have lived their day,

But keep on putting on their clothes

And putting things away. (5-8)

Brooks emphasizes how isolated the couple is by repeating "Two who."
Then she emphasizes how routine their life is by repeating "putting."

A pessimistic reading of this poem seems justified. The critic
Harry B. Shaw reads the lines just quoted as perhaps despairing: "they
are putting things away as if winding down an operation and readying
for withdrawal from activity" (80). However, Shaw observes, the word
but also indicates the couple's "determination to go on living, a refusal
to give up and let things go" (80). This dual meaning is at the heart of
Brooks's poem: the old people live a meager existence, yes, but their
will, their self-control, and their connection with another person--their
essential humanity--are unharmed.

52f

The truly positive nature of the poem is revealed in the last
stanza. In Brooks's words, the old couple remember with some
"twinges" perhaps, but also with "tinklings" (10), a cheerful image. As
Melhem says, these people are "strong in mutual affection and shared
memories" (123). And the final line, which is much longer than all the
rest and which catalogs the evidence of the couple's long life together,
is almost musically affirmative: "As they lean over the beans in their
rented back room that is full of beads and receipts and dolls and cloths,
tobacco crumbs, vases and fringes" (11).

What these people have is not much, but it is something.

[New page.]

Works Cited

Brooks, Gwendolyn. "The Bean Eaters." Literature: An Introduction to
Fiction, Poetry, and Drama. Ed. X. J. Kennedy and Dana Gioia.
8th ed. New York: Longman, 2001. 751.

Kent, George E. A Life of Gwendolyn Brooks. Lexington: UP of Kentucky, 1990.

Melhem, D. H. Gwendolyn Brooks: Poetry and the Heroic Voice. Lexington: UP of Kentucky, 1987.

Shaw, Harry B. Gwendolyn Brooks. Twayne's United States Authors
Ser. 395. Boston: Twayne, 1980.

3 ■ Writing about drama

Because plays—even some one-act plays—are relatively long, analytic essays on drama usually focus on only one aspect of the play, such as the structure of the play, the function of a single scene, or a character's responsibility for his or her fate. The essay's introduction indicates what the topic is and why it is of some importance, and the introduction may also state the thesis. The conclusion often extends the analysis, showing how a study of the apparently small topic helps to illuminate the play as a whole.

The "Questions for a literary analysis" on pages 792–93 will help you think about any work of literature, including a play, and find a topic to write on. The questions below provide additional prompts for thinking about drama. (You can download these questions from this book's Web site: see the box at the bottom of this page.)

Questions for analyzing drama

- **How does the plot (the sequence of happenings) unfold?** Does it seem plausible? If not, is the implausibility a fault? If there is more than one plot, are the plots parallel, or are they related by way of contrast?
- **Are certain happenings recurrent?** If so, how are they significant?
- **What kinds of conflict are in the play**—for instance, between two groups, two individuals, or two aspects of a single individual? How are the conflicts resolved? Is the resolution satisfying to you?
- **How does the author develop the characters?** How trustworthy are the characters when they describe themselves or others? Do some characters serve as **foils**, or contrasts, for other characters, thus helping to define the other characters? Do the characters change as the play proceeds? Are the characters' motivations convincing?
- **What do the author's stage directions add to your understanding and appreciation of the play?** If there are few stage directions, what do the speeches imply about the characters' manner, tone, and gestures?
- **What do you make of the setting, or location?** Does it help to reveal character or theme?
- **Do certain costumes** (dark suits, flowery shawls, stiff collars) **or properties** (books, pictures, candlesticks) **strike you as symbolic?**

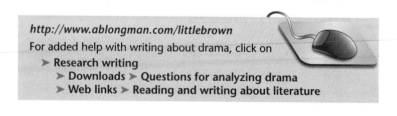

http://www.ablongman.com/littlebrown
For added help with writing about drama, click on
➤ Research writing
   ➤ Downloads ➤ Questions for analyzing drama
   ➤ Web links ➤ Reading and writing about literature

52f

The following essay on William Shakespeare's *Macbeth* focuses on the title character, examining the extent to which he is and is not a tragic hero. Although the writer bases the essay on his personal response to the play, he does not simply state a preference, as if saying he likes vanilla more than chocolate; instead, he argues a case and offers evidence from the play to support his claims.

The writer delays stating his thesis fully until the final paragraph: Macbeth is a hero even though he is a villain. But this thesis is nonetheless evident throughout the essay, from the title through the opening three paragraphs (which establish a context and the case the writer will oppose) through each of the five body paragraphs (which offer five kinds of evidence for the thesis).

Note The parenthetical citations in this essay include act, scene, and line numbers—MLA style for citations of verse plays (see p. 705).

52f

Michael Spinter

Professor Nelson

English 211, sec. 4

May 6, 2003

Macbeth as Hero

When we think of a tragic hero, we probably think of a fundamentally sympathetic person who is entangled in terrifying circumstances and who ultimately dies, leaving us with a sense that the world has suffered a loss. For instance, Hamlet must avenge his father's murder, and in doing so he performs certain actions that verge on the wrongful, such as behaving cruelly to his beloved Ophelia and his mother and killing Rosencrantz and Guildenstern; but we believe that Hamlet is fundamentally a decent man and that Denmark is the poorer for his death.

Macbeth, however, is different. He kills King Duncan and Duncan's grooms, kills Banquo, attempts to kill Banquo's son, and finally kills Lady Macduff and her children and her servants. True, the only people whom he kills with his own hands are Duncan and the grooms--the other victims are destroyed by hired murderers--but clearly Macbeth is responsible for all of the deaths. He could seem an utterly unscrupulous, sneaking crook rather than a tragic hero for whom a reader can feel sympathy.

Certainly most of the other characters in the play feel no sympathy for Macbeth. Macduff calls him a "hell-kite," or a hellish bird of prey (4.3.217), a "tyrant" (5.7.14), a "hell-hound" (5.8.3), and a "coward" (5.8.23). To Malcolm he is a "tyrant" (4.3.12), "devilish Macbeth" (4.3.117), and a "butcher" (5.8.69). Readers and spectators can hardly deny the truth of these characterizations. And yet Macbeth does not seem merely villainous. It would be going too far to say that we always sympathize with him, but we are deeply interested in him and do not dismiss him in disgust as an out-and-out monster. How can we account for his hold on our feelings? At least five factors play their parts.

First, Macbeth is an impressive military figure. In the first extended description of Macbeth, the Captain speaks of "brave Macbeth--well he deserves that name" (1.2.16). The Captain tells how Macbeth valiantly fought on behalf of his king, and King Duncan exclaims, "O valiant cousin! Worthy gentleman!" (1.2.2). True, Macbeth sometimes cringes, such as when he denies responsibility for Banquo's death: "Thou canst not say I did it" (3.4.51). But throughout most of the play, we see him as a bold and courageous soldier.

Of course, Macbeth's ability as a soldier is not enough by itself to explain his hold on us. A second reason is that he is in some degree a victim--a victim of his wife's ambition and a victim of the witches. Yes, he ought to see through his wife's schemes, and he ought to resist the witches, just as Banquo resists them, but surely Macbeth is partly tricked into crime. He is responsible, but we can imagine ourselves falling as he does, and his status as a victim arouses our sympathy.

A third source of his hold on us is that although Macbeth engages in terrible deeds, he almost always retains his conscience. For instance, after he murders Duncan he cannot sleep at night. When he tells Lady Macbeth that he has heard a voice saying, "Macbeth does murder sleep" (2.2.35), she ridicules him, but the voice is prophetic: he is doomed to sleepless nights. We in the audience are glad that Macbeth is tormented by his deed, since it shows that he knows he has done wrong and that he still has some decent human feelings.

A fourth reason why we retain some sympathy for Macbeth is that he eventually loses all of his allies, even his wife, and he stands before us a lonely, guilt-haunted figure. On this point, scene 2 of act 3 is

52f

especially significant. When Lady Macbeth asks Macbeth why he keeps to himself (line 8), he confides something of the mental stress that he is undergoing. But when she asks, "What's to be done?" (44), he cannot bring himself to tell her that he is plotting the deaths of Banquo and Fleance. Instead of further involving his wife, the only person with whom he might still have a human connection, Macbeth says, "Be innocent of the knowledge, dearest chuck . . ." (45). The word chuck, an affectionate form of chick, shows warmth and intimacy that are touching, but his refusal or his inability to confide in his wife and former partner in crime shows how fully isolated he is from all human contact. We cannot help feeling some sympathy for him.

52f

Finally, Macbeth holds our interest, instead of disgusting us, because he speaks so wonderfully. The greatness of his language compels us to listen to him with rapt attention. Some speeches are very familiar, such as "My way of life / Is fall'n into the sear, the yellow leaf . . ." (5.3.23-24) and "Tomorrow and tomorrow and tomorrow / Creeps in this petty pace from day to day . . ." (5.5.19-20). But almost every speech Macbeth utters is equally memorable, from his first, "So foul and fair a day I have not seen" (1.3.38), to his last:

> Before my body
> I throw my warlike shield. Lay on, Macduff:
> And damned be him that first cries, "Hold, enough!"
>
> (5.8.32-34)

If we stand back and judge Macbeth only by what he does, we of course say that he is a foul murderer. But if we read the play attentively, or witness a performance, and give due weight to Macbeth's bravery, his role as a victim, his tormented conscience, his isolation, and especially his moving language, we do not simply judge him. Rather, we see that, villain though he is, he is not merely awful but also awesome.

[New page.]

Work Cited

Shakespeare, William. The Tragedy of Macbeth. Ed. Sylvan Barnet. Rev. ed. New York: NAL, 1987.

CHAPTER 53

Writing in Other Humanities

The humanities include literature, the visual arts, music, film, dance, history, philosophy, and religion. The preceding chapter discusses the particular requirements of reading and writing about literature. This chapter concentrates on history. Although the arts, religion, and other humanities have their own concerns, they share many important goals and methods with literature and history.

53a Using the methods and evidence of the humanities

Writers in the humanities record and speculate about the growth, ideas, and emotions of human beings. Based on the evidence of written words, artworks, and other human traces and creations, humanities writers explain, interpret, analyze, and reconstruct the human experience.

The discipline of history focuses particularly on reconstructing the past. In Greek the word for history means "to inquire": historians inquire into the past to understand the events of the past. Then they report, explain, analyze, and evaluate those events in their context, asking such questions as what happened before or after the events or how the events were related to then existing political and social structures.

Historians' reconstructions of the past—their conclusions about what happened and why—are always supported with reference to the written record. The evidence of history is mainly primary

http://www.ablongman.com/littlebrown
For added help with writing in history, the visual arts, and other humanities, click on
➤ Research writing ➤ Web links
➤ Writing in the disciplines
➤ Sources in literature and other humanities

sources, such as eyewitness accounts and contemporary documents, letters, commercial records, and the like. For history papers, you might also be asked to support your conclusions with those in secondary sources.

In reading historical sources, you need to weigh and evaluate their evidence. If, for example, you find conflicting accounts of the same event, you need to consider the possible biases of the authors. In general, the more a historian's conclusions are supported by public records such as deeds, marriage licenses, and newspaper accounts, the more reliable the conclusions are likely to be.

53b Understanding writing assignments in the humanities

Papers in the humanities generally perform one or more of the following operations:

- *Explanation:* for instance, showing how a painter developed a particular technique or clarifying a general's role in a historical battle.
- *Analysis:* examining the elements of a philosophical argument or breaking down the causes of a historical event.
- *Interpretation:* inferring the meaning of a film from its images or the significance of a historical event from contemporary accounts of it.
- *Synthesis:* finding a pattern in a historical period or in a composer's works.
- *Evaluation:* judging the quality of an architect's design or a historian's conclusions.

Most likely, you will use these operations in combination—say, interpreting and explaining the meaning of a painting and then evaluating it. (These operations are discussed in more detail in Chapter 5.)

53c Using the tools and language of the humanities

The tools and language of the humanities vary according to the discipline. Major reference works in each field, such as those listed on the next five pages, can clarify specific tools you need and language you should use.

1 ■ Writing tools

A useful tool for the arts is to ask a series of questions to analyze and evaluate a work. (A list of such questions for reading literature appears on pp. 792–93.) In any humanities discipline, a journal—a log of questions, reactions, and insights—can help you discover and record your thoughts. (See pp. 120–21 and 607–08.)

In history the tools are those of any thorough and efficient researcher, as discussed in Chapters 44–46: a system for finding and tracking sources; a methodical examination of sources, including evaluating and synthesizing them; a system for gathering source information; and a separate system, such as a research journal, for tracking one's own evolving thoughts.

2 ▪ Language considerations

53c

Historians strive for precision and logic. They do not guess about what happened or speculate about "what if." They avoid trying to influence readers' opinions with words having strongly negative or positive connotations, such as *stupid* or *brilliant*. Instead, historians show the evidence and draw conclusions from that. Generally, they avoid using *I* because it tends to draw attention away from the evidence and toward the writer.

Writing about history demands some attention to the tenses of verbs to maintain consistency. Generally, historians use the past tense to refer to events that occurred in the past. They reserve the present tense only for statements about the present or statements of general truths. For example:

> Franklin Delano Roosevelt died in 1945. Many of Roosevelt's economic reforms persist in programs such as Social Security, unemployment compensation, and farm subsidies.

3 ▪ Research sources

The following lists give resources in the humanities. (Resources for literature appear on pp. 796–97.)

Specialized encyclopedias, dictionaries, and bibliographies

The arts

Architecture: From Prehistory to Post-Modernism
Dance Encyclopedia
Dictionary of Art
Encyclopedia of Pop, Rock, and Soul
Encyclopedia of World Art
Film Research: A Critical Bibliography
Film Review Annual
Guide to the Literature of Art History
International Cyclopedia of Music and Musicians
International Encyclopedia of Communications
International Television and Video Almanac

New Grove Dictionary of Music and Musicians
New Grove Dictionary of Opera
New Harvard Dictionary of Music
Oxford Companion to Twentieth-Century Art
Variety's Film Reviews

History

Afro-American Reference
American Heritage Encyclopedia of American History
American Indian Studies: A Bibliographic Guide
Cambridge Ancient History
Cambridge History of China
Dictionary of American History
Dictionary of American Immigration History
Dictionary of the Middle Ages
Encyclopedia of American History
Encyclopedia of Asian History
Encyclopedia of Latin-American History
Encyclopedia of World History
Guide to American Foreign Relations Since 1700
Harvard Guide to American History
History: Illustrated Search Strategy and Sources
Middle East Bibliography
Modern Encyclopedia of Russian and Soviet History
New Cambridge Modern History
Oxford Classical Dictionary
The Study of the Middle East: Research and Scholarship in the Humanities and Social Sciences

53c

Philosophy and religion

Catholic Encyclopedia
Concise Encyclopedia of Islam
Dictionary of the History of Ideas
Encyclopedia Judaica
Encyclopedia of Asian Philosophy
Encyclopedia of Ethics
Encyclopedia of Philosophy
Encyclopedia of Religion
Interpreter's Dictionary of the Bible
Library Research Guide to Religion and Theology
New Standard Jewish Encyclopedia
Oxford Dictionary of the Christian Church
Research Guide to Philosophy

Periodical indexes

America: History and Life
Art Index
Avery Index to Architectural Periodicals
Film Literature Index
Humanities Index

Musical Literature International
Music Index
Philosopher's Index
Religion Index

Abstracts and citation indexes

America: History and Life
Arts and Humanities Citation Index
Art Index
Dissertation Abstracts International (doctoral dissertations). Before 1969, the title was *Dissertation Abstracts.*
Historical Abstracts (world history)

Book reviews

Book Review Digest
Book Review Index

53c

Web sources

For updates of these sources and addresses, see this book's Web site (box on p. 812).

General

Arts and Humanities Data Service
http://ahds.ac.uk
BUBL Humanities Resources
http://bubl.ac.uk/link/hum.html
EDSITEment
http://edsitement.neh.gov
Humbul Humanities Hub
http://www.humbul.ac.uk
Internet Public Library
http://www.ipl.org/div/subject/browse/hum00.00.00
Voice of the Shuttle Humanities Gateway
http://vos.ucsb.edu

Art

artnet.com
http://www.artnet.com
BUBL Creative Arts Resources
http://bubl.ac.uk/link/art.html
Librarians' Index Arts, Crafts, and Humanities Resources
http://lii.org/search/file/artscraftshum
World Wide Arts Resources
http://wwar.com/browse.html

Dance

BUBL Dance Resources
http://bubl.ac.uk/link/d/dance.htm
Google Web Directory Dance Links
http://directory.google.com/Top/Arts/Performing_Arts/Dance

Film

ArtandCulture Film Resources
   http://www.artandculture.com/cgi-bin/WebObjects/ACLive.woa/
   wa/movement?id=371
CinemaSpot
   http://www.cinemaspot.com
Definitive Online Film Resource
   http://www.tdfilm.com
Internet Movie Database
   http://www.imdb.com

History

American and British History Resources on the Internet
   http://www.libraries.rutgers.edu/rul/rr_gateway/research_guides/
   history/history.shtml
Best of History Web Sites
   http://www.besthistorysites.net
Librarians' Index History Links
   http://lii.org/search/file/history
National Women's History Project
   http://www.nwhp.org

53c

Music

American Music Resource
   http://www.uncg.edu/~flmccart/amrhome.html
MusicMoz
   http://musicmoz.org
Music Theory Online
   http://www.societymusictheory.org/mto
Web Resources for Study and Research in Music
   http://www.ucc.ie/ucc/depts/music/online

Philosophy

Guide to Philosophy on the Internet
   http://www.earlham.edu/~peters/philinks.htm
Philosophy Documentation Center
   http://www.pdcnet.org
Philosophy Pages
   http://www.philosophypages.com
Social Science Information Gateway Philosophy Resources
   http://www.sosig.ac.uk/roads/subject-listing/World-cat/philos.html

Religion

Internet Resources for the Academic Study of Religion
   http://www.academicinfo.net/religindex.html
Pluralism Project
   http://www.pluralism.org/directory/index.php
Religious Studies Web Guide
   http://www.acs.ucalgary.ca/~lipton
Virtual Religion Index
   http://religion.rutgers.edu/vri

Theater

McCoy's Guide to Theater and Performance Studies
  http://www.stetson.edu/departments/csata/thr_guid.html
Theater Connections
  http://www.uncc.edu/jvanoate/theater
TheatreHistory.com
  http://www.theatrehistory.com
theatre-link.com
  http://www.theatre-link.com

53d   Citing sources in Chicago style

Writers in the humanities generally rely on one of the following guides for source-citation style:

The Chicago Manual of Style. 14th ed. 1993.
Gibaldi, Joseph. *MLA Handbook for Writers of Research Papers.* 6th ed. 2003.
Turabian, Kate L. *A Manual for Writers of Term Papers, Theses, and Dissertations.* 6th ed. Rev. John Grossman and Alice Bennett. 1996.

The recommendations of the *MLA Handbook* are discussed and illustrated in Chapter 49. Unless your instructor specifies otherwise, use these recommendations for papers in English and foreign languages. In history, art history, and many other disciplines, however, writers rely on *The Chicago Manual of Style* or the student reference adapted from it, *A Manual for Writers.*

Both books detail two documentation styles. One, used mainly by scientists and social scientists, closely resembles the style of the American Psychological Association, covered in Chapter 54. The other style, used more in the humanities, calls for footnotes or endnotes and an optional bibliography. This style is described below.

1 ■ Using Chicago notes and a list of works cited

In the Chicago note style, a raised numeral in the text refers the reader to source information in endnotes or footnotes. In these notes, the first citation of each source contains all the information readers need to find the source. Thus your instructor may consider a list of works cited optional because it provides much the same information. Ask your instructor whether you should use footnotes or endnotes and whether you should include a list of works cited.

http://www.ablongman.com/littlebrown
For added help with using Chicago style, click on
  ➤ **Documentation in the disciplines ➤ Chicago style**

Footnotes

In 1901, Madras, Bengal, and Punjab were a few of the huge Indian

1″ provinces governed by the British viceroy.⁶ British rule, observes   1″

Stuart Cary Welch, "seemed as permanent as Mount Everest."⁷

———————————————— ←— Line
5 spaces
6. Martin Gilbert, *Atlas of British History* (New York: Dorset] Single-
Press, 1968), 96.   space
←———————————— Double-space
7. Stuart Cary Welch, *India: Art and Culture* (New York: Met-] Single-
ropolitan Museum of Art, 1985), 421.   space

↕ 1″

Endnotes

Works cited

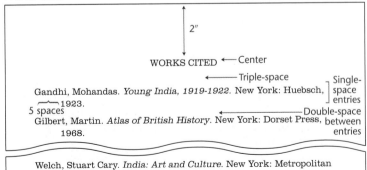

Whether providing footnotes or endnotes, use single spacing for each note and double spacing between notes, as shown in the samples on the previous page. Separate footnotes from the text with a short line. Place endnotes directly after the text, beginning on a new page. For the list of sources at the end of the paper, use the format on the previous page. Arrange the sources alphabetically by the authors' last names.

The examples below illustrate the essentials of a note and a works-cited entry.

Note

> 6. Martin Gilbert, *Atlas of British History* (New York: Dorset Press, 1968), 96.

Works-cited entry

Gilbert, Martin. *Atlas of British History.* New York: Dorset Press, 1968.

Notes and works-cited entries share certain features:

- Italicize or underline the titles of books and periodicals. Ask your instructor for his or her preference.
- Enclose in quotation marks the titles of parts of books or articles in periodicals.
- Do not abbreviate publishers' names, but omit "Inc.," "Co.," and similar abbreviations.
- Do not use "p." or "pp." before page numbers.

Notes and works-cited entries also differ in important ways:

Note	Works-cited entry
Start with a number (typed on the line and followed by a period) that corresponds to the note number in the text.	Do not begin with a number.
Indent the first line five spaces.	Indent the second and subsequent lines five spaces.
Give the author's name in normal order.	Begin with the author's last name.
Use commas between elements such as author's name and title.	Use periods between elements, followed by one space.
Enclose publication information in parentheses, with no preceding punctuation	Precede the publication information with a period, and don't use parentheses.
Include the specific page number(s) you borrowed from, omitting "p." or "pp."	Omit page numbers except for parts of books or articles in periodicals.

You can instruct your word processor to position footnotes at the bottoms of appropriate pages. It will also automatically number notes and renumber them if you add or delete one or more.

2 ■ Following Chicago models

In these models for common sources, notes and works-cited entries appear together for easy reference. Be sure to use the numbered note form for notes and the unnumbered works-cited form for works-cited entries.

Books

Chic
53d

1. A book with one, two, or three authors

1. Carol Gilligan, *In a Different Voice: Psychological Theory and Women's Development* (Cambridge: Harvard University Press, 1982), 27.

Gilligan, Carol. *In a Different Voice: Psychological Theory and Women's Development*. Cambridge: Harvard University Press, 1982.

1. Dennis L. Wilcox, Phillip H. Ault, and Warren K. Agee, *Public Relations: Strategies and Tactics,* 4th ed. (New York: HarperCollins, 1995), 182.

Wilcox, Dennis L., Phillip H. Ault, and Warren K. Agee. *Public Relations: Strategies and Tactics*. 4th ed. New York: HarperCollins, 1995.

2. A book with more than three authors

2. Geraldo Lopez and others, *China and the West* (Boston: Little, Brown, 2000), 461.

Lopez, Geraldo, Judith P. Salt, Anne Ming, and Henry Reisen. *China and the West*. Boston: Little, Brown, 2000.

3. A book with an editor

3. Hendrick Ruitenbeek, ed., *Freud as We Knew Him* (Detroit: Wayne State University Press, 1973), 64.

Ruitenbeek, Hendrick, ed. *Freud as We Knew Him*. Detroit: Wayne State University Press, 1973.

4. A book with an author and an editor

4. Lewis Mumford, *The City in History,* ed. Donald L. Miller (New York: Pantheon, 1986), 216-17.

Mumford, Lewis. *The City in History*. Edited by Donald L. Miller. New York: Pantheon, 1986.

Chicago note and works-cited models

5. A translation

5. Dante Alighieri, *The Inferno*, trans. John Ciardi (New York: New American Library, 1971), 51.

Alighieri, Dante. *The Inferno*. Translated by John Ciardi. New York: New American Library, 1971.

6. An anonymous work

6. *The Dorling Kindersley World Reference Atlas* (London: Dorling Kindersley, 2003), 150-51.

The Dorling Kindersley World Reference Atlas. London: Dorling Kindersley, 2003.

7. A later edition

7. Dwight L. Bollinger, *Aspects of Language,* 2d ed. (New York: Harcourt Brace Jovanovich, 1975), 20.

Bollinger, Dwight L. *Aspects of Language.* 2d ed. New York: Harcourt Brace Jovanovich, 1975.

8. A work in more than one volume

Citation of one volume without a title:

8. Abraham. Lincoln, *The Collected Works of Abraham Lincoln,* ed. Roy P. Basler (New Brunswick: Rutgers University Press, 1953), 5:426-28.

Lincoln, Abraham. *The Collected Works of Abraham Lincoln.* Edited by Roy P. Basler. Vol. 5. New Brunswick: Rutgers University Press, 1953.

Citation of one volume with a title:

8. Linda B. Welkin, *The Age of Balanchine,* vol. 3 of *The History of Ballet* (New York: Columbia University Press, 1969), 56.

Welkin, Linda B. *The Age of Balanchine.* Vol. 3 of *The History of Ballet.* New York: Columbia University Press, 1969.

9. A selection from an anthology

9. Rosetta Brooks, "Streetwise," in *The New Urban Landscape,* ed. Richard Martin (New York: Rizzoli, 2001), 38-39.

Brooks, Rosetta. "Streetwise." In *The New Urban Landscape,* ed. Richard Martin, 37-60. New York: Rizzoli, 2001.

10. A work in a series

10. Ingmar Bergman, *The Seventh Seal,* Modern Film Scripts Series, no. 12 (New York: Simon and Schuster, 1968), 27.

Bergman, Ingmar. *The Seventh Seal.* Modern Film Scripts Series, no. 12. New York: Simon and Schuster, 1968.

11. An article in a reference work

The abbreviation "s.v." in the first examples stands for the Latin *sub verbo,* "under the word."

11. *Merriam-Webster's Collegiate Dictionary,* 10th ed., s.v. "reckon."

Merriam-Webster's Collegiate Dictionary, 10th ed., s.v. "reckon."

11. Mark F. Herman, "Polymers," in *The New Encyclopaedia Britannica: Macropaedia*, 16th ed.

Herman, Mark F. "Polymers." In *The New Encyclopaedia Britannica: Macropaedia*, 16th ed.

Periodicals: Journals, magazines, newspapers

12. An article in a journal with continuous pagination throughout the annual volume

12. Janet Lever, "Sex Differences in the Games Children Play," *Social Problems* 23 (1976): 482.

Lever, Janet. "Sex Differences in the Games Children Play." *Social Problems* 23 (1976): 478-87.

13. An article in a journal that pages issues separately

13. June Dacey, "Management Participation in Corporate Buy-Outs," *Management Perspectives* 7, no. 4 (1998): 22.

Dacey, June. "Management Participation in Corporate Buy-Outs." *Management Perspectives* 7, no. 4 (1998): 20-31.

14. An article in a popular magazine

14. Mark Stevens, "Low and Behold," *New Republic*, 24 December 2000, 28.

Stevens, Mark. "Low and Behold." *New Republic*, 24 December 2000, 27-33.

15. An article in a newspaper

15. Gina Kolata, "Kill All the Bacteria!" *New York Times*, 7 January 2001, national ed., B1.

Kolata, Gina. "Kill All the Bacteria!" *New York Times*, 7 January 2001, national ed., B1, B6.

16. A review

16. John Gregory Dunne, "The Secret of Danny Santiago," review of *Famous All over Town*, by Danny Santiago, *New York Review of Books*, 16 August 1984, 25.

Dunne, John Gregory. "The Secret of Danny Santiago." Review of *Famous All over Town*, by Danny Santiago. *New York Review of Books*, 16 August 1984, 17-27.

Electronic sources

The Chicago Manual offers some models for documenting electronic sources, and *A Manual for Writers* updates these and adds a few more. For other models, the Web site of *The Chicago Manual* recommends MLA style (see pp. 721–32) or one of the links provided by the International Federation of Library Associates and Institutions at *http://www.ifla.org/I/training/citation/citing.htm.* You can adapt any of these sources to Chicago style as you see it here.

Note Follow MLA style when you must break an electronic address in a note or works-cited entry: break only after a slash, and do not hyphenate.

17. A source on a periodical CD-ROM

A source also published in print:

> 15. Gina Kolata, "Kill All the Bacteria!" *New York Times,* 7 January 2001, national ed., B1. *New York Times Ondisc* [CD-ROM], UMI-ProQuest, March 2001.

Kolata, Gina. "Kill All the Bacteria!" *New York Times,* 7 January 2001, national ed., B1, B6. *New York Times Ondisc* [CD-ROM]. UMI-ProQuest, March 2001.

Chic

53d

A source not published in print:

> 17. "Vanguard Forecasts," *Business Outlook* [CD-ROM], Information Access, March 2003.

"Vanguard Forecasts." *Business Outlook* [CD-ROM]. Information Access, March 2003.

18. A source on a nonperiodical CD-ROM

> 18. Mary Wollstonecraft Shelley, *Frankenstein, Classic Library* [CD-ROM] (Alameda, Calif.: Andromeda, 1993).

Shelley, Mary Wollstonecraft. *Frankenstein. Classic Library* [CD-ROM]. Alameda, Calif.: Andromeda, 1993.

19. An online book

> 19. Jane Austen, *Emma* [book online], ed. Ronald Blythe (Harmondsworth, Eng.: Penguin, 1972, accessed 15 December 2002), *Oxford Text Archive;* available from http://ota.ox.ac.uk/ public/english/Austen/emma.1519; Internet.

Austen, Jane. *Emma* [book online]. Edited by Ronald Blythe. Harmondsworth, Eng.: Penguin, 1972. Accessed 15 December 2002. *Oxford Text Archive.* Available from http://ota.ox.ac.uk/public/english/Austen/emma.1519; Internet.

20. An article in an online periodical

> 20. Andrew Palfrey, "Choice of Mates in Identical Twins," *Modern Psychology* 4, no. 1 (1996): par. 10 [journal online]; available from http://www.liasu.edu/modpsy/palfrey4(1).htm; Internet; accessed 25 February 2003.

Palfrey, Andrew. "Choice of Mates in Identical Twins." *Modern Psychology* 4, no. 1 (1996): 12 pars. [journal online]. Available from http://www.liasu.edu/modpsy/palfrey4(1).htm; Internet. Accessed 25 February 2003.

21. An online database

21. *Scots Teaching and Research Network* [database online], ed. John Corbett (Glasgow: University of Glasgow, 2 February 2002, accessed 5 March 2003); available from http://www.arts.gla.ac.uk/www/comet/starn.htm; Internet.

Scots Teaching and Research Network [database online]. Edited by John Corbett. Glasgow: University of Glasgow, 2 February 2002. Accessed 5 March 2003. Available from http://www.arts.gla.ac.uk/www/comet/starn.htm; Internet.

Other sources

22. A government publication

22. House, *Medicare Payment for Outpatient Physical and Occupational Therapy Services,* 107th Cong., 1st sess., 2001, H. Doc. 409, 12-13.

U.S. Congress. House. *Medicare Payment for Outpatient Physical and Occupational Therapy Services.* 107th Cong., 1st sess., 2001. H. Doc. 409.

23. A letter

A published letter:

23. Mrs. Laura E. Buttolph to Rev. and Mrs. C. C. Jones, 20 June 1857, *The Children of Pride: A True Story of Georgia and the Civil War,* ed. Robert Manson Myers (New Haven: Yale University Press, 1972), 334.

Buttolph, Mrs. Laura E. Letter to Rev. and Mrs. C. C. Jones, 20 June 1857. In *The Children of Pride: A True Story of Georgia and the Civil War,* ed. Robert Manson Myers. New Haven: Yale University Press, 1972.

A personal letter:

23. Ann E. Packer, letter to author, 15 June 1998.

Packer, Ann E. Letter to author. 15 June 1998.

24. An interview

24. Donald Rumsfeld, interview by William Lindon, *Frontline,* Public Broadcasting System, 10 October 2002.

Rumsfeld, Donald. Interview by William Lindon. *Frontline.* Public Broadcasting System, 10 October 2002.

25. A work of art

25. John Singer Sargent, *In Switzerland,* watercolor, 1908, Metropolitan Museum of Art, New York.

Sargent, John Singer. *In Switzerland,* watercolor, 1908. Metropolitan Museum of Art, New York.

26. A film or video recording

26. *Serenade,* George Balanchine, San Francisco Ballet, PBS Video, 1985, videocassette.

Serenade. George Balanchine. San Francisco Ballet. PBS Video, 1985. Videocassette.

27. A sound recording

27. Johannes Brahms, Piano concerto no. 2 in B-flat, Artur Rubinstein, Philadelphia Orchestra, Eugene Ormandy, RCA BRC4-6731, 1992.

Brahms, Johannes, Piano concerto no. 2 in B-flat. Artur Rubinstein. Philadelphia Orchestra. Eugene Ormandy. RCA BRC4-6731, 1992.

Two or more citations of the same source

To minimize clutter and give a quick sense of how often you cite a source, the Chicago style allows a shortened form for subsequent citations of a source you have already cited fully.

You may use the Latin abbreviation "ibid." (meaning "in the same place") to refer to the same source cited in the preceding note:

8. Janet Lever, "Sex Differences in the Games Children Play." *Social Problems* 23 (1976): 482.

9. Ibid., 483.

For any source already cited in your notes, not just immediately before, you may use the author's name and (if the author is responsible for more than one cited source) a shortened form of the title:

1. Carol Gilligan, *In a Different Voice: Psychological Theory and Women's Development* (Cambridge: Harvard University Press, 1982), 27.

2. Carol Gilligan, "Moral Development in the College Years," *The Modern American College,* ed. A. Chickering (San Francisco: Jossey-Bass, 1981), 286.

3. Gilligan, *In a Different Voice,* 47.

Omit the title if you are using only one source by the cited author.

The Chicago style recommends in-text parenthetical citations when you cite one or more works repeatedly. This practice allows you to avoid many notes saying "ibid." or giving the same author's name. In the example following, the note number refers to the complete source information in an endnote; the numbers in parentheses are page numbers in the same source.

> British rule, observes Stuart Cary Welch, "seemed as permanent as Mount Everest."[7] Most Indians submitted, willingly or not, to British influence in every facet of life (423-24).

53e   Formatting documents in Chicago style

The following guidelines for document format come mainly from Turabian's *Manual for Writers,* which offers more specific advice than *The Chicago Manual* on the format of students' papers. See page 819 for the format of footnotes, endnotes, and a list of works cited. And see pages 203–12 for advice on type fonts, lists, illustrations, and other elements of document design.

Margins and spacing

Use minimum one-inch margins on all pages of the body. (The first page of endnotes or works cited begins two inches from the top; see p. 819.) Double-space your own text and between notes and works-cited entries; single-space displayed quotations (see opposite) and each note and works-cited entry.

First page of paper

1″

1″   World War I was a transformative event for every partici-   1″

pant, not least for faraway India. Though at first unified strongly

resented were the Rowlatt Acts of 1919, by which the British Parliament withdrew juries from the trials of agitators.

1″

Paging

Number pages consecutively from the first text page through the end (endnotes or works cited). Use Arabic numerals (1, 2, 3) in the upper right corner.

Title page

On an unnumbered title page provide the title of the paper, your name, the course title, your instructor's name, and the date. Use all-capital letters, and center everything horizontally. Double-space between adjacent lines, and add extra space as shown below.

Title page

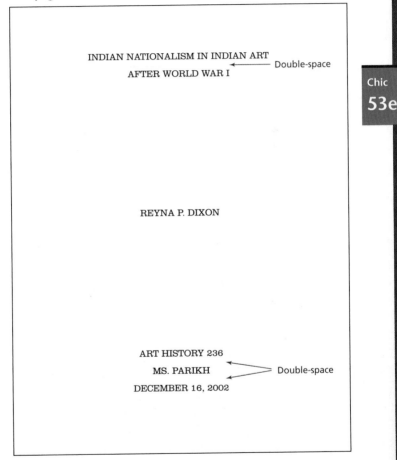

INDIAN NATIONALISM IN INDIAN ART
AFTER WORLD WAR I ⟵——— Double-space

REYNA P. DIXON

ART HISTORY 236
MS. PARIKH ⟵⟶ Double-space
DECEMBER 16, 2002

Poetry and long prose quotations

Display certain quotations separately from your text: three or more lines of poetry and two or more sentences of prose. Indent a displayed quotation four spaces from the left, single-space the quotation, and double-space both above it and below it. *Do not add quotation marks.*

Gandhi articulated the principles of his movement in 1922:

> I discovered that pursuit of truth did not permit violence being inflicted on one's opponent, but that he must be weaned from error by patience and sympathy. For what appears to be truth to one may appear to be error to the other. And patience means self-suffering.[9]

CHAPTER 54

Writing in the Social Sciences

The social sciences—including anthropology, economics, education, management, political science, psychology, and sociology—focus on the study of human behavior. As the name implies, the social sciences examine the way human beings relate to themselves, to their environment, and to one another.

54a Using the methods and evidence of the social sciences

Researchers in the social sciences systematically pose a question, formulate a **hypothesis** (a generalization that can be tested), collect data, analyze those data, and draw conclusions to support, refine, or disprove their hypothesis. This is the scientific method developed in the natural sciences (see p. 863).

Social scientists gather data in several ways:

- *They make firsthand observations of human behavior,* recording the observations in writing or on audio- or videotape.
- *They interview subjects about their attitudes and behavior,* recording responses in writing or on tape. (See pp. 648–49 for guidelines on conducting an interview.)
- *They conduct broader surveys using questionnaires,* asking people about their attitudes and behavior. (See the box on the next page.)

http://www.ablongman.com/littlebrown
For added help with writing in the social sciences, click on

➤ **Research writing**
   ➤ **Web links**
      ➤ **Writing in the disciplines**
      ➤ **Sources in the social sciences**

> ■ *They conduct controlled experiments,* structuring an environment in which to encourage and measure a specific behavior.

In their writing, social scientists explain their own research or analyze and evaluate others' research.

The research methods of social science generate two kinds of data:

> ■ *Quantitative data are numerical,* such as statistical evidence based on surveys, polls, tests, and experiments. When public-opinion pollsters announce that 47 percent of US citizens polled approve of the President's leadership, they are offering quantitative data gained from a survey. Social science writers present quantitative data in graphs, charts, and other illustrations that accompany their text.

> ■ *Qualitative data are not numerical but more subjective:* they are based on interviews, firsthand observations, and inferences, taking into account the subjective nature of human experience. Examples of qualitative data include an anthropologist's description of the initiation ceremonies in a culture she is studying or a psychologist's interpretation of interviews he conducted with a group of adolescents.

Conducting a survey

- **Decide what you want to find out—what your hypothesis is.** The questions you ask should be dictated by your purpose.
- **Define your population.** Think about the kinds of people your hypothesis is about—for instance, college men, or five-year-old children. Plan to sample this population so that your findings will be representative.
- **Write your questions.** Surveys may contain closed questions that direct the respondent's answers (checklists and multiple-choice, true/false, or yes/no questions) or open-ended questions allowing brief, descriptive answers. Avoid loaded questions that reveal your own biases or make assumptions about subjects' answers, such as "Do you want the United States to support democracy in China?" or "How much more money does your father make than your mother?"
- **Test your questions.** Use a few respondents with whom you can discuss the answers. Eliminate or recast questions that respondents find unclear, discomforting, or unanswerable.
- **Tally the results.** Count the actual numbers of answers, including any nonanswers.
- **Seek patterns in the raw data.** Such patterns may confirm or contradict your hypothesis. Revise the hypothesis or conduct additional research if necessary.

54b   Understanding writing assignments in the social sciences

Depending on what social science courses you take, you may be asked to complete a variety of assignments:

- A *summary or review of research:* reports on the available research literature on a subject, such as infants' perception of color.
- A *case analysis:* explains the components of a phenomenon, such as a factory closing.
- A *problem-solving analysis:* explains the components of a problem, such as unreported child abuse, and suggests ways to solve it.
- A *research paper:* interprets and sometimes analyzes and evaluates the writings of other social scientists about a subject, such as the effect of national appeals in advertising. An example appears in Chapter 50, pages 742–74.
- A *research report:* explains the author's own original research or the author's attempt to replicate someone else's research. A research report begins on page 859.

Many social science disciplines have special requirements for the content and organization of each kind of paper. The requirements appear in the style guides of the disciplines, listed on page 838. For instance, the American Psychological Association specifies the outline for research reports that is illustrated on pages 856–58. Because of the differences among disciplines and even among different kinds of papers in the same discipline, you should always ask your instructor what he or she requires for an assignment.

54c   Using the tools and language of the social sciences

The following guidelines for tools and language apply to most social sciences. However, the particular discipline you are writing in, or an instructor in a particular course, may have additional requirements. Many of the research sources listed on pages 834–38 can tell you more about your discipline's conventions.

1 ■ Writing tools

Many social scientists rely on a **research journal** or **log**, in which they record their ideas throughout the research-writing process. Even if a research journal is not required in your courses, you may want to use one. As you begin formulating a hypothesis, you can record preliminary questions. Then in the field (that is, when conducting research), you can use the journal to react to the evidence you are collecting, to record changes in your perceptions and ideas, and to assess your progress. (See pp. 120–21 and 607–08 for more on journals.)

To avoid confusing your reflections on the evidence with the evidence itself, keep records of actual data—notes from interviews, observations, surveys, and experiments—separately from the journal.

2 ■ Language considerations

54c

Each social science discipline has specialized terminology for concepts basic to the discipline. In sociology, for example, the words *mechanism, identity,* and *deviance* have specific meanings different from those of everyday usage. And *identity* means something different in sociology, where it applies to groups of people, than in psychology, where it applies to the individual. Social scientists also use precise terms to describe or interpret research. For instance, they say *The subject expressed a feeling of* rather than *The subject felt* because human feelings are not knowable for certain; or they say *These studies indicate* rather than *These studies prove* because conclusions are only tentative.

Just as social scientists strive for objectivity in their research, so they strive to demonstrate their objectivity through language in their writing. They avoid expressions such as *I think* in order to focus attention on what the evidence shows rather than on the researcher's opinions. (However, many social scientists prefer *I* to the artificial *the researcher* when they refer to their own actions, as in *I then interviewed the subjects.* Ask your instructor for his or her preferences.) Social scientists also avoid direct or indirect expression of their personal biases or emotions, either in discussions of other researchers' work or in descriptions of research subjects. Thus one social scientist does not call another's work *sloppy* or *immaculate* and does not refer to his or her own subjects as *drunks* or *innocent victims.* Instead, the writer uses neutral language and ties conclusions strictly to the data.

3 ■ Research sources

Specialized encyclopedias, dictionaries, and bibliographies

General

International Bibliography of the Social Sciences
International Encyclopedia of the Social and Behavioral Sciences
The Social Science Encyclopedia

Business and economics

Accountant's Handbook
Dictionary of Business and Economics
Encyclopedia of Advertising
Encyclopedia of Banking and Finance
Encyclopedia of Business Information Sources
Encyclopedia of Management
Handbook of Modern Marketing
McGraw-Hill Encyclopedia of Economics
The MIT Dictionary of Modern Economics
The New Palgrave Dictionary of Economics and the Law

Education

Bibliographic Guide to Education
Encyclopedia of American Education
Encyclopedia of Education
Encyclopedia of Educational Research
The Philosophy of Education: An Encyclopedia

54c

Political science and law

Black's Law Dictionary
Guide to American Law
Index to Legal Periodicals and Books
Information Sources of Political Sciences
Political Science: A Guide to Reference and Information Sources

Psychology, sociology, and anthropology

African American Encyclopedia
Afro-American Reference
Asian American Studies
Bibliographic Guide to Psychology
Encyclopedia of Anthropology
Encyclopedia of Crime and Justice
Encyclopedia of Psychology
Encyclopedia of Sociology
Guide to Research on North American Indians
Library Use: A Handbook for Psychology
Macmillan Dictionary of Anthropology
A Native American Encyclopedia: History, Culture, and Peoples
Race and Ethnic Relations: A Bibliography
Sociology: A Guide to Reference and Information Sources
Sourcebook of Hispanic Culture in the United States

Periodical indexes

ABC: Pol Sci
ABI/INFORM (business)
Business Periodicals Index
Business Publications Index and Abstracts
Criminal Justice Periodicals Index
Education Index

ERIC (Education Resources Information Center). *Current Index to Journals in Education*
Index to Legal Periodicals
Journal of Economic Literature
PAIS International in Print (government publications and political science journals)
Psychological Abstracts
Social Sciences Index
Sociofile
Sociological Abstracts

Abstracts and citation indexes

Abstracts in Anthropology
Business Publications Index and Abstracts
Criminal Justice and Police Science Abstracts
Dissertation Abstracts International (doctoral dissertations). Before 1969, the title was *Dissertation Abstracts.*
Human Resources Abstracts
Index to Legal Periodicals
International Political Science Abstracts
Journal of Economic Literature
PAIS International in Print (government publications and political science journals)
Psychological Abstracts or *PsychLIT*
Social Sciences Citation Index
Social Sciences Index
Sociological Abstracts
Urban Affairs Abstracts
Wilson Business Abstracts

Book reviews

Index to Book Reviews in the Social Sciences

Web sources

For updates of those sources and addresses, see this book's Web site (box on p. 831).

General

National Council for the Social Sciences
http://www.ncss.org
Social Science Data on the Internet
http://odwin.ucsd.edu/idata
Social Science Information Gateway
http://www.sosig.ac.uk
Virtual Library: Social Sciences
http://web.clas.ufl.edu/users/gthursby/socsci

Anthropology

American Anthropological Association
http://www.aaanet.org

American Folklife Center
  http://lcweb.loc.gov/folklife
Anthro.Net
  http://www.anthro.net
Anthropology Resources on the Internet
  http://www.anthropologie.net

Business and economics

Biz/ed
  http://www.bized.ac.uk
Business Administration Resources
  http://www.academicinfo.net/bus.html
Resources for Economists on the Internet
  http://rfe.wustl.edu/EconFAQ.html
Virtual International Business and Economic Sources
  http://library.uncc.edu/display/
    ?dept=reference&format=open&page=68

54c

Education

AskERIC
  http://www.askeric.org
Learner.org
  http://www.learner.org
Social Science Information Gateway Education Resources
  http://www.sosig.ac.uk/roads/subject-listing/World/educ.html
US Department of Education
  http://www.ed.gov

Ethnic and gender studies

Diversity and Ethnic Studies Websites and Guides
  http://www.public.iastate.edu/~savega/divweb2.htm
Diversity Database
  http://www.inform.umd.edu/EdRes/Topic/Diversity
Voice of the Shuttle Gender Studies Page
  http://vos.ucsb.edu/browse.asp?id=2711
Women's and Gender Studies Database
  http://www.uni-koeln.de/phil-fak/englisch/datenbank/e_index.htm

Political science and law

Legal Information Institute
  http://www.law.cornell.edu
Librarians' Index Law Resources
  http://lii.org/search/file/law
Political Science Resources
  http://www.psr.keele.ac.uk
Ultimate Political Science Links Page
  http://www.rvc.cc.il.us/faclink/pruckman/PSLinks.htm

Psychology

Encyclopedia of Psychology
  http://www.psychology.org

PsychCrawler
http://www.psychcrawler.com
Psychology Online Resource Central
http://www.psych-central.com
PsychWeb
http://www.psywww.com

Sociology

Social Science Information Gateway Sociology Resources
http://www.sosig.ac.uk/roads/subject-listing/World/sociol.html
SocioSite
http://www.pscw.uva.nl/sociosite
SocioWeb
http://www.socioweb.com/~markbl/socioweb
WWW Virtual Library: Sociology
http://socserv2.mcmaster.ca/w3virtsoclib

54d Citing sources in APA style

Some of the social sciences publish style guides that advise practitioners how to organize, document, and type papers. The following is a partial list:

American Anthropological Association. *AAA Style Guide.* 2002. *http://www.aaanet.org/pubs/style_guide.htm*
American Political Science Association. *Style Manual for Political Science.* 2001.
American Psychological Association. *Publication Manual of the American Psychological Association.* 5th ed. 2001.
American Sociological Association. *ASA Style Guide.* 2nd ed. 1997.
Linguistic Society of America. "LSA Style Sheet." Published every December in *LSA Bulletin.*
A Uniform System of Citation (law). 17th ed. 2001.

By far the most widely used style is that of the American Psychological Association (APA), so we detail it here. Always ask your instructor in any discipline what style you should use.

Note If you use APA style frequently and write on a computer, you may want to obtain APA-Style Helper, a student's companion to the *Publication Manual of the American Psychological Association* that formats source citations in APA style. It can be downloaded (for a fee) from the APA Web site, which can be reached through

http://www.ablongman.com/littlebrown
For added help with using APA style, click on
➤ **Research writing** ➤ **Exercises** ➤ **Exer. 11**
➤ **Documentation in the disciplines** ➤ **APA style**

this book's Web site: see the box on the facing page. Other bibliography programs can also help with APA style. See page 689 for more on such programs.

1 ■ Using APA parenthetical text citations

In the APA documentation style, parenthetical citations within the text refer the reader to a list of sources at the end of the text. A parenthetical citation contains the author's last name, the date of publication, and sometimes the page number from which material is borrowed. See below for an index to the models for various kinds of sources.

1. Author not named in your text

One critic of Milgram's experiments insisted that the subjects

"should have been fully informed of the possible effects on them"

(Baumrind, 1968, p. 34).

When you do not name the author in your text, place in parentheses the author's name and the date of the source. Separate the elements with commas. Position the reference so that it is clear what material is being documented *and* so that the reference fits as smoothly as possible into your sentence structure. (See pp. 706–08 for guidelines.) The following would also be correct:

In the view of one critic of Milgram's experiments (Baumrind,

1968), the subjects "should have been fully informed of the possi-

ble effects on them" (p. 34).

Unless none is available, the APA requires a page or other identifying number for a direct quotation (as in the preceding examples) and recommends an identifying number for a paraphrase. Use an appropriate abbreviation or symbol before the number—for instance, "p." for *page* and "¶" for *paragraph* (or "para." if you do not

---

APA parenthetical text citations

have the symbol). The identifying number may fall with the author and date (first example) or by itself in a separate pair of parentheses (second example). See also model 11, page 842.

2. Author named in your text

Baumrind (1968) insisted that the subjects in Milgram's study "should have been fully informed of the possible effects on them" (p. 34).

APA
54d

When you use the author's name in the text, do not repeat it in the reference. Place the source date in parentheses after the author's name. Place any page or paragraph reference either after the borrowed material (as in the example) or with the date: (1968, p. 34). If you cite the same source again in the paragraph, you need not repeat the reference as long as it is clear that you are using the same source and the page number (if any) is the same. Here is a later sentence from the paragraph containing the preceding example:

Baumrind also criticized the experimenters' rationale.

3. A work with two authors

Pepinsky and DeStefano (1997) demonstrated that a teacher's language often reveals hidden biases.

One study (Pepinsky & DeStefano, 1997) demonstrated the hidden biases often revealed in a teacher's language.

When given in the text, two authors' names are connected by "and." In a parenthetical citation, they are connected by an ampersand, "&."

4. A work with three to five authors

Pepinsky, Dunn, Rentl, and Corson (1999) further demonstrated the biases evident in gestures.

In the first citation of a work with three to five authors, name all the authors, as in the example above.

In the second and subsequent references to a work with three to five authors, generally give only the first author's name, followed by "et al." (Latin abbreviation for "and others"):

In the work of Pepinsky et al. (1999), the loaded gestures included head shakes and eye contact.

However, two or more sources published in the same year could shorten to the same form—for instance, two references shortening to Pepinsky et al., 1999. In that case, cite the last names of as many authors as you need to distinguish the sources, and then give "et al.": for instance, (Pepinsky, Dunn, et al., 1999) and (Pepinsky, Bradley, et al., 1999).

5. A work with six or more authors

One study (Rutter et al., 1996) attempted to explain these geographical differences in adolescent experience.

For six or more authors, even in the first citation of the work, give only the first author's name, followed by "et al." If two or more sources published in the same year shorten to the same form, give additional names as explained with model 4, above.

6. A work with a group author

An earlier prediction was even more somber (Lorenz Research, 1997).

APA
54

For a work that lists an institution, agency, corporation, or other group as author, treat the name of the group as if it were an individual's name. If the name is long and has a familiar abbreviation, you may use the abbreviation in the second and subsequent citations. For example, you might abbreviate American Psychological Association as APA.

7. A work with no author or an anonymous work

One article ("Right to Die," 1976) noted that a death-row inmate may crave notoriety.

For a work with no named author, use the first two or three words of the title in place of an author's name, excluding an initial *The*, *A*, or *An*. Italicize book and journal titles, place quotation marks around article titles, and capitalize the significant words in all titles cited in the text. (In the reference list, however, do not use quotation marks for article titles, and capitalize only the first word in all but periodical titles. See pp. 843 and 844.)

For a work that lists "Anonymous" as the author, use this word in the citation: (Anonymous, 1999).

8. One of two or more works by the same author(s)

At about age seven, most children begin to use appropriate gestures to reinforce their stories (Gardner, 1973a).

When you cite one of two or more works by the same author(s), the date will tell readers which source you mean—as long as your reference list includes only one source published by the author(s) in that year. If your reference list includes two or more works published by the same author(s) *in the same year*, the works should be lettered in the reference list (see p. 847). Then your parenthetical citation should include the appropriate letter: "1973a" in the preceding example.

9. Two or more works by different authors

Two studies (Herskowitz, 1994; Marconi & Hamblen, 1999) found that periodic safety instruction can dramatically reduce employees' accidents.

List the sources in alphabetical order by the first author's name. Insert a semicolon between sources.

APA

54d

10. An indirect source

Supporting data appeared in a study by Wong (cited in Marconi & Hamblen, 1999).

The phrase "cited in" indicates that the reference to Wong's study was found in Marconi and Hamblen. Only Marconi and Hamblen then appears in the list of references.

11. An electronic source

Ferguson and Hawkins (2002) did not anticipate the "evident hostility" of participants (¶ 6).

Electronic sources can be cited like printed sources, usually with the author's last name and the publication date. When quoting or paraphrasing electronic sources that number paragraphs instead of pages, provide the paragraph number preceded by the symbol "¶" if you have it, or by "para." Even if the source does not number its paragraphs, you can still direct readers to a specific location by listing the heading under which the quotation appears and then (counting paragraphs yourself) the number of the paragraph in which the quotation appears—for example, (Morrison & Lee, 2001, Method section, ¶ 4). When the source does not number pages or paragraphs or provide frequent headings, omit any reference number.

2 ▪ Using an APA reference list

In APA style, the in-text parenthetical citations refer to the list of sources at the end of the text. This list, titled References, includes full publication information on every source cited in the paper. The list falls at the end of the paper, numbered in sequence with the preceding pages.

The following sample shows the format of the first page of the APA reference list:

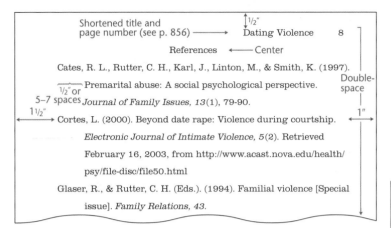

APA

54d

Arrangement

Arrange sources alphabetically by the author's last name or, if there is no author, by the first main word of the title.

Spacing

Double-space everything in the references, as shown in the sample, unless your instructor requests single-spacing. (If you do single-space the entries themselves, always double-space *between* them.)

Indention

As illustrated in the sample above, begin each entry at the left margin, and indent the second and subsequent lines five to seven spaces or one-half inch. Most word processors can produce this so-called hanging indent automatically.

Punctuation

Separate the parts of the reference (author, date, title, and publication information) with a period and one space. Do not use a final period in references to electronic sources, which conclude with an electronic address (see pp. 850–52).

Authors

For works with up to six authors, list all authors with last name first, separating names and parts of names with commas. Use initials for first and middle names even when names are listed fully on the source itself. Use an ampersand (&) before the last author's name. See model 3, page 846, for the treatment of seven or more authors.

Publication date

Place the publication date in parentheses after the author's or authors' names, followed by a period. Generally, this date is the year only, though for some sources (such as magazine and newspaper articles) it includes month and sometimes day as well.

Titles

In titles of books and articles, capitalize only the first word of the title, the first word of the subtitle, and proper nouns; all other words begin with small letters. In titles of journals, capitalize all significant words (see p. 519 for guidelines). Italicize the titles of books and journals. Do not italicize or use quotation marks around the titles of articles.

APA

54d

City of publication

For sources that are not periodicals (such as books or government publications), give the city of publication. The following US cities do not require state names as well: Baltimore, Boston, Chicago, Los Angeles, New York, Philadelphia, and San Francisco. Follow their names with a colon. For most other cities, add a comma after the city name, give the two-letter postal abbreviation of the state, and then add a colon. (You may omit the state if the publisher is a university whose name includes the state name, such as "University of Arizona.")

Publisher's name

Also for nonperiodical sources, give the publisher's name after the place of publication and a colon. Use shortened names for many publishers (such as "Morrow" for William Morrow), and omit "Co.," "Inc.," and "Publishers." However, give full names for associations, corporations, and university presses (such as "Harvard University Press"), and do not omit "Books" or "Press" from a publisher's name.

Page numbers

Use the abbreviation "p." or "pp." before page numbers in books and in newspapers. Do *not* use the abbreviation for journals and magazines. For inclusive page numbers, include all figures: "667–668."

Note If the following pages don't provide a model for a kind of source you used, try to find one that comes close, and provide ample information so that readers can trace the source. Often, you will have to combine models to cite a source accurately—for instance, combining "A book with two to six authors" (model 2) and "An article in a journal" (model 12) for a journal article with two or more authors.

APA References

APA

54

Books

1. A book with one author

Rodriguez, R. (1982). *A hunger of memory: The education of Richard Rodriguez.* Boston: Godine.

The initial "R" appears instead of the author's first name, even though the author's full first name appears on the source. In the title, only the first words of title and subtitle and the proper name are capitalized.

2. A book with two to six authors

Nesselroade, J. R., & Baltes, P. B. (1999). *Longitudinal research in behavioral studies*. New York: Academic Press.

An ampersand (&) precedes the last author's name.

3. A book with seven or more authors

Wimple, P. B., Van Eijk, M., Potts, C. A., Hayes, J., Obergau, W. R., Zimmer, S., et al. (2001). *Case studies in moral decision making among adolescents*. San Francisco: Jossey-Bass.

Substitute "et al." (Latin abbreviation for "and others") for all authors' names after the first six.

APA
54d

4. A book with an editor

Dohrenwend, B. S., & Dohrenwend, B. P. (Eds.). (1999). *Stressful life events: Their nature and effects*. New York: Wiley.

List the editors' names as if they were authors, but follow the last name with "(Eds.)."—or "(Ed.)." with only one editor. Note the periods inside and outside the final parenthesis.

5. A book with a translator

Trajan, P. D. (1927). *Psychology of animals* (H. Simone, Trans.). Washington, DC: Halperin.

The name of the translator appears in parentheses after the title, followed by a comma, "Trans.," a closing parenthesis, and a final period. Note also the absence of periods in "DC."

6. A book with a group author

Lorenz Research. (2000). *Research in social studies teaching*. Baltimore: Arrow Books.

For a work with a group author—such as a research group, government agency, or corporation—begin the entry with the group name. In the references list, alphabetize the work as if the first main word (excluding *The, A,* and *An*) were an author's last name.

7. A book with no author or an anonymous book

Merriam-Webster's collegiate dictionary (10th ed.). (2001). Springfield, MA: Merriam-Webster.

When no author is named, list the work under its title, and alphabetize it by the first main word (excluding *The, A, An*).

For a work whose author is actually given as "Anonymous," use this word in place of the author's name and alphabetize it as if it were a name:

> Anonymous. (2002). *Teaching research, researching teaching.*
>
> New York: Alpine Press.

8. Two or more works by the same author(s) published in the same year

> Gardner, H. (1973a). *The arts and human development.* New York:
>
> Wiley.
>
> Gardner, H. (1973b). *The quest for mind: Piaget, Lévi-Strauss, and*
>
> *the structuralist movement.* New York: Knopf.

When citing two or more works by exactly the same author(s), published in the same year—as in the examples above—arrange them alphabetically by the first main word of the title and distinguish the sources by adding a letter to the date. Both the date *and* the letter are used in citing the source in your text (see pp. 841–42).

When citing two or more works by exactly the same author(s) but *not* published in the same year, arrange the sources in order of their publication dates, earliest first.

9. A later edition

> Bollinger, D. L. (1975). *Aspects of language* (2nd ed.). New York:
>
> Harcourt Brace Jovanovich.

The edition number in parentheses follows the title and is followed by a period.

10. A work in more than one volume

> Lincoln, A. (1953). *The collected works of Abraham Lincoln* (R. P.
>
> Basler, Ed.). (Vol. 5). New Brunswick, NJ: Rutgers University
>
> Press.
>
> Lincoln, A. (1953). *The collected works of Abraham Lincoln* (R. P.
>
> Basler, Ed.). (Vols. 1-8). New Brunswick, NJ: Rutgers Univer-
>
> sity Press.

The first entry cites a single volume (5) in the eight-volume set. The second cites all eight volumes. Use the abbreviation "Vol." or "Vols." in parentheses, and follow the closing parenthesis with a period. In the absence of an editor's name, the description of volumes would follow the title directly: *The collected works of Abraham Lincoln* (Vol. 5).

11. An article or chapter in an edited book

Paykel, E. S. (1999). Life stress and psychiatric disorder: Applications of the clinical approach. In B. S. Dohrenwend & B. P. Dohrenwend (Eds.), *Stressful life events: Their nature and effects* (pp. 239-264). New York: Wiley.

Give the publication date of the collection (1999 above) as the publication date of the article or chapter. After the article or chapter title and a period, say "In" and then provide the editors' names (in normal order), "(Eds.)" and a comma, the title of the collection, and the page numbers of the article in parentheses.

Periodicals: Journals, magazines, newspapers

12. An article in a journal with continuous pagination throughout the annual volume

Emery, R. E. (2001). Marital turmoil: Interpersonal conflict and the children of discord and divorce. *Psychological Bulletin, 92,* 310-330.

See page 634 for an explanation of journal pagination. Note that you do not place the article title in quotation marks and that you capitalize only the first words of the title and subtitle. In contrast, you italicize the journal title and capitalize all significant words. Separate the volume number from the title with a comma, and italicize the number. Do not add "pp." before the page numbers.

13. An article in a journal that pages issues separately

Dacey, J. (1998). Management participation in corporate buy-outs. *Management Perspectives, 7*(4), 20-31.

Consult page 634 for an explanation of journal pagination. In this case, place the issue number in parentheses after the volume number without intervening space. Do *not* italicize the issue number.

14. An abstract of a journal article

Emery, R. E. (1992). Marital turmoil: Interpersonal conflict and the children of discord and divorce. *Psychological Bulletin, 92,* 310-330. Abstract obtained from *Psychological Abstracts, 1992, 69,* Item 1320.

When you cite the abstract of an article, rather than the article itself, give full publication information for the article, followed by Abstract obtained from and the information for the collection of ab-

stracts, including title, date, volume number, and either page number
or other reference number ("Item 1320" in the example).

15. An article in a magazine

Williams, N. (2002, October 24). Beethoven's late quartets. *The
New York Review of Books*, 16-18.

If a magazine has volume and issue numbers, give them as in models 12 and 13. Also give the full date of the issue: year, followed by a comma, month, and day (if any). Give all page numbers even when the article appears on discontinuous pages, without "pp."

16. An article in a newspaper

Kolata, G. (2001, January 7). Kill all the bacteria! *The New York
Times*, pp. B1, B6.

APA
54

Give month *and* day along with year of publication. Use *The* in the newspaper name if the paper itself does. Precede the page number(s) with "p." or "pp."

17. An unsigned article

The right to die. (1976, October 11). *Time, 121*, 101.

List and alphabetize the article under its title, as you would a book with no author (model 7, p. 846).

18. A review

Dinnage, R. (1987, November 29). Against the master and his men
[Review of the book *A mind of her own: The life of Karen
Horney*]. *The New York Times Book Review*, 10-11.

If the review is not titled, use the bracketed information as the title, keeping the brackets.

Electronic sources

In general, the APA's electronic-source references begin as those for print references do: author(s), date, title. Then you add information on when and where you retrieved the source—for example, Retrieved January 8, 2003, from http://www.isu.edu/finance-dl/46732 (in APA style, no period follows an electronic address at the end of the reference).

Using the following models for electronic sources, you may have to improvise to match your source to a model. Try to locate all the information required by a model, referring to pages 618–20 for help. However, if you search for and still cannot find some information, then give what you can find. If a source has no publication date, use "n.d." (for *no date*) in place of a publication date (see model 28, p. 852).

Note When you need to divide an electronic address from one line to the next, APA style calls for breaking *only* after a slash or before a period. Do not hyphenate an electronic address.

19. A journal article that is published online and in print

Palfrey, A. (1996). Choice of mates in identical twins [Electronic

  version]. *Modern Psychology, 4*(1), 26-40.

APA
54d

If you consulted the online version of a journal article that appears the same way both online and in print, follow model 12 or 13 (p. 848) for a print journal article, and insert [Electronic version] between the article title and the following period.

If you believe that the online version you consulted differs in some way from the print version, omit the bracketed insert and provide a retrieval statement with the date of your access and the complete electronic address for the article:

Grady, G. F. (2000). The here and now of hepatitis B immunization.

  Today's Medicine, 13, 145-151. Retrieved December 27, 2002,

  from http://www.fmrt.org/todaysmedicine/Grady050293

  .html

20. An article in an online journal

Wissink, J. A. (2000). Techniques of smoking cessation among

  teens and adults. *Adolescent Medicine, 2*. Retrieved August

  16, 2002, from http://www.easu.edu/AdolescentMedicine/

  2-Wissink.html

If the article has an identifying number, give it after the volume number and a comma.

21. A journal article retrieved from an electronic database

Wilkins, J. M. (1999). The myths of the only child. *Psychology

  Update, 11*(1), 16-23. Retrieved December 20, 2002, from

  ProQuest Direct database.

Many reference works and periodicals are available full-text from electronic databases to which your library subscribes, such as ProQuest Direct or LexisNexis. Your reference need not specify how you reached the database—for instance, through a Web site or on a CD-ROM. However, it should provide the appropriate information for the source itself—in the example here, for a journal article—and it should conclude with a retrieval statement giving the date of your access and the name of the database.

22. An abstract retrieved from an electronic database

Wilkins, J. M. (1999). The myths of the only child. *Psychology Update, 11*(1), 16-23. Abstract retrieved December 20, 2002, from ProQuest Direct database.

23. An article in an online newspaper

Pear, R. (2003, January 23). Gains reported for children of welfare to work families. *The New York Times on the Web.* Retrieved January 23, 2003, from http://www .nytimes.com/2003/01/23/national/23/WELF.html

24. An entire Web site (text citation)

The APA's Web site provides answers to frequently asked questions about style (http://www.apa.org).

Cite an entire Web site (rather than a specific page or document) by giving the electronic address in your text.

25. An independent document on the Web

Anderson, D. (2002, May 1). *Social constructionism and MOOs.* Retrieved August 6, 2002, from http://sites.unc.edu/ ~daniel/social_constructionism

Treat the title of an independent Web document like the title of a book. If the document has no named author, begin with the title and place the publication date after the title.

26. A document from the Web site of a university or government agency

McConnell, L. M., Koenig, B. A., Greeley, H. T., & Raffin, T. A. (2001, August 17). *Genetic testing and Alzheimer disease: Has the time come?* Retrieved September 1, 2002, from Stanford University, Project in Genomics, Ethics, and Society Web site: http://scbe.stanford.edu/ pges

Provide the name of the host organization and any sponsoring program as part of the retrieval statement.

APA

54d

27. An online government report

U.S. Department of Commerce. National Telecommunications
and Information Administration. (2001, October). *Falling
through the net: Toward digital inclusion.* Retrieved
April 12, 2002, from http://www.ntia.doc.gov/ntiahome/
fttn00/contents00.html

28. A multipage online document

Elston, C. (n.d.). *Multiple intelligences.* Retrieved June 6, 2002,
from http://education.com/teachspace/intelligences

APA
4d

For an Internet document with multiple pages, each with its own
electronic address, give the address of the document's home page.
Note the use of "n.d." after the author's name to indicate that the
document provides no publication date.

29. A part of an online document

Elston, C. (n.d.). Logical/math intelligence. In *Multiple intelligences.* Retrieved June 6, 2002, from http://education.com/
teachspace/intelligences/logical.jsp

If the part of a document you cite has a label (such as "chapter 6" or
"section 4"), provide that in parentheses after the document title:
Multiple intelligences (chap. 6).

30. A retrievable online posting

Tourville, M. (2003, January 6). European currency reform. Message posted to International Finance electronic mailing list,
archived at http://www.isu.edu/finance-dl/46732

Include postings to discussion lists and newsgroups in your list of
references *only* if they are retrievable by others. The source above is
archived (as the reference makes plain) and is thus retrievable at
the address given.

31. Electronic mail or a nonretrievable online posting (text citation)

At least one member of the research team has expressed reserva-
tions about the design of the study (L. Kogod, personal communication, February 6, 2003).

Personal electronic mail and other online postings that are not retrievable by others should be cited only in your text, as in the example above.

32. Software

Project scheduler 9000 [Computer software]. (2003). Orlando, FL:
 Scitor.

Provide an author's name for the software if an individual has the rights to the program. If you obtain the software online, you can generally replace the producer's city and name with a retrieval statement that includes the electronic address.

Other sources

33. A report

Gerald, K. (1998). *Medico-moral problems in obstetric care* (Report
 No. NP-71). St. Louis, MO: Catholic Hospital Association.

Treat the report like a book, but provide any report number in parentheses immediately after the title, with no punctuation between them.

For a report from the Educational Resources Information Center (ERIC), provide the ERIC document number in parentheses at the end of the entry:

Jolson, M. K. (1991). *Music education for preschoolers* (Report No.
 TC-622). New York: Teachers College, Columbia University.
 (ERIC Document Reproduction Service No. ED 264488)

34. A government publication

Hawaii. Department of Education. (2002). *Kauai district schools,
 profile 2000-01.* Honolulu, HI: Author.

Stiller, A. (1996). *Historic preservation and tax incentives.*
 Washington, DC: U.S. Department of the Interior.

U.S. House. Committee on Ways and Means. (2001). *Medicare
 payment for outpatient physical and occupational therapy
 services.* 107th Cong., 1st Sess. Washington, DC: U.S. Government Printing Office.

If no individual is given as the author, list the publication under the name of the sponsoring agency. When the agency is both the author and the publisher, use "Author" in place of the publisher's name.

35. A doctoral dissertation

A dissertation abstracted in DAI *and obtained from UMI:*

> Steciw, S. K. (1986). Alterations to the Pessac project of Le
>
> Corbusier. *Dissertation Abstracts International, 46,* 565C.
>
> (UMI No. 6216202)

A dissertation abstracted in DAI *and obtained from the university:*

> Chang, J. K. (2000). Therapeutic intervention in treatment of
>
> injuries to the hand and wrist (Doctoral dissertation,
>
> University of Michigan, 2000). *Dissertation Abstracts
>
> International, 50,* 162.

An unpublished dissertation:

> Delaune, M. L. (2001). *Child care in single-mother and single-
>
> father families: Differences in time, activity, and stress.*
>
> Unpublished doctoral dissertation, University of California,
>
> Davis.

36. An abstract of a dissertation

> Steciw, S. K. (1986). Alterations to the Pessac Project of Le
>
> Corbusier. *Dissertation Abstracts International, 46,*
>
> 565C.

37. An interview

> Brisick, W. C. (1998, July 1). [Interview with Ishmael Reed].
>
> *Publishers Weekly,* 41-42.

List a published interview under the interviewer's name. Provide the publication information for the kind of source the interview appears in (here, a magazine). Immediately after the date, in brackets, specify that the piece is an interview and give the subject's name if necessary. For an interview with a title, add the title (with an initial capital letter, no quotation marks, and no closing period) before the bracketed information.

   An interview you conduct yourself should not be included in the list of references. Instead, use an in-text parenthetical citation, as shown in model 31 (p. 852) for a nonretrievable online posting.

38. A motion picture

Spielberg, S. (Director). (1993). *Schindler's list* [Motion picture].

    United States: Viacom.

American Psychological Association (Producer). (2001).

    Ethnocultural psychotherapy [Motion picture]. (Available

    from the American Psychological Association, 750 First

    Street, NE, Washington, DC 20002-4242, or online from

    http://www.apa.org/videos/4310240.html)

A motion picture may be a film or a video. Depending on whose work you are citing, begin with the name or names of the creator, director, producer, or primary contributor, followed by his or her function in parentheses. (The first model above would begin with the producer's name if you were citing the motion picture as a whole, not specifically the work of the director.) Add [Motion picture] after the title. For a motion picture in wide circulation (first example), give the country of origin and the name of the organization that released the picture. For a motion picture that is not widely circulated (second example), give the distributor's name and address in parentheses.

39. A musical recording

Siberry, J. (1993). Sweet incarnadine. *When I was a boy* [CD]. Bur-

    bank, CA: Reprise.

Begin with the name of the writer or composer. (If you cite another artist's recording of the work, provide this information after the title of the work—for example, [Recorded by E. Davila].) Give the medium in brackets ([CD], [Cassette recording], and so on). Finish with the city and name of the recording label.

40. A television series or episode

Taylor, C., Cleveland, R., & Andries, L. (Producers). (2002). *Six feet*

    under [Television series]. New York: HBO.

Cleveland, R. (Writer), & Engler, M. (Director). (2002). Dillon

    Michael Cooper [Television series episode]. In C. Taylor, R.

    Cleveland, & L. Andries (Producers), *Six feet under*. New

    York: HBO.

For a television series, begin with the producers' names and identify their function in parentheses. Add [Television series] after the series title, and give the city and name of the network. For an episode, begin with the writer and then the director, identifying the function of each in parentheses, and add [Television series episode] after the episode title. Then provide the series information, beginning with "In" and the producers' names and function, giving the series title, and ending with the city and name of the network.

54e Formatting documents in APA style

The APA *Publication Manual* distinguishes between documents intended for publication (which will be set in type) and those submitted by students (which are the final copy). The guidelines below apply to most undergraduate papers. Check with your instructor for any modifications to this format.

Note See pages 842–44 for the APA format of a reference list. And see pages 203–12 for guidelines on type fonts, lists, tables and figures, and other elements of document design.

Margins

Use one-inch margins on the top, bottom, and right side. Add another half-inch on the left to accommodate a binder.

Spacing and indentions

Double-space your text and references. (See pp. 858–59 for spacing of displayed quotations.) Indent paragraphs and displayed quotations one-half inch or five to seven spaces.

Paging

Begin numbering on the title page, and number consecutively through the end (including the reference list). Type Arabic numerals (1, 2, 3) in the upper right, about one-half inch from the top.

Place a shortened version of your title five spaces to the left of the page number.

Title page

Include the full title, your name, the course title, the instructor's name, and the date. Type the title on the top half of the page, followed by the identifying information, all centered horizontally and double-spaced. Include a shortened form of the title along with the page number at the top of this and all other pages.

Abstract

Summarize (in a maximum of 120 words) your subject, research method, findings, and conclusions. Put the abstract on a page by itself.

Body

Begin with a restatement of the paper's title and then an introduction (not labeled). The introduction concisely presents the

Title page

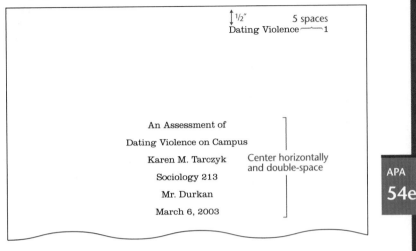

½″
5 spaces
Dating Violence ⌐ 1

An Assessment of

Dating Violence on Campus

Karen M. Tarczyk

Sociology 213

Mr. Durkan

March 6, 2003

Center horizontally
and double-space

APA
54e

Abstract

½″
5 spaces
Dating Violence ⌐ 2

No indention

Abstract ← Center

Double-
space

Little research has examined the patterns of abuse and violence

occurring within couples during courtship. With a questionnaire

1½″

administered to a sample of college students, the extent and na-

1″

First page of body

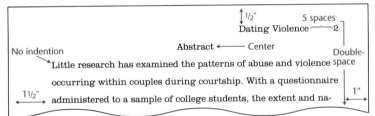

½″
5 spaces
Dating Violence ⌐ 3

An Assessment of

Dating Violence on Campus

Center

Double-
space

½″ or
5–7 spaces

In recent years, a great deal of attention has been devoted

1½″

to family violence. Numerous studies have been done on spouse

1″

Cates et al. concluded that premarital violence was a problem of

"abusive relationships" as well as "abusive individuals" (p. 90).

1″

problem you researched, your research method, the relevant background (such as related studies), and the purpose of your research.

The next section, labeled "Method," provides a detailed discussion of how you conducted your research, including a description of the research subjects, any materials or tools you used (such as questionnaires), and the procedure you followed. In the illustration below, the label "Method" is a first-level heading and the label "*Sample*" is a second-level heading.

Later page of body

> Dating Violence 4
>
> All the studies indicate a problem that is being neglected.
> My objective was to gather data on the extent and nature of pre-
> marital violence and to discuss possible interpretations.
>
> Method ← Double-
> ― space
> *Sample* ←
>
> I conducted a survey of 200 students (134 females, 66
> males) at a large state university in the northeastern United
> States. The sample consisted of students enrolled in an intro-

Format headings (including a third level, if needed) as follows:

First-Level Heading

Second-Level Heading

Third-level heading. Run this heading into the text

paragraph.

The "Results" section (labeled with a first-level heading) summarizes the data you collected, explains how you analyzed them, and presents them in detail, often in tables, graphs, or charts.

The "Discussion" section (labeled with a first-level heading) interprets the data and presents your conclusions. (When the discussion is brief, you may combine it with the previous section under the heading "Results and Discussion.")

The "References" section, beginning a new page, includes all your sources. See pages 842–44 for an explanation and sample.

Long quotations

Run into your text all quotations of forty words or less, and enclose them in quotation marks. For quotations of more than forty words, set them off from your text by indenting all lines one-half inch or five spaces, double-spacing above and below. For student papers, the APA allows single-spacing of displayed quotations:

Echoing the opinions of other Europeans at the time, Freud (1961) had a poor view of Americans:

> The Americans are really too bad. . . . Competition is much more pungent with them, not succeeding means civil death to every one, and they have no private resources apart from their profession, no hobby, games, love or other interests of a cultured person. And success means money. (p. 86)

Do not use quotation marks around a quotation displayed in this way.

Illustrations

Present data in tables and figures (graphs or charts), as appropriate. (See the sample on p. 861 for a clear table format to follow.) Begin each illustration on a separate page. Number each kind of illustration consecutively and separately from the other (Table 1, Table 2, etc., and Figure 1, Figure 2, etc.). Refer to all illustrations in your text—for instance, "(see Figure 3)." Generally, place illustrations immediately after the text references to them. (See pp. 208–11 for more on illustrations.)

54f   Examining a sample social science paper

On the following pages are excerpts from a sociology paper. The student followed the organization described on the preceding pages both in establishing the background for her study and in explaining her own research. She also followed the APA style of source citation and document format, although page borders and running heads are omitted here and only the required page breaks are indicated. See page 857 for spacing and other format details.

Excerpts from a research report (sociology)

[Title page. See also pp. 856–57.]

An Assessment of

Dating Violence on Campus

Karen M. Tarczyk

Sociology 213

Mr. Durkan

March 6, 2003

[New page.]

Abstract

Little research has examined the patterns of abuse and violence occurring within couples during courtship. With a questionnaire administered to a sample of college students, the extent and nature of such abuse and violence were investigated. The results, some interpretations, and implications for further research are discussed.

[New page.]

An Assessment of

Dating Violence on Campus

In recent years, a great deal of attention has been devoted to family violence. Numerous studies have been done on spouse and child abuse. However, violent behavior occurs in dating relationships as well, yet the problem of dating violence has been relatively ignored by sociological research. It should be examined further since the premarital relationship is one context in which individuals learn and adopt behaviors that surface later in marriage.

The sociologist James Makepeace (1989) contended that courtship violence is a "potential mediating link" between violence in one's family of orientation and violence in one's later family of procreation (p. 103). Studying dating behaviors at Bemidji State University in Minnesota, Makepeace reported that one-fifth of the respondents had had at least one encounter with dating violence. He then extended these percentages to students nationwide, suggesting the existence of a major hidden social problem.

More recent research supports Makepeace's. Cates, Rutter, Karl, Linton, and Smith (1997) found that 22.3% of respondents at Oregon State University had been either the victim or the perpetrator of premarital violence. Another study (Cortes, 2000) found that so-called date rape, while much more publicized and discussed, was reported by many fewer woman respondents (2%) than was other violence during courtship (21%).

[The introduction continues.]

All these studies indicate a problem that is being neglected. My objective was to gather data on the extent and nature of premarital violence and to discuss possible interpretations.

Method

Sample

I conducted a survey of 200 students (134 females, 66 males) at a large state university in the northeastern United States. The sample consisted of students enrolled in an introductory sociology course.

[The explanation of method continues.]

The Questionnaire

A questionnaire exploring the personal dynamics of relationships was distributed during regularly scheduled class. Questions were answered anonymously in a 30-minute time period. The survey consisted of three sections.

[The explanation of method continues.]

Section 3 required participants to provide information about their current dating relationships. Levels of stress and frustration, communication between partners, and patterns of decision making were examined. These variables were expected to influence the amount of violence in a relationship. The next part of the survey was adopted from Murray Strauss's Conflict Tactics Scales (1982). These scales contain 19 items designed to measure conflict and the means of conflict resolution, including reasoning, verbal aggression, and actual violence.

APA
54

Results

The questionnaire revealed significant levels of verbal aggression and threatened and actual violence among dating couples. A high number of students, 50% (62 of 123 subjects), reported that they had been the victim of verbal abuse. In addition, almost 14% (17 of 123) of respondents admitted being threatened with some type of violence, and more than 14% (18 of 123) reported being pushed, grabbed, or shoved. (See Table 1.)

[The explanation of results continues.]

[Table on a page by itself.]

Table 1

Incidence of Courtship Violence

Type of violence	Number of students reporting	Percentage of sample
Insulted or swore	62	50.4
Threatened to hit or throw something	17	13.8
Threw something	8	6.5
Pushed, grabbed, or shoved	18	14.6
Slapped	8	6.5
Kicked, bit, or hit with fist	7	5.7
Hit or tried to hit with something	2	1.6
Threatened with a knife or gun	1	0.8
Used a knife or gun	1	0.8

Discussion

Violence within premarital relationships has been relatively ignored. The results of the present study indicate that abuse and force do occur in dating relationships. Although the percentages are small, so was the sample. Extending them to the entire campus population would mean significant numbers. For example, if the nearly 6% incidence of being kicked, bitten, or hit with a fist is typical, then 300 students of a 5,000-member student body might have experienced this type of violence.

[The discussion continues.]

APA
54f

If the courtship period is characterized by abuse and violence, what accounts for it? The other sections of the survey examined some variables that appear to influence the relationship. Level of stress and frustration, both within the relationship and in the respondent's life, was one such variable. The communication level between partners, both the frequency of discussion and the frequency of agreement, was another.

[The discussion continues.]

The method of analyzing the data in this study, utilizing frequency distributions, provided a clear overview. However, more tests of significance and correlation and a closer look at the social and individual variables affecting the relationship are warranted. The courtship period may set the stage for patterns of married life. It merits more attention.

[New page.]

References

Cates, R. L., Rutter, C. H., Karl, J., Linton, M., & Smith, K. (1997). Premarital abuse: A social psychological perspective. *Journal of Family Issues, 13*(1), 79-90.

Cortes, L. (2000). Beyond date rape: Violence during courtship. *Electronic Journal of Intimate Violence, 5*(2). Retrieved February 16, 2003, from http://www.acast.nova.edu/health/psy/file-disc/file50.html

Glaser, R., & Rutter, C. H. (Eds.). (1994). Familial violence [Special issue]. *Family Relations, 43.*

Makepeace, J. M. (1989). Courtship violence among college students. *Family Relations, 28,* 97-103.

Strauss, M. L. (1982). *Conflict Tactics Scales.* New York: Sociological Tests.

CHAPTER 55

Writing in the Natural and Applied Sciences

The natural and applied sciences include biology, chemistry, physics, mathematics, engineering, computer science, and their branches. Their purpose is to understand natural and technological phenomena. (A *phenomenon* is a fact or event that can be known by the senses.) Scientists conduct experiments and write to explain the step-by-step processes in their methods of inquiry and discovery.

55a Using the methods and evidence of the sciences

Scientists investigate phenomena by the **scientific method**, a process of continual testing and refinement.

The scientific method

- **Observe carefully.** Accurately note all details of the phenomenon being researched.
- **Ask questions about the observations**.
- **Formulate a** *hypothesis,* or preliminary generalization, that explains the observed facts.
- **Test the hypothesis** with additional observation or controlled experiments.
- **If the hypothesis proves accurate, formulate a** *theory,* or unified model, that explains *why.*
- **If the hypothesis is disproved, revise it or start anew.**

Scientific evidence is almost always quantitative—that is, it consists of numerical data obtained from the measurement of phenomena. These data are called **empirical** (from a Greek word for "experience"): they result from observation and experience, generally in a controlled laboratory setting but also (as sometimes in astronomy or biology) in the natural world. Often the empirical evidence for scientific writing comes from library research into other people's reports of their investigations. Surveys of known data or existing literature are common in scientific writing.

55b Understanding writing assignments in the sciences

No matter what your assignment, you will be expected to document and explain your evidence carefully so that anyone reading can check your sources and replicate your research. It is important for your reader to know the context of your research—both the previous experimentation and research on your particular subject (acknowledged in the survey of the literature) and the physical conditions and other variables surrounding your own work.

Assignments in the natural and applied sciences include the following:

- *A summary:* distills a research article to its essence in brief, concise form. (Summary is discussed in detail on pp. 123–24.)
- *A critique:* summarizes and critically evaluates a scientific report.
- *A laboratory report:* explains the procedure and results of an experiment conducted by the writer. (An example begins on p. 879.)
- *A research report:* reports on the experimental research of other scientists and the writer's own methods, findings, and conclusions.
- *A research proposal:* reviews the relevant literature and explains a plan for further research.

A laboratory report has four or five major sections:

1. *Abstract:* a summary of the report.
2. *Introduction* or *Objective:* a review of why the study was undertaken, a summary of the background of the study, and a statement of the problem being studied.
3. *Method* or *Procedure:* a detailed explanation of how the study was conducted, including any statistical analysis.
4. *Results:* an explanation of the major findings (including unexpected results) and a summary of the data presented in graphs and tables.

5. *Discussion:* an interpretation of the results and an explanation of how they relate to the goals of the experiment. This section also describes new hypotheses that might be tested as a result of the experiment. If the section is brief, it may be combined with the previous section in a single section labeled *Conclusions.*

In addition, laboratory or research reports may include a list of references (if other sources were consulted). They almost always include tables and figures (graphs and charts) containing the data from the research (see p. 881).

55c Using the tools and language of the sciences

Tools and language concerns vary from discipline to discipline in the sciences. Consult your instructor for specifics about the field in which you are writing. You can also discover much about a discipline's tools and language from the research sources listed on pages 866–69.

1 ■ Writing tools

In the sciences a **lab notebook** or **scientific journal** is almost indispensable for accurately recording the empirical data from observations and experiments. Use such a notebook or journal for these purposes:

- *Record observations* from reading, from class, or from the lab.
- *Ask questions and refine hypotheses.*
- *Record procedures.*
- *Record results.*
- *Keep an ongoing record of ideas and findings* and how they change as data accumulate.
- *Sequence and organize your material* as you compile your findings and write your report.

Make sure that your records of data are clearly separate from your reflections on the data so that you don't mistakenly confuse the two in drawing your conclusions.

2 ■ Language considerations

Science writers prefer to use objective language that removes the writer as a character in the situation and events being explained, except as the impersonal agent of change, the experimenter. Although usage is changing, scientists still rarely use *I* in their reports and evaluations, and they often resort to the passive voice of verbs, as in *The mixture <u>was</u> then <u>subjected</u> to centrifugal* *force*. This conscious objectivity focuses attention (including the writer's) on the empirical data and what they show. It discourages the writer from, say, ascribing motives and will to animals and plants. For instance, instead of asserting that the sea tortoise *evolved* its hard shell *to protect* its body, a scientist would write only what could be observed: that the hard shell *covers and thus protects* the tortoise's body.

Science writers typically change verb tenses to distinguish between established information and their own research. For established information, such as that found in journals and other reliable sources, use the present tense (*Baroreceptors monitor blood pressure*). For your own and others' research, use the past tense (*The bacteria died within three hours. Marti reported some success*).

Each discipline in the natural and applied sciences has a specialized vocabulary that permits precise, accurate, and efficient communication. Some of these terms, such as *pressure* in physics, have different meanings in the common language and must be handled carefully in science writing. Others, such as *enthalpy* in chemistry, have no meanings in the common language and must simply be learned and used correctly.

3 ▪ Research sources

The following lists give resources in the sciences.

Specialized encyclopedias, dictionaries, and bibliographies

American Medical Association Encyclopedia of Medicine
Bibliographic Guide to the History of Computing, Computers, and the Information Processing Industry
Concise Oxford Dictionary of Mathematics
Dorland's Illustrated Medical Dictionary
Encyclopedia of Bioethics
Encyclopedia of Chemistry
Encyclopedia of Computer Science and Technology
Encyclopedia of Ecology
Encyclopedia of Electronics
Encyclopedia of Oceanography
Encyclopedia of Physics
Encyclopedic Dictionary of Mathematics
Grzimek's Animal Life Encyclopedia
Information Sources in the Life Sciences
Introduction to Reference Sources in Health Sciences
McGraw-Hill Encyclopedia of Engineering
McGraw-Hill Encyclopedia of the Geological Sciences
McGraw-Hill Encyclopedia of Science and Technology
Science and Technology in World History
Space Almanac
Van Nostrand's Scientific Encyclopedia
World Resources (environment)

55c

Periodical indexes

> *ACM Guide to Computing Literature*
> *Applied Science and Technology Index*
> *Bibliography and Index of Geology*
> *Biological and Agricultural Index*
> *Computer Literature Index*
> *Cumulative Index to Nursing and Allied Health Literature*
> *Engineering Index*
> *Environment Abstracts*
> *General Science Index*
> *Index Medicus*
> *MathSciNet: Mathematical Reviews*

Abstracts and citation indexes

> *Applied Science and Technology Index*
> *Bibliography and Index of Geology*
> *Biological Abstracts*
> *Chemical Abstracts*
> *Computer Abstracts*
> *Cumulative Index to Nursing and Allied Health Literature*
> *Dissertation Abstracts International* (doctoral dissertations). Before 1969, the title was *Dissertation Abstracts.*
> *Ecology Abstracts*
> *Engineering Index*
> *Environment Abstracts*
> *General Science Index*
> *MathSciNet: Mathematical Reviews*
> *Physics Abstracts*
> *Science Citation Index*

55c

Book reviews

> *Technical Book Review Index*

Web sources

For updates of these sources and addresses, see this book's Web site (box on p. 863).

General

Google Web Directory Science Links
   http://directory.google.com/Top/Science
Librarians' Index Science Resources
   http://lii.org/search/file/scitech
National Academy of Sciences
   http://www.nas.edu
Virtual Library: Science
   http://www.vlib.org/Science.html

Biology

BioMedNet
   http://www.bmn.com

Biology Online
http://biology-online.org
Biology Project
http://www.biology.arizona.edu/default.html
National Biological Information Infrastructure
http://www.nbii.gov/index.html

Chemistry

BUBL Chemistry Resources
http://link.bubl.ac.uk/ISC7023
Chemistry.org
http://www.chemistry.org/portal/Chemistry
University of Houston's Chemistry Resources
http://info.lib.uh.edu/indexes/chem.htm
WWW Virtual Library Links for Chemists
http://www.liv.ac.uk/Chemistry/Links/links.html

55c

Computer science

BUBL Computer Science Resources
http://link.bubl.ac.uk/computerscience
IEEE Computer Society
http://www.computer.org
University of Texas Virtual Computer Library
http://www.utexas.edu/computer/vcl
Virtual Library: Computing
http://www.vlib.org/Computing.html

Engineering

American Society of Civil Engineers' Resources
http://www.pubs.asce.org
BUBL Engineering Resources
http://link.bubl.ac.uk/engineering
Engineering Virtual Library
http://www.eevl.ac.uk/wwwvl.html
National Academy of Engineering
http://www.nae.edu

Environmental science

CIES Information Network
http://www.ciesin.org
EE-Link
http://eelink.net
EnviroLink
http://www.envirolink.org
Environmental Organization WebDirectory
http://www.webdirectory.com

Geology

American Geological Institute
http://www.agiweb.org
Digital Library for Earth Science Education
http://www.dlese.org

GeoSource
http://www.library.uu.nl/geosource/index.html
USGS Library
http://library.usgs.gov

Health sciences
American Medical Association
http://www.ama-assn.org
Centers for Disease Control and Prevention
http://www.cdc.gov
Hardin Medical Information Hub
http://www.lib.uiowa.edu/hardin/md
World Health Organization
http://www.who.int/en

Mathematics
AMS Math on the Web
http://www.ams.org/mathweb
BUBL Mathematics Resources
http://link.bubl.ac.uk/mathematics
Internet Mathematics Library
http://mathforum.com/library
Mathematical Atlas
http://www.math-atlas.org

Physics and astronomy
American Institute of Physics
http://www.aip.org
astronomyLINKS
http://astronomylinks.com
NASA Space Science Resources
http://spacescience.nasa.gov
PhysicsWeb
http://www.physicsweb.org

55d Citing sources in CSE style

Within the natural and applied sciences, practitioners use one of two styles of documentation, varying slightly from discipline to discipline. Following are some of the style guides most often consulted:

American Chemical Society. *ACS Style Guide: A Manual for Authors and Editors.* 2nd ed. 1997.
American Institute of Physics. *Style Manual for Guidance in the Preparation of Papers.* 4th ed. 1990.
American Mathematical Society. *A Manual for Authors of Mathematical Papers.* Rev. ed. 1990.
American Medical Association. *Manual of Style.* 9th ed. 1998.
Council of Biology Editors. *Scientific Style and Format: The CBE Manual for Authors, Editors, and Publishers.* 6th ed. 1994.

The most thorough and widely used of these guides is the last one, *Scientific Style and Format*. Its sponsoring organization, the Council of Science Editors, was until 2000 called the Council of Biology Editors, so the style is abbreviated either CSE (as here) or CBE.

Scientific Style and Format details both styles of scientific documentation: one using author and date and one using numbers. Both types of text citation refer to a list of references at the end of the paper (see opposite). Ask your instructor which style you should use.

1 ■ Using CSE name-year text citations

In the CSE name-year style, parenthetical text citations provide the last name of the author being cited and the source's year of publication. At the end of the paper, a list of references, arranged alphabetically by authors' last names, provides complete information on each source. (See opposite.)

The CSE name-year style closely resembles the APA name-year style detailed on pages 839–42. You can follow the APA examples for in-text citations, making several notable changes for CSE:

- *Do not use a comma to separate the author's name and the date:* (Baumrind 1968, p. 34).
- *Separate two authors' names with "and" (not "&"):* (Pepinsky and DeStefano 1997).
- *Use "and others" (not "et al.") for three or more authors:* (Rutter and others 1996).
- *List unnamed or anonymous authors as "Anonymous,"* both in the citation and in the list of references: (Anonymous 1976).

2 ■ Using CSE numbered text citations

In the CSE number style, raised numbers in the text refer to a numbered list of references at the end of the paper.

Two standard references[1,2] use this term.

These forms of immunity have been extensively researched.[3]

According to one report,[4] research into some forms of viral immunity is almost nonexistent.

Hepburn and Tatin[2] do not discuss this project.

---

http://www.ablongman.com/littlebrown
For added help with using CSE style, click on
➤ **Documentation in the disciplines** ➤ **CSE style**

Assignment of numbers

The number for each source is based on the order in which you cite the source in the text: the first cited source is 1, the second is 2, and so on.

Reuse of numbers

When you cite a source you have already cited and numbered, use the original number again (see the last example on the facing page, which reuses the number 2 from the first example).

This reuse is the key difference between the CSE numbered citations and numbered references to footnotes or endnotes. In the CSE style, each source has only one number, determined by the order in which the source is cited. With notes, in contrast, the numbering proceeds in sequence, so that each source has as many numbers as it has citations in the text.

Citation of two or more sources

When you cite two or more sources at once, arrange their numbers in sequence and separate them with a comma and no space, as in the first example on the facing page.

3 ■ Using a CSE reference list

For both the name-year and the number styles of in-text citation, provide a list, titled "References," of all sources you have cited. Format the page as shown for APA references on page 843 (but you may omit the shortened title before the page number).

Follow these guidelines for references, noting the important differences in name-year and number styles:

Spacing

Single-space each entry, and double-space between entries.

Arrangement

The two styles differ in their arrangement of entries:

Name-year style

Arrange entries alphabetically by authors' last names.

Number style

Arrange entries in numerical order—that is, in order of their citation in the text.

Format

In both styles, begin the first line of each entry at the left margin and indent subsequent lines:

Name-year style

Hepburn PX, Tatin JM. 2002. Human physiology. New York: Columbia Univ Pr. 1026 p.

Number style

2. Hepburn PX, Tatin JM. Human physiology. New York: Columbia Univ Pr; 2002. 1026 p.

Authors

List each author's name with the last name first, followed by initials for first and middle names. (See the examples above.) Do not use a comma after the last name or periods or space with the initials. Do use a comma to separate authors' names.

Placement of dates

The two styles differ, as shown in the examples at the top of the page.

Name-year style

The date follows the author's or authors' names.

Number style

The date follows the publication information (for a book) or the title (for a periodical).

Journal titles

Do not underline or italicize journal titles. For titles of two or more words, abbreviate words of six or more letters (without periods) and omit most prepositions, articles, and conjunctions. Capitalize each word. For example, *Journal of Chemical and Biochemical Studies* becomes J Chem Biochem Stud, *Developmental Biology* becomes Dev Biol, and *Annals of Medicine* becomes Ann Med. See the Rowell examples on the facing page.

Book and article titles

Do not underline, italicize, or quote a book or an article title. Capitalize only the first word and any proper nouns. See the Rowell examples opposite and model 2 on page 874.

Publication information for journal articles

Both the name-year and the number styles give the journal's volume number, a colon, and the inclusive page numbers of the article: 28:329-33 in the examples opposite. (If the journal has an issue number, it follows the volume number in parentheses: 62(2):26-40.) However, the styles differ in the punctuation as well as the placement of the date:

CSE References

Books

1. A book with one author *874*
2. A book with two to ten authors *874*
3. A book with more than ten authors *874*
4. A book with an editor *874*
5. A selection from a book *874*
6. An anonymous work *874*
7. Two or more cited works by the same author published in the same year *875*

Periodicals

8. An article in a journal with continuous pagination throughout the annual volume *875*
9. An article in a journal that pages issues separately *875*
10. An article in a newspaper *875*
11. An article in a magazine *875*

CSE
55d

Electronic sources

12. A source on CD-ROM *876*
13. An online journal article *876*
14. An online book *876*
15. A source retrieved from an online database *876*
16. A Web site *877*
17. Electronic mail *877*
18. A posting to a discussion list *877*
19. Computer software *877*

Other sources

20. A government publication *878*
21. A nongovernment report *878*
22. A sound recording, video recording, or film *878*

Name-year style

The date, after the author's name and a period, is followed by a period:

> Rowell LB. 1996. Blood pressure regulation during exercise. Ann Med 28:329-33.

Number style

The date, after the journal title and a space, is followed by a semicolon:

> 3. Rowell LB. Blood pressure regulation during exercise. Ann Med 1996;28:329-33.

The following examples show both a name-year reference and a number reference for each type of source.

Books

1. A book with one author

Gould SJ. 1987. Time's arrow, time's cycle. Cambridge: Harvard Univ Pr. 222 p.

1. Gould SJ. Time's arrow, time's cycle. Cambridge: Harvard Univ Pr; 1987. 222 p.

2. A book with two to ten authors

Hepburn PX, Tatin JM. 2002. Human physiology. New York: Columbia Univ Pr. 1026 p.

2. Hepburn PX, Tatin JM. Human physiology. New York: Columbia Univ Pr; 2002. 1026 p.

3. A book with more than ten authors

Evans RW, Bowditch L, Dana KL, Drummond A, Wildovitch WP, Young SL, Mills P, Mills RR, Livak SR, Lisi OL, and others. 1998. Organ transplants: ethical issues. Ann Arbor: Univ of Michigan Pr. 498 p.

3. Evans RW, Bowditch L, Dana KL, Drummond A, Wildovitch WP, Young SL, Mills P, Mills RR, Livak SR, Lisi OL, and others. Organ transplants: ethical issues. Ann Arbor: Univ of Michigan Pr; 1998. 498 p.

4. A book with an editor

Jonson P, editor. 2003. Anatomy yearbook. Los Angeles: Anatco. 628 p.

4. Jonson P, editor. Anatomy yearbook. Los Angeles: Anatco; 2003. 628 p.

5. A selection from a book

Krigel R, Laubenstein L, Muggia F. 2002. Kaposi's sarcoma. In: Ebbeson P, Biggar RS, Melbye M, editors. AIDS: a basic guide for clinicians. 2nd ed. Philadelphia: WB Saunders. p 100-26.

5. Krigel R, Laubenstein L, Muggia F. Kaposi's sarcoma. In: Ebbeson P, Biggar RS, Melbye M, editors. AIDS: a basic guide for clinicians. 2nd ed. Philadelphia: WB Saunders; 2002. p 100-26.

6. An anonymous work

[Anonymous]. 2000. Health care for multiple sclerosis. New York: US Health Care. 86 p.

6. [Anonymous]. Health care for multiple sclerosis. New York: US Health Care; 2000. 86 p.

CSE

55d

7. Two or more cited works by the same author published in the same year

Gardner H. 1973a. The arts and human development. New York: J Wiley. 406 p.

Gardner H. 1973b. The quest for mind: Piaget, Lévi-Strauss, and the structuralist movement. New York: AA Knopf. 492 p.

(The number style does not require such forms.)

Periodicals: Journals, magazines, newspapers

8. An article in a journal with continuous pagination throughout the annual volume

Ancino R, Carter KV, Elwin DJ. 1999. Factors contributing to viral immunity: a review of the research. Dev Biol 30:156-9.

8. Ancino R, Carter KV, Elwin DJ. Factors contributing to viral immunity: a review of the research. Dev Biol 1999;30:156-9.

9. An article in a journal that pages issues separately

Kim P. 1996 Feb. Medical decision making for the dying. Milbank Quar 64(2):26-40.

9. Kim P. Medical decision making for the dying. Milbank Quar 1996 Feb;64(2):26-40.

10. An article in a newspaper

Kolata G. 2001 Jan 7. Kill all the bacteria! New York Times;Sect B:1(col 3).

10. Kolata G. Kill all the bacteria! New York Times 2001 Jan 7;Sect B:1(col 3).

11. An article in a magazine

Scheiber N. 2002 June 24. Finger tip: why fingerprinting won't work. New Republic:15-6.

11. Scheiber N. Finger tip: why fingerprinting won't work. New Republic 2002 June 24:15-6.

Electronic sources

Scientific Style and Format includes a few formats for citing electronic sources, derived from *National Library of Medicine Recommended Formats for Bibliographic Citation.* For additional formats, the CSE Web site recommends the NLM 2001 supplement for Internet sources. The following models adapt these NLM formats to CSE name-year and number styles. For more information, consult the links at this book's Web site: see the box on page 870.

Note Since neither the CSE nor the NLM specifies how to break electronic addresses at the ends of lines, follow MLA style: break only after slashes, and do not hyphenate.

12. A source on CD-ROM

Reich WT, editor. 2002. Encyclopedia of bioethics [CD-ROM]. New York: Co-Health.

12. Reich WT, editor. Encyclopedia of bioethics [CD-ROM]. New York: Co-Health; 2002.

13. An online journal article

Grady GF. 2000. The here and now of hepatitis B immunization. Today's Med [Internet] [cited 2002 Dec 27];6(2):39-41. Available from: http://www.fmrt.org/todaysmedicine/ Grady050293.pdf6

13. Grady GF. The here and now of hepatitis B immunization. Today's Med [Internet] 2000 [cited 2002 Dec 27];6(2):39-41. Available from: http://www.fmrt.org/todaysmedicine/ Grady050293.pdf6

Give the date of your access, preceded by "cited," in brackets: [cited 2002 Dec 27] in the models above. If the article has no reference numbers (pages, paragraphs, and so on), estimate the length in brackets—for instance, [about 15 p.] or [about 6 screens].

14. An online book

Ruch BJ, Ruch DB. 1999. Homeopathy and medicine: resolving the conflict [Internet]. New York: Albert Einstein Coll of Medicine [cited 2003 Jan 28]. [about 50 p.]. Available from: http://www.einstein.edu/medicine/books/ruch.html

14. Ruch BJ, Ruch DB. Homeopathy and medicine: resolving the conflict [Internet]. New York: Albert Einstein Coll of Medicine; 1999 [cited 2003 Jan 28]. [about 50 p.]. Available from: http://www.einstein.edu/medicine/books/ruch.html

As with an online journal article, give the date of your access, preceded by "cited," in brackets. If the source uses page or other reference numbers, provide the total as in model 1 on page 874. If no reference numbers are provided, you may estimate them in brackets, as in the examples above.

15. A source retrieved from an online database

McAskill MR, Anderson TJ, Jones RD. 2002. Saccadic adaptation in neurological disorders. Prog Brain Res 140:417-31. In: PubMed [Internet]. Bethesda (MD): National Library of Medicine; [cited 2003 Mar 6]. Available from: http:// www.ncbi.nlm.nih.gov/PubMed; PMID: 12508606.

15. McAskill MR, Anderson TJ, Jones RD. Saccadic adaptation in neurological disorders. Prog Brain Res 2002;140:417-31. In: PubMed [Internet]. Bethesda (MD): National Library of Medicine; [cited 2003 Mar 6]. Available from: http://www.ncbi.nlm.nih.gov/PubMed; PMID: 12508606.

After "In," provide information on the database: title, place of publication, and publisher. (If the database author is different from the publisher, give the author's name before the title.) If you see a date of publication or copyright date for the database, give it after the publisher's name. Add the date of your access, preceded by "cited," in brackets. After the availability statement, add any identifying number the database uses for the source.

16. A Web site

American Medical Association [Internet]. 2003. Chicago: American Medical Association; [cited 2003 Jan 2]. Available from: http://ama-assn.org

16. American Medical Association [Internet]. Chicago: American Medical Association; 2003 [cited 2003 Jan 2]. Available from: http://ama-assn.org

17. Electronic mail

Millon M. 2003 May 4. Grief therapy [Internet]. Message to: Naomi Sakai. 3:16 pm [cited 2003 May 4]. [about 2 screens].

17. Millon M. Grief therapy [Internet]. Message to: Naomi Sakai. 2003 May 4, 3:16 pm [cited 2003 May 4]. [about 2 screens].

18. A posting to a discussion list

Stalinsky Q. 2002 Aug 16. The hormone-replacement study. In: Women Physicians Congress [Internet]. [Chicago: American Medical Association]; 9:26 am [cited 2002 Aug 17]. [about 8 paragraphs]. Available from: ama-wpc@ama-assn.org

18. Stalinsky Q. The hormone-replacement study. In: Women Physicians Congress [Internet]. [Chicago: American Medical Association]; 2002 Aug 16, 9:26 am [cited 2002 Aug 17]. [about 8 paragraphs]. Available from: ama-wpc@ama-assn.org

19. Computer software

Project scheduler 9000 [computer program]. 2003. Version 5.1. Orlando (FL): Scitor. CD-ROM. Accompanied by: 1 manual. System requirements: IBM PC or fully compatible computer; Windows 98 or higher; 8 MB RAM; hard disk with a minimum of 18 MB of free space.

19. Project scheduler 9000 [computer program]. Version 5.1. Orlando (FL): Scitor; 2003. CD-ROM. Accompanied by: 1 manual. System requirements: IBM PC or fully compatible computer; Windows 98 or higher; 8 MB RAM; hard disk with a minimum of 18 MB of free space.

Other sources

20. A government publication

Committee on Science and Technology, House (US). 1999. Hearing on procurement and allocation of human organs for transplantation. 106th Cong., 1st Sess. House Doc. nr 409.

20. Committee on Science and Technology, House (US). Hearing on procurement and allocation of human organs for transplantation. 106th Cong., 1st Sess. House Doc. nr 409; 1999.

21. A nongovernment report

Warnock M. 1998. Report of the Committee on Fertilization and Embryology. Baylor University, Department of Embryology. Waco (TX): Baylor Univ. Report nr BU/DE.4261.

21. Warnock M. Report of the Committee on Fertilization and Embryology. Baylor University, Department of Embryology. Waco (TX): Baylor Univ; 1998. Report nr BU/DE.4261.

22. A sound recording, video recording, or film

Teaching Media. 2000. Cell mitosis [videocassette]. White Plains (NY): Teaching Media. 1 videocassette: 40 min, sound, black and white, 1/2 in.

22. Cell mitosis [videocassette]. White Plains (NY): Teaching Media; 2000. 1 videocassette: 40 min, sound, black and white, 1/2 in.

55e Formatting documents in CSE style

Scientific Style and Format is not specific about margins, spacing for headings, and other elements of document format. Unless your instructor specifies otherwise, you can use the format of the APA (pp. 856–59). The CSE exception to this style is the list of references, which is described on pages 871–73.

The most troublesome aspects of manuscript preparation in the sciences are equations or formulas, tables, and figures. When typing equations or formulas, be careful to reproduce alignments, indentions, underlining, and characters accurately. If your word processor lacks special characters, write them in by hand. (Stationery and art-supply stores also have sheets of transfer type with special characters in different sizes that can be applied to your document by rubbing.)

Because you will be expected to share your data with your readers, most of your writing for the sciences is likely to require illustrations to present the data in concise, readable form. Tables usually summarize raw data (see p. 881 for an example), whereas figures (mainly charts and graphs) recast the data to show noteworthy comparisons or changes. Follow the guidelines on pages 208–11 for preparing tables and figures.

55f   Examining a sample science paper

The following biology paper illustrates the CSE number style for documenting sources. On page 882 passages from the paper and a reformatted list of references show the name-year style. Except for the citations and the references, the paper is formatted in APA style because CSE does not specify a format.

A laboratory report: CSE number style

[Title page.]

Exercise and Blood Pressure

Liz Garson

Biology 161

Ms. Traversa

December 13, 2002

[New page.]

Abstract

The transient elevation of blood pressure following exercise was demonstrated by pressure measurements of twenty human subjects before and after exercise.

[New page.]

Exercise and Blood Pressure

Introduction

The purpose of this experiment was to verify the changes in blood pressure that accompany exercise, as commonly reported.[1,2] A certain blood pressure is necessary for the blood to supply nutrients to the body tissues. Baroreceptors near the heart monitor pressure by determining the degree to which blood stretches the wall of the blood vessel.

[The introduction continues.]

During exercise, the metabolic needs of the muscles override the influence of the baroreceptors and result in an increase in blood pressure. This increase in blood pressure is observed uniformly (irrespective of sex or race), although men demonstrate a higher absolute systolic pressure than do women.[3] During strenuous exercise, blood pressure can rise to 40 percent above baseline.[1]

Method

The subjects for this experiment were twenty volunteers from laboratory classes, ten men and ten women. All pressure measurements were performed using a standard sphygmomanometer, which was tested for accuracy. To ensure consistency, the same sphygmomanometer was used to take all readings. In addition, all measurements were taken by the same person to avoid discrepancies in method or interpretation.

The first pressure reading was taken prior to exercise as the subject sat in a chair. This pressure was considered the baseline for each subject. All subsequent readings were interpreted relative to this baseline.

In the experiment, the subjects ran up and down stairs for fifteen minutes. Immediately after exercising, the subjects returned to the laboratory to have their pressure measured. Thirty minutes later, the pressure was measured for the final time.

Results

Table 1 contains the blood pressure measurements for the male and female subjects. With the exception of subjects 3 and 14, all subjects demonstrated the expected post-exercise increase in blood pressure, with a decline to baseline or near baseline thirty minutes after exercise. The data for subjects 3 and 14 were invalid because the subjects did not perform the experiment as directed.

Discussion

As expected, most of the subjects demonstrated an increase in blood pressure immediately after exercise and a decline to near baseline levels thirty minutes after exercise. The usual pressure increase was 20-40 mmHg for the systolic pressure and 5-10 mmHg for the diastolic pressure.

[Table on a page by itself.]

Table 1. Blood pressure measurements for all subjects (mmHg)

Subject	Baseline[a]	Post-exercise	30-minute reading
Male			
1	110/75	135/80	115/75
2	125/80	140/90	135/85
3	125/70	125/70	125/70
4	130/85	170/100	140/90
5	120/80	125/95	120/80
6	115/70	135/80	125/75
7	125/70	150/80	130/70
8	130/80	145/85	130/80
9	140/75	180/85	155/80
10	110/85	135/95	115/80
Female			
11	110/60	140/85	115/60
12	130/75	180/85	130/75
13	125/80	140/90	130/80
14	90/60	90/60	90/60
15	115/65	145/70	125/65
16	100/50	130/65	110/50
17	120/80	140/80	130/80
18	110/70	135/80	120/75
19	120/80	140/90	130/80
20	110/80	145/90	120/80

CSE
55f

[a]Normal blood pressure at rest: males, 110-130/60-90; females, 110-120/50-80.

In the two cases in which blood pressure did not elevate with exercise (subjects 3 and 14), the subjects simply left the laboratory and returned fifteen minutes later without having exercised. The experimental design was flawed in not assigning someone to observe the subjects as they exercised.

[New page.]

References

1. Guyton AC. Textbook of medical physiology. Philadelphia: WB Saunders; 1997. 998 p.

2. Rowell LB. Blood pressure regulation during exercise. Ann Med 1996;28:329-33.

3. Gleim GW, Stachenfeld NS. Gender differences in the systolic blood pressure response to exercise. Am Heart J 1991;121:524-30.

A laboratory report: CSE name-year style

These excerpts from the preceding paper show documentation in CSE name-year style:

The purpose of this experiment was to verify the changes in blood pressure that accompany exercise, as commonly reported (Guyton 1997; Rowell 1996).

This increase in blood pressure is observed uniformly (irrespective of sex or race), although men demonstrate a higher absolute systolic pressure than do women (Gleim and Stachenfeld 1991). During strenuous exercise, blood pressure can rise to 40 percent above baseline (Guyton 1997).

References

Gleim GW, Stachenfeld NS. 1991. Gender differences in the systolic blood pressure response to exercise. Am Heart J 121:524-30.

Guyton AC. 1997. Textbook of medical physiology. Philadelphia: WB Saunders. 998 p.

Rowell LB. 1996. Blood pressure regulation during exercise. Ann Med 28:329-33.

CSE
55f

PART XII

Special Writing Situations

CHAPTER 56

Essay Examinations

In writing an essay for an examination, you summarize or analyze a topic, usually in several paragraphs or more and usually within a time limit. An essay question not only tests your knowledge of a subject (as short-answer and objective questions do) but also tests your ability to think critically about what you have learned. (If you have not already done so, read this book's Chapter 5 on critical thinking, reading, and writing.)

56a   Preparing for an essay examination

To do well on an essay exam, you will need to understand the course content, not only the facts but also the interpretation of them and the relations between them.

- *Take careful lecture notes.*
- *Thoughtfully, critically read the assigned texts or articles.*
- *Review regularly.* Give the material time to sink in and stimulate your thinking.
- *Create summaries.* Recast others' ideas in your own words, and extract the meaning from notes and texts. (See pp. 123–24 for instructions on summarizing.)
- *Prepare notes or outlines to reorganize the course material around key topics or issues.* One technique is to create and answer likely essay questions. For instance, in a business course you might focus on the advantages and disadvantages of several approaches to management. In a short-story course you might locate a theme running through all the stories you have read by a certain author or from a certain period. In a psychology course you might outline various theorists' views of what

http://www.ablongman.com/littlebrown
For added help with preparing for essay exams, click on
➤ Special writing situations ➤ Web links ➤ Essay exams

causes a disorder such as schizophrenia. Working through such topics can help you anticipate questions, master the material, and estimate your time during the actual exam.

 If you have the opportunity to compose your essay exams on a computer, you'll also need to know the basic operations of computers and your instructor's procedure for submitting exams. While writing your exam, save your work frequently.

56b Planning your time and your answer

When you first receive an examination, take a few minutes to get your bearings and plan an approach. The time spent will not be wasted.

56b

- *Read the exam all the way through at least once.* Don't start answering any questions until you've seen them all.
- *Weigh the questions.* Determine which questions seem most important, which ones are going to be most difficult for you, and approximately how much time you'll need for each question. (Your instructor may help by assigning a point value to each question as a guide to its importance or by suggesting an amount of time for you to spend on each question.)

Planning continues when you turn to an individual essay question. Resist the temptation to rush right into an answer without some planning, for a few minutes can save you time later and help you produce a stronger essay.

- *Read the question at least twice.* You will be more likely to stick to the question and answer it fully.
- *Examine the words in the question and consider their implications.* Look especially for words such as *describe, define, explain, summarize, analyze, evaluate,* and *interpret,* each of which requires a different kind of response. Here, for example, is an essay question whose key term is *explain:*

Question
Given humans' natural and historical curiosity about themselves, why did a scientific discipline of anthropology not arise until the 20th century? Explain, citing specific details.

See the box on the next page and consult earlier discussions of such terms on pages 92–101 and 125–32.
- *Make a brief outline of the main ideas you want to include in your essay.* Use the back of the exam sheet or booklet for scratch paper. In the brief outline on page 887, a student planned her answer to the anthropology question above.

Sample instructions for essay examinations

Sample instructions	Key terms	Strategies for answers	Examples of wrong answers
Define *dyslexia* and compare and contrast it with two other learning disabilities.	Define	Specify the meaning of *dyslexia*—distinctive characteristics, ways the impairment works, etc.	Feelings of children with dyslexia. Causes of dyslexia.
	Compare and contrast	Analyze similarities and differences (severity, causes, treatments, etc.).	Similarities without differences, or vice versa.
Analyze the role of Horatio in *Hamlet*.	Analyze	Break Horatio's role into its elements (speeches, relations with other characters, etc.).	Plot summary of *Hamlet*. Description of Horatio's personality.
Explain the effects of the drug Thorazine.	Explain	Set forth the facts and theories objectively.	Argument for or against Thorazine.
	Effects	Analyze the consequences.	Reasons for prescribing Thorazine.
Discuss term limits for elected officials.	Discuss	Explain and compare the main points of view on the issue.	Analysis of one view. Argument for or against one view.
Summarize the process that resulted in the Grand Canyon.	Summarize	Distill the subject to its main points, elements, or steps.	Detailed description of the Grand Canyon.
How do you evaluate the Laffer curve as a predictor of economic growth?	Evaluate	Provide your opinion of significance or value, supported with evidence.	Explanation of the Laffer curve, without evaluation. Comparison of the Laffer curve and another predictor, without evaluation.

56b

1. Unscientific motivations behind 19th-c anthro.

   Imperialist/colonialist govts.
   Practical goals
   Nonobjective and unscientific (Herodotus, Cushing)

2. 19th-c ethnocentricity (vs. cultural relativism)

3. 19th-c anthro. = object collecting

   20th-c shift from museum to univ.
   Anthro. becomes acad. disc. and professional (Boas, Malinowski)

- *Write a thesis statement for your essay that responds directly to the question and represents your view of the topic.* (If you are unsure of how to write a thesis statement, see pp. 31–35.) Include key phrases that you can expand with supporting evidence for your view. The thesis statement of the student whose outline appears above concisely previews a three-part answer to the sample question:

Anthropology did not emerge as a scientific discipline until the 20th century because of the practical and political motivations behind 19th-century ethnographic studies, the ethnocentric bias of Western researchers, and a conception of culture that was strictly material.

56d

56c Starting the essay

An essay exam does not require a smooth and inviting opening. Instead, begin by stating your thesis immediately and giving an overview of the rest of your essay. Such a capsule version of your answer tells your reader (and grader) generally how much command you have and also how you plan to develop your answer. It also gets you off to a good start.

The opening statement should address the question directly and exactly, as it does in the successful essay answer beginning on the next page. In contrast, the opening of the unsuccessful essay (pp. 889–90) restates the question but does not answer it, nor does the opening provide any sense of the writer's thesis.

56d Developing the essay

Develop your essay as you would develop any piece of sound academic writing:

- *Observe the methods, terms, or other special requirements of the discipline in which you are writing* (see Chapters 51–55).

- *Support your thesis statement with solid generalizations,* each one perhaps the topic sentence of a paragraph.
- *Support each generalization with specific, relevant evidence.*

If you observe a few *don't*s as well, your essay will have more substance:

- *Avoid filling out the essay by repeating yourself.*
- *Avoid other kinds of wordiness that pad and confuse,* whether intentionally or not. (See pp. 564–71.)
- *Avoid resorting to purely subjective feelings.* Keep focused on analysis, or whatever is asked of you. (It may help to abolish the word *I* from the essay.)

The following essays illustrate a successful and an unsuccessful answer to the sample essay question on page 885 about anthropology. Both answers were written in the allotted time of forty minutes. Marginal comments on each essay highlight their effective and ineffective elements.

Successful essay answer

56d

Anthropology did not emerge as a scientific discipline until the 20th century because of the practical and political motivations behind 19th-century ethnographic studies, the ethnocentric bias of Western researchers, and a conception of culture that was strictly material.

[Gets right to the point with thesis statement]

[Answers question directly and previews three-part response]

Before the 20th century, ethnographic studies were almost always used for practical goals. The study of human culture can be traced back at least as far as Herodotus's investigations of the Mediterranean peoples. Herodotus was like many pre-20th-century "anthropologists" in that he was employed by a government that needed information about its neighbors, just as the colonial nations in the 19th century needed information about their newly conquered subjects. The early politically motivated ethnographic studies that the colonial nations sponsored tended to be isolated projects, and they aimed less to advance general knowledge than to solve a specific problem. Frank Hamilton Cushing, who was employed by the American government to study the Zuni tribe of New Mexico, and who is considered one of the pioneers of anthropology, didn't even publish his findings. The political and practical aims of anthropologists and the nature of their research prevented their work from being a scholarly discipline in its own right.

[Point 1 of thesis: practical aims]

[Example]

[Example]

Anthropologists of the 19th century also fell short of the standards of objectivity needed for truly scientific study. This partly had to do with anthropologists' close connection to imperialist governments. But even independent researchers were hampered by the prevailing assumption that Western cultures were inherently superior. While the modern anthropologist believes that a culture must be studied in terms of its own values, early ethnographers were ethnocentric: they judged "primitive" cultures by their own "civilized" values. "Primitive" peoples were seen as uninteresting in their own right. The reasons to study them, ultimately, were to satisfy curiosity, to exploit them, or to prove their inferiority. There was even some debate as to whether so-called savage peoples were human.

Point 2 of thesis: ethnocentricity

Finally, the 19th century tended to conceive of culture in narrow, material terms, often reducing it to a collection of artifacts. When not working for a government, early ethnographers usually worked for a museum. The enormous collections of exotica still found in many museums today are the legacy of this 19th-century object-oriented conception of anthropology, which ignored the myths, symbols, and rituals the objects related to. It was only when the museum tradition was broadened to include all aspects of a culture that anthropology could come into existence as a scientific discipline. When anthropologists like Franz Boas and Bronislaw Malinowski began to publish their findings for others to read and criticize and began to move from the museum to the university, the discipline gained stature and momentum.

Point 3 of thesis (with transition *Finally*): focus on objects

56d

Examples

In brief, anthropology required a whole series of ideological shifts to become modern. Once it broke free of its purely practical bent, the cultural prejudices of its practitioners, and the narrow conception that limited it to a collection of objects, anthropology could grow into a science.

Conclusion restates thesis supported by essay

Unsuccessful essay answer

The discipline of anthropology, the study of humans and their cultures, actually began in the early 20th century and was strengthened by the Darwinian revolution, but the discipline did not begin to take shape until people like

Introduction does not answer question

No thesis statement or sense of direction

Franz Boas and Alfred Kroeber began doing scientific research among nonindustrialized cultures. (Boas, who was born in Germany but emigrated to the US, is the father of the idea of historical particularism.)

Since the dawn of time, humans have always had a natural curiosity about themselves. Art and literature have always reflected this need to understand human emotions, thought, and behavior. Anthropology is yet another reflection of this need. Anthropologists have a different way of looking at human societies than artists or writers. Whereas the latter paint an individualistic, impressionistic portrait of the world they see, anthropologists study cultures systematically, scientifically. They are thus closer to biologists. They are *social scientists*, with the emphasis on both words.

Another reason why anthropology did not develop until the 20th century is that people in the past did not travel very much. The expansion of the automobile and the airplane has played a major role in the expansion of the discipline.

Cushing's important work among the Zuni Indians in New Mexico is a good example of the transition between 19th-century and 20th-century approaches to anthropology. Cushing was one of the first to develop the method of *participant observation.* Instead of merely coming in as an outsider, taking notes, and leaving, Cushing actually lived among the Zuni, dressing like them and following their customs. In this way, he was able to build a relationship of trust with his informants, learning much more than someone who would have been seen as an outsider.

Franz Boas, as mentioned earlier, was another anthropology pioneer. A German immigrant, Boas proposed the idea of *historical particularism* as a response to the prevailing theory of *cultural evolution.* Cultural evolution is the idea that cultures gradually evolve toward higher levels of efficiency and complexity. Historical particularism is the idea that every culture is unique and develops differently. Boas developed his theory to counter those who believed in cultural evolution. Working with the Kwakiutl Indians, he was also

56d

Irrelevant information

Adds cliché to the language of the question without answering the question

Wheel spinning by positioning contemporary anthropology as a scientific discipline

Not *Another reason* but the first reason given

Assertion without support

Next three paragraphs: discussion of pioneers shows familiarity with their work but does not answer question

Repetition pads

one of the first anthropologists to use a native assistant to help him gain access to the culture under study.

Information has unclear relevance to subject

A third pioneer in anthropology was Malinowski, who developed a theory of *functionalism*—that culture responds to biological, psychological, and other needs. Malinowski's work is extremely important and still influential today.

Vague assertion without support

Anthropologists have made great contributions to society over the course of the past century. One can only hope that they will continue the great strides they have made, building on the past to contribute to a bright new future.

Irrelevant and empty conclusion

56e Rereading the essay

The time limit on an essay examination does not allow for the careful rethinking and revision you would give an essay or research paper. You need to write clearly and concisely the first time. But try to leave yourself a few minutes after finishing the entire exam for rereading the essay (or essays) and doing touch-ups.

56e

- *Correct mistakes:* illegible passages, misspellings, grammatical errors, and accidental omissions.
- *Verify that your thesis is accurate*—that it is, in fact, what you ended up writing about.
- *Ensure that you have supported all your generalizations.* Cross out irrelevant ideas and details, and add any information that now seems important. (Write on another page, if necessary, keying the addition to the page on which it belongs.)

CHAPTER 57

Business Writing

When you write in business, you are addressing busy people who want to see quickly why you are writing and how they should respond to you. A wordy, incoherent letter or memo full of errors in grammar and spelling may prevent you from getting what you want, either because the reader cannot understand your wish or because you present yourself poorly. In business writing, follow these general guidelines:

- *State your purpose right at the start.*
- *Be straightforward, clear, concise, objective, and courteous.*
- *Observe conventions of grammar and usage,* which make your writing clear and impress your reader with your care.

Writing in business demands efficiency, but efficiency does not mean haste. Developing, drafting, and revising—the three overlapping stages of the writing process discussed in Chapters 1–3—apply in business writing as much as in academic writing. Except for brief or routine letters and memos, plan what you want to say; work out your meaning freely, unself-consciously, without stopping to edit; and then revise and edit your draft so that it will achieve your purpose with your reader.

Note A word processor's wizards or templates can help you format common business documents, such as letters or résumés. Before using such a tool, be sure the format is appropriate for your writing situation. And remember that a formatting tool can do nothing to help you express your ideas effectively.

CULTURE LANGUAGE Business writing in the United States favors efficiency and may seem abrupt or impolite compared with such writing in your native culture. For instance, business writers elsewhere may be expected to begin with polite questions about the addressee or with compliments for the addressee's company. US business writers, in contrast, get right to the point. See the sample documents in this chapter for examples of appropriate openings and other features of US business writing.

57a Writing business letters and job applications

The formats of business letters and résumés are fairly standardized and are thus expected by your correspondents. For more on the specific elements of document design (type fonts and sizes, headings, and so on), see pages 203–12.

1 ■ Using a standard form for letters

Use either unlined white paper measuring 8½" × 11" or what is called letterhead stationery with your address printed at the top of the sheet. Type the letter single-spaced, with double space between elements, on only one side of a sheet. (Unlike the double-spaced papers for your courses, business documents are almost always single-spaced.)

The two most common forms for business letters—the full block and the modified block—are illustrated and described on the following pages.

The letter

Return-address heading

Unless you're using letterhead stationery, the **return-address heading** of the letter gives your address (but not your name) and the date. If you are using letterhead, you need add only the date. Place your heading at least an inch from the top of the page, or place the date two lines below the letterhead if there is one. Align all lines of the heading on the left. In the block style, the return-address heading falls at the left margin (see the next page). In the modified block style, it falls to the right of the center of the paper (see p. 898).

Inside address

The **inside address** shows the name, title, and complete address of the person you are writing to. (See p. 896 for abbreviations of state names.) Place the address at least two lines below the return-address heading. In both block and modified block styles, the address falls at the left margin of the page.

Salutation

The **salutation** greets the addressee. In both styles it falls at the left margin, two lines below the inside address and two lines above

Business letter in block style

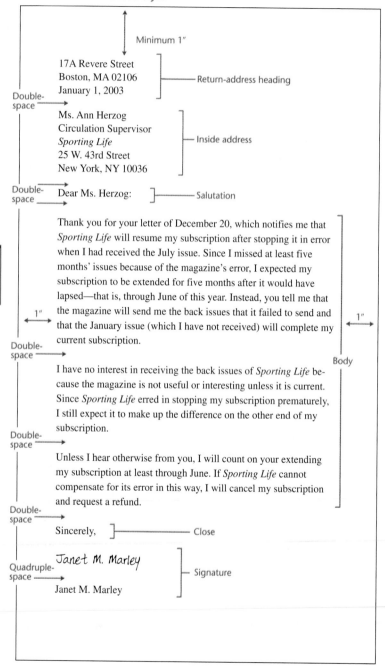

Minimum 1″

17A Revere Street
Boston, MA 02106 ——————— Return-address heading
January 1, 2003

Double-space →

Ms. Ann Herzog
Circulation Supervisor
Sporting Life — Inside address
25 W. 43rd Street
New York, NY 10036

Double-space →

Dear Ms. Herzog: ——————— Salutation

Thank you for your letter of December 20, which notifies me that
Sporting Life will resume my subscription after stopping it in error
when I had received the July issue. Since I missed at least five
months' issues because of the magazine's error, I expected my
subscription to be extended for five months after it would have
lapsed—that is, through June of this year. Instead, you tell me that
the magazine will send me the back issues that it failed to send and
that the January issue (which I have not received) will complete my
current subscription.

Double-space →

Body

I have no interest in receiving the back issues of *Sporting Life* because the magazine is not useful or interesting unless it is current.
Since *Sporting Life* erred in stopping my subscription prematurely,
I still expect it to make up the difference on the other end of my
subscription.

Double-space →

Unless I hear otherwise from you, I will count on your extending
my subscription at least through June. If *Sporting Life* cannot
compensate for its error in this way, I will cancel my subscription
and request a refund.

Double-space →

Sincerely, ——————— Close

Janet M. Marley

Quadruple-space →

Janet M. Marley ——————— Signature

1″

the body of the letter. Follow the salutation with a colon. Whenever possible, address your letter to a specific person. (Call the company or department to ask whom to address.) If you can't find a person's name, then use a job title (*Dear Human Resources Manager, Dear Customer Service Manager*) or use a general salutation (*Dear Smythe Shoes*). Use *Ms.* as the title for a woman when she has no other title, when you don't know how she prefers to be addressed, or when you know that she prefers to be addressed as *Ms.* If you know a woman prefers to be addressed as *Mrs.* or *Miss,* use the appropriate title.

Body

The **body** of the letter, containing its substance, begins at the left margin in both letter styles. Instead of indenting the first line of each paragraph, place an extra line of space between paragraphs so that they are readily visible.

Close

The letter's **close** begins two lines below the last line of the body and aligns with the return-address heading. That is, in the block style the close falls at the left margin (see the facing page), whereas in the modified block style it falls to the right of the center of the page (p. 898). The close should reflect the level of formality in the salutation. For formal letters, *Cordially, Yours truly,* and *Sincerely* are common closes. For less formal letters, you may choose to use *Regards, Best wishes,* or the like. Only the first word of the close is capitalized, and the close is followed by a comma.

57a

Signature

The **signature** of a business letter falls below the close and has two parts. One is your name typed on the fourth line below the close. The other is your handwritten signature, which fills the space between the close and your typed name. The signature should consist only of your name, as you sign checks and other documents.

Other information

Below the signature at the left margin, you may want to include additional information such as *Enc. 3* (indicating that there are three enclosures with the letter); *cc: Margaret Newton* (indicating that a copy is being sent to the person named); or *CHC/enp* (the initials of the author/the initials of the typist).

The envelope

The envelope of the letter should show your name and address in the upper-left corner and the addressee's name, title, and address in the center. Use an envelope that will adequately accommodate the letter once it is folded horizontally in thirds.

```
JANET M MARLEY
17A REVERE ST
BOSTON MA 02106


                        MS ANN HERZOG
                        CIRCULATION SUPERVISOR
                        SPORTING LIFE
                        25 W 43RD ST
                        NEW YORK NY 10036
```

The United States Postal Service recommends a format for envelopes that makes them easy for machines to read. As illustrated above, use all capital letters and no punctuation (spaces separate the elements on a line).

The following are the common Postal Service abbreviations for addresses:

57a

Street names

Avenue	AVE	Expressway	EXPY	Road	RD
Boulevard	BLVD	Freeway	FWY	Square	SQ
Circle	CIR	Lane	LN	Street	ST
Court	CT	Parkway	PKY	Turnpike	TPKE

Compass points

North	N	West	W	Southwest	SW
East	E	Northeast	NE	Northwest	NW

State names

Alabama	AL	Kentucky	KY	North Dakota	ND
Alaska	AK	Louisiana	LA	Ohio	OH
Arizona	AZ	Maine	ME	Oklahoma	OK
Arkansas	AR	Maryland	MD	Oregon	OR
California	CA	Massachusetts	MA	Pennsylvania	PA
Colorado	CO	Michigan	MI	Puerto Rico	PR
Connecticut	CT	Minnesota	MN	Rhode Island	RI
Delaware	DE	Mississippi	MS	South Carolina	SC
District of		Missouri	MO	South Dakota	SD
Columbia	DC	Montana	MT	Tennessee	TN
Florida	FL	Nebraska	NE	Texas	TX
Georgia	GA	Nevada	NV	Utah	UT
Hawaii	HI	New		Vermont	VT
Idaho	ID	Hampshire	NH	Virginia	VA
Illinois	IL	New Jersey	NJ	Washington	WA
Indiana	IN	New Mexico	NM	West Virginia	WV
Iowa	IA	New York	NY	Wisconsin	WI
Kansas	KS	North Carolina	NC	Wyoming	WY

2 ■ Writing requests and complaints

Letters requesting something—for instance, a pamphlet, information about a product, a T-shirt advertised in a magazine—must be specific and accurate about the item you are requesting. The letter should describe the item completely and, if applicable, include a copy or description of the advertisement or other source that prompted your request.

Letters complaining about a product or a service (such as a wrong billing from the telephone company) should be written in a reasonable but firm tone. (See the sample letter on p. 894.) Assume that the addressee is willing to resolve the problem when he or she has the relevant information. In the first sentence of the letter, say what you are writing about. Then provide as much background as needed, including any relevant details from past correspondence (as in the sample letter). Describe exactly what you see as the problem, sticking to facts and avoiding discourses on the company's social responsibility or your low opinion of its management. In the clearest and fewest possible words and sentences, proceed directly from one point to the next without repeating yourself. Always include your opinion of how the problem can be solved. Many companies are required by law to establish a specific procedure for complaints about products and services. If you know of such a procedure, be sure to follow it.

57a

3 ■ Writing a job application and résumé

In applying for a job or requesting a job interview, send both a résumé and a cover letter. If you need to submit your application electronically, see page 899.

The cover letter

The cover letter should follow the format guidelines on pages 893–95 and the content guidelines below. See the sample letter on the next page.

- *Interpret your résumé for the particular job.* Don't detail your entire résumé, reciting your job history. Instead, highlight and reshape only the relevant parts.
- *Announce at the outset what job you seek and how you heard about it.*

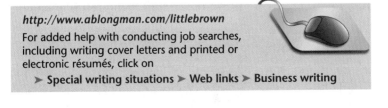

http://www.ablongman.com/littlebrown
For added help with conducting job searches, including writing cover letters and printed or electronic résumés, click on
➤ **Special writing situations** ➤ **Web links** ➤ **Business writing**

Job-application letter in modified block style

3712 Swiss Avenue
Dallas, TX 75204
March 2, 2003

Raymond Chipault
Human Resources Manager
Dallas News
Communications Center
Dallas, TX 75222

Dear Mr. Chipault:

In response to your posting in the English Department of Southern Methodist University, I am applying for the summer job of part-time editorial assistant for the *Dallas News*.

I am now enrolled at Southern Methodist University as a sophomore, with a dual major in English literature and journalism. My courses so far have included news reporting, copy editing, and electronic publishing. I worked a summer as a copy aide for my hometown newspaper, and for two years I have edited and written sports stories and features for the university newspaper. My feature articles cover subjects as diverse as campus elections, parking regulations, visiting professors, and speech codes.

As the enclosed résumé and writing samples indicate, my education and practical knowledge of newspaper work prepare me for the opening you have.

I am available for an interview at your convenience and would be happy to show more samples of my writing. Please e-mail me at ianirv@mail.smu.edu or call me at 214-744-3816.

Sincerely,

Ian M. Irvine

Ian M. Irvine

Enc.

57a

- *Include any special reason you have for applying,* such as a specific career goal.
- *Summarize your qualifications for this particular job,* including relevant facts about education and employment and emphasizing notable accomplishments. Mention that additional information appears in an accompanying résumé.
- *Describe your availability.* At the end of the letter, mention that you are free for an interview at the convenience of the addressee, or specify when you will be available (for instance, when your current job or classes leave you free).

The résumé

For the résumé that accompanies your letter of application, you can use the guidelines below and on page 902 as well as the samples on the next two pages.

- *Provide the appropriate information in table form:* your name and address, career objective, education, employment history, any special skills or awards, and information about how to obtain your references.
- *Use headings to mark the various sections of the résumé.* Space around the headings and within sections so that important information stands out.
- *Use capital letters conventionally.* Keep in mind that passages with many capitals can be hard to read. Definitely use capitals for proper nouns (pp. 520–22), but consider dropping them for job titles, course names, department names, and the like.
- *Limit your résumé to one page* so that it can be quickly reviewed. However, if your experience and education are extensive, a two-page résumé is preferable to a single cramped, unreadable page.
- *For a printed résumé, use techniques of document design.* Readable type fonts, lists, and some other elements discussed on pages 203–12 can make your résumé clearer and more attractive.

Employers often want an electronic version of a résumé so that they can add it to a computerized database of applicants. The employers may scan your printed résumé to convert it to an electronic file, or they may request electronic copy from you in the first place. If you think a potential employer may use an electronic version of your résumé, follow these additional guidelines:

- *Keep the design simple for accurate scanning or electronic transmittal.* Avoid images, unusual type, more than one column, vertical or horizontal lines, and highlighting (boldface, italic, or

(Text continues on p. 902)

57a

Résumé (traditional design)

Ian M. Irvine
3712 Swiss Avenue
Dallas, TX 75204
214-744-3816
ianirv@mail.smu.edu

POSITION DESIRED

Part-time editorial assistant.

EDUCATION

Southern Methodist University, 2001 to present.
Current standing: sophomore.
Major: English literature and journalism.
Journalism courses: news reporting, copy editing, electronic
publishing, communications arts, broadcast journalism.

Abilene (Texas) Senior High School, 1997-2001.
Graduated with academic, college-preparatory degree.

EMPLOYMENT HISTORY

2001 to present. Reporter, *Daily Campus*, student newspaper
of Southern Methodist University.
Write regular coverage of baseball, track, and soccer teams.
Write feature stories on campus policies and events. Edit
sports news, campus listings, features.

Summer 2002. Copy aide, *Abilene Reporter-News*.
Routed copy, ran errands, and assisted reporters with research.

Summer 2001. Painter, Longhorn Painters, Abilene.
Prepared and painted exteriors and interiors of houses.

SPECIAL SKILLS

Fluent in Spanish.
Proficient in Internet research and word processing.

REFERENCES

Available on request:

Placement Office
Southern Methodist University
Dallas, TX 75275

57a

Résumé (contemporary design)

Ian M. Irvine

3712 Swiss Avenue
Dallas, TX 75204
214-744-3816
ianirv@mail.smu.edu

Position desired   Part-time editorial assistant.

Education   *Southern Methodist University,* 2001 to present.
Current standing: sophomore.
Major: English literature and journalism.
Journalism courses: news reporting, copy editing,
electronic publishing, communications arts, broad-
cast journalism.

Abilene (Texas) Senior High School, 1997-2001.
Graduated with academic, college-preparatory
degree.

Employment history   2001 to present. Reporter, *Daily Campus,* student
newspaper of Southern Methodist University.
Write regular coverage of baseball, track, and soccer teams. Write feature stories on campus policies
and events. Edit sports news, campus listings,
features.

Summer 2002. Copy aide, *Abilene Reporter-News.*
Routed copy, ran errands, and assisted reporters
with research.

Summer 2001. Painter, Longhorn Painters, Abilene.
Prepared and painted exteriors and interiors of
houses.

Special skills   Fluent in Spanish.
Proficient in Internet research and word processing.

References   Available on request:

Placement Office
Southern Methodist University
Dallas, TX 75275

57a

(Continued from p. 899)

underlining). If its italics were removed, the traditionally designed sample on page 900 could probably be scanned or transmitted electronically. The two-column sample on page 901 perhaps could not.

- *Use concise, specific words to describe your skills and experience.* The employer's computer may use keywords (often nouns) to identify the résumés of suitable job candidates, and you want to ensure that your résumé includes the appropriate keywords. Name your specific skills—for example, the computer programs you can operate—and write concretely with words like *manager* (not *person with responsibility for*) and *reporter* (not *staff member who reports*). Look for likely keywords in the employer's description of the job you seek.

57b Writing business memos

Unlike business letters, which address people in other organizations, business memorandums (memos, for short) address people within the same organization. A memo can be quite long, but more often it deals briefly with a specific topic, such as an answer to a question, a progress report, or an evaluation. Both the content and the format of a memo aim to get to the point and dispose of it quickly, as indicated below and in the sample opposite.

Content

- *State your reason for writing in the first sentence.* You might outline a problem, make a request, refer to a request that prompted the memo, or briefly summarize new findings. Do not, however, waste words with expressions like "The purpose of this memo is. . . ."
- *Devote the first paragraph to a succinct presentation of your solution, recommendation, answer, or evaluation.* The first paragraph should be short, and by its end your reader should know precisely what to expect from the rest of the memo: the details and reasoning that support your conclusion.
- *Deliver the support in the body of the memo.* The paragraphs may be numbered or bulleted so that the main divisions of your

---

http://www.ablongman.com/littlebrown
For added help with writing memos,
click on
➤ **Special writing situations** ➤ **Web links** ➤ **Business writing**

Bigelow Wax Company

TO: Aileen Rosen, Director of Sales
FROM: Patricia Phillips, Territory 12 *PP*
DATE: March 17, 2003
SUBJECT: 2002 sales of Quick Wax in Territory 12

Since it was introduced in January 2002, Quick Wax has been unsuccessful in Territory 12 and has not affected the sales of our Easy Shine. Discussions with customers and my own analysis of Quick Wax suggest three reasons for its failure to compete with our product.

1. Quick Wax has not received the promotion necessary for a new product. Advertising—primarily on radio—has been sporadic and has not developed a clear, consistent image for the product. In addition, the Quick Wax sales representative in Territory 12 is new and inexperienced; he is not known to customers, and his sales pitch (which I once overheard) is weak. As far as I can tell, his efforts are not supported by phone calls or mailings from his home office.

2. When Quick Wax does make it to the store shelves, buyers do not choose it over our product. Though priced competitively with our product, Quick Wax is poorly packaged. The container seems smaller than ours, though in fact it holds the same eight ounces. The lettering on the Quick Wax package (red on blue) is difficult to read, in contrast to the white-on-green lettering on the Easy Shine package.

3. Our special purchase offers and my increased efforts to serve existing customers have had the intended effect of keeping customers satisfied with our product and reducing their inclination to stock something new.

Copies: L. Mendes, Director of Marketing
J. MacGregor, Customer Service Manager

57b

message are easy to see. In a long memo, you may need headings (see pp. 206–07).

- *Suit your style and tone to your audience.* For instance, you'll want to address your boss or a large group of readers more formally than you would a coworker who is also a friend.
- *Write concisely.* Keep your sentences short and your language simple, using technical terms only when your readers will understand them. Say only what readers need to know.

Format

- *Use a conventional memo heading.* A memo has no return address, inside address, salutation, or close. Instead, as shown in the sample memo on the previous page, the heading typically consists of the company's name, the addressee's name, the writer's name, the date, and a subject description or title.
- *Type the body single-spaced.* Double-space between paragraphs, and do not indent paragraphs.
- *Initial your name in the heading.* Otherwise, do not sign the memo.
- *List any recipients of copies.* If you're sending copies of the memo to people not included in the "TO" line, list those people two spaces below the last line.

Note See page 213 for a sample of a business report, which is more formal in expression and format than a memo.

57c Communicating electronically

Communicating via electronic devices, especially electronic mail and fax machines, speeds up correspondence but also creates new challenges. E-mail now plays such a prominent role in communication of all sorts that we discuss it extensively as part of essential computer skills (see pp. 192–96). Generally, the standards for business e-mail are the same as for other business correspondence.

Faxes follow closely the formats of print documents, whether letters (p. 893) or memos (p. 902). But there are some unique concerns:

- *Consider legibility.* Small type, photographs, horizontal lines, and other elements that look fine on your copy may not be legible to the addressee.
- *Include a cover sheet.* Most faxes require a cover sheet with fax-specific information: the addressee's name, company, and fax number; the date, time, and subject; your own name and fax and telephone numbers (the telephone number is important in case something goes wrong with the transmission); and the total number of pages (including the cover sheet) in the fax.
- *Advise your addressee to expect a fax.* Fax transmissions can go astray. The advice is essential if the fax is confidential because the machine is often shared.
- *Consider urgency.* Transmission by fax can imply that the correspondence is urgent. If yours isn't, you may want to use the mail instead. (Swamping your correspondents with needless faxes can make you the child who cried wolf when you really have an urgent message to transmit.)

CHAPTER 58

Oral Presentations

At some point during your education or your work, you will probably be called upon to speak to a group. Oral presentation can be anxiety producing, even for those who are experienced at it. This chapter shows you how you can apply your experiences as a writer to public speaking, and it offers some techniques that are uniquely appropriate for effective oral presentations.

58a Writing and speaking

Writing and speechmaking have much in common: both require careful consideration of your subject, purpose, and audience. Thus the mental and physical activities that go into the writing process can also help you prepare and deliver a successful oral presentation.

Despite many similarities, however, writing for readers is not the same as speaking to listeners. Whereas a reader can go back and reread a written message, a listener cannot stop a speech to rehear a section. Several studies have reported that immediately after hearing a short talk, most listeners cannot recall half of what was said.

Effective speakers adapt to their audience's listening ability by reinforcing their ideas through repetition and restatement. They use simple words, short sentences, personal pronouns, contractions, and colloquial expressions. In formal writing, these strategies might seem redundant and too informal; but in speaking, they improve listeners' comprehension.

http://www.ablongman.com/littlebrown
For added help with oral presentations, click on
➤ **Special writing situations**
  ➤ **Video tutorials**
    ➤ **Designing a *PowerPoint* presentation**
  ➤ **Web links**
    ➤ **Oral presentations**
    ➤ **Collections of effective speeches**

Checklist for an oral presentation

- **Purpose:** What do you want your audience to know or do as a result of your presentation? How can you achieve your purpose in the time and setting you've been given? (See below.)
- **Audience:** What do you know about the characteristics and opinions of your audience? How can this information help you adapt your presentation to your audience's interests, needs, and opinions? (See below.)
- **Organization and content:** How are your ideas arranged? Where might listeners have difficulty following you? What functions do your introduction and conclusion perform? How relevant and interesting is your supporting material for your topic and your audience? (See opposite.)
- **Method of delivery:** What method of delivery do you plan: extemporaneous? reading from a text? memorized? a mixture? How does your method suit the purpose, setting, and occasion of your presentation? (See pp. 909–10.)
- **Vocal and physical delivery:** In rehearsing your presentation, what do you perceive as your strengths and weaknesses? Is your voice suitably loud for the setting? Are you speaking clearly? Are you able to move your eyes around the room so that you'll be making eye contact during the presentation? Is your posture straight but not stiff? Do your gestures reinforce your ideas? Do you use visual aids appropriately? (See pp. 910–12.)
- **Confidence and credibility:** What techniques will you use to overcome the inevitable anxiety about speaking? How will you project your confidence and competence? (See pp. 912–13.)

58b

58b Considering purpose and audience

The most important step in developing an oral presentation is to identify your purpose: what do you want your audience to know or do as a result of your speech? Topic and purpose are *not* the same thing. Asking "What am I talking about?" is not the same as asking "Why am I speaking?"

In school and work settings, oral presentations may include anything from a five-minute report before a few peers to an hour-long address before a hundred people. Whatever the situation, you're likely to be speaking for the same reasons that you write in school or at work: to explain something to listeners or to persuade listeners to accept your opinion or take an action. See pages 13–14 for more on these purposes.

Adapting to your audience is a critical task in public speaking as well as in writing. You'll want to consider the questions about audience on page 10. But a listening audience requires additional considerations as well:

- *Why is your audience assembled?* Is it because these people want to hear you, because they are interested in your topic, because they have been required to attend, or because they always meet in this time and place? Listeners who are required to attend may be more difficult to interest and motivate than listeners who attend because they want to hear you and your ideas.
- *How large is your audience?* With a small group you can be informal. If you are speaking to a hundred or more people, you may need a public address system, a lectern, special lighting, and audiovisual equipment.
- *Where will you speak?* Your approach should match the setting—more casual for a small classroom, more formal for an auditorium. If the room is large and the audience small, you may ask the audience to fill in the front section of the room.
- *How long are you scheduled to speak and when?* A long speech early in the morning or late in the afternoon may find your audience too sleepy to listen well. And keep in mind that audiences lose patience with someone who speaks longer than the assigned time.

When speaking, unlike when writing, you can see and hear your audience's responses during your presentation. Thus you have the luxury and challenge of adapting your presentation to an audience as you speak. If you sense that an audience is bored, try to spice up your presentation. If an audience is restless, consult your watch to make sure you have not gone overtime. If you sense resistance, try to make midspeech adjustments to respond to that resistance.

58c

58c Organizing the presentation

An effective oral presentation, like an effective essay, has a recognizable shape. The arrangement of sections guides listeners through a presentation and helps them see how ideas and details are related to each other. The advice in Chapter 2 for organizing and outlining an essay serves the speechmaker as well as the writer (see pp. 35–45). Here are additional considerations for the introduction, conclusion, and supporting material.

1 ■ The introduction

First impressions count. A strong beginning establishes an important relationship among three elements in an oral presentation: you, your topic, and your audience. More specifically, the beginning of an oral presentation should try to accomplish three goals:

- *Gain the audience's attention and interest.* When you begin to speak, your listeners may not be ready to pay attention: they may be talking to neighbors or be preoccupied with other thoughts. To attract listeners' attention, begin with a question, an unusual example or statistic, or a short, relevant story.
- *Put yourself in the speech.* If you demonstrate your expertise, experience, or concern, your audience will be more interested in what you say and more trusting of you.
- *Introduce and preview your topic and purpose.* By the time your introduction is over, listeners should know what your topic is and the direction in which you wish to take them as you develop your ideas. This information will give them expectations for your speech on which they can pin the specific points that follow.

In addition to these guidelines for beginning a speech, there are some important pitfalls to avoid:

- *Don't try to cram too much into your introduction.* Giving only a sneak preview of your speech can pique your audience's curiosity about what you have to say.
- *Don't begin with an apology.* A statement such as "I wish I'd been given more time to get ready for this presentation" will only undermine your listeners' confidence in you.
- *Don't begin with "My speech is about. . . ."* The statement is dull, and it does little to clarify purpose.

2 ▪ Supporting material

Just as you do when writing, you can and should use facts, statistics, examples, and expert opinions to support spoken arguments (see pp. 147–49). In addition, as a speaker you can draw on other kinds of supporting material:

- *Use vivid description.* Paint a mental image of a scene, a concept, an event, or a person.
- *Use well-chosen quotations.* They can add an emotional or humorous moment to your speech.
- *Use true or fictional stories.* A narrative can rivet the audience's attention and illustrate your point. Most listeners remember a good story long after they have forgotten other details from a speech.
- *Use analogies.* Comparisons between essentially unlike things, such as a politician and a tightrope walker, link concepts memorably. (For more on analogy, see p. 98.)

Use a variety of supporting material in your speech. A presentation that is nothing but statistics can bore an audience. Nonstop storytelling may interest listeners but fail to achieve your purpose.

58c

3 ▪ The conclusion

Last impressions count as much as first impressions. You may hope that listeners will remember every detail of your speech, but they are more likely to leave with a general impression and a few ideas about you and your message. You want your conclusion to be clear, of course, but you also want it to be memorable. Remind listeners of how your topic and main idea connect to their needs and interests. If your speech was motivational, tap an emotion that matches your message. If your speech was informational, give some tips on how to remember important details.

58d Delivering the presentation

Writing and speaking differ most obviously in the form of delivery: the writer is represented in print; the speaker is represented in person. This section describes the methods and techniques of oral presentation as well as some ways of coping with stage fright.

58d

1 ▪ Methods of delivery

An oral presentation may be delivered impromptu, extemporaneously, from a text, or from memory. No one technique is best for all speeches; indeed, a single speech may include two or more forms or even all four—perhaps a memorized introduction, an extemporaneous body in which quotations are read from a text, and an impromptu response to audience questions during or after the speech.

Speaking impromptu

Impromptu means "without preparation": an impromptu presentation is one you deliver off-the-cuff, with no planning or practice. You may be called on in a class to express your opinion or to summarize something you've written. You may speak up at a neighborhood meeting. An audience member may ask you a question at the end of an oral presentation. The only way to prepare for such incidents is to be well prepared in general—to be caught up on course reading, for instance, or to know the facts in a debate.

Speaking extemporaneously

Extemporaneous speaking—that done with some preparation, but without reading from a text—is the most common form of presentation, typical of class lectures and business briefings. With extemporaneous speaking, you have time to prepare and practice in advance. Then, instead of following a script of every word, you speak from notes that guide you through the presentation. You can look and sound natural while still covering all the material you want to convey.

Speaking from a text

Delivering a presentation from a text involves writing the text out in advance and then reading aloud from it. With a text in front of you, you're unlikely to lose your way. However, a reading speaker can be dull for an audience. Try to avoid this form of delivery for an entire presentation.

If you do use a text, write it so that it sounds spoken (less formal) rather than written (more formal): for instance, the sentence *Although costs rose, profits remained steady* would sound fine in writing but stiff and awkward in speech because in conversation we rarely use such a structure. In addition, rehearse thoroughly so that you can read with expression and can look up frequently to make eye contact with listeners (see the facing page).

Speaking from memory

58d

A memorized presentation has a distinct advantage: complete freedom from notes or a text. That means you can look at your audience every minute and can move away from a lectern and even into the audience. However, you may be like most speakers in seeming less relaxed, not more relaxed, when presenting from memory: your mind is too busy retrieving the next words to attend to the responses of the audience. Further, you risk forgetting your place or a whole passage.

For these reasons, many experts discourage memorization. At least reserve the method for the introduction, perhaps, or some other part with which you want to make a strong impression. Rehearse not only to memorize the words but, beyond that, to deliver the words fresh, as if for the first time.

2 ■ Vocal delivery

The sound of your voice will influence how your listeners receive you. When rehearsing, consider volume, speed, and articulation.

- *Speak loudly.* In a meeting with five other people, you can speak in a normal volume. As your audience grows in size, so should your volume. Most speakers can project to as many as a hundred people, but a larger audience may require a microphone. If you can rehearse in the room where you'll be speaking, ask a friend or colleague to sit at the back and tell you what volume is easy to hear. It may seem like shouting to you, but to your audience it will sound confident and clear.
- *Speak slowly enough to be understandable.* Most audiences prefer speech that's a little fast, around 150 words a minute; but

they have difficulty following too-rapid speech at, say, 190 words a minute.

- *Speak clearly and correctly.* To avoid mumbling or slurring words, practice articulating. Sometimes it helps to open your mouth a little wider than usual. And to avoid mispronouncing words and names, look up questionable ones or ask someone for the correct pronunciation. (See also the next page for tips on practicing your presentation.)

3 ■ Physical delivery

You are more than your spoken words when you make an oral presentation. Your face and body also play a role in how your speech is received.

- *Make eye contact with listeners.* Looking directly in your listeners' eyes conveys your honesty, your confidence, and your control of your material. Don't look above the heads of the audience or at one friendly face. Instead, move your gaze around the entire room, settle on someone, and establish direct eye contact; then move on to someone else.
- *Stand up.* Always stand for a presentation, unless it takes place in a small room where standing would be inappropriate. You can see more audience members when you stand, and they in turn can hear your voice and see your gestures more clearly.
- *Stand straight, and move around.* Turn your body toward one side of the room and the other, step out from behind any lectern or desk, and gesture appropriately, as you would in conversation. Let your gestures and movement support and draw attention to important words and ideas.

58d

4 ■ Visual aids

You can supplement an oral presentation with visual aids such as posters, models, slides, or videos. Visual aids can emphasize key points, organize interrelated concepts, and illustrate complex procedures. They can gain the attention of listeners and improve their understanding and memory. With the *PowerPoint* software program, you can integrate visual aids with your speaking notes distilled as pointers for the audience. (Learn about using *PowerPoint* at this book's Web site: see the box on p. 905.)

The following guidelines can help you create effective and appropriate visual aids:

- *Use visual aids to underscore your points.* Short lists of key ideas, illustrations such as graphs or photographs, or objects such as models can make your presentation more interesting and memorable. But use visual aids judiciously: a battery of illustrations or objects will bury your message rather than amplify it.

- *Match visual aids and setting.* An audience of five people may be able to see a photograph and share a chart; an audience of a hundred will need projected images.
- *Coordinate visual aids with your message.* Time each visual aid to reinforce a point you're making. Tell listeners what they're looking at—what they should be getting from the aid. Give them enough viewing time so they don't mind turning their attention back to you.
- *Show visual aids only while they're needed.* To regain your audience's attention, remove or turn off any aid as soon as you have finished with it.

5 ▪ Practice

58d

Practicing an oral presentation is the speechmaker's equivalent of editing and proofreading a written text. You won't gain much by practicing silently in your head; instead, you need to rehearse out loud, with the notes you will be using. For your initial rehearsals, you can gauge your performance by making an audio- or videotape of yourself or by practicing in front of a mirror. A recording will let you hear mumbling, too-rapid delivery, grammatical errors, mispronounced words, and unclear concepts. A mirror or video will reveal your stance, your gestures, and your eye contact. Any of these practice techniques will tell you if your presentation is running too long or too short.

If you plan to use visual aids, you'll need to practice with them, too, preferably in the room where you'll make the presentation and certainly with the help of anyone who will be assisting you. Your goal is to eliminate hitches (upside-down slides, missing charts) and to weave the visuals seamlessly into your presentation.

6 ▪ Stage fright

Many people report that speaking in front of an audience is their number-one fear. Even many experienced and polished speakers have some anxiety about delivering an oral presentation, but they use this nervous energy to their advantage, letting it propel them into working hard on each presentation, preparing well in advance, and rehearsing until they're satisfied with their delivery. They know that once they begin speaking and concentrating on their ideas, enthusiasm will quell anxiety. They know, too, that the symptoms of anxiety are usually imperceptible to listeners, who cannot see or hear a racing heart, upset stomach, cold hands, and worried thoughts. Even speakers who describe themselves as nervous usually appear confident and calm to their audiences.

Several techniques can help you reduce your level of anxiety:

- *Use simple relaxation exercises.* Deep breathing or tensing and relaxing your stomach muscles can ease some of the physical symptoms of speech anxiety—stomachache, rapid heartbeat, and shaky hands, legs, and voice.
- *Think positively.* Try to convert any negative and irrational thoughts about speaking into positive ones about yourself and your behavior. Instead of worrying about the mistakes you might make, concentrate on how well you've prepared and practiced your presentation and how significant your ideas are.
- *Don't avoid opportunities to speak in public.* Practice and experience build speaking skills and offer the best insurance for success.

58d

Glossary of Usage

This glossary provides notes on words or phrases that often cause problems for writers. The recommendations for standard American English are based on current dictionaries and usage guides such as the ones listed on pp. 573–76. Items labeled **nonstandard** should be avoided in academic and business settings. Those labeled **colloquial** and **slang** occur in speech and in some informal writing but are best avoided in formal college and business writing. (Words and phrases labeled *colloquial* include those labeled by many dictionaries with the equivalent term *informal*.) See Chapters 38 and 39 for further discussion of word choice and for exercises in usage. See p. 578 for a description of dictionary labels. Also see pp. 590–91 for a list of commonly confused words that are pronounced the same or similarly. The words and definitions provided there supplement this glossary.

The glossary is necessarily brief. Keep a dictionary handy for all your writing, and make a habit of referring to it whenever you doubt the appropriateness of a word or phrase.

a, an   Use *a* before words beginning with consonant sounds, including those spelled with an initial pronounced *h* and those spelled with vowels that are sounded as consonants: *a historian, a one-o'clock class, a university.* Use *an* before words that begin with vowel sounds, including those spelled with an initial silent *h: an orgy, an L, an honor.*

The article before an abbreviation depends on how the abbreviation is read: *She was once an AEC undersecretary (AEC* is read as three separate letters); *Many Americans opposed a SALT treaty (SALT* is read as one word, *salt).*

For the use of *a/an* versus *the,* see pp. 340–43.

accept, except   *Accept* is a verb meaning "receive." *Except* is usually a preposition or conjunction meaning "but for" or "other than"; when it is used as a verb, it means "leave out." *I can accept all your suggestions except the last one. I'm sorry you excepted my last suggestion from your list.*

adverse, averse   *Adverse* and *averse* both mean "opposed" or "hostile." But *averse* describes the subject's opposition to something, whereas *adverse* describes something opposed to the subject: *The President was averse to adverse criticism.*

advice, advise   *Advice* is a noun, and *advise* is a verb: *Take my advice; do as I advise you.*

affect, effect   Usually *affect* is a verb, meaning "to influence," and *effect* is a noun, meaning "result": *The drug did not affect his driving; in* *fact, it seemed to have no effect at all.* But *effect* occasionally is used as a verb meaning "to bring about": *Her efforts effected a change.* And *affect* is used in psychology as a noun meaning "feeling or emotion": *One can infer much about affect from behavior.*

aggravate   *Aggravate* should not be used in its colloquial meaning of "irritate" or "exasperate" (for example, *We were aggravated by her constant arguing*). *Aggravate* means "make worse": *The President was irritated by the Senate's indecision because he feared any delay might aggravate the unrest in the Middle East.*

agree to, agree with   *Agree to* means "consent to," and *agree with* means "be in accord with": *How can they agree to a treaty when they don't agree with each other about the terms?*

ain't   Nonstandard for *am not, isn't,* or *aren't.*

all, all of   Usually *all* is sufficient to modify a noun: *all my loving, all the things you are.* Before a pronoun or proper noun, *all of* is usually appropriate: *all of me, in all of France.*

all ready, already   *All ready* means "completely prepared," and *already* means "by now" or "before now": *We were all ready to go to the movie, but it had already started.*

all right   *All right* is always two words. *Alright* is a common misspelling.

all together, altogether   *All together* means "in unison" or "gathered in one place." *Altogether* means "entirely." *It's not altogether true that our family never spends vacations all together.*

allusion, illusion   An *allusion* is an indirect reference, and an *illusion* is a deceptive appearance: *Paul's constant allusions to Shakespeare created the illusion that he was an intellectual.*

almost, most   *Almost* means "nearly"; *most* means "the greater number (or part) of." In formal writing, *most* should not be used as a substitute for *almost: We see each other almost* [not *most*] *every day.*

a lot   *A lot* is always two words, used informally to mean "many." *Alot* is a common misspelling.

among, between   Use *among* for relationships involving more than two people or things. Use *between* for relationships involving only two or for comparing one thing to a group to which it belongs. *The four of them agreed among themselves that the choice was between New York and Los Angeles.*

amongst   Although common in British English, in American English *amongst* is an overrefined substitute for *among.*

amount, number   Use *amount* with a singular noun that names something not countable (a noncount noun): *The amount of food varies.* Use *number* with a plural noun that names more than one of something countable (a plural count noun): *The number of calories must stay the same.*

an, and   *An* is an article (see *a, an*). *And* is a coordinating conjunction.

and etc. *Et cetera* (*etc.*) means "and the rest"; *and etc.* therefore is redundant. See also *et al., etc.*

and/or *And/or* indicates three options: one or the other or both (*The decision is made by the mayor and/or the council*). If you mean all three options, *and/or* is appropriate. Otherwise, use *and* if you mean both, *or* if you mean either.

and which, and who *And which* or *and who* is correct only when used to introduce a second clause beginning with the same relative pronoun: *Jill is my cousin who goes to school here and who calls me constantly.* Otherwise, *and* is not needed: *WCAS is my favorite AM radio station, which* [not *and which*] *I listen to every morning.*

ante-, anti- The prefix *ante-* means "before" (*antedate, antebellum*); *anti-* means "against" (*antiwar, antinuclear*). Before a capital letter or *i*, *anti-* takes a hyphen: *anti-Freudian, anti-isolationist.*

anxious, eager *Anxious* means "nervous" or "worried" and is usually followed by *about. Eager* means "looking forward" and is usually followed by *to. I've been anxious about getting blisters. I'm eager* [not *anxious*] *to get new running shoes.*

anybody, any body; anyone, any one *Anybody* and *anyone* are indefinite pronouns; *any body* is a noun modified by *any; any one* is a pronoun or adjective modified by *any. How can anybody communicate with any body of government? Can anyone help Amy? She has more work than any one person can handle.*

any more, anymore *Any more* means "no more"; *anymore* means "now." Both are used in negative constructions: *He doesn't want any more. She doesn't live here anymore.*

anyplace Colloquial for *anywhere.*

anyways, anywheres Nonstandard for *anyway* and *anywhere.*

apt, liable, likely *Apt* and *likely* are interchangeable. Strictly speaking, though, *apt* means "having a tendency to": *Horace is apt to forget his lunch in the morning. Likely* means "probably going to": *Horace is leaving so early today that he's likely to catch the first bus.*

   Liable normally means "in danger of" and should be confined to situations with undesirable consequences: *Horace is liable to trip over that hose.* Strictly, *liable* means "responsible" or "exposed to": *The owner will be liable for Horace's injuries.*

are, is Use *are* with a plural subject (*books are*), *is* with a singular subject (*book is*).

as Substituting for *because, since,* or *while, as* may be vague or ambiguous: *As we were stopping to rest, we decided to eat lunch.* (Does *as* mean "while" or "because"?) *As* should never be used as a substitute for *whether* or *who. I'm not sure whether* [not *as*] *we can make it. That's the man who* [not *as*] *gave me directions.*

as, like See *like, as.*

as, than In comparisons, *as* and *than* precede a subjective-case pronoun when the pronoun is a subject: *I love you more than he* [*loves you*].

As and *than* precede an objective-case pronoun when the pronoun is an object: *I love you as much as* [*I love*] *him.* (See also p. 279.)

assure, ensure, insure   *Assure* means "to promise": *He assured us that we would miss the traffic. Ensure* and *insure* often are used interchangeably to mean "make certain," but some reserve *insure* for matters of legal and financial protection and use *ensure* for more general meanings: *We left early to ensure that we would miss the traffic. It's expensive to insure yourself against floods.*

as to   A stuffy substitute for *about: The suspect was questioned about* [not *as to*] *her actions.*

at   The use of *at* after *where* is wordy and should be avoided: *Where are you meeting him?* is preferable to *Where are you meeting him at?*

at this point in time   Wordy for *now, at this point,* or *at this time.*

averse, adverse   See *adverse, averse.*

awful, awfully   Strictly speaking, *awful* means "awe-inspiring." As intensifiers meaning "very" or "extremely" (*He tried awfully hard*), *awful* and *awfully* should be avoided in formal speech or writing.

a while, awhile   *Awhile* is an adverb; *a while* is an article and a noun. Thus *awhile* can modify a verb but cannot serve as the object of a preposition, and *a while* is just the opposite: *I will be gone awhile* [not *a while*]. *I will be gone for a while* [not *awhile*].

bad, badly   In formal speech and writing, *bad* should be used only as an adjective; the adverb is *badly. He felt bad because his tooth ached badly.* In *He felt bad,* the verb *felt* is a linking verb and the adjective *bad* is a subject complement. (See also pp. 334–35.)

being as, being that   Colloquial for *because,* the preferable word in formal speech or writing: *Because* [not *Being as*] *the world is round, Columbus never did fall off the edge.*

beside, besides   *Beside* is a preposition meaning "next to." *Besides* is a preposition meaning "except" or "in addition to" as well as an adverb meaning "in addition." *Besides, several other people besides you want to sit beside Dr. Christensen.*

better, had better   *Had better* (meaning "ought to") is a verb modified by an adverb. The verb is necessary and should not be omitted: *You had better* [not just *better*] *go.*

between, among   See *among, between.*

bring, take   Use *bring* only for movement from a farther place to a nearer one and *take* for any other movement. *First, take these books to the library for renewal, then take them to Mr. Daniels. Bring them back to me when he's finished.*

bunch   In formal speech and writing, *bunch* (as a noun) should be used only to refer to clusters of things growing or fastened together, such as bananas and grapes. Its use to mean a group of items or people is colloquial; *crowd* or *group* is preferable.

Usage

burst, bursted; bust, busted   *Burst* is a standard verb form meaning "to fly apart suddenly." Its main forms are *burst, burst, burst;* the form *bursted* is nonstandard. The verb *bust* (*busted*) is slang.

but, hardly, scarcely   These words are negative in their own right; using *not* with any of them produces a double negative (see p. 338). *We have but* [not *haven't got but*] *an hour before our plane leaves. I could hardly* [not *couldn't hardly*] *make out her face.*

but, however, yet   Each of these words is adequate to express contrast. Don't combine them. *He said he had finished, yet* [not *but yet*] *he continued.*

but that, but what   These wordy substitutes for *that* and *what* should be avoided: *I don't doubt that* [not *but that*] *you are right.*

calculate, figure, reckon   As substitutes for *expect* or *imagine* (*I figure I'll go*), these words are colloquial.

can, may   Strictly, *can* indicates capacity or ability, and *may* indicates permission: *If I may talk with you a moment, I believe I can solve your problem. May* also indicates possibility: *You may like what you hear.*

can't help but   This idiom is common but redundant. Either *I can't help wishing* or the more formal *I cannot but wish* is preferable to *I can't help but wish.*

case, instance, line   Expressions such as *in the case of, in the instance of,* and *along the lines of* are usually unnecessary padding and should be avoided.

censor, censure   To *censor* is to edit or remove from public view on moral or some other grounds; to *censure* is to give a formal scolding. *The lieutenant was censured by Major Taylor for censoring the letters her soldiers wrote home from boot camp.*

center around   *Center on* is more logical than, and preferable to, *center around.*

climatic, climactic   *Climatic* comes from *climate* and refers to weather: *Last winter's temperatures may indicate a climatic change. Climactic* comes from *climax* and refers to a dramatic high point: *During the climactic duel between Hamlet and Laertes, Gertrude drinks poisoned wine.*

complement, compliment   To *complement* something is to add to, complete, or reinforce it: *Her yellow blouse complemented her black hair.* To *compliment* something is to make a flattering remark about it: *He complimented her on her hair. Compliment* also functions as a noun: *She thanked him for the compliment.* The adjective *complimentary* can also mean "free": *complimentary tickets.*

compose, comprise   *Compose* means "to make up": *The parts compose the whole. Comprise* means "to consist of": *The whole comprises the parts.* Thus, *The band comprises* [not *is comprised of*] *twelve musicians. Twelve musicians compose* [not *comprise*] *the band.*

conscience, conscious   *Conscience* is a noun meaning "a sense of right and wrong"; *conscious* is an adjective meaning "aware" or "awake." *Though I was barely conscious, my conscience nagged me.*

contact   Often used imprecisely as a verb instead of a more exact word such as *consult, talk with, telephone,* or *write to.*

continual, continuous   *Continual* means "constantly recurring": *Most movies on television are continually interrupted by commercials.* *Continuous* means "unceasing": *Some cable channels present movies continuously without commercials.*

convince, persuade   In the strictest sense, to *convince* someone means to change his or her opinion; to *persuade* someone means to move him or her to action. *Convince* is thus properly followed by *of* or *that,* whereas *persuade* is followed by *to*: *Once he convinced Othello of Desdemona's infidelity, Iago easily persuaded him to kill her.*

could care less   The expression is *could not* [*couldn't*] *care less. Could care less* indicates some care, the opposite of what is intended.

could of   See *have, of.*

couple of   Used colloquially to mean "a few" or "several."

credible, creditable, credulous   *Credible* means "believable": *It's a strange story, but it seems credible to me. Creditable* means "deserving of credit" or "worthy": *Steve gave a creditable performance. Credulous* means "gullible": *The credulous Claire believed Tim's lies.* See also *incredible, incredulous.*

criteria   The plural of *criterion* (meaning "standard for judgment"): *Our criteria are strict. The most important criterion is a sense of humor.*

data   The plural of *datum* (meaning "fact"): *Out of all the data generated by these experiments, not one datum supports our hypothesis.* Usually, a more common term such as *fact, result,* or *figure* is preferred to *datum.* Though *data* is often used as a singular noun, most careful writers still treat it as plural: *The data fail* [not *fails*] *to support the hypothesis.*

device, devise   *Device* is the noun, and *devise* is the verb: *Can you devise some device for getting his attention?*

different from, different than   *Different from* is preferred: *His purpose is different from mine.* But *different than* is widely accepted when a construction using *from* would be wordy: *I'm a different person now than I used to be* is preferable to *I'm a different person now from the person I used to be.*

differ from, differ with   To *differ from* is to be unlike: *The twins differ from each other only in their hair styles.* To *differ with* is to disagree with: *I have to differ with you on that point.*

discreet, discrete   *Discreet* (noun form *discretion*) means "tactful": *What's a discreet way of telling Maud to be quiet? Discrete* (noun form *discreteness*) means "separate and distinct": *Within a computer's memory are millions of discrete bits of information.*

disinterested, uninterested   *Disinterested* means "impartial": *We chose Pete, as a disinterested third party, to decide who was right. Uninterested* means "bored" or "lacking interest": *Unfortunately, Pete was completely uninterested in the question.*

Usage

don't   *Don't* is the contraction for *do not*, not for *does not: I don't care, you don't care,* and *he doesn't* [not *don't*] *care.*

due to   *Due* is an adjective or noun; thus *due to* is always acceptable as a subject complement: *His gray hairs were due to age.* Many object to *due to* as a preposition meaning "because of" (*Due to the holiday, class was canceled*). A rule of thumb is that *due to* is always correct after a form of the verb *be* but questionable otherwise.

due to the fact that   Wordy for *because.*

each and every   Wordy for *each* or *every.* Write *each one of us* or *every one of us,* not *each and every one of us.*

eager, anxious   See *anxious, eager.*

effect   See *affect, effect.*

elicit, illicit   *Elicit* is a verb meaning "bring out" or "call forth." *Illicit* is an adjective meaning "unlawful." *The crime elicited an outcry against illicit drugs.*

emigrate, immigrate   *Emigrate* means "to leave one place and move to another" (the Latin prefix *e-* means "out of": "migrate out of"): *The Chus emigrated from Korea. Immigrate* means "to move into a place where one was not born" (the Latin prefix *im-* means "into": "migrate into"): *They immigrated to the United States.*

ensure   See *assure, ensure, insure.*

enthused   Used colloquially as an adjective meaning "showing enthusiasm." The preferred adjective is *enthusiastic: The coach was enthusiastic* [not *enthused*] *about the team's victory.*

especially, specially   *Especially* means "particularly" or "more than other things"; *specially* means "for a specific reason." *I especially treasure my boots. They were made specially for me.*

et al., etc.   Use *et al.,* the Latin abbreviation for "and other people," only in source citations: *Jones et al.* Avoid *etc.,* the Latin abbreviation for "and other things," in formal writing, and do not use it to refer to people or to substitute for precision, as in *The government provides health care, etc.* See also *and etc.*

everybody, every body; everyone, every one   *Everybody* and *everyone* are indefinite pronouns: *Everybody* [or *Everyone*] *knows Tom steals. Every one* is a pronoun modified by *every,* and *every body* a noun modified by *every.* Both refer to each thing or person of a specific group and are typically followed by *of: The game commissioner has stocked every body of fresh water in the state with fish, and now every one of our rivers is a potential trout stream.*

everyday, every day   *Everyday* is an adjective meaning "used daily" or "common"; *every day* is a noun modified by *every: Everyday problems tend to arise every day.*

everywheres   Nonstandard for *everywhere.*

except   See *accept, except.*

except for the fact that Wordy for *except that*.

explicit, implicit *Explicit* means "stated outright": *I left explicit instructions. The movie contains explicit sex.* Implicit means "implied, unstated": *We had an implicit understanding. I trust Marcia implicitly.*

farther, further *Farther* refers to additional distance (*How much farther is it to the beach?*), and *further* refers to additional time, amount, or other abstract matters (*I don't want to discuss this any further*).

feel Avoid this word in place of *think* or *believe: She thinks* [not *feels*] *that the law should be changed.*

fewer, less *Fewer* refers to individual countable items (a plural count noun), *less* to general amounts (a noncount noun, always singular): *Skim milk has fewer calories than whole milk. We have less milk left than I thought.*

field The phrase *the field of* is wordy and generally unnecessary: *Margaret plans to specialize in* [not *in the field of*] *family medicine.*

figure See *calculate, figure, reckon.*

fixing to Avoid this colloquial substitute for "intend to": *The school intends* [not *is fixing*] *to build a new library.*

flaunt, flout *Flaunt* means "show off": *If you have style, flaunt it. Flout* means "scorn" or "defy": *Hester Prynne flouted convention and paid the price.*

flunk A colloquial substitute for *fail.*

former, latter *Former* refers to the first-named of two things, *latter* to the second-named: *I like both skiing and swimming, the former in the winter and the latter all year round.* To refer to the first- or last-named of three or more things, say *first* or *last: I like jogging, swimming, and hang gliding, but the last is inconvenient in the city.*

fun As an adjective, *fun* is colloquial and should be avoided in most writing: *It was a pleasurable* [not *fun*] *evening.*

further See *farther, further.*

get This common verb is used in many slang and colloquial expressions: *get lost, that really gets me, getting on. Get* is easy to overuse; watch out for it in expressions such as *it's getting better* (substitute *improving*) and *we got done* (substitute *finished*).

go As a substitute for *say* or *reply, go* is colloquial: *He says* [not *goes*], *"How do you do, madam?"*

good, well *Good* is an adjective, and *well* is nearly always an adverb: *Larry's a good dancer. He and Linda dance well together. Well* is properly used as an adjective only to refer to health: *You look well.* (*You look good*, in contrast, means "Your appearance is pleasing.")

good and Colloquial for "very": *I was very* [not *good and*] *tired.*

had better See *better, had better.*

had ought The *had* is unnecessary and should be omitted: *He ought* [not *had ought*] *to listen to his mother.*

half Either *half a* or *a half* is appropriate usage, but *a half a* is redundant: *Half a loaf* [not *A half a loaf*] *is better than none. I'd like a half-gallon* [not *a half a gallon*] *of mineral water, please.*

hanged, hung Though both are past-tense forms of *hang*, *hanged* is used to refer to executions and *hung* is used for all other meanings: *Tom Dooley was hanged* [not *hung*] *from a white oak tree. I hung* [not *hanged*] *the picture you gave me.*

hardly See *but, hardly, scarcely*.

have, of Use *have*, not *of*, after helping verbs such as *could, should, would, may,* and *might: You should have* [not *should of*] *told me.*

he, she; he/she Convention has allowed the use of *he* to mean "he or she": *After the infant learns to creep, he progresses to crawling.* However, many writers today consider this usage inaccurate and unfair because it seems to exclude females. The construction *he/she*, one substitute for *he*, is awkward and objectionable to most readers. The better choice is to make the pronoun plural, to rephrase, or, sparingly, to use *he or she*. For instance: *After infants learn to creep, they progress to crawling. After learning to creep, the infant progresses to crawling. After the infant learns to creep, he or she progresses to crawling.* (See also pp. 329–30 and 549.)

herself, himself See *myself, herself, himself, yourself*.

hisself Nonstandard for *himself*.

hopefully *Hopefully* means "with hope": *Freddy waited hopefully for a glimpse of Eliza.* The use of *hopefully* to mean "it is to be hoped," "I hope," or "let's hope" is now very common; but since many readers continue to object strongly to the usage, you should avoid it. *I hope* [not *Hopefully*] *the law will pass.*

idea, ideal An *idea* is a thought or conception. An *ideal* (noun) is a model of perfection or a goal. *Ideal* should not be used in place of *idea: The idea* [not *ideal*] *of the play is that our ideals often sustain us.*

if, whether For clarity, use *whether* rather than *if* when you are expressing an alternative: *If I laugh hard, people can't tell whether I'm crying.*

illicit See *elicit, illicit*.

illusion See *allusion, illusion*.

immigrate, emigrate See *emigrate, immigrate*.

impact Both the noun and the verb *impact* connote forceful or even violent collision. Avoid the increasingly common diluted meanings of *impact:* "an effect" (noun) or "to have an effect on" (verb). The diluted verb (*The budget cuts impacted social science research*) is bureaucratic jargon.

implicit See *explicit, implicit*.

imply, infer Writers or speakers *imply*, meaning "suggest": *Jim's letter implies he's having a good time.* Readers or listeners *infer*, meaning "conclude": *From Jim's letter I infer he's having a good time.*

in, into   *In* indicates location or condition: *He was in the garage. She was in a coma. Into* indicates movement or a change in condition: *He went into the garage. She fell into a coma.* Generally avoid the slang sense of *into* meaning "interested in" or "involved in": *I am into Zen.*

in . . .   A number of phrases beginning with *in* are needlessly wordy and should be avoided: *in the event that* (for *if*); *in the neighborhood of* (for *approximately* or *about*); *in this day and age* (for *now* or *nowadays*); *in spite of the fact that* (for *although* or *even though*); and *in view of the fact that* (for *because* or *considering that*). Certain other *in* phrases are nothing but padding and can be omitted entirely: *in nature, in number, in reality,* and *in a very real sense.* (See also pp. 566–67.)

incredible, incredulous   *Incredible* means "unbelievable"; *incredulous* means "unbelieving": *When Nancy heard Dennis's incredible story, she was frankly incredulous.* See also *credible, creditable, credulous.*

individual, person, party   *Individual* should refer to a single human being in contrast to a group or should stress uniqueness: *The US Constitution places strong emphasis on the rights of the individual.* For other meanings *person* is preferable: *What person* [not *individual*] *wouldn't want the security promised in that advertisement? Party* means "group" (*Can you seat a party of four for dinner?*) and should not be used to refer to an individual except in legal documents. See also *people, persons.*

infer   See *imply, infer.*

in regards to   Nonstandard for *in regard to, as regards,* or *regarding.* See also *regarding.*

inside of, outside of   The *of* is unnecessary when *inside* and *outside* are used as prepositions: *Stay inside* [not *inside of*] *the house. The decision is outside* [not *outside of*] *my authority. Inside of* may refer colloquially to time, though in formal English *within* is preferred: *The law was passed within* [not *inside of*] *a year.*

instance   See *case, instance, line.*

insure   See *assure, ensure, insure.*

irregardless   Nonstandard for *regardless.*

is, are   See *are, is.*

is because   See *reason is because.*

is when, is where   These are faulty constructions in sentences that define: *Adolescence is a stage* [not *is when a person is*] *between childhood and adulthood. Socialism is a system in which* [not *is where*] *government owns the means of production.* (See also p. 395.)

its, it's   *Its* is the pronoun *it* in the possessive case: *That plant is losing its leaves. It's* is a contraction for *it is* or *it has*: *It's* [*It is*] *likely to die. It's* [*It has*] *got a fungus.* Many people confuse *it's* and *its* because possessives are most often formed with *-'s;* but the possessive *its,* like *his* and *hers,* never takes an apostrophe.

-ize, -wise   The suffix *-ize* changes a noun or adjective into a verb: *revolutionize, immunize.* The suffix *-wise* changes a noun or adjective

Usage

into an adverb: *clockwise, otherwise, likewise.* Avoid the two suffixes except in established words: *The two nations are ready to settle on* [not *finalize*] *an agreement. I'm highly sensitive* [not *sensitized*] *to that kind of criticism. Financially* [not *Moneywise*], *it's a good time to invest in real estate.*

kind of, sort of, type of   In formal speech and writing, avoid using *kind of* or *sort of* to mean "somewhat": *He was rather* [not *kind of*] *tall.*

Kind, sort, and type are singular and take singular modifiers and verbs: *This kind of dog is easily trained.* Agreement errors often occur when these singular nouns are combined with the plural adjectives *these* and *those: These kinds* [not *kind*] *of dogs are easily trained. Kind, sort,* and *type* should be followed by *of* but not by *a: I don't know what type of* [not *type* or *type of a*] *dog that is.*

Use *kind of, sort of,* or *type of* only when the word *kind, sort,* or *type* is important: *That was a strange* [not *strange sort of*] *statement.*

later, latter   *Later* refers to time; *latter* refers to the second-named of two items. See also *former, latter.*

lay, lie   *Lay* means "put" or "place" and takes a direct object: *We could lay the tablecloth in the sun.* Its main forms are *lay, laid, laid. Lie* means "recline" or "be situated" and does not take an object: *I lie awake at night. The town lies east of the river.* Its main forms are *lie, lay, lain.* (See also p. 290.)

leave, let   *Leave* and *let* are interchangeable only when followed by *alone; leave me alone* is the same as *let me alone.* Otherwise, *leave* means "depart" and *let* means "allow": *Julia would not let Susan leave.*

less   See *fewer, less.*

let   See *leave, let.*

liable   See *apt, liable, likely.*

lie, lay   See *lay, lie.*

like, as   In formal speech and writing, *like* should not introduce a full clause (with a subject and a verb) because it is a preposition. The preferred choice is *as* or *as if: The plan succeeded as* [not *like*] *we hoped. It seemed as if* [not *like*] *it might fail. Other plans like it have failed.*

When *as* serves as a preposition, the distinction between *as* and *like* depends on meaning. *As* suggests that the subject is equivalent or identical to the description: *She was hired as an engineer. Like* suggests resemblance but not identity: *People like her do well in such jobs.* See also *like, such as.*

like, such as   Strictly, *such as* precedes an example that represents a larger subject, whereas *like* indicates that two subjects are comparable. *Steve has recordings of many great saxophonists such as Ben Webster and Lee Konitz. Steve wants to be a great jazz saxophonist like Ben Webster and Lee Konitz.*

Many writers prefer to keep *such* and *as* together: *Steve admires saxophonists such as . . .* rather than *Steve admires such saxophonists as. . . .*

likely   See *apt, liable, likely.*

line See *case, instance, line.*

literally This word means "actually" or "just as the words say," and it should not be used to qualify or intensify expressions whose words are not to be taken at face value. The sentence *He was literally climbing the walls* describes a person behaving like an insect, not a person who is restless or anxious. For the latter meaning, *literally* should be omitted.

lose, loose *Lose* means "mislay": *Did you lose a brown glove? Loose* means "unrestrained" or "not tight": *Ann's canary got loose. Loose* also can function as a verb meaning "let loose": *They loose the dogs as soon as they spot the bear.*

lots, lots of Colloquial substitutes for *very many, a great many,* or *much.* Avoid *lots* and *lots of* in college or business writing. When you use either one informally, be careful to maintain subject-verb agreement: *There are* [not *is*] *lots of fish in the pond.*

may, can See *can, may.*

may be, maybe *May be* is a verb, and *maybe* is an adverb meaning "perhaps": *Tuesday may be a legal holiday. Maybe we won't have classes.*

may of See *have, of.*

media *Media* is the plural of *medium* and takes a plural verb: *All the news media are increasingly visual.* The singular verb is common, even in the media, but most careful writers still use the plural verb.

might of See *have, of.*

moral, morale As a noun, *moral* means "ethical conclusion" or "lesson": *The moral of the story escapes me. Morale* means "spirit" or "state of mind": *Victory improved the team's morale.*

most, almost See *almost, most.*

must of See *have, of.*

myself, herself, himself, yourself The *-self* pronouns refer to or intensify another word or words: *Paul helped himself; Jill herself said so.* The *-self* pronouns are often used colloquially in place of personal pronouns, but that use should be avoided in formal speech and writing: *No one except me* [not *myself*] *saw the accident. Our delegates will be Susan and you* [not *yourself*]. See also p. 276 on the unchanging forms of the *-self* pronouns in standard American English.

nohow Nonstandard for *in no way* or *in any way.*

nothing like, nowhere near These colloquial substitutes for *not nearly* are best avoided in formal speech and writing: *That program is not nearly* [not *nowhere near*] *as expensive.*

nowheres Nonstandard for *nowhere.*

number See *amount, number.*

of, have See *have, of.*

off of *Of* is unnecessary. Use *off* or *from* rather than *off of: He jumped off* [or *from,* not *off of*] *the roof.*

Usage

OK, O.K., okay   All three spellings are acceptable, but avoid this collo-quial term in formal speech and writing.

on, upon   In modern English, *upon* is usually just a stuffy way of say-ing *on*. Unless you need a formal effect, use *on*: *We decided on* [not *upon*] *a location for our next meeting.*

on account of   Wordy for *because of.*

on the other hand   This transitional expression of contrast should be preceded by its mate, *on the one hand*: *On the one hand, we hoped for snow. On the other hand, we feared that it would harm the animals.* However, the two combined can be unwieldy, and a simple *but, how-ever, yet,* or *in contrast* often suffices: *We hoped for snow. Yet we feared that it would harm the animals.*

outside of   See *inside of, outside of.*

owing to the fact that   Wordy for *because.*

party   See *individual, person, party.*

people, persons   In formal usage, *people* refers to a general group: *We the people of the United States. . . . Persons* refers to a collection of indi-viduals: *Will the person or persons who saw the accident please notify. . . .* Except when emphasizing individuals, prefer *people* to *persons.* See also *individual, person, party.*

per   Except in technical writing, an English equivalent is usually preferable to the Latin *per*: *$10 an* [not *per*] *hour; sent by* [not *per*] *parcel post; requested in* [not *per* or *as per*] *your letter.*

percent (per cent), percentage   Both these terms refer to fractions of one hundred. *Percent* always follows a numeral (*40 percent of the vot-ers*), and the word should be used instead of the symbol (%) in general writing. *Percentage* stands alone (*the percentage of votes*) or follows an adjective (*a high percentage*).

person   See *individual, person, party.*

persons   See *people, persons.*

persuade   See *convince, persuade.*

phenomena   The plural of *phenomenon* (meaning "perceivable fact" or "unusual occurrence"): *Many phenomena are not recorded. One phenomenon is attracting attention.*

plenty   A colloquial substitute for *very: The reaction occurred very* [not *plenty*] *fast.*

plus   *Plus* is standard as a preposition meaning *in addition to: His income plus mine is sufficient.* But *plus* is colloquial as a conjunctive adverb: *Our organization is larger than theirs; moreover* [not *plus*], *we have more money.*

practicable, practical   *Practicable* means "capable of being put into practice"; *practical* means "useful" or "sensible": *We figured out a practical new design for our kitchen, but it was too expensive to be practicable.*

precede, proceed   The verb *precede* means "come before": *My name precedes yours in the alphabet.* The verb *proceed* means "move on": *We were told to proceed to the waiting room.*

prejudice, prejudiced   *Prejudice* is a noun; *prejudiced* is an adjective. Do not drop the *-d* from *prejudiced*: *I knew that my parents were prejudiced* [not *prejudice*].

pretty   Overworked as an adverb meaning "rather" or "somewhat": *He was somewhat* [not *pretty*] *irked at the suggestion.*

previous to, prior to   Wordy for *before.*

principal, principle   *Principal* is an adjective meaning "foremost" or "major," a noun meaning "chief official," or, in finance, a noun meaning "capital sum." *Principle* is a noun only, meaning "rule" or "axiom." *Her principal reasons for confessing were her principles of right and wrong.*

proceed, precede   See *precede, proceed.*

provided, providing   *Provided* may serve as a subordinating conjunction meaning "on the condition (that)"; *providing* may not. *The grocer will begin providing food for the soup kitchen provided* [not *providing*] *we find a suitable space.*

question of whether, question as to whether   Wordy substitutes for *whether.*

raise, rise   *Raise* means "lift" or "bring up" and takes a direct object: *The Kirks raise cattle.* Its main forms are *raise, raised, raised. Rise* means "get up" and does not take an object: *They must rise at dawn.* Its main forms are *rise, rose, risen.* (See also p. 290.)

real, really   In formal speech and writing, *real* should not be used as an adverb; *really* is the adverb and *real* an adjective. *Popular reaction to the announcement was really* [not *real*] *enthusiastic.*

reason is because   Although colloquially common, this expression should be avoided in formal speech and writing. Use a *that* clause after *reason is*: *The reason he is absent is that* [not *is because*] *he is sick.* Or: *He is absent because he is sick.*

reckon   See *calculate, figure, reckon.*

regarding, in regard to, with regard to, relating to, relative to, with respect to, respecting   Stuffy substitutes for *on, about,* or *concerning: Mr. McGee spoke about* [not *with regard to*] *the plans for the merger.*

respectful, respective   *Respectful* means "full of (or showing) respect": *Be respectful of other people. Respective* means "separate": *The French and the Germans occupied their respective trenches.*

rise, raise   See *raise, rise.*

scarcely   See *but, hardly, scarcely.*

sensual, sensuous   *Sensual* suggests sexuality; *sensuous* means "pleasing to the senses." *Stirred by the sensuous scent of meadow grass and* *flowers, Cheryl and Paul found their thoughts growing increasingly sensual.*

set, sit   *Set* means "put" or "place" and takes a direct object: *He sets the pitcher down.* Its main forms are *set, set, set. Sit* means "be seated" and does not take an object: *She sits on the sofa.* Its main forms are *sit, sat, sat.* (See also p. 290.)

shall, will   *Will* is the future-tense helping verb for all persons: *I will go, you will go, they will go.* The main use of *shall* is for first-person questions requesting an opinion or consent: *Shall I order a pizza? Shall we dance?* (Questions that merely inquire about the future use *will: When will I see you again?*) *Shall* can also be used for the first person when a formal effect is desired (I *shall* expect you around three), and it is occasionally used with the second or third person to express the speaker's determination (*You shall do as I say*).

should, would   *Should* expresses obligation: *I should fix dinner. You should set the table. Jack should wash the dishes. Would* expresses a wish or hypothetical condition: *I would do it. Wouldn't you?* When the context is formal, however, *should* is sometimes used instead of *would* in the first person: *We should be delighted to accept.*

should of   See *have, of.*

since   *Since* mainly relates to time: *I've been waiting since noon.* But *since* is also often used to mean "because": *Since you ask, I'll tell you.* Revise sentences in which the word could have either meaning, such as *Since you left, my life is empty.*

sit, set   See *set, sit.*

situation   Often unnecessary, as in *The situation is that we have to get some help* (revise to *We have to get some help*) or *The team was faced with a punting situation* (revise to *The team was faced with punting* or *The team had to punt*).

so   Avoid using *so* alone as a vague intensifier: *He was so late.* So needs to be followed by *that* and a clause that states a result: *He was so late that I left without him.*

some   *Some* is colloquial as an adverb meaning "somewhat" or "to some extent" and as an adjective meaning "remarkable": *We'll have to hurry somewhat* [not *some*] *to get there in time. Those are remarkable* [not *some*] *photographs.*

somebody, some body; someone, some one   *Somebody* and *someone* are indefinite pronouns; *some body* is a noun modified by *some;* and *some one* is a pronoun or an adjective modified by *some. Somebody ought to invent a shampoo that will give hair some body. Someone told Janine she should choose some one plan and stick with it.*

someplace   Informal for *somewhere.*

sometime, sometimes, some time   *Sometime* means "at an indefinite time in the future": *Why don't you come up and see me sometime? Sometimes* means "now and then": *I still see my old friend Joe sometimes. Some time* means "a span of time": *I need some time to make the payments.*

somewheres Nonstandard for *somewhere*.

sort of, sort of a See *kind of, sort of, type of*.

specially See *especially, specially*.

such Avoid using *such* as a vague intensifier: *It was such a cold winter. Such* should be followed by *that* and a clause that states a result: *It was such a cold winter that Napoleon's troops had to turn back.*

such as See *like, such as*.

supposed to, used to In both these expressions, the *-d* is essential: *I used to* [not *use to*] *think so. He's supposed to* [not *suppose to*] *meet us.*

sure Colloquial when used as an adverb meaning *surely: James Madison sure was right about the need for the Bill of Rights.* If you merely want to be emphatic, use *certainly: Madison certainly was right.* If your goal is to convince a possibly reluctant reader, use *surely: Madison surely was right. Surely Madison was right.*

sure and, sure to; try and, try to *Sure to* and *try to* are the correct forms: *Be sure to* [not *sure and*] *vote. Try to* [not *Try and*] *vote early to avoid a line.*

take, bring See *bring, take*.

than, as See *as, than*.

than, then *Than* is a conjunction used in comparisons, *then* an adverb indicating time: *Holmes knew then that Moriarty was wilier than he had thought.*

that, which *That* always introduces an essential clause: *We should use the lettuce that Susan bought* (*that Susan bought* limits *lettuce* to a particular lettuce). *Which* can introduce both essential and nonessential clauses, but many writers reserve *which* only for nonessential clauses: *The leftover lettuce, which is in the refrigerator, would make a good salad* (*which is in the refrigerator* simply provides more information about the lettuce we already know of). Essential clauses (with *that* or *which*) are not set off by commas; nonessential clauses (with *which*) are. (See also pp. 459–61.)

that, who, which Use *that* to refer to most animals and to things: *The animals that escaped included a zebra. The rocket that failed cost millions.* Use *who* to refer to people and to animals with names: *Dorothy is the girl who visits Oz. Her dog, Toto, who accompanies her, gives her courage.* Use *which* only to refer to animals and things: *The river, which runs more than a thousand miles, empties into the Indian Ocean.* (See also p. 372.)

their, there, they're *Their* is the possessive form of *they: Give them their money. There* indicates place (*I saw her standing there*) or functions to postpone the sentence subject (*There is a hole behind you*). *They're* is a contraction for *they are: They're going fast.*

theirselves Nonstandard for *themselves*.

them In standard American English, *them* does not serve as an adjective: *Those* [not *Them*] *people want to know.*

then, than   See *than, then.*

these kind, these sort, these type, those kind   See *kind of, sort of, type of.*

this, these   *This* is singular: *this* car or *This* is the reason I left. *These* is plural: *these* cars or *These* are not valid reasons.

this here, these here, that there, them there   Nonstandard for *this, these, that,* or *those.*

thru   A colloquial spelling of *through* that should be avoided in all academic and business writing.

thusly   A mistaken form of *thus.*

till, until, 'til   *Till* and *until* have the same meaning; either is acceptable. *'Til,* a contraction of *until,* is an old form that has been replaced by *till.*

time period   Since a *period* is an interval of time, this expression is redundant: *They did not see each other for a long time* [not *time period*]. *Six accidents occurred in a three-week period* [not *time period*].

to, too, two   *To* is a preposition; *too* is an adverb meaning "also" or "excessively"; and *two* is a number. *I too have been to Europe two times.*

too   Avoid using *too* as an intensifier meaning "very": *Monkeys are too mean.* If you do use *too,* explain the consequences of the excessive quality: *Monkeys are too mean to make good pets.*

toward, towards   Both are acceptable, though *toward* is preferred. Use one or the other consistently.

try and, try to   See *sure and, sure to; try and, try to.*

type of   See *kind of, sort of, type of.* Don't use *type* without *of: It was a family type of* [not *type*] *restaurant.* Or, better: *It was a family restaurant.*

uninterested   See *disinterested, uninterested.*

unique   *Unique* means "the only one of its kind" and so cannot sensibly be modified with words such as *very* or *most: That was a unique* [not *a very unique* or *the most unique*] *movie.*

until   See *till, until, 'til.*

upon, on   See *on, upon.*

usage, use   *Usage* refers to conventions, most often those of a language: *Is "hadn't ought" proper usage? Usage* is often misused in place of the noun *use: Wise use* [not *usage*] *of insulation can save fuel.*

use, utilize   *Utilize* can be used to mean "make good use of": *Many teachers utilize computers for instruction.* But for all other senses of "place in service" or "employ," prefer *use.*

used to   See *supposed to, used to.*

wait for, wait on   In formal speech and writing, *wait for* means "await" (*I'm waiting for Paul*), and *wait on* means "serve" (*The owner of the store herself waited on us*).

ways   Colloquial as a substitute for way: *We have only a little way* [not *ways*] *to go.*

well   See *good, well.*

whether, if   See *if, whether.*

which, that   See *that, which.*

which, who, that   See *that, who, which.*

who, whom   *Who* is the subject of a sentence or clause (*We don't know who will come*). *Whom* is the object of a verb or preposition (*We do not know whom we invited*). (See also pp. 280–81.)

who's, whose   *Who's* is the contraction of *who is* or *who has: Who's* [*Who is*] *at the door? Jim is the only one who's* [*who has*] *passed. Whose* is the possessive form of *who: Whose book is that?*

will, shall   See *shall, will.*

wise   See *-ize, -wise.*

with regard to, with respect to   See *regarding.*

would   See *should, would.*

would have   Avoid this construction in place of *had* in clauses that begin *if* and state a condition contrary to fact: *If the tree had* [not *would have*] *withstood the fire, it would have been the oldest in town.* (See also p. 313.)

would of   See *have, of.*

you   In all but very formal writing, *you* is generally appropriate as long as it means "you, the reader." In all writing, avoid indefinite uses of *you,* such as *In one ancient tribe your first loyalty was to your parents.* (See also p. 372.)

your, you're   *Your* is the possessive form of *you: Your dinner is ready. You're* is the contraction of *you are: You're bound to be late.*

yourself   See *myself, herself, himself, yourself.*

Usage

Glossary of Terms

This glossary defines terms of grammar, rhetoric, literature, and Internet research. Page numbers in parentheses refer you to sections of the text where the term is explained more fully.

absolute phrase   A phrase consisting of a noun or pronoun plus the *-ing* or *-ed* form of a verb (a participle): *Our accommodations arranged, we set out on our journey. They will hire a local person, other things being equal.* An absolute phrase modifies a whole clause or sentence (rather than a single word), and it is not joined to the rest of the sentence by a connector. (See pp. 257–58.)

abstract and concrete   Two kinds of language. **Abstract** words refer to ideas, qualities, attitudes, and conditions that can't be perceived with the senses: *beauty, guilty, victory.* **Concrete** words refer to objects, persons, places, or conditions that can be perceived with the senses: *Abilene, scratchy, toolbox.* See also *general and specific.* (See pp. 555–56.)

acronym   A pronounceable word formed from the initial letter or letters of each word in an organization's title: NATO (North Atlantic Treaty Organization).

active voice   See *voice.*

adjectival   A term sometimes used to describe any word or word group, other than an adjective, that is used to modify a noun. Common adjectivals include nouns (*wagon train, railroad ties*), phrases (*fool on the hill*), and clauses (*the man that I used to be*).

adjective   A word used to modify a noun (*beautiful morning*) or a pronoun (*ordinary one*). (See Chapter 16.) Nouns, some verb forms, phrases, and clauses may also serve as adjectives: *book sale; a used book; sale of old books; the sale, which occurs annually.* (See *clauses, prepositional phrases,* and *verbals and verbal phrases.*)
Adjectives come in several classes:

- A **descriptive adjective** names some quality of the noun: *beautiful morning, dark horse.*
- A **limiting adjective** narrows the scope of a noun. It may be a **possessive** (*my, their*); a **demonstrative adjective** (*this train, these days*); an **interrogative adjective** (*what time? whose body?*); or a number (*two boys*).
- A **proper adjective** is derived from a proper noun: *French language, Machiavellian scheme.*

932

Adjectives also can be classified according to position:

- An **attributive adjective** appears next to the noun it modifies: *full moon*.
- A **predicate adjective** is connected to its noun by a linking verb: *The moon is full*. See also *complement*.

adjective clause   See *adjective*.

adjective phrase   See *adjective*.

adverb   A word used to modify a verb (*warmly greet*), an adjective (*only three people*), another adverb (*quite seriously*), or a whole sentence (*Fortunately, she is employed*). (See Chapter 16.) Some verb forms, phrases, and clauses may also serve as adverbs: *easy to stop, drove by a farm, plowed the fields when the earth thawed*. (See *clause, prepositional phrase*, and *verbals and verbal phrases*.)

adverb clause   See *adverb*.

adverbial   A term sometimes used to describe any word or word group, other than an adverb, that is used to modify a verb, an adjective, another adverb, or a whole sentence. Common adverbials include nouns (*This little piggy stayed home*), phrases (*This little piggy went to market*), and clauses (*This little piggy went wherever he wanted*).

adverbial conjunction   See *conjunctive adverb*.

adverb phrase   See *adverb*.

agreement   The correspondence of one word to another in person, number, or gender. A verb must agree with its subject (*The chef orders egg sandwiches*), a pronoun must agree with its antecedent (*The chef surveys her breakfast*), and a demonstrative adjective must agree with its noun (*She likes these kinds of sandwiches*). (See Chapter 15.)

Logical agreement requires consistency in number between other related words, usually nouns: *The students brought their books* [not *book*]. (See p. 376.)

analogy   A comparison between members of different classes, such as a nursery school and a barnyard or a molecule and a pair of dancers. Usually, the purpose is to explain something unfamiliar to readers through something familiar. (See p. 98.)

analysis   The separation of a subject into its elements. Sometimes called **division**, analysis is fundamental to critical thinking, reading, and writing (pp. 125–27, 134) and is a useful tool for developing essays (p. 28) and paragraphs (p. 98).

antecedent   The word to which a pronoun refers: *Jonah, who is not yet ten, has already chosen the college he will attend* (*Jonah* is the antecedent of the pronouns *who* and *he*). (See pp. 326–27.)

APA style   The style of documentation recommended by the American Psychological Association and used in many of the social sciences. (For discussion and examples, see pp. 838–56.)

appeals   Attempts to engage and persuade readers. An **emotional appeal** touches readers' feelings, beliefs, and values. An **ethical appeal**

Terms

presents the writer as competent, sincere, and fair. **A rational appeal** engages readers' powers of reasoning. (See pp. 172–74.)

appositive   A word or phrase appearing next to a noun or pronoun that renames or identifies it and is equivalent to it: *My brother Michael, the best horn player in town, won the state competition* (*Michael* identifies which brother is being referred to; *the best horn player in town* renames *Michael*). (See pp. 263–64.)

argument   Writing whose primary purpose is to convince readers of an idea or persuade them to act. (See Chapters 6–7.)

article   The word *a, an,* or *the.* Articles are sometimes called **determiners** because they always signal that a noun follows. (See pp. 340–43 for when to use *a/an* versus *the.* See p. 915 for when to use *a* versus *an.*)

assertion   See *claim.*

assumption   A stated or unstated belief or opinion. Uncovering assumptions is part of critical thinking, reading, and writing (see pp. 127–29, 134–36). In argument, assumptions connect claims and evidence (see pp. 151–52).

audience   The intended readers of a piece of writing. Knowledge of the audience's needs and expectations helps a writer shape writing so that it is clear, interesting, and convincing. (See pp. 9–12, 172–75.)

auxiliary verb   See *helping verb.*

balanced sentence   A sentence consisting of two clauses with parallel constructions: *Do as I say, not as I do. Befriend all animals; exploit none.* Their balance makes such sentences highly emphatic. (See p. 410.)

belief   A conviction based on morality, values, or faith. Statements of belief often serve as assumptions and sometimes as evidence, but they are not arguable and so cannot serve as the thesis in an argument. (See p. 145.)

body   In a piece of writing, the large central part where ideas supporting the thesis are presented and developed. See also *conclusion* and *introduction.*

bookmark   In Internet use, an electronic address you save for later reference. (See p. 642.)

brainstorming   A technique for generating ideas about a subject: concentrating on the subject for a fixed time (say, fifteen minutes), you list every idea and detail that comes to mind. (See pp. 24–26.)

browser   A computer program that makes it possible to search the World Wide Web. (See p. 197.)

cardinal number   The type of number that shows amount: *two, sixty, ninety-seven.* Contrast *ordinal number* (such as *second, sixtieth, ninety-seventh*).

case   The form of a noun or pronoun that indicates its function in the sentence. Most pronouns have three cases:

- The **subjective case** (*I, she*) for the subject of a verb or for a subject complement.

- The **objective case** (*me, her*) for the object of a verb, verbal, or preposition.
- The **possessive case** to indicate ownership, used either as an adjective (*my, her*) or as a noun (*mine, hers*).

(See p. 276 for a list of the forms of personal and relative pronouns.)

Nouns use the subjective form (*dog, America*) for all cases except the possessive (*dog's, America's*).

cause-and-effect analysis The determination of why something happened or what its consequences were or will be. (See pp. 28 and 99.)

characters The people in a literary work, including the narrator of a story or the speaker of a poem. (See p. 792.)

Chicago style A style of documentation recommended by *The Chicago Manual of Style* and used in history, art, and other humanities. (For discussion and examples, see pp. 818–28.)

chronological organization The arrangement of events as they occurred in time, usually from first to last. (See pp. 43, 81.)

citation In research writing, the way of acknowledging material borrowed from sources. Most systems of citation are basically similar: a number or brief parenthetical reference in the text indicates that particular material is borrowed and directs the reader to information on the source at the end of the work. The systems do differ, however. (See pp. 700–35 for MLA style, pp. 818–28 for Chicago style, pp. 838–56 for APA style, and pp. 870–78 for CSE style.)

claim A positive statement or assertion that requires support. Claims are the backbone of any argument. (See pp. 144–46.)

classification The sorting of many elements into groups based on their similarities. (See pp. 28 and 96–97.)

clause A group of related words containing a subject and predicate. A **main (independent) clause** can stand by itself as a sentence. A **subordinate (dependent) clause** serves as a single part of speech and so cannot stand by itself as a sentence.

Main clause   We can go to the movies.
Subordinate clause   We can go if Julie gets back on time.

A subordinate clause may function as an adjective (*The car that hit Fred was speeding*), an adverb (*The car hit Fred when it ran a red light*), or a noun (*Whoever was driving should be arrested*). (See pp. 260–62.)

clichés See *trite expressions*.

climactic organization The arrangement of material in order of increasing drama or interest, leading to a climax. (See pp. 44, 83.)

clip art Drawings and icons available on word processors, CD-ROMs, and the Web, generally used to embellish documents. (See p. 211.)

clustering A technique for generating ideas about a subject: drawing and writing, you branch outward from a center point (the subject) to pursue the implications of ideas. (See p. 26.)

Terms

coherence The quality of an effective essay or paragraph that helps readers see relations among ideas and move easily from one idea to the next. (See pp. 45 and 77–78.)

collaborative learning In a writing course, students working together in groups to help each other become better writers and readers. (See pp. 65–67, 231–36.)

collective noun See *noun.*

colloquial language The words and expressions of everyday speech. Colloquial language can enliven informal writing but is generally inappropriate in formal academic or business writing. See also *formal and informal.* (See p. 545.)

comma splice A sentence error in which two main clauses are separated by a comma with no coordinating conjunction. (See Chapter 18.)

Comma splice	The book was long, it contained useful data.
Revised	The book was long; it contained useful data.
Revised	The book was long, and it contained useful data.

common noun See *noun.*

comparative See *comparison.*

comparison The form of an adverb or adjective that shows its degree of quality or amount.

- The **positive degree** is the simple, uncompared form: *gross, shyly.*
- The **comparative degree** compares the thing modified to at least one other thing: *grosser, more shyly.*
- The **superlative degree** indicates that the thing modified exceeds all other things to which it is being compared: *grossest, most shyly.*

The comparative and superlative degrees are formed either with the endings *-er* and *-est* or with the words *more* and *most, less* and *least.* (See pp. 336–37.)

comparison and contrast The identification of similarities (comparison) and differences (contrast) between two or more subjects. (See pp. 28, 97–98.)

complement A word or word group that completes the sense of a subject, an object, or a verb. (See pp. 245–46.)

- A **subject complement** follows a linking verb and renames or describes the subject. It may be an adjective, noun, or pronoun. *I am a lion tamer, but I am not yet experienced* (the noun *lion tamer* and the adjective *experienced* complement the subject *I*). Adjective complements are also called **predicate adjectives.** Noun complements are also called **predicate nouns** or **predicate nominatives.**
- An **object complement** follows and modifies or refers to a direct object. The complement may be an adjective or a noun. *If you elect me president, I'll keep the students satisfied* (the noun *president* complements the direct object *me,* and the adjective *satisfied* complements the direct object *students*).

■ **A verb complement** is a direct or indirect object of a verb. It may be a noun or pronoun. *Don't give the <u>chimp</u> that <u>peanut</u>* (*chimp* is the indirect object and *peanut* is the direct object of the verb *give;* both objects are verb complements).

complete predicate   See *predicate.*

complete subject   See *subject.*

complex sentence   See *sentence.*

compound construction   Two or more words or word groups serving the same function, such as a **compound subject** (*<u>Harriet and Peter</u> poled their barge down the river*), **compound predicate** (*The scout <u>watched and waited</u>*) or parts of a predicate (*She grew <u>tired and hungry</u>*), and **compound sentence** (*<u>He smiled, and I laughed</u>*). (See pp. 265–68.) **Compound words** include nouns (*featherbrain, strip-mining*) and adjectives (*two-year-old, downtrodden*).

compound-complex sentence   See *sentence.*

compound predicate   See *compound construction.*

compound sentence   See *sentence.*

compound subject   See *compound construction.*

conciseness   Use of the fewest and freshest words to express meaning clearly and achieve the desired effect with readers. (See Chapter 40.)

conclusion   The closing of an essay, tying off the writer's thoughts and leaving readers with a sense of completion. (See pp. 106–08 for suggestions.)

A *conclusion* is also the result of deductive reasoning. See *deductive reasoning* and *syllogism.*

concrete   See *abstract and concrete.*

conditional statement   A statement expressing a condition contrary to fact and using the subjunctive mood of the verb: *If she <u>were</u> mayor, the unions would cooperate.* See also *mood.*

conjugation   A list of the forms of a verb showing tense, voice, mood, person, and number. The conjugation of the verb *know* in present tense, active voice, indicative mood is *I know, you know, he/she/it knows, we know, you know, they know.* (See p. 304 for a fuller conjugation.)

conjunction   A word that links and relates parts of a sentence.

■ **Coordinating conjunctions** (*and, but, or, nor, for, so, yet*) connect words or word groups of equal grammatical rank: *The lights went out, <u>but</u> the doctors <u>and</u> nurses kept caring for patients.* (See p. 265.)

■ **Correlative conjunctions** or correlatives (such as *either . . . or, not only . . . but also*) are two or more connecting words that work together: *He was certain that <u>either</u> his parents <u>or</u> his brother would help him.* (See p. 266.)

■ **Subordinating conjunctions** (*after, although, as if, because, if, when,* and so on) begin subordinate clauses and link them to main clauses: *The seven dwarfs whistle <u>while</u> they work.* (See p. 259.)

conjunctive adverb (adverbial conjunction)   An adverb (such as *besides, consequently, however, indeed,* and *therefore*) that relates two main clauses in a sentence: *We had hoped to own a house by now; however, housing costs have risen too fast.* (See pp. 267–68.) The error known as a comma splice results when two main clauses related by a conjunctive adverb are separated only by a comma. (See pp. 361–62.)

connector (connective)   Any word or phrase that links words, phrases, clauses, or sentences. Common connectors include coordinating, correlative, and subordinating conjunctions; conjunctive adverbs; and prepositions.

connotation   An association called up by a word, beyond its dictionary definition. Contrast *denotation.* (See pp. 553–54.)

construction   Any group of grammatically related words, such as a phrase, a clause, or a sentence.

contraction   A condensation of an expression, with an apostrophe replacing the missing letters: for example, *doesn't* (for *does not*), *we'll* (for *we will*). (See p. 491.)

contrast   See *comparison and contrast.*

coordinate adjectives   Two or more adjectives that equally modify the same noun or pronoun: *The camera panned the vast, empty desert.* (See pp. 465–66.)

coordinating conjunction   See *conjunction.*

coordination   The linking of words, phrases, or clauses that are of equal importance, usually with a coordinating conjunction: *He and I laughed, but she was not amused.* Contrast *subordination.* (See pp. 416–18.)

correlative conjunction (correlative)   See *conjunction.*

count noun   See *noun.*

courseware   A program for online communication and collaboration among the teacher and students in a course. (See p. 236.)

critical thinking, reading, and writing   Looking beneath the surface of words and images to discern meaning and relationships and to build knowledge. (See Chapter 5.)

CSE style   Either of two styles of documenting sources recommended by the Council of Science Editors (formerly the Council of Biology Editors) and frequently used in the natural and applied sciences and in mathematics. (For discussion and examples, see pp. 870–78.)

cumulative (loose) sentence   A sentence in which modifiers follow the subject and verb: *Ducks waddled by, their tails swaying and their quacks rising to heaven.* Contrast *periodic sentence.* (See pp. 407–08.)

dangling modifier   A modifier that does not sensibly describe anything in its sentence. (See pp. 388–90.)

Dangling	Having arrived late, the concert had already begun.
Revised	Having arrived late, we found that the concert had already begun.

data In argument, a term used for *evidence*. See *evidence*.

database A collection and organization of information (data). A database may be printed, but the term is most often used for electronic sources.

declension A list of the forms of a noun or pronoun, showing inflections for person (for pronouns), number, and case. See p. 276 for a declension of the personal and relative pronouns.

deductive reasoning Applying a generalization to specific circumstances in order to reach a conclusion. See also *syllogism*. Contrast *inductive reasoning*. (See pp. 167–70.)

definition Specifying the characteristics of something to establish what it is and is not. (See pp. 28, 94–95, and 146.)

degree See *comparison*.

demonstrative adjective See *adjective*.

demonstrative pronoun See *pronoun*.

denotation The main or dictionary definition of a word. Contrast *connotation*. (See pp. 552–53.)

dependent clause See *clause*.

derivational suffix See *suffix*.

description Detailing the sensory qualities of a thing, person, place, or feeling. (See pp. 27 and 93.)

descriptive adjective See *adjective*.

descriptor See *keyword(s)*.

determiner A word that marks and precedes a noun: for example, *a, an, the, my, your*. See also *article*. (See pp. 340–44 for the uses of determiners before nouns.)

developing (planning) The stage of the writing process when one finds a subject, explores ideas, gathers information, focuses on a central theme, and organizes material. Compare *drafting* and *revising*. (See Chapters 1–2.)

dialect A variety of a language used by a specific group or in a specific region. A dialect may be distinguished by its pronunciation, vocabulary, and grammar. (See pp. 17–18 and 542–44.)

diction The choice and use of words. (See Chapters 38–40.)

dictionary form See *plain form*.

direct address A construction in which a word or phrase indicates the person or group spoken to: *Have you finished, John? Farmers, unite.*

direct object See *object*.

direct question A sentence asking a question and concluding with a question mark: *Do they know we are watching?* Contrast *indirect question*.

direct quotation (direct discourse) See *quotation*.

Terms

discussion list   A mailing list of subscribers who use e-mail to converse on a particular subject.

division   See *analysis.*

documentation   In research writing, supplying citations that legitimate the use of borrowed material and support claims about its origins. Contrast *plagiarism.* (See pp. 688–89.)

document design   The control of a document's elements to achieve the flow, spacing, grouping, emphasis, and standardization that are appropriate for the writing situation. (See Chapter 9.)

domain   The part of a Web address (or URL) that gives the organization sponsoring the site. (See pp. 653–54.)

double negative   A generally nonstandard form consisting of two negative words used in the same construction so that they effectively cancel each other: *I don't have no money.* Rephrase as *I have no money* or *I don't have any money.* (See pp. 338–39.)

double possessive   A possessive using both the ending *-'s* and the preposition *of: That is a favorite expression of Mark's.*

double talk (doublespeak)   Language intended to confuse or to be misunderstood. (See p. 546.)

download   To transfer data from another computer.

drafting   The stage of the writing process when ideas are expressed in connected sentences and paragraphs. Compare *developing (planning)* and *revising.* (See pp. 47–50.)

editing   A distinct step in revising a written work, focusing on clarity, tone, and correctness. Compare *revising.* (See pp. 58–61.)

ellipsis   The omission of a word or words from a quotation, indicated by the three spaced periods of an **ellipsis mark:** *"that all . . . are created equal."*

elliptical clause   A clause omitting a word or words whose meaning is understood from the rest of the clause: *David likes Minneapolis better than* [*he likes*] *Chicago.* (See p. 261.)

emoticon   Sideways faces made up of punctuation, used to convey emotion or irony in electronic communication. (See p. 196.)

emotional appeal   See *appeals.*

emphasis   The manipulation of words, sentences, and paragraphs to stress important ideas. (See Chapter 23.)

essay   A nonfiction composition of multiple paragraphs, focused on a single subject and with a central idea or thesis.

essential element   A word or word group that is necessary to the meaning of a sentence because it limits the thing it refers to: removing it would leave the meaning unclear or too general. Also called a **restrictive element,** an essential element is not set off by punctuation: *The keys to the car are on the table. That man who called about the apartment said he'd try again tonight.* Contrast *nonessential element.* (See pp. 459–62, 473–74.)

Terms

ethical appeal See *appeals.*

etymology The history of a word's meanings and forms.

euphemism A presumably inoffensive word that a writer or speaker substitutes for a word deemed possibly offensive or too blunt—for example, *passed beyond* for "died." (See p. 546.)

evaluation A judgment of the quality, value, currency, bias, or other aspects of a work. (See pp. 131–32, 136–37, 651–59.)

evidence The facts, examples, expert opinions, and other information that support the claims in an argument. (See pp. 147–51, 171.)

expletive A sentence that postpones the subject by beginning with *there* or *it* and a form of the verb *be: It is impossible to get a ticket. There should be more seats available.* (See p. 271.)

exposition Writing whose primary purpose is to explain something about a subject.

fallacies Errors in reasoning. Some evade the issue of the argument; others oversimplify the argument. (See pp. 156–62.)

faulty predication A sentence error in which the meanings of subject and predicate conflict, so that the subject is said to be or do something illogical: *The installation of air bags takes up space in a car's steering wheel and dashboard.* (See pp. 394–95.)

figurative language (figures of speech) Expressions that suggest meanings different from their literal meanings in order to achieve special effects. (See pp. 560–61.) Some common figures:

- **Hyperbole,** deliberate exaggeration: *The bag weighed a ton.*
- **Metaphor,** an implied comparison between two unlike things: *The wind stabbed through our clothes.*
- **Personification,** the attribution of human qualities to a thing or idea: *The water beckoned seductively.*
- **Simile,** an explicit comparison, using *like* or *as,* between two unlike things: *The sky glowered like an angry parent.*

A **mixed metaphor** is a confusing or ludicrous combination of incompatible figures: *The wind stabbed through our clothes and shook our bones.*

finite verb Any verb that makes an assertion or expresses a state of being and can stand as the main verb of a sentence or clause: *The moose eats the leaves.* (See p. 349.) Contrast *verbal,* which is formed from a finite verb but is unable to stand alone as the main verb of a sentence: *I saw the moose eating the leaves.*

first person See *person.*

flame To attack an online correspondent personally, as in a discussion list or newsgroup. (See p. 195.)

foil A character in a literary work who contrasts with another character and thus helps to define that other character. (See p. 808.)

formal and informal Levels of usage achieved through word choice and sentence structure. More informal writing, as in a letter to an

Terms

acquaintance or a personal essay, resembles some speech in its colloquial language, contractions, and short, fairly simple sentences. More
formal writing, as in academic papers and business reports, avoids
these attributes of speech and tends to rely on longer and more complicated sentences.

format   In a document such as an academic paper or a business letter,
the arrangement and spacing of elements on the page. See also *document design*.

fragment   See *sentence fragment*.

frame   A window on a computer screen. With two or more frames on
the same screen, a Web designer can show two or more documents at
once.

freewriting   A technique for generating ideas: in a fixed amount of
time (say, fifteen minutes), you write continuously without stopping to
reread. (See pp. 23–24.)

function word   A word, such as an article, conjunction, or preposition, that serves primarily to clarify the roles of and relations between
other words in a sentence: *We chased the goat for an hour but finally
caught it.* Contrast *lexical word*.

fused sentence (run-on sentence)   A sentence error in which two
main clauses are joined with no punctuation or connecting word between them. (See p. 363.)

> **Fused**   I heard his lecture it was dull.
> **Revised**   I heard his lecture; it was dull.

future perfect tense   See *tense*.

future tense   See *tense*.

gender   The classification of nouns or pronouns as masculine (*he,
boy, handyman*), feminine (*she, woman, actress*), or neuter (*it, typewriter, dog*).

general and specific   Terms designating the relative number of instances or objects included in a group signified by a word. The following list moves from most **general** (including the most objects) to most
specific (including the fewest objects): *vehicle, four-wheeled vehicle,
automobile, sedan, Ford Taurus, blue Ford Taurus, my sister's blue Ford
Taurus named Hank.* See also *abstract and concrete*. (See pp. 555–56.)

generalization   A claim inferred from evidence. See also *inductive reasoning*.

generic he   *He* used to mean *he or she*. For ways to avoid *he* when you
intend either or both genders, see pp. 329–30 and 549.

generic noun   A noun that refers to a typical member of a group
rather than to a specific person or thing: *Any person may come. A
student needs good work habits. A school with financial problems may
shortchange its students.* A singular generic noun takes a singular pronoun (*he, she,* or *it*). (See pp. 329–30.)

genitive case   Another term for possessive case. See *case*.

gerund   A verbal that ends in *-ing* and functions as a noun: *Working is all right for killing time* (*working* is the subject of the verb *is; killing* is the object of the preposition *for*). See also *verbals and verbal phrases*. (See p. 254.)

gerund phrase   A word group consisting of a gerund plus any modifiers or objects. See also *verbals and verbal phrases*.

grammar   A description of how a language works.

grounds   A term used for *evidence* in argument. See *evidence*.

helping verb (auxiliary verb)   A verb used with another verb to convey time, obligation, and other meanings: *You should write a letter. You have written other letters.* The **modals** include *can, could, may, might, must, ought, shall, should, will, would.* The other helping verbs are forms of *be, have,* and *do.* (See pp. 286, 292–97.)

homonyms   Words that are pronounced the same but have different spellings and meanings, such as *heard/herd* and *to/too/two.* (See pp. 590–91 for a list.)

HTML (hypertext markup language)   A computer language used for creating Web pages. An **HTML editor** is a program for coding documents in HTML. (See pp. 222–23.)

hyperbole   See *figurative language*.

hypertext   Text such as that on the Web that provides links allowing users to move easily and variously within and among documents. Contrast *linear text.* (See pp. 220–21.)

idiom   An expression that is peculiar to a language and that may not make sense if taken literally: for example, *dark horse, bide your time,* and *by and large.* See p. 558 for a list of idioms involving prepositions, such as *agree with them* and *agree to the contract.*

illustration or support   Supplying examples or reasons to develop an idea. (See pp. 27–28 and 93–94.)

imagery   Pictures created by words that appeal to the sense of sight, hearing, touch, taste, or smell.

imperative   See *mood*.

indefinite pronoun   See *pronoun*.

independent clause   See *clause*.

indicative   See *mood*.

indirect object   See *object*.

indirect question   A sentence reporting a question, usually in a subordinate clause, and ending with a period: *Writers wonder whether their work must be lonely.* Contrast *direct question*.

indirect quotation (indirect discourse)   See *quotation*.

inductive reasoning   Inferring a generalization from specific evidence. Contrast *deductive reasoning.* (See p. 167.)

Terms

infinitive A verbal formed from the plain form of the verb plus the **infinitive marker** *to: to swim, to write.* Infinitives and infinitive phrases may function as nouns, adjectives, or adverbs. See also *verbals and verbal phrases.* (See p. 255.)

infinitive marker See *infinitive.*

infinitive phrase A word group consisting of an infinitive plus any subject, objects, or modifiers. See also *verbals and verbal phrases.*

inflection The variation in the form of a word that indicates its function in a particular context. See *declension,* the inflection of nouns and pronouns; *conjugation,* the inflection of verbs; and *comparison,* the inflection of adjectives and adverbs.

inflectional suffix See *suffix.*

informal See *formal and informal.*

intensifier A modifier that adds emphasis to the word(s) it modifies: for example, *very slow, so angry.*

intensive pronoun See *pronoun.*

interjection A word standing by itself or inserted in a construction to exclaim or command attention: *Hey! Ouch! What the heck did you do that for?*

interpretation The determination of meaning or significance—for instance, in a work such as a poem or photograph or in the literature on some issue such as job discrimination. (See pp. 127–29, 134–36.)

interrogative Functioning as or involving a question.

interrogative adjective See *adjective.*

interrogative pronoun See *pronoun.*

intransitive verb A verb that does not take a direct object: *The woman laughed.* (See p. 343.)

introduction The opening of an essay, a transition for readers between their world and the writer's. The introduction often contains a statement of the writer's thesis. (See pp. 103–06 for suggestions.)

invention The discovery and exploration of ideas, usually occurring most intensively in the early stages of the writing process. (See pp. 19–30 for invention techniques.)

inversion A reversal of usual word order in a sentence, as when a verb precedes its subject or an object precedes its verb: *Down swooped the hawk. Our aims we stated clearly.*

IRC See *synchronous communication.*

irony The use of words to suggest a meaning different from what the words say literally: *What a happy face!* (said to someone scowling miserably); *With that kind of planning, prices are sure to go down* (written with the expectation that prices will rise).

irregular verb A verb that forms its past tense and past participle in some other way than by the addition of *-d* or *-ed* to the plain form: for example, *go, went, gone; give, gave, given.* Contrast *regular verb.* (See pp. 287–89 for a list of irregular verbs.)

jargon In one sense, jargon is the specialized language of any group, such as doctors or baseball players. In another sense, jargon is vague, pretentious, wordy, and ultimately unclear writing such as that found in some academic, business, and government publications. (See p. 570.)

journal A personal record of observations, reactions, ideas, and other thoughts. Besides providing a private place to think in writing, a journal is useful for making notes about reading (pp. 120–21, 607–08, 787–88), discovering ideas for essays (pp. 20–22), and keeping track of research (pp. 607–08, 814, 833–34, 865).

journalist's questions A set of questions useful for probing a subject to discover ideas about it. (See pp. 26–27.)

keyword(s) A word or words that define a subject, used for searching databases such as library catalogs and periodical indexes and for searching the Web. (See pp. 623–26.)

lexical word A word, such as a noun, verb, or modifier, that carries part of the meaning of language. Contrast *function word.*

linear text Text such as a conventional printed document that is intended to be read in sequence. Contrast *hypertext.* (See pp. 220–21.)

linking verb A verb that relates a subject to its complement: *Julie is a Democrat. He looks harmless. The boy became a man.* Common linking verbs are the forms of *be;* the verbs relating to the senses, such as *look* and *smell;* and the verbs *become, appear,* and *seem.* (See p. 245.)

listserv See *discussion list.*

logical agreement See *agreement.*

logical fallacies See *fallacies.*

lurking Reading but not participating in an Internet discussion list, newsgroup, or Web forum. (See p. 645.)

main clause See *clause.*

main verb The part of a verb phrase that carries the principal meaning: *had been walking, could happen, was chilled.* See also *verb phrase.*

mass noun Another term for noncount noun. See *noun.*

mechanics The use of capital letters, underlining or italics, abbreviations, numbers, and divided words. (See Chapters 33–37.)

metaphor See *figurative language.*

misplaced modifier A modifier so far from the term it modifies or so close to another term it could modify that its relation to the rest of the sentence is unclear. (See Chapter 21.)

Misplaced	The boys played with firecrackers that they bought illegally in the field.
Revised	The boys played in the field with firecrackers that they bought illegally.

Terms

A **squinting modifier** could modify the words on either side of it: *The plan we considered <u>seriously</u> worries me.*

mixed construction A sentence containing two or more parts that do not fit together in grammar or in meaning. (See pp. 392–95.)

mixed metaphor See *figurative language.*

MLA style The style of documenting sources recommended by the Modern Language Association and used in many of the humanities, including English. (For explanation and examples, see Chapter 49.)

modal See *helping verb.*

modifier Any word or word group that limits or qualifies the meaning of another word or word group. Modifiers include adjectives and adverbs as well as words, phrases, and clauses that act as adjectives and adverbs.

MOO See *synchronous communication.*

mood The form of a verb that shows how the speaker or writer views the action. (See pp. 312–14.)

- The **indicative mood,** the most common, is used to make statements or ask questions: *The play <u>will be performed</u> Saturday. Did you <u>get</u> the tickets?*
- The **imperative mood** gives a command: *Please <u>get</u> good seats.*
- The **subjunctive mood** expresses a wish, a condition contrary to fact, a recommendation, or a request: *I wish George <u>were coming</u> with us. Did you suggest that he <u>join</u> us?*

narration Recounting a sequence of events, usually in the order of their occurrence. (See pp. 27 and 92–93.) Literary narration tells a story. (See Chapter 52.)

narrator The speaker in a poem or the voice who tells a story. (See p. 792.)

neologism A word coined recently and not in established use. (See p. 546.)

netiquette Conventions and courtesies for Internet communication. (See pp. 195–96.)

newsgroup An Internet discussion group with a common site where all postings are recorded. (See p. 646.)

nominal A noun, a pronoun, or a word or word group used as a noun: *<u>Joan</u> and <u>I</u> talked. The <u>rich</u> owe a debt to the <u>poor</u>* (adjectives acting as subject and object). *<u>Baby-sitting</u> can be exhausting* (gerund acting as subject). *I like <u>to play with children</u>* (infinitive phrase acting as object).

nominative Another term for subjective case. See *case.*

noncount noun See *noun.*

nonessential element A word or word group that does not limit the term or construction it refers to and thus is not essential to the meaning of the sentence. Also called a **nonrestrictive element,** a nonessential element is set off by punctuation, usually commas: *The new apartment* *building, in shades of tan and gray, will house fifty people* (nonessential adjective phrase). *Sleep, which we all need, occupies a third of our lives* (nonessential adjective clause). *His wife, Patricia, is a chemist* (nonessential appositive). Contrast *essential element*. (See pp. 459–62.)

nonfinite verb   See *verbals and verbal phrases*.

nonrestrictive element   See *nonessential element*.

nonstandard   Words and grammatical forms not conforming to standard American English. (See pp. 543–44.)

noun   A word that names a person, place, thing, quality, or idea: *Maggie, Alabama, clarinet, satisfaction, socialism.* Nouns normally form the possessive case by adding *-'s* (*Maggie's*) and the plural by adding *-s* or *-es* (*clarinets, messes*), although there are exceptions (*men, women, children*). The forms of nouns depend partly on where they fit in certain overlapping groups:

- **Common nouns** name general classes and are not capitalized: *book, government, music.*
- **Proper nouns** name specific people, places, and things and are capitalized: *Susan, Athens, Fenway Park.*
- **Count nouns** name things considered countable in English (they form plurals): *ounce/ounces, camera/cameras, person/people.*
- **Noncount nouns** name things not considered countable in English (they don't form plurals): *chaos, fortitude, silver, earth, information.*
- **Collective nouns** are singular in form but name groups: *team, class, family.*

noun clause   A word group containing a subject and a verb and functioning as a subject, object, or complement: *Everyone wondered how the door opened. Whoever opened it had left.*

number   The form of a noun, pronoun, demonstrative adjective, or verb that indicates whether it is singular or plural: *woman, women; I, we; this, these; runs, run.*

object   A noun, pronoun, or word group that receives the action of or is influenced by a transitive verb, a verbal, or a preposition.

- **A direct object** receives the action of a verb or verbal and frequently follows it in a sentence: *We sat watching the stars. Emily caught whatever it was you had.* (See p. 244.)
- An **indirect object** tells for or to whom something is done: *I lent Stan my car. Reiner bought us all champagne.* (See pp. 245–46.)
- An **object of a preposition** usually follows a preposition and is linked by it to the rest of the sentence: *They are going to New Orleans for the jazz festival.* (See p. 250.)

object complement   See *complement*.

objective   See *case*.

opinion   A conclusion based on facts; an arguable, potentially changeable claim. Claims of opinion form the backbone of any argument. (See p. 145.)

Terms

ordinal number   The type of number that shows order: *first, eleventh, twenty-fifth*. Contrast *cardinal number* (such as *one, twenty-five*).

paragraph   Generally, a group of sentences set off by a beginning indention and developing a single idea. That idea is often stated in a **topic sentence**. (See Chapter 4.)

parallelism   Similarity of grammatical form between two or more coordinated elements: *Rising prices and declining incomes left many people in bad debt and worse despair.* (See Chapter 25.)

paraphrase   The restatement of source material in one's own words and sentence structures, useful for borrowing the original author's line of reasoning but not his or her exact words. Paraphrases must always be acknowledged in source citations. (See pp. 668–70.)

parenthetical citation   In the text of a paper, a brief reference, enclosed in parentheses, indicating that material is borrowed and directing the reader to the source of the material. See also *citation*.

parenthetical expression   A word or construction that interrupts a sentence and is not part of its main structure, called *parenthetical* because it could (or does) appear in parentheses: *Childe Hassam (1859–1935) was an American painter and etcher. The book, incidentally, is terrible.* (See pp. 508–09.)

participial phrase   A word group consisting of a participle plus any objects or modifiers. See also *verbals and verbal phrases*.

participle   A verbal showing continuing or completed action, used as an adjective or part of a verb phrase but never as the main verb of a sentence or clause. (See p. 254.)

- A **present participle** ends in *-ing: My heart is breaking* (participle as part of verb phrase). *I like to watch the rolling waves* (participle as adjective).
- A **past participle** most commonly ends in *-d, -ed, -n,* or *-en* (*wished, shown, given*) but sometimes changes the spelling of the verb (*sung, done, slept*): *Jeff has broken his own record* (participle as part of verb phrase). *The closed door beckoned* (participle as adjective).

See also *verbals and verbal phrases*.

particle   A preposition or adverb in a two-word verb: *look up, catch on*. (See pp. 300–01.)

parts of speech   The classes into which words are commonly grouped according to their form, function, and meaning: nouns, pronouns, verbs, adjectives, adverbs, conjunctions, prepositions, and interjections. See separate entries for each part of speech.

passive voice   See *voice*.

past participle   See *participle*.

past perfect tense   See *tense*.

past tense   See *tense*.

patterns of development   Ways of thinking that can help you develop and organize ideas in essays and paragraphs. (See pp. 27–28 and 92–101.)

perfect tenses See *tense.*

periodic sentence A suspenseful sentence in which modifiers precede the main clause, which falls at the end: *Postponing decisions about family while striving to establish themselves in careers, many young adults are falsely accused of greed.* Contrast *cumulative sentence.* (See p. 408.)

person The form of a verb or pronoun that indicates whether the subject is speaking, spoken to, or spoken about. In English only personal pronouns and verbs change form to indicate difference in person. In the **first person**, the subject is speaking: *I am* [or *We are*] *planning a party.* In the **second person**, the subject is being spoken to: *Are you coming?* In the **third person**, the subject is being spoken about: *She was* [or *They were*] *going.*

personal pronoun See *pronoun.*

personification See *figurative language.*

phrase A group of related words that lacks a subject or a predicate or both and that acts as a single part of speech. See *absolute phrase, prepositional phrase, verbals and verbal phrases,* and *verb phrase.*

plagiarism The presentation of someone else's ideas or words as if they were one's own. Whether accidental or deliberate, plagiarism is a serious and often punishable offense. (See pp. 680–88.)

plain case Another term for the subjective case of nouns. See *case.*

plain form The dictionary form of a verb: *make, run, swivel.* See also *verb forms.*

planning See *developing (planning).*

plot The pattern of events in a work of literature. (See p. 792.)

plural More than one. See *number.*

point of view The perspective or attitude of the narrator or speaker in a work of literature. See also *person.* (See p. 792.)

positive degree See *comparison.*

possessive See *case.*

predicate The part of a sentence that makes an assertion about the subject. A predicate must contain a finite verb and may contain modifiers, objects of the verb, and complements. The **simple predicate** consists of the verb and its helping verbs: *A wiser person would have made a different decision.* The **complete predicate** includes the simple predicate and any modifiers, objects, and complements: *A wiser person would have made a different decision.* See also *intransitive verb, linking verb,* and *transitive verb.* (See pp. 239, 243–46.)

predicate adjective See *complement.*

predicate noun (predicate nominative) See *complement.*

prefix A letter or group of letters (such as *sub, in, dis, pre*) that can be added at the beginning of a root or word to create a new word: *sub + marine = submarine; dis + grace = disgrace.* Contrast *suffix.* (See pp. 583–85.)

Terms

premise   Generally, a claim or assumption basic to an argument. In a deductive syllogism, one premise applied to another leads logically to a conclusion. See also *syllogism*. (See pp. 168–70.)

preposition   A word that forms a noun or pronoun (plus any modifiers) into a prepositional phrase: *about love, down the steep stairs*. The common prepositions include these as well as *after, before, by, for, from, in, on, to,* and many others. (See pp. 250–51.)

prepositional phrase   A word group consisting of a preposition and its object, plus any modifiers. A prepositional phrase usually functions as an adjective (*The boy in green stood up*) or as an adverb (*He walked to the speaker's platform*). (See pp. 250–52.)

present participle   See *participle.*

present perfect tense   See *tense.*

present tense   See *tense.*

pretentious writing   Writing that is more elaborate than the writing situation requires, usually full of fancy phrases and showy words. (See pp. 546–47.)

primary source   Firsthand information, such as an eyewitness account of events; a diary, speech, or other historical document; a work of literature or art; a report of a survey or experiment; and one's own interview, observation, or correspondence. Contrast *secondary source.* (See p. 614.)

principal clause   A main or independent clause. See *clause.*

principal parts   The plain form, past-tense form, and past participle of a verb. See *verb forms.* (See pp. 284–85.)

problem-solution organization   The arrangement of material to state and explain a problem and then to propose and explain a solution. (See pp. 44, 82–83.)

process analysis   The explanation of how something works or how to do something. (See pp. 28, 100–01.)

progressive tense   See *tense.*

pronoun   A word used in place of a noun. There are eight types of pronouns:

- **Personal pronouns** refer to a specific individual or to individuals: *I, you, he, she, it, we, they.* (See p. 276.)
- **Indefinite pronouns,** such as *everybody* and *some,* do not refer to specific nouns (*Everybody speaks*). (See pp. 322–23.)
- **Relative pronouns**—*who, whoever, which, that*—relate groups of words to nouns or pronouns (*The book that won is a novel*). (See pp. 260, 276.)
- **Interrogative pronouns**—*who, whom, whose, which, what*—introduce questions (*Who will contribute?*).
- **Intensive pronouns**—personal pronouns plus *-self* or *-selves*—emphasize a noun or other pronoun (*He himself asked that question*). (See pp. 276, 925.)

- **Reflexive pronouns** have the same form as intensive pronouns. They indicate that the sentence subject also receives the action of the verb (*They injured themselves*). (See pp. 276, 925.)
- **Demonstrative pronouns** such as *this, that,* and *such* identify or point to nouns (*This is the problem*).
- **Reciprocal pronouns**—*each other* and *one another*—are used as objects of verbs when the subjects are plural (*They loved each other*).

proofreading   Reading and correcting a final draft for misspellings, typographical errors, and other mistakes. (See p. 62.)

proper adjective   See *adjective.*

proper noun   See *noun.*

purpose   For a writer, the chief reason for communicating something about a subject to a particular audience. Purposes are both general (usually explanation or persuasion) and specific (taking into account the subject and desired outcome). (See pp. 13–15.)

quotation   Repetition of what someone has written or spoken. In **direct quotation (direct discourse)**, the person's words are duplicated exactly and enclosed in quotation marks: *Polonius told his son, Laertes, "Neither a borrower nor a lender be."* An **indirect quotation (indirect discourse)** reports what someone said or wrote but not in the exact words and not in quotation marks: *Polonius advised his son, Laertes, not to borrow or lend.*

rational appeal   See *appeals.*

reciprocal pronoun   See *pronoun.*

reflexive pronoun   See *pronoun.*

regional language   Expressions common to the people in a particular geographical area. (See p. 544.)

regular verb   A verb that forms its past tense and past participle by adding *-d* or *-ed* to the plain form: *love, loved, loved; open, opened, opened.* Contrast *irregular verb.* (See pp. 286–87.)

relative clause   A subordinate clause beginning with a relative pronoun such as *who* or *that* and functioning as an adjective.

relative pronoun   See *pronoun.*

restrictive element   See *essential element.*

revising   The stage of the writing process in which one considers and improves the meaning and underlying structure of a draft. Compare *developing (planning)* and *drafting.* (See pp. 51–58.)

rhetoric   The principles for finding and arranging ideas and for using language in speech or writing to achieve the writer's purpose in addressing his or her audience.

rhetorical question   A question asked for effect, with no answer expected. The person asking the question either intends to provide the answer or assumes it is obvious: *If we let one factory pollute the river, what does that say to other factories that want to dump wastes there?*

Terms

run-on sentence   See *fused sentence.*

sans serif   See *serifs.*

search engine   A computer program that conducts Internet searches from keywords or directories. (See pp. 640–45.)

secondary source   A source reporting or analyzing information in other sources, such as a critic's view of a work of art or a sociologist's summary of others' studies. Contrast *primary source.* (See p. 614.)

second person   See *person.*

sentence   A complete unit of thought, consisting of at least a subject and a predicate that are not introduced by a subordinating word. Sentences can be classed on the basis of their structure in one of four ways. A **simple sentence** contains one main clause: *I'm leaving.* A **compound sentence** contains at least two main clauses: *I'd like to stay, but I'm leaving.* A **complex sentence** contains one main clause and at least one subordinate clause: *If you let me go now, you'll be sorry.* A **compound-complex sentence** contains at least two main clauses and at least one subordinate clause: *I'm leaving because you want me to, but I'd rather stay.* (See pp. 272–73.)

sentence fragment   A sentence error in which a group of words is set off as a sentence even though it begins with a subordinating word or lacks a subject or a predicate or both. (See Chapter 17.)

Fragment	She lost the race. Because she was injured. [*Because,* a subordinating conjunction, makes the underlined clause subordinate.]
Revised	She lost the race because she was injured.
Fragment	He could not light a fire. Thus could not warm the room. [The underlined word group lacks a subject.]
Revised	He could not light a fire. Thus he could not warm the room.

sentence modifier   An adverb or a word or word group acting as an adverb that modifies the idea of the whole sentence in which it appears rather than any specific word: *In fact, people will always complain.*

series   A sequence of three or more items of equal importance: *The children are named John, Hallie, and Nancy.* The items in a series are separated with commas. (See p. 465.)

serifs   Small lines on the characters in type fonts, such as the lines along the bottom of this A. **Sans serif** type, such as Arial, does not have serifs. (See p. 205.)

server   A computer that links other computers in a network. Servers transfer data and store files.

setting   The place where the action of a literary work happens. (See p. 793.)

sexist language   Language expressing narrow ideas about men's and women's roles, positions, capabilities, or value. (See pp. 548–50.)

signal phrase Words that indicate who is being quoted: *"In the future," said Andy Warhol, "everyone will be world-famous for fifteen minutes."* (For punctuating signal phrases, see pp. 468–70. For using signal phrases to integrate quotations, see pp. 676–79.)

simile See *figurative language.*

simple predicate See *predicate.*

simple sentence See *sentence.*

simple subject See *subject.*

simple tense See *tense.*

singular One. See *number.*

slang Expressions used by the members of a group to create bonds and sometimes exclude others. Most slang is too vague, short-lived, and narrowly understood to be used in any but very informal writing. (See pp. 544–45.)

source A place where information or ideas may be found: book, article, Web site, work of art, television program, and so on.

spam To send an irrelevant and unsolicited electronic message to many recipients at once, such as all the subscribers to a discussion list.

spatial organization In a description of a person, place, or thing, the arrangement of details as they would be scanned by a viewer—for instance, from top to bottom or near to far. (See pp. 42–43 and 80–81.)

specific See *general and specific.*

split infinitive The often awkward interruption of an infinitive and its marker *to* by an adverb: *Management decided to immediately introduce the new product.* (See p. 385.)

squinting modifier See *misplaced modifier.*

standard American English The dialect of English used and expected by educated writers and readers in colleges and universities, businesses, and professions. (See pp. 17–18, 542–44.)

subject In grammar, the part of a sentence that names something and about which an assertion is made in the predicate. The **simple subject** consists of the noun alone: *The quick brown fox jumps over the lazy dog.* The **complete subject** includes the simple subject and its modifiers: *The quick brown fox jumps over the lazy dog.* (See p. 239.)

subject complement See *complement.*

subjective See *case.*

subjunctive See *mood.*

subordinate clause See *clause.*

subordinating conjunction See *conjunction.*

subordination The use of grammatical constructions to de-emphasize one element in a sentence by making it dependent on rather than equal to another element: *Although I left six messages for him, the doctor failed to call.* Contrast *coordination.* (See pp. 419–23.)

Terms

substantive   A word or word group used as a noun.

suffix   A **derivational suffix** is a letter or group of letters that can be added to the end of a root word to make a new word, often a different part of speech: *child, childish; shrewd, shrewdly; visual, visualize*. (See p. 585.) An **inflectional suffix** adapts a word to different grammatical relations: *boy, boys; fast, faster; tack, tacked*.

summary   A condensation and restatement of source material in one's own words and sentence structures, useful in reading for comprehending the material (see pp. 123–24) and in research writing for presenting the gist of the original author's idea (pp. 667–68). Summaries appearing in a paper must always be acknowledged in source citations.

superlative   See *comparison*.

syllogism   A form of deductive reasoning in which two premises stating generalizations or assumptions together lead to a conclusion. *Premise:* Hot stoves can burn me. *Premise:* This stove is hot. *Conclusion:* This stove can burn me. See also *deductive reasoning*. (See pp. 168–69.)

symbolism   The use of a concrete thing to suggest something larger and more abstract, as a red rose may symbolize passion or romance. (See p. 793.)

synchronous communication   Real-time, simultaneous communication over the Internet, analogous to a conference call on a telephone. Instant messaging, MOOs, and IRC (Internet relay chat) are examples. (See p. 646.)

synonyms   Words with approximately but not exactly the same meanings, such as *snicker, giggle,* and *chortle*. (See p. 554.)

syntax   In sentences, the grammatical relations among words and the ways those relations are indicated.

synthesis   Drawing connections among the elements within a work (such as the images in a poem) or among entire works (entire poems). Synthesis is an essential skill in critical thinking, reading, and writing (see pp. 129–31, 136) and in research writing (pp. 660–62).

tag question   A question attached to the end of a statement and consisting of a pronoun, a helping verb, and sometimes the word *not: It isn't raining, is it? It is sunny, isn't it?*

template   A word-processing form for a letter, memo, or other document. (See p. 203.)

tense   The form of a verb that expresses the time of its action, usually indicated by the verb's inflection and by helping verbs.

- The **simple tenses** are the **present** (*I race, you go*), the **past** (*I raced, you went*), and the **future,** formed with the helping verb *will* (*I will race, you will go*).
- The **perfect tenses,** formed with the helping verbs *have* and *had,* indicate completed action. They are the **present perfect** (*I have raced, you have gone*), the **past perfect** (*I had raced, you had gone*), and the **future perfect** (*I will have raced, you will have gone*).

- The **progressive tenses,** formed with the helping verb *be* plus the present participle, indicate continuing action. They include the **present progressive** (*I am racing, you are going*), the **past progressive** (*I was racing, you were going*), and the **future progressive** (*I will be racing, you will be going*).

(See p. 304 for a list of tenses with examples.)

theme   The main idea of a work of literature. (See p. 793.)

thesis   The central, controlling idea of an essay, to which all assertions and details relate. (See p. 31.)

thesis statement   A sentence or more that asserts the central, controlling idea of an essay and perhaps previews the essay's organization. (See pp. 31–35.)

third person   See *person.*

thread   In a discussion list, newsgroup, or Web forum, a series of messages on the same topic.

tone   The sense of a writer's attitudes toward self, subject, and readers revealed by words and sentence structures as well as by content. (See pp. 11–12, 152–53, 173–74, 792.)

topic   The subject of an essay or paragraph.

topic sentence   See *paragraph.*

transitional expression   A word or phrase, such as *thus* or *for example,* that links sentences and shows the relations between them. (See p. 87 for a list.) The error known as a comma splice occurs when two main clauses related by a transitional expression are separated only by a comma. (See pp. 361–62.)

transitive verb   A verb that requires a direct object to complete its meaning. (See pp. 244–45.)

trite expressions (clichés)   Stale expressions that dull writing and suggest that the writer is careless or lazy. (See p. 562.)

two-word verb   A verb plus a preposition or adverb that affects the meaning of the verb: *jump off, put away, help out.* (See pp. 300–01.)

uniform resource locator (URL)   An address for a document on the World Wide Web. (See pp. 653–54.)

unity   The quality of an effective essay or paragraph in which all parts relate to the central idea and to each other. (See pp. 45 and 73–76.)

upload   To transfer data or files from your local computer to another computer.

variety   Among connected sentences, changes in length, structure, and word order that help readers see the importance and complexity of ideas. (See Chapter 26.)

verb   A word or group of words indicating the action or state of being of a subject. The inflection of a verb and the use of helping verbs with it

Terms

indicate its tense, mood, voice, number, and sometimes person. See separate listings for each aspect and for *predicate*. (See Chapter 14.)

verbals and verbal phrases   Verbals are verb forms used as adjectives (*swimming children*), adverbs (*designed to succeed*), or nouns (*addicted to running*). The verbals in the preceding examples are a participle, an infinitive, and a gerund, respectively. (See separate entries for each type.) Verbal phrases consist of verbals plus objects or modifiers: *Swimming fast, the children reached the raft. Willem tried to unlatch the gate. Running in the park is his only recreation.* (See pp. 253–56.)

A verbal is a **nonfinite verb**: it cannot serve as the only verb in the predicate of a sentence. For that, it requires a helping verb. (See p. 349.)

verb forms   Verbs have five distinctive forms. The first three are the verb's **principal parts:**

- The **plain form** is the dictionary form: *live, swim.*
- The **past-tense form** adds *-d* or *-ed* to the plain form if the verb is regular: *live, lived.* If the verb is irregular, the plain form changes in some other way, such as *swim, swam.*
- The **past participle** is the same as the past-tense form for regular verbs. For irregular verbs, the past participle may differ (*swum*).
- The **present participle** adds *-ing* to the plain form: *living, swimming.*
- The **-s form** adds *-s* or *-es* to the plain form: *lives, swims.*

verb phrase   A verb consisting of a helping verb and a main verb: *has started, will have been invited.* A verb phrase can serve as the predicate of a clause: *The movie has started.*

voice   The form of a verb that tells whether the sentence subject performs the action or is acted upon. In the active voice the subject acts: *We made the decision.* In the passive voice the subject is acted upon: *The decision was made by us.* (See pp. 314–16.)

warrant   A term used for *assumption* in argument. See *assumption.*

Web forum   A discussion group on the Web, open to everyone and organized around subjects.

wizard   A file on many word processors and most desktop publishers that guides the user in designing documents. (See p. 203.)

word order   The arrangement of the words in a sentence, which plays a large part in determining the grammatical relation among words in English.

writing process   The mental and physical activities that go into producing a finished piece of writing. The overlapping stages of the process—developing or planning, drafting, and revising—differ for different writers and even for the same writer in different writing situations. (See Chapters 1–3.)

writing situation   The unique combination of writer, subject, audience, purpose, and other elements that defines an assignment or occasion and helps direct the writer's choices. (See pp. 3–5.)

Terms

Credits

Index

Index-1

Index-2

Index-4

Index

Index-6

Index

Index-8

Index-10

Index-12

Index

Index

Index-20

Index-22

Index

Index

Index-34

Index-46

Index-50

Index

Index-56

USEFUL LISTS AND SUMMARIES

GUIDE TO ⟨CULTURE LANGUAGE⟩ TOPICS

Throughout the handbook, the symbol ⟨CULTURE LANGUAGE⟩ signals topics for writers who are using standard American English as a second language or a second dialect. This guide indexes all these topics, with * marking exercises.